T0331737

Emerging Trends in the Development and Application of Composite Indicators

Veljko Jeremic
University of Belgrade, Serbia

Zoran Radojicic
University of Belgrade, Serbia

Marina Dobrota
University of Belgrade, Serbia

A volume in the Advances in Data Mining and
Database Management (ADMDM) Book Series

www.igi-global.com

Published in the United States of America by
    IGI Global
    Information Science Reference (an imprint of IGI Global)
    701 E. Chocolate Avenue
    Hershey PA, USA 17033
    Tel: 717-533-8845
    Fax: 717-533-8661
    E-mail: cust@igi-global.com
    Web site: http://www.igi-global.com

Library of Congress Cataloging-in-Publication Data

Names: Jeremic, Veljko, 1985- editor. | Radojicic, Zoran, 1967- editor. |
  Dobrota, Marina, 1984- editor.
Title: Emerging trends in the development and application of composite
  indicators / Veljko Jeremic, Zoran Radojicic, and Marina Dobrota, editors.
Description: Hershey, PA : Information Science Reference, [2017] | Includes
  bibliographical references and indexes.
Identifiers: LCCN 2016024314| ISBN 9781522507147 (hardcover) | ISBN
  9781522507154 (ebook)
Subjects: LCSH: Statistics. | Economic indicators. | Social indicators. |
  Political indicators. | Science indicators.
Classification: LCC HA155 .E46 2017 | DDC 300.72/7--dc23 LC record available at https://lccn.loc.gov/2016024314

This book is published in the IGI Global book series Advances in Data Mining and Database Management (ADMDM) (ISSN: 2327-1981; eISSN: 2327-199X)

British Cataloguing in Publication Data
A Cataloguing in Publication record for this book is available from the British Library.

All work contributed to this book is new, previously-unpublished material. The views expressed in this book are those of the authors, but not necessarily of the publisher.

For electronic access to this publication, please contact: eresources@igi-global.com.

Advances in Data Mining and Database Management (ADMDM) Book Series

David Taniar
Monash University, Australia

ISSN: 2327-1981
EISSN: 2327-199X

Mission

With the large amounts of information available to organizations in today's digital world, there is a need for continual research surrounding emerging methods and tools for collecting, analyzing, and storing data.

The **Advances in Data Mining & Database Management (ADMDM)** series aims to bring together research in information retrieval, data analysis, data warehousing, and related areas in order to become an ideal resource for those working and studying in these fields. IT professionals, software engineers, academicians and upper-level students will find titles within the ADMDM book series particularly useful for staying up-to-date on emerging research, theories, and applications in the fields of data mining and database management.

Coverage

- Profiling Practices
- Text Mining
- Predictive analysis
- Information Extraction
- Enterprise systems
- Customer Analytics
- Association Rule Learning
- Quantitative Structure–Activity Relationship
- Heterogeneous and Distributed Databases
- Neural Networks

IGI Global is currently accepting manuscripts for publication within this series. To submit a proposal for a volume in this series, please contact our Acquisition Editors at Acquisitions@igi-global.com or visit: http://www.igi-global.com/publish/.

Titles in this Series

For a list of additional titles in this series, please visit: www.igi-global.com

Web Usage Mining Techniques and Applications Across Industries
A.V. Senthil Kumar (Hindusthan College of Arts and Science, India)
Information Science Reference • copyright 2017 • 424pp • H/C (ISBN: 9781522506133) • US $200.00 (our price)

Social Media Data Extraction and Content Analysis
Shalin Hai-Jew (Kansas State University, USA)
Information Science Reference • copyright 2017 • 493pp • H/C (ISBN: 9781522506485) • US $225.00 (our price)

Collaborative Filtering Using Data Mining and Analysis
Vishal Bhatnagar (Ambedkar Institute of Advanced Communication Technologies and Research, India)
Information Science Reference • copyright 2017 • 309pp • H/C (ISBN: 9781522504894) • US $195.00 (our price)

Effective Big Data Management and Opportunities for Implementation
Manoj Kumar Singh (Adama Science and Technology University, Ethiopia) and Dileep Kumar G. (Adama Science and Technology University, Ethiopia)
Information Science Reference • copyright 2016 • 324pp • H/C (ISBN: 9781522501824) • US $195.00 (our price)

Data Mining Trends and Applications in Criminal Science and Investigations
Omowunmi E. Isafiade (University of Cape Town, South Africa) and Antoine B. Bagula (University of the Western Cape, South Africa)
Information Science Reference • copyright 2016 • 386pp • H/C (ISBN: 9781522504634) • US $210.00 (our price)

Intelligent Techniques for Data Analysis in Diverse Settings
Numan Celebi (Sakarya University, Turkey)
Information Science Reference • copyright 2016 • 353pp • H/C (ISBN: 9781522500759) • US $195.00 (our price)

Managing and Processing Big Data in Cloud Computing
Rajkumar Kannan (King Faisal University, Saudi Arabia) Raihan Ur Rasool (King Faisal University, Saudi Arabia) Hai Jin (Huazhong University of Science and Technology, China) and S.R. Balasundaram (National Institute of Technology, Tiruchirappalli, India)
Information Science Reference • copyright 2016 • 307pp • H/C (ISBN: 9781466697676) • US $200.00 (our price)

Handbook of Research on Innovative Database Query Processing Techniques
Li Yan (Nanjing University of Aeronautics and Astronautics, China)
Information Science Reference • copyright 2016 • 625pp • H/C (ISBN: 9781466687677) • US $335.00 (our price)

www.igi-global.com

701 E. Chocolate Ave., Hershey, PA 17033
Order online at www.igi-global.com or call 717-533-8845 x100
To place a standing order for titles released in this series, contact: cust@igi-global.com
Mon-Fri 8:00 am - 5:00 pm (est) or fax 24 hours a day 717-533-8661

Table of Contents

Detailed Table of Contents

Chapter 1

Teemu Makkonen, University of Surrey, UK & University of Southern Denmark, Denmark

Earlier quantitative studies on cross-border regional integration processes have commonly neglected Science, Technology, and Innovation (STI) indicators: even the most notable example of a composite indicator approach to measuring cross-border regional integration, i.e. the Oresund index, lacks a sub-category for STI. Consequently, by ignoring cross-border innovation and knowledge flows, the Oresund integration index fails to take into account one of the most important drivers of economic growth in cross-border regions. Therefore, a new composite STI indicator (sub-category) was introduced to strengthen the Oresund integration index. This was compiled from patent, publication and collaborative R&D project data. The findings show that this index performs reasonably well in depicting STI integration, while at the same time remaining simple and straightforward enough to be adopted in other cross-border regions.

Chapter 2

Yongjun Shen, Hasselt University, Belgium
Elke Hermans, Hasselt University, Belgium

Sustainability is a multi-dimensional concept that can be assessed by means of constructing a composite indicator or index. In doing so, a scientifically sound and appropriate index methodology is required. The research proposed in this chapter aims to provide a guideline for developing a sustainability index that is able to assess the impact of mobility on the urban quality of life. By studying the index development process in other domains critically and taking the specific sustainable urban mobility context into account, this study investigates the different methodological steps that are essential in the construction of a sustainable urban mobility index. The main challenges and potential options when developing such an index are discussed.

Chapter 3

Milica Jovanovic, University of Belgrade, Serbia
Jovana Rakicevic, University of Belgrade, Serbia
Maja Levi Jaksic, University of Belgrade, Serbia
Jasna Petkovic, University of Belgrade, Serbia
Sanja Marinkovic, University of Belgrade, Serbia

This chapter focuses on composite indices used in Technology Management (TM). It provides a critical comparative analysis of 5 indices, summarizes their structure, weighting process and emphasizes technology related components of indices as well as their advantages and disadvantages. The second part of the chapter examines the ranks of OECD and BRICS countries for Global Competitiveness Index (GCI), Global Innovativeness Index (GII) and Global Entrepreneurship Index (GEI), and further, we analyzed the correlations of GCI and GII pillars and clusters with the final ranks of countries. The research proved the presence and the importance of TM in the construction of the selected indices, but also identified that there is a lack of composite indicators used exclusively for TM performance which are measured globally by official institutions.

Chapter 4

Norsiah Abdul Hamid, Universiti Utara Malaysia, Malaysia
Mohd Sobhi Ishak, Universiti Utara Malaysia, Malaysia
Norhafezah Yusof, Universiti Utara Malaysia, Malaysia
Halimah Badioze Zaman, Universiti Kebangsaan Malaysia, Malaysia

The concept of Knowledge Society (KS) began due to recognition of the importance of knowledge and information in the development of a society. This chapter proposes a holistic view of knowledge society based on the development of composite indicators in nine different dimensions. The objective of the study is to propose a multi-dimensional approach comprising human capital, ICT, spirituality, economy, social, institutional and sustainability as determinants towards achieving a KS. These dimensions are discussed in-depth by the experts in semi-structured interviews and also validated by using Exploratory Factor Analysis (EFA) and Confirmatory Factor Analysis (CFA). The semi-structured interview data are presented in a verbatim manner so as to provide readers with in-depth feedback from the experts, while the EFA and CFA results of composite indicators are presented in graphics. Thus, this chapter contributes to the understanding of composite indicators of a knowledge society which can then be used by policy makers for future policy-making decision.

Chapter 5

Gordana Savić, University of Belgrade, Serbia
Milan Martić, University of Belgrade, Serbia

Composite indicators (CIs) are seen as an aggregation of a set of sub-indicators for measuring multi-dimensional concepts that cannot be captured by a single indicator (OECD, 2008). The indicators of development in different areas are also constructed by aggregating several sub-indicators. Consequently, the construction of CIs includes weighting and aggregation of individual performance indicators. These steps in CI construction are challenging issues as the final results are significantly affected by the method used in aggregation. The main question is whether and how to weigh individual performance indicators. Verifiable information regarding the true weights is typically unavailable. In practice, subjective expert opinions are usually used to derive weights, which can lead to disagreements (Hatefi & Torabi, 2010). The disagreement can appear when the experts from different areas are included in a poll since they can value criteria differently in accordance with their expertise. Therefore, a proper methodology of the derivation of weights and construction of composite indicators should be employed. From the operations research standpoint, the data envelopment analysis (DEA) and the multiple criteria decision analysis (MCDA) are proper methods for the construction of composite indicators (Zhou & Ang, 2009; Zhou, Ang, & Zhou, 2010). All methods combine the sub-indicators according to their weights, except that the MCDA methods usually require a priori determination of weights, while the DEA determines the weights a posteriori, as a result of model solving. This chapter addresses the DEA as a non-parametric technique, introduced by Charnes, Cooper, and Rhodes (1978), for efficiency measurement of different non-profitable and profitable units. It is lately adopted as an appropriate method for the CI construction due to its several features (Shen, Ruan, Hermans, Brijs, Wets, & Vanhoof, 2011). Firstly, individual performance indicators are combined without a priori determination of weights, and secondly, each unit under observation is assessed taking into consideration the performance of all other units, which is known as the 'benefit of the doubt' (BOD) approach (Cherchye, Moesen, Rogge, & van Puyenbroeck, 2007). The methodological and theoretical aspects and the flaws of the DEA application for the construction of CIs will be discussed in this chapter, starting with the issues related to the application procedure, followed by the issues of real data availability, introducing value judgments, qualitative data, and non-desirable performance indicators. The procedure of a DEA-based CI construction will be illustrated by the case of ranking of different regions of Serbia based on their socio-economic development.

Chapter 6

Composite indicators are emerging in several fields and disciplines as appealing method to synthesize a multitude of information, in a compact, single, and unique way. The process of aggregating heterogeneous information is itself very challenging and exposed to numerous threats. The chapter deepens on the methodological challenges that scientists, analysts, and final users must be aware of for a correct interpretation of the composite indexes. By mean of a worked example on the construction of composite indicators for food security, the chapter concludes that while different normalization and weighting approaches do not alter composite indicators, data imputation and aggregation methods are the most crucial steps: different methods convey very different results. For instance, the adoption of different aggregation procedures may largely alter the rankings based on composite indicators. In sum, the analysis shows that the index construction decisions matter and comment on policy and practical implications for the construction of composite indicators.

Chapter 7

Development is a complex and multidimensional phenomenon. The quantification of such a phenomenon requires indicators that may capture its most important components. In this chapter we present an extensive list of composite indicators of development, identifying their main possible common dimensions: income, income distribution, education, health, employment, infrastructures, values, and environment. We also discuss in detail five recent indices characterized by their comprehensiveness: 1) Regional Quality of Development Index (QUARS) of Sbilanciamoci!; 2) Wellbeing Index (WI) and Wellbeing/Stress Index (WSI) for measuring sustainable development; 3) Gross National Happiness (GNH) from the Center for Bhutan Studies; 4) Bertelsmann Transformation Index (BTI) of Bertelsmann Stiftung; and 5) World competitiveness scoreboard from the Institute for Management Development (IMD).

Chapter 8

The chapter focuses on the development of a socioeconomic index (SEI) using a Principal Components Analysis (PCA) of 26 variables at the Dissemination Area (DA) level for Alberta. First, the importance of socioeconomic factors in understanding child development outcomes is discussed, addressing the micro-macro level influences. Second, a description of the framework is provided along with the statistical procedures. Third, the results are presented, followed by a discussion of the benefits of having a summary measure in understanding kindergartners' developmental outcomes. The five components of SEI explained 56 per cent of the total variation in the overall index. The SEI patterns across Alberta were examined and the index was validated for its associations to the five domains of early child developmental outcomes, physical, social, emotional, language and cognitive skills, and communication and general knowledge. The index emerged as a strong correlate of all five domains with the strength of relationships varying across developmental domains and geography. A major strength of the procedure presented in the study is that it can be applied to different levels of geography and provides meaningful information to developmental research.

Chapter 9

The indicator-based scientific research has recently become a valuable source of information for policymakers, scholars and eventually, civil society. Many socioeconomic spheres are evaluated using composite indicators, whereas governance has not been left behind. Among several assessment measurements oriented on the rule of law and law enforcement, the Rule of Law Index devised by the World Justice Program stands out. Namely, it is a comprehensive and methodologically consistent index which measures the extent to which the countries follow the principles of the rule of law. However, the controversial question of the justification of its equal weighting scheme emerges. The presented study addresses this issue by applying the twofold I-distance approach to propose unbiased weights and an in-depth analysis of the index dynamics. Consequently, the aim of this paper is to scrutinize the Rule of Law Index and to shed light on its methodology. Furthermore, the proposed approach can serve as a foundation for future research on weighting schemes, which are enveloped with subjectivity.

Despite the intensive research on human capital, the debate regarding its measurement is ongoing. In this context, the objective of the present study is to underline the distinction between input and output indicators in human capital measurement, which has not attracted sufficient attention, and to present the importance of indicator selection by explaining the findings obtained. To that end, separate indexes will be developed for input and output indicators to measure the level of human capital for Turkey, and it will be analyzed whether the two index groups developed exhibit significant differences between provinces. In accordance with the purpose of this study, index estimations are made using the PCA method with the 2013 data of 81 provinces in Turkey. Province-based estimations demonstrate that the index values estimated by the input and output indicators produce significantly different conclusions. Therefore, selecting appropriate indicators according to the purpose of the study will enable the analyses to produce more accurate policy implications.

In the context of growing concern over the global environment and related sustainability issues, the purpose of this research is to stimulate discussion about the Environmental Performance Index (EPI) and its necessary role not only in measuring postgraduate students' attitudes about EPI, and its nine categories underpinned, but also, their important role in the development of appropriate curriculum of programs that are about environmental management and sustainable development as well. Further on, the obtained results of the presented research in the paper broaden the understanding of the opportunities for not only the Republic of Serbia but every country as well, in using the EPI methodology as it has a wide applicability in improving environmental pillars of their future sustainability.

Chapter 12

The chapter introduces the Age-friendly City Index as a way of measuring the age-friendliness of urban environments. The proposed index assesses the dimensions of outdoor spaces and transportation as they are perceived and evaluated by older people, residents of the fourteen biggest towns in the Czech Republic. The dimensions and items included in the index are constructed upon the theoretical framework proposed by the World Health Organisation Global Age-friendly Cities Project. Validation of the results of the index is based on experimental open-ended question analysis. The resulting categories confirm the importance of greenery and aesthetics for the age-friendly concept, and confirm the rankings of cities obtained via the composite index. In addition, comparison with similar measures tested in Canada and Hong Kong are discussed, and the necessity of backing up index measures with policy analysis and general structural support is argued for.

Chapter 13

Paulo Nocera Alves Junior, University of São Paulo (USP), Brazil
Enzo Barberio Mariano, São Paulo State University (UNESP), Brazil
Daisy Aparecida do Nascimento Rebelatto, University of São Paulo (USP), Brazil

This chapter addresses problems related to methodological issues, such as data normalization, weighting schemes, and aggregation methods, encountered in the construction of composite indicators to measure socio-economic development and quality of life. It also addresses the use of several Data Envelopment Analysis (DEA) models to solve these problems. The models are discussed and applied in constructing a Human Development Index (HDI), derived from the most recent raw and normalized data, using arithmetic and geometric means to aggregate the indices. Issues related to data normalization and weighting schemes are emphasized. Kendall Correlation was applied to analyze the relationship between ranks obtained by DEA models and HDI. Recommendations regarding the advantages and disadvantages of using DEA models to construct HDI are offered.

Chapter 14

Maja Mitrović, University of Belgrade, Serbia
Maja Marković, University of Belgrade, Serbia
Stefan Zdravković, University of Belgrade, Serbia

This chapter will explore the impact of cognitive skills on education. In the case of OECD (Organisation for Economic Co-operation and Development) countries, it will be examined the relation between the level of education to the economic situation of a state. Case study work is based on a statistical approach of OECD countries ranking, based on The Global Index of Cognitive Skills and Educational Attainment (GICSES) and Ivanovic distance (I-distance). The chapter will be presented to rank these countries based on the value of the global index. Using I-distance method it will be formed a new order, and then it will be carried out a comparative analysis of these two ways of ranking. The aim of the chapter is to present a new approach to the evaluation of a composite indicator based on the multivariate statistical analysis.

Preface

Composite Indicators (CIs) represent an emerging field of study, which occupied the attention of broad academic and general public. In essence, CI represents a compilation of several indicators into one value. This approach proved to be of great use for both policy-makers and public since the results are easily understood; observed entities are ranked, thus making the CI even more appealing. Still, CI could also fail to provide an in-depth performance of observed entities. Also, if the CI is methodologically faulted (data normalization, weighting factors, aggregating procedures, etc.) drawing an inaccurate conclusion is a possible, to say at least. Precisely those are the issues that the Emerging Trends in the Development and Application of Composite Indicators are striving to overcome, making this book a valuable contribution to the everyday policy making activities in the area of composite indicators. The impact of publications to our readers is reflected in building a critical look at the problem to expand their knowledge and establish an unbiased opinion about the observed phenomena. The book induces users' need to create broad ideas and to build their independent views. Critical thinking, developed by our readers, is a real value. Reduction of complex systems to simpler through the use of composite indicators allows us to view a more realistic picture of the problem. A proactive attitude of the users towards the measurement and statistical management is the additional value of this publication. The target audience of this book comprises researchers, developers, university teachers and students, public officials of different countries and governments who are inclined to gain more understanding of the relevance of composite indicators. Throughout the development of methodological issues and their successful implementation in a vast number of applications, government officials and policy makers can redefine and continue to shape the future of composite indicators.

In first chapter, "Measuring Cross-Border Regional Integration with Composite Indicators: The Oresund Integration Index" author points out that earlier papers which aimed at elaborating cross-border regional integration processes have commonly neglected science, technology and innovation (STI) indicators. In particular, probably the most popular composite indicator approach to measuring cross-border regional integration, i.e. the Oresund index, lacks a sub-category for STI. Consequently, by ignoring cross-border innovation and knowledge flows, the Oresund integration index fails to take into account one of the most important drivers of economic growth in cross-border regions. Therefore, a new composite STI indicator (sub-category) was introduced to strengthen the Oresund integration index. The STI indicator itself has been compiled by the author using data concerning from patents, publications, and collaborative R&D projects. The author showed that revised composite indicator was quite capable compared to the existing index. Another contribution is that paper revealed that the Oresund region prospered in STI indicators after the opening of the Bridge. The findings show that this index performs reasonably well in depicting

STI integration, while at the same time remaining simple and straightforward enough to be adopted in other cross-border regions. The author concludes with addressing the need for policy makers to shift its focus on the strongest industries which are present on both sides of the border.

In second chapter "Developing a Sustainable Urban Mobility Index: Methodological Steps" authors emphasize the importance of sustainable urban mobility. Still, mobility considerations are still excessively simplified or even ignored in current sustainability evaluation studies. As a potential remedy to the issue, authors propose a thorough understanding and assessment of the overall performance of the current urban transport system. In this respect, developing a sound sustainable urban mobility index is a must, although by no means an easy task. Authors pinpoint the crucial challenges which range from ascertaining the theoretical framework to making final policy decisions regarding best practices. They provide a guideline for developing such an index, including the essential steps of the methodology. All of the proposed measures must be studied with extra care since they represent the fundamental conditions for making a meaningful evaluation. Authors emphasize the use of the '3Ps' (Planet, People, and Profit) as the triple bottom line for sustainable urban mobility indicator development. In future directions of study, authors state that all these methodological steps will be followed to construct a sustainable urban mobility index for different cities of the world. The idea behind this approach is to verify the feasibility in practice. This is an issue of great concern as such an index will be used to serve as a practical instrument for city governments, transport policy makers, and inhabitants to show the level of sustainability on urban mobility. Consequently, policy makers will be able to identify which aspects cities are doing well, and for which aspects they are falling behind and need further development towards sustainability.

The third chapter titled "Composite Indices in Technology Management: A Critical Approach" discusses the advantages and disadvantages of application of Composite Indicators in the field of Technology Management (TM). By today's continuous and exponential technological growth and development, it is important to manage and follow the trends of technological changes, making technology and innovation management indispensable for achieving sustainable competitiveness at different levels in the economy. The chapter provides a critical comparative analysis of 5 indices concerning the Technology Management, regarding their structure, weighting, and individual components. It also clarifies the role of technology and innovation management performance indicators in the construction of these global indices. Another important focus of the chapter is the analysis of ranks of OECD and BRICS countries for Global Competitiveness Index (GCI), Global Innovativeness Index (GII), and Global Entrepreneurship Index (GEI). Authors analyzed the correlations of GCI and GII component pillars and clusters with the final ranks of countries. One of the key findings was that there is a lack of composite indicators used exclusively for TM performance and that there is an apparent necessity for a globally measured composite index which would be measured independently from other indices. This index could be used as a tool for improving global performance of countries and other entities, which would enable them to achieve high sustainability level.

In fourth chapter "Composite Indicators of a Knowledge Society: Triangulation of Experts Interviews and Factor Analyses", authors point out that the concept of knowledge society (KS) began due to the recognition of the importance of knowledge and information in the development of society. Active knowledge activities such as access, generation, sharing and disseminating are deemed crucial in the knowledge society. These activities which then expanded and multiplied the knowledge determine the vision towards transforming society. This chapter proposes a holistic view of knowledge society based on the development of composite indicators in nine different dimensions. A multi-dimensional approach is comprising human capital, ICT, spirituality, economy, social, institutional and sustainability are proposed as determinants towards achieving a KS. These dimensions are discussed in-depth by the experts in semi-structured interviews and also validated by using Exploratory Factor Analysis (EFA) and Confirmatory Factor Analysis (CFA). The semi-structured interview data are presented in a verbatim manner so as to provide readers with in-depth feedback from the experts. Results of the critical analysis of the interviews showed that the ICT and human capital are two most mentioned terms throughout the interviews with two experts, while the third expert emphasized more on the human development, rather than human capital. As the authors state, the critical dimension of proposed composite indicator is spirituality and the need to look at KS from a religious view. One of the conclusions is that a KS should have a good value system and a healthy culture, a society that uses knowledge to achieve sustainable growth and development, and where there is respect for human rights and human dignity. Results of the EFA and CFA showed that all nine dimensions of Malaysia's KS are statistically significant (ranging from the Human Capital dimension, all the way to Spirituality dimension). Consequently, this chapter contributes to the understanding of composite indicators of knowledge society which can then be used by policy makers for future policy making process.

In fifth chapter "Composite Indicators Construction by Data Envelopment Analysis: Methodological Background", authors give a comprehensive overview of Composite Indicators construction by using the particular method that measures the efficiency of entities, Data Envelopment Analysis (DEA). Besides the dilemma on normalization and aggregation method, one of the main issues that the process of constructing CIs faces is whether and how to weigh individual performance indicators. Verifiable information regarding the real weights of individual indicators is typically unavailable, and in practice subjective expert opinions are usually used to derive weights. However, disagreements on these subjective weights can appear since the experts from different areas are often included in a poll since they can value criteria differently by their expertise. From the operations research standpoint, the Data Envelopment Analysis is a proper method for the construction of Composite Indicators because it combines sub-indicators according to their weights which are determined a posteriori, as a result of model solving. Authors address the Data Envelopment Analysis as a non-parametric technique for efficiency measurement of different non-profitable and profitable units, which is lately adopted as an appropriate method for the CI construction due to its several aspects. Authors illustrated the procedure of a DEA-based CI construction by the case of ranking of different regions of Serbia based on their socio-economic development.

Sixth chapter "Methodological Challenges in Building Composite Indices: Linking Theory to Practice" presents an effort in determining composite indicators for measuring food security. The author underlines composite indicators as a holistic tool to measure complex phenomenon. Still, additional efforts in obtaining substantial theoretical and methodological foundations are needed. The chapter presents an overview of the methods embedded in the construction of composite indexes and pinpoints strengths and weaknesses of different techniques. Measuring complex phenomena such as food security requires not only a broad set of indicators but right methods to integrate all of them into one value. In the chapter, the author emphasizes how suitable may be the analyst's choice of algorithms to compute composite indicators by comparing different techniques to build composite indexes of food security. Results showed that different methods have different impacts on rankings: normalization and weighting are (relatively) less crucial decisions, whereas particular attention has to be paid in choosing the data imputation and aggregation methods. The author also addresses the issue of incorporating the proposed approach in other composite indicators. Also, the author emphasizes the reduced number of alternatives (for each step in the construction of the composite indicator) which have analyzed as a viable future direction study. Authors suggest that, when proposing new composite indexes, the United Nations, the international agencies, academics, and researchers, should pay careful attention to documenting how they transformed raw data into a single index.

Authors of the seventh chapter "Composite Indicators of Development: Some Recent Contributions" present a broad area of potential regarding the application of Composite Indicators in different areas of interest, as well as the diversity of methodologies used to construct them. The primary focus of the chapter is the use of Composite Indicators in measuring the development which is a complex and multidimensional phenomenon. The chapter presents an extensive list of composite indicators of development, identifying their main possible typical dimensions: income, income distribution, education, health, employment, infrastructures, values, and the environment. Among mentioned composite indicators of development, the majority does not completely reflect the multidimensionality inherent in the development phenomenon: 15 and 11 indices out of 54 included only two and three of the different dimensions of development, respectively. Moreover, only five indices out of 54 were characterized by their comprehensiveness regarding dimension coverage, thereby including the crucial dimensions of development. Authors discuss in detail five recent indices, identified by their comprehensiveness: (1) Regional Quality of Development Index (QUARS) of Sbilanciamoci!; (2) Wellbeing Index (WI) and Wellbeing/Stress Index (WSI) for measuring sustainable development; (3) Gross National Happiness (GNH) from the Center for Bhutan Studies; (4) Bertelsmann Transformation Index (BTI) of Bertelsmann Stiftung; and (5) World Competitiveness Scoreboard from the Institute for Management Development (IMD).

In eight chapter, "Constructing a Multidimensional Socioeconomic Index and the Validation of It with Early Child Developmental Outcomes", the author focuses on the development of a socioeconomic index (SEI) using a Principal Components Analysis (PCA) of 26 variables at the Dissemination Area (DA) level for Alberta. First, the importance of socioeconomic factors in understanding child development outcomes is discussed, addressing the micro-macro level influences. Second, a description of the framework is provided along with the statistical procedures. Third, the results are presented, followed by a discussion of the benefits of having a summary measure in understanding kindergartners' developmental outcomes. The SEI patterns across Alberta were examined, and the index was validated for its associations to the five domains of early child developmental outcomes, physical, social, emotional, language and cognitive skills, and communication and general knowledge. The index emerged as a strong correlate of all five domains with the strength of relationships varying across developmental domains and geography. A major strength of the procedure presented in the study is that it can be applied to different levels of geography and provides meaningful information to developmental research. The author anticipates that the model developed in this study will be a valuable tool for judging and deciding on the contextually-based SEI, thereby helping researchers and policymakers in the development of a summary index and application of it in early child development research in Canada. The index, undoubtedly, will significantly predict early child developmental outcomes of physical, social, emotional, language and cognitive skills, and communication and general knowledge in the province at both the smaller and larger levels of geography.

Authors of the ninth chapter "The Rule of Law Index: Is It Really Impartial? A Twofold Multivariate I-Distance Approach" describe the application of composite indicators in the field of law. They highlight that many socioeconomic spheres are evaluated using Composite Indicators, whereas governance being among them. Namely, governments acknowledged the benefits of statistical data and are now turning towards and relying on them. Authors single out the Rule of Law Index devised by the World Justice Program, as a comprehensive and methodologically consistent index which measures the extent to which the countries follow the principles the rule of law. However, they raise the controversial question of the justification of its equal weighting scheme. The chapter addresses this issue by applying the twofold I-distance approach to propose unbiased weights and an in-depth analysis of the index dynamics. The newly proposed weighting scheme gives justification for equal weighting of the index factors of the Rule of Law Index but provides evidence that the same does not apply for index sub-factors. Authors nominate the approach as a foundation for future research on weighting schemes of composite indices.

In the tenth chapter, "Comparison of Input and Output Indicators in Measuring Human Capital: An Analysis at Provincial Level for Turkey" authors point out that despite the intensive research on human capital, the debate regarding its measurement is ongoing. In particular, the distinction between input and output indicators in human capital measurement has not attracted sufficient attention in the current literature on the matter. Author aimed at presenting the importance of indicator selection and thus developed separate indexes for input (HCI) and output indicators (HCO) to measure the level of human capital for Turkey. Chapter demonstrated that input and output indicators may produce different results in measuring human capital. In the analysis conducted in 81 provinces in Turkey, the results showed that regions with a higher level of income and a higher standard of industrialization have high scores on the output index. Surprisingly, those are provinces with the lower scores on the input index. The majority of the provinces that have lower scores on the HCI, despite having far higher rankings on the HCO, are in the Marmara Region. Another remarkable point is that provinces are ranking in the bottom positions based on HCI scores also rank in the bottom positions based on HCO scores. In other words, no change is observed in provinces ranking in the bottom positions base on both indices. The findings of the study are expected to contribute significantly regarding a better analysis of the current situation and development of policy proposals.

The eleventh chapter "The Delphi Method Application in the Analysis of Postgraduate Students' Attitudes on the Environmental Performance Index" suggests that one of the suitable fields of application of Composite Indicators is the endless strive towards the preservation and sustaining the environment. The purpose of this chapter is to stimulate discussion about the Environmental Performance Index (EPI) and its necessary role in measuring postgraduate students' attitudes about EPI and its nine categories underpinned. Authors also address EPI's significant role in the development of appropriate curriculums of programs that are about environmental management and sustainable development. The analyses were performed by using the Delphi survey, which can be a useful tool for gaining the results of judgment in ranking categories of EPI by postgraduate students, in circumstances where certain limits exist in their knowledge about EPI, existing empirical methods and data, and their practical environmental knowledge and knowledge for sustainable development. Authors imply that the obtained results of the presented research broaden the understanding of the opportunities in using the EPI methodology because it is widely applicable in improving environmental pillars of their future sustainability.

In twelfth chapter, "How Age-Friendly Are Cities? Measuring Age-Friendliness with a Composite Index", the author introduces the Age-friendly City Index as a way of measuring the age-friendliness of urban environments. The need for measurement of age-friendliness in urban areas proved to be of great concern for policy makers. All of it is done to form a supportive physical and social environments within aging societies. The case study, a survey conducted on residents of the fourteen biggest towns in the Czech Republic, pointed out the assessment of outdoor spaces and transportation as they are perceived and evaluated by older people. Throughout the process, the theoretical framework proposed by the World Health Organisation Global Age-friendly Cities Project has been used as a guideline. The results confirm the importance of greenery and aesthetics for the age-friendly concept. Still, considerable variability among Czech towns in these respects was highlighted. Results suggested that the cities in leading positions have pro-active policy actors. They are fully committed to encapsulating the local government and social policy departments. Consequently, they are maximizing the use of their authority and political support for the development and innovation of social services and support for the active aging activity. Authors outline that additional efforts are needs, so the index is backed with policy analysis and government support. Also, the proposed approach of ranking of cities proved to be a good option in a quest for formulating age-friendly policies. Moreover, age-friendly index measurement must be repeated over time to understand the dynamics of development within the city.

The authors of thirteenth chapter, "Using Data Envelopment Analysis to Construct Human Development Index", focused on addressing the issues related to methodological obstacles encountered in the construction of composite indicators to measure socio-economic development and quality of life. The need for employment of quantitative methods, such as data envelopment analysis, to solve these problems proved to be of great concern. As a case study, the models are discussed and applied in constructing a human development index. In the chapter, both most recent raw and normalized data has been used, while as aggregation method, authors used both arithmetic and geometric means. Empirical evidence has shown that the aggregation method has the least while the weighting scheme has the most influence on the rankings. Also, authors noted that a data type has a significant effect on rankings. Authors pinpointed important factors to consider while selecting and adapting a prospective alternative to the present methodology for calculating the Human Development Index. As outlined in the chapter, main findings of the case study can be easily applied in the construction of any composite indicator, thus providing the options for incorporating obtained outcomes in other composite indicators guidelines.

In the final chapter "Statistical Approach for Ranking OECD Countries Based on Composite GICSES Index and I-Distance Method" authors present one of the many possibilities regarding the application and the enhancement of Composite Indicators, by exploring the impact of cognitive skills on education. Authors examined the influence that the level of education had to the economic situation of a state, by performing the research on the set of OECD (Organisation for Economic Co-operation and Development) countries. The case study in this chapter is based on a statistical approach of OECD countries ranking, based on The Global Index of Cognitive Skills and Educational Attainment (GICSES) and Ivanovic distance (I-distance) method. The OECD countries are initially ranked based on the results of investment in education by the concept of a composite index, whose indicators are integrated in order of their evaluation, according to an equal weighting scheme. Authors applied the I-distance method as an alternative to GICSES, in a view to improving the ranking of the observed countries, since it eliminates subjectivity in rankings. The countries are ranked based on the values of the GICSES, and the I-distance method is used to form a new order of variables. The aim of the chapter is to point out potential shortcomings of subjectively chosen weighting factors of the GICSES ranking methodologies and to present a new approach to the evaluation of Composite Indicators. Authors' approach provides detailed information on how each of the GICSES indicators contributes to the final positions and emphasizes crucial indicators in the process of classification.

Veljko Jeremic
University of Belgrade, Serbia

Zoran Radojicic
University of Belgrade, Serbia

Marina Dobrota
University of Belgrade, Serbia

Chapter 1
Measuring Cross–Border Regional Integration with Composite Indicators:
The Oresund Integration Index

Teemu Makkonen
University of Surrey, UK & University of Southern Denmark, Denmark

ABSTRACT

Earlier quantitative studies on cross-border regional integration processes have commonly neglected Science, Technology, and Innovation (STI) indicators: even the most notable example of a composite indicator approach to measuring cross-border regional integration, i.e. the Oresund index, lacks a sub-category for STI. Consequently, by ignoring cross-border innovation and knowledge flows, the Oresund integration index fails to take into account one of the most important drivers of economic growth in cross-border regions. Therefore, a new composite STI indicator (sub-category) was introduced to strengthen the Oresund integration index. This was compiled from patent, publication and collaborative R&D project data. The findings show that this index performs reasonably well in depicting STI integration, while at the same time remaining simple and straightforward enough to be adopted in other cross-border regions.

INTRODUCTION

Cross-border regions (CBRs) and their integration processes have been in the eye of political and scholarly debates for decades. However, measurement problems, related to data availability issues (not the lack of data *per se*, but the laborious process of gathering this data) and the choice of appropriate indicators to describe integration, have persistently hampered the quantitative investigation of these regions. Therefore, most quantitative studies on the subject have been restricted to studying a distinct feature of integration (with a limited set of individual indicators) including such aspects as the impacts of infrastructure projects on cross-border accessibility (Knowles & Matthiessen, 2009), labour market dynamics and commuting behaviour (Schmidt, 2005) or the more intangible issues of cultural and linguistic similarity (Bucken-

DOI: 10.4018/978-1-5225-0714-7.ch001

Knapp, 2001; Gregersen, 2003). An interesting exception has been developed in the Danish-Swedish CBR of Oresund (Öresund for Swedes and Øresund for Danes); namely the Oresund integration index (Öresundskomiteen, 2013) – henceforward referred to as "the Index" – calculated largely on the basis of the raw values of indicators in the Öresund database (Örestat, 2015).

The local authorities (that is, the Oresund Committee) responsible for raising awareness as well as studying and facilitating cross-border regional integration have collected data on various sub-categories of cross-border regional integration dating back to 2000, when the Oresund bridge (and a tunnel) – henceforward "the Bridge" – crossing the Oresund strait – henceforward "the Strait" – was opened, which significantly reduced travel times across the Strait, compared to ferry-traffic. In addition to the Oresund region being one of the most commonly used examples of cross-border regional integration (Nauwelaers, Maguire & Ajmone Marsan, 2013), the Index is exceptional since it is the only example of a CBR, where a time-series approach has been employed to study cross-border regional integration, together with composite indicators. In contrast, the other existing examples of studies focusing on cross-border regional integration commonly apply a cross-sectional approach with fixed years of analysis and a limited number of indicators (e.g. BAK Basel Economics, 2008; Decoville, Durand, Sohn & Walther, 2013). The Index uses a weighting scheme that allows the inclusion of various indicators of integration into a single composite indicator. This Index is then compared to the base year, 2000, to indicate, whether the region has moved towards, what can be labelled, a more integrated CBR or has drifted apart despite the improvements in infrastructure, as well as the political will and emphasis laid on promoting integration. The Index consists of five distinct sub-categories of integration, containing from three up to five individual indicators, including:

1. Labour markets,
2. Housing markets,
3. Business,
4. Culture, and
5. Transport and communication.

Despite being a notable example of time-series data and composite indicator approaches to cross-border regional integration, the Index still lacks a component (or sub-category) that takes into account what is arguably one of the most important drivers of regional economic development and competitiveness, namely the component (or sub-category) of *science, technology and innovation (STI)*. In short, as noted by Nauwelears et al. (2013), the Index fails to capture cross-border knowledge and innovation flows, against a background of STI in cross-border regional integration and economic development in CBRs having been highlighted as essential in, for example the emerging field of cross-border regional innovation systems (CBRIS) (Lundquist & Trippl, 2009). However, despite the well-developed conceptual background which can potentially guide the measuring of the innovativeness of CBRs, the literature on CBRIS has rarely quantified cross-border regional integration in terms of scientific and innovation collaboration.

Therefore, the aim of this paper is to strengthen the Index by adding a new sub-category, which specifically addresses the essential parts of the economy related to STI indicators in a cross-border context. The new sub-category was constructed from relevant indicators, also recommended by the OECD (2013), collected from existing databases, including:

1. Cross-border co-patents [OECD's Regional Patent (REGPAT) database (see OECD, 2008)],
2. Cross-border co-publications [Web of Science (WoS) database (see Thompson Reuters, 2015)] and
3. Cross-border research and development (R&D) projects [Community Research and Development Information Service (CORDIS) database (see European Commission, 2015)].

In line with this, an appropriate weighting scheme was suggested. Data was gathered from the year 2000 onwards corresponding to the Index. Subsequently, the composition, weighting scheme and limitations of the Index and the new STI sub-category are discussed, followed by the findings from the composite STI index. The results are presented together with comparisons to existing data on cross-border regional integration in the Oresund region. Thus, the paper aims at improving the Index and function as a reference for other regions and researchers interested in further quantitative works on CBRIS to apply, improve and develop composite indicators for measuring cross-border regional integration. This directly corresponds to the research agenda set by Nauwelaers et al. (2013) who stated that: "a more innovation-driven Oresund would need to be supported by an extension of the coverage of the Öresund database and a deepening of Örestat's work to cover innovation" (p. 10).

BACKGROUND: CROSS-BORDER REGIONAL INTEGRATION IN THE ORESUND REGION

According to the CBRIS literature, integration is one of the most important success factors for CBRs in relation to sustainable economic development, innovativeness and competiveness. Such cross-border regional integration should proceed throughout the economy, and not just in a few selective parts or segments, within both public and private institutions (Lundquist & Trippl, 2009; 2013; Trippl, 2010). It includes, for example, such dimensions as accessibility and mobility, labour markets, innovation networking and R&D collaboration as well as integration at the economic (e.g. trade), social (e.g. community or sense of obligation), and cultural (e.g. language understanding) levels. It also includes institutions and governance, for example accommodating common formal and informal rules and establishing collective cross-border decision making mechanisms (Nye, 1968; Nelles, 2011; Lundquist & Trippl, 2013). While it would take a long time for any conscious attempts or initiatives to have an impact on the more intangible aspects of integration such as institutional changes, social acceptance of integration or cultural coherence, one of the most visible symbols and straightforward ways of initiating integration in CBRs is building new, or improving existing, transportation infrastructure links (Westlund & Bygvrå, 2002; Lundquist & Trippl, 2013; Durand & Nelles, 2014). In the Oresund region (consisting of three administrative regions – the Capital Region of Denmark (including Copenhagen) and Region Zealand (including Roskilde) on the Danish side, and Scania County (including Malmö and Lund) on the Swedish side (Figure 1) – this kind of process was manifested in the Bridge connecting Denmark and Sweden, for the first time, via a fixed transportation link. Prior to the opening of the 16 km long fixed link between Copenhagen and Malmö in 2000, direct transportation between the two countries, and the 3 785 000 inhabitants of the Oresund region, was only possible via ferries and aircrafts (Örestat, 2013).

In terms of transport and labour markets, already during the first few years after the Bridge was opened Matthiessen (2004) and Schmidt (2005) indicated that there had been a modest positive post-bridge shift in functional cross-border integration in terms of transportation flows, migration patterns and commuting behaviour. However, there were sharp national differences in the level of support from the local inhabit-

Figure 1. Map of the Oresund region (highlighted in grey)

ants on the opposing sides of the border; Swedes being more pro than Danes towards the construction of a bi-national city (Bucken-Knapp, 2001; 2002; Nauwelaers et al., 2013). Additionally, as stated by Lundquist and Winther (2006), due to totally different national development paths and the positions of Copenhagen and Malmö in the urban and regional systems of their respective countries: "only a limited part of the development in the Oresund region can be linked to the effects of economic integration" (p. 126). Subsequently, the increased interaction across the Strait was much lower than expected and failed to meet the ("over-optimistic") rail and road traffic forecasts that were envisioned prior to the opening of the Bridge (Matthiessen, 2004; Knowles, 2006). The same applies to tourism and cross-border shopping behaviour, where only a modest increase, mostly due to differences in alcohol taxes, was observed in the number of travellers and shopping trips after the opening of the Bridge (Westlund & Bygvrå, 2002; Bygvrå & Westlund, 2005). These notions have given rise to a body of literature discussing the mismatch between the branding of the Oresund region as a highly integrated "cross-border hub" contra the reality of the majority of European CBRs being "regions (*only*) on paper" (Paasi, 2002). For example Hospers (2006) has maintained that in reality the Oresund region is merely a loosely integrated "imagined space".

Notwithstanding this critique, there has been subsequent growth in traffic volumes across the Bridge. Knowles and Matthiessen (2009) have attributed this growth to tax agreements encouraging commuting, discounted tolls/prices for crossing the Bridge and complementary labour and housing market opportunities (discussed in greater detail below). Nowadays an average of 91,500 individuals, about 18,000 commuters and 24,700 vehicles travel across the Strait each day; 76 per cent of the individual journeys are via the Bridge, while the ferry link between Elsinore (Helsingør in Danish) and Helsingborg accounts for the remainder. However, the cross-border regional integration in the Oresund region seems to have reached its peak just before the economic crisis of 2008 (Nauwelaers et al., 2013; Öresundskomiteen, 2013) and since then the number of border crossings have gradually declined (Örestat, 2013). Nevertheless, a recent socio-economic assessment of the benefits of the Bridge (Knudsen & Rich, 2013) revealed that it has generated significant consumer benefits, largely driven by labour market effects, i.e. business travel and commuting. As a side note, commuting is heavily one-sided in the Oresund region; it is primarily directed from Sweden to Denmark (Örestat, 2013). This is mainly due to two reasons:

1. Labour markets, i.e. Danish companies' labour shortages, higher salaries in Denmark and higher unemployment in Scania; and
2. Housing markets, i.e. significant housing price differences prompting many Danes to move to Sweden while still continuing to work in (and commute to) Denmark.

In the near future, commuting behaviour in the CBR is expected to be driven increasingly by real labour market integration rather than housing market integration due to the contemporary rise in unemployment in Denmark and the flattening of house price differentials across the Strait (Nauwelaers et al., 2013; Örestat, 2013).

However when it comes to the business sector of the CBR, a case study of the Oresund medi-tech plastics industry (Sornn-Friese & Sørensen, 2005) has shown that the development of cross-border inter-firm collaboration has remained tardy due to high (real or perceived) switching costs associated with changing collaboration partners, suppliers etc. Accordingly, in terms of STI: the long-term vision of the region includes the theme of "knowledge and innovation" (Öresundskomiteen, 2010), but this vision has not been fully implemented by the local authorities (Nauwelaers et al., 2013). Therefore, it is not all that surprising that studies of the cross-border Medicon Valley biotech cluster (Coenen, Moodysson & Asheim, 2004; Moodysson & Jonsson, 2007) have shown only limited rates of cross-border innovation collaboration, measured in terms of cross-border co-publications and co-patents among the biotech firms of the Oresund region. Nevertheless, T. Hansen and R. Hansen (2006) have observed an overall rate of growth in the number of cross-border co-authored scientific articles, which, in comparison to selected benchmark regions, indicate: "a growing integration of the biotech sector in the Oresund region" (p. 241). Accordingly, Lundquist and Trippl (2009) have pinpointed that there already seem to be relatively high levels of cross-border knowledge sharing in the Oresund region, at least in distinctive high-tech fields such as biotechnology and life sciences.

More recently, however, T. Hansen (2013) has shown that the observed "growing integration" seems to hold only within these few specific industries and scientific fields. In fact, when taking into account the total number of cross-border co-publications between the Danish and Swedish part of the Oresund region, the growth has remained relatively low; firstly, compared to the development of collaboration with other major research hubs; and secondly, compared to the much higher increase in Oresund's intra-regional cross-border co-authorships in the biotech sector. Accordingly, Oresund's biotech industry has been supported by a targeted policy effort "channelled" through the Medicon Valley Alliance, which had actually started operating a few years before the Bridge was constructed. The Medicon Valley Alliance is a non-profit, Oresund-based, membership organisation, which originally started as an Interreg II project, promoting collaboration within the CBR in the biotech and life sciences. It has 250 members, including universities, hospitals, businesses, regional governments, etc., that together employ circa 140,000 workers. Consequently, T. Hansen (2013) concluded his study by indicating that improvements in the physical infrastructure connecting opposing sides of the border can significantly enhance the cross-border regional integration of (at least certain) industries and scientific domains in CBRs, but only when accompanied by designated cross-border policies. These efforts should be sustained, since the temporal character of policy support measures is one of the main barriers hindering the development of innovations, for example within Oresund's cleantech industry (Kiryushin, Mulloth & Iakovleva, 2013; Nauwelaers et al., 2013). To conclude, here the focus was explicitly placed on the case study region at hand, i.e. the Oresund region; for comparative discussions summing up research on other CBRs *vis-à-vis* integration see, for example, van Houtum (2000), De Sousa (2013) and Sohn (2014).

MAIN FOCUS: THE ORESUND INTEGRATION INDEX

The Index allows the inclusion of various different indicators of integration in a single composite indicator. Thus, when compared to the base year, i.e. index year $2000 = 100$, it is possible to draw conclusion concerning the integration processes in the CBR, i.e. whether the Oresund region has become more or less integrated in the cross-border context in terms of the five sub-categories of the Index, namely:

1. Labour markets,
2. Housing markets,
3. Business,
4. Culture, and
5. Transport and communication.

Each of these sub-categories has between three to five individual indicators. The statistics applied to compile the basic indices are mainly derived from the Öresund database. Additionally, to remove spurious trends and cyclical movements, the indices are adjusted by comparable indices that reflect the overall domestic developments in Denmark/Sweden (Table 1). In short, the basic index is divided by the comparable index to obtain the adjusted basic index (OECD, 2013; Öresundskomiteen, 2013). Furthermore, the five sub-categories have equal weights in the total Index. To avoid situations whereby a change in an individual indicator, covering only a few units/persons, could dramatically alter the whole sub-category, the individual indicators are assigned a weight reflecting their importance (Table 1). Justifications for the weighting scheme can be found in the publications by OECD (2013) and Öresundskomiteen (2013).

Despite being an excellent example of measuring cross-border regional integration by utilising a time-series approach and composite indicators, the Index also has some critical shortcomings in relation to the contemporary state of the art CBRIS literature. First, while having the aim of reflecting all the relevant areas of cross-border regional integration, in reality the choice of the individual indicators is actually based on and heavily restricted by data availability (OECD, 2013). Thus, it could be argued that in many cases the choice of the individual indicators is less than optimal. Secondly, the Index fails to capture cross-border knowledge and innovation flows that could be measured with STI indicators. Since, enhanced cross-border innovation collaboration has been deemed essential for successful cross-border development futures in the CBRIS literature (Lundquist & Trippl, 2009), the fact that they are not taken into account in the Index hinders the development and monitoring of a more innovation-driven Oresund region (Nauwelaers et al., 2013). By introducing a new STI sub-category (discussed below), this paper aims to make an original contribution to tackling the latter shortcoming.

Table 1. Basic and comparable indices of the Oresund integration index

Weights	Basic Indices	Comparable Indices
20%	**Labour Market**	
40%	Commuters across the Oresund strait	Number of domestic commuters across the municipal borders
15%	Interest in working on the other side of the Oresund	Interest in taking a new job
40%	Number of Danes and Swedes working and living in the neighbouring country	Number of persons working and living in the Oresund region
5%	Number of Danish and Swedish students in the neighbouring country	Total numbers of students in the Oresund region
20%	**Housing Market**	
15%	Migration over the Oresund strait	Domestic migration between municipalities in the Oresund region
15%	Interest in migrating to the other side of the Oresund strait	Difference in housing prices
70%	Number of Danes and Swedes living in the other country	Population in the Oresund region
20%	**Business**	
25%	Trade between Denmark and Sweden	Total foreign trade in Denmark and Sweden
25%	Lorries across the Oresund strait	Domestic transport by lorries
25%	Investments, Danish in Sweden and Swedish in Denmark	Consumption price index
25%	Number of companies owned by the neighbouring country	Total foreign-owned companies in Denmark and Sweden
20%	**Culture**	
20%	Language understanding	
20%	Use of the neighbouring country's TV channels	Total TV use in Denmark and Sweden
20%	Danish-Swedish new marriages registered	Total new Danish or Swedish marriages registered
40%	Nights spent at hotels in the neighbouring country	Total nights spent in the Oresund region
20%	**Transport and Communication**	
41%	Personal cars on the Oresund bridge	Domestic development in road traffic
31%	Train travellers on the Oresund bridge	Number of passenger-kilometres in train in Denmark and Sweden
22%	Travellers between Elsinore and Helsingborg	Domestic development in road traffic
5%	Passengers from Southern Sweden at Copenhagen Airport	Total passengers at Copenhagen Airport
1%	Danish passengers travelling from Malmö Airport	Total passengers at Malmö Airport

OECD, 2013; Öresundskomiteen, 2013.

SOLUTIONS AND RECOMMENDATIONS: THE COMPOSITE STI INDEX

Cross-Border Co-Patents

Cross-border co-patents measure the level of technological cross-border collaboration among firms, R&D centres and organisations in a given CBR (OECD, 2013). While cross-border co-patents are commonly utilized as an indicator of cross-border innovation collaboration at the regional level in Europe (Lata, Scherngell & Brenner, 2013; 2015), it has been rarely used when discussing the cross-border regional integration process of the Oresund region (Moodysson & Jonsson, 2007). This is probably largely due to data availability issues related to the geographical scope of the Oresund region, which does not fit well with comparison made on the "official" NUTS-regions level: the Danish side has two NUTS-2 regions comprised of six NUTS-3 regions whereas the Swedish side is covered by a single NUTS-3 region. Therefore, this kind of data is not readily available from, for example, Eurostat's statistical databases. Here the data for basic and comparable indices were gathered by using the REGPAT database. By searching the address details in the inventor field of patents applications, the REGPAT database was utilized to identify first, cross-border co-patents between the Danish and Swedish sides of the CBR and second, the total number of cross-border co-patents between Denmark and Sweden (Table 2).

Cross-Border Co-Publications

Cross-border co-publications measure the level of scientific cross-border collaboration among research institutions in a given CBR (OECD, 2013). The indicator has been in a wide use, largely due to the existence of convenient publication databases, when measuring cross-border regional integration processes in certain industries and scientific fields in the Oresund region (Coenen et al., 2004; Hansen, T. & Hansen, R., 2006; Moodysson & Jonsson, 2007; Hansen, T., 2013). Here the data for basic and comparable indices were collected from the WoS database. The names of the municipalities and towns belonging to the Oresund region were used to identify first, cross-border co-publications between the Danish and the Swedish side of the CBR and second, the total number of scientific article publications in the CBR (Table 2).

Cross-Border Collaborative R&D Projects

Cross-border collaborative R&D projects measure the intensity of cross-border collaboration among research organisations in a given CBR (OECD, 2013). While having several European benchmarks to take advantage of (Lata et al., 2013; 2015), to the best of the author's knowledge this type of data has not been utilized previously in analyses of cross-border regional integration in the Oresund region. As with patents, this is probably principally due to data availability issues (caused not by the lack of R&D project data *per se*, but by the laborious nature of data gathering). However, the data can be mined from existing sources. Here the primary public repository comprising information on European Union (EU) funded R&D projects, i.e. the CORDIS database, was utilized to produce the basic and comparable indices. The geographical locations and names of the participating organisations were used to identify first, the number of (starting) cross-border collaborative R&D-projects between the Danish and Swedish side of the CBR and second, the total number of (starting) R&D projects in the CBR (Table 2).

Table 2. Basic and comparable indices of the science, technology, and innovation sub-category

Weights	Basic Index	Comparable Index
N/A	Science, Technology, and Innovation	
50%	Cross-border co-patents across the Oresund strait	Cross-border co-patents between Denmark and Sweden
25%	Cross-border co-publications (scientific articles) across the Oresund strait	Total number of scientific article publications in the Oresund region
25%	Cross-border collaborative R&D projects across the Oresund strait	Total participation in R&D projects in the Oresund region

Weighting Scheme

As in the case of the Index, the individual indicators in the STI sub-category were assigned weights to reflect their importance (see also Freudenberg, 2003) *vis-à-vis* innovation and (potential) further regional economic development. Based on existing knowledge of the "pay-offs" from innovation related activities, the weighting scheme takes into account that while patents are not necessarily linked to actual innovations, introduced into the market, they have been commonly utilized to depict the output side of innovation in economic analyses on the geography of innovation. In contrast, R&D and scientific publications have usually been seen as input indicators of innovation (Hagerdoorn & Cloodt, 2003; Makkonen & van der Have, 2013; Carvalho, N., Carvalho, L. & Nunes, 2015). Therefore, while acknowledging the simplicity of the solution, the individual indicators of the new STI sub-category receive the following weights: co-patents; 50%, co-publications; 25% and collaborative R&D projects; 25% (Table 2). The weighting scheme applied here is generally in line with the existing literature: for example, with the weighting scheme, based on fuzzy set theory and survey results of expert opinions in the field of STI, proposed by Moon and Lee (2005).

As stated by Frenken (2002), an increase in "the number of collaborations is, in itself, not an indication of integration". Rather the question is whether the increase is explained by general phenomenon or whether it truly signals "a more integrated pattern of collaborations" (pp. 347–348). For example, if the total number of scientific publications in the Oresund region is increasing, a similar increase in the number of cross-border co-publications would be more likely to be explained by this general trend than by a process of integration. Therefore, similar to the Index, the composite STI index for 2000–2012 (index year 2000 = 100) was derived by adjusting (dividing) the basic index with comparable one, then weighting and adding them together. Additionally, the STI sub-category was merged into the Index with equal weights (the combined index in Figure 3).

Limitations

The limitations of the new STI sub-category include the following well-known shortcomings common to composite STI indicators:

- Firstly, not all innovative activities captured by the proxy indicators used in this study actually lead to successful innovations. Thus, rather than measuring the collaboration that has actually led to cross-border innovations, the STI sub-category measures more the input side of innovation. However, data on actual innovations is hard to come by. For example, while in Sweden researchers from Lund University have compiled an extensive database on actual regional innovation counts (Sjöö, Taalbi, Kander & Ljungberg, 2014), as reported in trade and industrial journals, Denmark lacks this type of rich data. The European Community Innovation Surveys also do not provide data at the detailed geographical scales required to compile statistics that could be used in the Oresund region.
- Secondly, regional patent statistics suffer from a commonly identified limitation: patents are normally applied by headquarters and, thus, not necessary by the subsidiaries where the R&D activities leading to the invention were actually conducted (Etemad & Séguin Dulude, 1987). Therefore, a decision was made to use the inventor (instead of applicant) level in identifying cross-border patents. The inventor level is not free of its own shortcomings, e.g. "false" cross-border patents

caused by inventor movement can potentially skew the numbers of genuine international collaboration (Bergek & Bruzelius, 2010). However, it helps to overcome the "headquarter-bias" by focusing on the inter-personal knowledge flows between people who have *de facto* worked on the patent.

- Thirdly, bibliometric indicators, such as publications data, are error-prone (Luukkonen, Tijssen, Persson & Sivertsen, 1993). This is due, for example, to typographical errors and different name variants of towns. However, it is also quite straightforward to include several name variants in the data collection procedures in geographically limited case study contexts such as the Oresund region.

- Fourthly, as in the case of the Index (Table 1), the weighting scheme of this study (Table 2) can be considered to be arbitrary even though it is in line with earlier studies (e.g. Moon & Lee, 2005). However, after compiling the dataset, and given that new knowledge would arise to suggest otherwise, i.e. differing weights for the individual indicators, the analysis is simple enough to be replicated relatively easily with alternative weights.

In short: the choice of which innovation indicators to incorporate, errors in the data collection process, the weighting scheme and the methods to construct composite indicators will all have substantial consequences on the results of the analysis (Kleinknecht, van Montfort & Brouwer, 2002; Grupp & Mogee, 2004; Grupp & Schubert, 2010; Makkonen & van der Have, 2013; Kozłowski, 2015). However, due to the lack of convenient output indicators for innovation, the applied indicators and databases utilized here, which are all in common use in STI studies (Lata et al., 2015), present a generally acceptable "compromise". Furthermore, every step of the bibliometric data collection processes was taken with utmost care to minimize errors: considering the sheer total number of identified publications (over 130,000) and R&D-projects (over 3,000) in the dataset, the remaining errors can be considered trivial. In addition, when applying composite innovation indicators and commonly accepted input (and output) indicators of innovation, as in the study at hand, one can be fairly confident that, at the very least, the selected indicators will contain information on differing phases of the innovation process. Thus, when combined, they are likely to lead to a more comprehensive picture and more robust conclusions than if relying solely on a single indicator (Hagerdoorn & Cloodt, 2003; Paas & Poltimäe, 2012).

The Composite STI Index with Comparisons to the Oresund Integration Index

Figure 2 presents the individual basic, comparable and adjusted scores for co-patents, co-publications and collaborative R&D projects. This demonstrates the importance of adjusting the basic indices by talking into account comparable ones. Otherwise, there is the problem that general (national) trends could be confused with the actual effects of integration (Lundquist & Winther, 2006): for example, if there is a steady year-to-year increase in a comparable index, a corresponding increase in a basic index could mostly be explained by this general trend, hence the need to adjust it. As a general observation, there has been an almost steady increase in cross-border co-publications, while there has been more year-to-year variation in cross-border co-patents and collaborative R&D projects. This variation, which is in line with fluctuations in the sub-categories of the Index (Öresundskomiteen, 2015), will influence the composite STI index, as discussed below.

In general, the composite STI index follows the Index, but with some notable exceptions (Figure 3). It seems that the integration effects, which were (likely) associated with the opening of the Bridge, were

Figure 2. The basic, comparable and adjusted scores for cross-border A) co-patents, B) co-publications and C) collaborative R&D projects in the Oresund region (index year 2000 = 100)

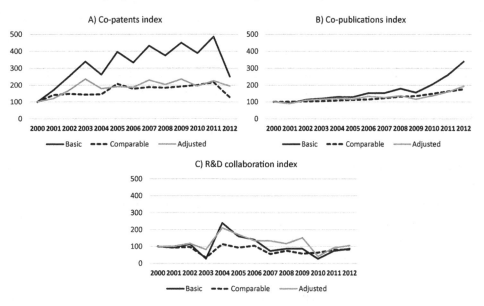

more straightforwardly transferred to STI than to overall cross-border regional integration. According to T. Hansen (2013) this is partly due to the supporting policy measures which facilitated STI integration in the Oresund region. There was already a significant upsurge in the composite STI index in 2001–2003, while overall cross-border regional integration moved more steadily towards its peak in 2008 (index

Figure 3. The Oresund integration index (Öresundskomiteen, 2013) and the composite science, technology, and innovation (STI) index compared (index year 2000 = 100)

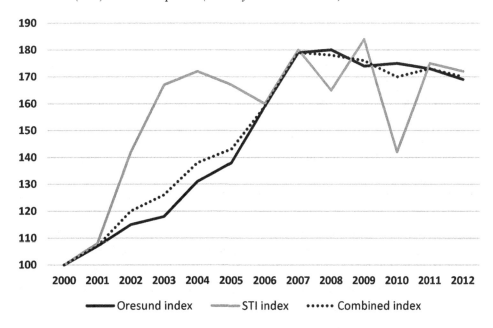

score = 180). The composite STI index reached its peak a year later in 2009 (index score = 184). The combined index peaks in 2007 with a value of 179. After 2008–2009, the Index and the composite STI index declined to 169 and 172 respectively in 2012, while the combined index decreased to 170 in the same period. Adding the composite STI index into the picture shows that when cross-border innovation collaboration is taken into account, the process of integration in the Oresund region seems to accelerate somewhat more quickly in the early years (2001–2003) of the observation period, but then slows down to follow the general pattern of the overall Index. This has raised concerns that the integration of the Oresund region could be in crisis, although the most recent data and forecasts provide cautious signs that integration is likely to start deepening in the near future after years of downturn and stagnation (Öresundskomiteen, 2015).

Additionally, there was a sudden year-long downward surge in the composite STI index in 2010. It would be tempting to consider that this indicates a definite sign of weaknesses in the methodology inherent to composite indicators, or is the result of random variations in the dataset. However, the downward surge was mainly caused by the record-low number of new cross-border collaborative R&D projects at the same time as there was a relative slowdown in cross-border co-patents and a (gradual) recovery from a decrease in the number of cross-border co-publications a year earlier (Figure 2). Therefore, 2010 really was a period of exceptionally low cross-border STI collaboration rather than an anomaly resulting from methodological or data issues. Furthermore, the fact that the most recent decrease in the number of cross-border co-patents in 2012 is not obviously evident in the composite STI index supports the notion (cf. Paas & Poltimäe, 2012) that utilising composite indicators is a way of overcoming some of the limitations of using single indicators. Firstly, this drop was also an EU-wide trend (Eurostat, 2015) and, thus, was already absorbed, to a certain degree, by adjusting the index. Secondly, since individual indicators can be prone to arbitrary year-to-year variations, the weighting scheme ensured that this abrupt downturn did not dramatically alter the entire STI index.

FUTURE RESEARCH DIRECTIONS AND CONCLUSION

Earlier studies on cross-border regional integration processes have largely been restricted to studying the more tangible features of integration (e.g. labour markets dynamics, commuting, etc.), while neglecting STI integration mainly due to not so much the lack of STI data *per se*, but the laborious nature of the data collection. Moreover, even the most notable example of a composite indicator approach to measuring cross-border regional integration, i.e. the Oresund integration index, lacks a sub-category for STI. This is regrettable since, by omitting innovation and knowledge flows, the Index fails to take into account one of the most important drivers of regional economic growth. Therefore, this paper has introduced a new composite indicator (sub-category) in order to measure STI integration in the case of the Oresund region; this was compiled from patent, publication and collaborative R&D project data.

The shortcomings common to composite STI indicators were discussed together with ways of coping with these. The findings show that the revised composite indicator is relatively effective in depicting the process of integration *vis-à-vis* STI indicators, as well as when it is compared to the existing overall Index. Accordingly, while not entirely consistent with earlier industry-specific case studies (e.g. Moodysson & Jonsson, 2007; T. Hansen, 2013) showing only limited rates of cross-border innovation collaboration in the Oresund region, the findings of this paper clearly show that in terms of STI the Oresund region has become more integrated after the opening of the Bridge.

In terms of the implications for other CBRs, the findings of this and earlier papers on the Oresund region suggest that policy should focus initially on the strongest industries which are present on both sides of the border. There is a need to set up organizations to facilitate cross-border collaboration in a similar fashion to the Medicon Valley Alliance, an existing example of a successful platform for this kind of development (T. Hansen, 2013). At a later stage, these industries could provide important role models for further integration in other sectors and segments of the economy (Lundquist & Trippl, 2013). Additionally, it is important that other CBRs, which are contemplating using infrastructure projects to increase integration, should be aware of the over-optimistic impact and traffic demand forecasts that are commonly produced by "fixed link project promoters" (Knowles & Matthiessen, 2009).

To conclude, while the data collection processes for the composite STI index developed in this paper are somewhat laborious, they are sufficiently straightforward to be updated relatively easily on a regular bases in the case of the Oresund region, and to be applied in other CBRs. The latter would facilitate conducting comparable cross-country analyses for the benefit of the empirical CBRIS literature. Unfortunately, a lack of national funding support for updating the database (Nauwelaers et al., 2013) constitutes a threat to the longevity of the Öresund database which was utilized in compiling the Index. This is a major concern for continued development of the methodology for measuring cross-border regional integration.

ACKNOWLEDGMENT

I am grateful to Mr Sebastian Zimmer from the Europa-Universität Flensburg for providing me with the patent data and for our discussions on the potential limitations of using regional patent statistics. I would also like to extend my gratitude to Professor Allan Williams from the University of Surrey and to the anonymous reviewers for their comments on improving the paper; any remaining errors are mine alone.

This work was funded by the Marie Curie Actions: Intra-European Fellowship for career development within the Seventh Framework Programme (FP7) of the EU under Grant PIEFGA-2013-624930.

REFERENCES

BAKBasel Economics, (2008). *Top technology region benchmarking report 2008*. Basel: BAK Basel Economics.

Bergek, A., & Bruzelius, M. (2010). Are patents with multiple inventors from different countries a good indicator of international R&D collaboration? The case of ABB. *Research Policy*, *39*(10), 1321–1334. doi:10.1016/j.respol.2010.08.002

Bucken-Knapp, G. (2001). Just a train-ride away, but still worlds apart: Prospects for the Øresund region as a binational city. *GeoJournal*, *54*(1), 51–60. doi:10.1023/A:1021188631424

Bucken-Knapp, G. (2002). Testing our borders: Questions of national and regional identity in the Øresund region. *Journal of Baltic Studies*, *33*(2), 199 219. doi:10.1080/01629770200000051

Bygvrå, S., & Wetlund, H. (2005). Shopping behaviour in the Øresund region before and after the establishment of the fixed link between Denmark and Sweden. *GeoJournal*, *61*(1), 41–52. doi:10.1007/s10708-005-0876-6

Carvalho, N., Carvalho, L., & Nunes, S. (2015). A methodology to measure innovation in European Union through the national innovation system. *International Journal of Innovation and Regional Development, 6*(2), 159–180. doi:10.1504/IJIRD.2015.069703

Coenen, L., Moodysson, J., & Asheim, B. (2004). Nodes, networks and proximities: On the knowledge dynamics of the Medicon Valley biotech cluster. *European Planning Studies, 12*(7), 1003–1018. doi:10.1080/0965431042000267876

De Sousa, L. (2013). Understanding European cross-border cooperation: A framework for analysis. *Journal of European Integration, 35*(6), 669–687. doi:10.1080/07036337.2012.711827

Decoville, A., Durand, F., Sohn, C., & Walther, O. (2013). Comparing cross-border metropolitan integration in Europe: Towards a functional typology. *Journal of Borderland Studies, 28*(2), 221–237. doi:10.1080/08865655.2013.854654

Durand, F., & Nelles, J. (2014). Binding cross-border regions: An analysis of cross-border governance in Lille-Kortrijk-Tournai Eurometropolis. *Tijdschrift voor Economische en Sociale Geografie, 105*(5), 573–590. doi:10.1111/tesg.12063

Etemad, H., & Séguin Dulude, L. (1987). Patenting patterns in 25 large multinational enterprises. *Technovation, 7*(1), 1–15. doi:10.1016/0166-4972(87)90043-5

European Commission. (2015). *CORDIS: Community Research and Development Information Service.* Retrieved November 25, 2015, from http://cordis.europa.eu/home_en.html

Eurostat. (2015). *Statistics explained: Patent statistics.* Retrieved November 25, 2015, http://ec.europa.eu/eurostat/statistics-explained/index.php/Patent_statistics

Frenken, K. (2002). A new indicator of European integration and an application to collaboration in scientific research. *Economic Systems Research, 14*(4), 345–361. doi:10.1080/0953531022000024833

Freudenberg, M. (2003). Composite indicators of country performance: A critical assessment. *OECD STI Working Papers, 2003*(16).

Gregersen, F. (2003). Factors influencing the linguistic development in the Øresund region. *International Journal of the Sociology of Language*, (159), 139–152. doi:10.1515/ijsl.2003.003

Grupp, H., & Mogee, M. (2004). Indicators for national science and technology policy: How robust are composite indicators? *Research Policy, 33*(9), 1373–1384. doi:10.1016/j.respol.2004.09.007

Grupp, H., & Schubert, T. (2010). Review and new evidence on composite innovation indicators for evaluating national performance. *Research Policy, 39*(1), 67–78. doi:10.1016/j.respol.2009.10.002

Hagedoorn, J., & Cloodt, M. (2003). Measuring innovative performance: Is there and advantage in using multiple indicators? *Research Policy, 32*(8), 1365–1379. doi:10.1016/S0048-7333(02)00137-3

Hansen, T. (2013). Bridging regional innovation: Cross-border collaboration in the Øresund region. *Geografisk Tidsskrift – Danish Journal of Geography, 113*(1), 25–38. doi:10.1080/00167223.2013.781306

Hansen, T., & Hansen, R. (2006). Integration of the scientific community as exemplified by the biotech sector: An analysis based on bibliometric indicators in the Danish–Swedish border region. *GeoJournal*, *67*(3), 241–252. doi:10.1007/s10708-007-9057-0

Hospers, G.-J. (2006). Borders, bridges and branding: The transformation of the Øresund region into an imagined space. *European Planning Studies*, *14*(8), 1015–1033. doi:10.1080/09654310600852340

Kiryushin, P., Mulloth, B., & Iakovleva, T. (2013). Developing cross-border regional innovation systems with clean technology entrepreneurship: The case of Øresund. *International Journal of Innovation and Regional Development*, *5*(2), 179–195. doi:10.1504/IJIRD.2013.055237

Kleinknecht, A., van Montfort, K., & Brouwer, E. (2002). The non-trivial choice between innovation indicators. *Economics of Innovation and New Technology*, *11*(2), 109–121. doi:10.1080/10438590210899

Knowles, R. (2006). Transport impacts of the Øresund (Copenhagen to Malmö) fixed link. *Geography (Sheffield, England)*, *91*(3), 227–240.

Knowles, R., & Matthiessen, C. (2009). Barrier effects of international borders on fixed link traffic generation: The case of Øresundsbron. *Journal of Transport Geography*, *17*(3), 155–165. doi:10.1016/j.jtrangeo.2008.11.001

Knudsen, M., & Rich, J. (2013). Ex post socio-economic assessment of the Oresund Bridge. *Transport Policy*, *27*(1), 53–65. doi:10.1016/j.tranpol.2012.12.002

Kozłowski, J. (2015). Innovation indices: The need for positioning them where they properly belong. *Scientometrics*, *104*(3), 609–628. doi:10.1007/s11192-015-1632-4 PMID:26257448

Lata, R., Scherngell, T., & Brenner, T. (2013). Observing integration processes in European R&D networks: A comparative spatial interaction approach using project based R&D networks and co-patent networks. In T. Scherngell (Ed.), *The geography of networks and R&D collaboration* (pp. 131–150). Cham: Springer International Publishing. doi:10.1007/978-3-319-02699-2_8

Lata, R., Scherngell, T., & Brenner, T. (2015). Integration processes in European research and development: A comparative spatial interaction approach using project based research and development networks, co-patent networks and co-publication networks. *Geographical Analysis*, *47*(4), 349–375. doi:10.1111/gean.12079

Lundquist, K.-J., & Trippl, M. (2009). Towards cross-border innovation spaces: A theoretical analysis and empirical comparison of the Öresund region and the Centrope area. *Institut für Regional- und Umweltwirtschaft Discussion Papers, 2009*(5).

Lundquist, K.-J., & Trippl, M. (2013). Distance, proximity and types of cross-border innovation systems: A conceptual analysis. *Regional Studies*, *47*(3), 450–460. doi:10.1080/00343404.2011.560933

Lundquist, K.-J., & Winther, L. (2006). The interspace between Denmark and Sweden: The industrial dynamics of the Öresund cross-border region. *Geografisk Tidsskrift – Danish Journal of Geography*, *106*(1), 115–129. doi:10.1080/00167223.2006.10649549

Luukkonen, T., Tijssen, R., Persson, O., & Sivertsen, G. (1993). The measurement of international scientific collaboration. *Scientometrics*, *28*(1), 15–36. doi:10.1007/BF02016282

Makkonen, T., & van der Have, R. P. (2013). Benchmarking regional innovation performance: Composite measures and direct innovation counts. *Scientometrics, 94*(1), 247–262. doi:10.1007/s11192-012-0753-2

Matthiessen, C. (2004). The Öresund area: Pre- and post-bridge cross-border functional integration: The bi-national regional question. *GeoJournal, 61*(1), 31–39. doi:10.1007/s10708-005-5234-1

Moodysson, J., & Jonsson, O. (2007). Knowledge collaboration and proximity: The spatial organization of biotech innovation projects. *European Urban and Regional Studies, 14*(2), 115–131. doi:10.1177/0969776407075556

Moon, H.-S., & Lee, J.-D. (2005). A fuzzy set theory approach to national composite S&T indices. *Scientometrics, 64*(1), 67–83. doi:10.1007/s11192-005-0238-7

Nauwelaers, C., Maguire, K., & Ajmone Marsan, G. (2013). The case of Oresund (Denmark-Sweden). *OECD Regional Development Working Papers, 2013*(21).

Nelles, J. (2011). *Cooperation in crisis? An analysis of cross-border intermunicipal relations in the Detroit-Windsor region. Articulo – Journal of Urban Research*, (6). doi:10.4000/articulo.2097

Nye, J. (1969). Regional integration: Concept and measurement. *International Organization, 22*(4), 855–880. doi:10.1017/S0020818300013837

OECD. (2008). The OECD REGPAT database: A presentation. *OECD STI Working Papers, 2008*(2).

OECD. (2013). *Regions and innovation: Collaborating across borders*. Paris: OECD Publishing.

Örestat. (2013). *Øresund trends 2012*. Arbetsförmedlingen Scania, Employment Region Copenhagen & Zealand, Interreg Project Jobs & Education, Malmö City, Landskrona City, Lund Municipality, Helsingborg City, Capital Region, Region Zealand, Region Sania, Wonderful Copenhagen and Öresundskomiteen.

Örestat. (2015). *Öresundsdatabasen (engelsk)*. Retrieved November 25, 2015, from http://www.orestat.se/en/oresundsdatabasen-engelsk

Öresundskomiteen. (2010). *Oresund regional development strategy*. Copenhagen: Öresundskomiteen.

Öresundskomiteen. (2013). *The Oresund integration index*. Copenhagen: Öresundskomiteen.

Öresundskomiteen. (2015). *Öresundskomiteens integrationsindeks JUNI 2015*. Copenhagen: Öresundskomiteen.

Paas, T., & Poltimäe, H. (2012). Consistency between innovation indicators and national innovation performance in the case of small economies. *Eastern Journal of European Studies, 3*(1), 101–121.

Paasi, A. (2002). Regional transformation in the European context: Notes on regions, boundaries and identity. *Space and Polity, 6*(2), 197–201. doi:10.1080/1356257022000003626

Schmidt, T. D. (2005). Cross-border regional enlargement in Øresund. *GeoJournal, 64*(3), 249–258. doi:10.1007/s10708-006-6874-5

Sjöö, K., Taalbi, J., Kander, A., & Ljungberg, J. (2014). SWINNO: A database of Swedish innovations, 1970–2007. *Lund Papers in Economic History, 2014*(133).

Sohn, C. (2014). The border as a resource in the global urban space: A contribution to the cross-border metropolis hypothesis. *International Journal of Urban and Regional Research*, *38*(5), 1697–1711. doi:10.1111/1468-2427.12071

Sornn-Friese, H., & Sørensen, J. (2005). Linkage lock-in and regional economic development: The case of the Øresund medi-tech plastics industry. *Entrepreneurship & Regional Development*, *17*(4), 267–291. doi:10.1080/08985620500218695

Thompson Reuters. (2015). *Web of science*. Retrieved November 25, 2015, from http://wokinfo.com/products_tools/multidisciplinary/webofscience/

Trippl, M. (2010). Developing cross-border regional innovation systems: Key factors and challenges. *Tijdschrift voor Economische en Sociale Geografie*, *101*(2), 150–160. doi:10.1111/j.1467-9663.2009.00522.x

van Houtum, H. (2000). An overview of European geographical research on borders and border regions. *Journal of Borderland Studies*, *15*(1), 56–83. doi:10.1080/08865655.2000.9695542

Westlund, H., & Bygvrå, S. (2002). Short-term effects of the Öresund Bridge on crossborder interaction and spatial behavior. *Journal of Borderland Studies*, *17*(1), 57–77. doi:10.1080/08865655.2002.9695582

ADDITIONAL READING

Andersson, Å., Andersson, D., & Matthiessen, C. (2013). *Öresundsregionen: Den dynamiska metropolen*. Stockholm: Dialogos.

Asheim, B., Coenen, L., & Moodysson, J. (2009). The life science cluster of Medicon Valley, Scandinavia. In OECD (Ed.), *Clusters, innovation and entrepreneurship* (pp. 131–154). Paris: OECD Publishing. doi:10.1787/9789264044326-7-en

Collinge, C., & Gibney, J. (2010). Place-making and the limitations of spatial leadership: Reflections on the Øresund. *Policy Studies*, *31*(4), 475–489. doi:10.1080/01442871003723432

Edquist, C., & Lundvall, B.-Å. (1993). Comparing the Danish and Swedish systems of innovation. In R. Nelson (Ed.), *National innovation systems: A comparative analysis* (pp. 265–298). New York: Oxford University Press.

Falkheimer, J. (2005). Formation of a region: Source strategies and media images of the Sweden–Danish Öresund region. *Public Relations Review*, *31*(2), 293–295. doi:10.1016/j.pubrev.2005.02.023

Gullett, W. (2000). Environmental decision making in a transboundary context: Principles and challenges for the Denmark-Sweden Øresund fixed link. *Journal of Environmental Assessment Policy and Management*, *2*(4), 529–559. doi:10.1142/S1464333200000473

Hall, P. (2008). Opportunities for democracy in cross-border regions? Lessons from the Øresund region. *Regional Studies*, *42*(3), 423–435. doi:10.1080/00343400701281592

Hansen, P., & Serin, G. (2007). Integration strategies and barriers to co-operation in cross-border regions: Case study of the Øresund region. *Journal of Borderland Studies*, *22*(2), 39–56. doi:10.1080/08 865655.2007.9695676

Hansen, P., & Serin, G. (2010). Rescaling or institutional flexibility? The experience of the cross-border Øresund region. *Regional & Federal Studies*, *20*(2), 201–227. doi:10.1080/13597561003731646

Jauhiainen, J. S. (2014). Baltic Sea region innovation systems: Challenges and opportunities. *Baltic Sea Region Policy Briefing*, *2*(1), 63–73.

Koschatzky, K. (2000). A river is a river: Cross-border networking between Baden and Alsace. *European Planning Studies*, *8*(4), 429–449. doi:10.1080/713666422

Linnros, H., & Hallin, P. (2001). The discursive nature of environmental conflicts: The case of the Öresund link. *Area*, *33*(4), 391–403. doi:10.1111/1475-4762.00045

Löfgren, O. (2008). Regionauts: The transformation of cross-border regions in Scandinavia. *European Urban and Regional Studies*, *15*(3), 195–209. doi:10.1177/0969776408090418

Makkonen, T. (2015). Scientific collaboration in the Danish–German border region of Southern Jutland–Schleswig. *Geografisk Tidsskrift – Danish Journal of Geography*, *115*(1), 27–38. doi:10.1080/0 0167223.2015.1011180

Maskell, P., & Törnqvist, G. (1999). *Building a cross-border learning region: Emergence of the North European Øresund region*. Copenhagen: Copenhagen Business School Press.

Matthiessen, C. (2000). Bridging the Öresund: Potential regional dynamics: Integration of Copenhagen (Denmark) and Malmö–Lund (Sweden): A cross-border project on the European metropolitan level. *Journal of Transport Geography*, *8*(3), 171–180. doi:10.1016/S0966-6923(00)00007-7

Matthiessen, C., & Knowles, R. (2011). Scandinavian links: Mega bridges linking the Scandinavian Peninsula to the European Continent. In S. Brunn (Ed.), *Engineering earth: The impacts of megaengineering projects* (pp. 735–746). Dordrecht: Springer. doi:10.1007/978-90-481-9920-4_42

Moodysson, J., Coenen, L., & Asheim, B. (2008). Explaining spatial patterns of innovation: Analytical and synthetic modes of knowledge creation in the Medicon Valley life-science cluster. *Environment & Planning A*, *40*(5), 1040–1056. doi:10.1068/a39110

O'Dell, T. (2003). Øresund and the regionauts. *European Studies*, *23*(1), 31–53.

Pedersen, S. (2004). Place branding: Giving the region of Øresund a competitive edge. *Journal of Urban Technology*, *11*(1), 77–95. doi:10.1080/1063073042000341998

Skjött-Larsen, T., Paulsson, U., & Wandel, S. (2003). Logistics in the Öresund region after the bridge. *European Journal of Operational Research*, *144*(2), 247–256. doi:10.1016/S0377-2217(02)00391-0

Tangkjær, C., & Jonsson, O. (2015). Cross-bordering strategies for the Øresund region. In J. Valdaliso & J. Wilson (Eds.), *Strategies for shaping territorial competitiveness* (pp. 172–193). Abingdon: Routledge.

van den Broek, J., & Smulders, H. (2014). Institutional gaps in cross-border regional innovation systems: The horticultural industry in Venlo–Lower Rhine. In R. Rutten, P. Benneworth, D. Irawati, & F. Boekema (Eds.), *The social dynamics of innovation networks* (pp. 157–176). Abingdon: Routledge.

van den Broek, J., & Smulders, H. (2015). Institutional hindrances in cross-border regional innovation systems. *Regional Studies. Regional Science*, *2*(1), 115–121.

Weidenfeld, A. (2013). Tourism and cross border regional innovation systems. *Annals of Tourism Research*, *42*(1), 191–213. doi:10.1016/j.annals.2013.01.003

KEY TERMS AND DEFINITIONS

Composite Indicator: A set of indicators that are compiled into a single index to capture phenomena that cannot be described with a single indicator or to simplify the information enclosed in several individual indicators.

Cross-Border Collaboration: A concerted action that takes place between public and/or private institutions across borders to yield benefits or to reach common goals.

Cross-Border Region: An area consisting of neighbouring territories belonging to different nation states.

Cross-Border Regional Innovation System: An interactive knowledge generation (the public sector) and exploitation (the private sector) system that spans across national borders.

Cross-Border Regional Integration: A process where a cross-border region becomes functionally (more) interlinked and interdependent.

Oresund Region: A cross-border region between Denmark and Sweden comprising the Danish Capital region and Region Zealand and the Swedish Scania County.

Oresund Integration Index: A set of indices measuring the level of cross-border regional integration between the Danish and Swedish parts of the Oresund region.

Science, Technology, and Innovation Indicators: A set of indicators (including for example patent, research and development and scientific publication statistics) that can be utilized to measure the innovative capabilities and performance of given organisations, nations or regions.

Chapter 2
Developing a Sustainable Urban Mobility Index:
Methodological Steps

Yongjun Shen
Hasselt University, Belgium

Elke Hermans
Hasselt University, Belgium

ABSTRACT

Sustainability is a multi-dimensional concept that can be assessed by means of constructing a composite indicator or index. In doing so, a scientifically sound and appropriate index methodology is required. The research proposed in this chapter aims to provide a guideline for developing a sustainability index that is able to assess the impact of mobility on the urban quality of life. By studying the index development process in other domains critically and taking the specific sustainable urban mobility context into account, this study investigates the different methodological steps that are essential in the construction of a sustainable urban mobility index. The main challenges and potential options when developing such an index are discussed.

INTRODUCTION

The world's population is increasingly city-based. In 2014, the urban population accounted for 54% of the total global population, up from 30% in 1950, and is expected to reach 67% by 2050 (United Nations, 2014). This explosion in urban population has been accompanied by a massive growth in both passenger and freight transport. Today, 64% of all travel undertaken is within urban environments and the total number of urban kilometers travelled is expected to triple by 2050 (van Audenhove, Korniichuk, Dauby, & Pourbaix, 2014). Urban mobility has become a crucial component of modernity, and has generated a revolution in contemporary economic and social relations. However, rapid growth of urban mobility systems has also presented a big challenge to all major city authorities around the world, that is, how to enhance mobility while at the same time reducing congestion, accidents, and pollution (Camagni,

DOI: 10.4018/978-1-5225-0714-7.ch002

Gibelli, & Rigamonti, 2002; Mihyeon Jeon, & Amekudzi, 2005). Taking the European Union (EU) as an example, a large majority of European citizens live in an urban environment, with over 60% living in urban areas of over 10,000 inhabitants. As a consequence, congestion in the EU is often located in and around urban areas and costs nearly 100 billion Euro, or 1% of the EU GDP, annually. Moreover, urban mobility in the EU accounts for 40% of all CO_2 emissions of road transport and up to 70% of other pollutants from transport (European Commission, 2015). Under this circumstance, the European Commission proposed in its Action Plan on Urban Mobility of 2009 to accelerate the take-up of a Sustainable Urban Mobility Plan (SUMP) in Europe, which has the central goal of improving accessibility of urban areas and of providing high-quality and sustainable mobility and transport to, through and within the urban area (Wefering, Rupprecht, Buhrmann, & Bohler-Baedeker, 2014). In short, to preserve the liveability of urban environments, the mobility system needs to move towards sustainability. To this end, a thorough understanding and assessment of the current performance of the urban transport system is required (Black, Paez, & Suthanaya, 2002; Yigitcanlar, & Dur, 2010). However, because sustainability is a complex matter that is affected by numerous factors, no single indicator is capable of capturing the entire picture. Consequently, the development of a composite indicator (CI), which combines individual indicator values into an overall index score, is considered to be a valuable approach for evaluating urban mobility sustainability (Mori, & Christodoulou, 2012).

Theoretically, a CI is a mathematical aggregation of a set of individual indicators that usually has no common units of measurement. The main pros and cons of using CIs are summarized in Saisana & Tarantola (2002) and the Organization for Economic Co-operation and Development (2008). For instance, CIs enable users to compare complex realities effectively and are easier to interpret than trying to find a common trend in many separate indicators. However, they may also invite simplistic policy conclusions or be misused to support a desired policy. In general, "… it is hard to imagine that debate on the use of composite indicators will ever be settled…" (Saisana, Tarantola, & Saltelli, 2005). However, if the methodological process for creating an index is scientifically sound, transparent, and based on solid statistical and conceptual principles, then the construction of a CI over a set of indicators is worthwhile. The index can be utilized as a powerful tool for policy analysis and public communication (Shen, Hermans, Bao, Brijs, Wets, & Wang, 2015).

To develop a sustainable urban mobility index, a reasonable definition of the research framework, an appropriate selection of sustainability indicators, a harmonized data collection and processing procedure, and a scientifically sound approach for weighting and aggregation are indispensable. These are the fundamental conditions for meaningful evaluation, and also the key to designing more effective policies towards sustainability. In this chapter, by studying the index development process in other domains critically and focusing on the specific sustainable urban mobility case, we aim to offer some insight into the various steps of the methodology for the development of a sound sustainable urban mobility index. The different methodological aspects involved in the index construction process are elaborated, and the main challenges and potential options when developing such an index are discussed.

CURRENT STATUS

During the last decades, all the major international organizations such as the United Nations (UN), the Organisation for Economic Co-operation and Development (OECD), the World Health Organization (WHO), and so on, have been producing CIs in wide-ranging fields such as economy, society, governance, security, environment, globalization, innovation, and sustainable development (Saisana & Tarantola, 2002; Freudenberg, 2003; Munda, 2005; Organization for Economic Co-operation and Development, 2008). According to a comprehensive review by Bandura (2008), around 180 different CIs are available all over the world currently, and some of them are related to sustainability (Singh, Murty, Gupta, & Dikshit, 2012; Mori & Christodoulou, 2012). For instance, the *Environmental Sustainability Index* developed jointly by Yale University, Columbia University, the World Economic Forum, and the Joint Research Center of European Commission (Esty, Levy, Srebotnjak, & de Sherbinin, 2005) is a measure to assess environmental sustainability, developed for 146 countries. The index provides a composite profile of national environmental stewardship based on a compilation of 21 indicators derived from 76 underlying data sets. Coob & Daly (1989) proposed an *Index of Sustainable and Economic Welfare* (ISEW), which is to measure the component of economic activity that leads to welfare to the society, with a long-term goal of replacing GDP as an indicator of progress due to the ISEW's ability to demonstrate the relationship between economic activities and their direct impacts on the quality of life. Krajnc & Glavic (2005) identified key indicators for three dimensions of sustainability, and a *Composite Sustainable Development Index* was developed in order to track integrated information on the economic, environmental, and social performance of a company with real-time information. The Sustainable Society Foundation developed a *Sustainable Society Index* (SSI), which integrates human wellbeing, environmental wellbeing, and economic wellbeing. In its latest version (van de Kerk & Manuel, 2014), 21 indicators were considered to show the level of sustainability of 151 countries. In addition, there are still several widely used CIs that are related to sustainability evaluation, such as Environmental Policy Performance Indicator, Sustainable Asset Management, Sustainability Assessment Tool for Energy System, Ecological Footprint, etc.

With respect to sustainability indices for cities, Zhang (2002) developed an *Urban Sustainability Index* (USI) based on 22 individual indicators in the context of urban development in China. The index tries to capture the three key points of urban sustainability; that is, the urban development capacity, the urban coordination capacity, and the urban development potential. The Institute of Sustainable Development in Italy developed an *ISSI index* for measuring the sustainable performance of Italy. The index comprises three components, namely socioeconomic, environment, and resources categories. Each category consists of 10 indicators. It is a multidimensional vector presentation tool which allows comparisons between the Italian regions as well as between countries (Ronchi, Federico, & Musmeci, 2002). Forum for the Future (2007) identified three dimensions of 13 indicators and combined them further in order to rank the 20 largest cities of Britain. The three dimensions are: Environmental Impact of the city (which describes the impact of the city on the environment with respect to resource use and pollution), Quality of Life for residents (which shows the state of city to live in for all its citizens), and the third dimension is Future Proofing (which indicates how well the city is preparing itself for a sustainable future). Arthur D. Little, the Global Management Consultancy, released two versions of its "Future of Urban Mobility" study in 2011 and 2014, respectively. An *Urban Mobility Index* was developed, which assessed the mobility maturity and performance of 84 cities worldwide (van Audenhove et al., 2014). Recently, the ARCADIS and the Sustainable Society Foundation published their latest version of the *Sustainable City/Cities Index* (SCI), respectively. The former one examined 50 cities from 31 countries by using totally 20 input indicators, comprising nine for the People component, six for the Planet component, and six for the Profit component (property prices appearing twice) (ARCADIS, 2015). The latter one combined 24 indicators describing human wellbeing, environmental wellbeing, and economic wellbeing, respectively, with data from 393 Dutch cities (Manuel, 2015). Both studies contained overall lessons as well as detailed city profiles describing individual performances and best practices.

Overall, in most of the current sustainability evaluation studies, mobility considerations are often excessively simplified or excluded. For instance, in the *Sustainable Cities Index* developed by ARCADIS, four mobility indicators were considered for different transport modes. However, they were all related to transport infrastructure such as the density of public transport network, and no mobility impact was taken into account. In the *Sustainable City Index* proposed by the Sustainable Society Foundation, CO_2 emission from transport was considered. However, it was one of the only two indicators related to transport. In the *Urban Mobility Index* developed by Arthur D. Little, more attention was paid to the passenger transport, while the impact of freight transport or logistics was not studied in particular. Filling these gaps is essential, because a thorough understanding and evaluation of the overall performance of the current urban transport system enables local authorities to address adequately the pressing impact areas, evaluate progress accurately, and avoid grounding policy measures on an insufficient knowledge base.

TOWARDS A SUSTAINABLE URBAN MOBILITY INDEX

Regardless of the field, a general objective of most of the indices that can be found in the literature nowadays is the ranking of different entities (e.g., countries, cities, etc.) and benchmarking according to some aggregated dimensions. Therefore, the way these indices are constructed and used appears to be an important research issue. Specifically, the construction of an index involves a series of methodological steps, such as the development of a theoretical framework, the selection of appropriate indicators, data collection and processing, the assignment of weights, the choice of the aggregation model, uncertainty and sensitivity analysis, and so on. Each methodological step needs thorough study, and different possibilities need to be weighed against each other. In the following sections, each step is discussed in more detail.

Developing a Theoretical Framework

To assess the impact of both passenger and freight mobility on the urban quality of life, an inclusive sustainability evaluation framework is required, based on which a set of suitable indicators can be developed. Generally speaking, the framework should clearly define the phenomenon that is to be measured and its sub-components (Organization for Economic Co-operation and Development, 2008). It should be based ideally on what is desirable to measure, and not on which indicators are available. According to the EU SUMP (Wefering et al., 2014), to achieve sustainable urban mobility the following objectives– as a minimum–should be addressed:

- Offering all citizens with transport options that enable access to key destinations and services;
- Improving the cost-effectiveness and efficiency of the transportation of persons and goods;
- Reducing energy consumption, greenhouse gas emissions, and air and noise pollution;
- Improving safety and security;
- Enhancing the attractiveness and quality of the urban environment and urban design.

These objectives indicate the multi-dimensional concept of sustainable urban mobility, and outline what should be measured by the composite indicator. However, given the broad concept of sustainable urban mobility, other aspects could be added, such as achieving a balanced development and better integration of the different transport modes.

Moreover, Arthur D. Little released in 2014 the second version of its "Future of Urban Mobility" study (van Audenhove et al., 2014). It highlighted the mobility challenges city authorities face on a worldwide basis (see Table 1), which comprised three components referred to as 'p's', that stand for planet, people, and profit considerations. This implies making transport sustainable, environmentally friendly and competitive, while addressing social concerns of diverse forms. Although the detailed indicators were different, such a framework was in line with the *Sustainable City/Cities Index* developed by ARCADIS and the Sustainable Society Foundation, respectively, that is, using three dimensions of sustainability, i.e., economic, social, and environmental, as the triple bottom line for indicator development. This framework can therefore be considered as a valuable guideline for assessing the sustainability of urban mobility in practice.

Selecting Appropriate Indicators

Guided by the established theoretical framework for the composite indicator, the next step in the index methodology relates to indicator selection. It is highly important to carefully select the indicators that capture the totality of the system, so as to balance all impacts of the predefined dimensions (Sikdar, Sengupta, & Harten, 2012). A fragile match between simplification and complication on the one hand and convenience and comprehensiveness on the other hand is required (Hermans, 2009; Singh et al., 2012).

In order to assess urban mobility sustainability, a long list of possible indicators that describes the current status of the urban transport system could be identified based on literature review (see e.g., Rai, van Lier, & Macharis, 2015; van Lier, Rai, & Macharis, 2015). A set of selection criteria is therefore required to determine appropriate indicators for index construction. Hermans (2009) summarized from literature eight criteria for indicator selection, which are: relevant, measurable, understandable, data available, reliable, comparable, specific, and sensitive. Based on these criteria, so-called best available indicators could be deduced from the long list of possible indicators. These indicators may belong to different types, such as input, output, process, or context indicators, but they can be measured in some common terms such as a rate (e.g., energy consumption rate of freight vehicles registered), a percentage (e.g., percentage of passenger kilometres by sustainable mode), or as qualitative information (e.g., level of policy intervention: 'low', 'medium', and 'high'); They could also be proxy measures when the desired ones are unavailable or when cross-sectional comparability is limited. When the indicator in

Table 1. Mobility challenges that city authorities are facing

Planet	• Air pollution • CO_2 emissions • Noise • Increasing ecological footprint
People	• Traffic chaos • Traffic security • Traffic jam • Decreasing quality of life and convenience
Profit	• Overloaded infrastructures • Insufficient public transport capacities • Increasing motorization • Limited parking places

Source: van Audenhove et al., 2014.

question is dependent on size-related factors, such as the number of road fatalities, scaling is required normally to make meaningful comparisons. However, the usage of different size measures (e.g., population, land area, traffic volume, etc.) will lead up to different indicators, in both name and value. In addition, these indicators may belong to different categories and be linked further to one another thus constituting a multilayer hierarchical structure (e.g, the *Sustainable City/Cities Index*). Such a structure contains valuable information which should not be ignored in the index construction (Shen, Hermans, Brijs, & Wets, 2013).

Moreover, as briefly mentioned above, in the selection of best indicators a distinction could be made between best available indicators and best needed indicators (European Commission, 2005). In the determination of best needed indicators, no data-related criteria are considered. They can be seen therefore as the most ideal indicators among the ones evaluated, whereas for the best available indicators, data of an acceptable quality are available. In practice, best available indicators can be used for the index construction immediately, while best needed indicators are valuable for the improvement of the quality and accuracy of the index when data of these indicators become available.

Below a number of mobility-related indicators used for the construction of some sustainability indices are presented. In the *Sustainable Cities Index* developed by ARCADIS, four mobility indicators were considered for different transport modes. They are:

- Density of public transport network;
- One-way commute time;
- Kilometers of metro/light rail network per capita;
- Survey of customer satisfaction in airports.

In the *Sustainable City Index* proposed by the Sustainable Society Foundation, two indicators related to transport were selected:

- The percentage of the number of daily trips by public transport, bicycle or on foot;
- CO_2 emission from road transport.

In the *Urban Mobility Index* developed by Arthur D. Little, 19 indicators in total were used to measure the maturity and performance of the cities under examination. They are:

- Financial attractiveness of public transport;
- Share of public transport in modal split;
- Share of zero-emission (i.e., by bicycle and walking) in modal split;
- Roads density;
- Cycle path network density;
- Urban agglomeration density;
- Smart card penetration;
- Bike sharing;
- Car sharing;
- Public transport frequency;
- Qualitative evaluation of strategy and actions of public sector with regard to urban mobility;
- Transport related CO_2 emissions;

- Daily concentrations of NO_2;
- Daily concentrations of PM_{10};
- Traffic related fatalities;
- Increase of share of public transport in modal split;
- Increase of share of zero-emission in modal split;
- Mean travel time to work;
- Density of passenger motorized vehicles.

These indicators are all relevant to the assessment of urban mobility sustainability. However, it should be noted that since the main focus of the first two indices was on cities, rather than on urban mobility, only indicators related to transport infrastructure were considered in the *Sustainable Cities Index*, and only two mobility-related indicators were used for the *Sustainable City Index*. Concerning the *Urban Mobility Index*, although it is mobility oriented, more attention was paid to the passenger transport, while the impact of freight transport or logistics was not studied in particular. In this respect, some potential indicators are:

- Freight vehicles loading rate;
- Energy consumption rate of registered freight vehicles;
- Share of freight vehicles using alternative energy sources;
- Share of traffic accidents involving freight vehicles.

Collecting Indicator Data

To compute an index score, data are required. Depending on the specific purpose of the index, the data requirement is different. For instance, to benchmark the current performance of the urban transport system among different cities, a data set containing indicator values for a large set of cities referring to a particular, preferably recent, period is aimed at; While to assess the change in the urban transport system of a particular city over time, time series data for all indicators deduced in the previous step of the city under study are the target. In practice, no matter whether it is a cross-sectional study or a longitudinal study, the availability of high quality data is an important influential factor with respect to the final selection of indicators.

Data can be collected by a variety of means. First, various data sources from local authorities may be available for consultation. However, one overall data source having information on all aspects is non-existent. Indicator data from different sources therefore need to correspond to the same set of cities and the same time period. For many indicators, making direct measurements is normally the most accurate data collection method. For example, trends in the number of pedestrians can be determined by annual counts at key points in the city. However, this method is often expensive and time consuming. Carrying out a household survey or interviewing local officers and experts is an alternative way for collecting indicator data. In general, the choice of the data collection method depends on the resources available, the type of variables to include, the size of the city, and the level of accuracy required.

Based on different data collection methods, different types of data can be gathered. Although the obtainment of measurable and quantitative data is preferred commonly in any index research, under many conditions, they are inadequate or inappropriate to depict the whole real world situation due to the complexity and uncertainty of the reality. Therefore, it has become more and more popular to take into account the presence of qualitative data when making a decision. Very often it is the case that a sustainability indicator (such as passenger satisfaction of taking public transport, qualitative evaluation of strategy and actions of public sector with regard to urban mobility, and so on) can, at most, be specified with either ordinal measures from best to worst or with the help of experts' subjective judgments, such as 'high', 'medium', and 'low'. Treating them simply as quantitative ones would result in wrong conclusions. It is therefore necessary to distinguish between quantitative and qualitative data when constructing the sustainable urban mobility index. For instance, if the passenger satisfaction of taking public transport is to be represented in the form of ordered classes rated on a 0–10 scale (with 0 representing the worst score while 10 the best), then the value of 8 is not twice as large as the value of 4, and the most that can be judged is that the former one is preferred to or more important than the latter.

Data Processing and Analysis

Given the high number of potential sustainability indicators, a large data set has to be collected. A number of data errors are to be expected in spite of careful study design, conduct, and error-prevention strategies. In this step of the index process, several data processing and analysis procedures are performed with the intention to identify and correct these errors or to at least minimize their impact on the following index construction.

In any data analysis, one of the first steps is the detection of outlaying observations, or *outliers*. Hawkins (1980) defined an outlier as an observation that deviates so much from other observations as to arouse suspicion that it was generated by a different mechanism. Often, detected outliers are candidates for aberrant data that may otherwise lead adversely to model misspecification, biased parameter estimations, and incorrect results. It is therefore important to identify them prior to modeling and analysis (Liu, Shah, & Jiang, 2004). By means of visualization (to identify best performing cities easily with respect to a particular indicator) and basic summary statistics (such as the mean and the variance), an idea about the distribution of the indicator values can be obtained first. Afterwards, both univariate methods and multivariate methods can be applied to detect potential statistical outliers (Ben-Gal, 2005). It should be noted here that only if a detected outlier is in fact erroneous, which may lead to incorrect results, should the outlying value be deleted from the analysis.

To take as much of the available indicator information into account for the sustainable urban mobility index research, a certain risk in the form of missing values is always present because no data collection system grants perfect data sets. Moreover, removing incorrect outliers from the original data set leads to more missing values. Therefore, prior to the index construction, missing data imputation has to be performed. This is defined as the process by which missing values in a data set are estimated by appropriately computed values, thereby producing a complete data set (Rubin, 1987).

Over the past decades, a variety of imputation approaches have been proposed, ranging from extremely simple to rather complex (Howell, 2008; Wilmots, Shen, Hermans, & Ruan, 2011). One fundamental taxonomy is between single imputation and multiple imputation. The former one, including for example unconditional mean imputation, regression imputation, decision trees imputation, clustering imputation, neural networks imputation, etc., fills in a single value for each missing value. The latter one by comparison, replaces each missing value with a list of simulated values that represent the uncertainty about the correct value to impute. No imputation model is free from assumptions. The imputation results should therefore be checked thoroughly for their statistical properties (such as distributional characteristics), and heuristically for their meaningfulness (e.g., whether or not the imputed values could be negative for some indicators).

A possible following step (this is related to the methodological choices made in the index construction) is normalization. Given the fact that the collected indicator data might differ in magnitude and units, they may cause bias in the index. Standardization, rescaling, distance to a reference measure, and the use of rank numbers are commonly used methods for normalization (Freudenberg, 2003). Taking the *Sustainable Cities Index* developed by ARCADIS (2015) as an example, the highest-ranked city in each indicator was given a score of 100%, while the lowest-ranked city received 0%, so that each city's performance was measured relative to the other cities under study and higher scores always represented more sustainable cities.

Finally, some multivariate analysis techniques such as correlation analysis, principal components analysis and cluster analysis, could be applied when studying the indicator data set as a whole (Hermans, 2009). In this way, interesting insights into the degree of correlation between the various sustainability indicators, clusters of similar cities, etc., can be gained.

Weighting

After the indicator data have been pre-processed, the next step is to apply an appropriate weighting scheme in order to deduce a weight for each indicator. It plays a central role in the development of a composite indicator. Ideally, the weighting process should be acceptable for as many members of the public as possible. However, this is practically impossible. Different weighting methods have their own strengths and limitations, and often result in different final scores and rankings. In general, there is no best method to use in all circumstances. In the literature, weights based on statistical methods (such as principal components analysis/factor analysis), participatory methods (e.g., analytic hierarchy process and budget allocation), optimization methods (like data envelopment analysis), and equal weighting are examples of widely used techniques (see e.g., Bax, Wesemann, Gitelman, Shen, Goldenbeld, Hermans, Doveh, Hakkert, Wegman, & Aarts, 2012; Hermans, van den Bossche, & Wets, 2008; Organization for Economic Co-operation and Development, 2008).

In equal weighting, the same weight is assigned to all the indicators. Because the weights usually sum up to one, each indicator weight equals $1/k$ (k denotes the number of indicators in the analysis. Equal weighting is the simplest and also the most widely applied technique in current sustainability index studies. Examples are the *Environmental Sustainability Index,* the *Sustainable Society Index*, the *Sustainable City/Cities Index,* and so on. However, it has some major limitations. The most important drawback is that no difference in importance of the indicators can be established. As a result, equal weighting is often not of great value for policymakers. Moreover, when more than two indicators are selected for the same aspects, there is a risk of overweighting this aspect in relation to other aspects (see the *Sustainable Cities Index developed by* ARCADIS (2015)).

Budget allocation is a participatory or subjective weighting method. In this method, a group of experts is asked to allocate a given budget to the indicators, and more budget will be given to those indicators they intend to stress their importance. In practice, the experts with a wide spectrum of knowledge and experience are first selected. Next, each expert is asked to allocate the predetermined budget to the indicators. Weights are then calculated based on the share of budget allocated to an indicator. In addition, the above procedures can be iterated if necessary. Many index studies use budget allocation to determine indicator weights, such as the *National Health Care Systems Performance developed* by King's Fund

(2001). However, it also has some limitations. First, the selection of experts is crucial and should be well-considered. Second, the assigned wight may not capture the importance of a specific indicator but rather, the need for political intervention in that dimension (Organization for Economic Co-operation and Development, 2008). In addition, the maximum number of indicators over which to distribute the budget is limited to around ten, enabling the expert to keep an overview (Saisana & Tarantola, 2002).

Analytic hierarchy process (AHP), developed by Saaty in the early 1970s, is another widely used technique to deduce weights, and has been applied to a number of sustainability index studies, such as the *Index of Environmental Friendliness* (Puolamaa, Kaplas, & Reinikainen, 1996), the *Transportation Sustainability Index* (Al-Atawi, Kumar, & Saleh, 2015), and so on. Different from the budget alloca-tion, experts in AHP are asked to judge the relative contribution/importance of each indicator compared with another indicator. Very often values are given on a scale of 1 to 9, in which 1 indicates equality between two indicators, while 9 indicates that the indicator is much more important than the other one. We then obtain a comparison matrix. Based on the eigenvector of this matrix the weights of the indi-vidual indicators can be deduced (Saaty, 1980). As a subjective weighting method like budget allocation, the selection of a proper expert panel is crucial. Apart from that, consistency of judgment is important when applying this method in practice. It is advisable to limit the number of indicators and to define sufficiently different indicators.

Principal component analysis (PCA) and factor analysis (FA) are often used to reduce the dimensions of a problem (Sharma, 1996). They group together individual indicators which are collinear to form a factor that captures as much as possible the information common to individual indicators. The use of PCA/FA in the index field (either to examine the interrelationships between the indicators or to deter-mine weights) is not rare, such as the *Environmental Sustainability Index* (Esty, et al., 2005). However, the most important drawback of applying this method is that weights are based on correlations which do not correspond necessarily to the real-world links between the phenomena being measured (Saisana & Tarantola, 2002). In addition, to deduce weights from this method, a certain level of correlation among indicators is required in order to reduce the problem in a number of factors, and the number of factors should be determined with caution because it has certain influence on the final weights. In general, this weighting method is attractive in instances where several (sufficiently correlated) indicators per aspect are considered.

Data envelopment analysis, developed by Charnes, Cooper, & Rhodes (1978), is an optimization technique that determines the best possible weights for a decision making unit (DMU). Compared with the previously discussed weighting methods, DEA is different, in which different indicator weights are derived for each DMU individually, and the relative performance of a particular DMU is assessed by taking the performance of all other DMUs into account. When applying this method, expert opinions can be incorporated into the model leading to more acceptable weights. In addition, the layered hierarchy of the indicators can be taken into account by applying a multiple layer DEA model (Shen et al., 2012; 2013), and Imprecise DEA and Fuzzy DEA models are currently available to incorporate both quantita-tive and qualitative data (Shen, Ruan, Hermans, Brijs, Wets, & Vanhoof, 2011). However, the sum of the weights calculated from this method does not equal to one. Therefore, it is not possible to compare the weights with the ones derived from other methods directly. In short, DEA is a performance measurement technique in which the most favorable weights are selected, thereby satisfying the imposed restrictions and resulting in the most optimal score. The results are influenced by the DMUs considered in the data set, hence this approach is about relative performance. This weighting method is most valuable when some expert opinions are available and there is no agreement on the correct set of weights and therefore it is decided to 'let the data speak for themselves'.

To conclude, the weighting methods introduced above are all valuable and promising in the case of the sustainable urban mobility index. However, because each weighting method has its own advantages and limitations, and no weighting scheme is above criticism, it is suggested that the specific indicator and data characteristics be taken into account when selecting the most appropriate weighting method(s). If possible, different weighting methods could be applied to combine individual indicators into an index and to have the results compared subsequently.

Aggregation

The next step in the index process is to try to find an answer to the question about which aggregation method to use in the construction of the index. Among others, linear and geometric aggregations are the two most commonly used aggregation methods. Linear aggregation rewards indicators proportionally to the weights, while geometric aggregation rewards those entities with higher scores (Organization for Economic Co-operation and Development, 2008). In both methods, weights express trade-offs between indicators, that is, a deficit in one dimension can be compensated for by a surplus in another. The difference is that in a linear aggregation the compensability is constant, while in the case of a geometric aggregation compensability is lower for the composite indicators with low values. In other words, a city with low scores on one indicator will need a much higher score on the others in order to improve its sustainability performance when geometric aggregation is used. Therefore, geometric aggregation methods are better suited when some degree of non-compensability between individual indicators or dimensions is required, such as in the case of sustainable urban mobility assessment in which an increase in mobility performance (profit) cannot compensate for a loss in social cohesion (people) or a worsening in environmental sustainability (planet). In this case, another aggregation method, i.e., the non-compensatory multi-criteria approach proposed by Munda and Nardo (2009), is also suggested, which assures non-compensability by finding a compromise between two or more legitimate goals. However, applying this method could be computationally costly when the number of cities under study is large.

Robustness Test

Based on the previous steps, the sustainable urban mobility index scores of different cities or of one city being assessed over different time periods can be computed. The results can be influenced largely, however, by the decisions taken at the different stages of the index process. It is therefore important to test rigorously the robustness of the index to the assumptions and methodological choices made, by means of uncertainty and sensitivity analysis.

Uncertainty analysis focuses on how uncertainty in the input factors propagates through the structure of the index and how it affects the index values. Sensitivity analysis assesses the contribution of the individual source of uncertainty to the output variance. A combination of uncertainty and sensitivity analysis can help researchers gauge the robustness of the composite indicator and improve transparency.

In practice, the approach taken to assess uncertainties in the final index result could involve the following methodological decisions:

- Inclusion and exclusion of individual indicators;
- Considering different hierarchical structures of the indicators;
- Using imputed values from different imputation methods;
- Choosing alternative data normalization techniques;
- Applying different weighting schemes, and
- Selecting different aggregation systems.

CONCLUSION AND FUTURE RESEARCH

Given the fact that sustainable urban mobility has become more and more important to the urban quality of life, but mobility considerations are still excessively simplified or even ignored in current sustainability evaluation studies, a thorough understanding and evaluation of the overall performance of the current urban transport system is imperative. In this respect, composite indicators or indexes, due to their remarkable ability for large amounts of information to be integrated into understandable formats, are increasingly recognized as a useful tool in policy analysis and in public communication, and are considered to be a valuable approach for evaluating urban mobility sustainability in particular. However, developing a sound sustainable urban mobility index is by no means easy. Challenges exist from ascertaining the theoretical framework at the very beginning to making final policy decisions in terms of best practices and future directions. In this paper, we provided a guideline for developing such an index, and investigated the essential steps of the methodology with their various options, which include the development of an inclusive sustainability evaluation framework, the selection of appropriate sustainability indicators, the collection and preparation of a high quality data set, the assignment of acceptable indicator weights, the choice of proper aggregation operators, and the sensitivity and uncertainty analysis.

In summary, to develop a sustainable urban mobility index, the aforementioned aspects should be studied carefully. They are the fundamental conditions for making a meaningful evaluation, and also the key to designing more effective policies towards sustainability. In particular, it was highlighted in this paper to use the '3Ps' (Planet, People, and Profit) as the triple bottom line for sustainable urban mobility indicator development, coupled with detailed indicator selection criteria including relevant, measurable, understandable, data available, reliable, comparable, specific, and sensitive. Moreover, harmonized data processing procedures have to be performed, which should include at least, outlier detection and missing data treatment, and could be extended by normalization and multivariate analysis when necessary. Furthermore, different weighting methods apart from equal weighting (e.g., statistical methods, participatory methods, optimization methods, and so on) were suggested to apply when combining individual sustainable urban mobility indicators, and the geometric aggregation approaches were recommended in the case of sustainable urban mobility assessment.

In the next phase, all these methodological steps will be followed to construct a sustainable urban mobility index for different cities of the world so as to verify the feasibility in practice. Moreover, such an index will be used to serve as a practical instrument for city governments, transport policy makers, and inhabitants to show the level of sustainability on urban mobility as a whole and to identify on which aspects cities are doing well, and for which aspects they are falling behind and need further development towards sustainability.

REFERENCES

Al-Atawi, A. M., Kumar, R., & Saleh, W. (in press). Transportation sustainability index for Tabuk city in Saudi Arabia: An analytic hierarchy process. *Transport*. doi:10.3846/16484142.2015.1058857

ARCADIS. (2015). *Sustainable Cities Index 2015*. Retrieved November 21, 2015, from http://www.worldurbancampaign.org/resources/partners-resources/

Bandura, R. (2008). *A survey of composite indices measuring country performance: 2008 Update. United Nations Development Programme*. Office of Development Studies.

Bax, C., Wesemann, P., Gitelman, V., Shen, Y., Goldenbeld, C., Hermans, E., Doveh, E., Hakkert, S., Wegman, F., & Aarts, L. (2012). *Developing a road safety index*. Deliverable 4.9 of the EC FP7 project DaCoTA.

Ben-Gal, I. (2005). Outlier detection. In O. Maimon & L. Rockach (Eds.), *Data mining and knowledge discovery handbook: A complete guide for practitioners and researchers*. Boston: Kluwer Academic. doi:10.1007/0-387-25465-X_7

Black, J. A., Paez, A., & Suthanaya, P. A. (2002). Sustainable urban transportation: Performance indicators and some analytical approaches. *Journal of Urban Planning and Development*, *128*(4), 184–209. doi:10.1061/(ASCE)0733-9488(2002)128:4(184)

Camagni, R., Gibelli, M. C., & Rigamonti, P. (2002). Urban mobility and urban form: The social and environmental costs of different patterns of urban expansion. *Ecological Economics*, *40*(2), 199–216. doi:10.1016/S0921-8009(01)00254-3

Charnes, A., Cooper, W. W., & Rhodes, E. (1978). Measuring the efficiency of decision making units. *European Journal of Operational Research*, *2*(6), 429–444. doi:10.1016/0377-2217(78)90138-8

Coob, J., & Daly, H. (1989). *For the common dood. Redirecting the economy toward community, the environment and a sustainable future*. Boston: Beacon Press.

Esty, D. C., Levy, M., Srebotnjak, T., & de Sherbinin, A. (2005). *2005 environmental sustainability index: Benchmarking national environmental stewardship*. New Haven, CT: Yale Center for Environmental Law and Policy.

European Commission. (2005). *Sustainable development indicators to monitor the implementation of the EU sustainable development strategy*. Brussels: Commission of the European Communities.

European Commission. (2015). *Clean transport, Urban transport*. Retrieved July 10, 2015, from http://ec.europa.eu/transport/themes/urban/urban_mobility/index_en.htm

Forum for the Future. (2007). *The sustainable cities index, ranking the largest 20 British cities*. Retrieved August 1, 2015, from http://www.forumforthefuture.org.uk

Freudenberg, M. (2003). *Composite indicators of country performance: A critical assessment*. STI working paper 2003/16. Paris: Organization for Economic Co-operation and Development (OECD).

Hawkins, D. (1980). *Identification of outliers*. London: Chapman and Hall. doi:10.1007/978-94-015-3994-4

Hermans, E. (2009). *A methodology for developing a composite road safety performance index for cross-country comparison.* (Doctoral Dissertation). Hasselt University, Belgium.

Hermans, E., Van den Bossche, F., & Wets, G. (2008). Combining road safety information in a performance index. *Accident; Analysis and Prevention, 40*(4), 1337–1344. doi:10.1016/j.aap.2008.02.004 PMID:18606264

Howell, D. C. (2008). The analysis of missing data. In W. Outhwaite & S. Turner (Eds.), *Handbook of social science methodology.* London: Sage.

King's Fund. (2001). *The sick list 2000, the NHS from best to worst.* Retrieved December 2, 2014, from http://www.fulcrumtv.com/sick%20list.htm

Krajnc, D., & Glavic, P. (2005). A model for integrated assessment of sustainable development. *Resources, Conservation and Recycling, 43*(2), 189–208. doi:10.1016/S0921-3449(04)00120-X

Liu, H., Shah, S., & Jiang, W. (2004). On-line outlier detection and data cleaning. *Computers & Chemical Engineering, 28*(9), 1635–1647. doi:10.1016/j.compchemeng.2004.01.009

Manuel, A. (2015). *Sustainable city index 2015.* The Hague, The Netherlands: Sustainable Society Foundation.

Mihyeon Jeon, C., & Amekudzi, A. (2005). Addressing sustainability in transportation systems: Definitions, indicators, and metrics. *Journal of Infrastructure Systems, 11*(1), 31–50. doi:10.1061/(ASCE)1076-0342(2005)11:1(31)

Mori, K., & Christodoulou, A. (2012). Review of sustainability indices and indicators: Towards a new City Sustainability Index (CSI). *Environmental Impact Assessment Review, 32*(1), 94–106. doi:10.1016/j.eiar.2011.06.001

Munda, G. (2005). Multi-criteria decision analysis and sustainable development. In J. Figueira, S. Greco, & M. Ehrgott (Eds.), *Multiple-criteria decision analysis: State of the art surveys* (pp. 953–986). New York: Springer.

Munda, G., & Nardo, M. (2009). Non-compensatory/non-linear composite indicators for ranking countries: A defensible setting. *Applied Economics, 41*(12), 1513–1523. doi:10.1080/00036840601019364

Organization for Economic Co-operation and Development (OECD). (2008). *Handbook on constructing composite indicators: Methodology and user guide.* Paris: OECD.

Puolamaa, M., Kaplas, M., & Reinikainen, T. (1996). *Index of environmental friendliness: A methodological study.* Eurostat.

Rai, H. B., van Lier, T., & Macharis, C. (2015). Towards data-based mobility policies in Flemish cities: creating an inclusive sustainability index. In *Proceedings of the BIVEC/GIBET Transport Research Days 2015* (pp. 104-116).

Ronchi, E., Federico, A., & Musmeci, F. (2002). A system oriented integrated indicator for sustainable development in Italy. *Ecological Indicators, 2*(1-2), 197–210. doi:10.1016/S1470-160X(02)00045-6

Rubin, D. B. (1987). *Multiple imputation for non-response in surveys*. New York: John Wiley & Sons. doi:10.1002/9780470316696

Saaty, T. L. (1980). *The analytic hierarchy process*. New York: McGraw-Hill.

Saisana, M., & Tarantola, S. (2002). *State-of-the-art report on current methodologies and practices for composite indicator development*. EUR 20408 EN Report. Ispra: The Joint Research Center of European Commission.

Saisana, M., Tarantola, S., & Saltelli, A. (2005). Uncertainty and sensitivity techniques as tools for the analysis and validation of composite indicators. *Journal of the Royal Statistical Society A, 168*(2), 307–323. doi:10.1111/j.1467-985X.2005.00350.x

Sharma, S. (1996). *Applied multivariate techniques*. New York: John Wiley and Sons.

Shen, Y., Hermans, E., Bao, Q., Brijs, T., Wets, G., & Wang, W. (2015). Inter-national benchmarking of road safety: State of the art. *Transportation Research Part C, Emerging Technologies, 50*, 37–50. doi:10.1016/j.trc.2014.07.006

Shen, Y., Hermans, E., Brijs, T., & Wets, G. (2013). Data envelopment analysis for composite indicators: A multiple layer model. *Social Indicators Research, 114*(2), 739–756. doi:10.1007/s11205-012-0171-0

Shen, Y., Hermans, E., Ruan, D., Wets, G., Brijs, T., & Vanhoof, K. (2011). A generalized multiple layer data envelopment analysis model for hierarchical structure assessment: A case study in road safety performance evaluation. *Expert Systems with Applications, 38*(12), 15262–15272. doi:10.1016/j. eswa.2011.05.073

Shen, Y., Ruan, D., Hermans, E., Brijs, T., Wets, G., & Vanhoof, K. (2011). Modeling qualitative data in data envelopment analysis for composite indicators. *International Journal of Systems Assurance Engineering and Management, 2*(1), 21–30. doi:10.1007/s13198-011-0051-z

Sikdar, S. K., Sengupta, D., & Harten, P. (2012). More on aggregating multiple indicators into a single index for sustainability analyses. *Clean Technologies and Environmental Policy, 14*(5), 765–773. doi:10.1007/s10098-012-0520-3

Singh, R. K., Murty, H. R., Gupta, S. K., & Dikshit, A. K. (2012). An overview of sustainability assessment methodologies. *Ecological Indicators, 15*(1), 281–299. doi:10.1016/j.ecolind.2011.01.007

United Nations, Department of Economic and Social Affairs, Population Division (2014). *World urbanization prospects: The 2014 revision, Highlights*. ST/ESA/SER.A/352.

van Audenhove, F., Korniichuk, O., Dauby, L., & Pourbaix, J. (2014). *The future of urban mobility 2.0, Arthur D. Little and UITP*. Retrieved August 5, 2015, from http://www.adl.com/FUM2.0

van de Kerk, G., & Manuel, A. (2014). *Sustainable society index 2014*. The Hague, The Netherlands: Sustainable Society Foundation.

van Lier, T., Rai, H. B., & Macharis, C. (2015). Sustainable logistics in urban areas: What gets measured, gets managed. In *Proceedings of the NECTAR City Logistics and Sustainable Freight Transport Workshop* (pp. 1-37).

Wefering, F., Rupprecht, S., Buhrmann, S., & Bohler-Baedeker, S. (2014). *Guidelines-developing and implementing a sustainable urban mobility plan.* Brussels: European Platform on Sustainable Urban Mobility Plans.

Wilmots, B., Shen, Y., Hermans, E., & Ruan, D. (2011). *Missing data treatment: Overview of possible solutions.* Diepenbeek: Policy Research Centre Mobility and Public Works, track Traffic Safety, RA-MOW-2011-002.

Yigitcanlar, T., & Dur, F. (2010). Developing a sustainability assessment model: The sustainable infrastructure, land-use, environment and transport model. *Sustainability, 2*(1), 321–340. doi:10.3390/su2010321

Zhang, M. (2002). *Measuring urban sustainability in China.* (Doctoral Dissertation). Erasmus University, The Netherlands.

ADDITIONAL READING

Alonso, A., Monzon, A., & Cascajo, R. (2015). Comparative analysis of passenger transport sustainability in European cities. *Ecological Indicators, 48*, 578–592. doi:10.1016/j.ecolind.2014.09.022

Anderson, S., Allen, J., & Browne, M. (2005). Urban logistics---how can it meet policy makers' sustainability objectives? *Journal of Transport Geography, 13*(1), 71–81. doi:10.1016/j.jtrangeo.2004.11.002

Bao, Q., Ruan, D., Shen, Y., Hermans, E., & Janssens, D. (2012). Improved hierarchical fuzzy TOPSIS for road safety performance evaluation. *Knowledge-Based Systems, 32*, 84–90. doi:10.1016/j.knosys.2011.08.014

Bastos, J. T., Shen, Y., Hermans, E., Brijs, T., Wets, G., & Ferraz, A. C. P. (2015). Traffic fatality indicators in Brazil: State diagnosis based on data envelopment analysis research. *Accident; Analysis and Prevention, 81*, 61–73. PMID:25942692

Carse, A. (2011). Assessment of transport quality of life as an alternative transport appraisal technique. *Journal of Transport Geography, 19*(5), 1037–1045. doi:10.1016/j.jtrangeo.2010.10.009

Castillo, H., & Pitfield, D. E. (2010). ELASTIC – A methodological framework for identifying and selecting sustainable transport indicators. *Transportation Research Part D, Transport and Environment, 15*(4), 179–188. doi:10.1016/j.trd.2009.09.002

Cherchye, L., Moesen, W., Rogge, N., & Van Puyenbroeck, T. (2007). An introduction to 'Benefit of the doubt' composite indicators. *Social Indicators Research, 82*(1), 111–145. doi:10.1007/s11205-006-9029-7

Dempster, A. P., & Rubin, D. B. (1983). Introduction. In W.G., Madow, I. Olkin, & D.B. Rubin (Eds.), Incomplete data in sample surveys, Vol. 2: Theory and bibliography (pp.3-10). New York: Academic Press.

Echenique, M. H., Hargreaves, A. J., Mitchell, G., & Namdeo, A. (2012). Growing cities sustainably: Does urban form really matter? *Journal of the American Planning Association, 78*(2), 121–137. doi:10.1080/01944363.2012.666731

European Commission. (2006). *Keep Europe moving --- Sustainable mobility for our continent: Midterm review of the European Commission's 2001 transport white paper*. Commission of the European Communities, Brussels.

Li, T., Ruan, D., Shen, Y., Hermans, E., & Wets, G. (in press). A new weighing approach based on rough sets theory and granular computing for road safety indicator analysis. *Computational Intelligence*. doi:10.1111/coin.12061

Li, T., Zhang, H., Yuan, C., Liu, Z., & Fan, C. (2012). A PCA-based method for construction of composite sustainability indicators. *The International Journal of Life Cycle Assessment*, *17*(5), 593–603. doi:10.1007/s11367-012-0394-y

Litman, T. (2007). Developing indicators for comprehensive and sustainable transport planning. *Transportation Research Record: Journal of the Transportation Research Board*, *2017*(1), 10–15. doi:10.3141/2017-02

Maibach, M., Schreyer, C., Sutter, D., van Essen, H. P., Boon, B. H., Smokers, R., . . . Bak, M. (2008). Handbook on Estimation of External Costs in the Transport Sector. Internalisation Measures and Policies for All external Cost of Transport (IMPACT), Version 1.1, CE Delft.

Parris, T. M., & Kates, R. W. (2003). Characterizing and measuring sustainable development. *Annual Review of Environment and Resources*, *28*(1), 559–586. doi:10.1146/annurev.energy.28.050302.105551

Peat, J., & Bartion, B. (2005). *Medical Statistics: A Guide to Data Analysis and Critical Appraisal*. Oxford: Blackwell Publishing Ltd. doi:10.1002/9780470755945

Santos, G., Behrendt, H., Maconi, L., Shirvani, T., & Teytelboym, A. (2010). Part I: Externalities and economic policies in road transport. *Research in Transportation Economics*, *28*(1), 2–45. doi:10.1016/j.retrec.2009.11.002

Santos, G., Behrendt, H., Maconi, L., Shirvani, T., & Teytelboym, A. (2010). Part II: Policy instruments for sustainable road transport. *Research in Transportation Economics*, *28*(1), 46–91. doi:10.1016/j.retrec.2010.03.002

Schiffler, R. E. (1988). Maximum Z score and outliers. *The American Statistician*, *42*(1), 79–80.

Shen, Y. (2012). *International benchmarking of road safety performance and development using indicators and indexes: Data envelopment analysis based approaches*. (doctoral dissertation). Hasselt University, Belgium.

Shen, Y., Hermans, E., Bao, Q., Brijs, T., & Wets, G. (2013). Road safety development in Europe: A decade of changes (2001-2010). *Accident; Analysis and Prevention*, *60*, 85–94. doi:10.1016/j.aap.2013.08.013 PMID:24029218

Shen, Y., Li, T., Hermans, E., Ruan, D., Wets, G., Vanhoof, K., & Brijs, T. (2010). A hybrid system of neural networks and rough sets for road safety performance indicators. *Soft Computing*, *14*(12), 1255–1263. doi:10.1007/s00500-009-0492-3

Spiekermann, K., & Wegener, M. (2004). Evaluating urban sustainability using land-use transport interaction models. *European Journal of Transport and Infrastructure Research*, *4*(3), 251–272.

Sweeting, W. J., & Winfield, P. H. (2012). Future transportation: Life time considerations and framework for sustainability assessment. *Energy Policy*, *51*, 927–938. doi:10.1016/j.enpol.2012.09.055

van Bueren, E., Van Bohemen, H., Itard, L., & Visscher, H. (Eds.). (2011). *Sustainable Urban Environments: An Ecosystem Approach*. New York: Springer Science & Business Media.

Yigitcanlar, R. T., & Dur, F. (2010). Developing a sustainability assessment model: The sustainable infrastructure, land-use, environment and transport model. *Sustainability*, *2*(1), 321–340. doi:10.3390/su2010321

Zito, P., & Salvo, G. (2011). Toward an urban transport sustainability index: An European comparison. *European Transport Research Review*, *3*(4), 179–195. doi:10.1007/s12544-011-0059-0

KEY TERMS AND DEFINITIONS

Aggregation: A process of combining n-tuples of objects belonging to a given set into a single object of the same set.

Composite Indicator: A mathematical aggregation of a set of individual indicators that measures multi-dimensional concepts but usually has no common units of measurement.

Missing Data Imputation: A process by which missing values in a data set are estimated by appropriately computed values, thereby producing a complete data set.

Normalization: A process in which data attributes within a data model are organized to increase the cohesion of entity types.

Outlier Detection: A process of identifying from a data set the observations that deviates very much from other observations.

Sensitivity Analysis: A study of how the uncertainty in the output of a mathematical model or system can be apportioned to different sources of uncertainty in its inputs.

Sustainability: A capacity of something to be maintained or to sustain itself. It is about taking what we need to live now, without endangering the potential for people in the future to meet their needs.

Sustainable Urban Mobility: The sustainable movement of people and goods within an urban geography. Defined as contributing to cities being able to function in a way that enables good levels of mobility for people and goods, promotes economic development of the city, and meanwhile, minimises air and noise pollution, and contributes towards targets to reduce CO_2 emissions.

Uncertainty Analysis: A process of investigating the uncertainty of relevant variables that are used in decision-making problems.

Weighting: A process of emphasizing the contribution of some aspects of a phenomenon (or of a set of data) to a final effect or result by giving them more weight in the analysis.

Chapter 3
Composite Indices in Technology Management:
A Critical Approach

Milica Jovanovic
University of Belgrade, Serbia

Maja Levi Jaksic
University of Belgrade, Serbia

Jovana Rakicevic
University of Belgrade, Serbia

Jasna Petkovic
University of Belgrade, Serbia

Sanja Marinkovic
University of Belgrade, Serbia

ABSTRACT

This chapter focuses on composite indices used in Technology Management (TM). It provides a critical comparative analysis of 5 indices, summarizes their structure, weighting process and emphasizes technology related components of indices as well as their advantages and disadvantages. The second part of the chapter examines the ranks of OECD and BRICS countries for Global Competitiveness Index (GCI), Global Innovativeness Index (GII) and Global Entrepreneurship Index (GEI), and further, we analyzed the correlations of GCI and GII pillars and clusters with the final ranks of countries. The research proved the presence and the importance of TM in the construction of the selected indices, but also identified that there is a lack of composite indicators used exclusively for TM performance which are measured globally by official institutions.

DOI: 10.4018/978-1-5225-0714-7.ch003

INTRODUCTION

Today's global environment characterizes continuous and exponential technological growth and development. Thus, it is very important to manage technology and follow the trends of technological changes. This chapter argues that technology and innovation management is indispensable for achieving sustainable competitiveness at different levels in the economy. The chapter provides a clear overview of the selected composite indicators, criticises their methodological approaches and clarifies the role of technology and innovation management performance indicators in the construction of global indices.

The concept of technology management (TM) is evolving and now encompasses multiple dimensions and components. The interest of scholars in research of TM performance characteristics is rising. This results in a growing number of dimensions, relationships and aspects continuously being added and discovered, also resulting in multiple indicators, indices, models which show a rising complexity of TM. In the conceptual sense, this chapter approaches TM from the perspective of comparative analysis of the chosen development indices used for ranking countries with a dual objective:

1. To present the components of TM developed in different models for measuring competitive, innovative, technological, economic, development, etc., performance in order to establish TM performance indicators leading towards the creation of comprehensive and integral index and
2. To identify the position of TM, measured by its contribution and in relation to the chosen overall global, competitive, innovative, development indices.

The integral TM approach and concept involves many aspects and dimensions some of which are represented by the multiple indicators presented in the analysis.

Technology Management (TM) is alternatively referred to as Technology and Innovation Management (TIM) in both the literature and this chapter (Levi Jaksic et al, 2014a). The complexity of TM is reflected by the multiple definitions coming as a result of approaching TM from different angles, with the overall agreement of its central role in shaping the economic and social reality of firms, regions, countries, and the global world. Some authors list information management, innovation management, entrepreneurship, new product development, Research and Development (R&D) management, intellectual property, as the crucial components of TM that are "increasingly recognized as essential for continued corporate and societal well-being" (Atkinson & Correa, 2007). There is an ample evidence of a steep rise in the development of the scientific field of TM (Cunningham & Kwakkel, 2011) that corresponds to the practical need of "managing technology as the fundamental source of competitive advantage of firms and economies" (Eskandari et al., 2007). In this century, the technological innovations in areas such as materials, electronics, aerospace, computers, telecommunications, and biotechnology have influenced the rise of dominant forces in the world economy (Levi Jaksic et al., 2014a). Yet there are serious concerns about "our effectiveness in generating and exploiting technology" (Mallick & Chaudhury, 2000). The MIT Commission on Industrial Productivity cites weak technology management practice as a primary cause for the decline of competitiveness in many key US industries (Mallick & Chaudhury, 2000).

The perspectives of micro and macro-management of technology and innovation are becoming more closely related to an integral approach. Open and sustainable innovation with entrepreneurial action results in new business ventures transforming the economy and society towards sustainability (Levi Jaksic et al, 2014b). Also, Samara et al. (2012) emphasize that TM performance is an integral part of national innovation systems (NIS). NIS can be described as the set of institutions, which jointly and individually contribute to the development and diffusion of new technologies and which provide the framework, within which governments form and implement policies to influence the innovation process (Metcalfe, 1995; Samara et al., 2012). Dynamics of national systems is driven by the co-evolution of two main dimensions: innovative capability (innovative efforts and investments increase primary for imitation and reinvestment in the future) and absorptive capacity (enhancing productivity of the R&D sector and policy commitment to technological activities) (Castellacci & Natera, 2013). Regarding the composition of NIS, it is observed as a set of institutions that interact among each other (e.g., universities, industries, and governments). They produce and implement knowledge innovation. As Guan and Chen (2012) highlight, "these actors provide the national innovation production framework within which governments form and implement policies to influence the innovation process". Etzkowitz and Leydesdorff (1995) recognized the existence of interconnection between three subjects (universities, industries and governments) and created a Triple Helix concept which suggests that, in a knowledge-based economy, innovativeness and economic development are achieved by successful cooperation of these subjects in creation, transfer and application of knowledge. This concept supports the NIS concept, but it evolves further and emphasizes the collaboration of these subjects and its linkage and the possibility of taking each other's role in the innovation process (Etzkowitz et al. 1998).

Samara et al. (2012) decompose the NIS into seven subsystems, namely Knowledge and Human Resources, Research Activities, Market Conditions, Institutional Conditions, Financial System, Innovation Process and Technological Performance. From their study, we can clearly see the place of TM performance in NIS. Accordingly, Grupp and Mogee (2004) presented an overview of the development of science and technology indicators and their use in measuring national innovative performance and national policy making, related to innovation. They also showed how innovation scoreboards can be manipulated in the policymaking system, since composite scores and country rank positions can vary considerably depending on the selection process of indicators included. This is a question that raises a lot of doubts when considering composite indicators. However, even being aware of this fact, composite indices had become a very popular way of assessing large phenomena, and the race for a better country rank on different lists has taken its toll.

The concept of technological progress, through innovating activities and knowledge creation, is recognized as the main engine of economic growth many years ago. Soete and Weel (1999, 1999a) argue that even the classical economists such as Karl Marx or Joseph Schumpeter realised the crucial importance of innovation and knowledge accumulation for long-term growth. Katic et al. (2012) analyze the most relevant indices of competitiveness available and the position of the knowledge competitiveness within the indices. The authors conclude that existing models of knowledge are not appropriate for countries in transition. Current models of knowledge contain a large number of qualitative indicators, which are subject to manipulative influences of experts, while models based on quantitative indicators consists of a small number of parameters.

Sustainable technology and innovation management is specifically oriented at the aspects of efficient and effective technology and innovation management linked to sustainable business competitiveness, growth, and the overall sustainable development of the economy and society (Barney, 2004; Levi Jaksic & Marinkovic, 2012). The complexity of TM is shown by its dual perspective in treating strategic and operational issues, all relevant to achieving competitiveness, innovativeness, technological readiness and capability, and is defined as "the process of effective integration and utilization of the innovation, strategic, operational, and commercial missions of an enterprise for gaining competitive advantage" (Badawy, 2009).

TM deals with products, processes, and services integrated into the new value created and delivered. Besides, it focuses on both firms and economy as a whole. "TM's ultimate objective is to enhance competencies for creating and improving products, processes or services in the marketplace" (Horwitch & Stohr, 2012).

We could say that technology entrepreneurship is one of the indispensable components of TM discipline, while it is also interpreted as the broad concept encompassing technology management and innovation leadership. Technology entrepreneurship in the wide context of knowledge entrepreneurship is oriented at competitiveness based on strong links between scientific results, new technologies, learning and bringing new value to the customer in the form of advanced products and services brought to the market (Jaksic & Trifunovic, 2010). Technological entrepreneurship is the link between science and technology and the practical new value created for the customers upgrading their living conditions and standards contributing to the overall welfare of the economy and society (Etlie, 2000). As claimed by United Nations (United Nations, 2012), enterprises which activities are based on R&D are becoming the essence of the knowledge-based economy. In order to overpass the communication problem between industry and science, there is a need for developing technology entrepreneurship, because it is particularly based on creating a competitiveness established by the cooperation of science, new technologies, learning and creation of new values for the consumers through the improved goods and services (Jaksic et al., 2014a). This is one of the main reasons, why technological entrepreneurship is of great importance for TM.

The emphasis on sustainable TM is related to the role of technology and its position at the core of all the business operations with a focus on the primary operations delivering value to the customers, but also on satisfying the goals of the society, economy, local community while simultaneously developing profitable business results (Jaksic, 2007; Todorovic et al., 2011). The TIM, as a specific set of competencies in the competency-based competitiveness approach, is recognized as the critical success factor for firms, sectors, economies, and regions.

Sustainable TM as the challenging new concept is drawing the attention of scholars and there is a rising interest both in theory and practice to managing TM performance within the broad context of sustainable development. Some of the efforts are seen in the development of integrated indices for ranking countries according to their development characteristics and related to their performance in innovativeness, competitiveness, and economic results.

In the effort to create models of the integrated performance measures based on indicators and composite indices, different institutions are involved, and different methodologies are developed (Adams et al., 2006; Bandura, 2008). Measurement results and values obtained through data collection both from institutional sources and surveys involving different actors – firms, government agencies and bodies, academia, are precious in managing performance leading to better policies and strategy at various levels of the economy. Therefore, the focus of the research presented in this chapter is to examine the approaches of the existing methodologies for developing performance indices. We compare these methodologies and give a critical analysis, which is expected to contribute to their improvement. Research is based on a chosen set of global indices used for cross-country comparisons with technology management indicators included.

Choosing among multiple global integral indices available, and the ultimate selection of 6 composite indices, was based on the following selection criteria: integral/global country level performance indices/indicators, availability of information on the main characteristics of the global indices (structure, individual indicators, calculation methodology, data collection procedures), and TM indicators included within the integral indices or developed as independent entities.

In this research, 3 global integral indices of development, innovativeness, competitiveness that include TM were selected for detailed examination. In the first section, we present 6 composite indices – Global Competitiveness Index, Global Innovation Index, Global Entrepreneurship Index, Technology Achievement Index, Summary Innovation Index, and ArCo Technology Index, and give the overview of positive and negative sides of each index. Further, we examine the selected indices comparing their key characteristics especially about TM indicators. The discussion and results are mainly focused on determining inconsistencies and drawbacks of the existing models and methodologies, while developing a new improved model is left for further research.

METHODOLOGY AND COMPARATIVE ANALYSIS OF INDICES

The next section examines the 6 methodologies which use the level of technology development as one of the aspects analyzed through composite indices. These indices are used as a tool for ranking countries according to their innovativeness and development: Global Competitiveness Index, Global Innovation Index, Technology Achievement Index, Global Entrepreneurship Index, Summary Innovation Index and ArCo Technology Index.

The unique methodological approach applied in this chapter that presents and analyse the selected indices has been developed for a more clearly comparative analysis. The indices are presented by: 1. Description, 2. Index structure (presenting the indicators, grouping at different levels and criteria used for grouping, e.g. input/output or sophistication levels, presentation of hierarchical schema), 3. Data Collection, Index Calculation, and Weighting, and 4. Technology related indicators (if the index itself is not entirely technology related).

Further, we gathered data for three selected indices - GCI, GII and GEI. The data was collected for 2014 on the sample of 34 OECD and 5 BRICS countries. In order to examine the importance and impact of TM related component of the selected indices, we applied the following statistical tool and methods:

1. **Standard Deviation:** In order to detect the discrepancy of ranks regarding different methodological approaches for index construction,
2. **Pearson's Correlation Coefficient:** For determination of the impact that TM related components have on the final scores of the selected indices,
3. **Principal Component Analysis:** In order to examine the possibility of grouping similar components of the indices and reducing their number.

Composite Indices for Technology Management

The importance of measuring the overall management performance is well-explained by the famous sentence of Lord Kelvin *"If you can't measure it, you cannot improve it"*, which is applicable also for the management processes. In order to improve, it is important to be able to assess the current state. Also, the reasons for managing and measuring management performance are found in the efforts to answer the following questions (Lebas, 1995): What were our results in the past? Which possibilities do we have? What do we tend to achieve in the future? How can we reach our goals in the future? How will we know if we have achieved our goals? Measuring the TM performance arises as an important and complex problem and assessing the effect of technology (implicitly or explicitly) is in the focus of numerous organizations.

They measure these effects through individual indicators as well as composite indices which include a large number of individual indicators. OECD, Eurostat, World Bank and other organizations publish the values of individual indicators each year in their yearbooks and Internet pages. These indicators are easy to compare by years, and also by countries, but they do not measure all important technological aspects. Also, the causal discrepancy between indicators cannot be seen. What is more important, these indicators do not give a comprehensive evaluation of the technological performance of the entity, but the overview of the individual aspects of TM. These are the reasons why composite indices are more suitable for solving this measurement problem (Zhou et al., 2010).

The problem of TM performance certainly draws attention. Archibugi et al. (2009) presented an overview of the synthetic indicators used for assessing the technological capabilities of nations, highlighting that composite indices have become a sort of a medal in technology and innovation race. They consider nine different indices: the Summary Innovation Index and the Global Innovation Index (European Commission); the Technology Index, the Technological Readiness Index and the Technological Innovation Index (World Economic Forum); the Knowledge Index (World Bank); the Technological Activity Index (UNIDO); the Technological Advance Index (UNCTAD); and the ArCo (Archibugi & Coco, 2004). Katic et al. (2015) developed a new competitiveness model based on knowledge and predominantly expressed quantitative parameters. The model comprises six key parameters: general preconditions, using advanced technologies, education, R&D, innovation and sustainable development.

One of the methodologies which also offers a comprehensive conceptual model of innovation and technology management seen from the perspective of national innovation systems and sustainability is shown in Figure 1.

Figure 1. Triple helix technology management model
Adapted from Levi Jaksic et. al., 2015.

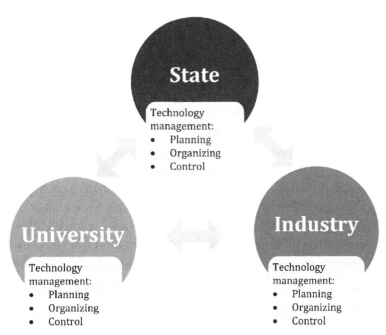

This model offers an overall approach to measuring the success of the national innovation systems regarding measuring the activities of TM at the national level (Levi Jaksic et al., 2015). Yet, the model is developed only as a conceptual approach, and is still not tested in practice, thus has only the scientific importance. But this chapter could be a step toward the implementation of the model.

Also, there are several methodologies that are not primarily focused on TM, but include it as an important aspect of overall performance of the observed entity. These indices differ by the aggregation method and the individual indicators used in the composition of the overall index. These kind of aggregate indicators are very suitable for measuring the complex economic issues such as competitiveness, sustainability, development, entrepreneurship and different criteria used for comparison. In this chapter, the authors want to present the current methodologies for measuring the performance of TM from the standpoint of sustainability and innovativeness, and give a critical analysis of current methodologies.

Methodological Introduction

The next section examines the 6 methodologies which use the level of technology development as one of the aspects analyzed through composite indices. These indices are used as a tool for ranking countries according to their innovativeness and development: Global Competitiveness Index, Global Innovation Index, Technology Achievement Index, Global Entrepreneurship Index, Summary Innovation Index and ArCo Technology Index.

The unique approach of presenting the selected indices has been developed for a more clearly comparative analysis. The indices are presented by: 1. Description, 2. Index structure (presenting the indicators, grouping at different levels and criteria used for grouping, e.g. input/output or sophistication levels, presentation of hierarchical schema), 3. Data Collection, Index Calculation and Weighting and 4. Technology related indicators (if the index itself is not entirely technology related).

Global Competitiveness Index (GCI)

Description

To measure competitiveness on a global level, since 2004 World Economic Forum (WEF) has published an annual report – Global Competitiveness Report for ranking countries based on a composite index – Global Competitiveness Index (GCI) (World Economic Forum, 2014). This index contains information about both macroeconomic and microeconomic aspects of an economy, since it is compounded by more than 100 single indicators which measure the central parts of these aspects. To get an overall picture of the competitiveness and sustainability of a country on a global market, it is crucial to include both of these aspects, since they have great influence on its positioning among other countries. This index "contributes to better understanding of key factors which determine economic development, helps explaining why are some countries more successful than others in increasing their income and providing new opportunities to its population and offers political subjects and business leaders an important tool for improving institutional reforms and economic politics" (World Economic Forum, 2014).

Index Structure

GCI includes more than 100 single indicators which are divided into 12 pillars. These pillars, shown in Figure 2 (adapted from World Economic Forum, 2014) are further classified among 3 sub-indices which are the key for the economies at different levels of development: Basic requirements sub-index, Efficiency enhancers sub-index and Innovation and sophistication factors sub-index (Figure 2). Economies are classified according to different economic development levels suggested by Porter: Factor-driven economies, Efficiency-driven economies and Innovation-driven economies (Porter, 2002). Each sub-index is influencing a particular economy type.

Although, from the Figure 2, it may seem that these pillars are totally independent and separate, it is very important to highlight that it is not the case. They may have an impact on each other, and the development of one pillar may influence categories from some other pillar e.g. it would be impossible to achieve a high development score in the innovation area (pillar 12) without sufficient development of the technology readiness area (pillar 9).

Indicators used for the construction of the pillars are measured in two ways: (1) based on quantitative data (such as GDP, population size, national development etc.) which are publicly available from other official institutions (World Bank, International Monetary Fund, statistical offices); (2) based on data gathered from *The Executive Opinion Survey* conducted by WEF. The participants in this survey are top managers in each country which provide answers related to their enterprises, economic conditions in the country, government institutions, and key national sectors – education, tourism, social aspects, health, etc. After data are collected, each pillar, and consequently sub-index, forms its own score. In the end, the final GCI score is calculated based on the scores of the sub-indices.

Figure 2. GCI structure

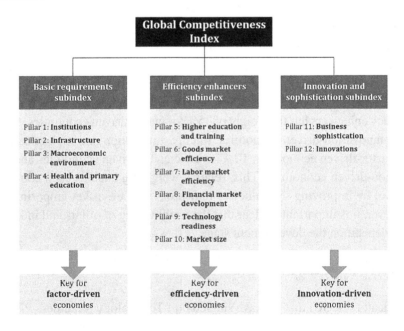

Data Collection, Index Calculation, and Weighting

By further examining the composition of GCI, it is obvious that differentiation should be introduced about some categories to better understand the structure of this index. There are 5 different terms used in defining the hierarchical structure of GCI.:

- Sub-index,
- Pillar,
- Group of clusters,
- Cluster of indicators, and
- Indicator.

At the highest level, there are 3 sub-indices. Each sub-index has a number of pillars, within which there are a cluster of indicators and a set of indicators, at the lowest level, interconnected to form a cluster at the higher level. Each of the pillars has at least 4, indicators and they form group clusters and further are organized into clusters. The importance of an indicator is evaluated on a scale ranging from 1 to 7, 7 being the most important, and the indicators are evaluated in such a manner. Otherwise, if not evaluated on a 1-7 scale, it is expressed by a value explained by each indicator. The difference in the way an indicator is estimated arises from differences in data collection: 1-7 scale is used if data is collected from Executive Opinion Survey, and if this is not the case, it is given in units that are specified for that type of data.

Indicators are grouped into clusters of indicators that are measured by weights which are "percentages" of importance within a pillar. The sum of clusters' weights in a pillar is 100%. Also, each pillar has importance weight within its own sub-index, and the sum of pillars' weights in each sub-index is 100%. Because of their complexity, two pillars (Institutions and Goods market efficiency) are divided into groups of clusters, which form the weights in the same way as the clusters, and the sum of their weights is 100% within a pillar.

It is important to emphasize that the final value of GCI is formed based on the values of the sub-indices, and the value of their weights differs depending on the stage of development of a specific country. Thus, Basic requirements sub-index is the most important for factor-driven economies, with 60% of overall GCI score; it has the weight of 40% for efficiency-driven economies and 20% for innovation-driven economies. Efficiency enhancers has the weight of 35% for factor-driven economies, 50% for efficiency-driven and 50% for innovation-driven economies. Finally, Innovation and sophistication sub-index has the 5% weight for factor-driven economies, 10% for efficiency-driven economies and the highest value of 30% for innovation-driven economies. This, relative weighting enables each country to improve its competitiveness level by improving the values of indicators that are of key importance for its stage of development. However, it is important to clear that the weightening of pillars and indicators remains the same and does not depend on the development stage.

Technology Related Indicators in GCI

There are 2 TM indicators in GCI that we have singled out: Technology Readiness Pillar and Innovation Pillar.

Technology Readiness Pillar

The first important TM related aspects of GCI is its 9th pillar – Technology readiness. In this pillar, the focus is on the capacity of a country to use ICT in everyday activities and production in order to increase the efficiency and provide innovation. This indicator can also be considered as a composite index, since it is compounded of 9 indicators, divided into 2 clusters: Technological adoption and ICT use. Technological adoption cluster has 3 indicators: Availability of latest technologies, Firm-level technology absorption and FDI and technology transfer, while ICT use has 6 indicators: Internet users, Broadband Internet subscriptions, Internet bandwidth, Mobile broadband subscription, Mobile telephone subscriptions and Fixed telephone lines. Both of the clusters have weight of 50%, while the value of indicators in Technological adoption is gathered from The Executive Opinion Survey, while the value of ICT use indicators is gathered from the official institutions. The value of this pillar has been used as a sort of independent index and the stage of development of a certain country has been analysed through the value of this index (Abdalla Alfaki & Ahmed, 2013). The score of the pillar is measuring the speed of existing technology adoption in an economy and the ability to use the technology in order to improve the productivity in a country. But, as indicators demonstrate, this pillar is focused on the usage of the existing technology in companies, not the R&D activities in evaluated countries. For this purpose, there is separated pillar – R&D innovation within Innovation and sophistication sub-index.

Innovation Pillar

As well as the Technology readiness, Innovation pillar (12th pillar) has been used as a composite index which compares the level of technology innovativeness achieved in an economy and is referred as Technology Innovation Index (Archibugi et al., 2009). This index is related not to the usage of the existing technologies, but to the research and development of new technologies and innovative expansion of knowledge. This pillar focuses on technology knowledge opposed to 11th pillar which relates to non-technological knowledge used for innovation. The focus of this pillar is on the investment in R&D activities. Indicators measured in this pillar are: Capacity for innovation, Quality of scientific research institutions, Company spending on R&D, University-industry collaboration in R&D, Government procurement of advanced technology products, Availability of scientists and engineers, PCT patent applications and Intellectual property protection. All of these indicators, except PCT patent application, are gathered from the Executives Opinions Survey.

Global Innovation Index (GII)

Description

In 2007, INSEAD business school presented Global Innovation Index – GII, as another composite index related to innovativeness and sustainability of a country. The authors of GII emphasize that this index is a "tool for decision makers whose goals are the improvement of innovative performance of a country" (Cornell University, INSEAD, & WIPO, 2014). GII tries to examine the suitability of the national environment for innovations, as well as the innovativeness of the outputs in examined country.

Index Structure

Similar as GCI, GII is also compounded of numerous single indicators. The list of indicators is evaluated each year, and the composition of GII varies year-to-year since new indicators are included in composition if they are marked as important for measuring innovativeness. However, the basic structure of GII remains the same and is shown in Figure 3: There are 2 sub-indices – Innovation Input sub-index and Innovation Output sub-index. Further, these sub-indices are decomposed on 7 pillars, 5 are related to innovation inputs, and 2 are related to innovation outputs. Each of the pillars is composed of 3 more clusters in which over 80 indicators are classified.

Data Collection, Index Calculation, and Weighting

Data collection is conducted in similar way as in GCI, based on the data from official institutions and based on the survey for the executives in the business sector. Also, some of the used data are also composite indices from international agencies. After data are gathered, the scores of clusters are calculated as the sum of weighted values of the indicators (the weights differ among indicators). Then, the value of each pillar is calculated as the average value of the cluster scores, and afterward, the value of each sub-index is also calculated as the average value of the pillars' scores. Finally, Innovation Efficiency Index is calculated as the ratio of Innovation outputs and Innovation inputs, while the final GII is also average of output and input sub-index.

Figure 3. GII structure
Adapted from Cornell University, INSEAD, & WIPO, 2014.

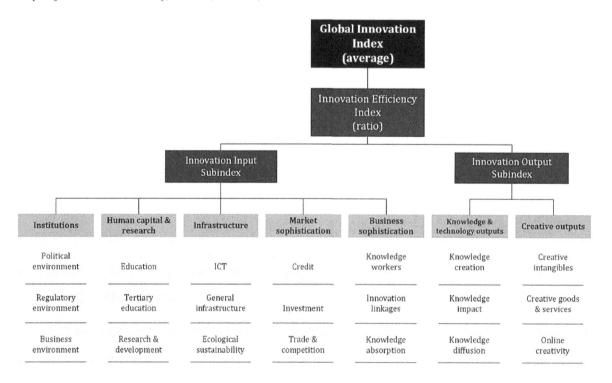

Technology Related Indicators in GII

There are 9 TM clusters in GII that we have singled out:

1. **Research and Development Cluster:** The R&D cluster measures the level and quality of R&D activities, with indicators on researchers (full-time equivalence), gross expenditure, and the quality of scientific and research institutions as measured by the average score of the top 3 universities in the QS World University Ranking of 2014. By design, this indicator aims at capturing the availability of at least 3 higher education institutions of quality within each economy (i.e., included in the global top 700), and is not aimed at assessing the average level of all institutions within a particular economy.

2. **ICT Cluster:** The ICTs cluster includes 4 indices developed by international organizations on ICT access, ICT use, online service by governments, and online participation of citizens (e-participation).

3. **Creative Goods and Services Cluster:** Cluster on creative goods and services includes proxies to get at creativity and the creative outputs of an economy. It includes 5 indices: Cultural and creative services exp., % total trade, National feature films/mn pop. 15-69, Global entertainment and media output/th pop. 15–69, Printing and publishing manufacture, and Creative goods exports, % total trade.

4. **Online Creativity Cluster:** On-line creativity includes 4 indicators, all scaled by population aged 15 through 69 years old: generic (biz, info, org, net, and com) and country-code top level domains, average monthly edits to Wikipedia; and video uploads on YouTube. Attempts made to strengthen this sub-pillar with indicators in areas such as blog posting, online gaming, the development of applications, and have so far proved unsuccessful.

5. **Creative Intangibles Cluster:** Creative intangible assets includes statistics on trademark applications by residents at the national office; trademark applications under the Madrid System by country of origin, and two survey questions regarding the use of ICTs in business and organizational models, new areas that are increasingly linked to process innovations in the literature.

6. **Innovation Linkage Cluster:** The Innovation linkages sub-pillar draws on both qualitative and quantitative data regarding business/university collaboration on R&D, the prevalence of well developed and deep clusters, the level of gross R&D expenditure (GERD) financed by abroad, and the number of deals on joint ventures and strategic alliances.

7. **Knowledge Workers Cluster:** This cluster includes 4 quantitative indicators on knowledge workers: employment in knowledge-intensive services; the availability of formal training at the firm level; R&D performed by business enterprise (GERD) as a percentage of GDP (i.e., GERD over GDP); and the percentage of total gross expenditure of R&D that is financed by business enterprise. In addition, the sub-pillar includes an indicator related to the percentage of females employed with advanced degrees.

8. **Knowledge Creation Cluster:** It includes 5 indicators that are the result of inventive and innovative activities: patent applications filed by residents both at the national patent office and at the international level through the PCT; utility model applications filed by residents at the national office; scientific and technical published articles in peer-reviewed journals; and an economy's number of articles (H) that have received at least H citations.

9. **Knowledge Diffusion Cluster:** It includes 4 statistics all linked to sectors with high-tech content or that are key to innovation: royalty and license fees receipts as a percentage of total trade; high-tech exports (net of re-exports) as a percentage of total exports (net of re-exports); exports of communication, computer and information services as a percentage of total trade; and net outflows of FDI as a percentage of GDP.

Technology Achievement Index (TAI)

Description

The main idea of creating Technology Achievement Index (TAI) is to assess the country's current situation in technological progress (UNDP, 2001; Desai et al., 2002). The TAI, a composite index of technological achievement, reflects the level of technological progress and the capacity of a country to participate in the network age. With this index a country can compare its technological performance with other countries. The TAI focuses on how well the country participates in creating and using technology.

Index Structure

TAI consists of 4 dimensions (each dimension consists of 2 indicators):

1. Creating new technology (Resident patent applications, Receipts of royalty and license fees),
2. Diffusing recent innovations (Internet hosts, Medium- and high- technology exports),
3. Diffusing old innovations (Telephone mainlines and cellular, Electricity consumption), and
4. Building a human skill base for the technological creation and adoption (Mean years of schooling, Gross tertiary science enrolment).

TAI index focuses on achievements rather than on efforts because it is not well known how inputs affect the outputs (for example: does the country that invests more in R&D also produce more patents?).

Data Collection, Index Calculation, and Weighting

The methodology used to calculate the TAI presents an average of the dimensions, which are calculated based on the selected indicators. The TAI has 8 indicators. Each dimension consists of 2 indicators.

When calculating the final TAI score, values of the indicators are normalized to a scale from 0 to 1 using goalposts. An indicator value that is equal to the upper goalpost will be normalized to 1 and a value equal to the lower goalpost will be normalized to 0.

Value for each dimension is calculated as the simple average of the indicators. The TAI is the simple average of these 4 dimensions. The indicators in each dimension are given equal weight, and the dimensions are given equal (one-quarter) weight in the final index. This means that diffusion of technology is given more weight since 2 of the 4 dimensions deal with this.

Global Entrepreneurship Index (GEI)

Description

The Global Entrepreneurship Index (GEI) combines individual data with institutional components in order to provide a detailed look at the entrepreneurial ecosystem of nations. This composite index of both individual- and country-level institutional data gives policymakers a tool for understanding the entrepreneurial strengths and weaknesses of their countries' economies.

This index aims to provide a deep understanding of the entrepreneurship concept, and also to measure both the quality and the scope of the entrepreneurial process. It is applied on 130 countries around the globe. GEI is designed to profile the national entrepreneurial systems unlike other output-based or process-based indices. GEI is definitely not a simple count of new businesses registered and is not focused on high-growth of entrepreneurship, but encounters the characteristics of entrepreneurship that enhance productivity, such as innovation, market expansion, being growth-oriented, and having an international outlook.

Index Structure

There are 4 levels of index-building:

1. Variables,
2. Pillars,
3. Sub-indexes, and,
4. The super-index.

The GEI is composed of 3 sub-indexes (called the 3As):

1. Entrepreneurial attitudes,
2. Entrepreneurial abilities, and
3. Entrepreneurial aspirations.

These 3 sub-indexes stand on 14 pillars. Each pillar contains an individual and an institutional variable that correspond to the micro- and the macro-level aspects of entrepreneurship. Unlike other indexes that incorporate only institutional or individual variables, the GEI pillars include both variables. All individual-level variables are from the Global Entrepreneurship Monitor (GEM) survey. The institutional variables are obtained from various sources. The pillars and variables of GEI are shown on Figure 4.

While Ability and Aspirations sub-indexes capture actual entrepreneurship abilities and aspirations, the entrepreneurial attitude sub-index identifies the attitudes of a country's population as they relate to entrepreneurship.

Data Collection, Index Calculation, and Weighting

GEI methodology captures the fact that systems consist of multiple components, and that these components co-produce system performance, by applying the penalty for bottleneck approach. Unlike this index,

Figure 4. GEI structure
Adapted from Acs et. al., 2015.

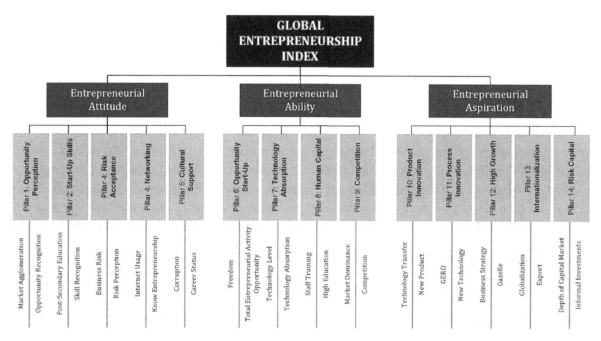

simple summative indexes fail to capture this main characteristic of any system. In a simple summative index, each system component contributes directly and independently to system performance. It would fail to recognize interactions, overlooking crucial aspects of system-level performance.

Regarding the *construction of the pillars* of GEI, they are calculated from the variables by using the interaction variable method (by multiplying the individual variable with the proper institutional variable). Index-building is based on a benchmarking principle. They selected the 95th percentile score adjustment, meaning that any observed value higher than the 95th percentile is lowered to the 95th percentile. The pillars are the basic building blocks of the 3 sub-indexes. The value of a *sub-index* is the arithmetic average of its pillars multiplied by 100. The *super-index* GEI is simply the average of the 3 sub-indexes. Theoretically, an available limit is 100, so the GEI points can also be interpreted as a measure of the efficiency of the entrepreneurship resources.

Technology Related Indicators in GEI

There are 3 TM pillars in GEI that we have singled out: Technology absorption, Product innovation, and Process innovation:

1. **Technology Absorption Pillar:** In the modern knowledge economy, ICT plays a crucial role in economic development. Technology Absorption Pillar includes 2 variables: Technology Level and Technology Absorption. The Technology Level variable is a measure of the businesses that are in technology sectors. The Tech Absorption institutional variable is a measure of a country's capacity for firm-level technology absorption, as reported by the World Economic Forum.

2. **Product Innovation Pillar:** New products play a crucial role in the economy of all countries. While rich countries for years were the source of most new products, developing countries today are producing products that are dramatically cheaper than their Western equivalents. Product Innovation Pillar includes Technology Transfer and New Product variable. New Product is a measure of a country's potential to generate new products and to adopt or imitate existing products. Technology Transfer is a complex measure of whether a business environment allows the application of innovations for developing new products.

3. **Process Innovation Pillar:** Process Innovation pillar includes 2 variables: Gross Domestic Expenditure on R&D and New Technology. Applying and/or creating new technology is another important feature of businesses with high growth potential. Most entrepreneurial businesses do not just apply new technology, they create it. GERD is the R&D percentage of GDP as reported by the Organisation for Economic Co-operation and Development.

Summary Innovation Index (SII)

Description

The Innovation Union Scoreboard (IUS) 2015 (European Comission, 2015) is the 14th edition since the introduction of the European Innovation Scoreboard (EIS) in 2001. The aim of publishing EIS each year was to assess the progress of the objectives concerning innovation set by the Lisbon Strategy in March 2000 (Archibugi et al., 2009). This last report 2015 follows the methodology of previous editions. The overall innovation performance of countries is measured using a composite indicator – the Summary Innovation Index (SII) – which summarizes the performance of a range of different indicators, and measures the strengths and weaknesses of the various national systems of innovation.

Index Structure

The Innovation Union Scoreboard classifies indicators into 3 main groups – Enablers, Firm activities and Outputs – separated into 8 innovation dimensions, and compounded from 25 indicators:

1. **Enablers:** Consist of the drivers which are crucial for innovation performance external to the firm and includes 3 innovation dimensions: Human resources, Open, excellent and attractive research systems, as well as Finance and support,
2. **Firm Activities:** Measure the innovation efforts within the firm, and includes 3 innovation dimensions: Firm investments, Linkages and entrepreneurship, and Intellectual assets, and
3. **Outputs:** Cover the effects of firms' innovation activities in 2 innovation dimensions: Innovators and Economic effects (European Comission, 2015).

Data Collection, Index Calculation, and Weighting

The detailed methodology for calculating SII is presented in the IUS report (European Comission, 2015, page 79). Innovation Union Scoreboard focuses its data sources primarily on the statistics of the official institutions, such as Eurostat, OECD and the United Nations, making its data highly reliable. Since some of the data could be missing, IUS replaces the missing data with the data from the last available year, which could somewhat affect the reliability of the final score. The index calculation methodology assumes 7-step approach to calculation a final SII score (European Comission, 2015, page 79):

1. **Identifying and Replacing Outliers:** Identification of positive and negative outliers, higher or lower than the mean across the observed countries;
2. **Setting Reference Years:** Based on data availability for all countries for which data availability is at least 75%;
3. **Imputing for Missing Values:** Replace missing values with the first available year. If there is no available data it will not be imputed and the indicators will be excluded from the calculation.
4. **Determining Maximum and Minimum Scores:** Highest or lowest score found for the whole period excluding outliers;
5. **Transforming Data if Data Are Highly Skewed:** Data is transformed for those indicators which are not on the 0% to 100% scale, by using a square root transformation;
6. **Calculating Re-Scaled Scores:** By subtracting the minimum score and dividing the result by the difference between the maximum and minimum score;
7. **Calculating Composite Innovation Indexes:** An average of re-scaled scores of all 25 indicators (for which data are available).

ArCo Technology Index

Description

ArCo is an index of technological capabilities applicable for a large number of both developed and developing countries, for two time periods. In addition to cross-country comparisons, it enables the time-series comparisons. The aim of creating this index was to include a larger number of countries, and to rely on dependable data sources. It analyzes 162 countries around the world, over the periods 1987–1990 and 1997–2000 and it is not updated since then.

Index Structure

ArCo index consists of 3 sub-indexes:

1. The creation of technology,
2. The technological infrastructures, and
3. The development of human skills.

It includes 8 basic indicators: 2 for the first sub-index (Patents registered at USPTO, Scientific and technical journal articles), 3 for the second (Internet penetration, Telephone penetration, Electricity consumption), and 3 for the third (Tertiary science and engineering enrolment, Mean years of schooling, Literacy rate).

Data Collection, Index Calculation, and Weighting

Standardized indicators from 0 to 1 were built according to the following formula:

$$\frac{Obs - Min}{Max - Min}$$

where *Obs* is observed value, *Min* is minimum observed value and *Max* is maximum observed value.

In order to enable the time-series comparisons, a maximum and a minimum value were fixed for ArCo, so that achieved scores for both periods would be on the same scale and thus comparable. Homogeneous indicators for all time periods were created with the certainty that no country would express a passed minimum value higher than the more recent one. The formula for this new indicator is presented below:

$$I_x = \frac{Obs_{present} - Min_{past}}{Max_{present} - Min_{past}}$$

The overall ArCo Technology Index is built by using equal weighting for the 3 sub-indexes:

$$ArCoTI = \sum_{i=1}^{3} \frac{1}{3} \cdot I_i$$

where I_i represents the 3 sub-indexes for each country. Each sub-index value is calculated by the same procedure used for the overall index, through the simple mean of the covered indicators.

CRITICAL ANALYSIS OF THE INDICES

Before proceeding to the analysis of specific advantages and disadvantages of each observed indicator, we should emphasize some problems that are common for all composite indices:

1. **Relevance and Quantification of the Qualitative Data:** When considering a global phenomenon, it should be a must to observe both the quantitative, and the qualitative data from surveys or policy review, in order to provide more precise insight and more accurate understanding of the problem (Freudenberg, 2003). The tendency to include "soft" qualitative data is another source of unreliability with regard to composites. However, including qualitative data always raises a question on the relevance and objectivity of the obtained results, and also a question on the quantification of the qualitative data. The best approach does not exist. When creating an index that includes qualitative data (GCI, GII, GEI, SII), it is a more comprehensive approach, but certainly not more accurate one. That is why a part of authors often observe only the quantitative data and solve the problem of accuracy (ArCo, TAI), but certainly come to the problem of incompleteness and missing elements.
2. **Standardization Problem:** A composite index is a group of indicators, indexes and other factors combined in a standardized way, which provides a useful statistical measure of overall performance over time. From the definition of a composite index we can anticipate the problem of standardization of data. If we could use the measures themselves, it would be more accurate and the difference in ranks might be more obvious, than in using scaled values. A lot of data is not available when

using standardization process, and also the process of standardization itself could be questionable (Jovanovic et al., 2012).

3. **What to Do with the Missing Data:** Generally, composite indices can deal with the problem of missing data in three ways (Foa & Tanner, 2012): The first and the simplest solution is to drop any country for which complete data does not exist; The second solution is to impute missing values using different methods (as in SII methodology); and third is to use only existing data in the estimation of the index, but supplement this with an estimated margin of error. For a detailed explanation see (Foa & Tanner, 2012).

4. **Aggregation Problem:** Besides choosing the relevant factors that will be included in the composite index, data aggregation is one of the most important steps in creating composite indices. Zhou et al. (2010) analyze the data aggregation problem in constructing composite indices from the perspective of information loss. Based on the "minimum information loss" principle, they present different aggregation models for constructing composite indices. As a part of the aggregation problem, there is a very commonly emphasized weighting problem. The easiest solution is to assign the same weight to all the components of a composite index. However, this leads us to many different questions regarding the reliability and accuracy of such a methodology. Secondly, experts may define the weights, but there is the problem of subjectivity. Finally, we can use 'objective' weighting, by choosing the right methodology that assigns a weight proportional to the variability of the indicator (Mazziota & Pareto, 2013).

The listed problems are general for all composite indicators, but further, we will focus on the advantages and disadvantages of the selected indices, and the summary is given in Table 1.

Indicators for determining such an important measure as competitiveness (GCI), innovativeness (GII) and entrepreneurship (GEI), must be selected very thoughtfully and precisely, must cover all relevant areas, and must be measured in a proper way. If we look at the list of indicators included in all 3 indices (World Economic Forum, 2014; Cornell University, INSEAD, & WIPO 2014; GEDI, 2014), we can see a wide scope of measures related to different areas. We can say that their creators really did consider all the areas relevant to international competitiveness, innovation and entrepreneurship. So, we conclude that these indicators are comprehensive, compounded by all the relevant sub-indicators. There is no problem regarding the selection of indicators; they are all logical and substantial components. Regarding GCI, there are groups of indicators related to every economy no matter what its development stage is. Having in mind the different weights of sub-indices which are assigned depending on the achieved development level, we could say that every country has the opportunity to build its position in accordance with its stage of development. Also, this kind of weighting by factors which are key for countries based on different level of development provides a better feedback for countries to determine which factors it has to be focused on in order to achieve a higher level of competitiveness.

Further, what could we say about the data collection for these components? Some data is collected from official reports and databases of official institutions, so the question of relevance and measuring this data cannot be raised. But, when it comes to data that is collected through different surveys, there are some doubts and there is a question of the relevance of the obtained data. This does not question the competence of the surveyed managers, but the existence of subjective attitudes towards certain areas, which can affect the final outcome of the index. Also, a number of indicators are qualitative, and there is a question if their quantification is done in a proper manner.

Table 1. Comparative analysis summary of global indices

Composite Index	Index Structure	Weighting	Techn. Related Component*	Advantages	Disadvantages
GCI	**Structure** • 3 sub-indices • 12 pillars • over 100 indicators **Data Collection** • Official data sources • Executive opinion Survey	• Relative weights for constructing index from sub-indices • Fixed weights for constructing sub-index from pillars and pillar from indicators	• Technology Readiness pillar • Innovation pillar	• A large number of indicators • Relative weights of sub-indices • Covers all important areas • Large scope of countries	• Subjectivity of survey • Fixed indicators and pillars weights • Quantification problem
GII	**Structure** • 2 sub-indices • 7 pillars • 3 clusters for each pillar • over 80 indicators **Data Collection** • Official data sources • Executive opinion Survey	• Average weighting for constructing index from sub-indices, sub-index from pillars and pillar from clusters • Fixed weights for constructing cluster from indicators	• Research & Development cluster • ICT cluster • Creative goods & services cluster • Online creativity cluster • Creative intangibles cluster • Innovation Linkage cluster • Knowledge workers cluster • Knowledge creation cluster • Knowledge diffusion cluster	• A large number of indicators • Covers all important areas • Input and output perspective • Annual update of indicators list • Large scope of countries	• Micro level focus • Subjectivity of survey • Input and output classification does not suit theoretical interpretation of efficiency • Average methodology • Fixed indicators weights
TAI	**Structure** • 4 dimensions • 8 indicators **Data Collection** • Official data sources	Average weighting for constructing index from dimensions and dimensions from indicators	All dimensions and components	• Enables the cross-country comparisons • Focus on TM performance • Relies on dependable data sources	• Not designed to measure change over time • Average methodology • Not updated on a yearly basis
GEI	**Structure** • 3 sub-indices • 14 pillars • 2 variables for each pillar • several sub-variables for each variable **Data Collection** • Official data sources • Global Entrepr. Monitor Survey	• Average weighting for constructing index from sub-indices and sub-index from pillars • Interaction variable method for constructing pillars from variables	• Technology Absorption pillar • Product Innovation pillar • Process Innovation pillar	• Incorporates both institutional and individual variables • Large scope of countries	• Average methodology • Subjectivity of survey • Quantification problem
SII	**Structure** • 3 types of indicators • 8 innovation dimensions • 25 indicators **Data Collection** • Official data sources	Average weighting for constructing index from indicators. Each indicator has 1/25 if the data is available.	All dimensions and components	• Relies on dependable data sources • It enables cross-country and time-series comparisons • Considers methodological changes • Focused on TTM performance • Classifies countries according to their innovative performance • Normalized data • There is no quantification problem	• Not designed to measure change over time • Average methodology • Covers only European countries
ArCo	**Structure** • 3 sub-indices • 8 indicators **Data Collection** • Official data sources	Average weighting for constructing index from sub-indices and sub-index from indicators	All dimensions and components	• Applicable for a large number of both developed and developing countries, for two time periods • It enables cross-country and time-series comparisons • Relies on dependable data sources • Focus on TM performance	• Not designed to measure change over time • Average methodology • Not updated on a yearly basis

*The lowest hierarchy level in index structure for which countries are ranked.

One of the questions that also arise is related to determining weights of indicators, pillars and sub-indices. As noticed, the weights of sub-indices are determined according to the stage of development of the observed country. But, when it comes to indicators, current weights are fixed set of values that are applied uniformly to data for each country, after which they are unified into observed indices (GII and GCI). Problem of uniform weighting must not be neglected (Bowen & Moesen, 2009), because the concepts of innovativeness and competitiveness imply that each country achieves higher by developing in one or multiple areas, depending on the circumstances of its environment and opportunities. Of course, other areas should not be neglected, but for this kind of problem it would be suitable to include a system of variable weighting. Also, a shortcoming of GII methodology is its micro-level focus, and even more important the classification of indicators on inputs and outputs. It has been noted that this perspective is a positive side because of the efficiency approach. However, the classification of indicators does not suit theoretical interpretation of efficiency in which the inputs should be minimized and outputs maximized. That also raises the question of the meaning of Innovation Efficiency Ratio which is a ratio between outputs and inputs. What does it represent if we do not maximize outputs and minimize inputs?

With all the advantages of the examined indices, there are clear shortcomings of the existing methodologies, and numerous improvements could be made. The comparative analysis summary of observed indices is presented in Table 1.

RESULTS AND DISCUSSION

Managing technological development is becoming a crucial aspect of the overall progress of a country, which is observed through competitiveness, innovativeness, and entrepreneurship – 3 important triggers of economic development (Acs et al., 2008, Brown & Ulijn, 2004, Mokyr, 2005). Thus, it is important to examine the indicators used for measuring TM and the role and presence of technology management in the creation of composite indices on a global level, used for cross-country comparisons. Therefore, in this section, we present the analysis of the selected countries' ranks according to GCI, GII and GEI. These 3 indices were selected because of the direct relationship with identified aspects of global development. Also, values of ArCo Technology Index and TAI were not updated since their construction, and have only scientific importance, as possible tools for monitoring technological capabilities of countries. Regarding Technology Readiness Index and Innovation Index, they were not examined as separated indices, but as components of GCI.

When it comes to the selection of the sample, OECD countries (34 countries – OECD, 2015) considered as the most developed countries, together with BRICS countries (Brazil, Russian Federation, India, South Africa) which represent the emerging economies, are observed. Data is collected for the year 2014, since this is the last year for which all the data are available.

In Table 2, there are the official ranks of the observed countries according to the 3 indices. However, because the total number of ranked countries differs, it was necessary to calculate relative rank of countries (R-GCI, R-GII and R-GEI – official rank divided by the total number of countries observed for each index). In this way the given ranks of different methodologies are comparable and on the same scale.

In order to examine the difference in rankings, we used standard deviation to determine how much ranks vary depending on the different methodological approach. The deviations were calculated for all 3 indices (ST. DEV. - 3) and between R-GCI and R-GII (ST. DEV. - 2), because of the analysis in the second part of the results. So, we can see that Slovenia has the greatest rank difference, with a standard

Table 2. Ranking of the countries and the deviation of the ranks

Country	GCI	GII	GEI	R-GCI	R-GII	R-GEI	St. Dev. - 3	St. Dev. - 2
Australia	22	17	2	15.28	11.89	1.67	7.09	2.40
Austria	21	20	17	14.58	13.99	14.17	0.31	0.42
Belgium	18	23	13	12.50	16.08	10.83	2.68	2.53
Brazil	57	61	80	39.58	42.66	66.67	14.83	2.17
Canada	15	12	-	10.42	8.39	-	1.43	1.43
Chile	33	46	15	22.92	32.17	12.50	9.84	6.54
China	28	29	46	19.44	20.28	38.33	10.67	0.59
Czech Republic	37	26	41	25.69	18.18	34.17	8.00	5.31
Denmark	13	8	4	9.03	5.59	3.33	2.87	2.43
Estonia	29	24	21	20.14	16.78	17.50	1.77	2.37
Finland	4	4	7	2.78	2.80	5.83	1.76	0.01
France	23	22	12	15.97	15.38	10.00	3.29	0.42
Germany	5	13	16	3.47	9.09	13.33	4.95	3.97
Greece	81	50	58	56.25	34.97	48.33	10.76	15.05
Hungary	60	35	42	41.67	24.48	35.00	8.67	12.16
Iceland	30	19	11	20.83	13.29	9.17	5.92	5.34
India	71	76	75	49.31	53.15	62.50	6.79	2.72
Ireland	25	11	18	17.36	7.69	15.00	5.04	6.84
Israel	27	15	20	18.75	10.49	16.67	4.30	5.84
Italy	49	31	48	34.03	21.68	40.00	9.34	8.73
Japan	6	21	35	4.17	14.69	29.17	12.55	7.44
Korea	26	16	32	18.06	11.19	26.67	7.76	4.86
Luxembourg	19	9	-	13.19	6.29	-	4.88	4.88
Mexico	61	66	57	42.36	46.15	47.50	2.66	2.68
Netherlands	8	5	8	5.56	3.50	6.67	1.61	1.46
New Zealand	17	18	-	11.81	12.59	-	0.55	0.55
Norway	11	14	14	7.64	9.79	11.67	2.02	1.52
Poland	43	45	26	29.86	31.47	21.67	5.26	1.14
Portugal	36	32	30	25.00	22.38	25.00	1.51	1.85
Russia	53	49	69	36.81	34.27	57.50	12.74	1.80
Slovak Republic	75	37	34	52.08	25.87	28.33	14.47	18.53
Slovenia	70	28	22	48.61	19.58	18.33	17.13	20.53
South Africa	56	53	50	38.89	37.06	41.67	2.32	1.29
Spain	35	27	31	24.31	18.88	25.83	3.65	3.84
Sweden	10	3	3	6.94	2.10	2.50	2.69	3.43
Switzerland	1	1	5	0.69	0.70	4.17	2.00	0.00
Turkey	45	54	39	31.25	37.76	32.50	3.46	4.60
United Kingdom	9	2	9	6.25	1.40	7.50	3.22	3.43
United States	3	6	1	2.08	4.20	0.83	1.70	1.49
No of countries observed	**144**	**143**	**120**			**Avg SD**	**5.70**	**4.43**

deviation of 17.13, which was achieved because of its very low rank of 70 for GCI in comparison to GII (28) and GEI (22). Next is Brazil, with the deviation of 14.83 which comes from its poorly developed entrepreneurship, while GCI and GII have close values. Also, Slovak Republic has GCI of 75, GII of 37 and GEI of 34 which gives a large deviation of 14.47. However, Austria and New Zealand have the similar values for each rank, and thus low deviation (<1). Also, Canada, Portugal, Netherlands, United States, Finland and Estonia have low values of deviations. In order to examine the different approaches of examined indices, and also include the perspective of technology management, we examined the correlation of pillars and ranks of GCI and GII. GEI was not examined because data was not available for the pillars for 2014.

Regarding GCI pillars and their correlation with GCI, the highest correlation is obtained for R&D Innovation r=0.8943, which implies strong positive correlation of R&D activities with the achieved competitiveness level. Also, business sophistication is highly positively correlated with the GCI rank, with coefficient value r=0.8571. Generally, what is the most surprising is that Market size has no correlation with the final GCI rank. This is somehow unexpected, having in mind that GCI measures the competitiveness of countries. It leads to the conclusion that the size of a market has no impact on competitiveness level of a country. However, this could also lead to the conclusion that small countries, despite their natural limitations, could reach a high level of competitiveness if they are successful in other areas. Regarding TM related areas, Technology readiness is also highly correlated, not at the same level as R&D Innovation and Business sophistication pillar, but still, has a great impact on the competitiveness level of a country. Generally, since GCI is oriented towards competitiveness, the institutional pillars have higher correlation, and technology management performance is recognized as an (important) aspect of measuring competitiveness level. Since management of technology should be a more important factor of innovativeness (Prajogo & Sohal, 2006), it is expected and should be incorporated in GII, with a higher impact than in GCI. Thus, we examined the correlation of pillars within GII with the final GII rank. The results showed that Human capital and research has the highest correlation with the GII, r=0.8835 and it is a strong positive linear correlation. From the results, it can be concluded that each pillar has a strong correlation with the rank, and the highest are assigned to Infrastructure, Creative outputs, Business sophistication and Knowledge and Technology output (all with r>0.8600).

When it comes to the presence of technology management, it is clear that all of the pillars related to this are highly correlated with the final GII rank. This proves the importance and the presence of technology management in reaching a higher level of innovativeness. Also, we can cross-examine the importance of the pillars of both indices with the final ranks (Table 3). We will focus primarily on TM related pillars. From the results, it is clear that GII has the highest correlation with Technological readiness and R&D Innovation, and Infrastructure, which are the TM pillars of GCI. That is one more proof of the TM presence in the global innovativeness. Also, if we focus on the relationship of TM-GII pillars and GCI, it can be seen that also TM pillars have a great correlation, and stand among the most correlated pillars.

Further, we wanted to examine the relationships between the components of both GCI and GII by applying principal component analysis (PCA) as the extraction method. This method helps to identify basic dimensions of the observed problem which are not evident at the first glance by grouping the similar elements and thus reducing the dimension of the problem (Jolliffe, 2002). The results (Table 4) of this analysis are correlated with the results of the previous analysis. Namely, for GCI, it extracted 3 components and even in the first component it explained the 58.225% of the total variance. This component is highly correlated with all three TM related pillars, with the correlation scores above 0.830. The second component was constructed mainly because of the Financial market development and Macroeconomic

Table 3. Correlations of GCI and GII pillars with GCI and GII ranks

	Pillar	Corr. with GCI Rank	Corr. Rank GCI	Corr. with GII Rank	Corr. Rank GII	Corr. Diff.
GCI	Technological readiness*	0.7344	8	0.8838	1	7
	Infrastructure*	0.7606	6	0.8429	2	4
	R&D Innovation*	0.8943	1	0.8398	3	2
	Higher education and training	0.7492	7	0.8089	4	3
	Labor market efficiency	0.8159	4	0.7806	5	1
	Health and primary education	0.6580	9	0.7608	6	3
	Goods market efficiency	0.7981	5	0.7582	7	2
	Business sophistication	0.8571	2	0.7487	8	6
	Institutions	0.8382	3	0.6974	9	6
	Financial market development	0.6540	10	0.4202	10	0
	Macroeconomic environment	0.3341	11	0.2607	11	0
	Market size	0.0480	12	-0.2302	12	0
GII	Infrastructure*	0.7699	1	0.8827	2	1
	Creative outputs*	0.7591	2	0.8810	3	1
	Business sophistication	0.7588	3	0.8731	4	1
	Human capital & research*	0.7317	4	0.8835	1	3
	Market sophistication	0.7290	5	0.6909	7	2
	Knowledge and technology output*	0.7112	6	0.8621	5	1
	Institutions	0.6023	7	0.7750	6	1

*TM related pillars.

Table 4. Principal component analysis results

GCI Component Matrix				GII Component Matrix	
GCI Pillars	1	2	3	GII Pillars	1
R&D Innovation*	0.889	0.047	0.229	Infrastructure*	0.920
Institutions	0.884	0.250	-0.035	Human capital & research*	0.904
Technology readiness*	0.875	-0.306	-0.111	Business sophistication	0.889
Goods market efficiency	0.868	0.184	-0.008	Creative outputs*	0.879
Higher education and training	0.852	-0.314	-0.099	Knowledge and technology output*	0.826
Labor market efficiency	0.846	0.191	-0.204	Institutions	0.824
Business sophistication	0.842	0.113	0.377	Market sophistication	0.734
Infrastructure*	0.830	-0.389	0.206		
Health and primary education	0.776	-0.474	-0.052		
Financial market development	0.576	0.743	0.069		
Macroeconomic environment	0.282	0.570	-0.426		
Market size	-0.207	0.205	0.867		
% of Variance	58.225	13.614	10.353	% of Variance	73.242
Cumulative %	58.225	71.839	82.192	Cumulative %	73.242

environment which have the highest correlation with this component, which added 13.614% of variance, explaining in a total of 71.839% of the variance with the first component. Finally, the last component was created due to the Market size pillar, which (having in mind that it is not correlated with the final GCI score) again raises the question of this variable, showing that this pillar is not related to the other variables and still not influencing the competitiveness level (GCI rank).

Considering GII component matrix, PCA resulted in only one component which explains 73.242% of variance, showing high correlations with all pillars, particularly with TM related pillars, which had the correlation of above 0.870.

In order to completely examine the TM presence, one more analysis was conducted and it was related to the clusters of GII (each pillar has 3 clusters) in order to have a closer insight into the areas that are most related to the GII rank. Correlation was also examined for both GII and GCI. We will emphasize that the same analysis of GCI would not be possible, because of the different structure on the lower level.

The results (Table 5) showed that within Human capital & research (the pillar most correlated with GII), R&D has the highest correlation, r=0.7874. In Infrastructure, the most correlated cluster is ICT, with the strong positive correlation of r=0.7725, while in Creative outputs, Online creativity has the role, r=0.7926. Business sophistication's cluster with the highest correlation is Knowledge workers, with the absolutely highest correlation among clusters, r=0.8951. Finally, as the last TM related pillar,

Table 5. Correlation of GII clusters with GCI and GII ranks

Pillar	Cluster	Corr. with GII	Corr. with GCI
Human capital & research	Education	0.6797	0.5251
	Research & Development*	**0.7874**	**0.7727**
	Tertiary education	0.6134	0.3886
Infrastructure	General infrastructure	0.4743	0.6764
	Ecological sustainability	0.5505	0.2922
	ICT*	**0.7725**	**0.6935**
Creative outputs	Creative goods & services*	0.5795	0.3000
	Online creativity*	**0.7926**	0.6072
	Creative intangibles*	0.5425	**0.6413**
Business sophistication	Innovation Linkage*	0.7370	0.7078
	Knowledge absorption	0.4223	0.3730
	Knowledge workers*	**0.8951**	**0.7427**
Knowledge and technology output (KTO)	Knowledge creation*	**0.8040**	**0.7359**
	Knowledge impact	0.6132	0.2894
	Knowledge diffusion*	0.5890	0.5408
Institutions	Political environment	**0.7546**	0.6005
	Regulatory environment	0.7226	0.5751
	Business environment	0.7431	**0.6102**
Market sophistication	Credit	**0.7703**	**0.6418**
	Investment	0.4802	0.6357
	Trade and competition	0.2218	0.4416

*TM related clusters.

KTO's most correlated pillar with GII is Knowledge creation. What is interesting is that the same clusters have similar relationships with GCI (although with slightly lower correlation score), except Creative outputs, where the most correlated cluster is Creative intangibles. But, what is more important is that all of these clusters are TM related. This shows that the TM is an essential part of both competitiveness and innovativeness, which emphasizes and proves its importance.

SOLUTIONS AND RECOMMENDATIONS

Indices which are formed for ranking economies at the global level must be carefully and precisely defined. Indicators that comprise indices must cover all relevant areas for the examined problem and their values must be accurately measured (Grupp & Mogee, 2004). If we look upon the structure of the presented indices, we can see that they include a whole range of indicators from different fields and that the authors of the indices include all the relevant areas. As for the GCI, the authors took into account the stage of development of each country and allowed each country to use all its advantages in order to achieve a better score. But the weighting problem of indicators still stands. For both GCI and GII, indicators have fixed weights used for determination of the value of indicator on the upper level (pillars in the case of GCI, groups of indicators in the case of GII). The problem of weighting is crucial (Decancq & Lugo, 2013) because fixed weights limit the ability of a country to improve its position if it is exceptional in one area, but is required to be equally good in all areas. Of course, other areas should not be neglected, but for this type of problem, the methodology should allow flexible weight coefficients. The authors believe that the weights which are not fixed would be a better solution for both indicators and sub-indices. One of the methods which allow the relative weights determination is Data Envelopment Analysis (DEA) (Cherchye et al., 2008) which measures the efficiency of the observed entities based on the output/input relations, and by allowing each unit to determine its combination of the importance of the used indicators, within the defined range. This would solve the weighting problem of the indicators. Also, in the literature (Jovanovic et al., 2012; Jeremic et al. 2013; Isljamovic et al., 2015) I-distance methodology was recognized as the proper one for weight determination. This is a multivariate statistical approach used originally for the socioeconomic country rank determination and ranks the units by using the variables which could be expressed through the different units (Ivanovic, 1977). The calculation of the rank is based on the distances between the entities on each criteria, where the final rank is created based on the distance from the referent entity which could be fictive or a real one and has the highest or the lowest score (depending on the type of indicator). This is also one of the methodologies that could solve the identified weighting problem.

On the other hand, GII uses the good perspective of inputs and outputs, which is suitable for efficiency approach. Nevertheless, in efficiency theory, inputs are values which should be minimized, while outputs are values with maximization goal, which is not the case in GII. Thus, there is a question: what represents the Innovative Efficiency Index calculated as the ratio between Innovation inputs and outputs. The recommendation is to re-examine this classification, and either re-classify the input and output indicators, or avoid the calculation of Innovative Efficiency Index since the countries are not ranked according to this index, and since the obtained result does not represent the efficiency score.

FUTURE RESEARCH DIRECTIONS

Future research will be directed towards examining the weighting problem, and testing methods that could solve this problem. Above all, the two of the listed methodologies will be tested for the selected countries in order to compare the ranking results and examine if the method of the official institutions could be improved.

This chapter examines how the current ranks and methodologies differ, and since some of the methodologies have been changed, it would be useful to examine how these methodological changes influenced the rank of the countries, and if the role of TM related pillars changed. Apart from that, the chronological analysis of the rank changes could and should be a subject of a new study, regardless of the methodological changes. This way we could go further from criticizing the methodology to capturing the changes that occur over years, with the aim to identify what leads to the better rank on different lists.

Also, in the chapter, the authors selected highly developed, OECD countries, and the emerging, BRICS countries, so the research and conclusions were based according to the results of these countries. In order to cover all development stages, the undeveloped countries should be included in the research. This way, it would be determined if the stage of development changes the observations of the authors, and if the presence of technology management is different with undeveloped countries included.

It would be useful to examine partial correlations of the pillars and clusters in order to see the mutual correlation between them, and examine their relationships. This way, it would also be possible to examine how TM areas influence each other and what is the intensity of that influence.

Furthermore, the interesting future research would be to examine if there is a difference in the presence of TM in countries with different levels of development. The samples of developed, emerging and undeveloped countries should be separated, and the existence of statistically significant difference should be determined.

CONCLUSION

The literature says that TM is becoming even more important than the technology characteristics itself (Levi Jaksic et. al., 2015). Thus, it is important to measure the performance of TM. This chapter had the goal to identify and critique the composite indices which are used in order to measure the TM performance on a global level. Composite indices are the measures compounded by numerous different indicators, whose values are the result of the aggregation process of indicators (Booysen, 2002). Since the indices can include various indicators, they can cover different aspects of the observed problem, which makes them suitable for usage as a tool of the comparison between countries. Also, because of the complexity of the problems, those indices are very sensitive on the selection of indicators and their importance, and are very often a subject of the scientific critiques (Jovanovic et. al., 2012; Cherchye et al., 2008; Seke et al., 2013). Through the research we have identified the lack of the composite indices used exclusively for TM. Technology Achievement Index and ArCo Technology Index were created for this purpose. However, they were only created for scientific purpose, and were not accepted widely as the important performance measures. Their creators should make a step towards their appliance, and update them annually. Management of technology is mostly included as an important component of other composite indices used for tracking the country performance from the perspective of other global phenomena (competitiveness, innovativeness etc.). The results of the research presented in the chapter showed a great correlation of TM related pillars with Global Competitiveness Index (GCI) ranks (the most related pillar is R&D Innovations), and also with Global Innovation Index (GII), where the results were even more convincing. Namely, all pillars which are TM related have the greatest relation with GII rank. Even further, the clusters that directly originate from the TM have the highest correlation score with both GII and GCI rankings. Principal component analysis also confirmed that the most of the variance could be explained by the component which is composed of TM related pillars (among others). This undoubtedly implies the importance of TM in contemporary global trends, in reaching a higher level of competitiveness and innovativeness. Further, it implies an unquestionable necessity for a globally measured composite index which would be measured independently from other indices. The index should be used as a tool for improving global performance of countries and other entities, which would enable them to achieve high sustainability level.

The chapter presents an overview of the existing methodologies for the creation of composite indices used for TM. Besides the unquestionable importance of TM, it identified the lack of the independent indices used for TM. The presented indices were carefully examined, and the shortcomings and the advantages of each were highlighted. Further, the authors conducted the analysis of the selected indicators in order to examine the different approaches of GCI and GII, and examine the presence of TM in their composition. The results showed that the TM indeed is a very important component (even the most important one) of the indices, which implied the necessity for an independent index used for measuring the performance of a complex process of management of technology.

REFERENCES

Abdalla Alfaki, I. M., & Ahmed, A. (2013). Technological readiness in the United Arab Emirates towards global competitiveness. World Journal of Entrepreneurship. *Management and Sustainable Development*, *9*(1), 4–13.

Acs, Z. J., Desai, S., & Hessels, J. (2008). Entrepreneurship, economic development and institutions. *Small Business Economics*, *31*(3), 219–234. doi:10.1007/s11187-008-9135-9

Acs, Z. J., Szerb, L., & Autio, E. (2015). *Global Entrepreneurship Index*. Powered by GEDI.

Adams, R., Bessant, J., & Phelps, R. (2006). Innovation management measurement: A review. *International Journal of Management Reviews*, *8*(1), 21–47. doi:10.1111/j.1468-2370.2006.00119.x

Archibugi, D., & Coco, A. (2004). A new indicator of technological capabilities for developed and developing countries (ArCo). *World Development*, *32*(4), 629–654. doi:10.1016/j.worlddev.2003.10.008

Archibugi, D., Denni, M., & Filippetti, A. (2009). The technological capabilities of nations: The state of the art of synthetic indicators. *Technological Forecasting and Social Change*, *76*(7), 917–931. doi:10.1016/j.techfore.2009.01.002

Atkinson, R. D., & Correa, D. K. (2007). *The 2007 State New Economy Index: Benchmarking Economic Transformation in the States*. The Information Technology and Innovation Foundation.

Badawy, A. M. (2009). Technology management simply defined: A tweet plus two characters. *Journal of Engineering and Technology Management*, *26*(4), 219–224. doi:10.1016/j.jengtecman.2009.11.001

Bandura, R. (2008). *A survey of composite indices measuring country performance: 2008 update.* New York: United Nations Development Programme.

Barney, J. B. (2004). Firm Resources and sustained competitive advantage. *Journal of Management,* *17*(1), 99–120. doi:10.1177/014920639101700108

Booysen, F. (2002). An overview and evaluation of composite indices of development. *Social Indicators Research,* *59*(2), 115–151. doi:10.1023/A:1016275505152

Bowen, H. P., & Moesen, W. (2009). Composite Competitiveness Indicators With Endogenous Versus Predetermined Weights: An Application To The World Economic Forum's Global Competitiveness Index. *Competitiveness Review: An International Business Journal Incorporating Journal of Global Competitiveness,* *21*(2), 129–151.

Brown, T. E., & Ulijn, J. M. (Eds.). (2004). *Innovation, entrepreneurship and culture: the interaction between technology, progress and economic growth.* Edward Elgar Publishing. doi:10.4337/9781845420550

Castellacci, F., & Natera, J. M. (2013). The dynamics of national innovation systems: A panel cointegration analysis of the coevolution between innovative capability and absorptive capacity. *Research Policy,* *42*(3), 579–594. doi:10.1016/j.respol.2012.10.006

Cherchye, L., Moesen, W., Rogge, N., Van Puyenbroeck, T., Saisana, M., Saltelli, A., & Tarantola, S. (2008). Creating composite indicators with DEA and robustness analysis: The case of the Technology Achievement Index. *The Journal of the Operational Research Society,* *59*(2), 239–251. doi:10.1057/palgrave.jors.2602445

Cornell University, INSEAD, & WIPO. (2014). *The Global Innovation Index 2014: The Human Factor In innovation.* Fontainebleau, Ithaca, and Geneva: Cornell University, INSEAD, WIPO.

Cunningham, S. W., & Kwakkel, J. (2011). Innovation forecasting: A case study of the management of engineering and technology literature. *Technological Forecasting and Social Change,* *78*(2), 346–357. doi:10.1016/j.techfore.2010.11.001

Decancq, K., & Lugo, M. A. (2013). Weights in multidimensional indices of wellbeing: An overview. *Econometric Reviews,* *32*(1), 7–34. doi:10.1080/07474938.2012.690641

Desai, M., Fukuda-Parr, S., Johansson, C., & Sagasti, F. (2002). Measuring the technology achievement of nations and the capacity to participate in the network age. *Journal of Human Development,* *3*(1), 95–122. doi:10.1080/14649880120105399

Eskandari, H., Sala-Diakanda, S., Furterer, S., et al. (2007). Enhancing the undergraduate industrial engineering curriculum, Defining desired characteristics and emerging topics. *Education + Training,* *49*(1), 45-55.

Etlie, J. E. (2000). *Managing Technological Innovation.* John Wiley & Sons.

European Comission, Directorate-General for Internal Market, Industry, Entrepreneurship and SMEs. (2015). *Innovation Union Scoreboard Report 2015.* Available at: http://ec.europa.eu/growth/industry/innovation/facts-figures/scoreboards/files/ius-2015_en.pdf

Foa, R., & Tanner, J. (2012). *Methodology of the Social Development Indices*. International Institute for Social Studies Working Paper # 2012-04. The Hague: International Institute of Social Studies.

Freudenberg, M. (2003). *Composite Indicators of Country Performance: A Critical Assessment*. OECD Science, Technology and Industry Working Papers, 2003/16. OECD Publishing. 10.1787/405566708255

GEDI. (2014). *The Global Entrepreneurship & Development Index*. Retrieved from http://www.thegedi. org/research/gedi-index/(Accessed 19 September 2015

Grupp, H., & Mogee, M. E. (2004). Indicators for national science and technology policy: How robust are composite indicators? *Research Policy*, *33*(9), 1373–1384. doi:10.1016/j.respol.2004.09.007

Guan, J., & Chen, K. (2012). Modeling the relative efficiency of national innovation systems. *Research Policy*, *41*(1), 102–115. doi:10.1016/j.respol.2011.07.001

Horwitch, M., & Stohr, E. A. (2012). Transforming technology management education: Value creation-learning in the early twenty-first century. *Journal of Engineering and Technology Management*, *29*(4), 489–507. doi:10.1016/j.jengtecman.2012.07.003

Isljamovic, S., Jeremic, V., Petrovic, N., & Radojicic, Z. (2015). Colouring the socio-economic development into green: I-distance framework for countries' welfare evaluation. *Quality & Quantity*, *49*(2), 617–629. doi:10.1007/s11135-014-0012-0

Ivanovic, B. (1977). *Classification theory*. Belgrade: Institute for Industrial Economics.

Jeremic, V., Jovanovic-Milenkovic, M., Martic, M., & Radojicic, Z. (2013). Excellence with Leadership: The crown indicator of SCImago Institutions Rankings IBER Report. *El Profesional de la Informacion*, *22*(5), 474–480. doi:10.3145/epi.2013.sep.13

Jolliffe, I. (2002). *Principal component analysis* (2nd ed.). New York: Springer.

Jovanovic, M., Jeremic, V., Savic, G., Bulajic, M., & Martic, M. (2012). How does the normalization of data affect the ARWU ranking? *Scientometrics*, *93*(2), 319–327. doi:10.1007/s11192-012-0674-0

Lebas, M. (1995). Performance measurement and performance management. *International Journal of Production Economics*, *41*(1-3), 23–35. doi:10.1016/0925-5273(95)00081-X

Levi Jaksic, M. (2007). Technology Innovation Management for Sustainable Business Development. In Contemporary Challenges of Theory and Practice in Economics, Section: Management and Marketing Under Globalization. University of Belgrade, Faculty of Economics.

Levi Jaksic, M., Jovanovic, M., & Petkovic, J. (2015). Technology Entrepreneurship in the Changing Business Environment – A Triple Helix Performance Model. *Amfiteatru Economic*, *17*(38), 422–440.

Levi Jaksic, M., & Marinkovic, S. (2012). *Menadžment održivog razvoja*. Beograd: FON.

Levi Jaksic, M., Marinkovic, S., & Kojic, J. (2014a). Technology Innovation Education in Serbia. In M. Levi Jaksic, S. Barjaktarovic Rakocevic, & M. Martic (Eds.), *Innovative Management and Firm Performance* (pp. 57–63). London: Palgrave, McMillan. doi:10.1057/9781137402226_2

Levi Jaksic, M., Marinkovic, S., & Kojic, J. (2014b). Open Innovation and Sustainable Technology Entrepreneurship. In M. Baćović (Ed.), *Entrepreneurship and Innovation as Precondition for Economic Development* (pp. 45–60). Podgorica: University of Montenegro.

Levi Jaksic, M., & Trifunovic, M. (2010). Leading Innovation Based on Knowledge Entrepreneurship. *Scientific Conference Proceedings, Fakulteta za organizacijske vede, Univerza v Mariboru.*

Makkonen, T. (2015). National innovation system capabilities among leader and follower countries: Widening gaps or global convergence? *Innovation and Development, 5*(1), 113–129. doi:10.1080/215 7930X.2014.992818

Mallick, D. N., & Chaudhury, A. (2000). Technology management education in MBA programs: A comparative study of knowledge and skill requirements. *Journal of Engineering and Technology Management, 17*(2), 153–173. doi:10.1016/S0923-4748(00)00019-9

Mazziotta, M., & Pareto, A. (2013). Methods For Constructing Composite Indices: One For All Or All For One? RIEDS-Rivista Italiana di Economia, Demografia e Statistica-Italian Review of Economics. *Demography and Statistics, 67*(2), 67–80.

Metcalfe, S. (1995). The economic foundations of technology policy: equilibrium and evolutionary perspectives. In P. Stoneman (Ed.), *Handbook of the Economics of Innovation and Technological Change* (pp. 409–512). London: Blackwell.

Mokyr, J. (2005). Long-term economic growth and the history of technology.Handbook of Economic Growth, 1, 1113-1180. doi:10.1016/S1574-0684(05)01017-8

National research Council. (1987). *Management of Technology: the hidden competitive advantage.* Washington, DC: National Academy press.

OECD. (2015). *OECD member countries.* Retrieved from http://www.oecd.org/about/membersandpartners/list-oecd-member-countries.htm

Porter, M. E. (2002). *Enhancing the Microeconomic Foundations of Prosperity: The Current Competitiveness Index.* World Economic Forum.

Prajogo, D. I., & Sohal, A. S. (2006). The integration of TQM and technology/R&D management in determining quality and innovation performance. *Omega, 34*(3), 296–312. doi:10.1016/j.omega.2004.11.004

Samara, E., Georgiadis, P., & Bakouros, I. (2012). The impact of innovation policies on the performance of national innovation systems: A system dynamics analysis. *Technovation, 32*(11), 624–638. doi:10.1016/j.technovation.2012.06.002

Seke, K., Petrovic, N., Jeremic, V., Vukmirovic, J., Kilibarda, B., & Martic, M. (2013). Sustainable development and public health: Rating European countries. *BMC Public Health, 13*(77), 1–7. doi:10.1186/1471-2458-13-77 PMID:23356822

Todorovic, M., Levi Jaksic, M., & Marinkovic, S. (2011). Sustainable technology management indicators: Objectives matrix approach. *African Journal of Business Management, 5*(28), 11386–11398.

UNDP. (2001). *Human Development Report, Making New Technologies Work for Human Development*. Oxford, UK: Oxford University Press.

United Nations. (2012). *Fostering innovative entrepreneurship: challenges and policy options / United Nations Economic Commission for Europe*. Geneva: United Nations New York.

World Economic Forum. (2014). *Global Competitiveness Report 2014-15*. Retrieved from http://www3. weforum.org/docs/WEF_GlobalCompetitivenessReport_2014-15.pdf

Zhou, P., Fan, L. W., & Zhou, D. Q. (2010). Data aggregation in constructing composite indicators: A perspective of information loss. *Expert Systems with Applications, 37*(1), 360–365. doi:10.1016/j. eswa.2009.05.039

ADDITIONAL READING

Archibugi, D., & Coco, A. (2005). Measuring technological capabilities at the country level: A survey and a menu for choice. *Research Policy, 34*(2), 175–194. doi:10.1016/j.respol.2004.12.002

Carayannis, E. G., & Provance, M. (2008). Measuring firm innovativeness: Towards a composite innovation index built on firm innovative posture, propensity and performance attributes. *International Journal of Innovation and Regional Development, 1*(1), 90–107. doi:10.1504/IJIRD.2008.016861

Cooke, P., & Leydesdorff, L. (2006). Regional Development in the Knowledge-Based Economy: The Construction of Advantage. *The Journal of Technology Transfer, 31*(1), 5–15. doi:10.1007/s10961-005-5009-3

Dobbie, M. J., & Dail, D. (2013). Robustness and sensitivity of weighting and aggregation in constructing composite indices. *Ecological Indicators, 29*, 270–277. doi:10.1016/j.ecolind.2012.12.025

Durand, M., & Giorno, C. (1987). Indicators of international competitiveness: Conceptual aspects and evaluation. *OECD Economic Studies, 9*, 147–182.

Etzkowitz, H., & Leydesdorff, L. (1995). The Triple Helix---University-Industry-Government: A Laboratory for Knowledge-Based Economic Development. *EASST Review, 14*, 14–19.

Etzkowitz, H., Webster, A., & Healey, P. (1998). Introduction. In H. Etzkowitz, A. Webster, & P. Healey (Eds.), *Capitalizing Knowledge*. Albany: State University of New York Press.

European Commission. (2008). *European Innovation Scoreboard 2008: Comparative Analysis of Innovation Performance*. Brussels: European Commission.

Gerpott, T., & Ahmadi, N. (2015). Composite indices for the evaluation of a country's information technology development level: Extensions of the IDI of the ITU. *Technological Forecasting and Social Change, 98*, 174–185. doi:10.1016/j.techfore.2015.03.012

Grigorovici, D. M., Schement, J. R., & Taylor, R. D. (2004). Weighing the intangible: towards a theory-based framework for information society indices. In E. Bohlin, S. Levin, N. Sung, & C.-H. Yoon (Eds.), *Global Economy and Digital Society* (pp. 169–199). Amsterdam: Elsevier.

Hagedoorn, J., & Cloodt, M. (2003). Measuring innovative performance: Is there an advantage in using multiple indicators? *Research Policy*, *32*(8), 1365–1379. doi:10.1016/S0048-7333(02)00137-3

Hollenstein, H. (1996). A composite indicator of a firm's innovativeness. An empirical analysis based on survey data for Swiss manufacturing. *Research Policy*, *25*(4), 633–645. doi:10.1016/0048-7333(95)00874-8

Katz, J. (2006). Indicators for complex innovation systems. *Research Policy*, *35*(7), 893–909. doi:10.1016/j.respol.2006.03.007

Martin, R. (2004). *A study on the factors of regional competitiveness – a draft final report for the European Commission Directorate-General Regional Policy (2004)*. Cambridge: Cambridge University Press.

Mitra, J. (2011). *Entrepreneurship, Innovation and Regional Development*. New York: Routledge.

Moesen, W., & Cherchye, L. (1998). *The Macroeconomic Performance of Nations: Measurement and Perception*. Centre for Economic Studies, Catholic University of Leuven.

Munda, G. (2012). Choosing aggregation rules for composite indicators. *Social Indicators Research*, *109*(3), 337–354. doi:10.1007/s11205-011-9911-9

Munda, G., & Nardo, M. (2005). *Constructing Consistent Composite Indicators: The Issue of Weights, JRC32434*. European Commission Joint Research Centre.

Nardo, M. (2005). *Handbook on Constructing Composite Indicators*. Methodology and User Guide. doi:10.1787/533411815016

Nardo, M. & Saisana, M. (2005). OECD/JRC Handbook on constructing composite indicators. Putting theory into practice.

Otoiu, A., Titan, E., & Dumitrescu, R. (2014). Are the variables used in building composite indicators of well-being relevant? Validating composite indexes of well-being. *Ecological Indicators*, *46*, 575–585. doi:10.1016/j.ecolind.2014.07.019

Parasuraman, A. (2000). Technology Readiness Index (TRI) a multiple-item scale to measure readiness to embrace new technologies. *Journal of Service Research*, *2*(4), 307–320. doi:10.1177/109467050024001

President's Commission on Industrial Competitiveness. (1985). *Global Competition: The New Reality, the Report of the President Commission on Industrial Competitiveness* (Vol. I-II). Washington, D.C.: U.S. Government Printing Office.

Saisana, M. (2004). Composite indicators: a review, Second workshop on composite indicators of country performance, OECD, Paris.

Salvati, L., & Carlucci, M. (2014). A composite index of sustainable development at the local scale: Italy as a case study. *Ecological Indicators*, *43*, 162–171. doi:10.1016/j.ecolind.2014.02.021

Santarelli, E., & Piergiovanni, R. (1996). Analyzing literature-based innovation output indicators: The Italian experience. *Research Policy*, *25*(5), 698–712. doi:10.1016/0048-7333(95)00849-7

Shao, B. B., & Lin, W. T. (2002). Technical efficiency analysis of information technology investments: A two-stage empirical investigation. *Information & Management*, *39*(5), 391–401. doi:10.1016/S0378-7206(01)00105-7

Soete, L. L., & Ter Weel, B. J. (1999a). Innovation, knowledge creation and technology policy: The case of the Netherlands. *De Economist, 147*(3), 293–310. doi:10.1023/A:1003797027548

Soete, L. L., & Weel, B. J. (1999). *Schumpeter and the knowledge-based economy: On technology and competition policy*. MERIT, Maastricht Economic Research Institute on Innovation and Technology.

Thoma, G. (2014). Composite value index of patent indicators: Factor analysis combining bibliographic and survey datasets. *World Patent Information, 38*, 19–26. doi:10.1016/j.wpi.2014.05.005

White, M. A., & Bruton, G. D. (2007). *The management of technology and innovation: a strategic approach*. Mason, OH: Thomson/South-Western.

Zhou, P., Ang, B. W., & Poh, K. L. (2006). Comparing aggregating methods for constructing the composite environmental index: An objective measure. *Ecological Economics, 59*(3), 305–311. doi:10.1016/j.ecolecon.2005.10.018

KEY TERMS AND DEFINITIONS

Competitiveness: Ability of a firm or a country to provide and sell goods and services under free and fair market conditions at competitive prices. It should provide an adequate return which maintains and/or expands the real long-term income of the people involved, in relation to the competitors.

Composite Index: A measure calculated by the aggregation of a number of indicators which can include different aspects of the observed problem, making it suitable for measuring complex phenomena (competitiveness, development etc.).

Innovativeness: Capacity to produce new products or processes, or introduce new ideas to the market. It is a capability of an entity (organization or nation) to be innovative.

Sustainable Development: Process of achieving a higher level of human development while simultaneously meeting environmental, economic and social challenges.

Technological Entrepreneurship: The link between science and technology and the practical new value created (by researching new technologies and developing existing) for upgrading customers' life quality and contributing to the overall society.

Technology Management: The process of connecting different disciplines in order to plan, organize, guide, direct and control all technological activities or operations for achieving strategic goals.

Weighting: The process of determining the importance of elements of the observed phenomenon and emphasizing the impact that the element has on the final result.

Chapter 4
Composite Indicators of a Knowledge Society:
Triangulation of Experts Interviews and Factor Analyses

Norsiah Abdul Hamid
Universiti Utara Malaysia, Malaysia

Norhafezah Yusof
Universiti Utara Malaysia, Malaysia

Mohd Sobhi Ishak
Universiti Utara Malaysia, Malaysia

Halimah Badioze Zaman
Universiti Kebangsaan Malaysia, Malaysia

ABSTRACT

The concept of Knowledge Society (KS) began due to recognition of the importance of knowledge and information in the development of a society. This chapter proposes a holistic view of knowledge society based on the development of composite indicators in nine different dimensions. The objective of the study is to propose a multi-dimensional approach comprising human capital, ICT, spirituality, economy, social, institutional and sustainability as determinants towards achieving a KS. These dimensions are discussed in-depth by the experts in semi-structured interviews and also validated by using Exploratory Factor Analysis (EFA) and Confirmatory Factor Analysis (CFA). The semi-structured interview data are presented in a verbatim manner so as to provide readers with in-depth feedback from the experts, while the EFA and CFA results of composite indicators are presented in graphics. Thus, this chapter contributes to the understanding of composite indicators of a knowledge society which can then be used by policy makers for future policy-making decision.

DOI: 10.4018/978-1-5225-0714-7.ch004

INTRODUCTION

The knowledge society concept began due to recognition of the importance of knowledge and information in the development of a society. Active knowledge activities such as access, generation, sharing and disseminating are deemed crucial in the knowledge society. These activities which then expanded and multiplied the knowledge determine the vision towards transforming a society. Thus, as stated by Mioara (2012), a "knowledge society" has always existed: "what is new now is the speed at which knowledge expands and innovates". Societies are no longer depending totally on resources such as land, labor and natural resources, but rather on the potential to produce, acquire, use and distribute knowledge (Economic Planning Unit Malaysia, 2001). Other scholars and researchers also agree that our society is now living in the age of information and knowledge, in which the most critical resources are both elements, and they have become the most important commodities for productivity (Al-Hawamdeh & Hart, 2002; Britz, Lor, Coetzee & Bester, 2006; Clarke 2003; Drucker 1993; Evans & Wurster, 1997; Evers, 2001; Lor & Britz, 2007), and major contributors towards economic and social growth (Rohrbach, 2007; Stehr, 1994).

Studies on KS are discussed more often in the western and developed countries. Governments and researchers in these countries put much effort into modelling and measuring the development of their societies so as to be acknowledged as a KS. They have long been aware of the importance of knowledge in developing their nations. In contrast to this situation, there are very few research coming from developing economies like Malaysia on this topic, particularly on the transformation of a society from the Industrial Age to the Knowledge Age (Amirudin, 2003). Acknowledgements on the importance of knowledge and information only begun in Malaysia around 1991 when the government proposed 'Vision 2020', in which Malaysia is targeted to be a fully developed nation by the year 2020. Since then, studies and initiatives have been undertaken to focus on the utilization and application of knowledge in every single human activity. However, it is evidenced that the initiative to define and benchmark KS in Malaysia is still lacking. The Malaysian government has realized the importance of knowledge (Economic Planning Unit Malaysia, 2005), but it has given priority to the economic growth of the nation, neglecting societal and human development.

Many governments in the Asia Pacific region such as Singapore, Japan, South Korea, Philippines and Thailand have undertaken the initiatives to enhance the economic, political and social aspects to achieve the knowledge society. For instance, Singapore is one of the earliest countries in the region to launch its KS vision in 1992 (Gerke & Evers, 2006). The Australian Knowledge-based Economy/Knowledge Society project started in early 2000 by the Australian Bureau of Statistics (ABS) (Roberts, 2002). The study posited that the concept of Knowledge Society has not been well explored in a statistical sense, as compared to Knowledge-based economy (Roberts, 2002, p. 3). The project presented a comprehensive framework for the measurement of well-being based on a rich set of key indicators, comprising of economics, social and environment dimensions. China formally made an effort to reform its economic structure to an open market and socialist market economy in 1993 (Gao, 2005). Gao further added that the essence of the transformation towards a KS is to transform the input-driven growth to knowledge-based growth. Hence, the importance of being a knowledge society to any nations can be seen in twofold. First, for the societal members, they would better appreciate knowledge as a source for development and human living. Second, for the government, a knowledge society means its society has achieve a level where the status of the society is at par with the developed nations, thus portrays the first class mentality of its citizens and high income nation.

In view of the knowledge era and the contribution of information and communications technology (ICT) to the development of a nation, the Malaysian government have formulated new national policies in the recent years. The most significant policies include the National Vision Policy (NVP – 2001-2020), the Third Outline Perspective Plan (OPP3), the National Development Policy (NDP), and the Malaysia Plan every five years (Rancangan Malaysia). The very recent 11th Malaysia Plan announced by the Prime Minister, Datuk Seri Najib Razak, also emphasized on the importance of the growth of people in a nation. Evidently, Malaysia is a country which requires her citizens to have faith and belief in God as a basic principle in life. The objective of this study is to propose a multi-dimensional approach comprising human capital, ICT, spirituality, economy, social, institutional and sustainability as determinants towards achieving a KS. These dimensions are discussed in-depth by the experts in semi-structured interviews.

Knowledge economy (KE) is an industry which focuses on the knowledge as a commodity. Malaysia is ranked 45th in the Knowledge Economy Index 2000, but has dropped to 48th in 2012 (World Bank, 2012). However, as a country that is aware about the importance of information and knowledge in the development, Malaysia has actually started the journey to become a high income nation since 1991 (Mahathir, 1991). In addition to KE, Knowledge Society (KS) is "a society in which its members appreciate knowledge, and knowledge is seen as a significant commodity of a nation's growth. A KS shows concern in the holistic development of the human capital and encompasses physical, intellectual, spiritual, economic, social, institutional and sustainable aspects of growth. A KS also propagates fairness and equality in all spheres of human lives which must take precedence. This includes the generation, access, use, sharing and dissemination of existing knowledge and the innovation of new knowledge through relevant ICT infrastructure and infostructure in tandem with the needs of that society" (Norsiah, 2011). Human capital in the context of this project is measured using four sub-factors namely education and training, research and development, skills, and knowledge sharing and dissemination, while social capital is defined as the social networks, groups, norms, values, and behaviors which are common and shared together in a community (Cohen & Prusak, 2001; Grootaert, Narayanan, Jones & Woolcock, 2004; Putnam & Goss, 2002). Putnam and Goss (2002) also recognized social capital to include technological change, which links social capital to the market and to changing patterns of production and consumption. Human development is about expanding the richness of human life, rather than simply the richness of the economy in which human beings live.

SEMI-STRUCTURED INTERVIEWS

Semi-structured interviews were conducted to elicit the crucial dimensions of the Malaysian KS. In this step, three prominent figures were invited to participate in the individual semi-structured interview in order to give their recommendations as well as to elaborate on the final definition of KS and the important dimensions of Malaysian KS. These three experts are prominent in the field of Knowledge Society and well-versed with Malaysia's policy planning and implementation. The face-to-face interviews were conducted separately and with their permission, they were voice-recorded. Prior to all the interviews, a list of questions that will be used as a guideline in the interview session were sent to all interviewees. The questions were aimed specifically at Malaysia's Vision 2020, important dimensions of Malaysia's KS and the definition of KS.

Table 1 shows the demographic profiles of the interview experts. The first prominent expert (Expert A) is a male and a former Prime Minister of Malaysia. He was the one who introduced the long-term Vision 2020 for Malaysia, to achieve a value-based knowledge society by the year 2020. The second prominent expert (Expert B) is a female and the former Executive Director of the Global Knowledge Partnership (GKP), an international NGO, and is currently a member of Malaysia's NITC. She has tremendous experience in KS and on the Malaysian policy especially in ICT, knowledge and human development. The interview sessions with the two experts were conducted face-to-face separately and voice-recorded. The last expert, Expert C, is also prominent in Malaysia's policy, and has more than 30 years working experience. He holds a PhD in Engineering. The interview with Expert C was conducted via email since he/she was not staying in Malaysia at the time of the fieldwork. The following part is the feedback of three interviews which were transcribed accordingly and meant to be shared verbatim with readers of this article. The *italicized statements* are the questions from the researcher.

Expert A

- *When you first introduced Vision 2020, what do you want to achieve?*

The main target when government introduced Vision 2020 is to become a developed country by the year 2020. And the developed country is by our own definition, not the definition that is given to, well, vaguely given, actually there is no definition for developed country. There are various rates from US, for example $36,000 per capita, to some countries in Europe which is not very high, maybe $15,000 per capita, so the range is there. But we want to be economically somewhere within that range, but there are other qualities that we want to preserve.

- *Do you think the government should give priority to the Knowledge Economy (KE) or the Knowledge Society, or both?*

Well, the KS will result in a knowledge-based economy. If the society has mastery of knowledge, that knowledge is going to be applied in his daily lives, including of course in the government and in the private sector, the knowledge is used. We all use knowledge, but the level of knowledge that we use differs between different societies. Even in our society, the knowledge of the village people for example,

Table 1. Demographic profiles of interview experts (n=3)

Profile	Expert A	Expert B	Expert C
Gender	Male	Female	Male
Race	Malay	Malay	Malay
Age	85	Unknown	62
Education	King Edward VII Medical College, Singapore	Master in Public Policy, Harvard University	PhD in Engineering
Job Position	Former Prime Minister of Malaysia (1981 to 2003 – 22 years); introduced Vision 2020 in 1991	Former Executive Director of the Global Knowledge Partnership (GKP) (2001-2008); *Current*: Member of Malaysia's NITC	Former Chief Executive Officer of MIMOS Berhad. *Current*: Self-employed; Strategic Management

villagers, is much lower, so their contribution of that knowledge to their living standard is lower, but where you have their children, getting educated and becoming even university professors and specialists and all that, obviously they now have more knowledge than their parents and therefore their knowledge brings them better quality of life, better income.

- *Should we achieved the KS first, and then the KE?*

It comes together, almost. What we mean by KS is a society that is highly educated in the modern knowledge. That means science, mathematics, and technologies, things like that, which will contribute towards his/her capacity to improve his/her quality of life. So the moment he/she improves in knowledge, he/she is in the position to improve his/her quality of life.

- *In your opinion, what is the meaning of 'a comprehensive/holistic human development'?*

Comprehensive means number one, of course the level of knowledge is high. So its capacity is....but then, human development actually involves also knowledge of the workings of society. For example, the economic working of a society. So supposing he is a trained economist, he must know the economic structure of the society to gain from it. If he is trained with a degree in management, then he has to fit with the structure of society to gain extract the benefits from that. If he may be of course a doctor or a lawyer, then his capacity to earn is more. A lawyer working in a poor country, he has the knowledge but the society is not a KS, and his earnings will not be high. So it is important that the society itself becomes knowledgeable, and therefore it improves its quality of life, and within that society, it's easy for someone with the knowledge to gain an advantage from the knowledge that is available to the society.

- *When we talk about the KS, we should in our own definition, integrate the Spiritual dimension. So, how do you think can we integrate the Spiritual dimension in the Malaysian KS?*

Well, that's why we say we want it in 'our own mold'. It's not just a matter of per capita income, and GDP. It is also the quality of the person, or the character of the person and this is influenced by his spiritual input into his life. So that he/she doesn't become too greedy, too materialistic. And we can see what has happened to America because he/she has forsaken spirituality, he/she has gone all the way in the direction of materialism, and they become very greedy, and they destroy themselves. It is a very good example currently because previously it is difficult for us to illustrate, but now it is happening in front of our eyes, how materialism contributes to us the destruction of human society.

- *When we say Human Capital, should we separate knowledge from it? Or should we combine the aspect of knowledge with the Human Capital dimension?*

We should not, unless you are talking in terms of numbers, where you have 300 university graduates and therefore you have source of human capital. But our view is that, 300 university graduates is not good enough with the knowledge in which he has graduated, but he must also be a person of quality, spiritually speaking. And the two together becomes a very good human capital.

- *Do you agree that we are now in the situation where knowledge is not replacing the traditional or natural resources (i.e. land, labor or other capital), instead knowledge is complementing them? We need the knowledge to operate.*

Well, knowledge is always complementing other assets that you have. Let's take our land for example. In the past, we had a lot of tin in the ground but the Malays did not know how to mine for tin. So the Chinese came, started mining for tin, and they enriched themselves. That shows the difference, we have resources, but we don't have knowledge. The Chinese don't have resources, but they have knowledge. Another example of course is the Arab countries. They have huge reserved reservoirs of oil but they have never studied on how to extract the oil. So they don't have the knowledge. People come from outside with the knowledge and exploit their oil. So you have resource without knowledge is no good. You have knowledge without resource, you can go somewhere to find the resource, and of course you can survive with knowledge.

- *Some people said that we can even become a KS without ICT while some said it can enable and facilitate towards KS. Do you think ICT can help in achieving KS? Or do you also believe that we could become a KS without ICT, or even without technology?*

Knowledge leads to KS, but the ability to acquire knowledge is limited because you acquire knowledge through book reading, through hearing a talk or lectures and all that. But once you have ICT, you have access to unlimited knowledge. Therefore, you did enhance your knowledge. The knowledge is there, the ability is there, but the source is not there. We used to have library, when we see people, the Greek civilization, all had great libraries and Muslims had great libraries, the store of knowledge. It is not available to everybody, limited number of people. Today, we have this Internet, and you can get anything, any information, even you want to make an atom bomb you can go to the Internet and get the knowledge. So the possibility for using knowledge to enhance your capability is much easier now than before. Therefore, you are many steps ahead of those who depend upon books, reading, and lectures, to get knowledge. Before this, we depend upon books, reading, lectures and all that, for people who can read. That's why in Islam says Iqra' (read) because when you read, you acquire knowledge. So we are told to acquire knowledge, not just to read for fun, you see, when you read, you acquire knowledge. Now, you not only can read, but you can access knowledge through the Internet, unlimited knowledge. ICT is an enhancer. It increases and enhances your capacity to use knowledge.

- *In identifying the important dimensions towards KS, do you agree that the Human Capital, Knowledge and ICT dimensions, plus the Spiritual, Economy, Social and Sustainability dimensions are the most important? We have to integrate all the dimensions together? Or do you have any other suggestion?*

Yes, all of them contribute, but the greatest contributor of course is knowledge, enhance through ICT, combine with a good value system, a good culture.

- *Could you please elaborate more on the 'good value system'?*

Well, what is culture? Culture consists also of your value system. What do you value most? The Japanese, they have a strong sense of shame. If you failed, you are ashamed. And sometimes the Japanese will commit hara-kiri if they failed, you see. But in some societies, failing is OK. OK, I failed, so what? Such people would not succeed. The Japanese, he doesn't want to kill himself, so he works hard to acquire skills, to make use of his knowledge, but I'm afraid Malays don't work hard because the sense of shame is not strong among us. We feel ashamed only if we are, say, somebody scolds us, in front of other people, feel ashamed, but when you fail, you are not ashamed. You know, you go and study, and you failed, it's alright. And nowadays, we have come to the stage where even if we are jailed, it's alright. You steal money, or you are corrupt, but you are not ashamed. You take money that doesn't belong to you, you steal, you corrupt, and there is no sense of shame. Even among the leaders now, there is no sense of shame. So if you don't have the right value system in your culture, then you cannot advance. Different people got different value system, you see. For example, some people say, if you can steal, why not? The thing is there, nobody is looking, I take it. Of course we are taught that even nobody is there, God is there to see what you are doing, you see. But that one you dismissed, you take it but there are some people, if you leave money on a taxi, for example, the taxi driver will not take the money, and he will strive to deliver it back. That is good value system. Such people will succeed.

- *What about the sustainability?*

Well, if you have this, it will be sustained. See, if we have this quality, this knowledge plus this quality (good value system) in your culture, it will be sustained. But if we have knowledge without the culture of high quality, it will not be sustained. If we have a culture, but no knowledge, also it cannot be sustained. So there is a need for the two to combine. Sustainability is sustained by the combination of your knowledge and your value system.

- *When people talked about sustainability, they also mentioned about the environment. Do you think that we have to consider this?*

Well, that is another aspect of sustainability, because we are living now in a very crowded world. In the past, if you burned some garbage behind your house, it doesn't matter, because the whole country had a population of 5 million only, during the Japanese time with the population about 5 million. So even if you burned the paddy fields, it doesn't pollute much. But when the numbers concentrated, like today we have about 8 million motor vehicles in Malaysia, population 27 million, 8 to 10 million motor vehicles, when you add up the exhaust from the 10 million, of course it is more polluting and therefore not sustainable.

- *How do you foresee the development so far? I mean the development of KS. Are we on the right track from the year that you introduced the Vision 2020?*

There is a consciousness about KS, but there is not enough effort put in to really acquire the knowledge. We are not really working hard to acquire the knowledge. 'We' here refers to Malaysians. If you go to the university, you see, most of the students are girls, not boys, you see, so the boys are not making any effort to acquire knowledge. They are not making any effort to acquire skills also. Skill is also part of knowledge. So, although we know that knowledge is important, we are not making the full effort to acquire the knowledge. The facilities are there, before we had only one university, now we have forty government universities, and sixty private universities. So the accessibility to knowledge is very good now, but we are not really making an effort to acquire knowledge. Of course if you compare Chinese and Malays, well Malays are very far backward.

- *Do you think that we can achieve a KS in the year 2020?*

Not 2020, I think, because we have fallen back quite a lot in the last five years. It may take a longer time, maybe 2030, 2040, I really don't know, I won't be around. So the thing is, we don't see the effort made, thus the passion, the desire to achieve is not there.

- *And how would you define the 'Knowledge Society' in your own words?*

Well, all human societies have some level of knowledge. But in modern times, your knowledge is very high. People are very learned in many areas, particularly in the field of science, they are very learned. But some are much more concerned about politics, economics, and all that, but they are not very learned, and therefore, although they understand these things, they are not able to manage because they are not learned in the area of administration, management and in priority areas. So we have to encourage more young people to involve in science and technology fields. They must acquire knowledge of science, basic sciences, satellite and all that, they must know. But the level of basic science now is already much higher than the level of basic science, say fifty years ago.

Expert B

- *I would like to get an in-depth knowledge about the philosophy and concept behind the KS, and what the government has targeted. Based on your past experience in the government, what is the government actually trying to achieve?*

If you go back to the description of Vision 2020, or even the speech that Dr. Mahathir delivered when he introduced the concept of Vision 2020 for the first time, I believe the intention was to position Malaysia at the level of development which is benchmarked against other developed countries. So there is an economic indicator of growth that Malaysia is being pegged to, but it is more than that. It is basically aiming for a developed Malaysian nation that is mature in every sense, politically, socially, economically, culturally, environmentally, very holistic perspective and vision.

- *How do we measure the 'maturity'?*

The maturity of the Malaysian nation, I think it depends on your worldview. For some people, spirituality is not a variable, but I think for Malaysia it is. To measure maturity, I think you have to look at democratic practices, how tolerant we are, how developed is our human capital, are our people well-educated, are they able to reason well, but it is not just a mental aspect of development, it is also about your heart, your mind and also your soul. That's why they say that a balanced human being, someone who is at peace with themselves spiritually, in terms of their faith-based or religious identity, and their other identities such as their ethnic-based identity, their nation-state-based identity, and various sub-groups within. So in terms of maturity, I think the best measure would be the development of people.

- *So we need to integrate all the mental, physical and spiritual aspects?*

Absolutely. If you are really aiming for holistic development. Because if you don't aim for that, if you pursue only economic growth, you would have gaps in development. And you may have moral problems that you cannot address, environmental degradation that you cannot address, corruption, etc. So you need to address development in a holistic way.

- *How do you define 'a comprehensive/holistic human development'?*

I would define it the same way if you were to look at the Millennium Development Goals that the United Nations has been advocating for many years. All the countries of the world signed the declaration on the MDG in the year 2000 and basically it is looking at education, health, poverty, all aspects of basic development. But I think there are also areas that they did not go into. They didn't really address rights per se, I mean it's embedded in the goals. Because when they looked at education, they are also looking at education as a basic human right, when they looking at poverty reduction, it's looking at freedom from poverty, so the rights layer is actually behind what they declared as their goal. For me, development means that people are free to choose, they can voice their opinions and they are mature enough to agree or disagree in a peaceful context.

- *And in terms of expressing the opinion, do you think that Malaysia is quite reserved?*

Yes, I do think so. I think it has to do with legacy because we have the Internal Security Act, and people don't feel free to voice their opinions, although you see some people doing it. But I think for the majority there is fear at the back of their minds, where they are thinking if they express themselves too freely, and if there is an opinion that goes against mainstream opinion or the powers that be, their safety could be jeopardized. You might somehow get detained with no due process, detained under the Internal Security Act, and you can't do anything about it. So I don't think that there is complete freedom of expression in Malaysia and I still think that we could do better and I think the reason that the government tries to, I use the word selectively, "clamp down" on the freedom of expression is because some people abused the freedom, where they may make assertions irresponsibly. So I think that you must have two things, if you want to have freedom, you must also assume responsibility.

- *And how can we integrate the spiritual dimension in our context?*

I think the people themselves integrate it into their daily lives. Because, you see, spirituality is a wide spectrum. One aspect of spirituality is embedded in institutionalized religion. So you define yourself as a Roman-Catholic, or a Sunni Muslim, or a Shia Muslim, or something like that. At the other end of spirituality are those who do not believe in institutionalized religion but they still believe in the Creator, in God or in Allah, or whatever it is that they believe to be the Supreme-being, but they do not believe in the institutionalizes religion. For mature and developed societies, you need to have tolerance that can accommodate all the differences, including the atheists, so to integrate the concept of spirituality into a knowledge-based society, it requires that you have knowledge of each other, what differentiates people, their belief system, and the ability to tolerate the differences, and to live together in harmony. So you choose what you believe in, and it's OK by me, and I choose what I believe in, and I practice what I believe in and it should be OK by you. If we can do that in Malaysia then I would say that we are developed. But at the moment, I think there are some Malaysians who are very narrow-minded, who believe that their way is the right way, and if people are different from them, they do not see it kindly. If you go to Bali, you will see people who look like Malays, same skin tone, same type of ethnic group, these are all Malay Polynesians that immigrated from South of Yunnan and spread out to populate the South Pacific Islands. The Hawaiians are our cousins, because we come from the same root or type of people. The South Pacific is actually full of Malay Polynesians, but they all have different religions, they have different beliefs. So if you go to Bali you'll see people who look Malay but they are Hindu instead of Muslim. In Indonesia, which is a very diverse country, thousands of islands, populations, espousing different beliefs, Islam is dominant because it is the religion of the majority. In Malaysia, it is similar.

- *Do you think that Human Capital is the most important dimension in the KS?*

Yes. In order to have knowledge, you need to develop your human capital. Of course you need infrastructure, you need other support systems to sustain the KS. But you need to have your human capital developed before you can do anything productive, or to sustain growth, or to grow in a sustainable way.

- *When we say Human Capital, should we separate knowledge from it? Or should we integrate the knowledge into the Human Capital dimension? Because when I read some literature, they tend to separate the knowledge from the HC.*

You can't have knowledge without developing your HC. On one hand you won't have the capacity to generate knowledge and on the other you won't be able to use that knowledge to produce more knowledge if your human capital is not developed. Human capital to me comprises all aspects of the human being, which includes his or her intellect, but it is more than that. It includes for example, human motivation, aspiration and values. You can have knowledge generated by people, but without vision and drive and effort, it goes nowhere or can be misused to do harmful things instead of good things for society. To generate knowledge you need to be able to learn. Learning is the essence of human capital development, which to me is also the root of the knowledge society.

- *Which one is more crucial, Human Capital, Intellectual Capital or Social Capital? There are lots of terms, so which one is more important to you?*

Intellectual Capital to me is part of Human Capital and Social Capital is developed through human interactions. So to me they are all interrelated and they are not mutually exclusive. You can't say which one is more important. Without one you can't have the other.

- *Do you agree that we are now living in a situation where knowledge is not replacing the traditional or natural resources (i.e. land, labor or other capital), instead knowledge is complementing them?*

To a certain extent, I would agree, but it's relative. In terms of resources, if you look at different countries, some countries are poorer than others. So by traditional measures of wealth, some have more and some have less. For those who do not have any kind of natural resources at all, what they have are their people. And if they develop their HC, they can actually make something. They can create a productive economy and it can be sustainable if managed well and powered by human beings. The thing about land and other types of physical assets, in terms of productive capacity, they are finite. So you are lucky if you have physical resources, but if you don't have them, your smart recourse would be knowledge and a service oriented economy. Malaysia is very rich in terms of natural resources. So if you complement that with HC development, so that development is a managed process that is knowledge-based, the intelligent use of these resources will lead to sustainability. You do not deplete your oil and gas without reason, without thinking about what's going to replace them; You do not pollute your water because you understand that it is a critical resource for health and economy, etc. In this regard knowledge resources complement physical resources. If you don't have any natural resources, then all you have is your people and so knowledge does not complement but is rather the main resource for development.

- *Some people said that we can even become a KS without the ICT. Do you agree on that?*

No, I don't agree. When you use the word society, it means everyone within a particular group. I generally associate society with populations bound within the borders of a nation-state. It's a limiting definition, but for the purpose of this discussion, this is what I will use. It is not possible to get the entire population of a country today to become a knowledge society or at least to involve a critical mass of people within the country without ICT (unless your country is really tiny in terms of population). If you look at history, there have been pockets of knowledge communities in different parts of the world, but they are reserved for the elites. Those who come from a certain class and can afford the time and the resources to accumulate knowledge and learn become part of the exclusive knowledge society. If you were in a traditional civilization of the past where you do not come from the ruling class, you don't stand a chance of being included, especially if you are a woman. Just think about when women around the world got the right to vote. The pockets of knowledge communities of the past are from the privileged class. But with ICT, you democratize access to knowledge, its creation and dissemination. You have the opportunity to have inclusive knowledge societies of a far wider scale, which can really be society-wide.

- *I have identified few dimensions, for example, human capital, ICT, spiritual, economy, social, sustainability and institutional. Do you think that all the dimensions should be integrated together?*

In terms of a holistic development, yes I do. But knowledge is an input. You use knowledge to produce something, a better way of life, and solutions for different challenges or problems. So it is an input to something. Yes, those dimensions are all integrated but they are of different degrees. Where you position them in your framework of holistic development is important. They don't all rank equally. I think the goal for every human society is sustainable development and growth. You want to be able to co-exist in harmony and to be able to live sustainably. So that your children and your children's children will have a planet to live on where they can find food and find productive ways of living in harmony. Because if you don't have that, then you know, what's the point?

- *How do you foresee the development so far? I mean the development of KS. Are we on the right track from the year that you introduced the Vision 2020?*

I think that you'd probably have to look at the people who track the indicators, but I think in terms of access to education, Malaysia does quite well. In terms of battling illiteracy, Malaysia does quite well as well. But that's just access to learning. In terms of quality of human capital and also maturity of people within the context of living in multi-ethnic, multi-religious society, that's where it needs to be improved. That's where you sort of like...you have to think of yourself as a human being who lives on a planet with other people who are different and you have to learn to live together and to co-exist, because if you think that only your way is correct then the way forward will always be paved by conflict and so you cannot have sustainable growth and development when you don't have peace. Without peace you cannot pursue your dream, your aspiration.

- *So you believe that we should spread the knowledge equally? Fairly and equally?*

I think access to knowledge is fundamental to life and fundamental to growth. If we want Malaysia to really develop well, then access to knowledge (learning) must be open to everyone. The only limitation is individual capacity. The principle should go as far as you can go where learning is concerned. Learning cannot be exclusive to those with means and resources. In fact Malaysia has done quite well in terms of giving people access to learning, especially the disadvantaged.

- *In your opinion, what should differentiate between our KS and other developed countries' KS?*

I think that knowledge societies everywhere would have the same root. They are all based on a learning culture, a sharing culture and a continuous cycle of knowledge generation.

- *Knowledge breeds knowledge?*

Yes, it's a cycle. That is why people say that knowledge based resources are infinite compared to physical resources. But what is different in terms of characteristic is what defines your nation and your culture based on the diversity within. So you just have to think about how Malaysia would be different in terms of its "packaging" than the United States. The United States is also multi-ethnic and multi-religious in composition. So are Indonesia, Sri Lanka and Nigeria. On what differentiates the knowledge societies of these countries? I would say that it depends on what the people decide, what they want to achieve as a nation and their shared values. Yes, the people. They should decide because they make up the society.

- *Do you have any suggestions on how do I define a KS? Or do you have your own definition?*

A knowledge-based society at its simplest level is a society that uses knowledge to achieve sustainable growth and development, and where there is respect for human rights and human dignity. Nevertheless, I think knowledge-based societies tend to think more about the collective rather than the individual though; collective as a unit. A KS is always thinking about the group, the interest of a group balanced against the interest of the individual, and trying to balance that in the best possible way (just way) by leveraging on the best knowledge that is available.

- *There are few definitions on KS proposed by some scholars but I think I need to look at the KS in terms of our country, to differentiate between the developed countries' and ours. I think because the target is to achieve the status of KS by the year 2020. But then we don't have any indicators, sort of indicators, and also the definition.*

I think indicators exist, but they are packaged differently depending on who is doing the packaging and using what frame to assess progress. The World Bank has the world development report and the Global ICT Report; UNESCO has its EFA and Knowledge Society reports. Some of the indicators tend to overlap, but it only matters if you are using the same frame. That's why you need to come up with your own definition and you have to identify your own indicators and then pick-and-choose the ones that are relevant based on your framework. KS is also about the culture of sharing, which is derived from mutual respect and trust. You don't share if you have no trust.

- *The previous models tend to focus more on the infrastructure, the ICT infrastructure. So I think I need to integrate the spiritual and human capital in the framework. The spiritual is broader than the religious. The religious is the subset of the spiritual. And I think I need to balance between the Muslim and the non-Muslim people.*

You must definitely integrate the human capital. When you say spiritual, you mean the values of the person. Exactly! You need to balance between the Muslim and the non-Muslim people especially when we are looking at a KS, because it includes everyone. And that's another principle of knowledge society. It's inclusive. It has all the wonderful values that make a society live in harmony, because they understand each other and they have knowledge about each other, and I believe also because they have a shared destiny, and that is what binds them, because otherwise there wouldn't be a society. For example, you could have a KS between a population of Malaysia and Indonesia as a collective, let's say a Malaysian-Indonesian KS. You could potentially have that. And that's a question of where do you want to set your boundary. And if you insist on putting it around the Malaysian boundary, then you have to look at the population as your unit and what binds them. So I would say the sense of shared destiny for Malaysians vs. other nations.

Expert C

- *Do you think technology is the major driver in knowledge society?*

Technology is NEVER the driver of social change. True, technology brings new opportunities for change, even new perceptions and inspirations for what we can be. But it does not determine what we want to be. Technology remains at most an enabler and facilitator of change. It is a tool to be used well and wisely. It does not change our basic principles or objectives in life. So what drives human thought and action? The objective of a change process is to achieve comprehensive human development. For the Malaysian case as conceptualized by the National IT Agenda, we have drawn key principles from Rukun Negara and Vision 2020, with suitable adaptations as already explained. That is how comprehensive human development was framed.

- *Do you have any other suggestion for a KS?*

I would also provide an Islamic perspective of comprehensive human development which applies the Maqasid al Shari'ah. There are similarities as well as differences between the two frames of reference. For example both frames see human pursuit of knowledge as crucial in achieving personal and societal well-being. Yet they are different in how each would treat the kinds of knowledge that should be pursued. The Islamic approach begins with individuals whose nafs (self) is driven by spiritual objectives of fulfilling his or her obligations to God, to himself and other fellow human beings and to the natural order. For Malaysia as a nation state, even if belief in God is recognized, the kinds of knowledge to be pursued are not necessarily conditioned by spiritual principles.

To take a simple example, let us consider pornography. According to the Maqasid framework, we would have anticipated the ease by which the net and the web would enable access to this kind of negative content. We would have developed infrastructure, laws, rules, regulations and technologies that would hinder development or distribution of such content. On the other hand, we would have put huge resources towards developing infrastructure, laws, rules, regulations and technologies that promote use of the net and web for education, learning and innovation. This shaping of human behavior is the objective of comprehensive human development, enabled by technology.

The alternative approach was taken by the world community, including Malaysia. Open the floodgates of the web, and then figure out how to protect the school-children and the young from negative content. Positive content development remains under discussion and debate even to this day. We can see from this illustration that the western notion of neutrality is dominant, whereas in Islam everything is subject to the exercise of human judgment, and therefore human values. Nothing is ever neutral and value-free.

- *Do you think knowledge and ICT development is important in our nation?*

The need for a systems view in knowledge and ICT development is greater than for any other discipline. First, knowledge is itself dynamic and interactive. "Knowledge begets more knowledge". Knowledge gets better when it is shared. The "network effects" brought by the net and the web promotes not just connectivity nationally, but across the globe without recognizing physical borders. The intellectual capacity of the entire world is being connected, as it were. Second, the quality and quantity of interaction between key human sub-systems determine the level of achievement possible for any society. Thus, effective models that describe to a good accuracy of what is actually happening in a highly complex process will help us to plan better development programs. Third, a systems view is an approximation of comprehensive human development. Without such a view we would be driving ahead in a state of blindness. In determining the purpose of the knowledge society, we cannot take the position that all dimensions are equal. If for example we claim that the purpose of a knowledge society is to achieve a knowledge economy, then it may be interpreted that as long as we have high added value it does not matter whether the additional wealth is equitably shared, or whether we have increased our level of corruption. There has to be a true purpose, and all other dimensions should be made subservient to fulfilling this purpose. It has to do with comprehensive human development. Both the key actor and the key beneficiary of the knowledge society must be the individual as a person and as a member of wider society. So what makes this individual to be a good learner (and unlearner and relearner)? And what makes him or her an effective member of a wider community capable of applying knowledge for human development? Even when speaking about technology, we must look at its human face.

To conclude on the results of the verbatim analysis of the interviews, ICT and human capital are two most mentioned terms throughout the interviews with Experts A and B, while Expert C emphasized more on the human development, rather than human capital. Another critical dimension is spiritual and the need to look at KS from the Islamic view. Experts A agreed that a KS should have a good value system and a good culture, so does Expert B when she mention KS is a society that uses knowledge to achieve sustainable growth and development, and where there is respect for human rights and human dignity. Nevertheless, she thinks that knowledge societies tend to think more about the collective rather than the individual. Interestingly, Expert C proposed an Islamic perspective of comprehensive human development which applies the Maqasid al Shari'ah and the need for a system view in knowledge and ICT, which he argued without such a view we would be driving ahead in a state of blindness.

FACTOR ANALYSES

The survey involved 450 respondents, comprised 235 males and 193 females; while 22 respondents did not report their gender. The age of the respondents ranged between 20 to 60 years and above (mean for age is 37.74 years old). The majority are Malays (78.4% or n=353) and majority works with the government sector (77.3%, n=348). The majority of the respondents obtained a Bachelor's degree (56.7% or n=255), and some of them hold a PhD (6% or n=27). The majority of the respondents have working experience between 1 and 10 years (mean=13.83). The demographic profiles of the respondents are summarized in Table 2.

Exploratory Factor Analysis (EFA)

Factor Analysis (FA) is a technique for simplifying a complex data set (Kline, 2005). Hair et al. (2010, p. 94) defined FA as "an interdependence technique whose primary purpose is to define the underlying structure among the variables in the analysis". Exploratory Factor Analysis (EFA) is a common statistical method that is used to group together items (manifest variables) that are related to a particular latent construct (factor) but relatively uncorrelated with other latent constructs. Steps to be employed in factor analysis as stated by SPSS (2005) are as follows:

1. Computation of the correlation matrix for the variables to be examined.
2. **Extraction of Factors:** Determining the number of factors necessary to represent the data.
3. **Rotation:** Adjusting the axes to make the factors more interpretable.
4. **Factor Score Calculations:** Scores for each factor are calculated for use in further analyses.

The correlation coefficients indicate factor loadings or the strength of association between the scales and factors (Smart, 2009). The cut-off point for selecting scales for interpretation of each factor was based on the calculated factor loadings of each scale. Several authors (Pallant, 2007; Tabachnick & Fidell, 2007) suggested that factor loadings of 0.30 and above are suitable for interpretation; while Hair et al. (2010) suggested interpretation should occur on scales with factor loadings of 0.50 or more. In the present research, a loading of 0.30 (Pallant, 2007; Tabachnick & Fidell, 2007) was used as the cut-off point for interpreting factor loadings.

Table 2. Demographic profiles of survey respondents (n=450)

Demographic Details	f	%	Demographic Details	f	%
Gender			Race		
Male	235	52.2	Malay	353	78.4
Female	193	42.9	Chinese	36	8.0
Not reported	22	4.9	Indian	26	5.8
Age			Sabah/Sarawak Ethnic group	10	2.2
20 - 29 years old	82	18.2	Not reported	25	5.6
30 - 39	143	31.8	Highest Level of Education		
40 - 49	71	15.8	PhD	27	6.0
50 - 59	64	14.2	Master's	128	28.4
60 and above	2	0.4	Bachelor's	255	56.7
Not reported	88	19.6	Not reported	40	8.9
Employer			Working Experience		
Government	348	77.3	1 - 10 years	184	40.9
Private	61	13.6	11 - 20 years	89	19.8
NGO	6	1.3	21 - 30 years	73	16.2
Not reported	35	7.8	31 - 40 years	22	4.9
			Not reported	82	18.2

Structural Equation Modelling (SEM)

Structural Equation Modelling (SEM) is a statistical methodology that takes a confirmatory (i.e. hypothesis-testing) approach to the analysis of a structural theory bearing on some phenomenon (Byrne, 2001; 2010). SEM has been substantially used in social sciences since it provides researchers with a comprehensive means for assessing and modifying theoretical models and thus, offers great potential for further theory development (Anderson & Gerbing, 1988). The term *structural equation modelling* conveys two important aspects of the procedure:

1. The causal processes under study are represented by a series of structural equations (i.e. regression), and
2. These structural relations can be modelled pictorially to enable a clearer conceptualization of the theory under study (Byrne, 2001; 2010).

SEM is valuable in inferential data analysis and hypothesis testing where the pattern of inter-relationships among the study constructs are specified *a priori* and grounded in established theory (Hoe 2008). Structural equation modelling is typically used in, and is appropriate for, non-experimental research, such as research conducted using questionnaires (Hair et al., 2010; Schumacker & Lomax, 2004).

Results of the hypotheses testing of the significant dimensions of Malaysia's KS showed that all the nine hypotheses can be accepted (Table 3). The highest loading coefficient was exhibited by the Human Capital dimension, with the value of 0.83 and followed by the Economy dimension, with loading coef-

Table 3. Hypotheses of significant dimensions of a KS and loading coefficient

Hypothesis	Loading Coefficient	Result
Human Capital is significantly related to the KS	0.83	Supported
Economy is significantly related to the KS	0.82	Supported
ICT is significantly related to the KS	0.77	Supported
Social is significantly related to the KS	0.76	Supported
Governance is significantly related to the KS	0.70	Supported
Environment is significantly related to the KS	0.70	Supported
Citizen Participation is significantly related to the KS	0.63	Supported
Culture is significantly related to the KS	0.55	Supported
Spirituality is significantly related to the KS	0.45	Supported

ficient of 0.82. ICT dimension had a loading coefficient of 0.77, followed by Social, Governance and Environment dimensions, each with loading coefficient of 0.76. 0.70 and 0.70. Citizen Participation had a loading coefficient of 0.63. The two lowest loading coefficients were Culture (0.55) and Spirituality dimension (0.45).

Knowledge Society Model

Malaysia's Knowledge Society model that can be observed in Figure 1 was based on the nine dimensions that emerged from the Exploratory Factor Analysis (EFA) along with their fit models and indicators of the survey data; and results from the Confirmatory Factor Analysis (CFA) as follows:

1.   Human Capital;
2.   ICT;
3.   Spirituality;
4.   Economic dimension;
5.   Social dimension;

Figure 1. Knowledge society model for Malaysia

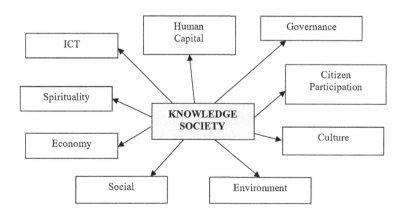

6. Governance;
7. Citizen Participation;
8. Culture; and
9. Environment.

The general model of KS provides evidence that the nine dimensions have significant importance to the development of Malaysia's KS. The results indicated that the general model of Malaysia's KS was a good fit model for guiding and explaining the development of KS in Malaysia. This supports the previous studies on the development of Knowledge Society and Knowledge-based Economy topics, particularly the use of the dimensions of Human Capital, ICT, Spirituality, Economic dimension, Social dimension, Governance, Citizen Participation, Culture and Environment. This study also supports previous findings on the important indicators pertaining to the status of a KS. The findings also support the New Economic Model (NEM) proposed by the Malaysian government (NEAC, 2010) which emphasized on the elements of high income earners, inclusiveness and sustainability.

The 131 indicators developed in this study were divided into nine significant dimensions that can be used as guidelines in determining the path towards the formation of a KS. It should also be noted that the indicators were paralleled to the government's recent policies such as the Government Transformation Program (GTP) containing six National Key Result Areas (NKRAs), Economic Transformation Program (ETP) containing National Key Economic Areas (NKEAs) and Strategic Reform Initiatives (SRIs), and Communications Content and Infrastructure (CCI) developed by Performance Management and Delivery Unit (PEMANDU) under the Prime Minister's Office of Malaysia. CCI for instance, emphasized on improving human capital and the paradigm shift from infrastructure to application and content (PEMANDU, 2010; 2012).

Perceived Importance Indicators of the Malaysia's Knowledge Society

This section lists the significant dimensions together with the final indicators of Malaysia's KS. The nine dimensions are Human Capital, ICT, Spirituality, Economy, Social, Governance, Citizen Participation, Culture and Environment.

1. **Human Capital:**
   a. **Education and Training (ET):** School education fulfils societal needs, Number of tertiary enrolments, Number of tertiary graduates, Tertiary students in Science, Technology, Engineering and Mathematics, Tertiary education fulfils societal needs, Total expenditure on training, Number of professional workers, Number of technical workers, Number of training courses for workers, Number of workers attending training course.
   b. **Research, Development and Innovation (RDI):** Total expenditure for Research, Development and Innovation (R&D&I), Number of researchers in R&D&I, Number of research institutions/ centers, Number of research projects awarded grant by local agency, Number of research projects awarded grant by foreign/international agency, Number of patents awarded to local researchers, Number of copyrights awarded to local researchers, Number of awards received by local researchers, Research cooperation between government-academia-industry-civil society-natural environments of society (Quintuple Helix), Effective protection system of intellectual property.

c. **Skills (SK):** Number of local professional workers coming back/immigrating to Malaysia (brain gain), Application of electronic learning, Application of mobile learning, Malay language proficiency as a national language, Intra-personal skills (e.g. motivation/perseverance, problem solving, self-discipline, capacity to make judgments based on goals in life), Inter-personal skills (e.g. teamwork, leadership), Consider experts' opinion in particular fields/areas.

d. **Knowledge Sharing and Dissemination (KSD):** Number of locally printed educational books sold, Number of locally published journals, Number of journal articles by local author, Number of printed newspapers sold daily, Number of locally sold educational magazines, Preservation of local and indigenous knowledge, Quality of knowledge shared and disseminated.

2. **ICT:**

a. **ICT Usage (ICTU):** Total population using the Internet, Total online newspaper readers, Number of electronic communities, Number of registered users on electronic communities, Number of Internet banking users, Number of Internet/online transactions (goods), Number of Internet/online transactions (services), Number of registered social media users.

b. **ICT Application (ICTA):** Implementation of e-Government, Implementation of e-Commerce, Implementation of e-Education, Implementation of e-Health, Implementation of e-Environment, Number of online sources for women, Number of online sources for marginalized groups, Number of online sources in local languages, Number of online sources in local languages, Number of media contents produced locally, Information censorship, Public awareness towards ICT and Cyber Laws.

c. **ICT Content (ICTC):** Number of local e-books published, Number of online local educational journals published, Number of application software produced by local developers, Number of public service portals providing information and knowledge, Number of public service portals providing transaction facilities (pay bills, summons, etc.), Quality of local content (e.g. documentary, educational software, animated film), Quality of knowledge acquired online.

d. **ICT Provision and Skill (ICTPS):** Total expenditure on ICT infrastructure, Total expenditure on ICT infostructure, Number of Internet hosts per 1,000 population, Number of public Internet access centers (including computerized and networked libraries / Community Internet Centre / Telecenters / Wireless access point / Community Broadband Centers), ICT literacy rate.

e. **ICT Adoption (ICTO):** Number of registered users for fixed line telephone, Number of registered users for cellular/mobile telephone services, Number of registered users for broadband, Number of personal computer buyers for every 1,000 population, Number of TV viewers, Number of radio listeners, Number of registered users of social networking sites.

3. **Spirituality (SPI):** Belief in God, Belief in transcendence and mystics (e.g. Prophets or God Messengers, angels, life after death, etc.), Give highest priority in life to religion/spirituality value, Obey the commands/errands of religion/spirituality (e.g. prayer, zikir/ritual chanting, practice good behavior, social service, voluntary service, give money to poor people, etc.), Avoid what is forbidden by the religion/spirituality (e.g. do not commit sin, don't be inhuman to other people, etc.), Apply the knowledge acquired from religion/spirituality into daily lives (in working, eating, dressing style, solving problem, etc.), Optimize the use of mosque/prayer place, Practice virtuous traits (honesty, trustworthiness, forgiveness, humility, etc.), Respect other people/religion/belief/culture/race (tolerance), Spirituality can improve the quality of life.

4. **Economy (ECON):** Gross National Index (GNI) per capita Purchasing Power Parity (PPP), Per capita income, Inequality in income distribution, Employment rates (ages 15-64), Adult unemployment rate (ages 25-54), Poverty rate, Inflation rate, Economic stability, Women involvement in workforce, Marginalized group involvement in workforce, High-technology exports.
5. **Social:**
   a. **Social Cohesion (SOCCO):** Life expectancy at birth, Marriage rate, Divorce rate, Household work hours (per person/week), Membership/participation in association, Life satisfaction index (aged 18 and above).
   b. **Social Fragmentation (SOCFR):** Number of crimes recorded, Number of adult prisoners, Number of corruptions recorded, Number of people living with HIV/AIDS, Number of drug addicts, Suicide rate recorded.
6. **Governance (GOV):** Political stability, Government effectiveness, Control of crimes, Control of corruption.
7. **Citizen Participation (CPAR):** Gender equality, Women participation in politics and decision/policy making, Marginalized group participation in politics and decision/policy making, Freedom of expression, Freedom of information.
8. **Culture (CUL):** Culture of innovation, Culture of lifelong learning, Acculturation of knowledge in life, Acculturation of creativity in life, Sustainable quality of life.
9. **Environment (ENV):** Freshwater quality, Freshwater resources, Forest resources, Fish resources, Energy resources, Environmental pollution index, Climate change, Ozone layer, Air quality, Waste generation, Biodiversity.

CONCLUSION

Principally, this research bridges the gap in previous research in literature within this area through an in-depth study on the construction of a Knowledge Society (KS) dimensions and important indicators and consequently validation of the model framework of Malaysia's KS. This framework contributes to current understanding of Malaysia's KS. The discussion that follows assumes the existence and viability of the significant dimensions of KS. The justification for this assumption is grounded within the findings of the literature review. This model serves as a theoretical foundation for empirical research, providing an initial step towards a theory on Knowledge Society. From an applied perspective, policy makers can take advantage of the proposed model, suggesting that nine dimensions should be considered in policy planning and decision making. It should be emphasized that all the dimensions are crucial in the development of a nation and have been stressed by various parties throughout the world. Besides the importance of economic growth, the social, cultural and human capital dimensions were also crucial in the national KS (Malhotra, 2003). The Millennium Development Goals (MDG) (United Nations, 2010), as agreed by 160 world leaders in 2000, also focused on eight goals, including the eradication of poverty and hunger, the achievement of universal primary education, the promotion of gender equality and empowerment of women, and ensuring environmental sustainability. These goals are among the indicators validated in this study. In addition, elements of religion, spirituality, values and belief system, the worldview and Maqasid al-Shari'ah all need to be blended and unified for Malaysia to be a KS. As human beings are dynamic and interactive, thus knowledge and wisdom are indeed important in this era.

REFERENCES

Abdul Wahab, A. (2003). *A complexity approach to national IT policy making: The case of Malaysia's Multimedia Super Corridor (MSC)*. (Doctoral thesis). School of Information Technology and Electrical Engineering (ITEE), University of Queensland, Queensland, Australia.

Ahmed, E. M. (2008). ICT and human capital intensities effects on Malaysian productivity growth. *International Research Journal of Finance and Economics, (13)*, 152-161.

Al-Hawamdeh, S., & Hart, T. L. (2002). *Information and knowledge society*. Singapore: McGraw-Hill.

Beniger, J. R. (1986). *The control revolution: Technological and economic origins of the information society*. Harvard University Press.

Britz, J. J., Lor, P. J., Coetzee, I. E. M., & Bester, B. C. (2006). Africa as a knowledge society: A reality check. *The International Information & Library Review, 38*, 25–40.

Byrne, B. M. (2001). *Structural equation modelling with AMOS: Basic concepts, applications and programming*. Mahwah, NJ: Lawrence Erlbaum Associates.

Byrne, B. M. (2010). *Structural equation modelling with AMOS: Basic concepts, applications and programming* (2nd ed.). New York: Routledge.

Clarke, M. (2003). e-Development? Development and the new economy. In UNU World Institute for Development Economics Research. Policy Brief No. 7. Helsinki: United Nations University.

Cohen, D., & Prusak, L. (2001). *In good company: How social capital makes organizations work*. Boston: Harvard Business School Press.

Creswell, J. W. (2003). *Research design: Qualitative, quantitative and mixed methods approaches* (2nd ed.). London: SAGE Publications.

Drucker, P. F. (1993). *Post-capitalist society*. New York: HarperCollins.

Duff, A. S. (2000). *Information society studies*. London: Routledge.

Economic Planning Unit Malaysia. (2001). *The third outline perspective plan 2001 - 2010*. Prime Minister's Department.

Economic Planning Unit Malaysia. (2005). *International comparison: The knowledge-based economy development index 2000/2004*. Retrieved from http://www.epu.gov.my/html/themes/epu/images/common/pdf/ME_2005_chapt_ 13.pdf

European Foundation for the Improvement of Living and Working Conditions. (2004). *European knowledge society foresight: The Euforia project synthesis*. Retrieved from http://www.eurofound.europa.eu/pubdocs/2004/04/en/1/ef0404en.pdf

Evans, P. B., & Wurster, T. S. (1997). Strategies and the new economics of information. *Harvard Business Review*, (September), 71–82. PMID:10170332

Evers, H. (2001). *Towards a Malaysian knowledge society.* Paper read at The 3rd International Malaysian Studies Conference (MSC3), Bangi, Selangor.

Gao, S. (2005). China's transformation into a knowledge-based economy. In *WBI Global Innovation Policy Dialogue: India and China.* Washington DC: World Bank Institute.

Gerke, S., & Evers, H. (2005). Local and global knowledge on Southeast Asia. In T. Menkhoff, H. Evers, & Y. W. Chay (Eds.), *Governing and managing knowledge in Asia.* London: World Scientific.

Gillham, B. (2000). *Developing a questionnaire.* London: Continuum.

Grootaert, C., Narayan, D., Jones, V. N., & Woolcock, M. (2004). *Measuring social capital: An integrated questionnaire.* The World Bank. Retrieved from http://books.google.com.my/books?id=2PLkjetXoC& dq='What+is+Social+Capital+world+bank+1999&printsec=frontcover&source=in&hl=en&ei=JsB mSqTFMZCG6AP8qajACQ&sa=X&oi=book_result&ct=result&resnum=12

Hair, J. F., Black, W. C., Babin, B. J., & Anderson, R. E. (2010). *Multivariate data analysis* (7th ed.). Upper Saddle River, NJ: Pearson Prentice Hall.

Hamid, N. A. (2011). *Development and validation of a knowledge society model and indicators in the Malaysian context.* (Unpublished Doctoral Thesis). Universiti Kebangsaan Malaysia.

Hurley, A. E., Scandura, T. A., Schriesheim, C. A., Brannick, M. T., Seers, A., Vandenberg, R. J., & Williams, L. J. (1997). Exploratory and confirmatory factor analysis: Guidelines, issues, and alternatives. *Journal of Organizational Behavior, 18*(6), 667–683. doi:10.1002/(SICI)1099-1379(199711)18:6<667::AID-JOB874>3.0.CO;2-T

Lor, P. J., & Britz, J. J. (2007). Is a knowledge society possible without freedom of access to information? *Journal of Information Science, 33*(4), 387–397. doi:10.1177/0165551506075327

Machlup, F. (1962). *The production and distribution of knowledge in the United States.* Princeton, NJ: Princeton University Press.

Mansell, R., & When, U. (1998). *Knowledge societies: Information technology for sustainable development.* New York: United Nations Commission on Science and Technology for Development.

Masuda, Y. (1980). *The information society as a post-industrial society.* World Future Society.

Miles, M. B., & Huberman, A. M. (1994). *Qualitative data analysis: An expanded sourcebook* (2nd ed.). California: SAGE.

Mioara, M. S. (2012). The impact of technological and communication innovation in the knowledge-based society. *Procedia: Social and Behavioral Sciences, 51,* 263–267. doi:10.1016/j.sbspro.2012.08.156

Mohamad, M. (1991). *Malaysia: The way forward.* Kuala Lumpur: Centre for Economic Research & Services, Malaysian Business Council. Retrieved from http://www.digitalibrary.my/dmdocuments/malaysiakini/007_malaysia_the%20way%20forward.pdf

National Economic Advisory Council (NEAC). (2010). *New economic model for Malaysia 2010.* Retrieved from http://www.neac.gov.my/content/download-option-new-economic-model-malaysia-2010

Pallant, J. (2007). *SPSS survival manual: A step by step guide to data analysis using SPSS*. Allen & Unwin.

Performance Management and Delivery Unit (PEMANDU). (2012). *Government Transformation Programme*. Retrieved from http://www.pemandu.gov.my/gtp/

Performance Management and Delivery Unit (PEMANDU) Malaysia. (2010). Retrieved from http://www.pemandu.gov.my/en/rural-basic-infrastructure/620.html

Putnam, R. D., & Goss, K. A. (2002). Introduction to democracies. In R. D. Putnam (Ed.), *Democracies in flux: The evolution of social capital in contemporary society*. Oxford, UK: Oxford University Press. doi:10.1093/0195150899.003.0001

Roberts, S. (2002). *A statistical framework for describing a knowledge-based economy/society*. In IAOS Conference 2002. Organised by Office for National Statistics, UK. London, UK.

Rohrbach, D. (2007). The development of knowledge societies in 19 OECD countries between 1970 and 2002. *Social Sciences Information. Information Sur les Sciences Sociales*, *46*(4), 655–689. doi:10.1177/0539018407082596

Sarosa, S. (2007). *The information technology adoption process within Indonesian small and medium enterprises*. (Doctoral thesis). University of Technology Sydney.

Smart, W. J. (2009). *Information system success: Evaluation of a carbon accounting and sequestration system*. (Doctoral thesis). School of Commerce and Management, Southern Cross University, Lismore, Australia.

Spangenberg, J. H. (2005). Will the information society be sustainable? Towards criteria and indicators for a sustainable knowledge society. *International Journal of Innovation and Sustainable Development*, *1*(1/2), 85–102. doi:10.1504/IJISD.2005.008082

Stehr, N. (1994). *Knowledge societies*. London: SAGE Publications.

Tabachnick, B., & Fidell, L. (2007). *Using multivariate statistics* (5th ed.). Boston: Pearson Education, Inc.

UNESCO. (2005). *World Report: Towards knowledge societies*. UNESCO Publishing. Retrieved from http://unesdoc.unesco.org/images/ 0014/001418/141843e.pdf

Webster, F. (1995). *Theories of the information society*. London: Routledge.

World Bank. (2012). *Knowledge Economy Index (KEI) 2012 Rankings*. Retrieved from http://www.siteresources.worldbank.org/INTUNIKAM/.../2012.pdf

Yin, R. (2003). *Case study research: Design and methods* (2nd ed.). Thousand Oaks, CA: Sage Publications.

ADDITIONAL READING

Abbas Ghanbari & Musa Abu Hassan. (2011). *Islamic understanding of information society: Interview with Muslim scholars*. Serdang: Universiti Putra Malaysia Press.

Abdul Rahim Anuar & Zulikha Jamaludin. (2005). *Agenda ICT ke arah pembangunan k-ekonomi Malaysia*. Sintok: Penerbit Universiti Utara Malaysia.

Bakry, S. H., & Al-Ghamdi, A. (2008). A framework for the knowledge society ecosystem: A tool for development. In M. D. Lytras, J. M. Carroll, E. Damiani, R. D. Tennyson, D. Avison, G. Vossen, & P. O. D. Pablos (Eds.), *The open knowledge society. A computer science and information systems manifesto*. Athens: Springer Berlin Heidelberg. doi:10.1007/978-3-540-87783-7_5

Barzilai-Nahon, K. (2006). Gaps and bits: Conceptualizing measurements for digital divide/s. *The Information Society*, *22*(5), 269–278. doi:10.1080/01972240600903953

Bell, D. (1973). *The coming of post-industrial society: A venture in social forecasting*. Harmondsworth: Penguin, Peregrine Books.

Bell, L. (2001). Preparing tomorrow's teachers to use technology: perspectives of the leaders of twelve national education associations. In *Contemporary issues in technology and teacher education. 1*(4): 517-534. Norfolk, VA: AACE. http://www.editlib.org/p/10740 [24th August 2008].

Britz, J. J., Lor, P. J., Coetzee, I. E. M., & Bester, B. C. (2006). Africa as a knowledge society: A reality check. *The International Information & Library Review*, *38*, 25–40.

Castells, M. (2000). *The rise of the network society: The information age: Economy, society and culture* (2nd ed., Vol. 1). Oxford: Blackwell Publishers.

Castells, M., & Himanen, P. (2004). *The information society and the welfare state: The Finnish model*. Oxford: Oxford University Press.

Davenport, T. H., & Prusak, L. (1997). *Information ecology: Mastering the information and knowledge environment*. Oxford: Oxford University Press.

Davenport, T. H., & Prusak, L. (1998). *Working knowledge: How organization manage what they know*. Boston: Harvard Business School Press.

Dordick, H. S., & Wang, G. (1993). *The information society - retrospective view*. Newbury Park, CA: Sage Publications.

Emmons, R. A. (1999). *The psychology of ultimate concerns: Motivation and spirituality in personality*. New York: Guilford.

Emmons, R. A. (2000). Is spirituality an intelligence? Motivation, cognition, and the psychology of ultimate concern. *The International Journal for the Psychology of Religion*, *10*(1), 3–26. doi:10.1207/S15327582IJPR1001_2

Institute of Strategic and International Studies Malaysia (ISIS). (2002). Knowledge-based economy master plan. Kuala Lumpur: ISIS Malaysia. http://unpan1.un.org/intradoc/groups/public/documents/APCITY/UNPAN013974.pdf [7th May 2009].

Kaldor, N. (1957). A model of economic growth. *The Economic Journal,67*(268 - Dec 1957), 591-624.

Krishnakumar, S., & Neck, C. P. (2002). The "what", "why' and "how" of spirituality in the workplace. *Journal of Managerial Psychology*, *17*(3), 153–164. doi:10.1108/02683940210423060

Lytras, M. D., & Sicilia, M. A. (2005). The knowledge society: A manifesto for knowledge and learning. *Int. J. Knowledge and Learning*, *1*(1/2), 1–11. doi:10.1504/IJKL.2005.006259

Mahathir Mohamad. (2008). Approaching 2020 – Major trends that will impact Malaysian business. Paper read at *Perdana Leadership Foundation Forum*. Organised by Perdana Leadership Foundation. Sime Darby Convention Centre, Kuala Lumpur, 8th August 2008.

Natoli, R. (2008). *Indicators of economic and social progress: An assessment and an alternative.* (Doctoral thesis).School of Applied Economics, Faculty of Business and Law, Victoria University, Melbourne, Australia.

Norsiah Abdul Hamid. (2011). *Development and validation of a knowledge society model and indicators in the Malaysian context*. (Unpublished Doctoral Thesis). Universiti Kebangsaan Malaysia.

Romer, P. M. (1986). Increasing returns and long-run growth. *Journal of Political Economy*, *94*(5), 1002–1037. doi:10.1086/261420

Romer, P. M. (1990). Endogenous technological change. *Journal of Political Economy*, *98*(5), 71–102. doi:10.1086/261725

United Nations Development Program (UNDP). (2015). Human Development Report 2015. Available at http://report.hdr.undp.org/

KEY TERMS AND DEFINITIONS

Economy: Economic-related activities that can measure the societal progress in the economy including income, poverty, economic stability and equal participation in workforce.

Human Capital: Inter-related elements of intellectual capital, knowledge, skills, competencies, and attributes, and its acquired activities such as education, training, R&D&I and supports from the government, private sector and NGOs.

Information and Communication Technology (ICT): Consists of the hardware, software, networks, and media for the collection, storage, processing, transmission and presentation of information (voice, data, text, images), as well as related services.

Institutional: Includes government efficiency, political stability, control of corruption, freedom of speech and information, and gender equality.

Knowledge: A combination of experience, value, context-based information, and expert opinion to assess and combine new information and experience.

Knowledge Society: A society in which its members appreciate knowledge, and knowledge is seen as a significant commodity of a nation's growth. A KS shows concern in the holistic development of the human capital and encompasses physical, intellectual, spiritual, economic, social, institutional and sustainable aspects of growth. A KS also propagates fairness and equality in all spheres of human lives which must take precedence. This includes the generation, access, use, sharing and dissemination of existing knowledge and the innovation of new knowledge through relevant ICT infrastructure and infostructure in tandem with the needs of that society.

Social: Social-related activities that contribute to the societal progress, including birth rate, marriage, people's participation in associations, crimes, corruption and life satisfaction index.

Spirituality: One's personal relation to the sacred or transcendent, a relation that informs other relationships and the meaning of one's own life.

Sustainability: The ability of a society to sustain itself in every aspect of living, including the environment, knowledge acculturation, culture of lifelong learning and innovation, and sustainable quality of life.

Chapter 5
Composite Indicators Construction by Data Envelopment Analysis:
Methodological Background

Gordana Savić
University of Belgrade, Serbia

Milan Martić
University of Belgrade, Serbia

ABSTRACT

Composite indicators (CIs) are seen as an aggregation of a set of sub-indicators for measuring multi-dimensional concepts that cannot be captured by a single indicator (OECD, 2008). The indicators of development in different areas are also constructed by aggregating several sub-indicators. Consequently, the construction of CIs includes weighting and aggregation of individual performance indicators. These steps in CI construction are challenging issues as the final results are significantly affected by the method used in aggregation. The main question is whether and how to weigh individual performance indicators. Verifiable information regarding the true weights is typically unavailable. In practice, subjective expert opinions are usually used to derive weights, which can lead to disagreements (Hatefi & Torabi, 2010). The disagreement can appear when the experts from different areas are included in a poll since they can value criteria differently in accordance with their expertise. Therefore, a proper methodology of the derivation of weights and construction of composite indicators should be employed. From the operations research standpoint, the data envelopment analysis (DEA) and the multiple criteria decision analysis (MCDA) are proper methods for the construction of composite indicators (Zhou & Ang, 2009; Zhou, Ang, & Zhou, 2010). All methods combine the sub-indicators according to their weights, except that the MCDA methods usually require a priori determination of weights, while the DEA determines the weights a posteriori, as a result of model solving. This chapter addresses the DEA as a non-parametric technique, introduced by Charnes, Cooper, and Rhodes (1978), for efficiency measurement of different non-profitable and profitable units. It is lately adopted as an appropriate method for the CI construction due to its several features (Shen, Ruan, Hermans, Brijs, Wets, & Vanhoof, 2011). Firstly, individual

DOI: 10.4018/978-1-5225-0714-7.ch005

performance indicators are combined without a priori determination of weights, and secondly, each unit under observation is assessed taking into consideration the performance of all other units, which is known as the 'benefit of the doubt' (BOD) approach (Cherchye, Moesen, Rogge, & van Puyenbroeck, 2007). The methodological and theoretical aspects and the flaws of the DEA application for the construction of CIs will be discussed in this chapter, starting with the issues related to the application procedure, followed by the issues of real data availability, introducing value judgments, qualitative data, and non-desirable performance indicators. The procedure of a DEA-based CI construction will be illustrated by the case of ranking of different regions of Serbia based on their socio-economic development.

INTRODUCTION

The purpose of this chapter is to introduce theoretical and methodological aspects of using a quantitative technique (Data envelopment analysis – DEA) in constructing composite indicators (CI). Composite indicators have recently become very popular and useful tools for comparing performance of countries. These indicators allow „simple comparisons of countries that can be used to illustrate complex and sometimes elusive issues in wide-ranging fields, e.g., education, environment, economy, society, or technological development" (OECD, 2008, p. 13). It often seems easier for the general public to interpret composite indicators than to identify common trends across many separate indicators; they have been also proven as a useful tool for benchmarking of the country performance (Saltelli, 2007). Numerous indicators have been constructed and introduced to cover all important areas of human and social development. A list of 178 composite indices can be found in the survey made by Bandura (2008).

However, composite indicators can send misleading messages if they are not properly constructed or calculated. Besides others techniques, such as multiple criteria decision analysis techniques of the equal weighted sum (Cherchye, Moesen, Rogge, & van Puyenbroeck, 2007), a statistical technique of composite I-distance indicator (Dobrota, Bulajic, Bornmann, & Jeremic, 2016), DEA is considered a suitable technique for constructing composite indicators. Detailed and structured literature reviews (Mariano, Sobreiro, & Rebelatto, 2015) indicate that DEA-based CIs are used in different areas covering different aspects of life, from economy and transportation to happiness.

The methodological and theoretical aspects, advantages and drawbacks of the DEA application to a CI construction will be discussed in detail in this chapter. The DEA theoretical background along the basic DEA models is given in the next two sections. The main focus of this chapter is put on the DEA-based CI discussed in the section "DEA-based composite indicators", followed by the models constructed for overcoming the DEA drawbacks. The procedure of a DEA-based CI construction is illustrated by the case study of the ranking of different regions of Serbia based on the socioeconomic development indicators. Finally, the concluding remarks are given.

BACKGROUND

Composite indicators (CIs) represent an aggregation of a set of sub-indicators for measuring multi-dimensional concepts that cannot be captured by a single indicator *e.g.* competitiveness, sustainability, single market integration, etc. (OECD, 2008). Dobrota, Savic, and Bulajic (2015) gave the example of using 12 single indicators for evaluating the European countries' educational structure development is given in the paper. The main focus of that paper is on the selection of indicators based on the defined research goals and available data, as well as the choice of an appropriate aggregation method. Thus, the construction of CIs includes several steps: defining a theoretical framework for creating a composite indicator, followed by data and individual performance indicators selection, the selection and imputation of missing data, data normalization, weighting and aggregation (OECD, 2008). The controversial issues can appear in any step of CI construction since results are significantly affected by the method used in data normalization, weighting, or aggregation. A decision maker is faced with a challenge to choose the right metrics for normalization (Cherchye, Moesen, Rogge, & van Puyenbroeck, 2007), the right weighting scheme (fixed or equal weighting), and the right method of aggregation (Munda, 2012).

Therefore, the main question is whether and how to weight individual performance indicators. Weights are usually given *a priori* and final measure is calculated by a simple additive weighting aggregation method. However, verifiable information regarding the true weights is typically not available. In practice, subjective expert opinions are used to derive weights, which can lead to disagreement (Hatefi & Torabi, 2010). The disagreement can appear when the experts from different fields are included in a poll since they can value criteria differently in accordance with their expertise. Therefore, a proper methodology of the derivation of weights and a construction of composite indicators should be employed. From operations research standpoint, data envelopment analysis (DEA) and multiple criteria decision analysis (MCDA) are appropriate methods for the construction of composite indicators (Zhou & Ang, 2009; Zhou, Ang, & Zhou, 2010). Both methods construct CI measure by assigning weights to variables but the principles are different. When assigning weights, MCDA method considers *a priori* experts' opinions, while DEA assigns weight to variables independently for each observed unit as a result of model solving.

The focus of this chapter is on DEA, a non-parametric technique, introduced by Charnes, Cooper and Rhodes (1978) for efficiency measurement of different non-profitable and profitable units. It has been recently broadened and adopted as an appropriate method for constructing CIs, using its several positive features (Shen, Ruan, Hermans, Brijs, Wets, & Vanhoof, 2011). Firstly, individual performance indicators are combined without *a priori* determined weights. Secondly, each unit under observation is assessed by taking into account the performance of all other units. Thirdly, the indicators used in the model can be expressed in different units of measurement, which means that normalization is not required. Finally, each unit in the observed set obtains its own best weights, without *a priori* determination, which puts each unit in the most favorable lights. The modified DEA method is also known as the 'benefit of the doubt' (BoD) approach (Cherchye, Moesen, Rogge, & van Puyenbroeck, 2007). Furthermore, the advantage of DEA is a possibility of incorporating the experts knowledge by weight restrictions, determining a common set of weights (Hatefi & Torabi, 2010) or performing a multiplicative aggregation of the indicators (Zhou, Ang, & Zhou, 2010). These positive features have led to an increased number of DEA-based CIs. On the other hand, numerous applications reveal several drawbacks of such indices and suggest alternative solutions given subsequently.

DATA ENVELOPMENT ANALYSIS

Data envelopment analysis (Charnes, Cooper, & Rhodes, 1978) was introduced for measuring relative efficiency of non-profit units, such as schools (Ruggerio & Vitaliano, 1999), whose performance depends on multiple inputs and multiple outputs. These inputs and outputs are usually not financial in nature and are difficult to measure. The DEA application areas are later expanded to the comparative analysis of efficiency for all types of non-profit units, profit-units, even to a comparative analysis of individual achievements e.g. as efficiency assessment of athletes (Cooper, Ruiz, & Sirvent, 2009; Radovanović, Radojičić, & Savić, 2014). Data envelopment analysis has lately received considerable attention in the construction of composite indicators due to its prominent advantages over other traditional methods such as equal or unequal weighting methods. The advantages and disadvantages will be discussed later, after presenting DEA basics.

DEA can be defined as a linear programming technique used to find the optimal set of relative weights (u, v) that will give the highest possible efficiency ratio of outputs to inputs for the decision-making units (DMUs) being evaluated. Let us suppose that the following parameters are known:

n – number of DMUs

m – number of inputs

s – number of outputs

x_{ij} – known amount of i-th input of DMU_j $\left(x_{ij} > 0, i = 1, 2, ..., m, j = 1, 2, ..., n\right)$

y_{rj} – known amount of r-th output of DMU_j $\left(y_{rj} > 0, r = 1, 2, ..., s, j = 1, 2, ..., n\right)$

Having known parameters given above, Charnes, Cooper, and Rhodes (1978) formulated mathematical model trying to maximize the relative efficiency h_k of DMU_k (k=1,..,n) by optimizing weight of inputs v_i $(i = 1, ..., m)$ and weight of outputs $u_r (r = 1, ..., s)$. The aim of relative efficiency maximization is completely achieved by setting objective function (1) in the mathematical model given below. The scaling problem (data normalization problem) is solved by introducing constraints (2) which say that no one of the evaluated DMUs will be more efficient than 1 (100%). There are n constraints of type (2) – one for each DMU in the observed set. The fractional model form is as follows:

$$\max h_k = \frac{\sum_{r=1}^{s} u_r y_{rk}}{\sum_{i=1}^{m} v_i x_{ik}} \tag{1}$$

s.t.

$$\frac{\sum_{r=1}^{s} u_r y_{rj}}{\sum_{i=1}^{m} v_i x_{ij}} \leq 1, j = 1, ..., n \tag{2}$$

$$u_1, ..., u_s \geq 0, v_1, ..., v_m \geq 0 \tag{3}$$

The model (1-3) should be solved n-times, once for each DMU. As a result, efficiency scores $h_k(k = 1,...,n)$, together with weights $v_i(i = 1,...,m)$ and u_r $(r = 1,...,s)$ will be obtained.

Input-Oriented CRS DEA Model

The calculation is more complicated if the model of fractional programming is used rather than the linear programming model. Therefore, the linear model (4-7) is created as an equivalent to the model (1-3) and it provides identical results assuming constant returns to scale (CRS).

$$(\max)h_k = \sum_{r=1}^{s} u_r y_{rk} \tag{4}$$

s.t.

$$\sum_{i=1}^{m} v_i x_{ik} = 1 \tag{5}$$

$$\sum_{r=1}^{s} u_r y_{rj} - \sum_{i=1}^{m} v_i x_{ij} \leq 0, j = 1, 2, ..., n \tag{6}$$

$$u_1,..., u_s \geq 0, v_1,..., v_m \geq 0 \tag{7}$$

In the model (4-7), DMU maximizes the virtual output under the constraint that its virtual input is equal to 1. The constraint given by eq. (6) indicates that the optimal weights for the DMU_k must satisfy the condition that the virtual output of each of n DMUs cannot be greater than its virtual input. If the objective function is equal to 1, then virtual outputs of all inefficient DMUs will be less than the virtual inputs. If the value of the objective function is less than 1, the efficiency reference set for DMU_k can be constituted. It consists of DMUs with virtual output equal to virtual input and it forms frontier for measuring the level of efficiency. As already mentioned, virtual inputs $\sum_{i=1}^{m} v_i x_{ik}$ and virtual outputs $\sum_{r=1}^{s} u_r y_{rk}$ of DMU_k, are calculated as the sum of the product of known inputs $x_{ik}, i = 1,...,m$ (outputs $y_{rk}, r = 1,...,s$) and assigned weights, considered as variables in the model (4-7).

A dual linear program (8-11) corresponding to the model (4-7):

$$(\min) Z_k \tag{8}$$

s.t.

$$\sum_{j=1}^{n} \lambda_j y_{rj} \geq y_{rk}, r = 1,...,s \tag{9}$$

$$Z_k x_{ik} - \sum_{j=1}^{n} \lambda_j x_{ij} \geq 0, i = 1,...,m \tag{10}$$

$$\lambda_j \geq 0, j = 1,...,n \tag{11}$$

The objective function (8) shows the efficiency level of DMU_k. Its value is the same as an objective function value of primal model (4-7). The variable Z_k is usually called intensity factor and indicates the level to which it is necessary to proportionally reduce the values of inputs of DMU_k to become efficient in producing the current level of outputs. Dual variables, $\lambda_j, (j = 1,...,n)$ show the importance that is assigned to DMU_j ($j = 1,...,n$), in defining the input-output mix of a hypothetical composite unit (efficiency reference set). The observed DMU_k is directly compared to a hypothetical composite unit. The variables $\lambda_j, (j = 1,...,n)$ are chosen so that virtual output value $\left(\sum_{j=1}^{n} \lambda_j y_{rj}, r = 1,...,s \right)$ of a hypothetical composite unit is not less than the corresponding actual output of DMU_k, and that virtual input $\left(\sum_{j=1}^{n} \lambda_j x_{ij}, i = 1,...,m \right)$ of each composite unit is not greater than the respective actual input of DMU_k. If DEA tries to minimize Z_k of DMU_k and it cannot find $\lambda_j, j = 1,...,n$ multipliers that will generate an efficiency level below 1 (100%), DMU_k is evaluated as a relatively efficient unit (Z_k=1). In such case, λ_k is the only multiplier with a value greater than 0 ($\lambda_j = 0, j = 1,...,n, j \neq k$). For inefficient units, Z_k is below 1 (100%), and there are groups of DMUs (efficiency reference set) that produce as much or more outputs and use fewer inputs offering a path to improve the efficiency of the inefficient units. The values of efficiency reference set multipliers $\lambda_j, j = 1,...,n$ are above 0.

Output-Oriented CRS DEA Model

Output-oriented DEA problem is created with the idea that DMU should achieve the maximal level of output using the current level of input.

Primal output-oriented DEA CRS model is:

$$(\min)h_k = \sum_{i=1}^{m} v_i x_{ik} \tag{12}$$

s.t.

$$\sum_{r=1}^{s} u_r y_{rk} = 1 \tag{13}$$

$$\sum_{i=1}^{m} v_i x_{ij} - \sum_{r=1}^{s} u_r y_{rj} \geq 0, j = 1, 2, \ldots, n \tag{14}$$

$$u_r \geq 0, r = 1, \ldots, s, v_i \geq 0, i = 1, \ldots, m \tag{15}$$

Dual output-oriented DEA CRS model is:

$$(\max) Z_k \tag{16}$$

s.t.

$$\sum_{j=1}^{n} \lambda_j x_{ij} \leq x_{ik}, i = 1, \ldots, m \tag{17}$$

$$Z_k y_{rk} - \sum_{j=1}^{n} \lambda_j y_{rj} \leq 0, r = 1, \ldots, s \tag{18}$$

$$\lambda_j \geq 0 \, j = 1, \ldots, n \tag{19}$$

The value of efficiency index obtained by primal CRS DEA model (12-15) or dual CRS DEA model (16-19) is greater or equal to 1 (reciprocal to the value obtained by models (4-7) or (8-11)).

Input-Oriented VRS Linear DEA Model

Banker, Charnes, and Cooper (1984) made the first extension of the basic DEA models by introducing the economic principle of variable returns to scale (VRS). The introduction of VRS principle has been achieved as slight modifications of the basic model. Primal DEA CRS model is modified by introducing a free-sign variable u^* that defines the returns to scale. Input-oriented primal DEA model is as follows:

$$(\max) h_k = \sum_{r=1}^{s} u_r y_{rk} + u^* \tag{20}$$

s.t.

$$\sum_{i=1}^{m} v_i x_{ik} = 1 \tag{21}$$

$$\sum_{r=1}^{s} u_r y_{rj} - \sum_{i=1}^{m} v_i x_{ij} + u^* \leq 0, j = 1, 2, \dots, n \tag{22}$$

$$u_r \geq 0, r = 1, \dots, s, v_i \geq 0, i = 1, \dots, m, u^* - free\text{-}sign \tag{23}$$

The optimization problem consists in finding values of weights $u_r \geq 0, (r = 1, \dots, s)$, $v_i \geq 0, (i = 1, \dots, m)$ and scale variables u^* to set the maximal value of objective function. The value u^* makes up a difference between CRS and VRS efficiency scores. According to primal-dual correspondence rules, dual model may be formulated:

$$(\min) \; Z_k \tag{24}$$

s.t.

$$\sum_{j=1}^{n} \lambda_j y_{rj} \geq y_{rk}, r = 1, \dots, s \tag{25}$$

$$Z_k x_{ik} - \sum_{j=1}^{n} \lambda_j x_{ij} \geq 0, i = 1, \dots, m \tag{26}$$

$$\sum_{j=1}^{n} \lambda_j = 1 \tag{27}$$

$$\lambda_j \geq 0, j = 1, \dots, n \tag{28}$$

The above VRS dual model differs from CRS dual model (8-11) only in adjunction of the constraint $\sum_{j=1}^{n} \lambda_j = 1, (j = 1, \dots, n)$ to ensure that the benchmark unit has a similar scope and similar input-output mix as the observed DMU_k.

Output-Oriented VRS Linear DEA Model

Output-oriented VRS DEA models are defined by a modification of output-oriented CRS DEA model. DEA CRS model is modified by introducing a free-sign variable u^* that defines the returns to scale. Output-oriented primal DEA model is as follows:

$$(\min)h_k = \sum_{i=1}^{m} v_i x_{ik} + u^* \tag{29}$$

s.t.

$$\sum_{r=1}^{s} u_r y_{rk} = 1 \tag{30}$$

$$\sum_{i=1}^{m} v_i x_{ij} - \sum_{r=1}^{s} u_r y_{rj} + u^* \geq 0, j = 1, 2, \ldots, n \tag{31}$$

$$u_r \geq 0, r = 1, \ldots, s, v_i \geq 0, i = 1, \ldots, m, u^* - free\text{-}sign \tag{32}$$

A dual output-oriented VRS DEA model is:

$$(\max)Z_k \tag{33}$$

s.t.

$$\sum_{j=1}^{n} \lambda_j x_{ij} \leq x_{ik}, i = 1, \ldots, m \tag{34}$$

$$Z_k y_{rk} - \sum_{j=1}^{n} \lambda_j y_{rj} \leq 0, r = 1, \ldots, s \tag{35}$$

$$\sum_{j=1}^{n} \lambda_j = 1 \tag{36}$$

$$\lambda_j \geq 0, j = 1, ..., n \tag{37}$$

The presented models are introduced for application in different contexts (constant or variable return to scale) and for different purposes (input or output orientation) of the analysis. The choice of the appropriate model is extremely important since efficiency scores depend on a model type and orientation. These models also make a basis for the development of new models and the expansion of DEA application in various fields, such as the development of DEA-based composite indicators.

DEA-BASED COMPOSITE INDICATORS

Solving any of the basic DEA models described in the previous chapter leads to the aggregated index of relative efficiency with the value scaled between 0 and 1. This means that the problem of normalization is resolved and a decision-maker does not have to opt for a specific method for data normalization (Cherchye, Moesen, Rogge, & van Puyenbroeck, 2007). The efficiency index h_k for each DMU_k, ($k=1,...$,n) is calculated based on the values of inputs and outputs and the weights assigned to them. The weights are not fixed in advance, but each DMU defines its own weighting scheme in order to achieve the best possible efficiency level. Thus, a weighting scheme is data-driven, as each DMU creates the best suitable weighting scheme. In this way, the problem of weighting data and aggregation of sub-indicators into one composite (efficiency) index is solved. As a result, the area of DEA application is widened to the area of construction of composite indicators.

'Benefit of the Doubt' DEA Model

Composite indicator Human Development Index (HDI) has been introduced by the UNDP (2000) as a measure of a socioeconomic development at a county level. The HDI is a composite index of socioeconomic indicators that reflect three major dimensions of human development: longevity, knowledge, and standard of living. Each dimension represents sub-indicators aggregated from several components. Similar logic is employed in creating CIs in other areas such as health, information society, environment and sustainability, education, etc. The common feature of all CIs is that sub-indicators are the results of performance in a specific country or region which is a member of the observed set. Thus, each sub-indicator is viewed as an output regardless of whether it has a positive or negative impact on future business, development, or the environment.

Therefore, DEA models are modified to adopt the CI components by introducing a dummy variable equal to 1 and several outputs with normalized or raw data. Each sub-component in the DEA terminology is considered as output since their increase favours the observed countries or regions. Therefore, a specific class of models, referred to as "benefit of the doubt" models, is created by Melyn and Moesen (1991), and Cherchye et al. (2007). The model is as follows (Shen, Ruan, Hermans, Brijs, Wets, & Vanhoof, 2011):

$$(\max)h_k = \sum_{r=1}^{s} u_r y_{rk} \tag{38}$$

s.t.

$$\sum_{r=1}^{s} u_r y_{rj} \leq 1, j = 1,...,n \tag{39}$$

$$u_1,...,u_s \geq 0 \tag{40}$$

This model provided the most favourable aggregated performance score for each DMU_k ($k=1,...,n$) in terms of all used component indicators. The resulting performance score h_k identifies the closeness of observed DMU_k to its best practice.

Another DEA-like model proposes the worst favourable weights for each DMU_k (Zhou, Ang, & Poh, 2007):

$$(\min) l_k = \sum_{r=1}^{s} u_r y_{rk} \tag{41}$$

s.t.

$$\sum_{r=1}^{s} u_r y_{rj} \geq 1, j = 1,...,n \tag{42}$$

$$u_1,...,u_s \geq 0 \tag{43}$$

The model (38-40) is very similar to an input minimizing multiplier DEA model with multiple inputs and a constant dummy output equal to 1. However, all the component indicators are of the benefit-type and are not appropriate for being considered as "inputs". Therefore, the model (**41-43**) measures how close the observed DMU_k is to the worst practice unit (inverse "benefit of the doubt" DEA model).

The 'benefit of the doubt' type DEA model is useful in the construction of CIs as it retains the advantages of DEA models and enables decision-makers to assess CIs only on the basis of the available data set of sub-indicators. *A priori* weights determination is not necessary, and performance of all DMUs is shown in the most favourable light. On the other hand, DEA-based CIs retain some disadvantages of DEA index, which will be discussed in the next chapter.

ADVANTAGES AND DRAWBACKS OF DEA MODELS

The proposed DEA-like models have their advantages and drawbacks. Some of the main advantages have already been highlighted. The advantages are:

1. The problem of selecting method of data normalization is solved by using the DEA model as it does not require normalization, and can work with raw data.
2. A common problem of *a priori* determination of weights for component indicators is solved by DEA models. They do not require *a priori* weights and treat them as variables. Consequently, a potential problem of disagreement among experts whose opinion should be taken into account in determining weights is solved.
3. The problem of selecting the aggregation method is also solved as the aggregation of component indicators and calculation of CIs is done simultaneously along the course of solving the DEA model.

On the other hand, several drawbacks of the DEA method are transferred to the DEA-like models for the construction of CIs. These drawbacks have been addressed in different ways in the literature and several of them are explored in this chapter:

1. The impossibility of distinction and ranking among efficient units i.e. all efficient units are located on the efficiency frontier and indices assigned to them are equal to 1.
2. The necessity to include an analysis of qualitative data, given that the basic DEA models work exclusively with non-negative quantitative data.
3. Basic DEA models do not take into account the undesirable outputs, i.e. outputs with a negative impact on the system performance and the environment.

Some of the ways to overcome these shortcomings found in the literature will be presented below.

Full Ranking of DMUs

Mahlberg and Obersteiner (2001) used the 'benefit of the doubt' model (38-40) for assessing the performance of 174 countries. The authors compare DEA-based indices with the HDI considering the four sub-indicators: life expectancy, adult literacy, enrolment rate, and GDP. The set of countries is divided into a set of efficient and a set of inefficient countries, but only the inefficient countries can be ranked according to the value of objective function h_k. Thus, the results have shown the inability of the model to make a difference between efficient units. The authors solved this problem by introducing weight restrictions. Other solutions are presented below.

In the first approach, the authors solved a problem of ranking the efficient units by introducing a two-phase CI calculation (Zhou, Ang, & Poh, 2007). The models (38-40) and (41-43) are used for a calculation of the best h_k and the worst l_k "benefit of the doubt" indicators for the observed DMU_k in the first phase. The second phase assumes the calculation of the final CI according to the following formula:

$$CI_k(\lambda) = \lambda \frac{h_k - h_k^-}{h_k^* - h_k^-} + (1 - \lambda) \frac{l_k - l_k^-}{l_k^* - l_k^-}, 0 \leq \lambda \leq 1 \tag{44}$$

where

$$h_k^* = \max h_j, j = 1, ..., n, h_k^- = \min h_j, j = 1, ..., n$$
$$l_k^* = \max l_j, j = 1, ..., n, l_k^- = \min l_j, j = 1, ..., n$$

Parameter λ is an adjusting parameter determined by a decision-maker, but the flexibility in the selection of λ value may also cause difficulty for a decision-maker to make the final subjective choice since there may not be enough evidence to support any choice of λ values. Moreover, different values of λ may lead to distinct and misleading results for CIs. Therefore, the alternative ways of solving the problem of full ranking are also given.

Super-Efficiency DEA Model

One of the first DEA-based CIs is created to assess a socioeconomic development level and human well-being in different regions of Serbia (Martić & Savić, 2001). The authors assessed 30 regions based on four inputs (arable area, active fixed asset, consumptions of the electricity, and population), treated as potentials and recourses, and four outputs (gross domestic products, total number of physicians, total number of students in primary school, and total number of students in secondary school), treated as indicators of development and living standard. Basic CRS DEA input-oriented model is employed for assessment of the regions efficiency. Furthermore, the sources of inefficiency and peer regions have been found for each inefficient region in the observed set. The authors were faced with a problem of setting realistic targets and solved it by introducing additional restrictions and region clustering with a linear discriminant analysis. A well-known Andersen-Petersen's super-efficiency DEA (Andersen & Petersen, 1993) is employed in the next phase as a tie-breaking method to allow a full ranking of the all 30 regions. A super-efficiency measure is obtained by excluding regions under evaluation form the production possibility set. The super-efficiency DEA model is very similar to the basic DEA model. For example, the modification of the input-oriented CRS DEA model (4-7) consists of excluding DMU_k from the production possibility set (set of units forming the efficient frontier) in the eq. (47). Super-efficiency CRS DEA model is as follows:

$$(\max)h_k = \sum_{r=1}^{s} u_r y_{rk} \tag{45}$$

s.t.

$$\sum_{i=1}^{m} v_i x_{ik} = 1 \tag{46}$$

$$\sum_{r=1}^{s} u_r y_{rj} - \sum_{i=1}^{m} v_i x_{ij} \le 0, j = 1, ..., n, j \ne k \tag{47}$$

$$u_1,...,u_s \geq 0, v_1,...,v_m \geq 0 \tag{48}$$

This model can easily be adapted to the 'benefit of the doubt' super-efficiency model:

$$(\max)h_k = \sum_{r=1}^{s} u_r y_{rk} \tag{49}$$

s.t.

$$\sum_{r=1}^{s} u_r y_{rj} \leq 1, j = 1,...,n, j \neq k \tag{50}$$

$$u_1,...,u_s \geq 0, v_1,...,v_m \geq 0 \tag{51}$$

Common Weights DEA-Like Approaches

Despotis (2005) used the model (29-32) to assess the Human development index (HDI) of countries in Asia and Pacific based on three components: life expectancy at birth, educational attainment, and GDP per capita. Three countries were top-ranked according to the HDI "efficiency" score. However, according to the authors, the h_k index, obtained by solving the proposed model, cannot be used to rank the countries in terms of human development, as it is obtained on the basis of a flexible scheme for assigning weights. Further steps in ranking human development refer to solving a tie-breaking model (52-55) based on common weights (w_r, $r = 1,...,s$), which ensures a fair assessment of all efficient DMU_j, $j \in E \subseteq \{1,...,n\}$.

$$(\min)(t/n)\sum_{j=1}^{n} d_j + (1-t)z \tag{52}$$

s.t.

$$\sum_{r=1}^{s} w_r y_{rj} + d_j \leq h_j^*, j \in E \tag{53}$$

$$d_j - z \leq 0, j \in E \tag{54}$$

$$u_1,...,u_s \geq 0, z \geq 0, d_j \geq 0, j \in E \tag{55}$$

where objective function represents the global efficiency score of DMU_k. It is calculated as a mean (L1 norm, $t=1$) or maximal deviation (L∞ norm, $t=0$) of the global efficiency score from the efficiency score $h_k^*, k \in E$ obtained by the solving model (38-40). The model was formulated in a goal-programming manner with deviation variables $d_j, (j = 1,...,n)$, and a non-negative variable z needs to be as small as possible. By varying the variable t between the two extreme values 0 and 1, the authors allowed the exploration of different sets of common weights - from those that minimize maximal deviation to the ones that maximize mean deviation. After obtaining the objective function value of the model (52-55), global efficiency score is obtained for DEA-efficient DMU_j ($j \in E$) assessed as efficient by solving the model (38-40) in the first phase. The same methodology has been employed for the reassessment of the HDI for the set of 174 countries (Despotis, 2005). This measure of human development is more objective than the HDI index obtained by a standard procedure (OECD, 2008) since the weights assigned to the component indicators are less arbitrary. They are actually assigned in an objective way in the first phase of solving the DEA-like "benefit of the doubt" model.

Another very similar approach based on goal programming is proposed in (Hatefi & Torabi, 2010). It is used for sustainable energy index and human development index of the APEC economies in 2002.

On the other hand, the arbitrariness in the weights assignment is reduced by introducing a multiple-layer hierarchal structure of the sub-indicators (Shen, Hermans, Brijs, & Wets, 2013). The main idea is to make a hierarchical structure of each sub-indicator and specify weights of each layer of each category of sub-indicators. The final CI is obtained as a sum product of weights of each layer of each category and values of sub-indicators at the lowest level of the hierarchy.

Modelling Qualitative Data

Precise, nonnegative, quantitative data are usually prerequisite for using the DEA model. But, today's world and performance evaluation require the introduction of factors that can only be expressed as qualitative data. Two models which can include quantitative data are proposed by Shen, Ruan, Hermans, Brijs, Wets, and Vanhoof (2011) for calculating CIs in the road safety management evaluation by creating a composite road safety policy performance index for 25 European countries. The results verify the robustness of the index scores computed from both models, and further imply the effectiveness and reliability of these two approaches.

The first approach assumes incorporating ordinal data into "benefit of the doubt" DEA model (38-40). A set of outputs is divided into a subset of s_1 numerical and s_2-s_1 ordinal indicators. Therefore, a modified model is as follows:

$$(\max)h_k = \sum_{r=1}^{s_1} u_r y_{rk} + \sum_{r=s_1+1}^{s_2} \sum_{l=1}^{L} y_{rlk} \tag{56}$$

s.t.

$$\sum_{r=1}^{s_1} u_r y_{rj} + \sum_{r=s_1+1}^{s_2} \sum_{l=1}^{L} y_{rlk} \leq 1, j = 1, ..., n \tag{57}$$

$$y_{rlj} > y_{rl+1j}, l = 1, ..., L-1, y_{rl+1j} > 0, r = 1, ..., s, j = 1, ..., n \tag{58}$$

$$u_1, ..., u_{s_1} \geq 0 \tag{59}$$

where y_{rlk} represents a virtual value of ordinal (qualitative) indicator $\left(r = s_1 + 1, ..., s_2 \right)$ of $DMU_k (k = 1, ..., n)$ at L-point scale $\left(l = 1, ..., L \right)$. The original ordinal values y_{rlk}^0 multiplied with position vector p_{rl} ($l=1,...,L$, $r=s_1+1,...,s_2$) under the condition $y_{r1k}^0 > y_{r2k}^0 > ... > y_{rL-1k}^0 > y_{rLk}^0$. Position vector p_{lr} is obtained by converting the ranking value of each DMU into its position. Therefore,

$$y_{rlk} = p_{lr} * y_{rlk}^0, \left(r = s_1 + 1, ..., s_2, k = 1, ..., n, l = 1, ..., L \right).$$

Another proposition considers using a fuzzy DEA model. Mathematical formulation of this model corresponds to the formulation of the DEA model (38-40), whereby the outputs y_{rk} are replaced by the equivalent fuzzy numbers $\widetilde{y}_{rk}$ ($r=1,...,s$, $k=1,..., n$). In the most common application, the symmetrical triangular simplification of fuzzy numbers $\widetilde{y}_{rk}$ is used to represent the uncertainty of information. Symmetrical triangular fuzzy number $\widetilde{y}_{rk}$ denoted by pairs of centers and spreads ($\widetilde{y}_{rk} = \left(y_{rk}, \alpha_{rk} \right)$, $r=1,...,s$, $k=1,...,n$). A corresponding model (Shen, Ruan, Hermans, Brijs, Wets, & Vanhoof, 2011; Shen, Hermans, Brijs, & Wets, 2013) is as follows:

$$(\max)h_k = \lambda \sum_{r=1}^{s} u_r \left(y_{rk} - (1-h)\alpha_{rk} \right) + (1-\lambda) \sum_{r=1}^{s} u_r \left(y_{rk} + (1-h)\alpha_{rk} \right) \tag{60}$$

s.t.

$$\sum_{r=1}^{s} u_r \left(y_{rk} + (1-h)\alpha_{rk} \right) \leq 1, j = 1, ..., n \tag{61}$$

$$u_1, ..., u_s \geq 0, 0 \leq h \leq 1, 0 \leq \lambda \leq 1 \tag{62}$$

The authors considered three situations of calculating fuzzy CI for DMU_k: optimistic ($\lambda = 0$), pessimistic, ($\lambda = 1$) and indifferent ($\lambda = 0.5$) approach.

After applying both models to the same case of constructing a composite road safety policy performance index, the authors concluded that the crisp index score achieved by the imprecise DEA-based CIs model is easy for interpretation and use while fuzzy index scores obtained based on the different possibility level ranking result verifies the robustness of both models.

Another approach in modelling imprecise data, when only the interval ($y_{rj} \in \left[\underline{y}_{rj}, \overline{y}_{rj} \right], r = 1,...,s, j = 1,...,n$) within the sub-indicator is believed to lie, is given in the paper by Cherchye, Moesen, Rogge, and Puyenbroeck (2011). By modifying the 'benefit of the doubt' model (38-40), the authors suggested solving the two models as alternative scenarios for each DMU_k. The model (63-66) is used for obtaining $\overline{h}_k$ as an upper bound and the model (67-70) for obtaining $\underline{h}_k$ as a lower bound of a CI value.

Upper bound CI model:

$$(\max)\overline{h}_k = \sum_{r=1}^{s} u_r \overline{y}_{rk} \tag{63}$$

s.t.

$$\sum_{r=1}^{s} u_r \overline{y}_{rj} \leq 1, j = 1,...,n \tag{64}$$

$$\sum_{r=1}^{s} u_r \underline{y}_{rj} \leq 1, j = 1,...,n, j \neq k \tag{65}$$

$$u_1,...,u_s \geq 0 \tag{66}$$

Lower bound CI model:

$$(\max)\underline{h}_k = \sum_{r=1}^{s} u_r \underline{y}_{rk} \tag{67}$$

s.t.

$$\sum_{r=1}^{s} u_r \underline{y}_{rj} \leq 1, j = 1,...,n \tag{68}$$

$$\sum_{r=1}^{s} u_r \bar{y}_{rj} \leq 1, j = 1,...,n, j \neq k \tag{69}$$

$$u_1,...,u_s \geq 0 \tag{70}$$

As a result, the CI value lies in the interval between its lower and higher bound $\left(h_k \in \left[\underline{h}_k, \bar{h}_k \right], k = 1,...,n \right)$. The length of the interval represents uncertainty in obtaining the real CI value. The certain CI value $\left(h_k = \underline{h}_k = \bar{h}_k \right)$ can be obtained for $y_{rk} = \underline{y}_{rk} = \bar{y}_{rk}$, $(r = 1,...,s)$ or if the DMU$_k$ is obtained as a benchmark in both calculation $\left(h_k = \underline{h}_k = \bar{h}_k = 1 \right)$. DMU$_k$ is considered as a potential benchmark when the upper bound of CI reaches a value equal to 1 $\left(\bar{h}_k = 1, \underline{h}_k < 1 \right)$. These models are used for evaluating countries according to a knowledge-based economy index consisting of 23 indicators.

Modelling Undesirable Outputs

As aforementioned, some outputs are cost-type and DMU$_k$ should reduce their values to improve the efficiency. There are a lot of approaches in the literature treating the undesirable outputs. One of them is proposed by Zanella, Camanho, and Dias (2015). They modified the model (12-15) to indirectly treat undesirable outputs:

$$(\min)h_k = \sum_{i=1}^{m} v_i x_{ik} \tag{71}$$

s.t.

$$\sum_{r=1}^{s} u_r y_{rk} + \sum_{q=1}^{l} p_q \left(M_q - b_{qk} \right) = 1 \tag{72}$$

$$\sum_{i=1}^{m} v_i x_{ij} - \sum_{r=1}^{s} u_r y_{rj} - \sum_{q=1}^{l} p_q \left(M_q - b_{qj} \right) \geq 0, j = 1,...,n \tag{73}$$

$$\begin{aligned} u_r &\geq 0, r = 1,...,s \\ p_q &\geq 0, q = 1,...,l \\ v_i &\geq 0, i = 1,...,m \end{aligned} \tag{74}$$

where b_{qj} represents undesirable output q for DMU$_j$ (q=1,..,l, j=1,...,n), p_q represents the weight attached to this undesirable output. A parameter M_q is a large positive number. It is introduced as an impact of an undesirable output on the final CI as nonnegative values satisfy a condition $M_q - b_{qj} \geq 0, \left(j = 1, ..., n \right)$. Each DMU will try to find out the set of suitable weights which put desirable outputs into a favourable position. This model could easily be adopted in a 'benefit of the doubt' manner. The input-oriented 'benefit of the doubt' model will be formulated as follows:

$$(\max)h_k = \sum_{r=1}^{s} u_r y_{rk} + \sum_{q=1}^{l} p_q \left(M_q - b_{qk} \right) \tag{75}$$

s.t.

$$\sum_{r=1}^{s} u_r y_{rj} + \sum_{q=1}^{l} p_q \left(M_q - b_{qj} \right) \leq 1, j = 1, ..., n \tag{76}$$

$$u_r \geq 0, r = 1, ..., s \tag{77}$$

$$p_q \geq 0, q = 1, ..., l \tag{78}$$

DEA-based models presented in this section are used for overcoming the weaknesses of the 'benefit of the doubt' DEA models. For this purpose, known techniques, such as super-efficiency fuzzy DEA modelling, are adopted for DEA-based CI constructions. On the other hand, several new approaches for full-ranking and including qualitative and imprecise data and undesirable outputs are also introduced.

CASE STUDY: RANKING OF REGIONS IN SERBIA

This section illustrates the procedure of constructing the socioeconomic development indicator for reassessing the regions evaluated in the paper by Martić and Savić (2001). The authors of the mentioned paper assessed 30 regions based on raw data on four inputs (arable area, active fixed asset, consumptions of the electricity, and population), treated as potentials and resources, and four outputs (gross domestic products, total number of physicians, total number of primary school pupils, and total number of secondary school pupils), treated as the indicators of development and standard of living. They created DEA efficiency and super-efficiency indices and ranked the regions according to their values.

The aim of this analysis is to rank regions according to the socioeconomic development indicator (SECI) capturing several sub-indicators which were created from raw data for the purpose of this illustration. The procedure of the SECI construction follows the five steps (OECD, 2008):

1. Defining theoretical framework,
2. Data and individual performance indicators selection,
3. Imputation of missing data and data normalization,
4. Weighting and aggregation,
5. Analysis of the results.

Defining Theoretical Framework

The theoretical framework of the analysis is defined by the SECI construction, and the DEA-CI construction methodology presented in the previous sections.

Data and Individual Performance Indicators Selection

Raw data on four inputs: arable area, active fixed asset, consumption of the electricity, and population, treated as potentials and resources, and four outputs: gross domestic product (GDP), the total number of physicians, the total number of primary school pupils, and the total number of employees in the public sector, for 30 regions is Serbia, are taken from the paper by Martić and Savić (2001). These inputs and outputs are treated as indicators of development and standard of living. The paper argues that the relation of some outputs to some of the inputs represents the development forces of production (gross domestic products or the total number of the employed in the public sector in relation to arable area, active fixed asset or population) or indicators of standard of living (the total number of physicians or total number of primary school pupils related to the population). Following this idea we have created seven sub-indicators that can be classified into three groups:

1. **Development Force Indicators (max):**
    a. GDP per population (I1),
    b. GDP per active fixed asset (I2),
    c. GDP per arable area (I3).
2. **Living Standard Indicators (max):**
    a. Total number of physicians per population (I4),
    b. Total number of pupils per population (I5),
    c. Total number of employees in the public sector per population (I6).
3. **Environmental Awareness Indicator (min):**
    a. Electricity consumption per population (I7).

The indicators of development forces and standard of living are created with a goal of their maximization, but the only indicator of environmental awareness can be defined as average electricity consumption. More than 60% of electrical energy in Serbia is produced by lignite-fired thermal power plants, which is not considered as a green production and should be reduced. Consequently, the electricity consumption should also be reduced. The descriptive statistics of these sub-indicator values is given in Table 1.

The indicators I1-I7 are treated separately with no *a priori* assumption which of them is more or less important, but whose weights are assigned freely in the process of model solving.

Table 1. Descriptive statistics of sub-indicators

	I1	I2	I3	I4	I5	I6	I7
Range	0.7970	0.1196	0.3873	3.4771	0.1088	0.2902	2.7760
Minimum	0.0836	0.0271	0.0112	0.7558	0.0145	0.0718	0.5455
Maximum	0.8807	0.1466	0.3985	4.2328	0.1233	0.3620	3.3215
Mean	0.4643	0.0789	0.0540	2.2713	0.0894	0.2348	1.6614
Standard Deviation	0.2492	0.0337	0.0703	0.8029	0.0323	0.0821	0.6709
Sample Variance	0.0621	0.0011	0.0049	0.6447	0.0010	0.0067	0.4501
Confidence Level (95.0%)	0.0931	0.0126	0.0262	0.2998	0.0121	0.0306	0.2505

Imputation of Missing Data and Data Normalization

The available database is used in this illustrative example. Therefore, there is neither missing data nor normalization as we will use the DEA-based models for data weighting and aggregation.

Weighting and Aggregation

Regarding the nature of the seven sub-indicators which need to be aggregated, we have opted for the DEA-based, 'benefit of the doubt' version of DEA model with an undesirable indicator (75-78). After that, several methods of ranking are deployed: full ranking method (44), super-efficiency DEA-based indicator (model (49-51)), and global efficiency indicator (common-weight DEA model (52-55)).

For the purpose of the analysis, DEA-solver software (Cooper, Seiford, & Tone, 2000) is employed for solving BoD best-favourable DEA-like models (75-78) and a similar worst-favourable model with undesirable indicator I7. In both cases, a parameter M is set as $M=\max(I7j, j=1,\ldots,30)$ and the model is solved as a standard DEA CRS model. All indicators are considered as outputs in the best-favourable model with the addition of one input with the fixed value 1 for all 30 regions. The results of the worst-favourable model are obtained when all indicators are transformed into inputs and one output with the fixed value set to 1 is added. The same software is used for solving the super-efficiency DEA model (49-51).

Global efficiency indicator is obtained by solving a common-weight DEA model (52-55) with an objective function defined as a mean deviation of global efficiency indicator from the DEA efficiency score, obtained by solving the model (38-40) with undesirable indicator I7. This means that parameter t is set to 1 ($t=1$). The common-weight DEA model (52-55) is solved by using spreadsheet modelling and *MS Excel Solver*.

Analysis of the Results

The obtained results are compared with the results obtained in the original paper (Martić & Savić, 2001). The SECI values for all regions are given in Table 2 and the rank of countries is shown in Table 3.

According to the original methodology, the number of efficient regions was 17 out of 30. Very similar results are obtained by the BoD best-favourable weights model. The differences are in that the Region of Rasina and the Region of Pirot are assessed as inefficient, but the Region of Kosovska Mitrovica is assessed as efficient. The results from the original paper can be directly compared with super-efficiency

Table 2. Indicator values of regions

No.	DMU	Martić, Savić Super-Efficiency	BoD SECI Best-Favorable	Global Efficiency SECI	Full Ranking Indifferent SECI	Super Efficiency SECI
1	Region of North Bačka	1.089	**1.000**	0.981	0.590	**1.045**
2	Region of Central Banat	1.186	**1.000**	**1.000**	0.500	**1.083**
3	Region of North Banat	0.939	0.939		0.793	0.939
4	Region of South Banat	0.987	0.992		0.734	0.992
5	Region of West Bačka	**1.075**	**1.000**	**1.000**	0.556	**1.029**
6	Region of South Bačka	**1.129**	**1.000**	**1.000**	0.604	**1.098**
7	Region of Srem	**1.070**	**1.000**	0.979	0.739	**1.047**
8	Region of Mačva	**1.282**	**1.000**	**1.000**	0.522	**1.068**
9	Region of Kolubara	**1.374**	**1.000**	**1.000**	1.000	**1.097**
10	Region of Danube	0.963	0.884		0.752	0.884
11	Region of Braničevo	0.692	0.767		0.500	0.767
12	Region of Šumadija	0.989	0.967		0.930	0.967
13	Region of Pomoravlje	0.805	0.778		0.525	0.778
14	Region of Bor	0.985	0.991		0.815	0.991
15	Region of Zaječar	**1.071**	**1.000**	0.901	0.916	**1.043**
16	Region of Zlatibor	**1.047**	**1.000**	0.993	0.737	**1.034**
17	Region of Morava	**1.095**	**1.000**	0.941	0.738	**1.058**
18	Region of Raška	**1.043**	**1.000**	0.918	0.877	**1.035**
19	Region of Rasina	**1.034**	0.963		0.524	0.963
20	Region of Nišava	**1.368**	**1.000**	0.858	0.818	**1.105**
21	Region of Toplica	0.914	0.943		0.875	0.943
22	Region of Pirot	**1.070**	0.970		0.935	0.970
23	Region of Jablanica	**1.326**	**1.000**	**1.000**	0.507	**1.110**
24	Region of Pčinj	**1.135**	**1.000**	0.974	0.668	**1.089**
25	Region of Kosovo	0.894	0.959		0.890	0.959
26	Region of Peć	0.741	0.952		0.897	0.952
27	Region of Prizren	0.555	0.864		0.708	0.864
28	Region of Kos. Mitrovica	0.862	**1.000**	0.703	1.000	**1.079**
29	Kosovo and Pomoravlje	0.822	0.989		0.976	0.989
30	City of Belgrade	**3.802**	**1.000**	**1.000**	1.000	**3.288**
Efficient regions count		17	16	7	3	16
Average		1.111	0.965	0.953	0.754	1.076
Max		3.802	1.000	1.000	1.000	3.288
Min		0.555	0.767	0.703	0.500	0.767
St. Dev.		0.542	0.063	0.079	0.171	0.427

Table 3. Ranks of regions

No.	DMU	Martić, Savić Super-Efficiency	BoD SECI Best-Favourable	Global Efficiency SECI	Full Ranking Indifferent SECI	Super Efficiency SECI
1	Region of North Bačka	10	1	9	23	12
2	Region of Central Banat	6	1	1	29	7
3	Region of North Banat	22	26	26	14	26
4	Region of South Banat	19	17	17	19	17
5	Region of West Bačka	11	1	1	24	16
6	Region of South Bačka	8	1	1	22	4
7	Region of Srem	13	1	10	16	11
8	Region of Mačva	5	1	1	27	9
9	Region of Kolubara	2	1	1	1	5
10	Region of Danube	21	27	27	15	27
11	Region of Braničevo	29	30	30	30	30
12	Region of Šumadija	18	21	21	6	21
13	Region of Pomoravlje	27	29	29	25	29
14	Region of Bor	20	18	18	13	18
15	Region of Zaječar	12	1	14	7	13
16	Region of Zlatibor	15	1	8	18	15
17	Region of Morava	9	1	12	17	10
18	Region of Raška	16	1	13	10	14
19	Region of Rasina	17	22	22	26	22
20	Region of Nišava	3	1	15	12	3
21	Region of Toplica	23	25	25	11	25
22	Region of Pirot	14	20	20	5	20
23	Region of Jablanica	4	1	1	28	2
24	Region of Pčinj	7	1	11	21	6
25	Region of Kosovo	24	23	23	9	23
26	Region of Peć	28	24	24	8	24
27	Region of Prizren	30	28	28	20	28
28	Region of Kos. Mitrovica	25	1	16	1	8
29	Kosovo and Pomoravlje	26	19	19	4	19
30	City of Belgrade	1	1	1	1	1

SECI values. They are also very similar. The Region of Belgrade is the most efficient according to the both methodology while the Region of Prizren (h=0.555) is the worst efficient according to the original methodology and the Region of Braničevo (h=0.767) is the worst according to the BoD SECI super efficiency value. Considering the other models, the number of 'efficient' regions has been reduced. The best discrimination is achieved by the full ranking method. Only three regions, the Region of Belgrade, the Region of Kosovska Mitrovica, and the Region of Kolubara maintain their efficiency at the highest level equal to 1. The ranks are shown in Table 3.

A non-parametric test of Spearman rank correlation shows that there is no correlation between a the full ranking indifferent SECI and other indicators at the level of significance 0.05 or 0.1 while the correlations between the other pairs of indicators are larger than 0.8 at the level of significance equal 0.05 (Table 4).

The correlations indicate that rankings obtained by the original analysis are comparable with the results obtained using the single-stage (super-efficiency) or the two-stage (global efficiency) BoD models. But results are not comparable with those obtained by the full ranking method since it takes into account the best and the worst favour scenarios for each DMU. On the other hand, this model shows the highest discrimination power. The 'efficient' regions are also highly ranked according to the results of the BoD model.

CONCLUSION

This chapter proposes a theoretical background of DEA-based composite indicators. Composite indicators capture multi-dimensional nature of performance measurement as opposed to traditional measures related to one dimension or ratio analysis.

Given that a CI is constructed on the basis of data on different sub-indicators whose valuable assets vary according to the scope and units of measurement, several issues could arise. For example, problems could be related to the selection of the appropriate methods for data normalization, the choice of weights and aggregation of sub-indicators. These problems were overcome by introducing a DEA-based CI. DEA is a mathematical programming technique for assessing the relative efficiency of observed units and determining their best practices on the basis of raw data of selected inputs and outputs. Aggregation is performed simultaneously with the determination of the weighting scheme for inputs and outputs, which is very flexible and may be different for each observed unit in order to put it in the best possible light. Accordingly, slight modifications of basic DEA models, by introducing a dummy input variable equal to 1, allow construction of a CI. Such models are known as "benefit of the doubt" DEA models, but this DEA-like CI construction also has its drawbacks. The drawbacks are primarily related to the inability to rank the efficient units with an index equal to 1, and the impossibility of turning qualitative data and undesirable outputs into the analysis.

The theoretical basis for the basic DEA models and "benefit of the doubt" DEA models for the construction of a CI is given in detail. The DEA fundamentals are used in the literature as a basis for the

Table 4. Spearman rank correlations

	Martić, Savić Super-Efficiency	BoD SECI Best-Favourable	Global Efficiency SECI	Full Ranking Indifferent SECI	Super Efficiency SECI
Martić, Savić super-efficiency	1				
BoD SECI best-favourable	0.8124*	1			
Global efficiency SECI	0.8626*	0.9271*	1		
Full ranking indifferent SECI	-0.0875	0.0297	-0.1015	1	
Super efficiency SECI	0.8701*	0.9213*	0.8903*	0.0617*	1

*Level of significance 0.05.

creation of models and approaches aimed at overcoming the mentioned disadvantages. The proposed models also use characteristics of the DEA and the ideas are captured from the DEA theory and practice. New modified models are also given in this chapter. And finally, the case study of ranking regions of Serbia according to the socioeconomic development gives insight into the procedure of constructing an overall CI capturing seven sub-indicators that were made from the raw data used in the original paper by Martić and Savić (2001). The model (75-78) presented in the previous sections is used for including undesirable indicators into the analysis and the full ranking of regions. The obtained results are comparable with the original results obtained by using basic DEA models with input and output-oriented indicators when the aim of the analysis is the same (efficiency maximization together with the best-favourable weighting of indicators). Otherwise, the result differs significantly as it is the case of the full ranking method which uses the best and the worst favourable weighting. Further study should analyse other drawbacks and shortcoming of a DEA-based CI and suggest possible solutions.

REFERENCES

Andersen, P., & Petersen, N. C. (1993). A procedure for ranking efficient units in data envelopment analysis. *Management Science*, *39*(10), 1261–1274. doi:10.1287/mnsc.39.10.1261

Bandura, R. (2008). *A Survey of Composite Indices Measuring Country Performance: 2008 Update.* UNDP.

Banker, R. D., Charnes, A., & Cooper, W. W. (1984). Some models for estimating technical and scale inefficiencies in data envelopment analysis. *Management Science*, *30*(9), 1078–1092. doi:10.1287/mnsc.30.9.1078

Charnes, A., Cooper, W. W., & Rhodes, E. (1978). Measuring the efficiency of decision making units. *European Journal of Operational Research*, *2*(6), 429–444. doi:10.1016/0377-2217(78)90138-8

Cherchye, L., Moesen, W., Rogge, N., & van Puyenbroeck, T. V. (2007). An introduction to 'benefit of the doubt' composite indicators. *Social Indicators Research*, *82*(1), 111–145. doi:10.1007/s11205-006-9029-7

Cherchye, L., Moesen, W., Rogge, N., & van Puyenbroeck, T. V. (2011). Constructing composite indicators with imprecise data: A proposal. *Expert Systems with Applications*, *38*(9), 10940–10949. doi:10.1016/j.eswa.2011.02.136

Cooper, W., Seiford, M. S., & Tone, K. (2000). *Introduction to Data Envelopment Analysis and its uses: With DEA-solver software and references.* New York: Springer.

Cooper, W. W., Ruiz, J. L., & Sirvent, I. (2009). Selecting non-zero weights to evaluate effectiveness of basketball players. *European Journal of Operational Research*, *195*(2), 563–574. doi:10.1016/j.ejor.2008.02.012

Despotis, D. K. (2005). A reassessment of the human development index via data envelopment analysis. *The Journal of the Operational Research Society*, *56*(8), 969–980. doi:10.1057/palgrave.jors.2601927

Despotis, D. K. (2005). Measuring human development via data envelopment analysis: The case of Asia and the Pacific. *Omega, 33*(5), 385–390. doi:10.1016/j.omega.2004.07.002

Dobrota, M., Bulajic, M., Bornmann, L., & Jeremic, V. (2016). A new approach to the QS University ranking using the composite I-distance indicator: Uncertainty and sensitivity analyses. *Journal of the Association for Information Science and Technology, 67*(1), 200–211. doi:10.1002/asi.23355

Dobrota, M., Savic, G., & Bulajic, M. (2015). A new approach to the evaluation of countries' educational structure and development: The European study. *European Review (Chichester, England), 23*(4), 553–565. doi:10.1017/S1062798715000277

Hatefi, S. M., & Torabi, S. A. (2010). A common weight MCDA–DEA approach to construct composite indicators. *Ecological Economics, 70*(1), 114–120. doi:10.1016/j.ecolecon.2010.08.014

Mahlberg, B., & Obersteiner, M. (2001). *Remeasuring the HDI by Data Envelopment Analysis, IR-01-069.* Luxemburg, Austria: International Institute for Applied System Analysis.

Mariano, E. B., Sobreiro, V. A., & Rebelatto, D. A. (2015). Human development and data envelopment analysis: A structured literature review. *Omega, 54*, 33–49. doi:10.1016/j.omega.2015.01.002

Martić, M., & Savić, G. (2001). An application of DEA for comparative analysis and ranking of regions in Serbia with regards to social-economic development. *European Journal of Operational Research, 132*(2), 343–356. doi:10.1016/S0377-2217(00)00156-9

Melyn, W., & Moesen, W. (1991). Towards a synthetic indicator of macroeconomic performance: Unequal weighting when limited information is available. *Public Economics Research Papers, 17*(1), 1–24.

Munda, G. (2012). Choosing aggregation rules for composite indicators. *Social Indicators Research, 109*(3), 337–354. doi:10.1007/s11205-011-9911-9

OECD. (2008). *Handbook on constructing composite indicators: Methodology and user guide.* OECD: OECD Publishing.

Radovanović, S., Radojicić, M., & Savić, G. (2014). Two-phased DEA-MLA approach for predicting efficiency of NBA players. *Yugoslav Journal of Operational Research, 24*(3), 347–358. doi:10.2298/YJOR140430030R

Ruggerio, J., & Vitaliano, D. F. (1999). Assessing the efficiency of public schools using data envelopment analysis and frontier regression. *Contemporary Economic Policy, 17*(3), 321–331. doi:10.1111/j.1465-7287.1999.tb00685.x

Saltelli, A. (2007). Composite indicators between analysis and advocacy. *Social Indicators Research, 81*(1), 65–77. doi:10.1007/s11205-006-0024-9

Shen, Y., Hermans, E., Brijs, T., & Wets, G. (2013). Data envelopment analysis for composite indicators: A multiple layer model. *Social Indicators Research, 114*(2), 739–756. doi:10.1007/s11205-012-0171-0

Shen, Y., Hermans, E., Brijs, T., & Wets, G. (2013). Fuzzy data envelopment analysis in composite indicator construction. In *Performance Measurement with Fuzzy Data Envelopment Analysis* (pp. 89–100). Springer Berlin Heidelberg.

Shen, Y., Ruan, D., Hermans, E., Brijs, T., Wets, G., & Vanhoof, K. (2011). Modeling qualitative data in data envelopment analysis for composite indicators. *International Journal and System Assurance and Engineering Management, 2*(1), 21–30.

Zanella, A., Camanho, A. S., & Dias, T. G. (2015). Undesirable outputs and weightings schemes in composite indicators based on data envelopment analysis. *European Journal of Operational Research, 245*(2), 517–530. doi:10.1016/j.ejor.2015.03.036

Zhou, P., & Ang, B. W. (2009). Comparing MCDA aggregation methods in constructing composite indicators using the Shannon-Spearman measure. *Social Indicators Research, 94*(1), 83–96. doi:10.1007/s11205-008-9338-0

Zhou, P., Ang, B. W., & Poh, K. L. (2007). A mathematical programming approach to constructing composite indicators. *Ecological Economics, 62*(2), 291–297. doi:10.1016/j.ecolecon.2006.12.020

Zhou, P., Ang, B. W., & Zhou, D. Q. (2010). Weighting and aggregation in composite indicators construction: A multiplicative optimization approach. *Social Indicators Research, 96*(1), 169–181. doi:10.1007/s11205-009-9472-3 PMID:19966916

ADDITIONAL READING

Adler, N., Yazhemsky, E., & Tarverdyan, R. (2010). A framework to measure the relative socio-economic performance of developing countries. *Socio-Economic Planning Sciences, 44*(2), 73–88. doi:10.1016/j.seps.2009.08.001

Athanassoglou A. (2015). Revisiting worst-case DEA for composite indicators. *Social Indices Research,* 1-14, doi .10.1007/s11205-015-1078-3

Bogetoft, P. (2012). *Performance Benchmarking: Measuring and Managing Performance.* New York: Springer. doi:10.1007/978-1-4614-6043-5

Booysen, F. (2002). An overview and evaluation of composite indices of development. *Social Indicators Research, 59*(2), 115–151. doi:10.1023/A:1016275505152

Cherchye, L., Moesen, W., Rogge, N., Puyenbroeck, T. V., Saisana, M., Saltelli, A., & Tarantola, S. et al. (2008). Creating composite indicators with DEA and robustness analysis: The case of the technology achievement index. *The Journal of the Operational Research Society, 59*(2), 239–251. doi:10.1057/palgrave.jors.2602445

Cook, W. D., & Kress, M. (1990). A data envelopment model for aggregating preference rankings. *Management Science, 36*(11), 1302–1310. doi:10.1287/mnsc.36.11.1302

Decancq, K., & Lugo, M. A. (2013). Weights in multidimensional indices of wellbeing: An overview. *Econometric Reviews, 32*(1), 7–34. doi:10.1080/07474938.2012.690641

Filippetti, A., & Peyrache, A. (2011). The patterns of technological capabilities of countries: A dual approach using composite indicators and data envelopment analysis. *World Development, 39*(7), 1108–1121. doi:10.1016/j.worlddev.2010.12.009

Gaaloul, H., & Khalfallah, S. (2014). Application of the "benefit-of-the-doubt" approach for the construction of a digital access indicator: A revaluation of the "Digital Access Index". *Social Indicators Research, 118*(1), 45–56. doi:10.1007/s11205-013-0422-8

Gor, S. O., & Gitau, C. M. W. (2010). Rethinking the HDI: A more theoretically consistent alternative. OIDA. *International Journal of Sustainable Development, 1*(5), 85–90.

Knox Lovell, C. A., Pastor, J. T., & Turner, J. A. (1995). Measuring macroeconomic performance in the OECD: A comparison of European and non-European countries. *European Journal of Operational Research, 87*(3), 507–518. doi:10.1016/0377-2217(95)00226-X

Martinez, E. R. (2013). Social and economic wellbeing in Europe and the Mediterranean basin: Building an enlarged human development indicator. *Social Indicators Research, 111*(2), 527–547. doi:10.1007/s11205-012-0018-8

Martinez, E. R., Limon, J. A. G., & Tadeo, A. J. P. (2011). Ranking farms with a composite indicator of sustainability. *Agricultural Economics, 42*(5), 561–575. doi:10.1111/j.1574-0862.2011.00536.x

Mizobuchi, H. (2014). Measuring world better life frontier: A composite Indicator for OECD better life index. *Social Indicators Research, 118*(5), 987–1007. doi:10.1007/s11205-013-0457-x

Nardo, M., Saisana, M., Saltelli, A., Tarantola, S., Hoffmann, A., & Giovannini, E. (2008). *Handbook on constructing composite indicators: Methodology and user guide*. Organization for Economic Cooperation and Development.

Oggioni, G., Riccardi, R., & Toninelli, R. (2011). Eco-efficiency of the world cements industry: A Data Envelopment Analysis. *Energy Policy, 39*(5), 2842–2854. doi:10.1016/j.enpol.2011.02.057

Pittman, R. W. (1983). Multilateral productivity comparisons with undesirable outputs. *The Economic Journal, 93*(372), 883–891. doi:10.2307/2232753

Rogge, N. (2012). Undesirable specialization in the construction of composite policy indicators: The environmental performance index. *Ecological Indicators, 23*, 143–154. doi:10.1016/j.ecolind.2012.03.020

Scheel, H. (2001). Undesirable outputs in efficiency evaluations. *European Journal of Operational Research, 132*(2), 400–410. doi:10.1016/S0377-2217(00)00160-0

Seiford, L. M., & Zhu, J. (2002). Modeling undesirable factors in efficiency evaluation. *European Journal of Operational Research, 142*(1), 16–20. doi:10.1016/S0377-2217(01)00293-4

Shen, Y., Hermans, E., Brijs, T., & Wets, G. (2013). Fuzzy data envelopment analysis in composite indicator construction. *Studies in Fuzziness and Soft Computing, 309*, 89–100. doi:10.1007/978-3-642-41372-8_4

Suri, T., Boozer, M. A., Ranis, G., & Stewart, F. (2011). Paths to success: The relationship between human development and economic growth. *World Development*, *39*(4), 506–522. doi:10.1016/j.worlddev.2010.08.020

Tofallis, C. (2013). An automatic-democratic approach to weight setting for the new human development index. *Journal of Population Economics*, *26*(4), 1325–1345. doi:10.1007/s00148-012-0432-x

UNDP. (2000). *Human Development Report 2000. UNDP*. United Nations Development Program.

Yamada, Y., Matui, T., & Sugiyama, M. (1994). New analysis of efficiency based on DEA. *Journal of the Operations Research Society of Japan*, *37*(1), 158–167.

KEY TERMS AND DEFINITIONS

Benefit of the Doubt: A favourable opinion or judgment adopted despite uncertainty i.e. optimistic assessment and aggregation of sub-indicators based on the most favourable weights.

CI: Composite indicator is an aggregation of a set of sub-indicators for measuring multi-dimensional concepts that cannot be captured by a single indicator.

DEA: Data envelopment analysis is a nonparametric mathematical programming technique developed to measure the relative efficiency of DMUs considering a set of units using multiple inputs to produce multiple outputs.

DMU: Decision Making Unit is a unit that transforms inputs into outputs.

Inputs: Resources that will be transformed in a process (expressed in units or financial form), as the amount of raw material and costs, i.e. resources that the DMU receives from the outside to start the process.

Outputs: The results of a transformation process, such as the amount of final goods, profit or other benefits, i.e. everything that is released by the DMU.

Qualitative Data: Data which cannot be expressed numerically but on the scale or as a fuzzy number.

Undesirable Outputs: The outputs with negative effects on the result such as pollution, costs, etc.

Chapter 6
Methodological Challenges in Building Composite Indexes:
Linking Theory to Practice

Fabio Gaetano Santeramo
University of Foggia, Italy

ABSTRACT

Composite indicators are emerging in several fields and disciplines as appealing method to synthesize a multitude of information, in a compact, single, and unique way. The process of aggregating heterogeneous information is itself very challenging and exposed to numerous threats. The chapter deepens on the methodological challenges that scientists, analysts, and final users must be aware of for a correct interpretation of the composite indexes. By mean of a worked example on the construction of composite indicators for food security, the chapter concludes that while different normalization and weighting approaches do not alter composite indicators, data imputation and aggregation methods are the most crucial steps: different methods convey very different results. For instance, the adoption of different aggregation procedures may largely alter the rankings based on composite indicators. In sum, the analysis shows that the index construction decisions matter and comment on policy and practical implications for the construction of composite indicators.

INTRODUCTION

Composite indicators are emerging in several fields and disciplines as appealing method to synthesize a multitude of information, in a compact, single, and unique way (Santeramo et al., 2012; Caracciolo and Santeramo, 2013; Dobrota et al., 2015; Mahadevan and Hoang, 2015; Santeramo, 2015a, 2016; Santeramo and Shabnam, 2015; Alam et al., 2016; Maricic et al., 2016). The process of aggregating heterogeneous information is itself very challenging and exposed to numerous threats. The chapter deepens on the methodological challenges that scientists, analysts, and final users must be aware of for a correct interpretation of the composite indices. The added value of this chapter is it builds on a worked example: the construction of composite indicators for food security. Food security is one of the most debated topic,

DOI: 10.4018/978-1-5225-0714-7.ch006

the main theme of the world EXPO 2015, and the first of the Millennium Goals. Needless to say, there has been much debate on food security (Wheeler and von Braun, 2013; Hertel, 2016). Numerous indicators of food security have been proposed aiming at establishing the level of food security at country level. Such a variety of indicators and the lack of consensus on how to evaluate policies (and outcomes) aimed at reducing food insecurity, have pushed international organizations to adopt composite indices to synthesize the information. From a practical point of view, the construction of composite indices consist of several steps: indeed, each choice is able to influence the composite indicator (Nardo et al., 2005a).

The chapter is intended to achieve two goals:

- First, I aim at providing a helicopter view of the process of building composite indicators, from the analyst point of view;
- Second, I provide a practical example of how heterogeneous information are synthesized in a single index and highlight the warnings that should be clear to analysts, policymakers, and audience, when computing, examining or reading results from composite indicators.

The chapter is divided in different sections. The methodological section, which follows the present section, presents the steps required to build a composite indicator; the worked example on Food Security puts the theory into practice; the paragraph is followed by a digression on how policymakers and the large audience should interpret composite indicators; the final section concludes with suggestions for future research.

In particular, the worked example provides insights on the challenges faced by analysts called to measure food security. The debate is hot as attested by the large number of articles published on this issue, and the large number of indicators on food security (Gabbert and Weikard, 2001; Carletto et al., 2013; Aurino, 2014; Cafiero et al. 2014;Santeramo, 2015a, 2015b; Svedberg, 2011; Carman et al., 2016; Ames et al., 2016). I provide a practical example by computing several composite indices for food security by using data provided by the Food and Agricultural Organization. I evaluate a set of techniques that are adopted in the construction of composite indicators. In particular I assess the relevance of methods to impute, homogenize, weight and aggregate data in order to compute composite indices are compared and the relevancy of the choices to be made will be discussed. I conclude that while different normalization and weighting approaches do not alter composite indicators, data imputation and aggregation methods are the most crucial steps: different methods convey very different results. In sum, I show that the index construction decisions matter. The last two sections go beyond the methodology and focus on the implications of my findings for practitioners, policymakers, and audience. In particular, I discuss how we should interpret the result of composite indices in order to minimize the impact of discretionary choices.

All in all, the chapter guides the reader to understand how theory and practice match (or not) when we synthesize composite/complex information into single indicators.

BACKGROUND AND METHODOLOGY

The process of building a composite indicator is challenged in many ways and in particular previous assessments of strategic objectives have been incorrectly conducted due the use of "indicators that were not systematically SMART [that is Specific, Measurable, Achievable, Relevant and Time-bound] and were often focusing on outputs and activities" (FAO, 2013). Moreover, composite indicators are inherently threatened by the low quality of indicators, the infeasibility of desired indicators, the necessity of homogenizing standards and frameworks. The FAO (2013) suggests that the entire process should "enhance capacities of data users to use information more effectively, and how data are used could even be monitored in order to justify enhancements and to allow for better prioritization. A continuous and joint assessment of data needs as well as of existing available data, is essential in order to identify gaps and agree on actions to address them". The above picture clarifies the challenges for the next future. Constructing composite indicators is only the first, yet crucial, step to be achieved to understand the phenomenon under analysis.

The present report summarizes the different phases involved in the realization of a composite index. An excellent reference is provided by Nardo *et al.* (2005). Following the handbook, I divide the process of building a composite indicator in six main points:

1. **Defining the Phenomenon:** The step consists in defining the theoretical basis for the selection and combination of single indicators into a composite indicator.
2. **Selecting Variables:** The second step is also very important is that the single indicators need to be picked on the basis of several features: analytical soundness, measurability, country coverage, relevance to the phenomenon being measured and relationship to each other. In addition, when direct data are not available, *ad hoc* proxy variables may be adopted.
3. **Filling the Gaps:** Consideration should be given to different approaches for imputing missing values. Extreme values should be examined as they can become unintended benchmarks.
4. **Homogenizing the Information:** Indicators should be normalized to render them comparable.
5. **Weighting and Aggregating:** Indicators should be aggregated and weighted according to the underlying theoretical framework. Multivariate analysis could be a preliminary or complementary step.
6. **Validating the Composite Indicator:** The validation of the composite indicator is aimed at the assessment of the robustness of the composite indicator. Finally, attempts should be made to correlate the composite indicator with other published indicators as well as to identify linkages through regressions.

The remainder of this chapter deepens on theoretical and empirical issues. The final goal is to present how to build a composite indicator and provide a worked example: the construction of a composite indicator for food security.

RESEARCH CONTEXT

The section aims at detailing the necessary steps to construct a composite indicator. Although not comprehensive, the described methodology should provide the minimum tools to construct a composite indicator to measure and evaluate a complex phenomenon. The first step *"Defining the phenomenon"* is the starting point of any composite indicators has to be the definition of the phenomenon under investigation and I aim at measuring.

A precise and concise definition of the complex phenomenon is a necessary, although not sufficient, prerequisites for constructing a useful composite index. It is very likely that a badly defined concept will be badly measured, monitored and evaluated, exactly as we would never be able to target a goal we have not clear in mind.

From a more practical perspective, the first step of the analysis consists in defining the concept under investigation (e.g. how do we define food security?), in determining sub-groups, or dimensions (e.g. determinants, outcome, and stability), and finally in identifying the indicators or variables that allow to measure all sub-components (e.g. determinants is measured by indicators of food availability, physical access, and so on).

The second step, "Selecting variables", consists in selecting the variables that will produce the composite indicator. Rely on variables of good quality is a major issue for constructing composite indices. Ideally, variables should be SMART, that is specific, measurable, accessible, relevant, and timeliness.

The data selection process is somehow subjective: it usually involves a set of heterogeneous indicators, from quantitative (hard) data, to qualitative (soft) data collected from surveys or policy reviews, or to proxies to convey into the index more information on the phenomenon when specific variables are unavailable.

The third step (*Filling the gaps*) consists in filling the gaps in the dataset. The vast majority of dataset are incomplete. When data are missing, it is important to establish if the lack of data is random or systematic: missing data at random depend on the variable itself or on other variables of the dataset (in other terms if that are randomly missing, this is likely to be due to the secific variable it has been adopted); systematic missing data are indeed due to the lack of information on the phenomenn under consideration. Unfortunately, despite the relevance of this distiction there are still no approaches to infer on the nature of the missing data: analystis should therefore adopt the most appropriare techniqes to deal with missing data somehow disregarding the nature of the missing.

Common approaches to impute missing data consist in deleting records that contain missing data, in imputing missing data by mean of ad hoc statistics (e.g. mean, median, regression imputation, etc.) or algorithms (e.g. Markov Chain, Monte Carlo algorithm, etc.). None of the approaches is exempt by drawbacks, therefore it is wise to carefully document the selected imputation procedures.

The fourth step is dedicated to "Homogenizing the information". Due to the heterogeneity of measurements units, the indicators in a data set need to be normalized prior to any data aggregation. The analysts may rely on a large set of normalization methods: the choice should be based on the data properties and the objectives of the index it has to be constructed (Freudenberg, 2003; Jacobs *et al.*, 2004).

Normalization methods include, among others, ranking, standardization, min-max, distance to a reference observation, score function, balance of opinions. All in all, normalization methods allow to compare indicators bringing different measurement units on a similar same dimension. Different methods imply different *pros* and *cons*. For instance, ranking method is extremely simple, robust to outliers and allow comparison among observations: a big disadvantage is that the method will eliminate information on levels. Balance of opinions is a different way to go: the metod is complex and useful in that missing primary data are imputed through the opinion of experts. As it is easy to imagine, the method is quite costly and of very difficult replication over time and space.

The next step, "Weighting and aggregating", is dedicated to the normalization of the information. The set of selected variables, whose data have been normalized and filled to reduce lack of information, constitute the ingredients of the composite indicator. The final step will be the synthesis of the overall information into few indices or a unique indicator. In particular, variables have to be properly aggregated and weighted.

As for previous step, a number of weighting techniques exists, none of which is exempt by a discretionary choice (Saaty, 2001). Statistical methods such as unobserved components models, or participatory methods, such as budget allocation, analytic hierarchy processes, and conjoint analysis are available alternatives. The theoretical framework underlying the composite indicator should mentor the selection of the technique. For instance, equal weighting implies that indicators (or dimensions) have similar importance, whereas principal components analysis or factor analysis rely on data variability and variables correlation: both methods allow to synthesize data variability through a reduced number of variables. Needless to say, if variables are not correlated (or low correlated) these methods cannot be applied.

Aggregation is the natural step following the weighting in that it condense the information conveyed by indicators into a single index. Two very common approaches are the linear aggregation and the geometric aggregation. The former, which is feasible when individual indicators have the same measurement unit, transfers the relative importance of single indicators to the composite index. In other terms, it is a conservative measure. On the contrary, geometric aggregations allows to take into account non compensability between indicators or dimensions.

The last step, "Validating the composite indicator", is aimed to ensuring the external validity of the composite indicator. The described process of constructing a composite indicator, required several judgment calls, in particular those involved in steps 2 - 4, that conflict with the goal of producing a scientific, objective, incontestable indicator of the complex phenomenon. The composite indicator, and the other results (e.g. rankings) should be validated through robustness checks and sensitivity analyses. The most common procedures are uncertainty analysis, focusing on how uncertainty in the input factors propagates through the structure of the composite indicator and affects the composite indicator values, and sensitivity analysis aiming at evaluate the contribution of the individual source of uncertainty to the output variance. Finally, the composite index should be compared to other proposed composite indicators.

DISCUSSION

Ensuring food security is "the challenge of feeding 9 billion people" (Godfray et al., 2010), the first Millennium Development Goal, and one of the most debated topic in Academia and International Organizations. Despite impressive achievements at the global level, with 700 million fewer people living in extreme poverty conditions in 2010 than in 1990, the United Nations estimates that 1.2 billion people are still living in extreme poverty. It is also true that governments are making every effort to eradicate hunger, poverty, and undernourishment, and policy interventions shooting for these targets are under the spotlight. On their side, the International Organizations, such as FAO or WB, reward governments successfully progressing in fighting food insecurity, and provide guidelines to policymakers. Thus, while Chile, China and Morocco have won recognition from FAO, on June the 16th 2014, for their outstanding progresses to reach elevate food security standards, scholars are animatedly debating on how to measure (and improve) food security status.

The most widely adopted definition of food security is 'a situation that exists when all people, at all time, have physical, social and economic access to sufficient, safe and nutritious food that meets their dietary needs and food preferences for an active and healthy life' (FAO, 2013).

However, how the definition can be translated into an actual measure of the level of food security is still debated. It has to be recognized that the existing indicators are not equivalent, indeed they convey different information on food security (Barrett, 2010). Further complexity arises when indicators are *complex*. Data quality, double counting, data aggregation are just few of the issues that researches need to deal with when computing food security composite indices. For instance, while existing indicators such as the Global Food Security Index, the Global Hunger Index, and the Poverty and Hunger Index, are already in use, there is no consensus on which methodology should be adopted to build food security composite indicators.

Based on the procedure described in previous sections, I present how to compute a composite indicator for food security: the variables used in the present analysis have been collected on FAOSTAT website.

The dataset FAO - FOOD SECURITY INDICATORS (released on October 9, 2012 and revised on March 15, 2013) is constructed by following the recommendation of experts gathered in the Committee on World Food Security (CFS) Round Table on hunger measurement, hosted at FAO headquarters in September 2011. In particular, I use all indicators provided by the FAO that have sufficient coverage to enable comparisons over time and space (Cafiero, 2013), and suggested as indicators of food security. The FAO has been recently expanded to introduce several new indicators to fill lack of information. I aim at introducing this new information to build a new index for food security.

Variables have been sub-divided in groups in order to reflect the theoretical framework. In particular, the first group consists of indicators of the determinants of food insecurity (structural conditions that are likely to worsen food security statust if no policy interventions is implemented); the second group merges variables on outcomes of food insecurity (e.g. inadequate food consumption or anthropometric failures); the third group provides information on the vulnerability to food insecurity (e.g. past variability of outcomes and conditions conducive to vulnerability to shocks). Within the first two groups, the indicators are further classified based on the dimension of food insecurity on which they provide information. The first set of variables comprises those capturing availability[1], physical access[2], economic access or affordability (Domestic Food Price Level Index), and utilization (e.g. Access to improved water sources; Access to improved sanitation facilities). The second group includes variables on Inadequate access to food[3], and Utilization[4]. The third group includes further important variables on price, and supply dynamics[5].

A variety of indicators for food security have been proposed. However, it is still unclear if "these different constructs equally represent the different domains of food security" (Jones *et al.*, 2013). Moreover, I believe any of such indicators are sufficient to measure and monitor the state of food security, in that "monitoring of food security should be [further] complemented by anthropometric measurements" (Pinstrup-Andersen, 2009).

I have identified four crucial "choice nodes" (Table 1): data filling, data transformation, weighting, and aggregation. The data filling (or data imputation) is the imputation is the process of replacing missing data with substituted values. The data transformation consists in the rescaling of data to a unique scale. The weighting and aggregation procedure are steps that allows to move from multiple indicators to a unique indicator (aggregation) attributing different relevance (weighting) to the single indicators.

In particular, I test for two methods to deal with missing data (multiple imputation and simple imputation), two methods to normalize data (by mean of z-score and by mean of the normalization adopted by intelligence unit to compute the Global Food Security Index 2013[6], namely the Min-Max method), four approaches to weight sub-indices (Equal weighting, empirical rank correlation, inverse correlation, and correlation by a shrinkage estimation), and three alternatives to aggregate information (linear aggregation, simple geometric aggregation, and CES aggregation[7]).

The variety of alternatives analyzed and compared provides, to the best of my knowledge, the first systematic attempt to assess (quantitatively) results from different indices.

Table 1. Different approaches for food security composite indicator

Scenarios	Imputation	Normalization	Weighting	Aggregation
1 - Baseline	Multiple	Z-score	Equal	Linear
2	Multiple	Z-score	Rank correlation	Linear
3	Multiple	Z-score	Inverse correlation	Linear
4	Multiple	Z-score	Shrinkage	Linear
5	Multiple	Normalization	Equal	Linear
6	Multiple	Z-score	Equal	Geometric
7	Multiple	Z-score	Equal	CES
8	Simple	Z-score	Equal	Linear

Supposing a two variables (x_1 and x_2) composite indicator, a linear aggregation would be $x_1 + x_2$, a geometric aggregation would be $(x_1 * x_2)^{(1/2)}$ and a CES aggregation would be $(x_1^y * x_2^y)^{(1/y)}$.

I compare eight different composite indicators, the baseline composite indicator and seven other composite indicators that differ from the baseline only for one method in one of the four "choice nodes". Although the set of potential alternatives is very large, I have focused on the alternatives proposed in other studies (*cfr*. Nardo et al., 2005a, 2005b). The baseline scenario has been obtained by adopting methods that are commonly adopted for composite indicators (Nardo et al., 2005a): multiple Imputation, normalization through z-score, equal weighting and linear aggregation. It is worth note that most of the proposed indices suche as the Global Food Security Index and the Global Hunger Index are a slight variant of the baseline scenario. Each indicator have been normalized to a 0-100 score to make them directly comparable with other indicators.

I compare the methods in terms of absolute deviations of ranking from the baseline scenario. He larger the deviation of ranking from the baseline scenario, the larger the distortion implied by the method for which the scenario under consideration differ from the baseline. It is worth emphasizing that the scenarios differ from the baseline only for one method. I apply the formula

SOLUTIONS AND RECOMMENDATIONS

I adopted different methodologies at four "choice nodes": filling missing data, homogenizing the information, weighting information and aggregating information. I compared changes in rankings obtained by eight different composite indices. The larger the differences in rankings induced by selecting alternative methods, the larger the importance of the choice, the wiser the decision-making process should be.

Choice of the methods to compute composite indices have different relevance: decisions on normalization and weighting methods are not very relevant; conversely, different techniques for data imputation seem to convey very heterogeneous outcomes. Lastly, the aggregation formula that is adopted is able to influence the entire composite indicator: different formulas provide very different composite indices. What this really imply for practitioners and policymakers?

Let me clarify with an emblematic examples may help the reader flavoring the relevance of choices. According to the baseline Index, Congo and Tanzania rank, respectively, 214 and 196 out of 228: their population (respectively 4 and 45 millions) are *food insecure*. However, if a different choice on the aggregation procedure would have been made, for instance if a geometric aggregation would have been adopted, these Countries would have been ranked 88th and 166th. Not only their overall rank would have been improved, but they would have also been reversed, implying that Tanzania would have been considered more food insecure than Congo!

The practical and policy implications are very important: the construction of composite indicators may substantially alter the rankings for food security. Is this opening the path of stategic behavior? Would different goverments prefer different indicators? Let me reply withan emblematic examples. Let 's consider Chile, China and Morocco. According to my results, each of these Country would prefer a different way to climb the ranking: Chile would be better off in the ranking if simple imputation, or inverse correlation would have been adopted; China would gain 7 positions in the world rank if I would have simply used a different normalization techniques; Morocco may have been better off if a different aggregation method would have been chosen. This poses the basis for a strategic behavior: governments are likely to target to be highly ranked depending on the specific composite indicator adopted by the International Organization. This is very far from the motivating aim for constructing a composite indicator. We may have left in the scientists and analysts' hands too flexible tools (and too many degrees of freedom): the current situation call for future research on how to build composite indicators for food security.

SUGGESTIONS FOR FUTURE RESEARCH AND CONCLUSION

Composite indicators have started to be applied in several contexts as holistic tool to measure complex phenomenon. While increasing in number and prominence, they still lack of solid theoretical and methodological foundations. Nardo (2005a) provides an excellent review of the methods embedded in the construction of composite indices, and pinpoints strengths and weaknesses of different techniques. Moving from the theory to the practice is a big jump, therefore analysts and final users, need to be aware of the practical implications that different choices may imply. In order to explore the methodological challenge to build composite indicators, with a fresher perspective, I have analyzed a practical example: the construction of a food security composite indicator.

The debate on food security is rapidly growing (Ouertani, 2016; Santeramo, 2015a, 2015b, 2015c, 2016), and it concerns a wide range of disciplines. A large set of indicators have been proposed. However, measuring the phenomenon as a whole is *per se* important and therefore how different single indicators should be aggregated is very important. I emphasize how relevant may be the analyst's choice of algorithms to compute composite indicators by comparing different techniques to build composite indices of food security. Different methods have different impacts on rankings: normalization and weighting are (relatively) less crucial decisions, whereas special attention has to be paid in choosing the data imputation and aggregation methods.

Needless to say, the research presented here is not exempt from limitations. In particular, the results cannot be generalized to other composite indicators. Different theoretical framework and different data may lead to diverse sensitiveness of their composite indicator to alternative methods. However, the validity of the present research is to highlight the importance of testing the robustness of the ranking obtained through composite indicators. A second limitation consists in the reduced number of alternatives (for each step in the construction of the composite indicator) I have analyzed. Indeed this represents a suggestion for future research.

Despite the limitations stated, the implications of the present study are very relevant as I showed that simply modifying the adopted data imputation technique or the aggregation method alter the rankings, and thus suggest to the governments of the therefore named "food insecure" Countries to take measures. The provocative question I raise is: to what extent analysts are able to synthesize a complex phenomenon such food security by mean of a single composite indicator? And how governments should interpret the message that existing food security indicators convey?

I suggest that, when proposing new composite indices, the United Nations, the international agencies, academics and researchers, should pay careful attention to emphasizing how they jumped from raw data into a single index. Without a clear and transparent procedure, no judgment or comparison with existing indicators can be made. As my simplified example shows, the political and practical implications of each choice are very relevant.

REFERENCES

Alam, M., Dupras, J., & Messier, C. (2016). A framework towards a composite indicator for urban ecosystem services. *Ecological Indicators*, *60*, 38–44. doi:10.1016/j.ecolind.2015.05.035

Ames, A., Ames, A., Houston, J., & Angioloni, S. (2016). Does Financial Literacy Contribute to Food Security? *International Journal of Food and Agriculture Economics*, *4*, 21–34.

Aurino, E. (2014). *Selecting a Core Set of indicators for Monitoring Global Food Security. A Methodological Proposal*. FAO Statistics Division Working Papers 14-06.

Cafiero, C. (2013). *What do we really know about food security?* National Bureau of Economic Research. doi:10.3386/w18861

Cafiero, C., Melgar-Quiñonez, H. R., Ballard, T. J., & Kepple, A. W. (2014). Validity and reliability of food security measures. *Annals of the New York Academy of Sciences*, *1331*(1), 230–248. doi:10.1111/nyas.12594 PMID:25407084

Caracciolo, F., & Santeramo, F. G. (2013). Price Trends and Income Inequalities: Will Sub-Saharan Africa Reduce the Gap? *African Development Review*, *25*(1), 42–54. doi:10.1111/j.1467-8268.2013.12012.x

Carletto, C., Zezza, A., & Banerjee, R. (2013). Towards better measurement of household food security: Harmonizing indicators and the role of household surveys. *Global Food Security*, *2*(1), 30–40. doi:10.1016/j.gfs.2012.11.006

Carman, K. G., & Zamarro, G. (2016). Does Financial Literacy Contribute to Food Security? *International Journal of Food and Agriculture Economics*, *4*, 1–19. PMID:26949563

Dobrota, M., Martic, M., Bulajic, M., & Jeremic, V. (2015). Two-phased composite I-distance indicator approach for evaluation of countries' information development. *Telecommunications Policy*, *39*(5), 406–420. doi:10.1016/j.telpol.2015.03.003

FAO. (2013). *New metrics to measure and monitor performance in agriculture and food security*. Paper presented at the FAO conference, Rome, Italy.

Freudenberg, M. (2003). *Composite indicators of country performance: a critical assessment.* Paris: OECD. doi:10.1787/405566708255

Gabbert, S., & Weikard, H. (2001). How widespread is undernourishment? A critique of measurement methods and new empirical results. *Food Policy, 26*(3), 209–228. doi:10.1016/S0306-9192(00)00043-9

Godfray, H. C. J., Beddington, J. R., Crute, I. R., Haddad, L., Lawrence, D., Muir, J. F., & Toulmin, C. et al. (2010). Food security: The challenge of feeding 9 billion people. *Science, 327*(5967), 812–818. doi:10.1126/science.1185383 PMID:20110467

Hertel, T. W. (2016). Food security under climate change. *Nature Climate Change, 6*(1), 10–13. doi:10.1038/nclimate2834

Jacobs, R., Smith, & Goddard. (2004). *Measuring performance: an examination of composite performance indicators.* Centre for Health Economics, Technical Paper Series 29.

Mahadevan, R., & Hoang, V. (2015). Is There a Link Between Poverty and Food Security? *Social Indicators Research*, 1–21.

Maricic, M., Bulajic, M., Dobrota, M., & Jeremic, V. (2016). Redesigning the Global Food Security Index: A Multivariate Composite I-Distance Indicator Approach. *International Journal of Food and Agricultural Economics, 4*(1), 69-86.

Nardo, M., Saisana, M., Saltelli, A., & Tarantola, S. (2005b). *Tools for composite indicators building.* Ispra: European Comission.

Nardo, M., Saisana, M., Saltelli, A., Tarantola, S., Hoffman, A., & Giovannini, E. (2005a). *Handbook on constructing composite indicators: methodology and user guide (No. 2005/3).* OECD Publishing. doi:10.1787/533411815016

Ouertani, E. (2016). Food Security in Tunisia within Water Scarcity the Relative Importance of the Meat Sector. *International Journal of Food and Agricultural Economics, 4*(1), 35-54.

Pinstrup-Andersen, P. (2009). Food security: Definition and measurement. *Food Security, 1*(1), 5–7. doi:10.1007/s12571-008-0002-y

Saaty, T. L. (2001). *Decision Making for Leaders: The Analytic Hierarchy Process for Decisions in a Complex World. 1999/2000 Edition* (Vol. 2). RWS publications.

Santeramo, F. G. (2014). *On the composite indicators for food security: Decisions matter!* MPRA Paper.

Santeramo, F. G. (2015a). On the composite indicators for food security: Decision matter! *Food Reviews International, 1*(1), 63–73. doi:10.1080/87559129.2014.961076

Santeramo, F. G. (2015b). Food security composite indices: Implications for policy and practice. *Development in Practice, 25*(4), 594–600. doi:10.1080/09614524.2015.1029439

Santeramo, F. G. (2015c). Indicatori compositi di Food Security: Quali implicazioni per i policymaker? *AgriregioniEuropa, 41*, 102–104.

Santeramo, F. G. (2016). Il consumo di calorie, micro e macro nutrienti: Cosa insegnano le elasticità al reddito? *AgriregioniEuropa, 44*, 101–102.

Santeramo, F. G., Di Pasquale, J., Contò, F., Tudisca, S., & Sgroi, F. (2012). Analyzing risk management in Mediterranean Countries: The Syrian perspective. *New Medit, 11*(3), 35–40.

Santeramo, F. G., & Shabnam, N. (2015). The income-elasticity of calories, macro-and micro-nutrients: What is the literature telling us? *Food Research International, 76,* 932–937. doi:10.1016/j. foodres.2015.04.014

Svedberg, P. (2011). How Many People are Malnourished? *Annual Review of Nutrition, 31*(1), 263–283. doi:10.1146/annurev-nutr-081810-160805 PMID:21756133

Wheeler, T., & von Braun, J. (2013). Climate change impacts on global food security. *Science, 341*(6145), 508–513. doi:10.1126/science.1239402 PMID:23908229

ADDITIONAL READING

Booysen, F. (2002). An overview and evaluation of composite indices of development. *Social Indicators Research, 59*(2), 115–151. doi:10.1023/A:1016275505152

Economist Intelligence Unit (2013). The Global Food Security Index 2013: An annual measure of the state of global food security.

IFPRI. (2011). Global hunger index – the challenge of hunger: price spikes and excessive food price volatility. Bonn, Washington, DC, Dublin.

Leys, C., Ley, C., Klein, O., Bernard, P., & Licata, L. (2013). Detecting outliers: Do not use standard deviation around the mean, use absolute deviation around the median. *Journal of Experimental Social Psychology, 49*(4), 764–766. doi:10.1016/j.jesp.2013.03.013

Malinowski, E. R. (2009). Determination of rank by median absolute deviation (DRMAD): A simple method for determining the number of principal factors responsible for a data matrix. *Journal of Chemometrics, 23*(1), 1–6. doi:10.1002/cem.1182

Munda, G. (2012). Choosing aggregation rules for composite indicators. *Social Indicators Research, 109*(3), 337–354. doi:10.1007/s11205-011-9911-9

Munda, G., & Nardo, M. (2003). *On the methodological foundations of composite indicators used for ranking countries.* Ispra, Italy: Joint Research Centre of the European Communities.

Munda, G., & Saisana, M. (2011). Methodological considerations on regional sustainability assessment based on multicriteria and sensitivity analysis. *Regional Studies, 45*(2), 261–276. doi:10.1080/00343401003713316

Paruolo, P., Saisana, M., & Saltelli, A. (2013). Ratings and rankings: Voodoo or science? *Journal of the Royal Statistical Society. Series A (General), 176*(3), 609–634. doi:10.1111/j.1467-985X.2012.01059.x

Pemberton, C., Patterson-Andrews, H., & De Sormeaux (2016) Relative Vulnerability of Selected Caribbean States to Changes in Food Security Due To Tropical Storms and Hurricanes. *International journal of food and agricultural economics, 4*(1), 125-136.

Saisana, M., & Saltelli, A. (2013). Joint Research Centre Statistical Audit of the 2014 Global Innovation Index. The Global Innovation Index 2014, 55. In Cornell University, INSEAD, and WIPO (Eds.), The Global Innovation Index 2014: The Human Factor In innovation. Fontainebleau, Ithaca, and Geneva.

Tate, E. (2012). Social vulnerability indices: A comparative assessment using uncertainty and sensitivity analysis. *Natural Hazards*, *63*(2), 325–347. doi:10.1007/s11069-012-0152-2

Zornic, N., Bornmann, L., Maricic, M., Markovic, A., Martic, M., & Jeremic, V. (2015). Ranking Institutions within a University based on their scientific performance: a percentile-based approach. *El profesional de la información*, 24(5), 551-566.

KEY TERMS AND DEFINITIONS

Aggregation: Process of synthesizing single variables and indices into a multidimensional indices.
Composite Index: A combination of simple variables or indices to measure a complex phenomenon.
FAO: The Food and Agriculture Organization of the United Nations is an agency leading international efforts to eradicate hunger and ensure food security.
Food Security: The condition existing of having access to adequate and safe food.
Imputation: Process of replacing missing data through different techniques.
Millennium Goals: World targets to reduce global poverty by the first two decades of 2000s
Validation: Process of demonstrating that the model is a reasonable representation of the phenomenon under consideration.

ENDNOTES

[1]   The group includes variables such as Average Dietary Energy Supply Adequacy; Average Value of Food Production; Share of dietary energy supply derived from cereals, roots and tubers; Average protein supply; Average supply of protein of animal origin

[2]   This set s would include variables such as Percent of paved roads over total roads; Rail-lines density; Road density

[3]   This set s would include variables such as Prevalence of undernourishment; Share of food expenditure of the poor; Depth of the food deficit; Prevalence of food inadequacy

[4]   The group includes variables such as Percentage of children under 5 years of age who are stunted; Percentage of children under 5 years of age affected by wasting; Percentage of children under 5 years of age who are underweight; Percent of adults who are underweight

[5]   This set (Vulnerability/stability) would include variables such as Domestic food price level index volatility, Per Capita food production variability, Per Capita food supply variability, Political stability and absence of violence/terrorism, Value of food imports over total merchandise exports, Percent of arable land equipped for irrigation, Cereal import dependency ratio.

[6]   The report is available at: http://foodsecurityindex.eiu.com/

7   Geometric aggregation is intended to capture the hierarchical structure of the phenomenon. As Barrett (2010) pointed out, "availability, access, and utilization *[…]* are inherently hierarchical, with availability necessary but not sufficient to ensure access, which is, in turn, necessary but not sufficient for effective utilization". The structure calls for further research on how to aggregate sub-index. An alternative, yet not empirically investigated, is to use a quasi-linear aggregation method, or to use a *Stone-Geary-type* function.

Chapter 7

Composite Indicators of Development:
Some Recent Contributions

Sandrina B. Moreira
Instituto Politécnico de Setúbal (ESCE – IPS), Portugal

Nuno Crespo
Instituto Universitário de Lisboa (ISCTE – IUL), Portugal

ABSTRACT

Development is a complex and multidimensional phenomenon. The quantification of such a phenomenon requires indicators that may capture its most important components. In this chapter we present an extensive list of composite indicators of development, identifying their main possible common dimensions: income, income distribution, education, health, employment, infrastructures, values, and environment. We also discuss in detail five recent indices characterized by their comprehensiveness: 1) Regional Quality of Development Index (QUARS) of Sbilanciamoci!; 2) Wellbeing Index (WI) and Wellbeing/Stress Index (WSI) for measuring sustainable development; 3) Gross National Happiness (GNH) from the Center for Bhutan Studies; 4) Bertelsmann Transformation Index (BTI) of Bertelsmann Stiftung; and 5) World competitiveness scoreboard from the Institute for Management Development (IMD).

INTRODUCTION

The most important issues emerging from the literature on economics of development in recent years are the complexity and multidimensionality of the concept of development. Consequently, income per capita – the reference indicator for ranking countries at different levels of development – hardly gives, by itself, a sufficient indication of the disparities that exist between countries and over time. Mainly since the 1990s, the emergence of a wide range of composite indicators of development comes as no surprise. The Human Development Index (HDI) is the most internationally known indicator that aims to overcome the narrow focus on income per capita. Nevertheless, the majority of index proposals (including the HDI) are not sufficiently comprehensive in capturing the main dimensions of the concept(s) of development.

DOI: 10.4018/978-1-5225-0714-7.ch007

The present chapter seeks to provide a broad set of composite indicators of development, highlighting the dimensions covered in each of the indices listed here. On the other hand, a more limited group of indices is assembled for detailed discussion. Thus, starting with a discussion of the relevance of composite indicators for measuring development, the main focus of the present chapter encompasses two parts:

1. First, a proposal to disaggregate the main dimensions of development, and an extensive list of indices as well as their coverage of the different dimensions of development identified here;
2. Second, a detailed presentation of five recent proposals whose multidimensional nature stands out.

BACKGROUND

For many years, and mainly after the Second Word War, there has been a close connection between economic growth and development. The first has been viewed as a necessary and sufficient condition for the latter and, therefore, measuring a country's level of development through indicators of economic activity, especially the level of income per capita, has become a common approach.

However, since the 1970s, there has been a turning point in the practices and approaches to development, and the notion of development has been expanded to consider new dimensions not exclusively centered on the economic perspective. As a whole, the new concepts of development – sustainable, human, and local development are the most frequently mentioned – have been allowing a more adequate understanding of the complexity and multidimensionality of the phenomenon at issue. Regarding the quantitative assessment of the performance of countries in terms of development, composite indicators have gained greater importance as a result.[1]

Composite indicators are mathematical combinations of a set of indicators. There are many conceptual and methodological arguments in favor of this measurement approach. According to Saisana and Tarantola (2002), the main pros of using composite indicators are:

*   Composite indicators synthesize complex or multidimensional issues;
*   They are easier to interpret than a battery of separate indicators;
*   They facilitate the task of comparing the performance across countries; and their progress over time, and thereby attract public interest;
*   They reduce the size of a list of indicators without losing basic information.

Nevertheless, there are also some important criticisms levelled at composite indicators. Booysen (2002) stresses the following arguments against composite indicators:

*   They always exclude one or more essential elements of the domain at issue;
*   Particular components of the index may be quantified with the aid of different variables (possibly better ones);
*   Composite indicators may be unable to reveal more than what a single variable alone reveals;
*   The selection process of the variables may be *ad hoc*, that is, politically or ideologically motivated, or simply determined by the availability and accuracy of data;
*   The data employed in composite indicators are often inaccurate and non-comparable;

- Often no clear rationale is presented for the selected weighting and aggregation techniques;
- Composite indicators may lack practical value if they give no specific or focused policy advice.

The main advantage of composite indicators is, indeed, their multidimensionality, since they represent aggregate and relatively simple measures of a combination of components of complex phenomena, as is the case of development. Currently, a great variety of composite indicators have been proposed to quantitatively assess country performance in a diverse set of topics that can, in general, be interpreted as measures of development (e.g. Booysen, 2000, 2002).

More recently, and especially after the call for action in the report of the Commission on the Measurement of Economic Performance and Social Progress, also known as the Stiglitz-Sen-Fitoussi Commission (Stiglitz, Sen, & Fitoussi, 2009), some indices have appeared as an attempt to give a more appropriate quantification of these phenomena. The Better Life Index from the Organization for Economic Cooperation and Development (OECD), for instance, is an interactive web-based tool that allows people to compare well-being across countries according to their own preferences in housing, income, jobs, community education, environment, governance, health, life satisfaction, safety, and work-life balance (OECD, 2015). First published in 2011, the OECD Better Life Index is updated annually and currently covers all OECD countries, as well as the Russian Federation and Brazil. In addition, the Social Progress Index, launched in 2013 by the Social Progress Imperative, is an aggregate measure of the social and environmental performance of 133 countries covering 94% of the world's population (Porter, Stern, & Green, 2015). Two key features of the index are the exclusive focus on social and environmental indicators, thereby excluding economic indicators, and the usage of outcomes of success rather than input measures. Both indices are good examples of initiatives newly advanced to amend, complement, or replace the income per capita as a summary measure of development, allowing for a more textured assessment of the phenomenon.

THE MULTIDIMENSIONALITY OF THE MEASUREMENT OF DEVELOPMENT: COMPOSITE INDICATORS

Given the multidimensional nature of the concept of development, an adequate quantitative assessment of the phenomenon requires the definition of its main constituent items. Even though the understanding of development may vary in time, among countries, or even among individuals, a range of dimensions representing the material standard of living of individuals usually underlies the concept of development and its meaning, such as freedom, equity, health, education, and a healthy environment, among others.

The disaggregation of development into its main dimensions has been attempted by many authors. For instance, Booysen (2000, 2002) illustrates the multidimensionality of the composite indicators, classifying them according to twelve different dimensions of development, which are:

1. Demographic dynamics;
2. Education, training, and knowledge;
3. Health, food, and nutrition;
4. Human settlement, infrastructure, and communication;
5. Political and social stability;

6. Culture, social fabric, and family values;
7. Environmental resources and pressures;
8. Political and civil institutions;
9. Income and economic growth;
10. Unemployment and labor utilization;
11. Poverty and inequality; and
12. Economic freedom.

Given the aim of the present chapter, and based on the criteria of intrinsic relevance and recurrent inclusion in alternative attempts of development disaggregation, we first propose nine crucial dimensions for the level of a country's development. They are:

*   Income;
*   Income distribution (poverty; inequality);
*   Education (knowledge; educational infrastructures; others);
*   Health (longevity; health infrastructures; others);
*   Employment (volume; quality);
*   Infrastructures (energy; transport; communication; housing; money and finance; justice; culture, sport, and recreation; others);
*   Values (economic freedom; socio-political freedom);
*   Environment (atmosphere; land; water; nature and biodiversity; others);
*   Others.

The last dimension has a residual character, including aspects of development not reflected in the earlier ones, and includes gender equality, cultural diversity, macroeconomic context, and political and social stability, among others.

The next step is the identification of a representative number of surveys on composite indicators of development or including lists of such indicators. The studies identified here are the following:

*   Booysen (2002);
*   Morse (2004);
*   Gadrey and Jany-Catrice (2007);
*   Goossens et al. (2007);
*   Afsa et al. (2008);
*   Bandura (2008);
*   Eurostat (2008);
*   Saisana (2008);
*   Soares and Quintella (2008);
*   Singh et al. (2009).

Finally, the development indices presented here combine the following criteria: (i) they are mentioned in at least two of the above studies; (ii) they include at least two of the above dimensions. The end result is a selection of 54 composite indicators of development.

The analysis of the dimensions covered in each selected index is summarized in Table 1.

Table 1. Multidimensionality of composite indicators of development

Author/Organization	Composite Indicators of Development	N.º of Dimensions	Dimensions of Development								
			A	B	C	D	E	F	G	H	I
Bennett (1951)	Index of relative consumption levels	4			√	√		√			√
Beckerman and Bacon (1966)	Index of relative real consumption per head	3			√			√			√
McGranahan et al. (1972)	General index of development	5			√	√	√	√			√
Nordhaus and Tobin (1972)	Measure of Economic Welfare (MEW)	5			√	√	√	√			√
Morris (1979)	Physical Quality of Life Index (PQLI)	2			√	√					
Zolotas (1981)	Economic Aspects of Welfare (EAW)	6			√	√	√	√		√	√
Ram (1982)	Indices of 'overall' development	3	√		√	√					
Commission of the European Communities (1984)	Relative intensity of regional problems in the community	2	√				√				
Ginsburg et al. (1986)	World standard distance scales	3	√			√		√			
Camp and Speidel (1987)	International human suffering index	5	√		√	√			√		√
Slottje (1991)	Aggregate indexes of quality of life	5	√		√	√		√	√		
Diener (1995)	Quality of life indices	6	√	√	√	√			√	√	
Estes (1998)	Weighted Index of Social Progress (WISP)	5	√		√	√			√		√
Goedkoop and Spriensma (2001)	Eco-indicator 99	2				√				√	
Prescott-Allen (2001)	Wellbeing Index (WI) e Wellbeing/Stress Index (WSI)	9	√	√	√	√	√	√	√	√	√
Randolph (2001)	G-Index	2						√			√
UNDP (2001)	Technology Achievement Index (TAI)	2			√			√			
Tarantola et al. (2002)	Internal Market Index World (IMI)	3						√	√		√
Smith (2003)	Index of Economic Well-Being (IEWB)	7	√	√	√	√	√			√	√
Tsoukalas and Mackenzie (2003)	Personal Security Index (PSI)	5	√	√		√	√		√		
UN et al. (2003)	Green GDP ou Environmentally adjusted NDP (eaNDP)	2	√							√	
Hagén (2004)	Welfare index	3	√			√				√	
NISTEP (2004)	General Indicator of Science and Technology (GIST)	2			√						√
Porter and Stern (2004)	National innovative capacity index	2			√				√		
The Economist (2004)	Quality-of-life index	5	√			√	√		√		√
European Commission (2005)	Investment in the knowledge-based economy	2			√			√			
European Commission (2005)	Performance in the knowledge-based economy	3	√		√			√			
Marks et al. (2006)	Happy Planet Index (HPI)	2				√				√	
Sbilanciamoci (2006)	Regional Quality of Development Index (QUARS)	8		√	√	√	√	√	√	√	√
World Bank (2006)	Adjusted net saving ou Genuine saving	3			√					√	√
ATK/FP (2007)	A.T. Kearney/FOREIGN POLICY Globalization Index	2						√			√
Gwartney and Lawson (2007)	Economic Freedom of the World (EFW) index	2							√		√
Miringoff and Opdycke (2007)	Index of social health	6	√	√	√	√	√		√		
Talberth et al. (2007)	Genuine Progress Indicator (GPI)	7		√	√			√	√	√	√
UNDP (2007)	Human Development Index (HDI)	3	√		√	√					

continued on following page

Table 1. Continued

Author/Organization	Composite Indicators of Development	N.° of Dimensions	Dimensions of Development								
			A	B	C	D	E	F	G	H	I
UNDP (2007)	Human Poverty Index (HPI-1) for developing countries	2			√	√					
UNDP (2007)	Human Poverty Index (HPI-2) for selected OECD countries	4		√	√	√	√				
Bertelsmann Stiftung (2008)	Bertelsmann Transformation Index (BTI)	9	√	√	√	√	√	√	√	√	√
Dreher *et al.* (2008)	KOF index of globalization	3						√	√		√
EIU (2008)	E-readiness rankings	6	√		√		√	√	√		√
Esty *et al.* (2008)	Environmental Performance Index (EPI)	2				√				√	
Holmes *et al.* (2008)	Index of economic freedom	2							√		√
IMD (2008)	World competitiveness scoreboard	9	√	√	√	√	√	√	√	√	√
Porter and Schwab (2008)	Global Competitiveness Index (GCI)	6	√		√	√		√	√		√
Roodman (2008)	Commitment to Development Index (CDI)	3							√	√	√
StC (2008)	Mothers' index	3			√	√					√
van de Kerk and Manuel (2008)	Sustainable Society Index (SSI)	7		√	√	√	√		√	√	√
Dutta and Mia (2009)	Networked Readiness Index (NRI)	4			√			√	√		√
EIU (2009)	Business environment rankings	7	√		√	√	√	√	√		√
UNU-MERIT (2009)	Summary Innovation Index (SII)	4			√		√	√			√
Center for Bhutanese Studies - website	Gross National Happiness (GNH) index	9	√	√	√	√	√	√	√	√	√
Friends of the Earth - website	Index of Sustainable Economic Welfare (ISEW)	7		√	√	√	√	√		√	√
Réseau d'Alerte sur les Inégalités (RAI) - website	Baromètre des Inégalités et de la Pauvreté (BIP40)	7	√	√	√	√	√		√		√
Social Indicators Department [n.a.]	Index of individual living conditions	7	√		√	√	√	√	√	√	

Notes: A = Income; B = Income Distribution; C = Education; D = Health; E = Employment; F = Infrastructures; G = Values; H = Environment; and I = Others (a residual dimension, including aspects of development not reflected in the previous dimensions such as gender equality, cultural diversity, macroeconomic context, and political and social stability).

As Table 1 reveals, the indices of development include a small number of dimensions. This is of special interest, since the development phenomenon requires a multidimensional assessment that does not exclude its main constituent elements. Indeed, almost half of the indicators presented in Table 1 (26 out of 54) include three or fewer of the various dimensions of development identified here.

Given the aim of the present chapter, five recent indicators were selected from Table 1, because of their comprehensiveness in terms of dimension coverage. They are:

- Regional Quality of Development Index (QUARS), Sbilanciamoci! (2006);
- Wellbeing Index (WI) and Wellbeing/Stress Index (WSI), Prescott-Allen (2001);
- Gross National Happiness (GNH) of the Center for Bhutanese Studies;
- Bertelsmann Transformation Index (BTI), Bertelsmann Stiftung (2008);
- World competitiveness scoreboard, IMD (2008).

The first index includes eight of the nine dimensions and the other four indices encompass all nine dimensions. Thus, they constitute a valid complement to the most widely used indicators in the literature of economics development, namely the income per capita and the HDI. The next section discusses their main characteristics and quantification approach, using the latest information available.

SOME RECENT PROPOSALS FOR COMPOSITE INDICATORS OF DEVELOPMENT

Regional Quality of Development Index (QUARS)

The QUARS is an initiative of a campaign entitled Sbilanciamoci!. This Italian campaign involves more than 40 associations and civil society networks sharing the purpose of suggesting alternatives to the Italian budgetary policies, highlighting environmental and social aspects. The Sbilanciamoci! campaign published its first report on the Qualità Regionale dello Sviluppo (QUARS; quality of regional development) in the year 2000. Sbilanciamoci!'s understanding of that concept is as follows:

A region in which the economic dimension (production, distribution, consumption) is sustainable and compatible with environmental and social factors, where the social and health services adequately meet the needs of all the citizens, where participation in cultural life is alive, where the conditions needed to guarantee economic, social and political rights and equal opportunities to all individuals regardless of income, sex or country of origin are present and where the environment and territory are protected. (Andreis, 2012, p. 9)

Sbilanciamoci! proposes a synthetic index – the QUARS – to evaluate the development quality of the Italian regions, encompassing seven macro-indicators and 45 variables (Andreis, 2012).

- Concerning the environmental dimension, 10 variables are identified to assess the environmental impact of production, distribution, and consumption, as well as proper steps taken to mitigate the negative effects on the environment.
- The macro-indicator on the economy and labor contains four variables that reflect the working conditions and income guaranteed by the economic system and redistribution policies.
- In the macro-indicator of rights and citizenship, Sbilanciamoci! analyses the social inclusion of young people, the elderly, immigrants, and other underprivileged people.
- In the field of equal opportunities, gender equality (in economic, political, and social life) is at focus.
- At the cultural and educational level, the following aspects are taken into account: participation in the school system; quality of the service; educational level of the population; and cultural demand and supply.
- The health macro-indicator encompasses such features as the quality and efficiency of the service, proximity, and general health of the population.
- Lastly, five indicators measure political and social participation of citizens.

The variables that make up the index are all standardized, and therefore differences in score represent the actual differences existing between regions in the various aspects considered in the index.[2] Positive (negative) values for the QUARS of each region represent a score above (below) the mean for the regions. The further away the values are from zero, the further away they are from the mean value.

After the normalization of the variables, the mean values of the macro-indicators are calculated and the QUARS corresponds to the average of these mean values:

$$QUARS = \frac{1}{N} \sum X_i \tag{2}$$

in which N is the number of macro-indicators and X_i the i-th macro-indicator.

The QUARS is computed to measure development quality and it questions, in the first place, GDP per capita as the conventional measure of the development level, and also alternative indicators to GDP such as the HDI or the Genuine Progress Indicator (GPI). According to Sbilanciamoci!, the measurement of the development quality goes beyond the simple consideration of the income level (measured by GDP/GNP per capita) or even other purely quantitative indicators. A distinguishing characteristic of the QUARS is thus its evaluation of the quality of the work, the quality of the social services (education, heath, and assistance), and the quality of the environment, among others.

On the other hand, regarding the database, the QUARS is specifically conceived to be adopted in the economic planning of regional governments in Italy. Indeed, it is already a reference indicator in Lazio (the region of Rome).

Wellbeing Index (WI) and Wellbeing/Stress Index (WSI)

Prescott-Allen (2001) proposes a new method to assess the sustainability of nations, given that "no country knows how to be green without going into the red" (p. 2). According to this author countries with a high standard of living impose excessive pressure on the environment, while nations with low demands on the ecosystem are poor. This dichotomy is more easily perceptible applying the well-being assessment method described in Prescott-Allen (2001) that, ultimately, allows the evaluation of countries' performance in four indices:[3]

- Human Wellbeing Index;
- Ecosystem Wellbeing Index;
- Wellbeing Index;
- Wellbeing/Stress Index.

Human Wellbeing Index (HWI)

The HWI comprehends 36 indicators that globally aim to give a more realistic picture of the socio-economic conditions than the one resulting from conventional indicators like GDP or the HDI. This index is an average of the values of the following dimensions:

- Health and population;
- Wealth;
- Knowledge and culture;

- Community;
- Equity.

The equity dimension is excluded if the average is lower without it.

Ecosystem Wellbeing Index (EWI)

The EWI synthesizes 51 indicators on the state of the environment with the purpose of being a broader measure than other global indices such as the Ecological Footprint (EF) or the Environmental Performance Index (EPI). This index is an average of the values of the following dimensions:

- Land;
- Water;
- Air;
- Species and genes;
- Resource use.

The resource use dimension is excluded if the average is lower without it.

Wellbeing Index (WI) and Wellbeing/Stress Index (WSI)

The WI and the WSI are both specific to the Prescott-Allen's (2001) well-being assessment method. The first index juxtaposes the two previous ones (HWI and EWI) so they can be compared, and the second index measures the ecological cost of human well-being. Both measure people and the ecosystem together, in order to compare their status, verify the impact of one on the other, and stress improvements in both.

The WI is the arithmetic average of the HWI and the EWI:

$$WI = \frac{HWI + EWI}{2} \tag{3}$$

In turn, the WSI is given by the ratio of human well-being to ecosystem stress:

$$WSI = \frac{HWI}{100 - EWI} \tag{4}$$

The dimensions of the indices that form both the WI and the WSI (i.e. HWI and EWI) are disaggregated in elements and/or sub-elements, represented by a single indicator whenever possible and in some cases by multiple indicators. Overall, there are 36 and 51 indicators, respectively.

The observed value of each indicator is transformed into a value that matches the performance scale of the so-called barometer of sustainability. The idea is as follows: (i) the barometer scale comprises five bands – bad, poor, medium, fair, and good – and the corresponding values range 20 points each on a scale of 0 to 100; (ii) for each indicator minimum and maximum values of performance are previously defined to each of the above bands;[4] (iii) the observed value of a given indicator determines the minimum and maximum values (of a given band) to be used in the normalization of the indicator by employing the following formula:

$$Z_i = \frac{\left[\left(X_i - \min W_{ij}\right)\left(\max W_{ij} - \min W_{ij}\right)\right] \cdot 20}{\min Y_j} \qquad (5)$$

in which Z_i is the normalized value of the i-th indicator, X_i is the original value of the i-th indicator, $\min W_{ij}$ and $\max W_{ij}$ are, respectively, minimum and maximum values of the j-th band of performance associated with the original value of the i-th indicator, and $\min Y_j$ expresses the minimum point of the j-th band of performance on the barometer scale.

The next step is to aggregate scores in hierarchy: indicator scores into sub-element scores; sub-element scores into element scores; and element scores into dimension scores. Finally, dimension scores are combined into two indices – HWI and EWI. Dimensions are given equal weight, but elements, sub-elements, and indicators are sometimes given different weights.[5]

Gross National Happiness (GNH) Index

The GNH is a complex concept that includes a set of inter-related human happiness conditions. The origins of the concept can be traced back to the early 1970s and are attributable to King Singye of Bhutan, who coined the phrase "Gross National Happiness is more important than Gross Domestic Product".[6] At the end of 2008, this Asian country officially adopted the GNH index developed by the non-governmental organization Center for Bhutan Studies.

Measures of happiness available in the literature are subjective well-being measures such as the satisfaction with life index proposed by White (2007). In general, individuals respond to a question like "how happy are you?" on an ordinal scale, ranging from one (the worst result) to "n" (the best result). Indicators of subjective well-being are then defined based on the mean, the median, or the variance of the distribution. On the other hand, a number of conventional measures of progress and development are multidimensional in nature but objective measures of well-being that do not reflect the Bhutanese understandings of happiness adequately. Based on these arguments, the Center for Bhutan Studies proposes an index – the GNH index – aimed to be a deeper representation of well-being than existing indicators and, in particular, a reflection of the happiness and general well-being of the Bhutanese population.

The GNH index includes nine core dimensions of human well-being, from traditional areas of social concern such as standard of living, education, and health to less traditional ones such as time use (work vs. leisure), emotional well-being, and community vitality (Ura, Alkire, Zangmo, & Wangdi, 2012).

- The first dimension is measured by the psychological well-being index comprising emotional balance indicators, spiritual indicators, and an indicator of general psychological distress.
- The second dimension is assessed through an index of time use that includes two variables – sleeping hours and total working hours.
- The third dimension is measured by a community vitality index consisting of indicators of family vitality, safety, reciprocity, social support, trust, socialization, and kinship density.

- The fourth dimension is captured by a culture index that gathers indicators of value transmission, basic precepts, community festivals, dialect use, traditional sports, and artisan skills.
- The fifth dimension has a health index that evaluates the health status of the population, its health knowledge, and the barriers to health care access.
- The sixth dimension is quantified through the education index, which analyzes the educational level of the population, its understanding of the district language, and its knowledge of history and local traditions.
- The seventh dimension corresponds to ecological diversity and resilience, capturing ecological degradation and ecological knowledge of the population, and its forestation practices.
- The standard of living index encompasses indicators linked to income, housing, food security, and hardship, and is the eighth dimension.
- Finally, the ninth component of happiness and well-being in Bhutan is good governance, which evaluates government performance, the degree of people's freedom, and their level of institutional trust.

The indicators that comprise the sub-indices of the GNH index are estimated from survey questionnaire data; given that individuals are interested in their own well-being and are thus the ones that can best judge the subject. This inquiry was conducted in different districts of Bhutan twice in 2007 and 2010 and included a mixture of objective, subjective, and open-ended questions.

The methodological approach followed in the calculation of the GNH index also has an innovative character and can be disaggregated in two steps (Ura, Alkire, Zangmo, & Wangdi, 2012). In the first instance, one applies a sufficiency cut-off or threshold to each indicator of the index, assuming a meaning similar to the concept of poverty line in the poverty measurement context. The poverty line separates the poor from the non-poor and, correspondingly, this divider line of sufficiency distinguishes the individuals who attain a sufficient level of achievement in a given indicator from those whose attainments fall short of sufficiency. Setting the exact sufficiency cut-off in a given indicator is a difficult task and certainly involves value judgments. Nevertheless, it is possible to identify some sufficient level of achievement on the different indicators of the index, the attainment of which would reflect a sufficient quality of life. Achievements above that level would hardly contribute to an improvement of the individual's quality of life, and thus an individual is considered happy if that person achieves sufficiency in all nine dimensions of the GNH index.

The procedure to accomplish this first step is to apply the following formula:

$$Z_{ik} = \begin{cases} \dfrac{C_i - X_{ik}}{C_i} & if \ X_{ik} < C_i \\ 0 & if \ X_{ik} \geq C_i \end{cases} \tag{6}$$

in which Z_{ik} is the normalized value of the i-th indicator and k-th individual, X_{ik} is the original value of the i-th indicator and k-th individual, and C_i represents the cut-off of sufficiency of the i-th indicator.

Therefore, distances from the cut-offs (Z_{ik}) take into account the depth of the insufficiency levels, that is, the further away from the cut-off, the greater the value obtained. Finally, the distances from the cut-offs are squared in order to take into account the severity of the insufficiency levels, and thus give more weight to poor achievements.

The second step to compute the GNH index is the aggregation of data (sample) population. Replicating the above procedure for all the individuals in the sample, one obtains, for each indicator, the average of the squared distances from the cut-offs. The difference between the value of one and a given average gives us the contribution of that indicator to the index. An equal weighting to these resulting values determines the value of the final index.

In brief:

$$GNH\ index = \frac{1}{N \cdot M} \sum \sum \left(1 - Z_{ik}^2\right) \tag{7}$$

in which N is the number of indicators and M the number of individuals.

The GNH index has been computed for the different districts considered in the analysis of happiness and well-being in Bhutan. The decomposition of the GNH index by dimension (or indicator) immediately reveals those dimensions that present the greatest shortfalls from sufficiency. Future surveys will allow a deeper analysis of the index and inherent dimensions over time.

Bertelsmann Transformation Index (BTI)

The transformation index of Bertelsmann Stiftung is a German initiative that assesses the development and transformation processes of countries that have yet to achieve a fully consolidated democracy and market economy. Here the distinctive mark is on the evaluation of developing and transformation countries from two perspectives: on the one hand, the state of democracy and market liberalization; on the other hand, the performance of political leaders in the management of these changes. The Bertelsmann Stiftung produces biannual world rankings on two indices: the status index and the management index. Both are computed on the basis of 17 criteria subdivided into 49 questions in total. The scores of the last survey are available in Bertelsmann Stiftung (2014).

Status Index

The status index scores represent the mean value of the democracy and market economy scores:

$$Status\ index = \frac{1}{O}\left(\frac{1}{P}\sum D_p + \frac{1}{Q}\sum ME_q\right) \tag{8}$$

in which O is the number of dimensions, D_p the p-th criterion of the democracy dimension, ME_q the q-th criterion of the market economy dimension, P the number of democracy criteria, and Q the number of market economy criteria.

The scores of the democracy dimension aggregate the scores of five equally weighted criteria:

- Stateness;
- Political participation;
- Rule of law;
- Stability of democratic institutions;
- Political and social integration.

The criteria scores, in turn, are the means of quality assessments by experts who respond on an ordinal scale ranging from one (worst) to 10 (best).

The scores of the market economy dimension are likewise the average of seven criteria scores and the scores of each criterion, in turn, correspond to the mean of the scores for the respective individual questions. The market economy dimensions are the following:

- The level of socio-economic development;
- The organization of the market and competition;
- Currency and price stability;
- Private property;
- Welfare regime;
- Economic performance;
- Sustainability.

Management Index

The management index reveals the quality of political management under given structural conditions. The index takes into account structural difficulties such as high levels of poverty or a history of violent conflicts, given that good governance under difficult conditions should be appreciated more than an equivalent performance under promising conditions. Therefore, the management index scores represent the mean value of four management criteria weighted by a fifth criterion, the level of difficulty, which captures such difficult structural conditions:

$$Management\ index = \frac{1}{R-1}\sum_{r=1}^{R-1} M_r \cdot \left[1 + (LD-1) \cdot \frac{0.25}{9}\right] \cdot \frac{10}{12.5} \tag{9}$$

in which R is the number of management criteria, M_r the r-th criterion of the management criteria, and LD corresponds to the fifth management criterion, known as the level of difficulty.

In other words, the experts evaluate through specific qualitative indicators the degree of accomplishment in the criteria of steering capability, resource efficiency, consensus-building, international cooperation, and the level of difficulty. The qualitative indicators of the last criterion are combined with quantitative indicators that reflect a country's level of economic development and education. The resulting mean level of difficulty scores are multiplied by the mean management criteria scores (after being converted to an appropriate scale) to compute the final index (management index).

World Competitiveness Scoreboard

The World Competitiveness Scoreboard (WCS) is an overall ranking published in the world competitiveness yearbook and developed by the IMD, a leading Swiss management school.

Similar to the Global Competitiveness Index (GCI) of the World Economic Forum (Schwab, 2014), the IMD produces an annual ranking on global competitiveness for various economies worldwide, from the most to the least competitive. According to the IMD (2014), the competitiveness of nations is their ability to create and maintain an environment that sustains more value creation for its enterprises and more prosperity for its people.

On the basis of the global competitiveness ranking there are four competitiveness factors that, in turn, are disaggregated into five sub-factors each:

- **Economic Performance:** Domestic economy, international trade, international investment, employment, and prices);
- **Government Efficiency:** Public finance, fiscal policy, institutional framework, business legislation, and societal framework;
- **Business Efficiency:** Productivity and efficiency, labor market, finance, management practices, and attitudes and values;
- **Infrastructure:** Basic, technological, scientific, health and environment, and education.

The criteria that form each sub-factor are a combination of hard and soft data. Hard data are quantitative data from regional and international organizations as well as private industries in a total of 135 criteria. Soft data are compiled from the IMD's Executive Opinion Survey, which gathers 118 questions conceived to measure competitiveness as it is perceived by business executives.

The starting point in designing the IMD's (2014) rankings is to compute the standardized value of each of the 253 criteria/indicators for the different economies under scrutiny.[7] The economies are then ranked by criterion, sub-factor, and factor, and finally the global competitiveness ranking is calculated. Quantitative data are weighted two-thirds in the overall ranking and survey data are weighted one-third. The remaining components of the final index (factors and sub-factors) are equally weighted:

$$WCS = \frac{1}{O}\left(\frac{1}{S}\sum EP_s + \frac{1}{T}\sum GE_t + \frac{1}{U}\sum BE_u + \frac{1}{V}\sum IS_v\right) \tag{10}$$

in which O is the number of factors, EP_s represents the s-th subfactor of the economic performance factor, GE_t the t-th subfactor of the government efficiency factor, BE_u the u-th subfactor of the business efficiency factor, IS_v the v-th subfactor of the infrastructure factor, and S, T, U, and V are, respectively, the number of economic performance, government efficiency, business efficiency, and infrastructure subfactors.

FUTURE RESEARCH DIRECTIONS

The five composite indicators discussed in this chapter represent good examples of recent proposals for the measurement of the complex and multidimensional phenomenon of development. Nonetheless, each index chosen has a different understanding and definition of the multidimensional concept to be measured. For example, the QUARS developed by Sbilanciamoci! is founded on the idea that a good quality of development is based on environmental sustainability, promotion of rights, and quality of life. Prescott-Allen's (2001) measurement of sustainable development has combined indicators of human well-being with those of environmental stability to generate a more comprehensive picture of the state of the world. The GNH index is developed to orient the people and the nation toward happiness and well-being, mainly by improving the conditions of people who are not-yet-happy. The Bertelsmann Stiftung's Transformation Index (BTI) is meant to study the transformation processes and political management of countries on their path toward democracy and a market economy. Finally, the IMD World competitiveness scoreboard has pioneered the study of world competitiveness based on factors that facilitate prosperity. These composite indicators in policy areas, such as competitiveness or sustainable development, might thus not have the direct purpose of measuring development. Moreover, even though some of the indices have an international dimension, BTI excludes all OECD countries, for instance, because it focuses on developing countries and countries in transition, while the QUARS and the GNH are case studies. Therefore, the development of new indicators that, in addition to their comprehensiveness, have a more universal application – facilitating more direct comparisons at the international level – is still to come.

The depth and breadth of the five indices chosen are undeniable, even though some limitations are present, primarily methodological aspects inherent in the construction of composite indicators. Taking as reference the four indices elaborated by Prescott-Allen (2001) and the QUARS, for instance, the literature stresses some of their most important limitations, mainly the following: (i) choosing the indicators that best represent the elements of the system as well as performance criteria for each indicator is a time consuming stage of the well-being assessment method (Prescott-Allen, 2001); (ii) treatment given to the equity and resource use dimensions is a problem of Prescott-Allen's indices (Eurostat, 2008); (iii) data availability is also an issue for both those well-being indices (Graymore, 2005) and the QUARS (Goossens, Mäkipää, Schepelmann, de Sand, Kuhndt, & Herrndorf, 2007); (iv) the normalization method chosen to build the QUARS (z-scores) does not allow determining the performance of a given region in absolute terms, but only in relation to the other regions taken into consideration (Sbilanciamoci!, 2006) (v) the lack of an explicit weighting method for the variables in the QUARS is considered to have been, in a certain way, arbitrary (Goossens, Mäkipää, Schepelmann, de Sand, Kuhndt, & Herrndorf, 2007).

Among the crucial methodological issues regarding composite indicators is the assignment of weights to the components (and possible sub-components) of the multidimensional concept at stake in order to have an aggregated indicator. The simplest method – equal weighting – is the common procedure in the literature and thus the composite indicator is determined by the average of the corresponding indicators (OECD & EC, 2008; Moreira, Simões, & Crespo, 2012). Nonetheless, the literature offers a variety of weighting methods alternatives, usually disaggregated into two general categories: statistical techniques of multivariate analysis, like the principal component analysis or the factor analysis; participatory methods, among which methodologies known as budget allocation or public opinion are well-known examples (OECD & EC, 2008).

Consequently, an extremely appealing avenue for further research would be to employ different weighting schemes, especially methods in which weights can be objectively formed, and assess whether there is correspondence to the most favored approach in the literature of assigning equal weight to each dimension of development. This procedure could be applied either to the composite indicators of development highlighted in this chapter or to a new index of development built from scratch.

Finally, there is still room for further research on the broad set of available composite indicators of development. The present chapter gives a list of 54 indices, using a selection criterion to identify the most representative indicators and thereafter discard the least consolidated contributions in the literature. However, an updated version would enrich the corpus of information available, with the inclusion of more recent initiatives such as the Multidimensional Poverty Index (Alkire, 2010, 2013), the Better Life Index (OECD, 2015), or the Social Progress Index (Porter, Stern, & Green, 2015). Furthermore, broadening the list of composite indicators of development would enable a more in-depth evaluation of those that are sufficiently comprehensive in terms of dimension coverage and thus may be a valid complement to internationally well-known indicators of development, either the income per capita or the HDI.

CONCLUSION

The concept of development is described as a complex phenomenon with a multidimensional content, and indicators that capture its multidimensional nature are needed for a quantitative evaluation of the domain. Composite indicators in the assessment of development are of great importance. These indicators share the most important advantage of summarizing an extensive volume of information on the different dimensions that characterize a given complex phenomenon.

A wide range of composite indicators of development is currently available in the literature. Based on a nomenclature that disaggregates development into their main common dimensions encompassing income, income distribution, education, health, employment, infrastructures, values, and environment, we have considered indicators that simultaneously include at least two of the different proposed dimensions and are mentioned in at least two of the studies selected on composite indicators of development. The purpose of the mentioned criteria is to identify the most representative indices of development from the literature.

However, we have evaluated the dimension coverage of that sample of 54 composite indicators of development, and the majority does not completely reflect the multidimensionality inherent in the development phenomenon. Indeed, 15 and 11 indices out of 54 included only two and three of the different dimensions of development, respectively. Moreover, only five indices out of 54 were characterized by their comprehensiveness in terms of dimension coverage, thereby including the crucial dimensions of development.

The few composite indicators that reflect the most important aspects of development were found to be the wellbeing index (WI) and wellbeing/stress index (WSI), the regional quality of development index (QUARS), the transformation index of Bertelsmann Stiftung (BTI), the world competitiveness scoreboard from the International Institute for Management Development (IMD), and the gross national happiness index (GNH). They are stressed out because they constitute complementary measures to the most frequently used indicators in the development assessment – the income per capita and the widely-used composite indicator HDI.

Nevertheless, a more in-depth analysis of the five indices has shown that an adequate quantification of the development phenomenon and its constituent elements should be further pursued. More recent initiatives in the development literature framework might accomplish this imperative goal.

REFERENCES

Afsa, C., Blanchet, D., Marcus, V., Pionnier, P-A., & Rioux, L. (2008). *Survey of existing approaches to measuring socio-economic progress*. Study prepared for Commission on the Measurement of Economic Performance and Social Progress, INSEE/OECD.

Alkire, S., & Santos, M. E. (2010). *Acute multidimensional poverty: A new index for developing countries*. Human Development Research Paper, 11.

Alkire, S., & Santos, M. E. (2013). A multidimensional approach: Poverty measurement & beyond. *Social Indicators Research, 112*(2), 239–257. doi:10.1007/s11205-013-0257-3

Andreis, S. (2012). *QUARS – Regional quality of development index: Building alternative measures for development/quality of life*. Project Wealth Kick-off Convention.

ATK/FP. (2007). *The Globalization Index 2007*. A.T. Kearney / Foreign Policy Magazine.

Bandura, R. (2008). *A survey of composite indices measuring country performance: 2008 Update*. New York: Office of Development Studies.

Beckerman, W., & Bacon, R. (1966). International comparisons of income levels: A suggested new measure. *The Economic Journal, 76*(303), 519–536. doi:10.2307/2229519

Bennett, M. K. (1951). International disparities in consumption levels. *The American Economic Review, 41*(4), 632–649.

Stiftung, B. (2008). *Bertelsmann transformation index 2008: Political management in international comparison*. Gütersloh: Bertelsmann Stiftung Verlag.

Stiftung, B. (2014). Transformation index. In *Political management in international comparison*. Gütersloh: Bertelsmann Stiftung Verlag.

Booysen, F. (2000). *The development of economic development: Alternative composite indices*. (Unpublished doctoral dissertation). University of Stellenbosch.

Booysen, F. (2002). An overview and evaluation of composite indices of development. *Social Indicators Research, 59*(2), 115–151. doi:10.1023/A:1016275505152

Camp & Speidel. (1987). The military burden, economic growth, and the human suffering index: Evidence from the LDCs. *Cambridge Journal of Economics, 13*(4), 497–515.

Commission of the European Communities. (1984). *The regions of Europe: Second periodic report on the social and economic situation of the regions of the community, together with a statement of the regional policy committee*. Luxembourg: OPOCE.

Diener, E. (1995). A value based index for measuring national quality of life. *Social Indicators Research, 36*(2), 107–127. doi:10.1007/BF01079721

Dreher, A., Gaston, N., & Martens, P. (2008). *Measuring globalization - Gauging its consequences*. New York: Springer.

Dutta, S., & Mia, I. (2009). *The global information technology report 2008–2009: Mobility in a networked world*. Geneva: World Economic Forum & INSEAD.

EIU. (2008). *E-readiness rankings 2008: Maintaining momentum*. A white paper from the Economist Intelligence Unit.

EIU. (2009). *Country forecast Eastern Europe*. London: Economist Intelligence Unit.

Estes, R. J. (1998). Trends in world social development, 1970-95: Development prospects for a new century. In P. K. Nandi & S. M. Shahidullah (Eds.), *Globalization and the evolving world society* (pp. 11–39). Leiden: Brill.

Esty, D., Levy, M., Kim, C., de Sherbinin, A., Srebotnjak, T., & Mara, V. (2008). *2008 environmental performance index*. New Haven, CT: Yale Center for Environmental Law and Policy.

European Commission. (2005). *Towards a European research area – science, technology and innovation – key figures 2005*. Luxembourg: Office for Publications of the European Communities.

Eurostat. (2008). *Feasibility study on the measure of wellbeing presentation of Eurostat work*. Brussels: Eurostat/Strategic Development Group.

Gadrey, J., & Jany-Catrice, F. (2007). *Les Nouveaux Indicateurs de Richesse*. Repères-La Découverte.

Ginsburg, N., Osborn, J., & Blank, G. (1986). *Geographic perspectives on the wealth of nations*. Department of Geography Research Paper No. 220. University of Chicago.

Goedkoop, M. & Spriensma, R. (2001). *The eco-indicator 99: A damage oriented method for life cycle assessment - methodology report*. Amersfoort: PRé Consultants.

Goossens, Y., Mäkipää, A., Schepelmann, P., de Sand, I., Kuhndt, M., & Herrndorf, M. (2007). *Alternative progress indicators to gross domestic product (GDP) as a means towards sustainable development. Study provided for the European Parliament's Committee on the Environment, Public Health and Food Safety*. PDESP/European Parliament.

Graymore, M. (2005). *Journey of sustainability: Small regions, sustainable carrying capacity and sustainability assessment methods*. (Unpublished doctoral dissertation). Griffith University.

Gwartney, J., & Lawson, R. (2007). Economic freedom of the world: 2007 annual report. Vancouver: Fraser Institute.

Hagén, H.-O. (2004). *Background facts on economic statistics 2004:15 - Comparing welfare of nations*. Stockholm: Department of Economic Statistics, Statistics Sweden.

Holmes, K. R., Feulner, E. J., & O' Grady, M. A. (2008). *2008 index of economic freedom*. Washington, DC: The Heritage Foundation & Dow Jones & Company, Inc.

IMD. (2008). *IMD world competitiveness yearbook 2008*. Lausanne: International Institute for Management Development.

IMD. (2014). *IMD world competitiveness yearbook 2014*. Lausanne: International Institute for Management Development.

Marks, N., Abdallah, S., Simms, A., & Thompson, S. (2006). *The (un)happy planet index: An index of human well-being and environmental impact*. London: New Economics Foundation.

McGranahan, D. V., Richard-Proust, C., Sovani, N. V., & Subramanian, M. (1972). *Contents and measurement of socioeconomic development*. New York: Praeger.

Miringoff, M.-L., & Opdycke, S. (2007). *America's social health: Putting social issues back on the public agenda*. Armonk, NY: M.E. Sharpe.

Moreira, S. B., Simões, N., & Crespo, N. (2012). Composite indicators of development – The importance of dimensional weights. *Global Economics and Management Review*, *2*(September), 79–95.

Morris, M. D. (1979). *Measuring the condition of the world's poor: The physical quality of life index*. New York: Pergamon Press.

Morse, S. (2004). *Indices and indicators in development*. London: Earthscan Publications Ltd.

NISTEP. (2004). *Science and technology indicators: 2004 – A systematic analysis of science and technology activities in Japan*. Japan: National Institute of Science and Technology Policy.

Nordhaus, W., & Tobin, J. (1972). Is growth obsolete? National Bureau of Economic Research, General Series No. 96.

OECD. (2015). *Better Life Index 2015: Definitions and medata*. OECD Statistics Online.

OECD & EC. (2008). Handbook on constructing composite indicators: Methodology and user guide. Paris & Ispra: OECD (the Statistics Directorate and the Directorate for Science, Technology and Industry) & European Commission (the Econometrics and Applied Statistics Unit of the Joint Research Center).

Porter, M. E., & Schwab, K. (2008). *The global competitiveness report 2008-2009*. Geneva: World Economic Forum.

Porter, M. E., & Stern, S. (2004). Ranking national innovative capacity: Findings from the national innovative capacity index. In X. Sala-i-Martin (Ed.), *The Global competitiveness report 2003-2004* (pp. 91–116). New York: Oxford University Press.

Porter, M. E., Stern, S., & Green, M. (2015). *Social progress index 2015: Executive summary*. Social Progress Imperative.

Prescott-Allen, R. (2001). *The wellbeing of nations: A country-by-country index of quality of life and the environment*. Washington, DC: Island Press.

Ram, R. (1982). Composite indices of physical quality of life, basic needs fulfilment, and income: A principal component representation. *Journal of Development Economics*, *11*(2), 227–247. doi:10.1016/0304-3878(82)90005-0

Randolph, J. (2001). *G-Index: Globalisation measured. Global Insight*. World Markets Research Center.

Roodman, D. (2008). *The commitment to development index: 2008 edition*. Washington, DC: Center for Global Development.

Saisana, M. (2008). *List of composite indicators*. Retrieved July 23, 2015, from http://composite-indicators. jrc.ec.europa.eu/

Saisana, M., & Tarantola, S. (2002). *State-of-the-art report on current methodologies and practices for composite indicator development*. Joint Research Center, European Commission.

Sbilanciamoci! (2006). *The QUARS: Assessing the quality of development in Italian regions*. Roma: Lunaria.

Schwab, K. (2014). *The global competitiveness report 2014-2015*. Geneva: World Economic Forum.

Singh, R. K., Murty, H. R., Gupta, S. K., & Dikshit, A. K. (2009). An overview of sustainability assessment methodologies. *Ecological Indicators*, *9*(2), 189–212. doi:10.1016/j.ecolind.2008.05.011

Slottje, D. J. (1991). Measuring the quality of life across countries. *The Review of Economics and Statistics*, *73*(4), 684–693. doi:10.2307/2109407

Smith, J. (2003). *Guide to the construction and methodology of the index of economic well-being*. Ottawa: Center for the Study of Living Standards.

Soares, J. Jr, & Quintella, R. H. (2008). Development: An analysis of concepts, measurement and indicators. *Brazilian Administration Review*, *5*(2), 104–124. doi:10.1590/S1807-76922008000200003

Social Indicators Department. (n.d.). *Calculation of composite index of individual living conditions*. Mannheim: Social Indicators Department, Center for Survey Research and Methodology (ZUMA), Leibniz Institute for the Social Sciences (GESIS).

StC. (2008). *State of the world's mothers 2008: Closing the survival gap for children under 5*. Westport, CT: Save the Children.

Stiglitz, J. E., Sen, A. & Fitoussi, J.-P. (2009). *Report by the commission on the measurement of economic performance and social progress*. Academic Press.

Talberth, J., Cobb, C., & Slattery, N. (2007). *The genuine progress indicator 2006: A tool for sustainable development*. Oakland, CA: Redefining Progress.

Tarantola, S., Saisana, M., & Saltelli, A. (2002). *Internal market index 2002: Technical details of the methodology*. European Commission Joint Research Center.

The Economist. (2004). *The economist intelligence unit's quality-of-life index*. Economist Online.

Tsoukalas, S., & Mackenzie, A. (2003). *The personal security index, 2003 - five years later*. Ottawa: Canadian Council on Social Development.

UN. (2015). *Transforming our world: The 2030 agenda for sustainable development*. United Nations.

UN, EC, IMF, OECD, & World Bank. (2003). Handbook of national accounting: integrated environmental and economic accounting 2003. Studies in Methods, Series F, No.61, Rev.1, United Nations, European Commission, International Monetary Fund, Organisation for Economic Co-operation and Development and World Bank.

UNDP. (2001). *Human development report 2001*. New York: Oxford University Press.

UNDP. (2007). *Human development report 2007*. New York: Oxford University Press.

UNU-MERIT. (2009). *European innovation scoreboard 2008: Comparative analysis of innovation performance*. Maastricht Economic and Social Research and Training Center on Innovation and Technology, Inno Metrics, Pro Inno Europe.

Ura, K., Alkire, S., Zangmo, T., & Wangdi, K. (2012). *A short guide to gross national happiness index*. Bhutan: The Center for Bhutan Studies.

Zolotas, X. (1981). *Economic growth and declining social welfare*. New York: New York University Press.

van de Kerk, G., & Manuel, A. (2008). *Sustainable society index SSI-2008*. Netherlands: Sustainable Society Foundation.

White, A. (2007). A global projection of subjective well-being: A challenge to positive psychology? *Psychtalk*, *56*, 17–20.

World Bank. (2006). *Where is the wealth of nations? Measuring capital for the 21st century*. Washington, DC: The World Bank.

ADDITIONAL READING

Atkinson, A. (2015). *Inequality – What can be done?* Cambridge, MA: Harvard University Press. doi:10.4159/9780674287013

Böhringer, C., & Jochemc, P. (2007). Measuring the immeasurable – A survey of sustainability indices. *Ecological Economics*, *63*(1), 1–8. doi:10.1016/j.ecolecon.2007.03.008

Cherchye, L., Ooghe, E., & Puyenbroeck, T. V. (2008). Robust human development rankings. *The Journal of Economic Inequality*, *6*(4), 287–321. doi:10.1007/s10888-007-9058-8

Chowdhury, S., & Squire, L. (2006). Setting weights for aggregate indices: An application to the commitment to development index and human development index. *The Journal of Development Studies*, *42*(5), 761–771. doi:10.1080/00220380600741904

Cobb, C., & Cobb, J. (1994). *The green national product: A proposed index of sustainable economic welfare*. Lanham: University Press of America.

Cobb, C., Halstead, T., & Rowe, J. (1995). *The genuine progress indicator: Summary of data and methodology*. San Francisco: Redefining Progress.

Cohen, A., & Saisana, M. (2014). Quantifying the qualitative: Eliciting expert input to develop the multidimensional poverty assessment tool. *The Journal of Development Studies*, *50*(1), 35–50. doi:10.1080/00220388.2013.849336

Despotis, D. K. (2005). A reassessment of human development index via data envelopment analysis. *The Journal of the Operational Research Society*, *56*(8), 960–980. doi:10.1057/palgrave.jors.2601927

Dreher, A., Gaston, N., & Martens, P. (2008). *Measuring globalization - Gauging its consequences.* New York: Springer.

Ewing, B., Goldfinger, S., Oursler, A., Reed, A., Moore, D., & Wackernagel, M. (2010). *The ecological footprint atlas 2010.* Oakland: Global Footprint Network.

Ferreira, F. (2011). Poverty is multidimensional - But what are we going to do about it? *The Journal of Economic Inequality, 9*(3), 493–495. doi:10.1007/s10888-011-9202-3

Hamilton, C. (2007). Measuring sustainable economic welfare. In G. Atkinson, S. Dietz, & E. Neumayer (Eds.), *Handbook of sustainable development* (pp. 307–317). Cheltenham: Edward Elgar. doi:10.4337/9781847205223.00030

Haughton, J., & Khandker, S. (2009). *Handbook on poverty and inequality.* Washington, D.C.: World Bank Publications.

Mazumbar, K. (2003). A new approach to human development index. *Review of Social Economy, 61*(4), 535–549. doi:10.1080/0034676032000160895

Mayer, A. L. (2008). Strengths and weaknesses of common sustainability indices for multidimensional systems. *Environment International, 34*(2), 277–291. doi:10.1016/j.envint.2007.09.004 PMID:17949813

Nardo, M., Saisana, M., Saltelli, A. E., & Tarantola, S. (2005). *Handbook on constructing composite indicators: Methodology and user guide.* Paris: OECD. doi:10.1787/533411815016

OECD-GPT (2009). *Measuring the progress of societies.* OECD-Global Project Team.

Peichl, A., & Pestel, N. (2010). *Multidimensional measurement of richness: Theory and an application to Germany.* IZA Discussion Paper No. 4825, Institute for the Study of Labor, Bonn.

Roodman, D. (2008). *The commitment to development index: 2008 edition.* Washington, D.C.: Center for Global Development.

Saisana, M. (2004, February). *Composite indicators: A review.* Paper presented at second workshop on composite indicators of country performance, OECD, Paris.

Samimi, P., Lim, G., & Buang, G. (2012). A critical review on synthetic globalization indexes. *International Journal of Fundamental Psychology and Social Science, 2*(1), 28–31.

Siche, J. R., Agostinho, F., Ortega, E., & Romeiro, A. (2008). Sustainability of nations by indices: Comparative study between environmental sustainability index, ecological footprint and the emergy performance indices. *Ecological Economics, 66*(4), 628–637. doi:10.1016/j.ecolecon.2007.10.023

Silber, J. (2007). Measuring poverty: Taking a multidimensional perspective. *Hacienda Pública Espanõla, 182*(3), 29–73.

UNDP. (2014). *Human development report 2014 – Sustaining human progress: Reducing vulnerabilities and building resilience.* New York: Oxford University Press.

Weziak-Bialowolska, D. M., & Dijkstra, L. (2014). *Monitoring multidimensional poverty in the regions of the European Union.* Luxembourg: Publications Office of the European Union.

KEY TERMS AND DEFINITIONS

Composite Indicators of Development or Development Indices: Aggregate a set of indicators into a single index of development and thus are largely multidimensional in nature.

Development: As opposed to economic growth constitutes a complex and multifaceted process of positive change in the wellbeing or the quality of life for individuals and society.

Development Indicators: Designed to capture just one aspect of development, either economic performance or poverty.

GDP: In per capita terms, is the most well-known of the indicators used to gauge standards of living.

HDI: Encompasses health, education, and income indicators for measuring the human development of nations.

Measurement: Means the use of indices and indicators to quantitatively assess a given concept/ phenomenon.

Multidimensionality: Characterizes a concept/phenomenon that can be disaggregated into several dimensions or components for measurement purposes.

ENDNOTES

[1]   A complementary measurement approach consists in assessing the different dimensions of development separately, using a number of indicators for each individual dimension. For instance, the new Sustainable Development Goals, adopted in 2015 to succeed and update the former Millennium Development Goals are a recent United Nations proposal comprising 17 goals, 169 targets, and 304 indicators (UN, 2015).

[2]   Standardization (or z-scores) means a replacement of the observed values of each indicator by the normalized values using the formula:

$$Z_i = \left(X_i - \bar{X} \right) \big/ \sigma \text{ (1)}$$

in which Z_i is the normalized value of the i-th indicator, X_i is the original value of the i-th indicator, $\bar{X}$ represents the average value, and σ the standard deviation.

[3]   Prescott-Allen's (2001) well-being assessment method encompasses six stages: (i) definition of the system and its goals; (ii) identification of the elements for each of the sub-systems (human system and the ecosystem) and their respective objectives; (iii) choice of both indicators that best represent the elements of the system and performance criteria for each indicator; (iv) collection of data and normalization of the indicators; (v) calculation of the four indices (mentioned above); (vi) revision of the results and policy proposals.

[4]   Performance criteria are available in Prescott-Allen, 2001, pp. 300-6.

[5]   Choices made for the different components of the indices at the weighting and aggregation level are summarized in Prescott-Allen, 2001, pp. 310-2.

[6]   [http://www.gnhcentrebhutan.org/], 22 July 2015.

[7]   Recall formula (1) at endnote 2.

Chapter 8
Constructing a Multidimensional Socioeconomic Index and the Validation of It with Early Child Developmental Outcomes

Vijaya Krishnan
University of Alberta, Canada

ABSTRACT

The chapter focuses on the development of a socioeconomic index (SEI) using a Principal Components Analysis (PCA) of 26 variables at the Dissemination Area (DA) level for Alberta. First, the importance of socioeconomic factors in understanding child development outcomes is discussed, addressing the micro-macro level influences. Second, a description of the framework is provided along with the statistical procedures. Third, the results are presented, followed by a discussion of the benefits of having a summary measure in understanding kindergartners' developmental outcomes. The five components of SEI explained 56 per cent of the total variation in the overall index. The SEI patterns across Alberta were examined and the index was validated for its associations to the five domains of early child developmental outcomes, physical, social, emotional, language and cognitive skills, and communication and general knowledge. The index emerged as a strong correlate of all five domains with the strength of relationships varying across developmental domains and geography. A major strength of the procedure presented in the study is that it can be applied to different levels of geography and provides meaningful information to developmental research.

DOI: 10.4018/978-1-5225-0714-7.ch008

INTRODUCTION

A decade or two ago, child development researchers focused on a child's biological characteristics in describing his or her development (Krishnan, 2011). However, in recent years, interest has shifted into a different direction by exploring children's developmental outcomes using a holistic approach. Thus, socioeconomic and cultural factors are incorporated into the research designs along with biological factors as predictors (Evans & Wachs, 2010; Lustig, 2010; Perreia & Smith, 2007; Program Effectiveness Data Analysis Coordinators of Eastern Ontario, 2009). Consequently, there is a growing theoretical and empirical literature making reference to several indicators and application of more sophisticated statistical procedures (e.g., Lee, 2014; Hoff, Laursen, & Bridges, 2012; Moore, Murphy, Bandy, & Lawner, 2014). In contrast, much of the early literature in the early 2000s made use of a composite involving few indicators or a single indicator as a proxy for defining socioeconomic status. In this context, the best-known are the Hollingshead four-factor index of social status (based on householder education and occupation) and the socioeconomic index of occupations (a measure of occupational prestige utilizing education and income data).[1] Researchers have argued that socioeconomic disadvantages (e.g., poverty) of communities and neighborhoods in which children live can be inversely related to such developmental outcomes as school readiness and educational performance (Crosnoe, 2007; Liu & Lu, 2008). Unfortunately however, based on studies of children and youth that appeared in three major journals over the period 1991-2000, researchers found the use of aggregate measures of socioeconomic status as a rare thing (Ensminger & Fothergill, 2003; see also, Hoff et al., 2012). In general, the literature lacks a contextually-based socioeconomic index in order to fully understand inequalities in early child developmental outcomes and a model that links it to the developmental outcome of interest.

This study fills the gap by developing a measure that summarizes multi-dimensional aspects of the socioeconomic conditions in a Canadian province at the Census Dissemination Area (DA) level as it allows for the possibility of comparing developmental outcomes across smaller as well as larger geographic areas in relation to the contexts in which children live. This exercise represents a significant departure from current strategies and the evidence might change the long-standing paradigm that a composite index will do it all; there may be situations where a particular component may be a better correlate of a certain domain of child development than others, and its relationship to development may vary across domains of development and at different geographic levels. Generally speaking, the approach used here in developing the index cannot be thought of as a radical departure from existing methodologies in index construction. However, it is anticipated that the index will add more value, especially when it becomes a generally acceptable yardstick to assess patterns and trends and also to monitor the relative position of communities and/or neighborhoods in developmental outcomes. The index would make it easier for tracking progress over time by developing a new and revised measure, with data collected through Censuses in the future, if necessary.

The chapter is organized as follows: First, the importance of socioeconomic factors in understanding child development outcomes is discussed. Second, the micro-macro level influences of socioeconomic factors on developmental health are outlined. This exercise is intended to make a case for adopting a macro approach in index construction. Third, a brief description of the framework for constructing the index is provided. This will help in rationalizing the use of a Principal Components Analysis (PCA) in order to construct the index. This is followed by a discussion of the computational procedures of the composite index utilizing the PCA approach. Then the results are discussed, both in terms of geographic distribution of the index and its component parts and their relationships to early child development outcome measures. Finally, the chapter concludes with some cautionary remarks on the index to help researchers in their evaluation of the index while highlighting the potential benefits of having a summary measure in understanding kindergartners' developmental outcomes.

SOCIOECONOMIC CONTEXT AS THE BASIS OF HEALTHY CHILD DEVELOPMENT

The 12 broad factors that have been identified by Public Health Agency of Canada (2015) as health determinants are:

1. Income and social status;
2. Social support networks;
3. Education and literacy;
4. Employment/working conditions;
5. Social environments;
6. Physical environments;
7. Personal health practices and coping skills;
8. Healthy child development;
9. Biology and genetic endowment;
10. Health services;
11. Gender; and
12. Culture (see also, Berkman & Kawachi, 2000; Health Canada, 1996).

The 12 factors form the key to conceptualizing health in general. When children's healthy development is considered, most or all of the remaining 11 factors influence and are also influenced by this factor. A detailed description of the 12 factors is beyond the scope of this chapter, and only the factor of healthy child development is the focus of our discussion here.

No doubt, it is important to consider the characteristics of parents and their backgrounds in order to fully understand the relationship between say, standard of living and early child developmental outcomes. For example, parents' own educational status can influence income and the purchasing power or commodity consumption of things like cars and housing. Education may also directly affect parents' awareness, choices and behaviors toward child-related resources and programs, determining children's overall wellbeing. Here, the possibility for an adverse effect of such factors as health problems and/or social discrimination on parents' ability to utilize their education to earn a living cannot be ruled out. In such instances, however, as some would argue (e.g., Fotso & Kuate-defo, 2005; Reed, Habicht, & Niameogo, 1996), quality child-care programs can at least partially mitigate the adverse effect of poor economic circumstances. At a community or neighborhood level, a higher proportion of educated individuals may translate into better services and programs available to children. In the paragraphs that follow, we discuss our rationale for a focus on a socioeconomic index at the contextual level through an examination of both micro- and macro-level factors. It is not the intention however, to question the choice of micro-level variables in any given analysis or to demonstrate that one level of measurement, say macro is superior to micro.

The Micro- and Macro-Level Influences of Socioeconomic Factors on Health

Theoretically speaking, a variable, such as wealth could influence health-outcomes differently, based on how it is being perceived and at what level it is being measured. For example, car-ownership reflects a different picture of wealth than that of homeownership, but both contribute to an understanding of a person's and, thereby an area's wealth. The interactions between two measures of a concept, such as wealth is also worthy of interest.

The reasons for differences in relationships to an outcome variable health, measured at two measurement levels can be due to, among other things, differences in size or nature of the geographic unit under consideration, and the conception(s) of variables themselves. There are evidences to suggest that the relationships between health outcomes and socioeconomic backgrounds are stronger when they are measured at the individual-level (e.g., Geronimus & Bound, 1998; Pampalon, Hamel, & Gamache, 2009). At the same time, there are evidences to suggest that the magnitude of relationships can be similar in both instances, for the entire or a sub-group of the population (e.g., Davey Smith & Hart, 1999; Subramanian, Chen, Rehkopf, Waterman, & Krieger, 2006). In addition to such conflicting evidences, one of the consistent arguments among researchers in general is that the two measurement levels of socioeconomic status do not reflect the same reality, and are based on different constructs, explaining the impact on the outcome variable differently and with varying strengths.

A study in the US by Steenland, Henley, Calle, and Thun (2004) examined the differences in the predictive value of socioeconomic status variables, measured at micro- and macro-levels, on mortality. Both types of variables, as the authors argued, acted through a complex array of intermediate risk factors, including the more conventional ones, such as smoking as well as factors affecting access to and quality of care. In their own words:

The fact that area-level socioeconomic status variables continue to retain some predictive power for vascular disease mortality even after adjustment for individual-level socioeconomic status variables would suggest either that they are capturing residual confounding at the individual level not fully controlled by individual-level socioeconomic status, or that ecologic variables themselves in fact have independent predictive power because they are capturing community-wide factors that influence mortality (e.g., access to medical care, stress resulting from community-wide poverty). (p. 1055)

A study in Canada by Mustard, Derksen, Berthelot, & Wolfson (1999) found the variations associated with income deciles as similar at the individual and area-based levels for all health outcomes, including, mortality, disability, and nursing home admissions), except for disability and the prevalence of mental health problems. As Pampalon et al., (2009) have noted, it is safer to conclude that, area-level socioeconomic status, not only reflects the characteristics of a population, but also of the physical and social contexts to which people belong.

Whether or not individual level variables exert a different relationship to health outcomes than area-level variables, and whether or not they are measured by one or many indicators, they can serve as a proxy for area-level socioeconomic conditions. Although it is convenient to split up micro and macro variables and also their impacts on a construct like socioeconomic status, we can conclude that it is to some extent an artificial divide and there is no clear distinction between the two because micro impacts macro and vice versa. For example, if individuals' income rises, there is a micro impact on the family/household, labor force, and economy. But, labor force (supply and demand) and economy are also macro variables that can influence macro-level policies and programs. However, it is to be mentioned that the type of aggregation bias (referred to as ecological fallacy) is common and unavoidable in situations where there is a shift from one level to another. The inclusion of both levels of socioeconomic variables or proxies of them cannot be as easy as one would think in any single study, because of lack of data, and this may probably explain the over-whelming use of just one level of variables, mostly area-level (Ackerman & Brown, 2010; Kershaw, Irwin, Trafford, & Hertzman, 2005; Lalloue et al., 2013). There is now a renewed interest in developmental studies to control area-level socioeconomic indicators in order to take care of the variations in different stressors, environmental/ecological in nature, on families and children. Such designs have revealed proportionately large numbers of developmentally at-risk children in socially and economically disadvantaged areas (Evans, 2004; 2006).

Making the Case for a Contextually-Based Socioeconomic Index (SEI)

Ideally, to measure any single concept, we need many variables, preferably both qualitative and quantitative, and also of some kind of relationships among variables, positive or negative. However, it is not only relevant, but also necessary to use quantitative data to draw policy conclusions, mainly because of cost-effectiveness. In particular, as earlier stated, since individuals' incomes can alter areas' incomes, area-level SEI can be equally important as individual-level SEI in explaining most health status variables, especially children's developmental domains.

In the absence of individual-level measures which are not routinely collected, in order to describe the social context of health, some researchers use just a single macro variable, such as poverty, education, or occupation (e.g., Perreira & Smith, 2007), while some others use a combination of a smaller number of several variables, such as housing, income, and occupation to create indices of the overall socioeconomic condition (Braveman et al., 2005; Diez-Roux, 2003). It is to be noted that the availability of aggregate and small area data through national censuses, especially in Europe and North America in the past two decades, resulted in the creation of numerous area-based indices. They are created from a variety of socioeconomic and demographic variables and are variously termed as, *socioeconomic deprivation index*, *index of multiple deprivation*, *human economic hardship*, or *healthy communities index*, to name a few (British Columbia, 2009; Canadian Institute for Health Information, 2005; Davis et al., 1999; Eibner & Sturm, 2006; Fukuda, Nakamura, & Takano, 2007; Pampalon & Raymond, 2000). Unfortunately, however, the variability in their approaches to compute indices, and the lack of conceptual frameworks linking such indices to health outcomes, make it a challenge to systematically assess their validity in developmental research. Moreover, as earlier noted, there is little or no evidence to suggest how different components of a composite index are associated to different outcomes of children's development. A single index summarizing the complex circumstances where children live, not only allows comparisons across groups of children with different developmental trajectories, but also helps to validate developmental theories, such as Bronfenbrenner's (1977) bio-ecological model of child development (see, Krishnan, 2010 for a conceptual framework of child development).

More specifically, there are at least three main reasons guiding this work. First, individual socioeconomic characteristics are not routinely collected or are difficult to obtain. By contrast, contextual data are easier to retrieve from existing databases and are cost-effective. Second, the increase in available information on demographic, economic, social and cultural variables reinforces the need for quantifying complex concepts such as socioeconomic status and assessing their impacts on population health for theoretical reasons. Third, a summary statistic, consolidating data that have already been collected can be extremely useful for policymakers to monitor changes, both in absolute and relative terms over time and across areas, reducing the burden of cost. Such a statistic could help to further illuminate the relationship between children's health and contextual factors by highlighting instances where intervention may be most needed, and thereby prioritize budget allocations.

It follows from our discussion above that the goal is to present a procedure for developing a composite socioeconomic index, derived from small area statistics, using many aspects that reflect the complex nature of the Canadian society (e.g., income, education, housing, and ethnicity). And, in order to assess the predictive ability and thereby generalizability, the index and its parts are analyzed in terms of their relationships to early child developmental outcome measures at different levels of geography.

Prior to providing a framework for developing a composite SEI, however, some thought should be devoted to the idea of constructing a composite index utilizing the various domains of child development. Although, in this chapter, we consider the development of SEI only, a reference to the child development index might provide an evidence base about how the methodology adopted here can contribute to the improvement of both the practice and science of a child development index. Indeed, the same methodology in constructing the composite SEI can be easily adapted to developing a child development index or child well-being index. The interested reader can find a detailed discussion on the construction of a composite called the School Preparedness Index (SPI) in Krishnan (2011). In brief, for SPI, the author used the Canadian Early Child Development Instrument (EDI) data to develop a single index comprised of the five core developmental domains or dimensions-physical health and wellbeing, social competence, emotional maturity, language and cognitive development, and anxiety and fearfulness- using PCA and a weighting system. According to the author, the very idea of incorporating the domains of EDI into a composite index has the potential to elucidate significant differences of developmental performances in preschoolers across communities. More specifically, by having a composite index, progress can be measured, monitored, and regularly debated and reviewed by policymakers and program planners. Additionally, this can lead to efforts at various levels and also aligning various stakeholders or agencies to standardize the data collection procedures so that progress in outcome measures can be monitored and tracked against a benchmark. Yet, such a summary index can be criticized on the ground that the indicators of development, especially that of children, change quickly over time and space, rendering current indicators useless in the future (Krishnan, 2011). Generally speaking, efforts to construct composite indices of child and youth well-being are in their infancy (Lamb & Land, 2013).[2] As a result, it is inappropriate to give further explanation on this topic, especially when our major goal is to develop a composite index of SEI that encompassed different contextual factors.

CONSTRUCTION OF THE SOCIOECONOMIC INDEX: A PRINCIPAL COMPONENTS ANALYSIS APPROACH

The basic steps involved in constructing the index are shown in Figure 1. Each of these steps is discussed in more detail in the sections that follow.

Data and Variables

The composite SEI was based on the 2006 Census of Canada data for the province of Alberta, supplied by the University of Alberta's data library. The index relates to the socioeconomic conditions in an area,

Figure 1. The Socioeconomic Index (SEI) algorithm

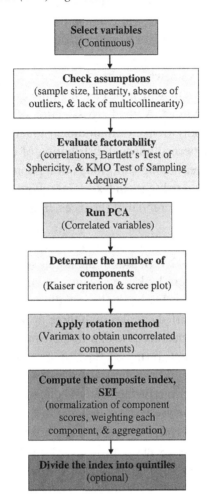

the smallest of which is the Dissemination Area (DA). The data covered 5,222 DAs in Alberta. 2006 Census was the latest available and most reliable source of information for analyzing many household characteristics at a small area level, at the time the index was developed. The three main reasons for using DA as the spatial unit of analysis were as follows. A DA is: the smallest unit where there are no substantial issues with confidentiality of information on characteristics of persons, families, and dwellings; the smallest standard geographic area for which all census data are disseminated; and a stable geographic unit that is composed of one or more adjacent dissemination blocks, so that a comparison of an up-dated index utilizing the most recent census data can be done easily.

In general, commonly used variables in socioeconomic index construction are: education, income (disparity), occupation, unemployment rate, poverty rate, value of home, single parent households, household crowding/ratio of number of people to the number of rooms, homeownership, language proficiency, race/ethnicity, foreign-born, residential instability, health, and crime (Fukuda, Nakamura, & Takano, 2007; Havard, Deguen, Bodin, Louis, & Laurent, 2008; Messer et.al., 2008; Pampalon et al., 2009; Singh, Miller, & Hankey, 2002; Vyas & Kumaranayake, 2006; Zagorski, 1985).[3] Before we proceed to discuss the variables involved in the index, it is important to recognize the fact that there exists no general rule or consensus about the number of variables needed, the type of statistical procedures, and/or the assumptions underlying such procedures. Therefore, our computation of the index is primarily based on, such aspects as data availability, good judgment, or some evidence of a relationships between variables and their underlying constructs (components, in this case), and developmental outcome measures. In many instances, the choice of variables is somewhat arbitrary.

Our goal was to identify variables by which we can, not only explain, but also map socioeconomic inequalities by different geographic units. A good cross-section of socioeconomic, demographic, and cultural variables were included not only to ensure a multidimensional design in unraveling socioeconomic inequities but also to reflect the patterned unequal distribution of infrastructure, resources, economic opportunities, advantages, and power among sub-groups of a population. Regardless of how they are being presented, classified or categorized (e.g., index scores, quintiles, high-medium-low), distinct socioeconomic groupings, may exhibit differential life chances, living standards and cultural and/or ethnic values and practices among Canadians.

Based on literature search, 26 theoretically important and policy-relevant variables were chosen for the present study out of a total of 42 variables in the initial selection.[4] In some instances, different computations of the same variable were looked at, mainly to choose the variable with the minimum number of missing cases and/or outliers. For example, initially, 'proportion of all couples with three or more children' and 'proportion of married couples with three or more children' were both considered, but only the second variable was retained because this variable had fewer missing values. It is possible that due to language barriers, immigrants from non-English-speaking countries are more likely to hold low-paying jobs, and thereby socially and economically disadvantaged. Although this variable was in our original selection, it was dropped from further analysis due to a large number of missing values. A description of variables used in the analyses is provided in Table 1.

Notwithstanding the complexities involved in explaining the role of each and every variable included in the study, a brief discussion of variables, age dependency ratio, public transit use, unpaid housework, and in-migration rate seems important. A comprehensive review of previous work is not within the scope of this chapter, but some of the key findings utilizing these variables are briefly noted. The importance of age dependency ratio in understanding socioeconomic inequities can be debatable and one could argue that in many populations, neither all nor most people do not stop being economically active after age 65, nor all persons aged 15-64 are economically active. However, age dependency ratio was included in the analysis based on the assumption that as populations age, increases in old-age dependency ratios in particular, are likely to cause added pressures on the social security as well as public health systems, especially in countries like Canada.

The important role that a public transit system can play in generating job accessibility for socially disadvantaged workers was noted by Foth, Manaugh, & El-Geneidy (2013). In their study utilizing census tract level socio-economic characteristics in the Toronto region, Foth et al. (2013) examined the relationships to social disadvantage of such factors as accessibility to jobs and transit travel time over a ten-year period, 1996-2006. The authors found the most socially disadvantaged census tracts as having better accessibility and thereby lower transit travel times relative to the rest of the region. In another context, Boschmann (2011) argued that, workers select home locations based on transportation, not work location, because modes of and time for travel could dictate their ability to reach work places. Although the direction of relationship between public transit use and socioeconomic status is difficult to predict, it can be argued that public transit use can impact quality of life, environment, health, activity patterns, accessibility, and social inclusion, to name a few. Further, on the basis of some previous stud-

Table 1. Definition of variables in Socioeconomic Index (SEI)

Variable	Description
1. Age dependency ratio[⊗]	Population aged under 15 or 65+ to population aged 15-64
2. Children under 5 years of age[ε]	Population aged 0-4 in the total population
3. Children 3+[ε]	Couple families married with 3 or more children
4. Divorced/Separated	Population 15 or older divorced/separated
5. Lone parents[ε]	Lone-parent families in Census families
6. Unattached elderly[ε]	Population aged 65 or older living alone
7. Dwelling size	Number of rooms per dwelling
8. Dwelling value[ε]	Value of owner-occupied private, non-farm/reserved dwelling
9. Owned house[ε]	Owner occupied private dwellings
10. House with major repair[ε]	Owner occupied private dwellings in need of major repair
11. Median income€	Median income in 2005 of population aged 15 or older
12. Income disparity[£]	Families with less than <$20000 or those with at least $50000
13. Low income[ε]	Economic families with a low income after tax in 2005
14. Government transfer[ε]	Government transfer payments in 2005 for all economic families
15. Unemployment rate[£]	Population 15 or older unemployed
16. Female participation rate[⊗]	Females 15 or older in the labour force
17. Education[ε]	Population aged 15 or older with no cert/diploma/degree
18. Managerial/Prof occupation[ε]	Population 15 or older in managerial or professional occupations
19. Immigrant[ε]	Recent immigrants in the population
20. Indian/Métis/Inuit [ε]	Population identified as Indian/Métis/Inuit
21. In-migration rate [ε]	In-migration rate
22. Unpaid housework [ε]	Population 15 or older doing 60+ hours unpaid work
23. Unpaid childcare [ε]	Population 15 or older doing 60+ hours unpaid childcare
24. British/French ethnicity[ε]	Population with British or French ethnic background
25. Foreign born[ε]	Population born outside of Canada
26. Public transit[ε]	Employed persons aged 15 or older using public transit

Source: Statistics Canada, 2006 Census.

[⊗]Reflect and square root transformation formula: New variable=SQRT (K-Old variable) where K= largest possible value +1.

[ε]Natural log transformation: New variable=Ln(1+Old variable).

[£]Log 10 transformation: New variable=Log_{10}(Old variable).

Note: All variables are in percentages, with the exception of dwelling size, dwelling value, and median income. The first two are in averages.

ies (e.g., Laroche, Toffoli, Kim, & Muller, 1996), it is safer to conclude that, at a micro-level, engaging in environmentally-friendly behaviors (e.g., use of public transportation or reducing the use of car fuel consumption) can have some relationship with culture.

Regardless of the fact that the gap between men's and women's performance of domestic work has narrowed, although only slightly, a greater share of housework like caregiving and domestic work in Canada continues to be performed by women (Marshall, 2006). Subsistence and/or survival-based activities (e.g., the cultivation of vegetables and the care of livestock animals) is another type of unpaid work performed predominantly by women and are vital to their livelihoods, especially in rural areas of Canada. According to Teitelbaum and Beckley (2006), in Canadian rural communities, subsistence activities (e.g., farming) are important not solely due to economic necessity; these also form part of communities' cultural identity, heritage and survival. Undoubtedly, men's and women's rates and patterns of participation in unpaid house work, could have an impact on their labour force status, age, and household composition, consequently impacting the socioeconomic landscape of families and communities.

Okonny-Myers (2010, p. 2) noted that,

... based on the population of immigrants who filed taxes in 2006, in a province other than the one to which they were originally destined, Alberta registered the highest proportional in-migration rate with 37% more immigrants moving in than were destined there. This was reflective of the mobility in the general population and this finding was echoed in a report by Statistics Canada which stated that in 2006, Alberta posted a record high net interprovincial migration.

This translated into a positive net change rate (in-migration minus out-migration) of 18 per cent (p.4), changing the socio-cultural landscape of Alberta.

Framework for Developing Composite Indices

As earlier noted, a number of indices have been developed around the globe over the years, and they include, *Duncan's index* that classifies occupation based on education and income (Oakes & Rossi, 2003), *Townsend's index* that explains health in terms of material deprivation (Morris & Castairs, 1991), and the *Living Conditions Index* that measures inequities in housing, health, etc. (Boelhouwer & Stoop, 1999; see also, Fotso & Kuate-defo, 2005 and Krishnan, 2015). The development of an index can be typically based on judgements or statistical procedures or both. Our computation procedures of the composite index were based within the context of PCA.

The Use of a Principal Components Analysis to Extract Components

Factor Analysis (FA) is a widely used statistical procedure in the behavioral and social sciences that allows a researcher to observe a group of variables that are correlated to one another and also to identify the underlying dimensions that make these correlations. There is a general consensus that FA is preferable to PCA mainly because it can come up with the least number of factors or dimensions which can account for the common variance shared by a set of variables with the factors reflecting the common variance of the variables, excluding unique (variable-specific) variance. Theoretically, the most important distinction between FA and PCA is that PCA is not a model based technique and involves no hypothesis or it does not involve the examination of interdependence between components.[5] FA, on the other hand, is a model based technique that involves interdependence between factors. It takes into account the relationships between many indicators, latent factors, and error. Also, FA is believed to generate consistent results mainly because of its recognition of error. In short, FA has the ability to show unique variance and has the ability to estimate error apart from shared variance, whereas PCA identifies all variance equally without regard to types of variance, shared, unique, and error (see Hooper, 2012 for a detailed discussion on FA and Beavers, et al., 2013 for practical considerations when employing factor analytic procedures).

Although PCA is often attributed to Hotelling (1933), the earliest description of it was given by Pearson (1901). PCA is a useful technique that extracts all the factors (components) underlying a set of variables and transforms a large number of variables into a smaller and more coherent set of uncorrelated (orthogonal) factors, called the principal components. In other words, it redistributes all variance into orthogonal components. The principal components account for much of the variance among the original variables with each component being a linear weighted combination of the initial measured variables. The weights for each principal component are given by the eigenvectors of the correlation matrix or the covariance matrix, when the data were standardized. The components are ordered and mathematically precise so that the first component accounts for the largest possible amount of variation, the second component is completely uncorrelated with the first component, and accounts for the maximum variation that is not accounted for by the first, and the third accounts for the maximum that the first and the second not accounted for and so on. The variance in the data accounted for by a component is represented by the eigenvalue of the corresponding eigenvector.

A major step in conducting PCA is rotation. Once the number of components is determined, the next step is to interpret them. The two approaches to rotation are orthogonal (uncorrelated) and oblique (correlated), where the orthogonal results in solutions that are easier to interpret (Tabachnick & Fidell, 2007). Within the two approaches, there are a number of rotational strategies: in orthogonal, varimax, quartimax, and equamax and in oblique, direct oblimin and promax. In general, the goal in utilizing a rotation strategy is to obtain a clear and simple pattern of high loadings for some variables and low for others so that the clusters of variables become less subjective (the factor loadings refer to the correlations between the variables and the factors.). A commonly used orthogonal approach is varimax, which is a variance maximizing strategy that maximizes the variance (variability) of the factor (component). Put another way, it aims to obtain a pattern of loadings on each component that is as diverse as possible. To repeat what we said earlier, the defining characteristic that distinguishes between FA and PCA is that, PCA uses all the variance in the observed variables without regard to the underlying structure, while FA recognizes both shared and unique variances and hypothesizes that a structure underlies the variables. In most situations, it is likely that the two procedures produce virtually similar results. Again, whereas PCA is a preferred method for data reduction while preserving the dimensions of the data with fewer components, FA is a preferred method for detecting structure.

In sum, in the absence of individual level variables, the approach of constructing area-based socioeconomic indices built from weights derived from PCA have the potential to understand socioeconomic disparities with readily available data that are comprehensive.[6] Unlike other approaches, PCA is not only computationally easy but also avoids many of the problems associated with the traditional methods, such as aggregation, standardization, and nonlinear relationships of variables influencing socioeconomic environments. In fact, Krishnan (2015) used three different approaches, PCA, Range Equalization (RE), and Division by Mean (DM) to assess the impact of different methods of weighting and standardization procedures on a composite called the Living Conditions Index (LCI). Between the two methods, the RE method was found better because it accounted for larger variations and stronger correlations to the PCA composite. Generally speaking, however, the PCA method appeared promising, particularly for cross-community comparisons as it is based on a weighting scheme.[7]

Identifying Outliers and Assessing Linearity and Normality

A number of issues related to the data being analyzed need to be considered when attempting a factor analysis (see, Nardo, Saisana, Saltelli, & Tarantola, 2005). These assumptions are outlined in the context of parametric tests in almost all statistical textbooks and SPSS manuals, but are often given little attention by researchers when developing composite indices, based on PCA. Although sample size, variable scaling (interval vs. categorical), and relevancy of sub-indicators that measure underlying dimensions are important assumptions in the application of PCA, in our context, however, we felt no need to discuss them because none of these assumptions pertain to our data; all variables were measured at the interval-level and they were the only variables included in the input for PCA.[8]

The presence of outliers can affect factor analysis results and their interpretations; outliers or values that are substantially lower/ higher than other values in the data set can impact correlations and thus distort PCA results. Therefore, they were checked using such SPSS procedures as the histogram or the actual shape of the distribution, normal Q-Q plot where the observed value for each score is plotted against the expected value, the box-plot of the distribution of scores, and the descriptive statistics (e.g., mean and 5% trimmed mean). Outliers are defined by the SPSS procedure as points that lay more than 1.5 box-lengths from the edge of the box. However, for our purposes, only the extreme points, those that extend more than three box-lengths (in most instances, two or three values) were detected in all variables and were removed before performing PCA.[9]

The use of a factor analysis assumes the relationship between variables as linear.[10] It is often tedious to check scatterplots of all variables with all others in a data-set, especially when the analysis is performed using a large number of variables. If two variables behave in a non-linear fashion, the correlation coefficient can bias the strength of the relationship. However, the problem can be critical when dealing with small samples.[11] Twenty variables, with the exception of six variables were transformed statistically, using such transformations as reflect and square root, natural logarithm or $\log_{10}$, after inspecting the nature or skewness of the distribution (Table 1).[12] The type of transformation recommended by Tabachnick and Fidell's (2007) was utilized (see also, Pallant, 2007 for a graphical representation of scores and suggested transformations). After removing the extreme values and performing the necessary transformations, the means and trimmed means were found very similar, indicating that there is no cause for further concern in terms of extreme cases (Table 2)[13].

In addition, descriptive statistics, such as skewness (a measure of symmetry) and kurtosis (a measure of 'peakedness') were used to detect the type of distribution. The results showed extremely small positive or negative values, providing a further validation of symmetry (Table 2). Despite having a large sample size, we inspected the shape of the distribution.[14] Additionally, two statistical measures, generated by SPSS were used to assess the factorability of the data. They are the Barlett's Test of Sphericity (Bartlett, 1954) that compares the observed correlation matrix to the identity matrix and the Kaiser-Meyer-Olkin (KMO) measure of sampling adequacy (Kaiser, 1970; 1974) that is indicative of whether or not we can factorize the observed variables efficiently. The results are presented in Table 3, and will be discussed in the next section.

Testing the Appropriateness of a Principal Components Analysis (PCA)

Recall that PCA does not rely on assumptions or hypotheses or it is not based on a model set *a priori*, like FA. In order for the PCA to yield meaningful results, the variables in the data set have to be related

Table 2. Descriptive statistics of variables in Socioeconomic Index (SEI)

Variable	Mean	5% Trimmed Mean	Skewness	Kurtosis	Range
Age dependency ratio	4.40	4.32	0.35	-0.68	8.92
Children under 5 years of age	1.85	1.86	-0.25	0.29	2.42
Children 3+	2.48	2.48	-0.24	-0.20	2.69
Divorced/Separated	2.38	2.40	-0.52	0.21	2.64
Lone parents	2.76	2.76	0.02	-0.62	2.77
Unattached elderly	3.44	3.43	-0.08	-0.44	2.63
Dwelling size	7.05	7.07	-0.26	0.90	2.15
Dwelling value	12.43	12.43	0.15	0.60	3.22
Owned house	4.27	4.33	-2.52	7.51	3.38
House with major repair	2.26	2.25	0.36	0.68	3.95
Median income	10.25	10.25	-0.26	0.90	2.15
Income disparity	0.21	0.19	0.65	0.78	2.05
Low income	2.48	2.46	-0.45	-0.17	3.04
Government transfer	2.13	2.14	-0.23	-0.07	3.71
Unemployment rate	0.70	0.70	0.61	0.85	1.55
Female participation rate	5.73	5.73	0.03	0.24	7.65
Education	3.14	3.16	-0.52	0.46	3.26
Managerial/Professional occupation	2.82	2.83	-0.24	-0.42	2.97
Immigrant	1.70	1.67	0.60	-0.39	3.13
Indian/Métis/Inuit	1.84	1.78	1.18	1.94	4.12
In- migration rate	3.67	3.69	-0.37	-0.46	3.39
Unpaid housework	1.78	1.76	0.60	0.27	3.20
Unpaid childcare	2.14	2.15	-0.07	-0.23	3.08
British/French ethnicity	3.63	3.66	-3.21	15.97	3.15
Foreign born	2.58	2.59	-0.18	-0.77	3.32
Public transit	2.51	2.52	-0.38	-0.56	3.29

Note: The statistics are based on the transformed variables wherever a transformation was necessary.

Table 3. KMO Measure of Sampling Adequacy (MSA) and Bartlett's Test of Sphericity

KMO Measure of Sampling Adequacy	Bartlett's Test of Sphericity		
	Chi-Square	df	Sig
0.857	17087.394	325	0.00

to one another. If the correlations between variables are large enough, the analysis is of some value and the variables share common components.[15] Therefore, before being submitted to a factor analysis (PCA, in this case), the correlations were checked. To test the correlations, the Bartlett's Test of Sphericity was conducted (Table 3).[16] The results of our analysis showed a significance level of 0.00, a value that is small enough to reject the hypothesis (the probability should be less than 0.05 to reject the null). It can be concluded that the strength of the relationship among the observed variables is strong or the correlation matrix is not an identity matrix as is required by PCA to be considered as a viable procedure.

Further, the data were checked for multicollinearity, that is, whether or not the variables are too closely linked in some way; a simple correlation between two variables, for example, if ± 0.9, the variables can be nearly equal and problematic. Multicollinearity could increase the standard error of factor loadings, making them less reliable and also difficult to label. There are some who either combine collinear variables or eliminate them prior to factor analysis. Some others forgo factor analysis altogether. In the present study, KMO, a Measure of Sampling Adequacy (MSA) was used to detect multicollinearity in the data so that the appropriateness of carrying out a PCA can be detected. More specifically, sampling adequacy predicts if data are likely to factor well, based on (partial) correlations. In reality, the KMO measure compares the magnitudes of the observed correlation coefficients to the magnitudes of the partial correlation coefficients. If the variables, in fact, have common factors, the partial correlation coefficients should be small, compared to the total correlation coefficient. For our data, it was 0.857, signaling that it is okay to proceed with a PCA of the variables (Table 3).[17] These diagnostic procedures indicated the appropriateness of PCA for the data.

From Observed Variables to Principal Components and then to a Composite

The 26 variables in Table 1 were included in the analyses. Since the correlation matrix is the standardized version of the covariance matrix, and because the variables were not standardized, the correlation matrix was used as an input to PCA to extract the components. The results from PCA were used to calculate the composite index as a linear combination of components. In order to identify the number of components that best represented the data or to check whether the components were statistically well-balanced, the correlations (so-called loadings) between the individual variables and their underlying component were examined. We started with oblimin rotation because it can provide information about the degree of correlation between the components. However, only the results from the orthogonal (varimax rotation) were used since our goal was to obtain a clear pattern of loadings, and more importantly, as we had stated earlier, varimax rotation gives a simple structure with unrelated components that are easy to interpret.

The number of factors extracted can be defined by the user, and there are techniques available in SPSS that can be used to help decide the number of factors. One of the most commonly used techniques is Kaiser's criterion, or the eigenvalue rule. Under the specified rule, only those components with an eigenvalue (the variances extracted by the factors) of 1.0 or more were retained. Using this criterion, our data revealed eight components in the first instance. We employed a graphical method, known as the Catell's (1966) scree test, as well.[18] After examining the screeplot, only five factors were needed to be extracted because a sharp change in slope was noticed after the fifth eigenvalue. The results from PCA are presented in Table 4.

Table 4. Results of Principal Components Analysis (PCA): Varimax rotation factor matrix

Variable	Component				
	1	**2**	**3**	**4**	**5**
Age Dependency ratio		0.839			
Children under 5 years of age					0.782
Children 3+				0.437	
Divorced/Separated		0.653			
Lone parents		0.518			
Unattached elderly		0.579			
Dwelling Size		-0.768			
Dwelling value	-0.738				
Owned house		-0.810			
House with major repair				0.629	
Median income	-0.726				
Income disparity	0.734				
Low income		0.491			
Government transfer	0.843				
Unemployment rate				0.570	
Female participation rate					-0.478
Education	0.748				
Managerial/Professional Occupation	-0.694				
Immigrant			0.573		
Indian/Métis/Inuit				0.629	
In-migration rate		-0.464			
Unpaid housework				0.555	
Unpaid childcare					0.699
British/French ethnicity			-0.647		
Foreign born			0.804		
Public transit			0.472		
Percent of variance (55.69%)	**16.25%**	**14.68%**	**9.15%**	**8.92%**	**6.69%**

Note: A variable with a positive loading indicates a negative association to the component and *vice versa*. Some variables needed adjustment later on to ease our interpretation. For instance, income disparity has a positive loading to the component it belongs. Therefore, this variable was reversed to mean that, the *lower* the disparity, the *better* the economic situation.

RESULTS FROM PRINCIPAL COMPONENTS ANALYSIS

The Five Components Resulting from the Principal Components Analysis

According to the set criteria (varimax rotation), the 26 variables were correlated with five components that were uncorrelated, which accounted for 55.7 per cent of the total variance. The first component accounted for 16.3 per cent of the total variation. For this component, income disparity, government transfer payments, and education showed markedly higher positive loadings, while dwelling value, median income, and occupation showed strong negative factor loadings.[19] A negative loading simply means that the results need to be interpreted in a different fashion; to avoid any confusion in the interpretation of relationships between variables and their underlying components, a reversal of signs can be done (see, note to Table 4). For example, since areas with a large proportion of expensive houses is an indication of richness, the negative sign on this variable means the higher the value of housing, the better the economic situation. The first component is a reasonable representation of the economic system. It means that better economic circumstances are associated with high dwelling value, high median income, and high percentage of population in managerial/professional occupations, and low income disparity, low government transfer payments, and low percentage of population with no certificate/diploma/degree. For the second component, age dependency ratio, divorced/separated, unattached elderly, lone parents, and low income showed strong positive loadings and dwelling size, owned house, and in-migration rate showed strong negative loadings. The component accounted for 14.7 per cent of the variance. We may interpret this factor as a measure of the social system. The study by Fukuda et al., (2007) in Japan found similar negative loadings for variables, dwelling size, income, and owned houses and positive loadings for unemployment rate and aged single dwellings in their study.

The third component accounted for 9.2 per cent of the variations and explains the variations in recent immigrants, British/French ethnicity, foreign-born population, and public transit. This is a measure of the cultural system because three out of the four cultural variables loaded high on this factor. The fourth component accounted for 8.9 per cent of the variance and explains the variations in house with major repair, Indian/Métis/Inuit, unemployment rate, unpaid housework, and couples with three or more children. The interpretation of this component or the labeling of it is less straightforward. However, the variables are indicative of some kind of vulnerability within the population or the component may be labelled as vulnerability. The fifth component accounted for 6.7 per cent of the variance explaining the differences in children under age five, unpaid child care, and female labor force participation. This component was labelled as child care for our purposes.

The Overall Socioeconomic Index and Component-Specific Indices

Building a composite index involves the use of a number of constituent parts or factors, which together represent an overall idea. For our purpose, the component-specific indices and the overall SEI were computed using the methodology described in Nardo et al., (2005). Specifically, the component scores were normalized and then aggregated to enable an overall comparison. That is, to make data comparable, the data were normalized using the equation: (actual value – minimum value)/ (maximum-minimum) where minimum and maximum values were, respectively, the lowest and highest values in the 5,222 DAs for any given variable. The normalized value was then transformed into a positive number on a scale of 0 to 100. A high value on a component thus meant greater SEI, with the vulnerability factor being an exception.

In order to construct component-specific indices and also the overall index SEI, a weighting scheme was applied, which in effect can correct for overlapping information between two or more correlated variables.[20] The five elements of the composite SEI were made stand-alone. First, a grouping of all individual variables (normalized values) with the loadings that are reported in Table 4 was done to develop components.[21] For instance, the first component, *economic system* was formed by grouping the six variables. The five components were then aggregated by assigning a weight to each one of them equal to the proportion of the explained variance in the data. For example, the weight for the first component was calculated as 0.29=16.25/55.69 (see Table 4). Thus, the aggregated SEI was calculated as a linear combination of the five component-specific scores with their normalized values.

The Five Levels of the Socioeconomic Index: Socioeconomic Status (SES)

Because we were interested in comparing the socioeconomic patterns at different levels of geography, we constructed the quintiles using the SEI scores for DAs and classified the 5222 DAs into five categories of Socioeconomic Status (referred to as SES), of approximately equal numbers of DAs within. Our decision to classify SEI into quintiles was based on Statistics Canada's approach. More specifically, Statistics Canada classifies income information into increasing levels, from the poorest to the richest, and divides into five groups, known as "quintiles," each representing 20 per cent of all families. The first quintile comprises the poorest families and the last quintile includes the richest. Once the quintiles are formed, the income of the families in each quintile is calculated in proportion to the income of all families. The percentage of income going to each group is also measured, and such a classification has been used to assess stability over time. It is important to note that, income has been found very stable over the past 30 years in Canada or the share of income going to each quintile has varied only slightly.

For our purpose, SES is being used to describe how an area's social hierarchy is structured, arrived at from quintiles (1=Low or least advantaged, 2=Medium low, 3=Medium, 4=Medium high, and 5=High or most advantaged). Our hypothesis is that the SEI distribution cannot be uniform across Alberta. This will become more clear when we examine the SES's five levels. For instance, the index values can be skewed to the left for urban areas and skewed to the right for rural areas. If the index is uniformly distributed, the difference in mean socioeconomic score between adjacent quintiles should be even. However, the difference in means between the fourth and fifth groups was found higher than any other adjoining quintile (Table 5).

Levene's test for homogeneity of variances was used to test whether the variance in scores is the same for each of the five SES groups.[22] The results of our analysis showed a significance level of 0.000, a value that is small enough to reject the hypothesis. Consistent with the assumption that the probability should be less than 0.05 to reject the null, the DAs demonstrated considerable socioeconomic variability.

Table 5. Mean standardized Socioeconomic Index (SEI) scores by quintile

Quintile	Mean	SD	95% CI
1	38.022	9.645	(37.44, 38.61)
2	52.219	2.298	(52.08, 52.36)
3	59.069	1.752	(58.96, 59.18)
4	65.643	2.104	(65.52, 65.77)
5	75.981	5.187	(75.67, 76.30)
Total	58.187	13.768	(57.81, 58.56)

Levene statistic: 639.02; df1 = 4; df2 = 5217; Sig = 0.000.

Patterns of Socioeconomic Index by Geography across Alberta

A major purpose of this section is to outline the facets of SEI across Alberta. More specifically, the intent is to present the results of an exploratory analysis, where SEI and its five component parts are stratified at three levels of geography, namely DA, sub-community, and community with a particular interest in looking at variation across communities. As the next section drills deeper into relationships between child development outcome measures and SEI, we reveal in this section, some of the findings from an analysis of patterns of SEI by geographic levels. However, before we do so, a brief outline of the EDI and the geographic level at which the EDI results are reported are in order. For ease of analysis and interpretation, SEI patterns are studied at the same geographic levels as the EDI.

The Early Child Development Instrument (EDI)

In 2009, the Government of Alberta launched the Early Child Development (ECD) Mapping Initiative as part of a five-year plan to gather information on the development of kindergarten-aged children in the province of Alberta. The purpose of the initiative, led by the provincial Ministry of Education, was to study children's developmental performance by the end of the formative first five years and to learn more about the contextual factors that may be influencing their development in five core areas of physical health and well-being, social competence, emotional maturity, language and thinking skills, and communication and general knowledge. The ECD Mapping Initiative was the first population-based study of Kindergarten children, encompassing the whole province (see ECMap, 2014 for a detailed discussion of the initiative.).

The Early Development Instrument (EDI), created by the Offord Centre for Child Studies at McMaster University in Hamilton, Ontario in 2000 (Janus & Offord, 2007) was selected as the tool to measure early development outcomes. The tool consists of 103 items/questions across five areas: physical health and well-being, social competence, emotional maturity, language and thinking skills, and communication and general knowledge.[23] EDI is primarily designed to assist and target communities at a local level, although data are collected through surveys. The data on Alberta's kindergarteners were collected by school authorities under the supervision of the provincial Ministry of Education (see, Krishnan, 2013 for a detailed discussion on the EDI and its psychometric properties.). The analysis of EDI data and community engagement were done by the Early Child Development Mapping Project (ECMap) in the Community-University Partnership for the Study of Children, Youth and Families (CUP), based at the University of Alberta. The childhood development data for this study came from a cohort of children aged 4 to 7 as part of a large database of the EDI (N=70,206), collected across years, 2009-2013.

Creating Early Child Development (ECD) Communities and Sub-Communities

There are, of course, many ways to define a community. For the purposes of Early Child Development (ECD) Mapping Initiative to which this author was part of, a community was defined as an urban or rural geographic area where people live, work, play, and raise their children, and where they identify with all or parts of the local geography, landmarks, institutions, and social groups (e.g., parks, schools, sport teams, places of worship and community centres) (ECMap, 2012).

As stated earlier, the results of analysis of EDI data are always reported at a macro-level. Establishing community boundaries, however was a particular challenge in Alberta. There exist no common administrative boundaries that encompass the entire province; school districts, health zones, federal and provincial constituencies, municipalities and regional bodies overseeing the operation of programs and services at the local level (Family and Community Support Services, for example) all have their own sets of administrative boundaries. To create boundaries that would be meaningful to those who reside in various communities across the province, community members and groups were approached for their inputs into determining the boundaries for their community with the assistance of ECMap's community development coordinators (CDCs), located at various parts of the province. Boundaries were then adjusted to match postal codes and Statistics Canada's own boundaries used in enumerations. Through this process, 100 communities, or early childhood development (ECD) communities as they are known were identified for the whole province. With the help of community members, communities were subdivided into sub-communities to reflect the diversity of their populations more closely, wherever necessary. This resulted in a total of 337 sub-communities across Alberta.[24]

The Spatial Pattern of Socioeconomic Index Components Across Three Levels of Geography

Table 6 shows the mean, lowest, and highest score values, both for overall and for each component of SEI with a comparison of scores at the DA, community and sub-community levels. The values show how the scores for DAs, communities, and sub-communities deviate from their means, and also point to differences between DAs, communities, and sub-communities. Statistically, the lowest and/or the highest values can be outliers. However, they can be meaningful in most instances and can be reflective of the real diversity in socioeconomic conditions across geographic areas in the province. While at the DA level, the scores ranged from 12.4 to 63.28 in the overall SEI, at the community level, they ranged from 23.56 to 50.22, and at the sub-community level, they ranged from 22.77 to 56.98.

The distributions of components varied substantially based on the level of aggregation. As one would expect, the gaps (or range) by geographic areas, however, proved to be smaller among communities, compared to sub-communities, regardless of what component was considered. Overall, economic component had the largest range (maximum-minimum), in absolute terms, namely 15.58 (i.e., 20.86-5.28) and 21.74 (i.e., 27.02-5.28), respectively for communities and sub-communities (Table 6). The results

Table 6. Minimum, maximum, and mean of scores on Socioeconomic Index (SEI) and its five components by three geographic units

	Alberta (N=5,222)*			Community (N=100)			Sub-Community (N=337)		
	Min	**Max**	**Mean**	**Min**	**Max**	**Mean**	**Min**	**Max**	**Mean**
Economic	0	29.18	13.06	5.28	20.86	11.74	5.28	27.02	13.06
Social	0	26.36	15.89	10.01	19.53	16.47	4.67	22.37	16.58
Cultural	0	16.43	10.7	5.87	13.55	11.52	4.51	15.24	10.84
Vulnerability	0	16.02	5.83	4.4	12.42	6.43	1.8	13.21	5.89
Childcare	0	12.01	6.11	3.97	7.34	5.72	2.81	8.26	5.84
SEI	**12.4**	**63.28**	39.93	**23.56**	**50.22**	39.02	**22.77**	**56.98**	40.44

* Provincial values were based on DAs, and community and sub-community values were based on aggregation of DAs that represented each community and sub-community.

Note: The higher the scores, the better the SEI, except for vulnerability; for vulnerability, the lower the score, the better the SEI.

suggest that level of geography plays an important role in detecting the impact of socioeconomic gradients in child development measures, and higher levels of aggregation possibly underscore the extent of variations in some areas of development more than others. More detailed estimates of variations, based on different geographic levels are necessary before drawing any firm conclusions on associations of the size of a geographic area and SEI.[25] The findings provide some indication that variations in SEI and its components across Alberta are wide. But, wide variations in SEI do not necessarily mean the extent of variations is uniform across all geographic levels and across all components.

Relative Dispersion of Socioeconomic Index within and between Communities

In addition to comparing geographic levels according to mean scores on SEI and its factors, it is equally important to examine distributions within geographic levels. More specifically, we were interested on the spatial patterning of SEI and the five components across 100 communities. This was achieved through the computation and graphing of the interquartile range (IQR).[26] This exercise, of course cannot tell the source of variation within or between communities, but it gives a different perspective to SEI variability. The information, not presented here, helped us to understand the relative dispersion within a community (in terms of the DAs within) and between communities better by ranking communities in ascending order of the IQR of the distribution of SEI and its components.[27]

Results indicated that even the top most community in terms of overall SEI, needed improvement because its within-variation exceeded much more than the critical value of two from the median IQR.[28] The component-specific IQR values differed substantially, although suggested relatively smaller inter-community variations in two components, namely social mobility and child care. Some communities are likely to be at a greater disadvantage as evidenced by their wide variations in SEI and component-specific IQR values, of course within and between others in the province. Because the SEI components produce widely varying pictures, it is difficult to put all of them together into a coherent trajectory of the socioeconomic spectrum. However, two major points should be noted here. First, there showed no universal model of pattern that can be followed provincially, in terms of both the overall SEI and its components. Second, average scores appeared to hide significant variations among communities because communities themselves were composed of different number of smaller geographic units or DAs to which original computations were made. The empirical evidence is that, both the individual components of SEI as well as size of geographic area matter.

Socioeconomic Index and Component Rankings of Communities

Based on community rankings of SEI, each community was positioned from 1 to 100, enabling us to get a better feel on how each community fared on the socioeconomic scale.[29] That is, whether Community A falls into low, medium low, medium, medium high, or high. Despite being at the top in the overall SEI ranking, the rankings were different with respect to the individual components for the same community. Thus, some communities did well on the overall SEI but poor on the components of the SEI. A closer look at the 10 top communities showed that, the factors driving their composite ranking tended to vary, especially in terms of the last three components. This finding suggests that the SEI will continue to shift as the various components change in the future.

A PRELIMINARY LOOK AT THE RELATIONSHIP BETWEEN EARLY CHILD DEVELOPMENT OUTCOMES AND SOCIOECONOMIC INDEX

As earlier noted, there was a marked divide between the top and bottom quintiles, and virtually every community suggested its own pattern for each of the component and the overall SEI. Will the SEI quintiles show any consistent pattern in terms of EDI outcome measures at the community level? This section attempts to flag the three derived EDI outcome measures across SEI quintiles.[30] It does not, however, attempt to answer the question, what component of SEI has the strongest or what component has the weakest link to EDI and why. A comprehensive multivariate analysis of the potential determinants of EDI is beyond the scope of this study. Additionally, we do not see this chapter as a place to review evidence regarding the influence of socioeconomic status on child development (See Krishnan, 2010 for a comprehensive review of theories of child development, intended at predicting diverse aspects of development). Given that there are volumes written on the topic (e.g., Bradley & Corwyn, 2002; Caro, 2009; Chen, 2007; Sirin, 2005), what follows should be viewed as a pragmatic summary.

Previous research (e.g., Bradley & Corwyn, 2002) has shown that socioeconomic status is associated with a wide array of health, cognitive, and socioemotional outcomes in children, with effects at multiple levels, including both family and neighborhood. In her overview of research on SES and physical health in childhood, Chen (2004) argued that there is a gradient relationship between SES and children's health, such that for each incremental increase in SES, there is a comparable benefit in children's health. As this author has noted, in order to fully understand the mechanisms that underlie in the SES-health relationship, there is a need for interdisciplinary collaborations and the examination of the degree to which societal (e.g., social capital), neighbourhood (e.g., residential segregation), and family-level variables (e.g., relationship quality), and individual-child factors (e.g., stress) contribute to this relationship. The model can probably be further improved by finding answers to, say will a low SEI community exacerbate developmental delays or provide fewer mechanisms for better developmental outcomes and/or vice versa? No attempt is made to answer this question as well, but a rudimentary attempt is made to flag the importance of SEI in understanding the EDI outcome measures, and also to explore the association of the overall SEI and its components at three geographic levels.

- **EDI-SEI Relationships at the Dissemination Area Level:** Dissemination areas characterized by high mean scores for all five development domains had significantly high overall SEI (Table 7). All four components, with the exception of vulnerability had positive linear relationships with development; vulnerability was unrelated to the EDI outcomes, at small-area level.
- **EDI-SEI Relationships at the Sub-Community Level:** The relationships between SEI and EDI showed similar pattern at the sub-community level as at the DA level, especially for the overall SEI and the two components of SEI, namely economic and social (Table 8). None of the EDI developmental domains, with the exception of communication and general knowledge, was significantly related to the cultural component, at the sub-community level. Child care was not significantly related to any one of the developmental domains.
- **EDI-SEI Relationships at the Community Level:** The relationships between EDI and SEI showed similar results at the community level as at the sub-community level, with few exceptions (Table 9). Whereas at least one developmental domain (communication and general knowledge) had a significant relationship to the cultural component at the sub-community level, none of the five domains had a significant relationship to the component at the community level. While child

Table 7. Correlations of Early Child Development Instrument (EDI) outcomes with Socioeconomic Index (SEI) and its components at the Dissemination Area (DA) level (N=4,236)

	SEI	Economic	Social	Cultural	Vulnerability	Child Care
Physical health and well-being	.340**	.264**	.222**	.052**	-.010	.059**
Social competence	.297**	.220**	.201**	.054**	.004	.068**
Emotional maturity	.278**	.233**	.178**	.008	-.023	.042*
Language and thinking skills	.352**	.284**	.186**	.090**	-.013	.079**
Communication and general knowledge	.376**	.243**	.216**	.216**	.008	.070**

Note: The total number of DAs was reduced to 4,236 due to missing cases on EDI.
*p<=0.05 **p<=0.001.

Table 8. Correlations of Early Child Development Instrument (EDI) outcomes with Socioeconomic Index (SEI) and its components at the sub-community level (N=337)

	SEI	Economic	Social	Cultural	Vulnerability	Child Care
Physical health and well-being	.418**	.263**	.349**	-.008	-.230**	.058
Social competence	.398**	.273**	.329**	.013	-.133*	.034
Emotional maturity	.414**	.328**	.315**	-.074	-.255**	-.045
Language and thinking skills	.505**	.406**	.272**	.024	-.260**	.036
Communication and general knowledge	.480**	.312**	.228**	.226**	-.189**	.086

*p<=0.01 **p<=0.001.

Table 9. Correlations of Early Child Development Instrument (EDI) outcomes with Socioeconomic Index (SEI) and its components at the community-level (N=100)

	SEI	Economic	Social	Cultural	Vulnerability	Child Care
Physical health and well-being	.301***	.030	.343***	-.002	-.317***	.257**
Social maturity	.362***	.188	.246**	-.004	-.284**	.139
Emotional maturity	.364***	.218*	.228*	-.082	-.359***	.063
Language and thinking skills	.537***	.408***	.132	-.045	-.429***	.180*
Communication and general knowledge	.371***	.178*	.159	.155	-.265***	.171*

*p<=0.05 **p<=0.01 ***p<=0.001.

care did not relate to EDI outcomes at the sub-community level, it was significantly related to physical health and well-being, language and thinking skills, and communication and general knowledge, at the community level.

- **Experiencing Great Difficulty (in One or More and in Two or More), and Developing Appropriately (in All Five) by SES:** Not surprisingly, as Figure 2 suggests, generally speaking, the higher the SES, the lower the percentages of children falling into EGD1+ and EGD2+, and consequently higher the percentages falling into Developing Appropriately (all five developmental domains). However, there is an indication of a nonlinear relationship between EDI and SES at some levels. For instance, areas with low SES levels performed better in terms of percentages of children falling into both EGD1+ and EGD2+, than those with medium levels of SES. This may mean that not only the pictures painted by components do not mirror each other but also, the overall SES may portray a picture of its own in its association with EDI outcomes. The five components although providing distinct sets of information about inequity in the distribution of economic, social, cultural, vulnerability, and child care across communities in Alberta, their impacts on EDI can be complex and varied in nature.

It is important to note that the performance of communities, in terms of percentage of children developing appropriately, did not show much variation in the higher four socioeconomic status levels, but the percentage was noticeably low at the lowest level of the socioeconomic spectrum. This may mean that there is no universal model that can be followed provincially, in terms of the SEI-EDI relationships.

Figure 2. EGD1+, EGD2+, and DA5 by SES levels

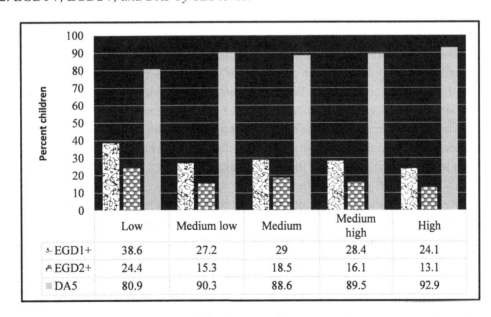

	Low	Medium low	Medium	Medium high	High
EGD1+	38.6	27.2	29	28.4	24.1
EGD2+	24.4	15.3	18.5	16.1	13.1
DA5	80.9	90.3	88.6	89.5	92.9

EGD1+: Experiencing great difficulty in one or more domains of development
EGD2+: Experiencing great difficulty in two or more domains of development
DA5: Developing appropriately in all five domains of development
SES: Socioeconomic status (measured as quintile categories, unlike SEI)

CONCLUSION AND DISCUSSION

The chapter focused on the topic of SEI development within a PCA framework. While component scores following PCA are relatively easy to create and may be useful for further data analyses, researchers using component scores need to be aware of the assumptions required by the procedure. While data screening and the checking of assumptions for outliers, normality, linearity, and homoscedasticity are part of most parametric tests, they need to be revisited in the context of PCA because they can determine whether or not a particular data set is suitable for index construction. For example, component scores may be skewed to the right or left and thereby non-normal, especially if the factorability of the correlation matrix as suggested by Bartlett's Test of Sphericity does not attain statistical significance. Clearly, there are methodological issues related to data quality that need to be addressed when developing PCA-based indices.

The multi-dimensional composite index developed here within the framework of a PCA procedure provides a better picture of economic, social, cultural, and related structural conditions, and thereby, socioeconomic stratification of areas across major SES groupings, such as quintiles. The differences in mean socioeconomic scores were found uneven in Alberta, at the small area level; the difference in mean was higher between the fourth and richest quintiles than any other adjacent quintiles. In other words, the disparity between medium-high- and high-SES categories is greater, compared to inequity between other SES categories. Communities varied substantially in the distribution of socioeconomic components. Even those communities that had a high (overall) SEI did poorly in terms of some of the components of SEI. The main message is, the size of a geographic area matters in understanding socioeconomic disparities. Since each child in the area contributes to the overall relationship, it is possible that larger geographic levels containing more children in the EDI population show similar patterns of relationships between EDI and SEI more than smaller geographic areas; sub-communities and communities mostly do have similar patterns of relationships in terms of the components of SEI and EDI developmental domains with comparatively higher mean scores for EDI in geographic areas where economic and social aspects of SEI are high, but vulnerability is low.

The overall composite SEI can serve as an important correlate of EDI for some communities. However, component-specific SEI may act as better correlates in some because communities differ in terms of their make-up of each of the components. Whether or not the components in SEI relate to EDI depends not only on the size of the geographic area but also on the developmental domain itself. At both the sub-community and community levels, the three main aspects of SEI that influence early child developmental outcomes are economic, social, and vulnerability. Economic factor has the largest contribution in the overall SEI, but in the EDI-SEI equation, this component exerts the greatest influence on the language and thinking skills area, at all geographic levels.

Researchers need to be cautioned about interpreting some of the results. First, the socioeconomic scores should not be generalized to those based on individual-level data. Second, socioeconomic groupings are obtained by classifying Dissemination Areas and ranking the scores prior to grouping. The index provides only a relative measure of inequality between areas, and it cannot provide information on absolute levels of economic, social, or cultural aspects within a community. It can be used for comparisons across areas, or over time, provided the computational procedures follow the same method and same set of variables. Third, the index came from the correlations in the data for Alberta at the DA level. The construction of an index at the community-level can risk our effort to capture urban-rural disparities. For example, in urban areas, property and housing value may emerge as important variables, whereas in rural areas, family size or accessibility to services may emerge as important. Fourth, the choice of variables included can have an impact on the index, thereby influencing early child development outcomes. For example, Houweling, Kunst, & Mackenbach (2003) noted the classification of socioeconomic groups as impacting child health outcomes, directly. Variables or their proxies require careful consideration, especially when socioeconomic indices are used as determinants of health outcomes. Finally, although there is no standard criterion to follow in terms of what percentage of variance can be considered as adequate in any analysis, the total explained variance of 56 per cent suggests that the efforts to understand the chosen set of 26 variables as five underlying concepts is an indication of a successful outcome.[31] However, omitted variables such as, durable assets (collected locally) and population density might prove to be important correlates of socioeconomic inequalities. In any case, socioeconomic status indicators, which vary by individuals, locations, or times, should take into account the complex nature and also the bio-ecological aspects of developmental outcomes. Given these cautionary notes, we suggest that in the absence of individual socioeconomic data on relevant variables, area measures such as the one developed here can be extremely useful for the purposes of monitoring disparities in health (e.g., infant mortality and cancer mortality) and developmental outcomes and for identifying communities that may be targeted for programs to improve access to services or infrastructure development and also specific interventions to improve overall quality of life and welfare.

The study presented here has some limitations, especially when the analysis of SEI-EDI relationships is only descriptive and preliminary. Although some of the associations of socioeconomic index can be derived from correlational analysis, a modeling of the EDI within a multivariate framework is important to understand the SEI effects adequately, direct and indirect[32] large scale EDI data bases, combined with sophisticated modeling techniques are beginning to untangle the relation between SEI and EDI outcomes (Mousavi & Krishnan, 2014). The findings, in general made it clear that SEI will serve as an important predictor of child developmental outcomes.

Since both SEI and EDI are summary measures of several variables or items/questions, from a policy point of view, we cannot map out the actual situation of the communities and the variables that most contribute to a specific developmental delay in young children. For example, fewer years of schooling or lack of it may be contributing to the low cognitive skills among young children. In other words, indicators when aggregated and converted to summary scores, they could obscure possible important effects (Mousavi & Krishnan, 2014). However, this may very well be the case with any indices or summary measures. Further, we analyzed associations between SEI and child outcomes without controlling for other contextual variables, such as community assets/resources (e.g., libraries, playgrounds, parks, etc.) and characteristics of children (e.g., sex, ethnicity, immigrant status, etc.). This may have biased our estimates; the estimates may have reflected some pre-existing differences in services and programs in a community or sub-community and also differences in children's ability to perform what is expected of their individual characteristics (e.g., ethnic background). However, this cannot be treated as a major limitation, since the set of selected variables in SEI included some features relevant to assets or resources in an area (e.g., home ownership). Given this and other limitations imposed by the data, it is anticipated that the model developed in this study will be a valuable tool for judging and deciding on the contextually-based SEI, thereby helping researchers and policymakers in the development of a summary index and application of it in early child development research in Canada. The index, undoubtedly, will significantly predict early child developmental outcomes of physical, social, emotional, language and cognitive skills, and communication and general knowledge in the province at both the smaller and larger levels of geography.

ACKNOWLEDGMENT

The author is indebted to Dr. Susan Lynch, former Project Director of Early Child Development Mapping Project (ECMap) Alberta and Dr. Amin Mousavi, Assistant Professor at University of Saskatchewan, Canada for their support, encouragement and helpful comments throughout the course of this project.

REFERENCES

Ackerman, B. P., & Brown, E. D. (2010). Physical and psychological turmoil in the home and cognitive development. In G. W. Evans & T. D. Wachs (Eds.), *Chaos and its Influence on Children's Development* (pp. 35–47). Washington, DC: American Psychological Association.

Antony, G. M., & Rao, K. V. (2007). A composite index to explain variations in poverty, health, nutritional status and standard of living: Use of multivariate statistical methods. *Public Health*, *121*(8), 578–587. doi:10.1016/j.puhe.2006.10.018 PMID:17467017

Bartlett, M. S. (1954). A note on the multiplying factors for various chi square approximations. *Journal of the Royal Statistical Society, 16*(Series B), 296-8.

Beavers, A. S., Lounsbury, J. W., Richards, J. K., Huck, S. W., Skolits, G. J., & Esquivel, S. L. (2013). Practical considerations for using exploratory factor analysis in educational research. *Practical Assessment, Research & Evaluation*, *18*(6), 1–13.

Berkman, L. F., & Kawachi, I. (2000). *Social Epidemiology*. New York: Oxford University Press.

Boelhouwer, J., & Stoop, I. (1999). Measuring well-being in the Netherlands: The SCP index from 1974 to 1997. *Social Indicators Research*, *48*(1), 51–75. doi:10.1023/A:1006931028334

Bolch, B. W., & Huang, C. J. (1974). *Multivariate Statistical Methods for Business and Economics*. Englewood Cliffs, NJ: Prentice Hall.

Bornstein, M. H., Hahn, C., Suwalsky, J. T. D., & Haynes, O. M. (2003). Socioeconomic status, parenting, and child development: The Hollingshead four-factor index of social status and the socioeconomic Index of occupations. In M. H. Bornstein & R. H. Bradley (Eds.), *Socioeconomic Status, Parenting, and Child Development* (pp. 29–82). Mahwah, NJ: Lawrence Erlbaum Associates.

Boschmann, E. (2011). Job access, location decision, and the working poor: A qualitative study in the Columbus, Ohio metropolitan area. *Geoforum*, *42*(6), 671–682. doi:10.1016/j.geoforum.2011.06.005

Bradley, R. H., & Corwyn, R. F. (2002). Socioeconomic status and child development. *Annual Review of Psychology*, *53*(1), 371–399. doi:10.1146/annurev.psych.53.100901.135233 PMID:11752490

Braveman, P. A., Cubbin, C., Egerter, S., Chideya, S., Marchi, K. S., Metzier, M., & Posner, S. (2005). Socioeconomic status in health research: One size does not fit all. *Journal of the American Medical Association*, *294*(22), 2879–2888. doi:10.1001/jama.294.22.2879 PMID:16352796

British Columbia. (2009). *British Columbia Regional Socio-Economic Indicators: Methodology*. British Columbia: Ministry of Labor & Citizens Services.

Bronfenbrenner, U. (1977). Toward an experimental psychology of human development. *The American Psychologist*, *32*(7), 513–532. doi:10.1037/0003-066X.32.7.513

Bryant, F. B., & Yarnold, P. R. (1995). Principal-components analysis and exploratory and confirmatory factor analysis. In L. G. Grimm & P. R. Yarnold (Eds.), *Reading and understanding multivariate statistics* (pp. 99–136). Washington, DC: American Psychological Association.

Canadian Institute for Health Information (2005). *Developing a healthy community's index: A collection of papers*. Author.

Caro, D. H. (2009). Socio-economic status and academic achievement trajectories from childhood to adolescence. *Canadian Journal of Education*, *32*(3), 558–590.

Catell, R. B. (1966). The scree test for numbers of factors. *Multivariate Behavioral Research*, *1*(2), 245–276. doi:10.1207/s15327906mbr0102_10 PMID:26828106

Chang, Y.-J., Schneider, L., & Finkbeiner, M. (2015). Assessing child development: A critical review and the Sustainable Child Development Index (SCDI). *Sustainability*, *7*(5), 4973–4996. doi:10.3390/su7054973

Chen, E. (2007). Why socioeconomic status affects the health of children: A psychosocial perspective. *American Psychological Society*, *13*(3), 112–114.

Crosnoe, R. (2007). Early child care and the school readiness of children from Mexican immigrant families.[Spring]. *IMR*, *41*(1), 152–181.

Davey Smith, G., Ben-Shlomo, Y., & Hart, C. (1999). Use of census-based aggregate variables to proxy for socioeconomic group: Evidence from national samples. *American Journal of Epidemiology*, *150*(9), 996–997. doi:10.1093/oxfordjournals.aje.a010109 PMID:10547146

Davis, P., McLeod, K., Ransom, M., Ongley, P., Pearce, N., & Howden-Chapman, P. (1999). The New Zealand Socioeconomic Index: Developing and validating an occupationally-derived indicator of socio-economic status. *Australian and New Zealand Journal of Public Health*, *23*(1), 27–33. doi:10.1111/j.1467-842X.1999.tb01201.x PMID:10083686

Diez-Roux, A. V. (2003). Residential environments and cardiovascular risk. *Journal of Urban Health*, *80*(4), 569–589. doi:10.1093/jurban/jtg065 PMID:14709706

ECMap. (2012). *Fact sheet*. Retrieved December 19, 2015, from http://www.ecmap.ca/images/EC-Map_FactSheets/ECMap_Communities_FactSheet_20120914.pdf

ECMap. (2014). *How are our young children doing? Final Report of the Early Child Development Mapping Project (ECMap) Alberta*. Retrieved December 19, 2015, from http://www.ecmap.ca/images/ECMap_Reports/ECMap_Final_Report_20141118.pdf

Eibner, C., & Sturm, R. (2006). US-based indices of area-level deprivation: Results from health care for communities. *Social Science & Medicine*, *62*(2), 348–359. doi:10.1016/j.socscimed.2005.06.017 PMID:16039764

Ensminger, M. E., & Fothergill, K. (2003). A decade of measuring SES: What it tells us and where to go from here? In M. H. Bornstein & R. H. Bradley (Eds.), *Socioeconomic Status, Parenting, and Child Development*. Lawrence Erlbaum Associates.

Evans, G. W. (2004). The environment of childhood poverty. *The American Psychologist*, *59*(2), 77–92. doi:10.1037/0003-066X.59.2.77 PMID:14992634

Evans, G. W. (2006). Child development and the physical environment. *Annual Review of Psychology*, *57*(1), 423–451. doi:10.1146/annurev.psych.57.102904.190057 PMID:16318602

Evans, G. W., & Wachs, T. D. (Eds.). (2010). Chaos and its Influence on Children's Development. Washington, DC: American Psychological Association.

Foth, N., Manaugh, K., & El-Geneidy, A. (2013). Towards equitable transit: Examining transit accessibility and social need in Toronto, Canada 1996-2006. *Journal of Transport Geography*, *29*, 1–10. doi:10.1016/j.jtrangeo.2012.12.008

Fotso, J., & Kuate-defo, B. (2005). Measuring socioeconomic status in health research in developing countries: Should we be focusing on households, communities, or both? *Social Indicators Research*, *72*(2), 189–237. doi:10.1007/s11205-004-5579-8

Fukuda, Y., Nakamura, K., & Takano, T. (2007). Higher mortality in areas of lower socioeconomic position measured by a single index of deprivation in Japan. *Public Health*, *121*(3), 163–173. doi:10.1016/j.puhe.2006.10.015 PMID:17222876

Geronimus, A. T., & Bound, J. (1998). Use of census-based aggregate variables to proxy for socioeconomic group: Evidence from national samples. *American Journal of Epidemiology*, *148*(5), 475–486. doi:10.1093/oxfordjournals.aje.a009673 PMID:9737560

Havard, S., Deguen, S., Bodin, J., Louis, K., Laurent, O., & Bard, D. (2008). A small-area index of socioeconomic deprivation to capture health inequalities in France. *Social Science & Medicine*, *67*(12), 2007–2016. doi:10.1016/j.socscimed.2008.09.031 PMID:18950926

Health Canada. (1996). *Toward a Common Understanding: Clarifying the Core Concepts of Population Health*. Ottawa: Health Canada.

Hoff, E., Laursen, B., & Bridges, K. (2012). Measurement and model building in studying the influence of socioeconomic status on child development. In L. Mayes & M. Lewis (Eds.), *The Cambridge Handbook of Environment in Human Development* (pp. 590–606). New York: Cambridge University Press. doi:10.1017/CBO9781139016827.033

Hooper, D. (2012). Exploratory Factor Analysis. In H. Chen (Ed.), *Approaches to Quantitative Research – Theory and its Practical Application: A Guide to Dissertation Students*. Cork, Ireland: Oak Tree.

Hotelling, H. (1933). Analysis of a complex of statistical variables into principal components. *Journal of Educational Psychology, 24*(6), 417–441. doi:10.1037/h0071325

Houweling, T. A. J., Kunst, A. E., & Mackenbach, J. P. (2003). Measuring health inequality among children in developing countries: Does the choice of the indicator of socioeconomic status matter? *International Journal for Equity in Health, 2*(1), 8. doi:10.1186/1475-9276-2-8 PMID:14609435

Janus, M., & Offord, D. (2007). Development and psychometric properties of the early development instrument (EDI): A measure of children's school readiness. *Canadian Journal of Behavioural Science, 39*(1), 1–22. doi:10.1037/cjbs2007001

Kaiser, H. (1970). A second generation little jiffy. *Psychometrika, 35*(4), 401–415. doi:10.1007/BF02291817

Kaiser, H. (1974). An index of factorial simplicity. *Psychometrika, 39*(1), 31–36. doi:10.1007/BF02291575

Kershaw, P., Irwin, L., Trafford, K., & Hertzman, C. (2005). *The British Columbia Atlas of Child Development* (Vol. 40). Human Early Learning Partnership, Western Geographical Press.

Krieger, N., Chen, J. T., & Waterman, P. D. (2002). Geocoding and monitoring of US socioeconomic inequalities in mortality and cancer incidence: Does the choice of area-based measure and geographic level matter? *American Journal of Epidemiology, 156*(5), 471–482. doi:10.1093/aje/kwf068 PMID:12196317

Krishnan, V. (2010, May). *Early child development: A conceptual model.* Presented at the Early Childhood Council Annual Conference 2010, Christchurch, New Zealand.

Krishnan, V. (2011). *Introducing a School Preparedness Index for a Canadian sample of preschoolers without special needs.* Retrieved January 26, 2016, from http://www.cup.ualberta.ca/wp-content/uploads/2013/04/IntroducingSPICUPWebsite_10April-13.pdf

Krishnan, V. (2013). *The Early Child Development Instrument (EDI) An item analysis using Classical Test Theory (CTT) on Alberta's data.* Retrieved January 26, 2016, from http://www.cup.ualberta.ca/wp-content/uploads/2013/04/ItemAnalysisCTTCUPWebsite_10April13.pdf

Krishnan, V. (2015). Development of a Multidimensional Living Conditions Index (LCI). *Social Indicators Research, 120*(2), 455–481. doi:10.1007/s11205-014-0591-0 PMID:25774072

Lai, D. (2003). Principal component analysis on human development indicators of China. *Social Indicators Research, 61*(3), 319–330. doi:10.1023/A:1021951302937

Lalloue, B., Monnez, J. M., Padilla, C., Kihal, W., Le Meur, N., Zmirou-Navier, D., & Deguen, S. (2013). A statistical procedure to create a neighborhood socioeconomic index for health inequalities analysis. *International Journal for Equity in Health, 2*(1), 12–21. PMID:23537275

Lamb, V. L., & Land, K. C. (2013). Methodologies Used in the Construction of Composite Child Well-Being Indices. In A. Ben-Arieh (Ed.), *Handbook of Child Well-Being.* New York: Springer.

Laroche, M., Toffoli, R., Kim, C., & Muller, T. E. (1996). The influence of culture on pro environmental knowledge, attitudes, and behavior: A Canadian perspective. *Advances in Consumer Research. Association for Consumer Research (U. S.), 23*, 196–202.

Lee, B. J. (2014). Mapping domains and indicators of children's well-being. In A. Ben-Arieh, F. Casas, I. Frønes, & J. E. Korbin (Eds.), *The Handbook of Child Well-Being—Theories, Methods and Policies in Global Perspective* (pp. 2797–2805). Dordrecht, The Netherlands: Springer.

Liu, X., & Lu, K. (2008). Student performance and family socioeconomic status. *Chinese Education & Society, 41*(5), 70–83. doi:10.2753/CED1061-1932410505

Lustig, S. L. (2010). An ecological framework for the refugee experience: What is the impact on child development? In G. W. Evans & T. D. Wachs (Eds.), *Chaos and its Influence on Children's Development* (pp. 239–251). Washington, DC: American Psychological Association. doi:10.1037/12057-015

Marshall, K. (2006). Converging gender roles. *Perspectives on Labour and Income, 18*(3), 7–19.

Messer, L. C., Vinikoor, L. C., Laraia, B. A., Kaufman, J. S., Eyster, J., Holzman, C., & O'Campo, P. et al. (2008). Socioeconomic domains and associations with preterm birth. *Social Science & Medicine, 67*(8), 1247–1257. doi:10.1016/j.socscimed.2008.06.009 PMID:18640759

Moore, K. A., Murphey, D., Bandy, T., & Lawner, E. (2014). Indices of child well-being and developmental contexts. In A. Ben-Arieh, F. Casas, I. Frønes, & J. E. Korbin (Eds.), *The Handbook of Child Well-Being—Theories, Methods and Policies in Global Perspective* (pp. 2807–2822). Dordrecht, The Netherlands: Springer. doi:10.1007/978-90-481-9063-8_139

Moore, K. A., Theokas, C., Lippman, L. H., Bloch, M., Vandivere, S., & O'Hare, W. P. (2008). A microdata child well-being index: Conceptualization, creation, and findings. *Child Indicators Research, 1*(1), 17–50. doi:10.1007/s12187-007-9000-4

Morris, R., & Castairs, V. (1991). Which deprivation? A comparison of selected deprivation indices. *Journal of Public Health Medicine, 13*, 318–326. PMID:1764290

Mousavi, A., & Krishnan, V. (2014). *Socioeconomic status as a determinant of early child developmental outcomes: A multi-level analysis on Early Development Instrument (EDI) data, ECMap, CUP.* Faculty of Extension, University of Alberta.

Mustard, C. A., Derksen, S., Berthelot, J. M., & Wolfson, M. (1999). Assessing ecologic proxies for household income: A comparison of household and neighborhood level income measures in the study of population health status. *Health & Place, 5*(2), 157–171. doi:10.1016/S1353-8292(99)00008-8 PMID:10670997

Nardo, M., Saisano, M., Saltelli, A., & Tarantola, S. (2005). *Tools for Composite Indicators Building.* European Commission Joint Research Centre, Institute for the Protection and Security of the Citizen Econometrics and Statistical Support to Antifraud Unit.

Nicoletti, G., Scarpetta, S., & Boylaud, O. (2000). *Summary indicators of product market regulation with an extension to employment protection legislation.* Economics department working papers No. 226. Paris: OECD. Retrieved Jan 20, 2016, from http://www.oecd.org/eco/eco100

Oakes, J. M., & Rossi, P. H. (2003). The measurement of SES in health research: Current practice and steps toward a new approach. *Social Science & Medicine, 56*(4), 769–784. doi:10.1016/S0277-9536(02)00073-4 PMID:12560010

Okonny-Myers, I. (2010). *The Interprovincial Mobility of Immigrants in Canada.* Ottawa: Citizenship and Immigration Canada. Retrieved January 27, 2016, from http://www.cic.gc.ca/english/pdf/research-stats/interprov-mobility.pdf

Pallant, J. (2007). *SPSS Survival Manual: A Step by Step Guide to Data Analysis Using SPSS for Windows* (3rd ed.). New York: McGraw Hill, Open University Press.

Pampalon, R., Hamel, D., & Gamache, P. (2009). A comparison of individual and area-based socioeconomic data for monitoring social inequalities in health (Statistics Canada, Catalogue no. 82-003-XPE). *Health Reports, 20*(3), 85–94. PMID:20108609

Pampalon, R., & Raymond, G. (2000). A deprivation index for health and welfare planning in Quebec. *Chronic Diseases in Canada, 21,* 104–113. PMID:11082346

Pearson, K. (1901). On lines and planes of closest fit to systems of points in space. *Philosophical Magazine, 2*(6), 559–572. doi:10.1080/14786440109462720

Perreira, K. M., & Smith, L. (2007). A cultural-ecological model of migration and development: Focusing on Latino immigrant youth. *Prevention Researcher, 14*(4), 6–9.

Planning Commission. (1993). *Report on the Expert Group on Estimation of Proportion and Number of Poor.* New Delhi: Perspective Planning Division.

Program Effectiveness Data Analysis Coordinators of Eastern Ontario. (2009). *Early Childhood Risks, Resources, and Outcomes in Ottawa.* Retrieved January 18, 2016, from http://parentresource.on.ca/DACSI_ e.html

Public Health Agency of Canada. (2015). Retrieved March 7, 2016, from http://www.phac-aspc.gc.ca/ph-sp/determinants/index-eng.php

Reed, B. A., Habicht, J. P., & Niameogo, C. (1996). The effects of maternal education on child nutritional status depend on socio-environmental conditions. *International Journal of Epidemiology, 25*(3), 585–592. doi:10.1093/ije/25.3.585 PMID:8671560

Rygel, L., O'Sullivan, D., & Yarnal, B. (2006). A method for constructing a social vulnerability index: An application to hurricane storm surges in a developed country. *Mitigation and Adaptation Strategies for Global Change, 11*(3), 741–764. doi:10.1007/s11027-006-0265-6

Saltelli, A., Nardo, M., Saisana, M., & Tarantola, S. (2004). *Composite indicators-The controversy and the way forward.* OECD World Forum on Key Indicators, Palermo.

Sekhar, C. C., Indrayan, A., & Gupta, S. M. (1991). Development of an Index of Need for Health Resources for Indian States Using Factor Analysis. *International Journal of Epidemiology, 20*(1), 246–250. doi:10.1093/ije/20.1.246 PMID:2066229

Shavers, V. L. (2007). Measurement of socioeconomic status in health disparities research. *Journal of the National Medical Association, 99*(9), 1013–1023. PMID:17913111

Singh, G. K., Miller, B. A., & Hankey, B. F. (2002). Changing area socioeconomic patterns in U.S. cancer mortality, 1950-1998: Part II-Lung and colorectal cancers. *Journal of the National Cancer Institute*, *94*(12), 916–925. doi:10.1093/jnci/94.12.916 PMID:12072545

Sirin, S. R. (2005). Socioeconomic status and academic achievement: A meta-analytic review of research. *Review of Educational Research*, *75*(3), 417–453. doi:10.3102/00346543075003417

Steenland, K., Henley, J., Calle, E., & Thun, M. (2004). Individual-and area-based socioeconomic status variables as predictors of mortality in a cohort of 179,383 persons. *American Journal of Epidemiology*, *159*(11), 1047–1056. doi:10.1093/aje/kwh129 PMID:15155289

Subramanian, S. V., Chen, J. T., Rehkopf, D. H., Waterman, P. D., & Krieger, N. (2006). Comparing individual and area-based socioeconomic measures for the surveillance of health disparities: A multilevel analysis of Massachusetts births, 1989-1991. *American Journal of Epidemiology*, *164*(9), 823–834. doi:10.1093/aje/kwj313 PMID:16968866

Tabachnick, B. G., & Fedell, L. S. (2007). *Using Multivariate Statistics* (5th ed.). Boston: Pearson Education.

Teitelbaum, S., & Beckley, T. (2006). Hunted, harvested and homegrown: The prevalence of self-provisioning in rural Canada. *Journal of Rural and Community Development*, *1*(2), 114–130.

Vyas, S., & Kumaranayake, L. (2006). Constructing socioeconomic status indices: How to use principal components analysis. *Advance Access Publication*, *9*, 459–468.

Warner, R. M. (2013). *Applied Statistics: from Bivariate through Multivariate Techniques* (2nd ed.). Thousand Oaks, CA: Sage Publications, Inc.

Zagorski, K. (1985). Composite measures of social, economic, and demographic regional differentiation in Australia: Application of multi-stage principal component methods to aggregate data analysis. *Social Indicators Research*, *16*, 131–156. doi:10.1007/BF00574614

ADDITIONAL READING

DiStefano, C., Zhu, M., & Mindrila, D. (2009). Understanding and using factor scores: Considerations for the applied researcher. *Practical Assessment, Research & Evaluation*, *14*(20), 1–7.

European Commission-JRC. (2008). Composite indicators: An information server on composite indicators and ranking systems. Italy: Institute for the Protection and Security of the Citizen. Retrieved January 10, 2016, from http://composite-indicators.jrc.ec.europe.eu/FAQ.htm

Jollands, N., Lermit, J., & Patterson, M. (2004). Aggregate eco-efficiency indices for New Zealand: A principal components analysis. *Journal of Environmental Management*, *73*(4), 293–305. doi:10.1016/j.jenvman.2004.07.002 PMID:15531388

Miranti, R., Cassells, R., Vidyattama, Y., & McNamara, J. (2009, June). Inequality in Australia: Does region matter? Paper Presented at the 2nd General Conference of the International Microsimulation Association, Ottawa, Canada.

Ott, W. R. (1978). *Environmental Indices: Theory and Practice*. Ann Arbor: Ann Arbor Science.

Patterson, M. (2002). *Headline Indicators for Tracking Progress to Sustainability in New Zealand*. Wellington, New Zealand: The Ministry of the Environment.

Reinstadler, A., & Ray, J. (2010). *Macro determinants of individual income poverty in 93 regions of Europe*. Luxembourg: Eurostat.

Saisana, M., & Tarantola, S. (2002). *State-of- the-art Report on Current Methodologies and Practices for Composite Indicator Development (EUR 20408 EN)*. Italy: European Commission-JRC.

Sharpe, A. (2004). *Literature review of frameworks for macro-indicators*. Ottawa: Centre for the Study of Living Standards.

Slocum-Gori, S. L., & Zumbo, B. D. (2010). Assessing the unidimensionality of psychological scales: Using multiple criteria from factor analysis. *Social Indicators Research*. doi:10.1007/s11205-010-9682-8

Trocmé, N., MacLaurin, B., Fallon, B., Shlonsky, A., Mulcahy, M., & Esposito, T. (2009). *National Child Welfare Outcomes Indicator Matrix (NOM)*. Montreal: Centre for Research on Children and Families, McGill University.

Yong, A. G., & Pearce, S. (2013). A beginner's guide to factor analysis: Focusing on exploratory factor analysis. *Tutorials in Quantitative Methods for Psychology*, *9*(2), 79–94.

KEY TERMS AND DEFINITIONS

Composite Index: Combines several variables or factors, utilizing some statistical procedures. It provides an alternative to individual characteristics and serves as a useful reference to measure performance over time.

Dissemination Area (DA): The smallest standard geographic area for which all census data are disseminated in Canada. It is a small and relatively stable geographic unit, composed of one or more adjacent dissemination blocks with a population ranging anywhere from 400 to 700 persons.

Early Child Development (ECD): Early childhood spans from birth to six years. This period is critical as the child attains skills in physical, social/emotional and language/cognitive domains, that sets the foundation for the entire life course.

Early Child Development Instrument (EDI): Developed in 1999 by McMaster University's Offord Centre for Child Studies, the EDI is a kindergarten teacher-competed questionnaire that measures a child's performance in five key domains of development: physical health and well-being, social competence, emotional maturity, language and cognitive development, and communication skills and general knowledge.

Principal Components Analysis (PCA): A statistical technique for identifying a smaller number of uncorrelated dimensions, called *principal components* in a large set of data, without much loss of information. The procedure helps to obtain the maximum amount of variance with the fewest number of principal components.

Quintiles: Used to create cut-off values. In the present context, five groups are created from all dissemination areas in terms of socioeconomic index scores. The four cut-off values thus divide the socioeconomic index scores into five classes (Low, Medium low, Medium, Medium high, and High) with approximately 20% of the dissemination areas in each group (quintile).

Socioeconomic Index (SEI): The SEI summarizes social and economic conditions over a wide variety of indicators into a single composite index for each dissemination area within the province of Alberta. The index has five components: economic, social, cultural, vulnerability, and child care, each being a weighted combination of three to eight variables.

Socioeconomic Status (SES): A measure based on quintiles. It is ranked from 1 (Low) to 5 (High), based on ranges of mean socioeconomic index scores across dissemination areas, grouped into five categories with each category assigned to approximately 20% of the dissemination areas.

Statistics Canada: Canada's central statistical office that produces information on the country's population, resources, economy, society, and culture, every five years and conducts about 350 surveys on virtually all aspects of Canadian's life.

ENDNOTES

[1]   A useful discussion on this can be found in Bornstein, Hahn, Suwalsky, & Haynes (2003).

[2]   Readers may refer to Chang, Schneider & Finkbeiner (2015) for a comprehensive review of child development in the context of sustainable development, identifying relevant aspects and gaps. See also, Moore et al., (2008) where the authors combined wellbeing and contextual measures to create an index of the overall condition of the child.

[3]   Readers are directed to Shavers (2007), for a discussion on the commonly used contextual variables.

[4]   A complete list of variables that were included in the initial selection is available upon request.

[5]   Although PCA, as the name tells, technically yields components, the term factor has been used interchangeably by many. We have followed the same in the discussion here, while acknowledging the fact that FA refers to the entire family of techniques, of which PCA is only one among them.

[6]   PCA was first used to combine socioeconomic indicators into a single index (Boelhouwer & Stoop, 1999). Acknowledging the inappropriateness of simple aggregation procedures, Lai (2003) modified the UNDP Human Development Index by using PCA to create a linear combination of indicators of development. Several researchers have used PCA, especially since late 1990s, to compute area socioeconomic indices (Antony & Rao, 2007; Fotso & Kuate-defo, 2005; Fukuda, et al., 2007; Havard et al., 2008; Messer et al., 2008; Rygel, O'Sullivan, & Yarnal, 2006; Sekhar, Indrayan, & Gupta, 1991; Vyas & Kumaranayake, 2006; Zagorski, 1985).

[7]   Readers may refer Vyas & Kumaranayake, (2006), for an assessment of advantages and disadvantages of PCA and Saltelli, Nardo, Saisana, & Tarantola (2004), for the pros and cons of composite indicators, in general.

8   Regardless of the fact that there is no scientific answer on the question of how many cases are necessary, our sample size satisfied both the cases-to-variables ratio and the rule of 200, as endorsed by Bryant & Yarmold (1995) (see also, Nardo et al., 2005).

9   The process of removing extreme outliers from a total of 5,222 Dissemination Areas, in no way would result in a loss of variability, but was considered as a necessary step because FA can be sensitive to outliers (Pallant, 2007).

10   When PCA is used, we have the option of using either the correlation or the covariance matrix. Because the procedure is sensitive to differences in the units of measurement of variables, as a general rule, it is better to standardize the variables before applying PCA (Bolch & Huang, 1974).

11   With an adequate sample size (at least five cases for each variable), unless there is a cause for concern about nonlinearity, it is safer to proceed without any mathematical transformation of variables, as some would suggest (e.g., Pallant, 2007).

12   There is, as Pallant (2007) had rightly said, there is controversy concerning transformation or mathematically modifying scores using formulas, with some strongly supporting, and others arguing against. Initially, we ran PCA without transforming the variables, but abandoned the idea and ran models with transformed variables. The correlation matrix formed our input, and the use of parametric tests warrants the use of normal distributions.

13   Note that the descriptive statistics were based on data from which the extreme values were removed. If any of the values are found different after the procedure, the data require further investigation.

14   For perfectly normal distributions, the skewness and kurtosis values will be 0, although it happens extremely rare in the social sciences (Pallant, 2007). In a large sample situation, as Tabachnick & Fidell (2007) noted, skewness "will not make a substantive difference" (p. 80). Kurtosis can result in an underestimate of the variance, but this will also be taken care of, if the sample size is large (200+ cases).

15   According to Tabachnick & Fidell (2007), to be considered suitable for factor analysis, the correlations should be at least 0.3 or greater.

16   The Bartlett's Test of Sphericity has the null hypothesis that the correlation matrix is an identity matrix (Bartlett, 1954). What it means is, while the diagonal elements in the correlation matrix are all 1, all off-diagonal elements are 0.

17   The maximum value of KMO can be 1.0, a value of 0.9 is considered as 'marvelous', 0.80, 'meritorious', 0.70, 'middling', 0.60, 'mediocre', 0.50, 'miserable' (Antony & Rao, 2007; see also, Planning Commission, 1993).

18   These are plots of each of the eigenvalues of the factors. We inspect the plot to find the place where the smooth decrease of eigenvalues shows to stabilize. To the right of this point, we can find nothing but only 'factorial scree' (meaning debris which collects on the lower part of a rocky slope).

19   Since the loadings, resulting from an orthogonal rotation are correlation coefficients of each variable with the component, they naturally range from -1 to +1.

20   Each component depends on a set of coefficients (loadings) where each coefficient measures the correlation between the individual variable and the underlying component. Therefore, if no correlation is found between the individual variables, then weights cannot make any sense. Also, the variables must be in the same measurement scale for them to be grouped.

21   Grouping the individual variables with the highest loadings into a component or composite is usually the adopted strategy in index construction (Nicoletti, Scarpetta, & Boylaud, 2000), and we followed the same strategy here. Using an alpha level of 0.01, for a sample size of at least 300, a rotated factor loading need to be 0.32 to be considered statistically meaningful (Tabachnick & Fidell, 2007).

22   The test assumes that the variances of the populations from which different samples are drawn are equal. In other words, it tests the null hypothesis that the population variances are equal. If the resulting p-value of Levene's test is less than the critical value, the differences in sample variances are unlikely to have occurred by chance.

23   The Offord Centre uses the term language and cognitive skills, but has been changed to language and thinking skills by Early Child Development Mapping Project (ECMap) in Alberta.

24   An interactive version of the community map can be found on the website, http://www.ecmap.ca

25   A discussion on whether or not the size of a geographic area matters in the association between socioeconomic inequalities on area-based measures in health outcomes can be found in Krieger et al., (2002).

26   When the data set has extreme values, as in our case, variability can be summarized by a statistic called the interquartile range (IQR), which is the difference between the first quartile (25th percentile) and the third (75th percentile) quartile. IQR spans 50 per cent of a data set and eliminates the influence of outliers because the highest and lowest quarters of the data are removed. The score point difference across IQR is a good measure of socioeconomic gaps at the community level. The 25th percentile is the score reached by 24 out of 25 DAs and the 50th percentile, also known as the median score, is defined as the score that half of the DAs in the community do not reach and the other half exceed. The 75th percentile is the score reached by 74 out of 75 DAs.

27   Charts containing IQRs for each component is available upon request.

28   Longer bars on a histogram plotting IQRs indicate more diverse backgrounds of SEI and its components within the community, the median being the score in the middle of the distribution of IQRs. As a general rule of thumb, a community with its IQR deviating, more than two from the median value deserves attention and by more than 3.5 from the median deserves even more attention, in terms of inequity.

29   Since we realize the sensational nature of community ranking in terms of their SEI and/or EDI, the discussion is limited to providing only part of the picture.

30   National cut-off values were set for each area of development corresponding to three classifications of *Experiencing Great Difficulty* (EGD), *Experiencing Difficulty* (ED), and *Developing Appropriately* (DA), based on percentages of children who scored at or below the 10th, between 10th and 25th, and above 25th percentiles. The terms EGD, ED, and DA, replace the Offord Centre's vulnerable, at-risk, and on-track categories, respectively. The term vulnerability has been subjected to a lot of concern and criticism because it carries a negative connotation, and a re-examination of the terms was thus necessary. EGD was further categorized into EGD1+ and EGD 2+, based on the number of domains of development. The two categories are not mutually exclusive, but we adhered to the definitions and terminologies strictly for comparative purposes. These are the labels that are in use in the province. Alberta results for developing appropriately cannot be compared with the Canadian norm, however, because a Canadian norm has not been established for this category (see ECMap, 2014).

31   Regardless of the fact that there exists no standard as to how much variance a solution must explain, Warner (2013) recommended the variance explained by retained components to be reasonably high or somewhere in the range 40% -70%·

32   Multivariate analyses, especially within the framework of a bioecological model, controlling for other community and/or neighborhood-level factors (e.g., resource) is needed to learn more about how socioeconomic status impact the development of children. It is also important to note that there is a lack of primary data to fully understand interactions at all levels of social ecology; data are largely drawn from a secondary source, thereby limiting the availability of variables to conduct multivariate analyses.

Chapter 9
The Rule of Law Index:
Is It Really Impartial? A Twofold Multivariate I–Distance Approach

Milica Maricic
University of Belgrade, Serbia

Milica Bulajic
University of Belgrade, Serbia

Milica Vasilijevic
University of Belgrade, Serbia

ABSTRACT

The indicator-based scientific research has recently become a valuable source of information for policymakers, scholars and eventually, civil society. Many socioeconomic spheres are evaluated using composite indicators, whereas governance has not been left behind. Among several assessment measurements oriented on the rule of law and law enforcement, the Rule of Law Index devised by the World Justice Program stands out. Namely, it is a comprehensive and methodologically consistent index which measures the extent to which the countries follow the principles of the rule of law. However, the controversial question of the justification of its equal weighting scheme emerges. The presented study addresses this issue by applying the twofold I-distance approach to propose unbiased weights and an in-depth analysis of the index dynamics. Consequently, the aim of this paper is to scrutinize the Rule of Law Index and to shed light on its methodology. Furthermore, the proposed approach can serve as a foundation for future research on weighting schemes, which are enveloped with subjectivity.

INTRODUCTION

Over the recent years, the interest of governments, donors, businesses, and civil society around the world in the quality of governance and the enforcement of the law and the rule of law increased. Therefore, ensuring the enforcement of the rule of law has become a unifying goal of all stakeholders (WJP, 2014).

DOI: 10.4018/978-1-5225-0714-7.ch009

In order to accurately determine the actions needed to achieve their goal, a need for a clear, easily understandable, statistically sound measure of the rule of law emerged.

As statistics and composite indices developed, they were, slowly, but surely, introduced in the sphere of social sciences, especially law. Namely, governments acknowledged the benefits of statistical data and are now turning towards and relying on them. The main purpose of such data (indicators, indices, time series,...) is to provide the needed initiative for reform (Merry, 2009). Also, composite indices of governance have the ability to captivate public interest (Michener, 2015). They have been widely accepted by the general public as they reduce a multidimensional phenomenon to a single dimension and provide an easily comparable number or rank. Moreover, they tend to provide the objective truth, they facilitate comparison between the entities and most importantly, they quantify accomplishments (Merry, 2009). Therefore, statistical data and composite indices became increasingly central to global reform and global governance.

In the recent years a daunting task has been put in front of policy makers, law experts, and statisticians: to measure the rule of law. Providing such a metric is not a straightforward task for multiple reasons (Bergman, 2012). One of the main issues is the definition of the rule of law as the concept itself which is highly complex and controversial (Skaaning, 2009). Adriaan Bedner (2010) provided a research titled "An elementary approach to the Rule of Law" in which he attempted to provide a conceptual framework for defining the rule of law. The main conclusion of his thorough review is that the rule of law has two main tasks: to protect the citizens against the power of the state and to protect citizens' property and lives from assaults by fellow citizens. Therefore, the rule of law aims to regulate not solely how the state treats its citizens, but also how citizens treat one another. Although the main ideas behind the concept are more or less clearly defined, its functions and elements remain unstandardized, unorganized, and difficult to envelop. Consequently, the different rule of law measurements produced dissimilar results (Møller & Skaaning, 2011). Therefore, debates sparked on the topic of the validity of the used data, indicator methodology, and later (mis)use of the measurement (Kaufman et al., 2007). Another, more general issue, is the fact that law, not just the rule of law, is difficult to measure in qualitative terms (Davis & Kruse, 2007). This issue draws the question of indicator choice and its ability to measure the desired phenomenon (Davis, 2004). Regardless their limitations, composite indices that measure the level of law implementation, rule of law, or results of policy reforms have not yet received the same amount of scrutiny as composite indices of sustainability, development, or university rankings (Bersch & Botero, 2014; Gisselquist, 2014). Up to lately, policy indices have not attracted enough attention from statisticians and methodologists, mostly because a large percent of their indicators are qualitative metrics that rely on expert opinion and judgment (Decancq & Lugo, 2013).

However, four rule of law related composite indices have attracted the attention of academics, politicians, and practitioners: *Freedom House, World Bank Worldwide Governance Indicators,* the *Bertelsmann Transformation Index,* and the *Rule of Law Index* (Merkel, 2012). The only thing in common for all these indexes is that they have an impressive country coverage. Although widely accepted, these indicators have several limitations. Namely, each of them is guided by another definition of the rule of law, which automatically makes their results incomparable. Further, some of them measure other phenomenon that rule of law is just a part of, such as political management, or quality of democracy. One that stands out for its broad-based approach, broad concept, and reliable, self-generated data is the *Rule of Law Index* (Merkel, 2012). What makes the added value of this index is its specialization and independent data collection (Merry et al., 2015). However, this composite index has two major drawbacks: first, its factors and sub-factors are equally weighted, making its results questionable and perceived as biased, and second, it is completely based on survey results (Saisana & Tarantola, 2002; Nardo et al., 2005a).

As mentioned above, many composite indices that are used for measuring law implementation or the rule of law have been described as biased due to the subjective nature of their indicators and their weighting scheme. Thus, the aim of this paper is to provide an in-depth analysis and to propose a new weighting scheme of the *Rule of Law Index*. Namely, the *Rule of Law Index* is solely based on the results of the examination polls and its weighting scheme can be classified as intuitive. Therefore, the index provides rankings of countries based on a subjective assessment of an individual towards a legal framework. To accomplish the initial task and to reduce the level of biasness of the *Rule of Law Index,* we propose the I-distance method, more precisely the twofold I-distance approach, which can significantly upgrade the measuring process in a composite index and reduce the level of its biasness (Dobrota et al., 2015). Namely, by employing the I-distance method a new weighting scheme can be obtained. The perk of the new weighting scheme is that it is based on the provided dataset and not on the expert opinion. The obtained results could justify the equal weighting proposed by the index creators or suggest a new, impartial one that will be less subjective and less dependent on the experts' knowledge and opinion.

The following chapter sees the introduction of the *Rule of Law Index* while the I-distance method and the twofold I-distance approach will be elaborated in detail in Section *Methodology*. Next the results are given, followed by the future research directions. The concluding remarks are provided in the final chapter.

RULE OF LAW INDEX

In 2008, the *World Justice Project* developed the *Rule of Law Index* - a quantitative measurement of the level up to which the county enforces the principles of the rule of law. The *Rule of Law Index,* which will be analysed in this paper is the seventh edition of the index (WJP, 2014).

The index, which puts an effort to measure the rule of law in 99 countries, comprises of nine factors and 47 sub-factors calculated using the data collected by the *World Justice Project*. However, not all factors enter the framework for final ranking of countries. *Informal Justice* (Factor 9) and its three sub-factors are not accounted in the overall score due to a severe lack of data. Therefore, this factor is used as a satellite factor for within country comparison. In our research, we will focus on the eight factors and their sub-factors. The structure of the *Rule of Law Index* and the codes assigned to its factors and sub-factors are given in Table 1.

The first factor, *Constraints on Government Powers,* measures the extent up to which the ones who govern are constrained by the constitution and laws. Such measurements are crucial for the economic development because only governments have the power not to follow their commitments, but, on the other hand, have incentives to do so at will (Haggard & Tiede, 2011). Besides governmental checks, this factor aims to include the non-governmental checks such as free and independent press (WJP, 2014). Factor 1 seeks to measure the constraints put on the governance through legislature (SF 1.1), judiciary (SF 1.2), review agencies (SF 1.3), sanctions to government officials (SF 1.4), non-government checks (SF 1.5), and the level of the governance power transferred by law (SF 1.6).

The following factor, *Absence of Corruption,* through four indicators, measures the level of corruption of government officials. Uslaner (2005) defines corruption as the act of transfer of resources from the mass public to the elite. Therefore, corruption creates inequality and fundamentally opposes the

Table 1. The Rule of Law Index factors, sub-factors, and assigned codes

Factor	Code	Sub-Factor	Code
Constraints on Government Powers	F1	Government powers are effectively limited by the legislature	SF1.1
		Government powers are effectively limited by the judiciary	SF1.2
		Government powers are effectively limited by independent auditing and review agencies	SF1.3
		Government officials are sanctioned for misconduct	SF1.4
		Government powers are subject to non-governmental checks	SF1.5
		Transition of power is subject to the law	SF1.6
Absence of Corruption	F2	Government officials in the executive branch do not use public office for private gain	SF2.1
		Government officials in the judicial branch do not use public office for private gain	SF2.2
		Government officials in the police and military do not use public office for private gain	SF2.3
		Government officials in the legislative branch do not use public office for private gain	SF2.4
Open Government	F3	The laws are publicized and accessible	SF3.1
		The laws are stable	SF3.2
		Right to petition the government and public participation	SF3.3
		Official information is available on request	SF3.4
Fundamental Rights	F4	Equal treatment and absence of discrimination	SF4.1
		The right to life and security of the person is effectively guaranteed	SF4.2
		Due process of law and rights of the accused	SF4.3
		Freedom of opinion and expression is effectively guaranteed	SF4.4
		Freedom of belief and religion is effectively guaranteed	SF4.5
		Freedom from arbitrary interference with privacy is effectively guaranteed	SF4.6
		Freedom of assembly and association is effectively guaranteed	SF4.7
		Fundamental labor rights are effectively guaranteed	SF4.8
Order and Security	F5	Crime is effectively controlled	SF5.1
		Civil conflict is effectively limited	SF5.2
		People do not resort to violence to redress personal grievances	SF5.3
Regulatory Enforcement	F6	Government regulations are effectively enforced	SF6.1
		Government regulations are applied and enforced without improper influence	SF6.2
		Administrative proceedings are conducted without unreasonable delay	SF6.3
		Due process is respected in administrative proceedings	SF6.4
		The government does not expropriate without lawful process and adequate compensation	SF6.5
Civil Justice	F7	People can access and afford civil justice	SF7.1
		Civil justice is free of discrimination	SF7.2
		Civil justice is free of corruption	SF7.3
		Civil justice is free of improper government influence	SF7.4
		Civil justice is not subject to unreasonable delay	SF7.5
		Civil justice is effectively enforced	SF7.6
		ADR is accessible, impartial, and effective	SF7.7

continued on following page

Table 1. Continued

Factor	Code	Sub-Factor	Code
Criminal Justice	F8	Criminal investigation system is effective	SF8.1
		Criminal adjudication system is timely and effective	SF8.2
		Correctional system is effective in reducing criminal behavior	SF8.3
		Criminal system is impartial	SF8.4
		Criminal system is free of corruption	SF8.5
		Criminal system is free of improper government influence	SF8.6
		Due process of law and rights of the accused	SF8.7
Informal Justice*	/	Informal justice is timely and effective	/
		Informal justice is impartial and free of improper influence	/
		Informal justice respects and protects fundamental rights	/

*Note: The factor *Informal Justice* is not included in the aggregated scores and rankings due to lack of data.

principles of the rule of law. This factor estimates the corruption of government officials in the executive branch (SF 2.1), judicial branch (SF 2.2), police and military (SF 2.3), and the legislative branch (SF 2.4).

The *Open Government* factor evaluates the openness of the government towards its citizens. The two-way communication between the citizens and the government can have a positive impact on the citizen's level of trust in the government (Welch & Hinnant, 2003). To enforce the relationship between the government and its citizens and to enable the rule of law, the country's laws should be publicized and accessible (SF 3.1), and most importantly stable (SF 3.2). Besides, citizens should be given the opportunity to participate and petition against the laws and government decisions they find improper (SF 3.3) and the right to demand official information on request (SF 3.4).

Human rights should be protected by the rule of law according to the Universal Declaration of Human Rights (UN, 2015). Accordingly, the *Fundamental Rights* factor is the most detailed factor as it encompasses a wide aspect of the rights protected by the rule of law. The fundamental rights should be guaranteed by the constitution. Therefore, this factor analyzes whether the Constitution grants the firmly established human rights such as freedom of opinion (SF 4.4) or labor rights (SF 4.8).

The *Order and Security* factor evaluates how the government assures the security of persons and property. This factor is highly important as it is a precondition for the realization of other rights that the rule of law is based on (WJP, 2014). Therefore, crime should be controlled through security forces and judiciary (SF 5.1), civil conflict should be limited (SF 5.2), and citizens should address to official bodies to resolve the issues, not to attempt to solve them by themselves (SF 5.3). These tasks are complex and require institutional development, credible security forces, adequate training of prosecutors, a criminal code, and many more (Samuels, 2006).

The government imposes laws, but it should also be capable of enforcing and implementing them accordingly. The sixth factor, *Regulatory Enforcement,* examines whether the regulations are effectively enforced (SF 6.1), without improper influence (SF 6.2), without delay (SF 6.3), respecting the administrative proceeding (SF 6.4), and that there is no expropriation of private property without compensation (SF 6.5). Besides creating laws, governments need to take notice on the quality of their enforcement by the regulators and courts, as the laws are essential elements of corporate governance (La Porta et al., 1998).

The seventh factor, *Civil Justice,* includes seven sub-factors in total. It measures whether the civil justice system can effectively resolve the issues citizens address. The rule of law promises justice and equality before the law. Therefore, access to legal services and legal representation are needed (Genn, 1997). The civil justice should be accessible (SF 7.1), free of discrimination (SF 7.2), free of corruption (SF 7.3), free of government influence (SF 7.4), timely (SF 7.5), effective (SF 7.6), and should allow alternative dispute resolution (ADR) (SF 7.7).

The eighth factor, *Criminal Justice,* aims to assess the criminal justice system that is expected to protect persons, property, and province (Braithwaite & Pettit, 1990). This factor makes an integral part of the rule of law, as it brings action against individuals who committed actions against the law. The criminal justice system should be efficient and timely (SF 8.2), impartial (SF 8.4), free of corruption (SF 8.5), free of government influence (SF 8.6). Also, criminal investigation should be effective (SF 8.1), the rights of the accused should be respected (SF 8.7), and the imposed correctional system should be effective in reducing the crime rates (SF 8.3).

Finally, the last factor, *Informal Justice,* concerns the informal justice systems such as tribal and religious courts that resolve disputes (WJP, 2014). Although *World Justice Project* has collected a certain amount of data regarding this factor, due to severe missing data this factor is not yet included in the overall index. However, the efforts put into measuring the informal justice should be recognized. Namely, in some parts of the world the informal ways of resolving disputes are widely accepted. UNDP is aware of that fact stating that informal justice systems should meet several criteria and that any intervention or initiative they propose "should work towards gradually enhancing the quality of dispute resolution" and "adhere to the human rights principles" (UNDP Oslo Governance Centre, 2006, p 10). The attempt to quantify the informal justice is a major step towards measuring as many aspects of the rule of law as possible.

After the detailed presentation of the *Rule of Law Index,* we can conclude that it is a comprehensive multistage composite index that has been recognized for having a normative definition of the rule of law and a clear theory of what the rule of law represents (Merry et al., 2015). As any composite index, it has issues with the indicator selection and data collection processes, weighting scheme, and the aggregation method employed (Saisana & D'Hombres, 2008).

The sub-factors and factors that make the *Rule of Law Index* were chosen in consultation with academics, practitioners, and community leaders from around the world (WJP, 2014). Accordingly, they have been chosen on subjective basis, with no proper justification. Therefore, the presented indicator selection process can easily be questioned. The *World Justice Project* conducts two polls in each country to collect the data for the calculation of the presented sub-factors: a general population poll (GPP) and qualified respondents' questionnaires (QRQ). The GPP is conducted in three major cities in each country on the representative sample of 1000 respondents. On the other hand, the QRQ is designed for in-country practitioners and academics with experience in law and public health. Although the data is collected through surveys, their results are highly reliable as the *World Justice Project* monitors the survey processes. Putting aside the fact that the survey process has been conducted under strict rules, the issue of subjectivity of the collected answers arises. Namely, they can still be viewed with skepticism and ambivalence as the respondents express their opinions (Turner and Martin, 1985). The next step in the index construction after data collection is normalization on the scale from 0 to 1 using the *Min-Max* method (WJP, 2014).

The aggregation method used to calculate the *Rule of Law Index* is the arithmetic average. The weights assigned to sub-factors to obtain factor values and to factors to obtain the overall score are equal weights. However, equal weights do not mean zero weighting (Nardo et al., 2005a). Equal weighting implies judgment on the observed phenomenon, whereas all core parts of the phenomenon are equally important. In the case of the *Rule of Law Index*, although the assigned weights are equal, the effective weights show discrepancies (Table 2).

The index consists of eight factors, so the weight assigned to each of them equals 0.125 (1/8). Looking at the sub-factors, their weights within factors can be calculated in the same way. After the weights within factors are obtained, the effective weights of sub-factors can be calculated. Effective weights of sub-factors show their importance for the ranking process. For example, in case of factor *Absence of Corruption,* the sub-factor weights are 0.031 (0.125 • 0.25). When calculating the *Rule of Law Index,* all sub-factors of the *Absence of Corruption* factor will be weighted by 0.031 and later summed with other weighted sub-factors. Using the same approach, the effective weights were calculated for all 44 sub-factors. The results presented in Table 2 point out that eventually the sub-factors are not given the same importance. Precisely, effective weights range from 0.016 (Sub-factors of *Fundamental Rights*) to 0.042 (Sub-factors of *Order and Security*). The presented result means that sub-factors of factors that consist of a larger number of components have smaller implicit weights than the sub-factors of factors grouping fewer components. Applying equal weighting within each factor leads to unequal weighting of sub-factors in the overall composite index (Nardo et al., 2005b) which is not based on contribution, whereas on the index framework.

Current weighting scheme, which at first glance places the same importance to all factors and sub-factors, in fact, creates an unbalanced composite index. First, the sub-factors are not weighted by their contribution or significance to the observed problem, whereas by the number of sub-factors within the factor they belong to. Secondly, the aggregation method employed is easily challenged due to its compensative nature (Munda, 2008). Finally, the users of the index could be misled thinking all sub-factors have the same importance in the overall index. The weighting scheme has a high impact on the overall results and eventually on the entity ranks, and as such it should not depend on the framework of the composite index. Therefore, the presented weighing scheme should be additionally analyzed to overcome the above-mentioned issues. We suggest employing the twofold I-distance approach to address the observed limitations. Namely, this approach can be used for both ranking countries by the level of which they follow the principles of the rule of law and for determining unbiased weighting factors of composite indices (Jovanovic-Milenkovic et al., 2015).

Table 2. Effective weights assigned to index sub-factors

Factor	Weights within *Rule of Law* (a)	Number of Sub-Factors	Weights within Factors (b)	Effective Weights of Sub-Factors (a•b)
1. Constrains on Government Powers	0.125	6	0.167	0.021
2. Absence of Corruption	0.125	4	0.250	0.031
3. Open Government	0.125	4	0.250	0.031
4. Fundamental Rights	0.125	8	0.125	**0.016**
5. Order and Security	0.125	3	0.333	**0.042**
6. Regulatory Enforcement	0.125	5	0.200	0.025
7. Civil Justice	0.125	7	0.143	0.018
8. Criminal Justice	0.125	7	0.143	0.018

METHODOLOGY

I-Distance Method

To create a new weighting scheme for the *Rule of Law Index*, we decided to employ the I-distance method. This statistical multivariate analysis was devised in the 70's when a need for socioeconomic ranking emerged. Ivanovic (1977) created a method that could answer to the chosen criteria: to rank entities using a large number of variables of different units. After being initially used for socioeconomic research, the I-distance method has been used with great success in many areas as presented in several scientific papers (for example Maricic & Kostic-Stankovic, 2014; Zornic et al., 2015; Dobrota, Savic & Bulajic, 2015).

What makes this method stand out is the fact that it is based on calculating the mutual distances between the entities being processed, whereupon they are compared to one another to create a rank (Seke et al., 2013). To measure the distance and rank countries, it is necessary to fix one entity as a reference in the observed set using the I-distance method. The ranking of entities in the set is based on the calculated distance from the referent entity (Jeremic et al., 2013; Jovanovic et al., 2012). The referent entity can be an actual or a fictive entity with the minimum or maximum values of all observed variables. In the performed analysis, the authors used a fictive entity with minimal indicator values as the referent entity.

For a selected set of variables $X^T = \left(X_1, X_2, \ldots X_k \right)$ chosen to characterize the entities, the I-distance between the two entities $e_r = \left(x_{1r}, x_{2r}, \ldots x_{kr} \right)$ and $e_s = \left(x_{1s}, x_{2s}, \ldots x_{ks} \right)$ is defined as:

$$D(r,s) = \sum_{i=1}^{k} \frac{\left| d_i\left(r,s \right) \right|}{\sigma_i} \prod_{j=1}^{i-1} \left(1 - r_{ji.12\ldots j-1} \right), \tag{1}$$

where $d_i(r,s)$ is the distance between the values of a variable X_i for e_r and e_s e.g. the discriminate effect:

$$d_i\left(r,s \right) = x_{ir} - x_{is} \quad i \in \left\{ 1, \ldots k \right\}. \tag{2}$$

σ_i is the standard deviation of X_i, and $r_{ji.12\ldots j-1}$ is a partial coefficient of the correlation between X_i and X_j, $\left(j < i \right)$.

The calculation of the I-distance is an iterative process, consisted of several steps. First, the value of the discriminate effect of the first variable (the most significant variable, which provides the largest amount of information on the phenomena upon which the entities will be ranked) is calculated. Then, the value of the discriminate effect of the second variable that is not covered by the first one is calculated. This procedure is repeated for the all observed variables in the data set (Jeremic & Jovanovic-Milenkovic, 2014).

To overcome the problem of negative coefficient of partial correlation, which can occur when it is not possible to achieve the same direction of variables, it is suitable to use the square I-distance (Jeremic et al., 2013). It is given as:

$$D^2(r,s) = \sum_{i=1}^{k} \frac{d_i^2(r,s)}{\sigma_i^2} \prod_{j=1}^{i-1} \left(1 - r_{ji.12...j-1}^2\right)$$

(3)

Another case when the square I-distance is recommended is when an index is comprised of a large number of variables. Namely, a certain amount of information of the least significant variables for the ranking process can be lost. Therefore, it is advisable to apply the square I-distance method as it can minimize the amount of the lost information. As the presented framework has up to 8 sub-factors, the square method was employed.

Twofold I-Distance Approach

The I-distance method can be applied to all variables that make a composite index, but it can also be applied to indicators in several stages. Namely, if the method was employed directly to all indicators, a certain amount of information could be lost. On the other hand, the method could be applied in stages following the structure of the analysed index. Besides reducing the amount of the information loss, such approach allows the analyst to gain insight into the entity rank dynamics not only overall but also by index dimensions. To better present how the twofold I-distance approach works in practice, we will explain its application on the *Rule of Law Index*.

Following the structure of the *Rule of Law Index,* our suggested approach for its reengineering was twofold: First, we applied the I-distance method on the sub-factors of each factor. By so we gained an insight of each factors' dynamics. Secondly, again the I-distance method was applied, but now on the previously obtained factor results to calculate the Total I-distance value i.e. the overall ranking of countries. Figure 1 shows the proposed framework for the in-depth analysis of the *Rule of Law Index*.

Figure 1. The proposed framework for the in-depth analysis of the Rule of Law Index

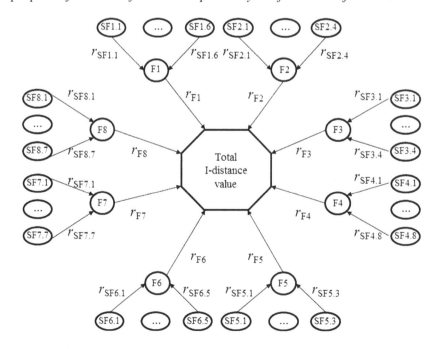

As one can note on Figure 1, the Pearson's correlation coefficients between sub-factors and factors and correlation coefficients between factors and the Total I-distance were calculated. Namely, I-distance method has a particular feature that is to present the importance of variables for the ranking process through Pearson's correlation coefficients (Maricic & Kostic-Stankovic, 2014). The obtained correlation coefficients do not represent the new weights of factors and sub-factors; they provide information on the key factors or sub-factors for the ranking process. Moreover, the correlation coefficients can be used to determine a new weighting scheme or to revise the number of indicators that make the composite index according to the Composite I-distance Methodology (CIDI) (Dobrota et al., 2016). Namely, new weights can be calculated using the following equation:

$$w_i = \frac{r_i}{\sum_{j=1}^{k} r_j} \tag{4}$$

where r_i $(i=1,...,k)$ is the Pearson's correlation coefficient of the i-th input variable and the I-distance value. The sum of weights acquired using this approach is 1 (Dobrota et al., 2015). The new weighting scheme we propose is unbiased in terms that it is solely based on the provided data and formed on the basis of the statistical I-distance method that has previously been used with great success. By applying weights based on the I-distance the overall level of subjectivity of the observed metric can be reduced, and the validity of the index can be increased.

RESULTS

As previously explained, our approach for the analysis of the *Rule of Law Index* was twofold. First, we applied the I-distance method on the sub-factors of each factor, and second, again we employed the I-distance but now on the previously obtained factor I-distance values to calculate the Total I-distance value. Such an approach gave us an insight to country rankings by factors and by the newly-obtained overall index values. Besides, we were able to obtain a new weighting scheme, which is unbiased on both index levels.

The analysis was conducted on the official *Rule of Law Index* dataset for the year 2014. The dataset was complete, so we were able to analyze all 99 countries covered by the index. The top 15 ranked countries by the twofold I-distance approach, their ranks by factors and their rank by the official *Rule of Law Index* are given in Table 3.

Comparing the ranks by the twofold I-distance approach and the official *Rule of Law* ranks one can see that the top three countries have not changed. However, several discrepancies can be noticed. For example, Austria and Singapore improved their ranks by three positions while Finland, on the other hand, dropped four positions. To statistically measure the differences in ranks between the official and the Total I-distance ranks, the Spearman's correlation coefficient was calculated. Spearman's correlation coefficient is based on the differences between ranks of two variables, whereas identical values of variables are assigned a rank equal to the average of their positions in the ascending order of the values (Ramsey, 1989). The correlation between the two ranks is large and statistically significant $r_s=0.890$ (p<0.01).

Table 3. The ranking of top 15 countries by the total I-distance ranking, their ranks by eight factors after applying the I-distance method, and their official Rule of Law Index ranks

Country	F1	F2	F3	F4	F5	F6	F7	F8	Total I-Distance Rank	Rule of Law Rank
Denmark	1	1	6	3	4	2	4	2	1	1
Norway	2	2	1	2	35	1	1	4	2	2
Sweden	4	6	5	1	8	3	6	6	3	3
Austria	8	9	4	5	10	7	8	5	4	7
Netherlands	6	7	8	7	18	4	2	9	5	5
New Zealand	3	4	2	6	12	6	10	11	6	6
Singapore	19	5	18	21	2	8	5	3	7	10
Finland	5	3	10	4	11	12	9	1	8	4
Australia	7	8	12	11	15	5	12	13	9	8
Japan	14	12	9	20	1	11	11	20	10	12
Germany	9	15	14	8	13	15	3	15	11	9
Canada	12	17	3	18	17	10	13	16	12	11
UK	10	11	11	14	23	9	15	12	13	13
Hong Kong, China	16	10	7	27	3	14	16	10	14	16
Republic of Korea	15	18	13	24	9	17	7	8	15	14

Analysing the obtained Total I-distance results, one can conclude that the Scandinavian countries (Denmark, Norway, and Sweden) top the list. These countries have national audit offices whose primary activity is to question whether the governments are enforcing the rule of law. For example, in Sweden, the Swedish National Audit Office (SNAO), a government-independent body, has the mandate to examine the work of the government agencies and the government itself (Grönlund, Svärdsten, & Öhman, 2011). Such agencies are an additional way of implementing the principles of the rule of law. Closely behind are Austria and the Netherlands, followed by New Zealand. Contrarily to the Scandinavian countries, Austria carried out a three-pronged Rule of Law Initiative for the years 2004-2008 (Buhler, 2008), while the New Zealand firmly incorporated the rule of law principles in its constitution legislature (WJP, 2014).

Looking at the presented results per factor, Norway's ranks are quite interesting. Namely, it is ranked 35th in Factor 5, while it is second in the overall. On the other hand, Singapore is ranked below top 10 in three factors (F1, F3, and F4), but is eventually in the 7th place. The same accounts for Japan, who is ranked below top 10 in six factors but enters the top 10 by the overall result. To better depict the observed phenomenon, we will focus our attention on the importance of sub-factors and factors for the ranking methodology.

As explained before, the I-distance method has a special feature: it can point out the importance of the analyzed indicators for the overall ranking. Therefore, the 2014 database was further examined, and the Pearson's correlation coefficients with the I-distance values were determined. First, the correlation coefficients between the sub-factors and factor I-distance values were obtained (Table 4).

The correlation coefficients within Factors 1, 2, 3, 6, and 8 are high, and their range within the factor is small. Namely, among the five factors, Factor 1 has the largest range of 0.151. This means that all

Table 4. Correlation between sub-factors and factors values obtained using the I-distance method

F1		F2		F3		F4		F5		F6		F7		F8	
SF	r	SF	r	SF	r	SF	r	SF	r	SF	r	SF	r	SF	r
1.2	0.954	2.1	0.970	3.2	0.921	4.2	0.916	5.2	0.834	6.2	0.925	7.6	0.887	8.7	0.938
1.3	0.887	2.4	0.907	3.3	0.851	4.3	0.904	5.1	0.685	6.1	0.893	7.3	0.856	8.3	0.900
1.4	0.885	2.2	0.888	3.4	0.841	4.6	0.894	5.3	0.591	6.4	0.886	7.4	0.817	8.5	0.885
1.1	0.855	2.3	0.876	3.1	0.841	4.8	0.877			6.3	0.840	7.7	0.791	8.2	0.854
1.6	0.847					4.4	0.811			6.5	0.814	7.2	0.78	8.4	0.818
1.5	0.803					4.1	0.790					7.1	0.758	8.6	0.796
						4.7	0.784					7.5	0.637	8.1	0.792
						4.5	0.729								

*Note: F – Index factor, SF – Index sub-factor, r – Pearson's correlation coefficient, $p < 0.01$ for all r.

of the indicators covered by these factors are important for the ranking process and that their structures are stable and coherent. The most important indicators per factor are 1.2 (*Government powers are effectively limited by the judiciary*), 2.1 (*Government officials in the executive branch do not use public office for private gain*), 3.2 (*The laws are stable*), 4.2 (*The right to life and security of the person is effectively guaranteed*), 5.2 (*Civil conflict is effectively limited*), 6.2 (*Government regulations are applied and enforced without improper influence*), 7.6 (*Civil justice is effectively enforced*), and 8.7 (*Due process of law and rights of the accused*). These results are in concordance with the previous research. Namely, initially, courts are endowed with formal powers to constrain governments (Staton & Moore, 2011). Therefore, the judiciary should be allowed to effectively check government and its governing bodies. When it comes to corruption, Warren (2004) states that the public trust is often given to the executive branch of the state, and corruption in it is seen as a violation of "public trust". Accordingly, government as the trustee and executor of collective purpose is loosing credentials if the corruption is perceived (Della Porta & Vannucci, 1999), which can be harmful for the democracy. Weingast (2008) believes that stabilizing the laws in all spheres would lead to the rise of wealth. The same author states that the rule of law requires the state to treat citizens equally and impersonally, not allowing bribery or private interests to influence the regulatory enforcement. The rule of law should be equally applied on all citizens. Therefore, the fundamental rights of criminal suspects should be enforced and respected (WJP, 2014).

More attention should be placed on Factors 4, 5, and 7. Namely, their correlation coefficients vary more than the latter ones. In the case of Factor 4, all sub-factors proved to be important as their correlation coefficient is above 0.6. However, not all sub-factors have the same importance. Their significance ranges from r=0.916 (SF 4.2) to r=0.784 (SF 4.5). Factor 5 raises concerns as sub-factor 5.3 has the correlation coefficient with the I-distance below 0.6. Correlation coefficients of this factor range from r=0.834 (SF 5.2) to r=0.591 (SF 5.3). Sub-factor 5.3 is still important for the ranking, but such a result indicates that Factor 5 (*Order and Security*) could be revised. The importance of the sub-factors of Factor 7 varies the most: 0.25. This clearly means that the structure of this indicator is not coherent, and that it should be revised. The presented results are in concordance with the previous detailed statistical analysis of the *Rule of Law Index* conducted by Saisana and Saltelli (2014). Namely, the authors stated that Factor 4 is the least coherent, that Factor 5 is the least robust one, and that Factor 7 has a low percent of variance explained.

Pearson's correlation coefficients between the factors and the Total I-distance value marked *Regulatory Enforcement* (Factor 6) as the most important for the ranking process, followed by *Absence of Corruption* (Factor 3) (Table 5). These results were confirmed in several studies. Namely, Haggard and Tiede (2011) found that in order to enable the rule of law and to initiate economic growth, governments need to be able to provide and enforce laws. As others have noted, the rule of law measures load heavily on the corruption dimension (Kaufmann, Kraay, & Mastruzzi, 2008, p. 21; Skaaning, 2009). The *Rule of Law Index* does not differ on this issue. On the other hand, *Order and Security* (Factor 5) was the least important factor for the ranking. The low importance of Factor 5 has been elaborated by Saisana and Saltelli (2014, pp. 191), who stated that it is "slightly less influential" than the other factors.

The final step in our research was to determine the unbiased weighting scheme that is based on the I-distance method. The weighting scheme was obtained using the Pearson's correlation coefficients, as explained in the previous section, using the formula (4). The proposed weighting scheme is given in Table 6.

Table 5. Correlation between factors and total I-distance

Factor	Coefficient of Correlation
6. Regulatory Enforcement	0.939**
2. Absence of Corruption	0.934**
8. Criminal Justice	0.927**
7. Civil Justice	0.915**
3. Open Government	0.905**
1. Constraints on Government Powers	0.875**
4. Fundamental Rights	0.841**
5. Order and Security	0.749**

Note: **p<0.01.

Table 6. The proposed weighting scheme for the Rule of Law Index

	Factor 1		Factor 2		Factor 3		Factor 4		Factor 5		Factor 6		Factor 7		Factor 8	
	SF	r	SF	r	SF	r	SF	r	SF	r	SF	r	SF	r	SF	r
Weights within factor	1.2	0.18	2.1	0.27	3.2	0.27	4.2	0.14	5.2	0.40	6.2	0.21	7.6	0.16	8.7	0.16
	1.3	0.17	2.4	0.25	3.3	0.25	4.3	0.14	5.1	0.33	6.1	0.21	7.3	0.16	8.3	0.15
	1.4	0.17	2.2	0.24	3.4	0.24	4.6	0.13	5.3	0.28	6.4	0.20	7.4	0.15	8.5	0.15
	1.1	0.16	2.3	0.24	3.1	0.24	4.8	0.13			6.3	0.19	7.7	0.14	8.2	0.14
	1.6	0.16					4.4	0.12			6.5	0.19	7.2	0.14	8.4	0.14
	1.5	0.15					4.1	0.12					7.1	0.14	8.6	0.13
							4.7	0.12					7.5	0.12	8.1	0.13
							4.5	0.11								
Weights among factors	0.12		0.13		0.13		0.12		0.11		0.13		0.13		0.13	

Looking at the weights assigned to factors, we can say that all of the factors are roughly equally important. Such result is in concordance with the official weighting scheme and with the in-depth study conducted by Saisana and Saltelli (2014). The newly proposed weighting scheme proves to be balanced and again statistically confirms the initial factor weights proposed by the indicator creators. However, the same does not account for the sub-factors. The newly proposed weighting scheme shows discrepancies within Factor 5, whose sub-factor weights significantly differ. Its weights vary from 0.28 to 0.4, meaning the indicator *Civil conflict is effectively limited* is almost as twice as important as *People do not resort to violence to redress personal grievances*. Factors 4, 7, and 8 also display weight inconsistencies, but they are not so large as in the case of Factor 5. This result implies that more attention should be placed on Factor 5 and its sub-factors. Our result is in concordance with the study conducted by Saisana and Saltelli (2014) who also marked Factor 5 as the factor that should be re-analysed. Also, the result implies that the overall index value of countries with high values of the sub-factor 5.2 might have been reduced due to the lower officially assigned weight to the sub-factor.

FUTURE RESEARCH DIRECTIONS

During our research, we identified four possible future directions of the study: inclusion of the ninth factor *Informal Justice* in the analysis, evaluating the new weighting scheme, reducing the number of indicators, and performing a hybrid weighting approach.

As mentioned before, the *Rule of Law Index* comprises of nine factors, whereas only eight of them are aggregated into the overall index value. The I-distance method highly depends on the number of the observed variables. Therefore, it would be interesting to see how will the weighting scheme change upon the inclusion of the factor *Informal Justice* in the official calculation of the index.

The newly obtained weighting scheme, presented in this paper, should be evaluated to ensure the reliability of the results. Suggested analyses to resolve the perceived issue are the uncertainty and sensitivity analysis. Uncertainty analysis tackles the question of the influence of input indicators on the overall result by creating alternative models of the analysed composite index. On the other hand, the sensitivity analysis measures the effect of each individual score of the uncertainty analysis. The results of both analyses can provide useful information on the impact of indicators and their weights to overall scores (Sasiana & D'Hombres, 2008). Uncertainty and sensitivity analysis have been previously used with great success in the assessment of composite indices (Dobrota et al., 2015; Saisana, 2008). Namely, if the new weighing scheme shows high sensitivity and less stability, the official weighting scheme would be signed as more trustworthy.

The third direction of the future studies concerns the number of indicators that enter the index framework. The analysis of the correlation coefficients and the new weights provided in the previous section showed that the structure of several factors is not coherent and that it could be refined. One of the possible statistical approaches that could be used to achieve such a task is the Post Hoc I-distance approach. This approach is an iterative process whereas indicators are removed from the framework based on their correlation coefficient with the I-distance value. In the first step, I-distance method is applied to all indicators. Then correlation coefficients of each indicator with the I-distance value are calculated. Based on the obtained value, the indicator with the least significance for the ranking process is excluded from the framework. The procedure is repeated until the sum of correlation coefficients starts to drop (Markovic et al., 2016). The *Rule of Law Index* consists of 44 indicators that are collected through detailed surveys. Therefore, a statistically justified reduction of sub-factors can significantly reduce the resources needed to acquire the data and obtain the index values.

Finally, the question of objectiveness in composite indices arises. Should the weighting scheme be completely unbiased? When analysing a weighing scheme, researchers, maybe, need not alter weights on all indicator levels. Namely, creating a composite index using just objective methods to assign weights creates a rigid metric. Also, a recent study showed that expert opinion should be taken into account when creating a composite measure (Zhou, Ang & Zhou, 2010). Therefore, we propose a fusion of biased and objective approach (Maricic et al., 2015). I-distance method could be applied just on sub-factors to create factors or just on already created factors. When it comes to devising objective weights, one approach can be to use the officially assigned weights, and the other would be to assemble a new expert group to suggest new weights. Another issue that should be also taken into account is the choice of experts who will take part in the process of assigning weights to a certain level of the composite measure. In the case of the *Rule of Law Index,* the new expert group could be formed by related academics, government representatives, and even non-governmental organizations representatives. Further, the question arises: which level of the composite index should be based on expert opinion and which should be impartial. Therefore, we propose two hybrid approaches: first, in which the weights on the lower level of the composite index will be impartial and on the upper level will be left unchanged, and second, which will be the other way around (Figure 2).

The hybrid approach has two benefits: First, it takes into account the expert opinion and secondly, it reduces the level of biasness of the composite measure.

DISCUSSION AND CONCLUSION

A recent study by Haggard and Tiede (2011, pp. 673) elaborated four distinct causal mechanisms through which the rule of law has been associated with economic growth: through the provision of security of person; through security of property and enforcement of contract; through checks on government; and through checks on corruption and private capture. Botero and Ponce (2010) state that the rule of law acts as an "assurance of stability, order, and economic development". Also, according to UNDP, the rule of law is an important mean of achieving sustainable human development. Clearly, it can be concluded

Figure 2. Hybrid approaches for scrutinizing the Rule of Law Index

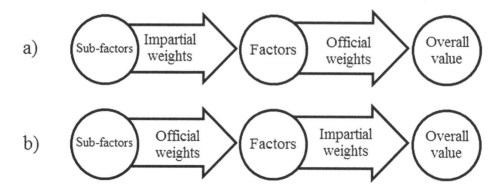

that the rule of law is an important concept for the human wellbeing and that precise and statistically sound measurements of its level of enforcement are needed.

As mentioned before, the concept of the rule of law is by itself difficult to define and conceptualize. Another issue that creators of the rule of law indices faced was the indicator selection. For example, Glaeser et al., (2004) argued that only the objective measurements should be used to reduce the potential bias. On the other hand, Rios-Figueroa and Staton (2008) advocated for the use of subjective indicators as they believe such measurements can capture interesting information on the rule of law. The *World Justice Project* stood out as the organization willing to provide a comprehensive answer to all the issues that emerged regarding a creation of a composite index of the rule of law. Since the publication of their *Rule of Law Index* in 2008, the index has gained the reputation of a multidimensional, reliable, and stable composite index. However, the robustness analysis by the *Joint Research Centre* experts (Saisana & Saltelli, 2014) provoked further analysis of this index's weighting scheme.

The aim of this study was to propose a new weighing scheme that will not be based on expert opinion and will try to reduce the level of biasness of the official *Rule of Law Index*. We decided to employ a statistical I-distance method to analyse and propose a direction to enhance the *Rule of Law Index* for the year 2014. As the observed composite index is multi-layered, we applied the twofold I-distance approach, which has been used with success in a previous studies (Maricic & Kostic-Stankovic, 2014; Jovanovic-Milenkovic et al., 2015). Except creating an objective ranking of the observed countries, we were able to obtain a new weighting scheme thanks to the ability of the I-distance to point out relevant variables for the ranking process (Dobrota et al., 2015; 2016). Our approach allows statistically based calculation of weighting schemes, which is a step forward from the subjectively based equal weighting.

The new weighting scheme is in accordance with the official weighing scheme on the factor level. Namely, our weights on the factor level are almost equal. Therefore, we can say that equal weighting on the upper index level is justified. Meanwhile, the results on the lower index level differ. According to the official weighting scheme, all sub-factors within factors have the same importance. The obtained weights within factors showed that the importance of sub-factors within a factor varies. Our analysis showed that three factors need in-depth analysis: *Fundamental Rights* (Factor 4), *Order and Security* (Factor 5) and *Civil Justice* (Factor 7). Interestingly, these factors have the lowest (Factor 5) or the highest (Factor 4) number of sub-factors. The correlation coefficient analysis proved that most of the sub-factors are important for their respective factor, whereas Factor 5 could be refined.

Finally, the effects of the application of the new weighting scheme should be noticed: possible policy implications. Unequal effective weights within Factors 5 and 7 might initiate specific reforms and additional audit of governmental institutions. In case of Factor 5, the sub-factor *Civil conflict is effectively limited* gained importance. The official methodology of the *Rule of Law Index* defines this sub-factor as a measure of political violence, including terrorism, armed conflict, and political unrest (WJP, 2014). Countries all over the world are aiming to reduce the level of political violence, especially in the turbulent political times such as today (Dragu & Polborn, 2014). Therefore, the sub-factor values of the analysed countries are expected to rise, leading to potential rank changes. On the other hand, more detailed inspection on the functioning of the civil system (Factor 7) might result in substantial reforms, reduction of corruption, higher efficiency, and more openness to the civil society. The new weighting scheme might, therefore, help governments around the world to more easily identify areas where policy improvements are need.

The presented paper has several benefits that should be pointed out. Firstly, it aims at introducing objective weights into the *Rule of Law Index*. Secondly, it employs the twofold I-distance approach that has previously been used for an in-depth analysis of a composite index (Jovanovic-Milenkovic et al., 2015). Thirdly, the newly proposed weighting scheme gives justification for equal weighting of the index factors but provides evidence that the same does not apply for index sub-factors. Nevertheless, it should be kept in mind that the weighting scheme presented here depends on the number of the factors and that it is susceptible to changes if the factor *Informal Justice* is included in the calculation of the index. We believe that the proposed methodology for scrutinizing composite indices employed on the *Rule of Law Index* can initiate further research on the index itself and the weighing schemes of composite indices.

REFERENCES

Bedner, A. (2010). An Elementary Approach to the Rule of Law. *Hague Journal on the Rule of Law*, *2*(1), 48–74. doi:10.1017/S1876404510100037

Bergman, M. (2012). The Rule, the Law, and the Rule of Law: Improving Measurement and Content Validity. *Justice System Journal*, *33*(2), 174–193. doi:10.1080/0098261X.2012.10768010

Bersch, K., & Botero, S. (2014). Measuring Governance: Implications of conceptual choices. *European Journal of Development Research*, *26*(1), 124–141. doi:10.1057/ejdr.2013.49

Botero, J. C., & Ponce, A. (2011). *Measuring the Rule of Law*. doi: 10.2139/ssrn.1966257

Braithwaite, J., & Pettit, P. (1990). *Not just deserts: A republican theory of criminal justice*. Oxford, UK: Clarendon Press.

Bühler, K. G. (2008). The Austrian Rule of Law Initiative 2004-2008. *The Panel Series, the Advisory Group and the Final Report on the UN Security Council and the Rule of Law. Max Planck UNYB*, *12*, 409.

Davis, K. E. (2004). What can the Rule of Law variable tell us about Rule of Law reforms? *NYU Law and Economics Research Paper*, 4-26. doi: 10.2139/ssrn.595142

Davis, K. E., & Kruse, M. B. (2007). Taking the measure of law: The case of the Doing Business project. *Law & Social Inquiry*, *32*(4), 1095–1119. doi:10.1111/j.1747-4469.2007.00088.x

Decancq, K., & Lugo, M. A. (2013). Weights in multidimensional indices of wellbeing: An overview. *Econometric Reviews*, *32*(1), 7–34. doi:10.1080/07474938.2012.690641

Della Porta, D., & Vannucci, D. (1999). *Corrupt exchanges: Actors, Resources, and Mechanisms of Political corruption*. New York: Walter de Gruyter.

Dobrota, M., Bulajic, M., Bornmann, L., & Jeremic, V. (2016). A new approach to QS University Ranking using composite I-distance indicator: Uncertainty and sensitivity analyses. *Journal of the Association for Information Science and Technology*, *67*(1), 200–211. doi:10.1002/asi.23355

Dobrota, M., Martic, M., Bulajic, M., & Jeremic, V. (2015). Two-phased composite I-distance indicator approach for evaluation of countries' information development. *Telecommunications Policy*, *39*(5), 406–420. doi:10.1016/j.telpol.2015.03.003

Dobrota, M., Savic, G., & Bulajic, M. (2015). A New Approach to the Evaluation of Countries' Educational Structure and Development: The European Study. *European Review (Chichester, England)*, *23*(4), 553–565. doi:10.1017/S1062798715000277

Dragu, T., & Polborn, M. (2014). The rule of law in the fight against terrorism. *American Journal of Political Science*, *58*(2), 511–525. doi:10.1111/ajps.12061

Genn, H. (1997). Understanding Civil Justice. *Current Legal Problems*, *50*(1), 155–187. doi:10.1093/clp/50.1.155

Gisselquist, R. M. (2014). Developing and evaluating governance indexes: 10 questions. *Policy Studies*, *35*(5), 513–531. doi:10.1080/01442872.2014.946484

Glaeser, E., LaPorta, R., Lopez-de-Silanes, F., & Shleifer, A. (2004). Do institutions cause growth? *Journal of Economic Growth*, *9*(3), 271–303. doi:10.1023/B:JOEG.0000038933.16398.ed

Grönlund, A., Svärdsten, F., & Öhman, P. (2011). Value for money and the rule of law: The (new) performance audit in Sweden. *International Journal of Public Sector Management*, *24*(2), 107–121. doi:10.1108/09513551111109026

Haggard, S., & Tiede, L. (2011). The rule of law and economic growth: Where are we? *World Development*, *39*(5), 673–685. doi:10.1016/j.worlddev.2010.10.007

Ivanovic, B. (1977). *Classification theory*. Belgrade: Institute for Industrial Economics.

Jeremic, V., & Jovanovic-Milenkovic, M. (2014). Evaluation of Asian university rankings: Position and perspective of leading Indian higher education institutions. *Current Science*, *106*(12), 1647–1653.

Jeremic, V., Jovanovic-Milenkovic, M., Martic, M., & Radojicic, Z. (2013). Excellence with Leadership: The crown indicator of SCImago Institutions Rankings IBER Report. *El Profesional de la Informacion*, *22*(5), 474–480. doi:10.3145/epi.2013.sep.13

Jovanovic, M., Jeremic, V., Savic, G., Bulajic, M., & Martic, M. (2012). How does the normalization of data affect the ARWU ranking? *Scientometrics*, *93*(2), 319–327. doi:10.1007/s11192-012-0674-0

Jovanovic-Milenkovic, M., Brajovic, B., Milenkovic, D., Vukmirovic, D., & Jeremic, V. (2015). (in press). Beyond the equal-weight framework of the Networked Readiness Index A multilevel I-distance methodology. *Information Development*. doi:10.1177/0266666915593136

Kaufmann, D., Kraay, A., & Mastruzzi, M. (2007). *The worldwide governance indicators: Answering the critics*. World Bank Policy Research Working Paper No. 4149. Washington, DC: World Bank.

Kaufmann, D., Kraay, A., & Mastruzzi, M. (2008). *Governance matters VII: Aggregate and individual governance indicators for 1996–2007*. World Bank Policy Research Working Paper No. 4654. Washington, DC: World Bank.

La Porta, R., Lopez de Silanes, F., Shleifer, A., & Vishny, R. (1998). Law and finance. *Journal of Political Economy*, *106*(6), 1113–1155. doi:10.1086/250042

Maricic, M., Bulajic, M., Martic, M., & Dobrota, M. (2015). Measuring the ICT Development: The Fusion of Biased and Objective Approach. In *Proceedings of the XII Balkan Conference on Operational Research (BALCOR 2015)*.

Maricic, M., & Kostic-Stankovic, M. (2016). Towards an impartial Responsible Competitiveness Index: A twofold multivariate I-distance approach. *Quality & Quantity*, *50*(1), 1–18. doi:10.1007/s11135-014-0139-z

Markovic, M., Zdravkovic, S., Mitrovic, M., & Radojicic, A. (2016). An Iterative Multivariate Post Hoc I-Distance Approach in Evaluating OECD Better Life Index. *Social Indicators Research*, *126*(1), 1–19. doi:10.1007/s11205-015-0879-8

Merkel, W. (2012). Measuring the Quality of Rule of Law. In M. Zurn, A. Nollkaemper, & R. Peerenboom (Eds.), *Rule of Law Dynamics: In an Era of International and Transnational Governance*. Cambridge University Press. doi:10.1017/CBO9781139175937.004

Merry, S. E. (2009, March). Measuring the world: indicators, human rights, and global governance. In *Proceedings of the 103rd Annual Meeting* (vol. 103, pp. 239-243). American Society for International Law.

Merry, S. E., Davis, K., Kingsbury, B., & Fisher, A. (2015). *The Quiet Power of Indicators: Measuring Governance, Corruption, and Rule of Law*. Cambridge University Press.

Michener, G. (2015). Policy Evaluation via Composite Indexes: Qualitative Lessons from International Transparency Policy Indexes. *World Development*, *74*, 184–196. doi:10.1016/j.worlddev.2015.04.016

Møller, J., & Skaaning, S. E. (2011). On the limited interchangeability of rule of law measures. *European Political Science Review*, *3*(3), 371–394. doi:10.1017/S1755773910000421

Munda, G. (2008). *Social multi-criteria evaluation for a sustainable economy*. Berlin: Springer. doi:10.1007/978-3-540-73703-2

Nardo, M., Saisana, M., Saltelli, A., & Tarantola, S. (2005a). *Input to Handbook of Good Practices for Composite Indicators' Development*. Ispra, Italy: Joint Research Centre.

Nardo, M., Saisana, M., Saltelli, A., Tarantola, S., Hoffman, A., & Giovannini, E. (2005b). *Handbook on constructing composite indicators*. Academic Press.

Ramsey, P. H. (1989). Critical values for Spearman's rank order correlation. *Journal of Educational and Behavioral Statistics*, *14*(3), 245–253. doi:10.3102/10769986014003245

Rios-Figueroa, J., & Staton, J. (2008). *Unpacking the rule of law: A review of Judicial independence measures*. Committee on concepts and measures working paper series. International Political Science Association.

Saisana, M. (2008). The 2007 Composite Learning Index: Robustness Issues and Critical Assessment. Report 23274. European Commission, JRC-IPSC.

Saisana, M., & D'Hombres, B. (2008). Higher Education Rankings: Robustness Issues and Critical Assessment. How much confidence can we have in Higher Education Rankings? EUR23487, Joint Research Centre, Publications Office of the European Union. doi:10.2788/92295

Saisana, M., & Saltelli, A. (2014). JCR statistical audit of the WJP Rule of Law index 2014. In *World Justice Project* (pp. 188–197). The World Justice Project Rule of Law Index.

Saisana, M., & Tarantola, S. (2002). State-of-the-art report on current methodologies and practices for composite indicator development. European Commission, Joint Research Centre, Institute for the Protection and the Security of the Citizen, Technological and Economic Risk Management Unit.

Samuels, K. (2006). Rule of Law in Post-Conflict Countries. Operational Initiatives and Lessons Learnt. Social Development Papers (37). Conflict Prevention and Reconstruction (CPR) Unit in the Social Development of the Sustainable Development Network of the World Bank.

Seke, K., Petrovic, N., Jeremic, V., Vukmirovic, J., Kilibarda, B., & Martic, M. (2013). Sustainable development and public health: Rating European countries. *BMC Public Health*, *13*(77). doi:10.1186/1471-2458-13-77 PMID:23356822

Skanning, S. (2009). Measuring the rule of law. *Political Research Quarterly*, *63*(2), 449–460. doi:10.1177/1065912909346745

Staton, J. K., & Moore, W. H. (2011). Judicial power in domestic and international politics. *International Organization*, *65*(03), 553–587. doi:10.1017/S0020818311000130

Turner, C., & Martin, E. (1985). *Surveying Subjective Phenomena*. Russell Sage Foundation.

UN. (2015). *The Universal Declaration of Human Rights*. Retrieved September 15, 2015, from http://www.un.org/en/documents/udhr/

UNDP Oslo Governance Centre. (2006). *How informal justice systems can contribute*. Oslo: United Nations.

Uslaner, E. M. (2005, November). The bulging pocket and the rule of law: Corruption, inequality, and trust. In *Conference on The Quality of Government: What It Is, How to Get It, Why It Matters* (pp. 17-19).

Warren, E. M. (2004). What does corruption mean in a democracy? *American Journal of Political Science*, *48*(2), 328–343. doi:10.1111/j.0092-5853.2004.00073.x

Weingast, B. R. (2008). Why developing countries prove so resistant to the rule of law. In Global Perspectives on the Rule of Law. Routledge.

Welch, E. W., & Hinnant, C. C. (2003, January). Internet use, transparency, and interactivity effects on trust in government. In *Proceedings of the 36th Annual Hawaii International Conference on System Sciences*. IEEE. doi:10.1109/HICSS.2003.1174323

WJP. (2014). *The World Justice Project Rule of Law Index 2014*. The World Justice Project.

Zhou, P., Ang, B. W., & Zhou, D. Q. (2010). Weighting and aggregation in composite indicator construction: A multiplicative optimization approach. *Social Indicators Research*, *96*(1), 169–181. doi:10.1007/s11205-009-9472-3 PMID:19966916

Zornic, N., Bornmann, L., Maricic, M., Markovic, A., Martic, M., & Jeremic, V. (2015). Ranking institutions within a university based on their scientific performance: A percentile-based approach. *El Profesional de la informacion*, *24*(5), 551-566. doi: 10.3145/epi.2015.sep.05

ADDITIONAL READING

Bovaird, T., & Löffler, E. (2003). Evaluating the quality of public governance: Indicators, models and methodologies. *International Review of Administrative Sciences*, *69*(3), 313–328. doi:10.1177/0020852303693002

Cherchye, L., Lovell, C. K., Moesen, W., & Van Puyenbroeck, T. (2007). One market, one number? A composite indicator assessment of EU internal market dynamics. *European Economic Review*, *51*(3), 749–779. doi:10.1016/j.euroecorev.2006.03.011

Christiane, A. (2006). *Development Centre Studies Uses and Abuses of Governance Indicators*. OECD Publishing.

Holcombe, R. G., & Rodet, C. S. (2012). Rule of law and the size of government. *Journal of Institutional Economics*, *8*(1), 49–69. doi:10.1017/S1744137411000348

Hoskins, B. L., & Mascherini, M. (2009). Measuring active citizenship through the development of a composite indicator. *Social Indicators Research*, *90*(3), 459–488. doi:10.1007/s11205-008-9271-2

Išljamović, S., Jeremić, V., Petrović, N., & Radojičić, Z. (2015). Colouring the socio-economic development into green: I-distance framework for countries' welfare evaluation. *Quality & Quantity*, *49*(2), 617–629. doi:10.1007/s11135-014-0012-0

Jeremic, V., Bulajic, M., Martic, M., & Radojicic, Z. (2011). A fresh approach to evaluating the academic ranking of world universities. *Scientometrics*, *87*(3), 587–596. doi:10.1007/s11192-011-0361-6

Kaufmann, D., Kraay, A., & Mastruzzi, M. (2011). The worldwide governance indicators: Methodology and analytical issues. *Hague Journal on the Rule of Law*, *3*(2), 220–246. doi:10.1017/S1876404511200046

Krever, T. (2013). Quantifying Law: Legal indicator projects and the reproduction of neoliberal common sense. *Third World Quarterly*, *34*(1), 131–150. doi:10.1080/01436597.2012.755014

Maricic, M., Jankovic, M., & Jeremic, V. (2014). Towards a Framework for Evaluating Sustainable Society Index. *Romanian Statistical Review*, *62*(3), 49–62.

Møller, J., & Skaaning, S. E. (2013). Sub-components of the Rule of Law: Reassessing the Relevance of Diminished Subtypes. *Comparative Sociology*, *12*(3), 391–421. doi:10.1163/15691330-12341259

Møller, J., & Skaaning, S. E. (2014). *The Rule of Law: Definitions, Measures, Patterns and Causes*. Palgrave Macmillan. doi:10.1057/9781137320612

Munda, G., & Nardo, M. (2003). *On the methodological foundations of composite indicators used for ranking countries*. Ispra, Italy: Joint Research Centre of the European Communities.

Munda, G., & Nardo, M. (2009). Noncompensatory/nonlinear composite indicators for ranking countries: A defensible setting. *Applied Economics*, *41*(12), 1513–1523. doi:10.1080/00036840601019364

Nardo, M., Saisana, M., Saltelli, A., & Tarantola, S. (2005). *Tools for composite indicators building*. Ispra: European Comission.

Paruolo, P., Saisana, M., & Saltelli, A. (2013). Ratings and rankings: Voodoo or science? *Journal of the Royal Statistical Society. Series A, (Statistics in Society), 176*(3), 609–634. doi:10.1111/j.1467-985X.2012.01059.x

Saisana, M., D'Hombres, B., & Saltelli, A. (2011). Rickety numbers: Volatility of university rankings and policy implications. *Research Policy, 40*(1), 165–177. doi:10.1016/j.respol.2010.09.003

Saisana, M., Saltelli, A., & Tarantola, S. (2005). Uncertainty and sensitivity analysis techniques as tools for the quality assessment of composite indicators. *Journal of the Royal Statistical Society. Series A, (Statistics in Society), 168*(2), 307–323. doi:10.1111/j.1467-985X.2005.00350.x

Saltelli, A., Nardo, M., Saisana, M., & Tarantola, S. (2005). Composite indicators: the controversy and the way forward. Statistics, Knowledge and Policy Key Indicators to Inform Decision Making: Key Indicators to Inform Decision Making, 359-372. OECD Publishing

Santos, A. (2012). The World Bank's Uses of the 'Rule of Law' Promise in Economic Development. The new law and economic development: A critical appraisal. Georgetown Public Law Research Paper No. 12-053, 253-300

Scully, G. W., & Slottje, D. J. (1991). Ranking economic liberty across countries. *Public Choice, 69*(2), 121–152. doi:10.1007/BF00123844

Tarantola, S., & Saltelli, A. (2007, November). *Composite indicators: the art of mixing apples and oranges.* Paper presented on Composite Indicators – Boon or Bane, 16th Scientific Colloquium by the German Federal Statistical Office and German Statistical Society. Weisbaden, Germany

Voigt, S. (2012). How to measure the rule of law. *Kyklos, 65*(2), 262–284. doi:10.1111/j.1467-6435.2012.00538.x

Zhou, P., Ang, B. W., & Poh, K. L. (2006). Comparing aggregating methods for constructing the composite environmental index: An objective measure. *Ecological Economics, 59*(3), 305–311. doi:10.1016/j.ecolecon.2005.10.018

Zurn, M., Nollkaemper, A., & Peerenboom, R. (Eds.). (2012). *Rule of law dynamics: in an era of international and transnational governance.* Cambridge University Press. doi:10.1017/CBO9781139175937

KEY TERMS AND DEFINITIONS

Composite I-Distance Methodology (CIDI): Multivariate statistical methodology based on the I-distance method used to create new composite indexes using data-driven weights.

Effective Weights: The actual weight a sub-indicator or indicator is assigned when aggregated into a composite index.

I-Distance Method: A multivariate statistical method used to rank entities based on a number of selected variables of same or different measurement units.

Robust: Statistically stable, insensitive to outliers, and not highly effected by different methodological assumptions.

Rule of Law: A multidimensional concept which aims at protecting the citizens from the government and from fellow citizens in a clear, publicized, stable, and equally applied manner.

Twofold I-Distance Approach: A multivariate statistical approach based on the application of the I-distance method following the twofold structure of the analysed composite index.

Weighting Scheme: The weighting scheme in a composite index aims at reflecting the relative importance of each of the sub-indicators and/or indicators. It is needed to combine in a meaningful way the preselected variables which make the composite index framework.

Chapter 10
Comparison of Input and Output Indicators in Measuring Human Capital:
An Analysis at Provincial Level for Turkey

Sibel Bali
Uludag University, Turkey

ABSTRACT

Despite the intensive research on human capital, the debate regarding its measurement is ongoing. In this context, the objective of the present study is to underline the distinction between input and output indicators in human capital measurement, which has not attracted sufficient attention, and to present the importance of indicator selection by explaining the findings obtained. To that end, separate indexes will be developed for input and output indicators to measure the level of human capital for Turkey, and it will be analyzed whether the two index groups developed exhibit significant differences between provinces. In accordance with the purpose of this study, index estimations are made using the PCA method with the 2013 data of 81 provinces in Turkey. Province-based estimations demonstrate that the index values estimated by the input and output indicators produce significantly different conclusions. Therefore, selecting appropriate indicators according to the purpose of the study will enable the analyses to produce more accurate policy implications.

INTRODUCTION

Because human capital is a multi-dimensional concept, it is difficult to find an appropriate single indicator to represent it as a whole. Studies in the relevant literature focus on the dimension of education and often use the indicators of enrollment rate or average years of schooling as proxies. Although education has a key role in the formation of human capital, focusing merely on a single proxy results in the omission of other dimensions of human capital, which may make it more difficult to see the actual effect of human capital. Thus, it would be more appropriate to create a composite indicator from indicators that

DOI: 10.4018/978-1-5225-0714-7.ch010

reflect the sub-dimensions of human capital and to use it as a proxy for human capital (Fraumeni, 2008; Dreger, Erber & Glocker, 2009; Furceri & Mourougane, 2010).

An important consideration related to human capital is that the variables used in measuring the level of human capital are categorized as input and output indicators. Input indicators include indicators such as investments that aim to enhance the level of human capital. Although input indicators are a good fit for representing the investment in the level of human capital, they might not fully reflect the current level of human capital. Output indicators are indicators that reflect the current level of human capital, in other words, the level that has been realized rather than the level expected to be realized. However, many studies select indicators without paying attention to this distinction. In empirical studies, the dataset selected significantly affects the results of the study. Numerous studies have remarked that analysis results vary depending on indicator used for measuring human capital.

In this context, the objective of the present study is to underline the distinction between input and output indicators, which has not attracted sufficient attention, and to present the importance of indicator selection by explaining the findings obtained. To that end, separate indexes will be developed for input and output indicators to measure the level of human capital for Turkey, and an analysis will be conducted regarding whether the two index groups developed exhibit significant differences between provinces. Because the education and health policies of countries have intrinsic differences, the appropriateness of cross-country comparisons should be debated further on this subject. It is thought that cross-regional analyses will be appropriate because countries have unitary policies regarding, e.g., education and health. In accordance with the purpose of this study, index estimations are made using the PCA method with the 2013 data of 81 provinces in Turkey.

The study is structured as follows: The introduction section explains the importance of the subject, the objective of the study. The second section briefly summarizes the development of the concept of human capital in the economic literature. The third section summarizes the relevant literature on the measurement and definitions of human capital. The fourth section gives brief information about principal component analysis (PCA), which is the empirical methodology employed in the study. The fifth section presents the indicators, discusses the main findings, and attempts to develop proposals in line with these findings.

BACKGROUND

The Importance of Human Capital

For a long time, the concept of human capital did not draw the attention it deserves in the economic literature. One of the underlying reasons it was overlooked was that before and during the initial phases of the Industrial Revolution, the basic qualities of the labor force were sufficient for the conditions of production at the time. Under those conditions, which could be described as primitive, there was no need to address matters related to the quality of labor. Additionally, labor was relatively homogenous in terms of quality as almost all labor was rural and low skilled in that period. Thus, studies in the economics literature long considered labor quantitatively and did not take into account the quality of labor (Folloni & Vittadini, 2010). However, there were a few significant studies on the importance of the quality of labor in that period, although they did not draw much attention.

It was Petty (1690) who first emphasized the economic importance of human beings in the 17th century, although he never used the term human capital. Petty (1690) regarded labor as the father of wealth, and he stated that the value of labor had to be taken into consideration in estimating the wealth of a nation (Le, Gibson & Oxley; 2005; Oxley, Trinh & John, 2008; Folloni & Vittadini, 2010; Bawumia, & Appiah-Adu, 2015). Smith (1776) noted in The Wealth of Nations that the skills acquired by members of a society cost a real expense, which is a capital fixed and realized in his person. In addition to the views of Petty (1690) and Smith (1776), Mill (1848) and Marshall (1890) emphasized individuals' level of knowledge and skills. However, this topic did not receive sufficient attention, and it took a long time for this topic to be comprehensively assessed under the umbrella of a theory in the economics literature.

With the acceleration of technological developments, the ramifications of the structure of production, and the increasing role of specialization and division of labor in production processes, the level of knowledge and skills of individuals has become a pivotal topic in the economics literature. As a result of these developments, the dominant discourse in Western Europe, particularly after World War I, was replaced by the idea that the competitive advantage of industrialized countries no longer merely stemmed from the cost advantage and that trade patterns focused on non-price competition (Andréosso-O'Callaghan, 2002). Today, companies have to improve their products, services and business processes on a continuous basis in the face of a rapidly changing, competitive and innovative environment. Such an environment can be achieved only with the knowledge, skills and creativity of human capital because individuals are both the creators and the beneficiaries of these developments.

Upon these developments, growth models relying on conventional production functions proved inadequate to explain economic growth through physical capital and labor. Schultz (1961) noted that it was necessary, under these new conditions, to follow an approach that covered the quality of labor in addition to the quantity of labor. Schultz (1961) stated that the expenditures for the education of individuals were not consumption but rather an investment and a form of capital; subsequently, the concept of human capital started to be used formally. Nevertheless, studies in the relevant literature long debated whether humans can be categorized as a form of capital. Those that were against this view considered that categorization of humans as a form of capital treated humans as a 'machine' and thus were unethical. Although the concept of human capital began to be used in 1960s, it was only in the 1970s that the concept eventually took its place in economic analyses. In the mid-1980s, it started to be intensively and comprehensively analyzed, particularly in new growth models (Andréosso-O'Callaghan, 2002).

Traditional growth models that were predominant until the 1980s regarded the basic actors of growth, including knowledge accumulation, technology and human capital, as exogenous. Rapid technological developments, however, quickly changed the production structures and trade patterns, indicating that the role of the concept of human capital in economic processes had become non-negligible. Traditional growth models faced harsh criticism on the grounds that they did not address factors such as knowledge, technology and human capital and that they assumed that capital had diminishing returns and thus that the economy would proceed to a steady state. The underlying reason for this criticism was that it neglected actors that took on pivotal roles in the modification process of economies, that there was an unexplained residual in growth, and that the income gaps between countries did not seem to be likely to be bridged (Bali Eryigit, Eryigit & Dulgeroglu, 2012).

Romer (1986) and Lucas (1988), pioneers of endogenous growth, argued that sustainable growth in the long term could possibly be achieved by increasing the accumulation of human capital. New growth models hold that increases in the accumulation of human capital boost not only the productivity of labor but also the productivity of other factors of production, technological developments and innovations by creating externalities. They assert that individuals with a high level of knowledge and skills can augment natural capital by utilizing existing resources more efficiently and finding new resources and develop new technologies that will eliminate environmental problems jeopardizing the global ecosystem (Sharpe, 2001). Eventually, with the development of new growth theories, human capital has become an important topic of research. However, despite such intensive research, debates on how to define and measure human capital are ongoing. The next section addresses the matters required to be taken into account in defining and measuring human capital.

The Definitions and Measurement of Human Capital

Numerous studies state that the explanatory power of the effect of human capital on economic growth is sensitive to the indicators used for human capital (Lindahl & Krueger, 2001; Andreosso-O'Callaghan, 2002; Le, Gibson & Oxley, 2005; Oxley, Trinh & John, 2008; Boarini, d'Ercole & Liu, 2012; Esteban, Lopez-Pueyo & Sanaú, 2015). One of the most substantial reasons for this is that human capital is poorly measured. Human capital is an intangible concept, and because it cannot be directly observed as physical capital can, human capital stock is measured indirectly. This raises debates over how to measure it. The multidimensionality of the concept of human capital and the vagueness of its definition make it more difficult to measure human capital. Considering that something defined poorly cannot be measured precisely, it is crucial to define the concept of human capital correctly (Romer, 1989; Le, Gibson & Oxley, 2005; Han, Lin & Chen, 2008; Dreger, Erber & Glocker, 2009; Folloni & Vittadini, 2010; Jones, 2014; Meier, Favero & Compton, 2016).

Becker (1964) noted that human capital can be defined individually at national, industrial and organizational levels. As the scale of definition becomes smaller, a more comprehensive measurement can be conducted for the human capital of individuals. However, assessments made at industrial and organizational levels may not be suitable for comparisons between countries or regions within a country due to the difficulty in collecting data and the poor availability and lack of continuity of data sets. Usually, no secondary data are available to assess human capital stock at this scale. Thus, researchers have to collect these data by themselves. Because the primary objective of this study is to emphasize the importance of the selection of indicators, human capital stock will be assessed based on the national definition to allow for the availability of data and comparisons between regions. Hence, other definitions are excluded from the scope of this study.

Becker (1962), one of the pioneers of human capital theory, defined human capital as a stock of skills and qualifications individuals acquire through, e.g., investments in education, on-the-job training, medical care, vitamin consumption and information about the economic system. Education and training are considered the most important investments in human capital. In his article 'Investment in human capital', Schultz (1961) explained investments in human capital with the following examples instead of directly defining human capital: "Much of what we call consumption constitutes investment in human capital. Direct expenditures on education, health, and internal migration to take advantage of better job opportunities are clear examples". The examples given by Schultz (1961) are also found in the definition given by Sharpe (2001), who conducted research on the measurement of human capital. Sharpe (2001) defined human capital as the aggregation of investments in such areas as education, health, on-the-job-training, and migration, which enhance an individual's productivity in the labor market and in non-market activities. Finally, the United Nations Development Programme (UNDP), which publishes the human development index, defines human capital as follows: "It is about creating an environment in which people can develop their full potential and lead productive, creative lives in accord with their needs and interests."

The definition of human capital contributes to its measurement, and as mentioned above, the intangibility of the concept makes it more difficult to measure. Although it is possible to directly measure physical capital, a tangible concept, it is not possible to directly measure human capital, an intangible concept. Additionally, it is noteworthy that as the scope of definition expands, it becomes more difficult to measure human capital (Krušinskas & Bruneckienė, 2015). For the abovementioned reasons, a correct definition of human capital would not end the debates over the indicators to be used. Moreover, the multidimensional nature of the concept is another reason for these ongoing debates.

Assessments made based on a single indicator may fall short and produce mixed results due to the multidimensionality of the concept. Human capital has sub-dimensions such as education, health, and living standards, each of which significantly contributes to the accumulation of human capital (Stroombergen, Rose & Nana, 2002; Boarini, d'Ercole & Liu, 2012). Studies in the relevant literature that assess the accumulation of human capital on the basis of a single indicator select the sub-dimension of education, which is considered to contribute most to the accumulation of human capital[1]. The reason behind this selection is the notion that education plays a key role in the accumulation of human capital (De la Fuente & Domenech, 2006). In addition, it would be more appropriate to use a dataset composed of more representative indicators rather than a single indicator for each sub-dimension in measuring the sub-dimensions of human capital (Sharpe, 2001; Dreger, Erber & Glocker, 2009). The most fundamental approaches for measuring the level of human capital are briefly mentioned below.

The education-based approach is an approach based on the notion that education plays a key role in the accumulation of human capital. It uses indicators such as investments for education, the rate of schooling, the percentage of the population that received a certain education, and the number of classrooms, teachers and schools per student. This approach is criticized on the grounds that it does not take into account the other sub-dimensions of human capital. However, researchers who adopt this approach advocate it based on the argument that education level nurtures the other sub-dimensions of human capital by creating externalities, such as the possibility of better jobs, a higher income, opportunity and awareness for healthier nutrition, and the possibility of receiving better health services (Haveman & Wolfe, 1984, Sharpe, 2001; Le, Gibson & Oxley, 2005; Fraumeni, 2008; Oxley, Trinh & John, 2008; Boarini, d'Ercole & Liu, 2012, De la Fuente & Domenech, 2015).

Another approach employed to measure the level of human capital is the cost-based approach, first introduced by Engel (1886). Studies by Schultz (1961), Kendrick (1976) and Eisner (1985) are example pioneer studies based on this approach. In the cost-based approach, calculations are made based on the costs of investments made to enhance the accumulation of human capital. This approach relies on information on all the costs incurred when producing human capital. The cost-based approach to measuring human capital is similar to that conventionally applied to measure economic capital. Therefore, it should be noted that this approach does not assess the intangible elements of human capital. Additionally, the difficulty of defining and pricing all elements contributing to the formation of human capital is one of the disadvantages of this approach (Mulligan & Sala-i-Martin, 1997; Le, Gibson & Oxley, 2005; Fraumeni, 2008; Oxley, Trinh & John, 2008; Kwon, 2009; Folloni & Vittadini, 2010Boarini, d'Ercole & Liu, 2012).

Another approach to measuring human capital is the income-based approach. The income-based approach measures human capital by summing the discounted values of all future income streams that all individuals in the population expect to earn throughout their lifetime. Petty (1690) employed this approach, which is based on the assumption that wages will exactly reflect productivity differences. However, wages may change with the influence of trade unions or during periods of economic crisis, without reflecting productivity differences. The poor availability of the dataset required for this approach is an important drawback (Weisbrod, 1961; Graham & Webb, 1979; Jorgenson & Fraumeni, 1989, 1992a, 1992b; Folloni & Vittadini, 2010, Boarini, d'Ercole & Liu, 2012).

In addition to the abovementioned approaches, it is possible to assess the accumulation of human capital through input and output indicators. According to this approach, indicators are categorized into two groups: input and output indicators. Input indicators represent the size and quality of investments in human capital, and output indicators represent the actual results of such investments (Sharpe, 2001). Thus, it is possible to say that whereas the cost-based approach focuses on the input side of human capital, the income-based approach assesses the output side of human capital (Boarini, d'Ercole & Liu; 2012). The education-based approach can assess both the input and the output side (see Vos, 1996; Sharpe, 2001; Scheerens, Luyten & van Ravens, 2011; Karahan, 2012.).

As in cost-based approaches, input indicators represent investments in human capital rather than the human capital stock. Investments constitute the basis of human capital formation, and in a sense, they represent future capital stock rather than existing capital stock. Additionally, it is not certain whether investments that promote the level of human capital will turn into human capital stock. For instance, human capital stock may be lower than expected if the number of schools or teachers per student is high but the number of students dropping out of school or the rate of schooling is low; if the graduates do not join the labor force; or if environmental dynamics have adverse effects on the average life expectancy even though the health infrastructure is well developed. Furthermore, the transformation of input indicators into human capital stock takes place in a delayed manner. For instance, it takes time for the effects of a new education program to be observed, for students starting school to graduate, and for the construction of a school to be completed (Psacharopoulos & Arriagada, 1986; Vos, 1996; Cohen & Soto; 2007). Although input indicators do not reflect the human capital stock thoroughly, they are crucial for determining the sustainability of human capital and thus should be watched closely. A decline in an input indicator will adversely affect the future human capital stock, which will, in turn, affect the output indicators. Nonetheless, a decline in an input indicator may not necessarily result in decreased level of human capital. If resources have started to be used more effectively, it is possible that the results will not deteriorate (Sharpe, 2001).

From the viewpoint of human capital, output indicators are indicators that represent the human capital stock possessed by the economy. They are shaped by the investments in human capital. Hence, one may say that input indicators are the determinants of output indicators. In this sense, output indicators demonstrate the extent to which the goals set and policies implemented are successful (Vos, 1996). These indicators can also be used to measure the quality and productivity of human capital stock. As mentioned, input indicators represent the investments made to enhance the accumulation of human capital. It is not certain whether these investments will contribute to the accumulation of human capital. For instance, a high number of schools or teachers per student may not ensure a high rate of schooling or a high number of graduates. Keeping girls from attending school in underdeveloped or developing countries despite the availability of education infrastructure is a good example. Women with a bachelor's degree withdrawing from the labor force after having a child is another example. Although the health investments of the U.S. are at the same level as those of other developed countries, the average life expectancy is higher in the U.S. than in other developed countries due to, e.g., environmental dynamics and nutrition; this fact indicates that investments in the field of health do not give the same level of results across time (Sharpe, 2001). For such reasons, when the level of human capital in a country or region is assessed merely by input indicators, one may find that the country/region has a higher level of human capital than expected.

By contrast, when the level of human capital is measured by the use of output indicators under the same circumstances, the level of human capital calculated will be lower.

For these and similar reasons, selecting indicators to represent human capital in accordance with the objective of the study may provide more accurate results and allow for development of effective policy recommendations. For example, one should compare the input and output indicator sets to assess the effectiveness of existing policies and the sustainability of the accumulation of human capital (Sharpe, 2001). Input indicators may be a wiser choice to conduct a projection of the effects of policies and investments in the coming years, and output indicators may be a more rational choice to assess the economic effects of the current level of human capital. If considerably different results are obtained when the level of human capital in a country is assessed individually by input and output indicators, this discrepancy should be noted. If these two groups of indicators give similar results, it will not matter which group of indicators is used in the empirical analyses. However, if the two groups of indicators give different results, the differences and the reasons behind these differences should be presented, and the necessary policy to ensure the sustainability of human capital measures should be implemented.

METHOD[2]

This study employs principal component analysis (PCA) to calculate a human capital index based on input and output indicators. PCA is a multivariate statistical technique that linearly transforms an original set of variables into a substantially smaller set of uncorrelated variables that represents most of the information in the original set of variables (Dunteman, 1989) The central idea of PCA is to reduce the dimensionality of a dataset consisting of a large number of interrelated variables while retaining as much of the variation present in the dataset as possible. A principal component analysis is concerned with explaining the variance–covariance structure of a set of variables through a few linear combinations of these variables. Its general objectives are data reduction and interpretation (Johnson & Wichern, 2014). This is achieved by transforming to a new set of variables the principal components (PCs), which are uncorrelated and ordered so that the first few retain most of the variation present in all of the original variables (Joliffe, 2002).

PCA is used to express a structure explained by p correlated variables through a smaller number of uncorrelated variables ($p>k$) than the number of original variables, which are the linear components of original variables. It uses the eigenvalue and eigenvectors of the covariance or correlation matrix to find the linear components of the p variable in the data matrix.

For PCA analysis, the following transformation should be performed:

$$Y = Xa \tag{1}$$

where p is the number of variables, n is the number of observations, Y is the principal component matrix of size *pxn*, a is the optimal weight vector, and X is the standardized data matrix of size *pxn*. For instance, the variance of Y is (for $p-3$)

$$\mathrm{var}\left(Y\right) = \mathrm{var}\left(a_1 X_1 + a_2 X_2 + a_3 X_3\right) \tag{2}$$

or

$$\mathrm{var}\left(Y\right) = \mathrm{var}\left(a_1^2 s_{11} + a_2^2 s_{22} + a_3^2 s_{33} + 2a_1 a_2 s_{12} + 2a_1 a_3 s_{13} + 2a_2 a_3 s_{23}\right) \tag{3}$$

where s_{ij} denotes the covariance between X_i and X_j. Equation (3) can be rewritten as follows:

$$\mathrm{var}\left(Y\right) = a'Sa \tag{4}$$

where S is the variance-covariance matrix of data matrix X. The first principal component maximizes $\mathrm{var}\left(Y\right) = a'Sa$ under normalization restriction $a'a = 1$. This process can be re-expressed as follows using the Lagrange multipliers technique:

$$L = a'Sa - \lambda\left(1 - a'a\right) \tag{5}$$

Accordingly, the necessary condition for optimization is satisfied to determine a:

$$\frac{\partial L}{\partial a} = \frac{\partial\left[a'Sa - \lambda\left(1 - a'a\right)\right]}{\partial a} = 0 \tag{6}$$

where the first-order condition is $2\left(Sa - \lambda a\right) = 0$ or $\left(S - \lambda I\right)a = 0$, and I denotes identity matrix. Here, the multiplier can be interpreted as an eigenvalue of the S variance-covariance matrix, and the solution to equation $\left(S - \lambda I\right)a = 0$ corresponds to eigenvalue a. Therefore, the roots are obtained from $\left|S - \lambda I\right| = 0$. Undoubtedly, there is more than one root. However, we address the highest root. If $\left(S - \lambda I\right)a = 0$ is multiplied by a':

$$a'Sa - a'\lambda Ia = 0 \tag{7}$$

where $a'a = 1$ denotes normalization, and λ is a scalar; this transforms equation (7) into

$$a'Sa = \lambda = \mathrm{var}\left(Y\right) \tag{8}$$

which is the determination of the highest eigenvalue to maximize $\mathrm{var}\left(Y\right)$.

By repeating this procedure, eigenvalues can be obtained up to principal component p through the use of $\lambda_i \left(i = 1, 2, ..., p\right)$. The values of the eigenvalues can be found in ascending order (Jolliffe, 2002). Here, what should be known is that the total variance of the original variables equals the total variance of the principal components, and the percentage of variance explained (δ_i) from the ith principal component (i=1,2,...,p) is as follows:

$$\delta_i = \frac{\lambda_i}{\lambda_1 + \lambda_2 + \ldots + \lambda_p}, \ (i = 1, 2, \ldots, p) \tag{9}$$

After obtaining the values of the principal components, significant principal components should be selected to calculate the index score. The Kaiser criterion is commonly used for this purpose. According to the Kaiser criterion, as many principal components as the number of eigenvalues higher than 1 are selected. Then, the percentages of variances explained of k number of principal components should be weighted, with their sum being equal to 1. These weighted principal components are used in the index calculation (Arsoy, Arabaci & Ciftcioglu, 2012).

$$end_{skr} = \sum_{i=1}^{k} \left[\frac{\delta_i}{\sum_{i=1}^{k} \delta_i} Y_i \right] \tag{10}$$

DATA AND FINDINGS

The datasets used in the study were obtained from the Turkish Statistical Institute. For the calculation of the human capital index, the input indicators used are the number of health-care personnel per 100,000 people *(Hlth_pr)*, the number of hospital beds per 100,000 people *(Hsp_bd)*, the number of students for vocational training school and undergraduate programs of higher education institutions *(Stn_ugr)*, the secondary-school enrollment rate *(Sec_en)*, the number of lecturers (Lec-nm), the number of teachers per student *(Tch_st)*, the ratio of population with access to the drinking and utility water network to the total population of the municipality *(Wtr_nw)*, and the ratio of population receiving waste services to the total population of the province *(Wst_sr)*.The output indicators used for the calculation of the human capital index are the literacy rate *(lit_rt)*, the ratio of graduates from secondary school *(sec_sch)*, the ratio of graduates from high school *(hgh_sch)*, the ratio of graduates from university *(unv_dgr)*, the ratio of people with a master's or a PhD degree *(up_grd)*, the average life expectancy *(lif_exp)*, the net infant mortality rate *(ninf_mor)*, the crude suicide rate *(sui_rt)*, and the ratio of deaths by tumor diseases to total deaths *(tum_dis)*.

Descriptive statistics of the indicators used in calculating the human capital index based on input indicators (hereinafter referred to as HCI) are given in Table 1, and the correlation matrix is given in Table 2. The Kaiser-Meyer-Olkin (KMO) test and Bartlett's test of sphericity are applied in an attempt to determine whether the relationship between indicators is significant and the data are suitable for PCA. The KMO value is found to be 0.648 (because 0.648 > 0.50). This value and the sample size can be said to be suitable for principal component analysis (Field, 2000; Hair, Black, Babin, Anderson, & Tatham, 2006). Bartlett's test of sphericity shows that the relationship between variables is significant (p<0.01) and that the correlation matrix of variables is different from the identity matrix. The KMO value and the results of the Bartlett's test indicate that principal component analysis can be applied.

The explained variances obtained from the application are given in Table 3. The coefficients in the table show that the variables with the highest explained variance are the number of health-care personnel per 100,000 people, the number of teachers per student in secondary education, and the number of lecturers per student. The variables with the lowest explained variance are the number of students enrolled

Table 1. Descriptive statistics of the indicators used in calculating the HCI

	Obs.	Mean.	Min.	Max.	Med.	Std. Dev.
Hlth_pr	81	835.33	476.12	1350.02	835.33	183.53
Hsp_bd	81	260.12	124.00	512.00	260.12	85.41
Stn_ugr	81	14600	742	468114	14600	53038
Sec_en	81	77.70	42.42	100.00	77.70	12.43
Lec-nm	81	1758	243	27092	1758	3639
Tch_st	81	0.0685	0.04	0.11	0.06	0.01
Wtr_nw	81	97.72	82.00	100.00	97.72	3.40
Wst_sr	81	73.65	37.00	99.00	73.65	12.70

Table 2. Correlation matrix of the indicators used in calculating the HCI

	Hlth_pr	Hsp-bd	Stn_ugr	Sec_en	Lec-nm	Tch_st	Wtr_nw	Wst_sr
Hlth_pr	1							
Hsp_bd	0.774	1						
Stn_ugr	0.208	0.278	1					
Sec_en	0.711	0.456	0.145	1				
Lec-nm	0.221	0.167	0.506	0.132	1			
Tch_st	0.606	0.327	0.021	0.667	.0.182	1		
Wtr_nw	0.265	0.514	0.116	0.205	0.135	0.252	1	
Wst_sr	0.277	0.176	0.270	0.382	0.441	0.051	0.170	1

Table 3. Communalities, HCI

	Initial	Extraction
Hlth_pr	1.000	0.862
Tch_st	1.000	0.802
Sec_en	1.000	0.738
Lec-nm	1.000	0.662
Wst_sr	1.000	0.576
Hsp-bd	1.000	0.559
Wtr_nw	1.000	0.554
Stn_ugr	1.000	0.510

in higher education and the ratio of people with access to the drinking and utility water network to the total population of the municipality.

Considering the eigenvalues of components for the calculation of the HCI and the ratio of the explained variances, the first component alone accounts for approximately 55.9% of the total variance, and the second principal component accounts for 23.3%. The first and second principal components together explain for approximately 79.2% of the total variance. This percentage of variance explained is usually suitable for PCA and can be considered a good ratio. In other words, it is possible to explain a dataset of 8 variables with only 2 variables. Out of 8 interrelated variables, 2 unrelated variables are obtained, thus eliminating the dependence and ensuring the reduction of dimensions, which is the purpose of the principal component analysis.

Table 4 presents the component matrix. It shows the weight of each indicator on each component. Within the first component, according to the scores given in Table 6, the variables with the greatest significance in absolute value are the number of health-care personnel per 100,000 people, the secondary-school enrollment rate, the number of hospital beds per 100,000 people, and the number of teachers per student, respectively. The second component is determined by the number of lecturers and the ratio of population receiving waste services to the total population and the number of students for vocational training school and undergraduate programs of higher education institutions.

Descriptive statistics of the indicators used in calculating human capital index based on output indicators (hereinafter referred to as HCO) are given in Table 5, and the correlation matrix is given in Table 6. The results of the Kaiser-Meyer-Olkin (KMO) test and Bartlett's test of sphericity are given in Table 9. The KMO value is found to be 0.767. Because the KMO value is higher than 0.50, the sample size can be said to be suitable for PCA. The results of Bartlett's test of sphericity indicate that the relationship between variables is significant ($p<0.01$) and that the correlation matrix of variables is different from the identity matrix. In conclusion, the KMO value and the results of Bartlett's test indicate that principal component analysis can be applied to calculate the HCO.

The explained variances obtained from the application are given in Table 7. The coefficients in the table show that the variables with a high explained variance are those that show the percentage of the population with a certain educational background in the total population, which represent human capital's dimension of education.

Table 4. Component matrix, HCI

	Component	
	1	**2**
Hlth_pr	0.917	
Sec_en	0.837	
Hsp_bd	0.747	
Tch_st	0.644	
Wtr_nw	0.490	
Lec-nm		0.746
Wst_sr		0.601
Stn_ugr		0.526

Table 5. Descriptive statistics, HCO

	Obs.	Mean.	Min.	Max.	Med.	Std. Dev.
lit_rt	81	0.9140	0.80861	0.9675	0.9220	0.0397
sec_sch	81	0.0344	0.0100	0.0592	0.0366	0.0099
hgh_sch	81	0.1515	0.0647	0.2252	0.1563	0.0359
unv_dgr	81	0.0765	0.0329	0.1427	0.0779	0.0205
up_grd	81	0.0061	0.0205	0.0227	0.0058	0.0031
lif_exp	81	78.786	74.925	80.729	78.092	1.1252
ninf_mor	81	0.1019	0.0403	0.1886	0.1000	0.0306
sui_rt	81	0.2526	0.1075	1.3389	0.2257	0.1483
tum_dis	81	0.1978	0.1039	0.2540	0.2000	0.0312

Table 6. Correlation matrix, HCO

	lit_rt	sec_sch	hgh_sch	unv_dgr	up_grd	lif_exp	ninf_mor	sui_rt	tum_dis
lit_rt	1								
sec_sch	0.7506	1							
hgh_sch	0.6518	0.8691	1						
unv_dgr	0.6969	0.8056	0.8926	1					
up_grd	0.5196	0.6160	0.6893	0.8557	1				
lif_exp	0.0874	0.2520	0.3667	0.3962	0.2488	1			
ninf_mor	0.4370	0.5467	0.5991	0.5687	0.3777	0.5013	1		
sui_rt	-0.0354	0.0860	0.1486	0.0033	0.0143	0.2869	0.2872	1	
tum_dis	0.4057	0.5193	0.5688	0.5790	0.5655	0.1744	0.4927	0.0879	1

Table 7. Communalities, HCO

	Initial	Extraction
unv_dgr	1.000	0.911
hgh_sch	1.000	0.860
sec_sch	1.000	0.805
up_grd	1.000	0.679
ninf_mor	1.000	0.674
lit_rt	1.000	0.668
sui_rt	1.000	0.627
lif_exp	1.000	0.620
tum_dis	1.000	0.582

Considering the eigenvalues of the components for the calculation of the HCO and the ratio of the explained variances, there are two main components. The first component accounts for approximately 63.4% of the total variance, whereas the second component accounts for 16.8%. The first and second components together explain approximately 80.2% of the total variance. This percentage of variance explained is usually suitable for PCA and can be considered a good ratio. In other words, it is possible to explain a dataset of 9 variables with only 2 variables. Out of 9 interrelated variables, 2 unrelated variables are obtained, thus eliminating the dependence and ensuring the reduction of dimensions, which is the purpose of the principal component analysis.

Table 8 shows the component matrix. Within the first component, according to the scores given in Table 8, the variables with the greatest significance in absolute value are the percentage of high-school graduates, the percentage of university graduates, the percentage of secondary-school graduates, the percentage of graduates with a master's or a PhD degree, the infant mortality rate, the literacy rate, and the ratio of deaths from tumor diseases to total deaths, respectively. The second principal component is determined by the crude suicide rate and average life expectancy.

In order to get an index from principal component scores, two principal components are weighted, as sum of their variance explanation ratio is equal to one. Then sum of these weighted principal components yields related index (Atabek, Cosar & Sahinoz, 2005; Arsoy, Arabaci & Ciftcioglu, 2012). Figure 1 presents HCI and HCO index scores.

The scores of the provinces according to the human capital index calculated by input indicators and according to the human capital index calculated by output indicators and the ranking of provinces based on the index scores are given in Figure 1. According to the HCI scores calculated, Eskisehir, Ankara, Istanbul, Isparta, Izmir, Edirne, Elazig, Trabzon, Bolu and Kayseri are the provinces with the top ten highest scores. The provinces with the lowest ten index scores are Siirt, Bitlis, Van, Mardin, Igdır, Sanlıurfa, Sırnak, Mus, Agri and Hakkari. According to the HCO scores, Ankara, Eskisehir, Izmir, Istanbul, Yalova, Tunceli, Edirne, Kocaeli, Trabzon and Rize have the top ten highest index scores, and Hakkari, Batman, Mardin, Van, Siirt, Mus, Hatay, Agrı, Sirnak and Sanliurfa have the ten lowest index scores.

Additionally, Figure 2 maps the rank differences obtained by extracting the HCO ranks of provinces from their HCI ranks. The purpose of calculating and mapping the rank differences between the two

Table 8. Component matrix, HCO

	Component	
	1	**2**
hgh_sch	0.945	
unv_dgr	0.927	
sec_sch	0.886	
up_grd	0.800	
lit_rt	0.753	
ınınf_mor	0.713	
tum_dis	0.693	
sui_rt		0.777
lif_exp		0.655

Figure 1. HCI and HCO index scores and ranks of provinces based on regions in 2013

Marmara Region	HCI		HCO	
	Score	Rank	Score	Rank
Balıkesir	-0,04	45	0,95	26
Bilecik	0,06	40	1,20	21
Bursa	0,52	23	1,51	12
Canakkale	0,50	24	1,32	18
Edirne	1,66	6	1,85	7
Istanbul	3,27	3	2,71	4
Kırklareli	0,31	30	1,51	13
Kocaeli	0,67	17	1,83	8
Sakarya	-0,21	51	1,04	24
Tekirdag	0,07	39	1,39	15
Yalova	0,16	36	2,51	5

Aegean Region	HCI		HCO	
	Score	Rank	Score	Rank
A.karahisar	0,03	42	-0,53	56
Aydın	0,28	31	0,65	30
Denizli	0,57	19	0,68	29
Izmir	1,73	5	2,94	3
Kutahya	0,47	25	0,27	40
Manisa	0,25	32	-0,36	52
Mugla	-0,18	49	1,36	16
Usak	0,05	41	-0,32	50

Mediterranean Region	HCI		HCO	
	Score	Rank	Score	Rank
Adana	0,57	20	0,34	38
Antalya	0,63	18	1,11	23
Burdur	0,42	27	0,23	41
Hatay	-0,64	62	-3,05	78
Isparta	2,29	4	1,12	22
K. Maras	-0,63	60	-1,34	63
Mersin	-0,32	55	0,12	43
Osmaniye	-0,34	56	-0,38	53

Southeastern Anatolia Region	HCI		HCO	
	Score	Rank	Score	Rank
Adiyaman	-1,02	65	-1,60	64
Batman	-1,21	69	-2,36	73
Diyarbakir	-0,63	61	-2,09	69
Gaziantep	-0,99	64	-2,05	68
Kilis	-0,27	53	-2,11	70
Mardin	-1,81	75	-2,52	74
Siirt	-1,44	72	-2,73	76
Sanliurfa	-2,00	77	-3,87	81
Sirnak	-2,04	78	-3,65	80

Black Sea Region	HCI		HCO	
	Score	Rank	Score	Rank
Amasya	0,23	33	0,73	27
Artvin	-0,15	47	1,23	20
Bartın	-1,02	66	-0,53	57
Bayburt	-0,23	52	-0,19	48
Bolu	1,32	9	0,99	25
Corum	-0,02	44	-0,63	59
Duzce	-0,53	59	0,53	33
Giresun	0,10	38	0,63	31
Gumushane	-0,49	58	0,41	35
Karabuk	0,68	16	1,52	11
Kastamonu	-0,20	50	-0,22	49
Ordu	-1,06	68	0,03	46
Rize	0,18	35	1,54	10
Samsun	0,54	22	0,41	36
Sinop	-0,29	54	-0,55	58
Tokat	0,31	29	-0,42	54
Trabzon	1,37	8	1,69	9
Zonguldak	0,33	28	0,44	34

Central Anatolia Region	HCI		HCO	
	Score	Rank	Score	Rank
Aksaray	-0,64	63	-0,72	61
Ankara	3,67	2	4,51	1
Cankırı	-0,08	46	0,29	39
Eskisehir	4,39	1	3,05	2
Karaman	0,13	37	-0,45	55
Kayseri	0,99	10	0,71	28
Kırıkkale	0,76	14	1,50	14
Kirsehir	0,46	26	1,29	19
Konya	0,99	11	-0,04	47
Nevsehir	-0,02	43	0,23	42
Nigde	-0,37	57	0,07	45
Sivas	0,78	12	0,11	44
Yozgat	-0,17	48	-0,70	60

Eastern Anatolia Region	HCI		HCO	
	Score	Rank	Score	Rank
Agri	-2,46	80	-3,42	79
Ardahan	-1,30	70	-0,95	62
Bingol	-1,06	67	-1,63	66
Bitlis	-1,65	73	-2,12	71
Elazig	1,44	7	0,59	32
Erzincan	0,57	21	1,33	17
Erzurum	0,77	13	-0,35	51
Hakkari	-2,48	81	-2,20	72
Igdir	-1,86	76	-1,84	67
Kars	-1,44	71	-1,62	65
Malatya	0,74	15	0,35	37
Mus	-2,33	79	-2,89	77
Tunceli	0,20	34	2,22	6
Van	-1,81	74	-2,63	75

indices of these provinces is to show the extent to which the two indices calculated based on input and output indicators produce different results. Negative values indicate that the province ranks higher based on HCI scores than on HCO scores. Positive values indicate that the province ranks higher based on HCO scores. For instance, the province of Erzurum, represented with a value of -38 on the map, ranks 38 places higher based on its HCI scores than on its HCO scores. By contrast, the province of Mugla, with a value of 33, ranks 33 places higher based on its HCO scores than on its HCI scores. Accordingly, Figure 2 shows that the provinces of Mugla, Yalova, Tunceli, Artvin, Sakarya, Duzce, Rize, Tekirdag, Gumushane and Ordu rank higher based on its HCO scores than on its HCI scores. By contrast, the provinces of Erzurum, Konya, Sivas, Elazig, Tokat, Malatya and Manisa have far higher human capital based on the HCI index than on the HCO index. The rankings of all provinces are different based on the two indices, but the abovementioned provinces have the highest difference. The analysis of these differences based on regions will produce more detailed results in terms of revealing the importance of indicator selection.

Figure 1 clearly shows that human capital indices calculated by input and output indicators in the Marmara Region present highly different results. Whereas the provinces in the Marmara Region rank lower based on HCI scores, they have high rankings based on HCO scores. It is possible to say that the provinces in this region are backward in terms of human capital investments but still have the highest rankings in terms of human capital stock. Marmara is the region of Turkey with the highest level of industrialization and level of GNP per capita (Filiztekin, 2012; Kalkinma Bakanligi, 2013). In fact, the region has the highest level of human capital if the human capital indicators are assessed in terms of aggregate figures. Nevertheless, the region's higher level of economic development compared to other regions makes it an attractive spot for immigrants. The insufficiency of human capital investments in the face of intensive immigration flows and the low level of human capital of immigrants result in a decreased regional average of human capital(Bulbul & Kose, 2010; Demir, Yasa, & Dagdemir, 2013; Kalkinma Bakanligi, 2013). The number of health-care personnel/hospital beds and the number teachers

Figure 2. Map of the differences between HCI and HCO index provincial rankings, 2013

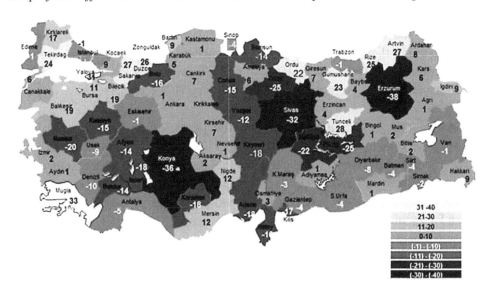

per student in the region are low. Nonetheless, it has higher values for indicators representing the ratio of the population with a certain educational background to the total population.

In the Aegean Region, the provinces of İzmir and Denizli rank in the top 20 based HCI scores. The provinces of İzmir and Mugla rank in the top 20 based HCO scores. The HCI rankings of the provinces in the Aegean Region, excluding İzmir, Mugla and Aydin are higher than their HCO rankings. Therefore, it is possible to say that there are problems in the transformation of human capital investments into human capital stock in the region. Another noteworthy result regarding the region is that Mugla ranks 49th based on HCI scores, whereas it ranks 16th based on HCO scores.

The Central Anatolia Region contains the provinces of Eskisehir and Ankara, which rank first and second based on both human capital indices. The provinces in the region have close rankings based on the two indices. However, whereas the provinces of Konya, Sivas, Kayseri, Karaman and Yozgat have high rankings based on HCI scores, their rankings are lower based on HCO scores. Therefore, one may say that there are problems in the transformation of human capital investments into human capital stock in these provinces. The results of Konya and Sivas are remarkable; they fell by 36 and 32 places in the ranking based on HCO scores compared to the ranking based on HCI scores. The results obtained from this region clearly show the importance of indicator selection in calculating the indices within the scope of this study. When the level of human capital is assessed merely based on input indicators, it will result in erroneous results and mistaken commentary because the level of human capital in these provinces will be found to be higher than it actually is.

In the Mediterranean Region, the provinces of Isparta, Antalya and Adana rank in the top 20 based on HCI scores, but no province in the Mediterranean Region ranks in the top 20 based on HCO scores. The HCO rankings of the provinces in the region, excluding Osmaniye and Mersin, are lower than their HCI rankings. Therefore, it is possible to say that there are problems in the transformation of human capital investments into human capital stock in the region. The score discrepancy is particularly remarkable in Isparta: Whereas Isparta ranks 4th based on HCI scores, it ranks 22nd based on HCO scores. Osmaniye and Mersin have higher rankings based on their HCO scores than on their HCI scores; they rank 3 and 12 positions higher, respectively, based on their HCO scores than on their HCI scores.

In the Black Sea Region, Trabzon, Bolu and Karabuk rank in the top 20 based on HCI scores, whereas Trabzon, Rize, Karabuk and Artvin rank in the top 20 based on HCO scores. Ordu, Gumushane, Rize, Duzce and Artvin rank approximately 20 places higher in the rankings based on HCO scores than those based on HCI scores. Kastamonu, Bayburt, Karabuk, Amasya, Giresun and Bartın have higher rankings based on HCO scores than on HCI scores; the differences in the rankings based on two indices are smaller than the differences between the rankings of Ordu, Gumushane, Rize, Duzce and Artvin based on two indices. Whereas Bolu, Corum and Samsun have higher HCI scores, they have remarkably lower HCO scores.

In the East Anatolia Region, Erzurum, Elazig and Malatya rank in the top 20 based on HCI scores. These provinces do not rank in the top 20 based on HCO scores. Tunceli and Erzincan rank in the top 20 based on HCO scores. All provinces in the region other than those that are mentioned above rank in the bottom 20 based on both HCI and HCO scores. In other words, there are no considerable differences between the scores of these provinces based on the two indices. However, Erzurum, Elazig and Malatya, which have high HCI scores, have far lower rankings based on HCO scores. Therefore, it is possible to say that there are problems in the transformation of human capital investments into human capital stock in these provinces. Another noteworthy result regarding the region is that Tunceli ranks 34th based on HCI scores, whereas it ranks 6th based on HCO scores. It can be noted that the high ratio of people with a high school, undergraduate or graduate diploma to the total population, a high average life expectancy, and a low infant mortality rate cause this province to have a high ranking based on HCO scores.

In the Southeast Anatolia Region, the provinces rank in the bottom 20 based on both indices. Moreover, there are no significant differences between the two index scores of the provinces. Only Kilis has a higher ranking based on HCI scores despite having a far lower ranking based on HCO. This is the region with the lowest scores in terms of both human capital investments and human capital stock.

FUTURE RESEARCH DIRECTIONS

This study aims to show the importance of indicator selection in creating composite indicators. In line with this objective, the analyses conducted indicate that input and output indicators may produce different results in measuring human capital. In fact, numerous studies dealing with the impact of human capital on economic growth state that findings vary depending on the selection of indicators. Thus, this study will contribute significantly to the literature as it suggests the importance of indicator selection, which is not addressed sufficiently in empirical analyses.

Besides its contributions, the study also has some constraints. These constraints may be addressed within the bounds of possibility, allowing for more accurate determination of the level of human capital. The first of these constraints is the data constraint, depending on the scope of the study. Calculation of different indices by using alternative measures representing human capital may ensure the development of studies in this field. The second constraint is that the scope of this study is limited to Turkey. Conducting analyses for countries in which socioeconomic differences exist between regions, such as Turkey, will allow for testing the findings of this study. In addition to comparisons between regions, comparisons between countries may provide significant benefits.

This study advocates that one should select input and output indicators in accordance with the purpose of the study in creating composite indicators. A composite indicator encompassing both sets of indicators is appropriate for testing the sustainability of human capital. Future studies that calculate three different indices addressing input indicators, output indicators and both sets of indicators, and analyse these results accordingly may substantially contribute to the development of this study.

Finally, the subject of this paper is an appropriate one for the data envelopment analysis (DEA), which is a useful technique for determining the efficiency of decision-making units. DEA analysis can be used to assess and benchmark the overall performance incorporating multiple measures, and enables one to assess how efficiently a unit uses the available inputs to generate a set of outputs relative to other units in the data set. Input and output indicators present considerably different results. Because province-based estimations present that the index values estimated by the input and output indicators lead to highly different conclusions for Turkey, DEA analysis enables policymakers to evaluate the efficiency of human capital investment.

CONCLUSION

Correct and accurate measurement is one of the fundamental requirements to establish economic relations properly and to formulate well-developed policy recommendations. Incorrect measurement prevents economic relations from being assessed properly and causes researchers to obtain mixed results. This study addresses the importance of measurement with respect to the concept of human capital. Many studies on the economic effects of human capital note that different results are obtained depending on the indicators used to represent human capital (Kruger & Lindahl, 2001; Le, Gibson & Oxley, 2005; Middendorf, 2005; Skare & Lacmonovic, 2015). One of the major reasons for these discrepancies is the measurement of human capital by a single indicator, although it is a multidimensional concept. Another reason is that researchers calculate the index without taking into account the distinction between input and output indicators for composite indicators.

In this context, this study calculates two different indices and compares their results in an attempt to demonstrate that input and output indicators may produce different results in measuring human capital. To the best of one's knowledge, no analysis has been conducted for such purpose regarding Turkey. Therefore, the findings of the study are expected to contribute significantly in terms of a better analysis of the current situation and development of policy proposals. In the analysis conducted on 81 provinces in Turkey, input and output indicators present considerably different results. Whereas provinces with a higher level of income and a higher level of industrialization have high scores on the output index, they have lower scores on the input index. The majority of the provinces that have lower scores on the HCI, despite having far higher rankings on the HCO, are in the Marmara Region. Unplanned immigration flows into this region cause human capital investments to be inadequate. Additionally, the fact that immigration flows are from regions with a low level of human capital causes the index scores to be calculated lower than expected. These provinces that have high rankings in terms of nominal figures have far lower rankings on the basis of the same figures per capita. Another remarkable point is that provinces ranking in the bottom positions based on HCI scores also rank in the bottom positions based on HCO scores. In other words, no change is observed in provinces ranking in the bottom positions based on both indices.

In conclusion, this study presents the importance of making a distinction between input and output indicators in selecting indicators for a study. This findings is consistent with the claims of Vos (1996), Stroombergen, Rose & Nana (2002), Folloni & Vittadini (2010) and Boarini, d'Ercole & Liu (2012), Karahan (2012). Calculations made at the provincial level show that index scores calculated based on input and output indicators give considerably different results. Developing an index that takes into account the groups of input and output indicators can ensure a more accurate measurement. It was previously mentioned that input indicators represent investment in human capital, and output indicators represent human capital stock. The selection of indicators that are suitable for the purpose of the study, taking into account the definitions of the indicators, may allow for obtaining more effective results from the analysis. In this regard, one may say that it would be more appropriate to select output indicators in assessing the economic effects of the accumulation of human capital and input indicators in assessing the human capital investments. It would be more appropriate to analyze both indicator groups in analyzing the sustainability of human capital.

REFERENCES

Andréosso-O'Callaghan, B. (2002). *Human Capital Accumulation and Economic Growth in Asia. National Europe Centre Paper No. 29*. Australian National University.

Arsoy, A. P., Arabaci, O., & Ciftcioğlu, A. (2012). Corporate social responsibility and financial performance relationship: The case of Turkey. *The Journal of Accounting and Finance*, *53*, 159–176.

Atabek, A., Cosar, E. E., & Sahinoz, S. (2005). A new composite leading indicator for Turkish economic activity. *Emerging Markets Finance and Trade*, *41*(1), 45–64. doi:10.1080/1540496X.2005.11052597

Bakanligi, K. (2013). *Bolgesel Gelisme Ulusal Stratejisi (2014-2023)*. Ankara: Kalkınma Bakanligi.

Bawumia, M., & Appiah-Adu, K. (Eds.). (2015). *Key Determinants of National Development: Historical Perspectives and Implications for Developing Economies*. Gower Publishing, Ltd.

Becker, G. (1962). Investment in human capital: A theoretical analysis. *Journal of Political Economy*, *70*(5, Part 2), 9–49. doi:10.1086/258724

Becker, G. (1964). *Human Capital: A Theoretical and Empirical Analysis, with Special Reference to Education*. National Bureau of Economic Research; doi:10.7208/chicago/9780226041223.001.0001

Boarini, R., d'Ercole, M. M., & Liu, G. (2012). *Approaches to Measuring the Stock of Human Capital: A Review of Country Practices (No. 2012/4)*. OECD Publishing. doi:10.1787/18152031

Bulbul, S., & Kose, A. (2010). Turkiye'de bolgelerarasi ic goc hareketlerinin cok boyutlu olcekleme yontemi ile incelenmesi. *Istanbul Universitesi Isletme Fakultesi Dergisi*, *39*(1), 75-94. Retrieved from http://www.journals.istanbul.edu.tr/iuisletme/index

De la Fuente, A., & Doménech, R. (2006). Human capital in growth regressions: How much difference does data quality make? *Journal of the European Economic Association*, *4*(1), 1–36. doi:10.1162/jeea.2006.4.1.1

De la Fuente, A., & Doménech, R. (2015). Educational attainment in the OECD, 1960–2010. Updated series and a comparison with other sources. *Economics of Education Review*, *48*, 56–74. doi:10.1016/j.econedurev.2015.05.004

Demir, N., Yasa, S., & Dagdemir, V. (2013). Duzey 1 Bolgelerine Gore Yoksulluk ve Goc Durumu. *Journal of the Faculty of Agriculture*, *44*(1), 99–102. Retrieved from http://dergipark.ulakbim.gov.tr/ataunizfd/

Dreger, C., Erber, G., & Glocker, D. (2009). *Regional measures of human capital in the European Union* (No. 3919). IZA Discussion Papers. doi: 10.2139/ssrn.1285563

Dunteman, G. H. (1989). *Principal Components Analysis*. Newbury Park, CA: SAGE Publications, Inc.; doi:10.4135/9781412985475

Eisner, R. (1985). The Total Incomes System of Accounts. *Survey of Current Business*, *65*(1), 24–48. doi:10.1111/j.1475-4991.1991.tb00385.x

Eryigit, S. B., Eryigit, K. Y., & Selen, U. (2012). The long-run linkages between education, health and defence expenditures and economic growth: Evidence from Turkey. *Defence and Peace Economics*, *23*(6), 559–574. doi:10.1080/10242694.2012.663577

Esteban, G. G., Lopez-Pueyo, C., & Sanaú, J. (2015). Human capital measurement in OECD countries and its relation to GDP growth and innovation. *Revista de economía mundial*, *39*, 77 108. Retrieved from http://rabida.uhu.es/dspace/handle/10272/10697

Field, A. (2000). *Discovering statistics using SPSS for Windows: Advanced techniques for beginners (Introducing Statistical Methods series)*. Sage Publications.

Filiztekin, A. (2012). *Bolgesel Buyume, Es-Hareketlilik ve Sektorel Yapı* (No. 2012/61). Discussion Paper, Turkish Economic Association.

Folloni, G., & Vittadini, G. (2010). Human capital measurement: A survey. *Journal of Economic Surveys*, *24*(2), 248–279. doi:10.1111/j.1467-6419.2009.00614.x

Fraumeni, B. M. (2008, November). *Human capital: From indicators and indexes to accounts.* Fondazione Giovanni Agnelli/OECD Workshop on the Measurement of Human Capital, Turin, Italy.

Furceri, D., & Mourougane, A. (2010). *Structural Indicators: A Critical Review*. OECD Publishing.

Graham, J. W., & Webb, R. H. (1979). Stocks and depreciation of human capital: New evidence from a present-value perspective. *Review of Income and Wealth*, *25*(2), 209–224. doi:10.1111/j.1475-4991.1979. tb00094.x

Hair, J. F., Black, W., Babin, B., Anderson, R. E., & Tatham, R. L. (2006). *Multivariate data analysis*. New Jersey: Pearson Prentice Hall.

Han, T. S., Lin, C. Y. Y., & Chen, M. Y. C. (2008). Developing human capital indicators: A three-way approach. *International Journal of Learning and Intellectual Capital*, *5*(3-4), 387–403. doi:10.1504/ IJLIC.2008.021018

Haveman, R., & Wolfe, B. (1984). Schooling and economic well-being: The role of non-markets effects. *The Journal of Human Resources*, *19*(3), 377–407. doi:10.2307/145879

Johnson, R. A., & Wichern, D. W. (2014). *Applied multivariate statistical analysis*. Essex, England: Pearson Prentice Hall.

Joliffe, I. T. (2002). *Principal Component Analysis* (2nd ed.). New York: Springer-Verlag, New York, Inc.; doi:10.1007/b98835

Jones, B. F. (2014). The Human Capital Stock: A Generalized Approach. *The American Economic Review*, *104*(11), 3752–3777. doi:10.1257/aer.104.11.3752

Jorgenson, D. W., & Fraumeni, B. M. (1989). Investment in education. *Educational Researcher*, *18*(4), 35–44. doi:10.3102/0013189X018004035

Jorgenson, D. W., & Fraumeni, B. M. (1992a). Investment in education and US economic growth. *The Scandinavian Journal of Economics*, *94*, 51–70. doi:10.2307/3440246

Jorgenson, D. W., & Fraumeni, B. M. (1992b). The output of the education sector. In *Output measurement in the service sectors* (pp. 303–341). University of Chicago Press.

Karahan, O. (2012). Input-output indicators of knowledge-based economy and Turkey. *Journal of Business Economics and Finance*, *1*(2), 21–36. Retrieved from http://dergipark.ulakbim.gov.tr/jbef/index

Kendrick, J. (1976). *The Formation and Stocks of Total Capital*. New York: Columbia University Press for NBER.

Krušinskas, R., & Bruneckienė, J. (2015). Measurement of intellectual capital of Lithuanian cities by a composite index. *Journal of Business Economics and Management*, *16*(3), 529–541. doi:10.3846/16 111699.2012.729155

Kwon, D. B. (2009). Human capital and its measurement. In *The 3rd OECD World Forum on 'Statistics, Knowledge and Policy' Charting Progress, Building Visions, Improving Life Busan*. OECD World Forum.

Le, T., Gibson, J., & Oxley, L. (2005). *Measures of human capital: A review of the literature (No. 05/10)*. New Zealand Treasury.

Lindahl, M., & Krueger, A. B. (2001). Education for Growth: Why and for Whom? *Journal of Economic Literature*, *39*(4), 1101–1136. doi:10.1257/jel.39.4.1101

Lucas, R. E. Jr. (1988). On the mechanics of economic development. *Journal of Monetary Economics*, *22*(1), 3–42. doi:10.1016/0304-3932(88)90168-7

Marshall, A. (1890). *Principles of political economy*. New York: Maxmillan.

Meier, K. J., Favero, N., & Compton, M. (2016). Social Context, Management, and Organizational Performance: When human capital and social capital serve as substitutes. *Public Management Review*, *18*(2), 258–277. doi:10.1080/14719037.2014.984621

Middendorf, T. (2006). Human capital and economic growth in OECD countries. *Jahrbucher fur Nationalokonomie und Statistik*, 670–686.

Mill, J. S. (1848). *Principles of Political Economy with Some of Their Applications to Social Philosophy*. Manchester, UK: George Routledge and Sons.

Mulligan, C. B., & Sala-i-Martin, X. (1997). A labor income-based measure of the value of human capital: An application to the states of the United States. *Japan and the World Economy*, *9*(2), 159–191. doi:10.1016/S0922-1425(96)00236-8

Nehru, V., Swanson, E., & Dubey, A. (1995). A new database in human capital stock in developing industrial countries: Sources, methodology and results. *Journal of Development Economics*, *46*(2), 379–401. doi:10.1016/0304-3878(94)00054-G

OECD. (2000). *Education at a Glance: OECD Indicators*. Paris: OECD. doi: 10.1787/eag-2015-en

Oxley, L., Trinh, L., & John, G. (2008). Measuring Human Capital: Alternative Methods and International Evidence. *The Korean Economıc Review*, *24*(2), 283-344. Retrieved from http://www.kereview.or.kr/main/?load_popup=1&filter=on

Petty, W. (1899). *Political Arithmetick* (London, 1690). *Economic Writings*, *1*, 245.

Psacharopoulos, G., & Arriagada, A. M. (1986). The educational composition of the labour force: An international comparison. *International Labour Review*, *125*(5), 561–574.

Romer, P. M. (1986). Increasing returns and long-run growth. *Journal of Political Economy*, *94*(5), 1002–1037. doi:10.1086/261420

Romer, P. M. (1989). *Human capital and growth: theory and evidence*. NBER Working Paper Series, 3173. doi: 10.3386/w3173

Scheerens, J., Luyten, H., & van Ravens, J. (2011). Measuring educational quality by means of indicators. In *Perspectives on Educational Quality* (pp. 35–50). Springer Netherlands; doi:10.1007/978-94-007-0926-3_2

Schultz, T. W. (1961). Investment in Human Capital. *The American Economic Review, 51*(1), 1–17.

Sharpe, A. (2001). *The development of indicators for human capital sustainability*. Annual Meeting of the Canadian Economics Association, Montreal, Canada.

Skare, M., & Lacmanovic, S. (2015). Human capital and economic growth: a review essay. *Amfiteatru Economic, 17*(39), 735-760. Retrieved from http://www.amfiteatrueconomic.ro/temp/Article_2422.pdf

Smith, A. (1776). *An inquiry into the nature and causes of the wealth of nations*. London: George Routledge and Sons. doi:10.1093/oseo/instance.00043218

Stroombergen, A., Rose, W. D., & Nana, G. (2002). *Review of the statistical measurement of human capital*. Statistics New Zealand working paper.

Vos, R. (1996). *Educational indicators: What's to be measured?* INDES Working Papers I-1. Washington, DC: Inter-American Development Bank.

Weisbrod, B. A. (1961). The valuation of human capital. *Journal of Political Economy, 69*(5), 425–436. doi:10.1086/258535

ADDITIONAL READING

Adler, N., Yazhemsky, E., & Tarverdyan, R. (2010). A framework to measure the relative socio-economic performance of developing countries. *Socio-Economic Planning Sciences, 44*(2), 73–88. doi:10.1016/j.seps.2009.08.001

Akay, E. C. (2016). Education Inequalities and Human Capital Formation in MENA Region. In M. Erdoğdu & B. Christiansen (Eds.), *Comparative Political and Economic Perspectives on the MENA Region* (pp. 151–179). Hershey, PA: Information Science Reference; doi:10.4018/978-1-4666-9601-3.ch007

Akinyemi, B. O. (2009). Human Capital Management for Sustainable Competitive Advantage in the New Economy. In T. Torres-Coronas & M. Arias-Oliva (Eds.), *Encyclopedia of Human Resources Information Systems: Challenges in e-HRM* (pp. 441–450). Hershey, PA: Information Science Reference; doi:10.4018/978-1-59904-883-3.ch065

Chambers, R. G. (1998). Input and output indicators. In *Index numbers: essays in honour of Sten Malmquist* (pp. 241–271). Springer Netherlands; doi:10.1007/978-94-011-4858-0_7

Cohen, D., & Soto, M. (2007). Growth and human capital: Good data, good results. *Journal of Economic Growth, 12*(1), 51–76. doi:10.1007/s10887-007-9011-5

Doménech, R. (2006). Human capital in growth regressions: How much difference does data quality make? *Journal of the European Economic Association, 4*(1), 1–36. doi:10.1162/jeea.2006.4.1.1

Fraumeni, B. M. (2015). *Choosing a Human Capital Measure: Educational Attainment Gaps and Rankings (No. w21283)*. National Bureau of Economic Research; doi:10.3386/w21283

Hamilton, K., & Liu, G. (2014). Human capital, tangible wealth, and the intangible capital residual. *Oxford Review of Economic Policy, 30*(1), 70–91. doi:10.1093/oxrep/gru007

Jeremic, V., Slovic, D., & Radojicic, Z. (2012). Measuring human capital: a statistical approach. *Actual Problems of Economics*, (5), 359-363.

Kesti, M., Leinonen, J., & Syväjärvi, A. (2016). A Multidisciplinary Critical Approach to Measure and Analyze Human Capital Productivity. In M. Russ (Ed.), *Quantitative Multidisciplinary Approaches in Human Capital and Asset Management* (pp. 1–22). Hershey, PA: Business Science Reference; doi:10.4018/978-1-4666-9652-5.ch001

Klomp, J. (2013). The measurement of human capital: A multivariate macro-approach. *Quality & Quantity, 47*(1), 121–136. doi:10.1007/s11135-011-9507-0

Kovacevic, M. (2010). *Review of HDI critiques and potential improvements*, UNDP. Human Development Reports, 33.

Lai, D. (2003). Principal component analysis on human development indicators of China. *Social Indicators Research, 61*(3), 319–330. doi:10.1023/A:1021951302937

Li, H., Liang, Y., Fraumeni, B. M., Liu, Z., & Wang, X. (2013). Human capital in China, 1985–2008. *Review of Income and Wealth, 59*(2), 212–234. doi:10.1111/j.1475-4991.2012.00517.x

Liu, G. (2011), *Measuring the Stock of Human Capital for Comparative Analysis: An Application of the Lifetime Income Approach to Selected Countries*, OECD Statistics Working Papers, No. 2011/06, OECD Publishing, Paris. doi: 10.1787/18152031

Liu, G. (2013). Measuring the Stock of Human Capital for International and Intertemporal Comparisons. In *Measuring Economic Sustainability and Progress* (pp. 493–544). University of Chicago Press; doi:10.7208/chicago/9780226121475.003.0015

Mamaqi, X., & Miguel, J. (2014). Human Capital and Business Performance: An Empirical Approach Using Structural Equation Modeling.[IJKSR]. *International Journal of Knowledge Society Research, 5*(2), 20–32. doi:10.4018/ijksr.2014040103

Põldaru, R., & Roots, J. (2014). A PCA–DEA approach to measure the quality of life in Estonian counties. *Socio-Economic Planning Sciences, 48*(1), 65–73. doi:10.1016/j.seps.2013.10.001

Reychav, I., & Weisberg, J. (2011). Human Capital in Knowledge Creation, Management, and Utilization. In D. Schwartz & D. Te'eni (Eds.), *Encyclopedia of Knowledge Management* (2nd ed., pp. 389–401). Hershey, PA: Information Science Reference; doi:10.4018/978-1-59904-931-1.ch037

Santos, M. E., & Santos, G. (2014). Composite Indices of Development. In *International development: ideas, experience, and prospects* (pp. 133–150). Oxford University Press; doi:10.1093/acprof:oso/9780199671656.003.0009

Škare, M., & Lacmanovic, S. (2015). Human capital and economic growth: A review essay. The *Amfiteatru. The Economic Journal*, *17*(39), 735–760. Retrieved from http://www.amfiteatrueconomic.ro/temp/Article_2422.pdf

Slottje, D. (2010). Human capital measurement: Theory and practice. *Journal of Economic Surveys*, *24*(2), 201–205. doi:10.1111/j.1467-6419.2009.00612.x

Soboleva, I. (2010). Paradoxes of the measurement of human capital. *Problems of Economic Transition*, *52*(11), 43–70. doi:10.2753/PET1061-1991521103

Tavakoli, M. M., & Shirouyehzad, H. (2013). Application of PCA/DEA method to evaluate the performance of human capital management: A case study. *Journal of Data Envelopment Analysis and Decision Science*, *2013*(1), 1-20. doi: 10.5899/2013/dea-00042

Thakur, S. K. (2010). Identification of Regional Fundamental Economic Structure (FES) of India: An Input-Output and Field of Influence Approach. In Santos-Paulino, A. U., & Wan (Eds), The Rise of China and India Impacts, Prospects and Implications (pp. 138-172). Palgrave Macmillan UK. doi:10.1016/j.strueco.2007.07.001

KEY TERMS AND DEFINITIONS

Composite Indicator: A group of specific individual indicators aggregated into a single measure of progress toward a defined objective.

Human Capital: An individual's well-being and health, knowledge, skills, and abilities.

Human Capital Investment: Any investment that allows individuals to raise their education, health and living standards.

Human Capital Stock: The current level of human capital of a society in a given period and the gains from human capital investments.

Input Indicator: The total resources for the attainment of the goals set in the beginning of the process.

Output Indicators: Output Indicators refer to the indicators representing the actual result at the end of a process.

Principal Component Analysis: A method of expressing the variance structure of P number variables with a less number of new variables that are the linear components of such variables.

ENDNOTE

[1] The most commonly used indicator to measure human capital is the secondary-school enrollment rate due to the easy availability and broad coverage of this dataset. However, it is not a perfect indicator for representing human capital; although it represents the investment in human capital,

human capital formation has not yet taken place because the individuals included in the rate have not yet graduated (De la Fuente & Domenech, 2006).

[2] In the method section, I drew on my doctoral thesis titled "The Institutional Determinants of Financial Development: A Cross-Country Analysis"

Chapter 11
The Delphi Method Application in the Analysis of Postgraduate Students' Attitudes on the Environmental Performance Index

Natasa Petrovic
University of Belgrade, Serbia

Dragana Makajic-Nikolic
University of Belgrade, Serbia

Jasna Petkovic
University of Belgrade, Serbia

Maja Levi Jaksic
University of Belgrade, Serbia

Marko Cirovic
University of Belgrade, Serbia

ABSTRACT

In the context of growing concern over the global environment and related sustainability issues, the purpose of this research is to stimulate discussion about the Environmental Performance Index (EPI) and its necessary role not only in measuring postgraduate students' attitudes about EPI, and its nine categories underpinned, but also, their important role in the development of appropriate curriculum of programs that are about environmental management and sustainable development as well. Further on, the obtained results of the presented research in the paper broaden the understanding of the opportunities for not only the Republic of Serbia but every country as well, in using the EPI methodology as it has a wide applicability in improving environmental pillars of their future sustainability.

DOI: 10.4018/978-1-5225-0714-7.ch011

INTRODUCTION

The world we have created today as a result of our thinking thus far has problems which cannot be solved by thinking the way we thought when we created them. – Albert Einstein

Despite the fact that "the environment provides numerous goods and services to humanity" (Radojicic, Isljamovic, Petrovic, & Jeremic, 2012), the stability of the Earth's ecology is undermined due to the activities carried out by the human species (Petrović, 2013), environmental problems reached their critical point in the 21st century (e.g. Bonnett, 2007; Mert, 2006; Flood, & Carson, 2013) and they continue to rapidly grow. This can be "documented" thanks to specific indicators, that define the "planet's health", which is unfortunately in its decay: global holocaust of all animal and plant species, destruction of forests, the disappearance of the main species of fish, coral reef destruction, destabilization of biological habitat, increasing number of diseases resistant to antibiotics, lack of fresh water sources, pollution of the air and water, increasing risk of chemicals, damage to land, rapidly declining biodiversity, dependence on pesticides and fertilizers, the increasing number of species resistant to pesticides, almost total dependence on non-renewable forms of energy sources, globally destabilized climates and increased production of weapons of mass destruction (Petrović, 2012). Parallel, the rise of the world population brought forward the inefficient consumption of natural resources (Symth, 2004), and the consequential environmental problems became the main subject of the world agenda (Young, 2009).

Therefore, the entire humankind is forced to overcome these problems if it wants to demonstrate its commitment to sustainability as a crucial ingredient for the survival of the planet Earth and the world as we know it. The urgency to deal with the sustainability issues has been putting pressure on all three basic pillars of sustainable development, which are being investigated and performed simultaneously. These three pillars are social, economic and environmental (e.g. WCED, 1987; UNCED, 1992; UNSD, 1992; Grubb, Koch, Thomson, Munson, & Sullivan, 1993; Panjabi, 1997; Earth Summit, 2002; UN, 2015). It must be noted that there is evidence of developments in all of the three pillars, but not always related in the adequate manner. Although this shows rising interest in the field of sustainability, problems may emerge that could inhibit commitments towards building an adequate and proper sustainable future. This is especially important when it comes to the complex issue of sustainable development, which refers to the environment: "We are in a state of planetary emergency, with environmental problems piling up high around us. Unless we address the various issues prudently and seriously, we are surely doomed for disaster. Current environmental problems require urgent attention" (CEF, 2015). In order to measure man's success in these efforts, various environmental metrics and indicators were developed. The task of these environmental metrics is to measure the influences on the environment caused by various technologies and human activities. One of them is the Environmental Performance Index.

The Environmental Performance Index (EPI) ranks how well countries perform on high-priority environmental issues in two broad policy areas: protection of human health from environmental harm and protection of ecosystems. EPI is constructed through the calculation and aggregation of 20 indicators reflecting national-level environmental data. These indicators are combined into nine issue categories, each of which fit under one of two overarching objectives: Environmental Health and Ecosystem Vitality. (EPI, 2015)

In light of the above, this paper presents two issues. Firstly, it presents the research on what the environmentally educated students think of certain categories of the Environmental Performance Index. This was done through the examination of students' evaluation of all the EPI categories and improvement possibilities for the Republic of Serbia within these categories. Secondly, it presents the comparison of the rankings made by the students (members of the panel group), with the rankings made by the experts (members of the design group) from the Centre for Environmental Management and Sustainable Development of the University of Belgrade - Faculty of Organizational Sciences, according to the EPI methodology results. This was done in order to obtain feedback for the purpose of the betterment of the educational process in the field of environmental education and the education for sustainable development within the higher education system, and more precisely within postgraduate studies.

For the panel group the authors chose postgraduate students enrolled at Master studies titled Environmental Management and Sustainable Development at the University of Belgrade – Faculty of Organizational Sciences. The authors picked postgraduate students as an example of environmentally educated panel/expert group in order to evaluate their levels of acquired knowledge at the Master studies. This was done in order to point out the importance of widespread approaches for improving students' environmental awareness, knowledge and understanding of environmental and sustainability issues (Petrovic, Jeremic, Petrovic, & Cirovic, 2014) in accordance with future role in the sustainable development of their country". This is especially important because the data about environmental educational curriculum and programs in Serbia has shown that there is an evident lack of formal and permanent environmental education at all levels of formal education" (Klemenovic, 2004; Trumic, Petrovic, & Radojicic, 2009; Petrovic, 2010; Pavlovic, 2011; Sakac, Cveticanin, & Sucevic, 2012; Petrovic et al., 2014).

For the purpose of this research, the authors used the Delphi method for gaining students' assessment of nine categories used for forming the 2014 Environmental Performance Index. This method has been developed by the Yale Center for Environmental Law & Policy (YCELP) and the Center for International Earth Science Information Network (CIESIN) at Columbia University, in collaboration with the World Economic Forum and with the support from the Samuel Family Foundation and the McCall MacBain Foundation (EPI, 2015). In addition, it should be noted that this kind of research, according to the authors' knowledge, is the very first. Therefore, it represents a pilot project in order to investigate the necessity of starting a wider project for the assessment of postgraduate students' attitudes about the EPI and gathering the data on possible improvement of formal higher environmental education in the Republic of Serbia.

BACKGROUND

Sustainable Development

We are witnessing intensive efforts of society looking for solutions leading to sustainable development. The evidence of these efforts is found in multiple activities of different actors, at multiple levels in diverse fields striving to answer the urgent sustainability issues and fulfill sustainability goals. The complex sustainability equation is referred to as the triple integrated equation, derived from a set of social, economic, and environmental equations, corresponding to the three basic pillars of sustainable development goals (Sempels & Hoffman, 2013. p.20). Sustainable development is most commonly defined as "the development that meets the needs of the present without compromising the ability of future generations to meet their own needs" (WCED, 1987). It requires an understanding of the complex interplay of environmental, economic, and social processes at different scales, from local to global. Since its establishment, the sustainable development concept has been developing, and countries, organizations, institutions worldwide are committed towards the goals, and incorporating shared principles, objectives, and instruments. Further on, the domains of the three equations represented by indicators of performance lead to "careful analysis of key drivers of performance and a measurement of both drivers and the link between them" (Epstein & Roy, 2001. p. 602).

In literature review and analysis, we have understood that social and environmental dimensions and goals (Field & Field, 2006) often enlarge the traditional economic equation represented by comparable economic performance indicators. In addition, a radical turnaround in prioritization of the environmental and social goals over economic ones can be foreseen, while at the same time not eliminating the economic equation. Some authors even postulate that the economic and the environmental equations are confronted, opposing, and contradictory, the solutions are looked for in the domain of coercion, legal acts, and regulations limiting, forbidding and constraining damaging actions to the environment. This could be understood as the reaction to urgent needs in a short time span only (Bardy & Massaro, 2013. p. 139). Moreover, the new philosophy of sustainable development is forcing radical changes in paradigms and calls for "re-engineering" our views. The micro and macro perspectives are interwoven and there is a widespread understanding of technology and business innovation becoming crucial as they drive the economy towards achieving the sustainable development goals (Levi Jakšić, 2011; Levi Jakšić, 2012; Levi Jakšić, Barjaktarović Rakočević, & Martić, 2014; Levi Jakšić, 2015; Levi Jakšić, Marinković, & Petković, 2015). The relationships between entrepreneurship, innovation, and sustainable development are a "subject of rising interest nowadays" (Kardos, 2012). Sustainable business development is approached through new sustainable business, technology, and innovation models (Delanghe & Muldur, 2014; Archibugi, Filippetti, & Frenz, 2012). "If the business model cannot align economic, environmental, and social issues, the only credible solution is to change it (...) the business model should be innovated by integrating sustainability in order to build or keep a competitive advantage in an ever changing economy" (Kardos, 2012). This also leads us to the conclusion that we witness a convergence of the 'non-profit' and 'business for profit' sector as leading to the "non-profit sector gearing towards more market-based solutions, mechanisms, and dynamics, (...) businesses in general have assumed social responsibilities in a broad array of their activities, as well as responsibilities for the natural environment and natural resource consumption. At the forefront is the preserving of the 'essential' or 'critical' natural capital and sustainable development is achieved if actions of producers and consumers do not harm – air, biodiversity, climate, soil, and water – and thus maintain the earth's ecosystem services." (Bardy & Massaro, 2013. p. 139)

The efforts are oriented in a broad front addressing complex objectives of sustainable development. Multiple actors are involved and it is emphasized that a wide range of instruments, i.e. education, communication, participation, legal acts and regulations, strategy, research and development, technology and innovation, business, etc. need to be developed in transforming sustainable goals, objectives and principles into concrete actions, behaviors and attitudes at all levels – micro and macro. These are strategic sustainable issues of a complex nature with high priorities in generating solutions in the shortest period, with implications and considerations for a long time span in the future.

The Environmental Performance Index (EPI)

Environmental performance indicators form the fundamental basis for understanding and assessing the organizational environmental performance. The International Organization for Standardization (ISO) issued a guideline of the environmental performance evaluation process as ISO 14031 - Environmental Performance Evaluation – Guidelines. This guideline establishes the concept and procedure for selection of environmental performance indicators, but it does not provide its own indicators. Environmental performance indicators are being developed by research organizations such as World Business Council for Sustainable Development (WBCSD) and Global Reporting Initiative (GRI). Moreover, the importance of organizational environmental performance reporting is increasingly rising (UN, 1972; WCED, 1987). Therefore, when it comes to organizations, for Environmental Performance Index we can say that they represent an organization method for the measurement and evaluation of its own environmental performance. More precisely, these indicators are quantifiable metrics that reflect the environmental performance of an organization. Environmental performance is measured in comparison to organizational goals. It can be concluded that environmental indicators are essential tools for monitoring environmental progress, environmental policies evaluation, and means for informing the wider public (EC, 2003).

One of the challenges facing utilization of Environmental Performance Indicators for creating a composite assessment of environmental impacts of organizational strategies is finding a meaningful common currency to describe different types of impacts. In answering many questions about environmental impacts, monetary values do not adequately describe non-market costs - such as the loss of an individual life, loss of biodiversity, impacts on 'non-game' species, disruption of an ecosystem, future costs of current soil erosion, or loss of non-replaceable resources (e.g. Daly, Cobb & Cobb, 1994; Riha, Levitan, & Hutson, 1996; Petrović & Slović, 2011; Petrović, Slović, & Ćirović, 2012; Ćirović, Petrović, & Slović, 2012). Another challenge of creating composite assessments of environmental impacts is the difficulty to select just one set of environmental indicators for evaluating all the impacts of an organisation (Becker, 2008; Cetin & Nisanci, 2010; Emil, 1994; Garetz, 1993; Cirovic, Petrovic, & Slovic, 2014).

One of the responses provided for this challenge is the methodology established at the Yale University by a joint project between the Yale Centre for Environmental Law & Policy (YCELP) and the Centre for International Earth Science Information Network (CIESIN) at Columbia University, in collaboration with the World Economic Forum and with support from the Samuel Family Foundation and the McCall MacBain Foundation. The goal of the project was to develop the composite set of environmental indicators that form the Environmental Performance Index. The idea for creating this Index was provided by the global need of environmental policy makers for scientific qualitative and quantitative data on environmental performance (Esty et al., 2006; Emerson et al., 2010; Emerson et al., 2012). This index for a year 2014 prioritizes Environmental Health and Ecosystem Vitality. Environmental Health is considered as a human health safety from the environmental harms, while Ecosystem Vitality measures environmental protection. These two issues are introspected through nine categories underpinned by 20 environmental indicators. The nine environmental issues are divided by these two categories as follows (EPI, 2015):

1. **Environmental Health:**
   a.   Health Impacts,
   b.   Air Quality,
   c.   Water and Sanitation.
2. **Ecosystem Vitality:**
   a.   Water Resources,
   b.   Agriculture,
   c.   Forests,
   d.   Fisheries,
   e.   Biodiversity and Habitat,
   f.   Climate and Energy.

Most of the research done in the field uses indicators that can portray only a part of properties of the environmental performance of an observed entity. That is the reason why researchers have tried finding appropriate ways by which a synthetic standardized EPI can be obtained. Environmental Performance Index (Esty et al., 2006; Tyteca, 1996; Olsthoorn et al., 2001) takes the most comprehensive combination of relevant environmental measures into account.

The EPI methodology has been evolving for more than 15 years now. The work on environmental performance measurements is constantly improved and in that period EPI has gone through six iterations. YCELP in partnership with CIESIN and the World Economic Forum, first published the Environmental Sustainability Index (ESI) (the older version of EPI) in 2000. Creating ESI was based on an idea of achieving long-term development goals, emphasized by the United Nations, Millennium Declaration, by the year 2015. Although the Declaration stressed environmental sustainability as an aim, no relevant quantitative metrics were available at that time. Plan was for ESI to address that challenge. ESI measured 76 sustainability indicators. This large number of factors faced a problem of a lack of targets to which these indicators would be compared with.

Yale-Columbia experts created pilot EPI in 2006 reducing this large number of indicators to carefully selected 16 indicators. This selection aimed to measure performance as outcome-oriented indicators, providing easily comparable results between the countries. Indicators were classified into two environmental objectives which basis persists in 2014 EPI: 1) reducing environmental stresses on human health and 2) promoting the vitality of the ecosystem and sound natural resource management. The EPI versions of 2008 and 2010 included small methodology changes in response to expert feedback gained on previous EPI reports. The number of indicators was raised to 25 in the 2008 and 2010 version of EPI. Additionally, weight for the climate change category was changed from 0.1 in the pilot version of EPI to 0.25 in 2008 and 2010 version of EPI. This was done due to international importance given to the climate issue. In 2010, the EPI methodology was modified further to allow making clearer distinctions when interpreting the results between countries ranking close to each other. In general, from 2006 to 2010, methodology stayed relatively the same. One of the major steps forward was introduced in 2012 version of EPI. This step included incorporation of time series data. Time series gave possibility of comparing the progress of countries through time and gave a basis for creating future predictions. Time series allowed analysts to create data trends, and data trends entered in the final EPI results gave a fuller insight into state of the matter (Esty et al., 2006; EPI, 2015)

Off course, although EPI has gone through 15 years of evolution, there is still room for improvements. It has been recognized that EPI is still lacking data on several quite important environmental issues such as (EPI, 2015):

- Freshwater quality,
- Toxic chemical exposures,
- Municipal solid waste management,
- Nuclear safety,
- Wetlands loss,
- Agricultural soil quality and degradation,
- Recycling rates,
- Adaptation, vulnerability, and resiliency to climate change,
- Desertification.

Nevertheless, EPI remains highly influential and recognized environmental metric. Moreover, it moves beyond the metrics trying to find correlation simply between the economic growth and the state of the environment. Additionally, studies by OECD (1991), Grossman & Krueger (1994), suggest that the strongest correlation between the economic growth and environmental affairs stays in the fact that once prosperity of the citizens' rises, they become more demanding toward their governments in dealing with the environmental issues.

The EPI methodology starts with gathering the data from the countries and transferring that data set into comprehensive, comparative performance indicators based on the population size, gross domestic product, and other denominations that characterize all the countries reporting on their environmental performance. Furthermore, these results are then placed on a scale from 0 to 100, in order to reach comprehensive output for wider audience and gaining the foundation for easier further environmental assessment. "Scores are then converted to a scale of 0 to 100 by simple arithmetic calculation, with 0 being the farthest from the target (worst observed value) and 100 being closest to the target (best observed value)" (EPI, 2015). Obtained data are then applied for computing the indicators that accumulate the index. Indicators that were selected for forming the index are utilized as a measure of a countries ability to achieve the targeted goals proclaimed by international treaties signed either by the countries or by countries national policies. This measure represents the extent to which the norms of these policies were fulfilled or the level of the success countries performed while implementing international standards in the above mentioned nine categories (Emerson et al., 2012; Hsu et al., 2014; EPI, 2015).

Each of the 20 indicators represents the fulfillment of one specific environmental policy. Their fulfillment is represented as a weighted measure of policy implementation. These weighted measures are corresponding to the relevance and quality of the data set provided for the specific policy meaning that it is proportional to the reliability of the data obtained for the observed environmental issue (Emerson et al., 2012; Hsu et al., 2014; EPI, 2015).

Environmental Performance Index testifies that combination and formation of composite set of indicators whose application could lead to viable assessment that can give relevant insight into countries or organizational performance on the issues that deal with their environmental impacts is possible. This is proven by the increased popularity in usage of Environmental Performance Index. Additionally EPI has become relevant consideration metric of the policy makers around the globe, which gives extra weight to the portrayed methodology.

Delphi Method

The Delphi method was developed during the Cold War with the underlining idea of gaining a new forecasting technique. The Delphi was initially created for forecasting the influence of development of new technologies in the war. Traditional forecasting methods, such as theoretical approach, quantitative model, extrapolation trend, were considered unsuitable because of their known shortcomings mostly regarding the lack of scientific data. As a remedy to these shortcomings Olaf Helmer and Norman Dalkei (Dalkey & Helmer, 1963; Brown, 1968; Sackman, 1974; Linstone & Turoff, 1975) created the Delphi through the project RAND during the 1950s. The Delphi method presents one of the most widespread methods for intuitive forecasting and one of the most commonly known forecasting methods (Popper, 2008), that is based on series of written questionnaires with feedback and re-voting (Popper, 2008). There are two participant roles:

- **Design Group:** (Sometimes just one person) That makes the questionnaires for the expert group and makes the consensus of the expert group, and
- **Expert Group:** Panel that answers the questionnaires.

The members of panel do not meet face-to-face; they are characterized by three important conditions: anonymity, iteration with controlled feedback, and statistical response. This is not an opinion survey, but rather, a way systematically asking and summarizing expert judgment in successive rounds of Delphi forecasts (Mulloen, 2003). In addition, Bramwell and Hykawy (1999) gave the first idea for applying the Delphi method in forecasting events in education. Despite some limitations, it has been recommended that studies employing the Delphi should be continued in order to further refine the technique and to explore its application. The Delphi method represents "a systematic procedure that collates the opinions of a diverse group of experts located in different geographical areas whose opinions are important for decision analyses. Through the Delphi technique, different responses and views are obtained on the underlying problem resulting in generating new ideas and unique suggestions, and eventually provides consensus on the findings among a panel of experts" (Eskandari et al., 2007).

Rowe and Wright (1999) characterize the classical Delphi method by four key features:

1. **Anonymity of Delphi Participants:** Allows the participants to freely express their opinions without undue social pressures to conform from others in the group. Decisions are evaluated on their merit, rather than who has proposed the idea,
2. **Iteration:** Allows the participants to refine their views in light of the progress of the group's work from round to round,
3. **Controlled Feedback:** Informs the participants of the other participant's perspectives, and provides the opportunity for Delphi participants to clarify or change their views,
4. **Statistical Aggregation of Group Response:** Allows for a quantitative analysis and interpretation of data.

Basic steps within Delphi method are as follows:

- The group of experts is formed, as well as a questionnaire concerning the forecasting theme,
- The first stage of interviewing is carried out by submitting the questionnaires to panel members,

- The answers are then analyzed and the results of these analyses are shown to experts in the second stage of interviewing. After that, they adjust their answers in line with these results, everything until they reach a consensus,
- In the end, the collected information are summed up and analyzed, and the results are presented.

The Delphi method has plenty of advantages. The process allows the collection of stances of great number of experts. In this way, we accomplish better statistical reliability and easier reaching of consensus. Delphi allows experts to freely and anonymously change their opinion and stances regarding some questions. The advantage is to be found in the fact that the researches that have been carried out and modified depending on the research field can be used in other countries as well. Back in the past, the most important deficiency of this method was recognized in the price and duration of forecasting since it involves great number of people in order to accomplish important goals (Porter et al., 2011). It is now possible to overcome these disadvantages by using modern information-communication technologies. Questionnaires could be sent via Internet to great number of experts in different parts of the world. The lack of Delphi method is the fact that the bad formulation of a questionnaire could lead to bad results, which is why it is necessary to dedicate great attention to production of questionnaires and proper conception of questions (Martino, 1993; Linstone & Turoff, 2002).

The Delphi method is applied for forecasting the probability and time of the emergence of future events. In order to give a prognosis, a group of experts identifies and defines the given event, the probability of its development and possible time of future event. Delphi method is also important because of the impartiality of participants bearing in mind that opinions and presumptions of forecasting experts are based on collecting data through polls, i.e. on filling out the questionnaires. Experts fill questionnaires independently of each other, which gives this method the impartial character when it comes to judgment (Makridakis, Wheelwright, & Hyndman, 1998).

The country with most experience in such forecasting is Japan. Scientific and technological institutions every five years starting from 1971 conducted the best-known researches. Their goal was to collect information that will help in easier decision making and introducing strategies on the level of government's agencies or private entrepreneurs. As a method of technology forecasting, Delphi method was also used in many other countries such as Germany, United Kingdom, Hungary, and France (Obradović, 2004). Also, the one of the more successful examples of the use of Delphi method that is commonly quoted in literature is its use in automobile industry (Levi Jakšić, Stošić, Marinković, & Obradović, 2007).

METHODOLOGY: RESEARCH CONTEXT

Previous studies have shown that "many educators feel that they should not only teach the science, but also engage students and encourage positive responsiveness about the environment and sustainability" (i.e. Mason & Santi, 1998; Cross & Price, 1999; Lester, Ma, Lee, & Lambert, 2006; Petrovic et al., 2014), as well as that good environmental higher education "engages formal, non-formal, and informal education and uses a variety of pedagogical techniques that promote participatory learning and higher-order thinking skills" (UNESCO, 2012; Petrovic et al., 2014).

The Master studies selected for our research were Environmental Management and Sustainable Development studies that are a presented study group at Master program Management at the University of Belgrade – Faculty of Organizational Sciences, the Republic of Serbia. At this study group, a framework and a curriculum for good environmental higher education are developed on a wide scale of scientific and practical knowledge of environmental science and sustainable development as a good benchmark for the adequate improvement of students' knowledge at postgraduate level, as well as a promotion of higher order thinking skills in a cooperative context for learning and evaluation (Petrovic et al., 2014). The study group Environmental management and sustainable development consists of three obligatory courses, two elective courses, and internship for a period of a two semesters. The obligatory courses are Management and Organization, Integrated Environmental Management and Sustainable Development. Students chose two elective courses from the list of elective courses: Eco Marketing - Selected chapters, Environmental Risk Management, Management of Environmental Suitability of Products, Eco-Innovation Project Management, Statistics for Management - Selected chapters, Intellectual Property Management, Technological Forecasting, and Strategic Technological Cooperation (FOS, 2015a). The course programs are "based on a strong pedagogical methodology, requiring participants to turn their environmental and management knowledge and understanding into appropriate environmental actions and into behavior change for sustainability" (Petrovic, 2010; Petrovic et al., 2014).

In this paper, we discussed the application of the Delphi method in evaluation of postgraduate students' attitudes about nine issue categories of The 2014 Environmental Performance Index by model that we used in our research. We suggested the usage of the Delphi method, having in mind that Bramwell and Hykawy (1999) have suggested that the Delphi method seemed to have promising application as a tool for teaching people to think and discuss about the future in a more complex way than they ordinarily would. It can be concluded that this method has high applicability for sustainability foresight, as well as it is one of the best-known qualitative methods of forecasting in the long run, especially when quantitative methods are not adequate, as it happened in this case.

The model of used and modified Delphi method in this research consists of:

Round 1: Selected experts from the Centre for Environmental Management and Sustainable Development (members of the design group) composed the questionnaire based on The 2014 Environmental Performance Index – EPI and its nine categories: Health Impacts, Air Quality, Water & Sanitation, Climate & Energy, Biodiversity & Habitat, Fisheries, Forests, Agriculture, and Water Resources.

Round 2: The first questionnaire was handed out to the students and they anonymously filled it. They evaluated the significance of the given categories of EPI based on their attitudes and knowledge.

Round 3: Based on the obtained questionnaire results, the arithmetic means and dispersions (variance and standard deviation) of nine categories of The 2014 Environmental Performance Index were calculated. A new questionnaire comprised of only the categories that had the biggest dispersion in answers has been made.

Round 4: The participants were handed out the new questionnaire with the categories from the round 3. Final results are gained as combination of results of the first and the second questionnaire.

Round 5: Based on arithmetic means from round 4, members of the design group have assigned ranks to all nine categories of EPI. The three highest ranked categories have been used in the new questionnaire. This third questionnaire represents a classical Delphi application, and it was focused on forecasting in the next ten years, that is from the year 2015 up to 2025. For this, precise questions were created.

Round 6: The participants were handed out the final questionnaire.

Round 7: The filled out questionnaire was processed using the software UT and the forecasts were calculated and shown.

Round 8: The experts from the design group ranked the nine of EPI categories from the viewpoint of EPI methodology results for the Republic of Serbia.

Round 9: Assigned ranks from the round 8 were compared with the ranks from the round 5. The goal of this round was to determine the differences between these ranks, and consequentially give more attention to categories with the biggest differences, during future generations' classes at study group Environmental Management and Sustainable development.

Participants and Design

The research was performed on the postgraduate students attending the study group Environmental Management and Sustainable Development at master studies Management of the 2014/2015 academic year.

Main goal of the research was to gain answers to the following questions:

Q1: What are the most important categories of Environmental Performance Index in the Republic of Serbia in the postgraduate students' opinions?

Q2: What are the attitudes of the postgraduate students and the educators with expertise in Environmental Performance Index and sustainable development on the priority of individual categories for EPI in the Republic of Serbia?

Q3: In which fields and courses should we improve both scientific and practical environmental knowledge of postgraduate students?

The curriculum of the studies program has provided basic knowledge on the investigated area and needed terminology that secured the relevance of the questioned group of students used for this research. All of the enrolled students (total number of students was 13, while seven of them were female and six of them were male) participated in the survey, and all of the students completed the survey and the results for each of them were then calculated. The questionnaire was a part of the expert monitoring of the Centre for environmental management and sustainable development from the Faculty of Organizational Sciences, and its results have been used solely in scientific and academic purposes. Participation in the questionnaire and the responses given were classified and available only to the research team, without the involvement of third parties or other panelists.

In June, after the classes have finished and the students passed their exams with passing marks, the students accessed the first round of the Delphi research. In order for the students to fill out the questionnaire, a meeting was organized at the Faculty of Organizational Sciences, where the respondents, i.e. students, were seated in a large conference hall, with enough space apart from each student, so that they could not influence the opinions of their fellow respondents. Also, according to the propositions of the Delphi questionnaire, it was explained to them beforehand that they are not allowed to communicate with each other while they are filling out the form, that their filled out forms will be used solely in academic purposes, and that after the analysis of the forms from the first round, they will get the arithmetic mean and the variances of the responses. Two days after that, the students were asked to come in again for another meeting. Based on the results gained from the first round, for certain questions (where $\sigma_n^2 > 1$) the research process was repeated. After the data from the second round were analyzed, the results obtained showed a significant agreement of the responses from the round two with the responses from the round one. With that, the role of the experts of the Delphi research, in our case – the students, was over. This way, we gained the results of the students' opinions on the ranked categories of EPI (see Table 1.). After a week has passed, when the members of the design group have calculated all the results, the students were asked to come back once again for a classical Delphi forecast for a period of 10 years, for the chosen, highest ranked indicators.

Instruments

In order to evaluate the results of the survey, we used statistical analysis for calculation of the arithmetic mean rating, variance and standard deviation:

- Calculation of the arithmetic mean rating (t_n) was done using the following equation:

$$t_n = \frac{1}{n} \sum_{i=1}^{k} f_i \cdot t_i \tag{1}$$

where k is the number of different rating scores, f_i is a number of experts that evaluated observed item with rating score t_i, and n represents the total number of experts $\left(n = \sum_{i=1}^{k} f_i \right)$.

- Calculation the variance and standard deviation were made using the following equations:

$$\sigma^2 = \frac{1}{n} \sum_{i=1}^{k} f_i \left(t_i - t_n \right)^2 \tag{2}$$

Table 1. The results of the first and the second questionnaire

Environmental Performance Index Categories	Arithmetic Mean (t_n)	Variance (σ_n^2)
Health Impacts (Child Mortality)	1.23	0.34
Air Quality (Household Air Quality, Air Pollution)	1.54	0.4
Water and Sanitation (Access to Drinking Water, Access to Sanitation)	1.62	0.38
Agriculture (Agricultural Subsidies, Pesticide Regulation)	1.92	0.48
Climate and Energy (Trend in CO2 Emissions, Change of Trend in Carbon Intensity, Trend in Carbon Intensity)	2.15	0.15
Water Resources (Wastewater Treatment)	2.23	0.18
Biodiversity and Habitat (National Biome Protection, Global Biome Protection, Marine Protected Areas, Critical Habitat Protection)	2.54	0.4
Forests (Change in Forest Cover)	2.54	0.4
Fisheries (Coastal Shelf Fishing Pressure, Fish Stocks)	3.23	0.34

$$\sigma_n = \sqrt{\sigma_n^2} \tag{3}$$

where σ_n^2 is variance and σ_n is standard deviation.

In addition, we used a developed software package for the Delphi method used in forecasting at University of Belgrade - Faculty of Organizational Sciences.

RESULTS

In the round 2, the postgraduate students who voluntarily participated in the survey had the task of answering three questionnaires regarding the priorities in choosing nine categories of Environmental Performance Index – EPI, which should, in their opinion, reflect national priorities of the Republic of Serbia. In the first round, the questionnaire consisted of 14 questions in total. The first three questions were general. From question four to twelve, the examinees were asked to rank the listed categories of EPI by using a five point scale (1 – *the most significant*, 2 – *very significant*, 3 – *significant*, 4 – *not so significant*, 5 – *the least significant/insignificant*). These questions (questions four to twelve) are considered the most important ones because they directly refer to the main goals of our research. In the next question (question thirteen), the examinees had to choose three EPI categories they thought represent the most significant environmental issues for the Republic of Serbia, while simultaneously elaborating the reasons why they chose them. In question fourteen, they had to choose three categories they thought are of the least significance for the total EPI rank of Serbia.

After calculating the results of students from the first questionnaire, arithmetic mean and variance were calculated. In three EPI categories, great deviations were found: Climate & Energy, Agriculture and Water Resources. In order to obtain better concurrence for these categories, a new questionnaire was made in round three. Summarized results of the first and the second questionnaires are given in Table 1.

Experts from the design group now drew up a new questionnaire for conducting classical Delphi method for forecasting which relates to EPI categories best rated by students (round 5). Those are the following categories: Health Impacts, Air Quality, and Water & Sanitation. The results of round seven are shown in Figures 1, 2, and 3.

It is quite obvious that the examinees in the first round, when it comes to EPI category that refers to Health Impacts, have reached a weak agreement to this question, saying that the total load of children diseases caused by outdoor air pollution will be five times less in the first half of 2024 (P = 0.4809), as can be seen from the arithmetic mean ($t_n = 9.0769$). Further on, $\sigma_n^2 = 1.6095$, which is no small deviation. Standard deviation is 1.2686, which is understandable since the question is very specific and trespasses the forecasting domain in medicine field, while at the same time examinees are not expert enough and are poorly educated in this matter (FOS, 2015b). Still, having in mind that this question is a part of EPI methodology, it has been included in the questionnaire for its global, regional and national significance in relation to societies' birthrates and prosperity.

When it comes to Air Quality category and the question 'When will the measures for prevention and reduction of air pollution while at the same time improving air quality will meet 50 percent of European standards?', the respondents reached even better agreement that resulted in a statement that this event will happen in 7.3846 years, that is, in the first half of 2022 (P = 0.3259). Variance is $\sigma_n^2 = 0.8521$, while the standard deviation is 0.9231. Therefore, it can be concluded that the respondents have reached

Figure 1. The forecasting results for question "When do you think the total load of children diseases caused by outdoor air pollution will be five times less?"

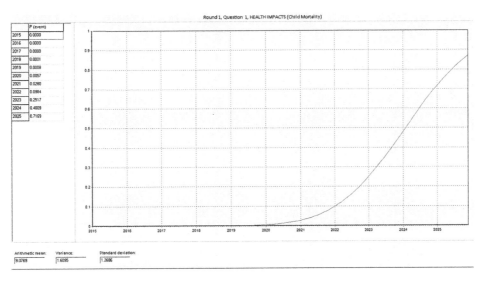

higher level of agreement than in the previous question, which proves that not only the respondents are aware of the significance of water, but also the question précised by 50 percent probability gave them a reason to provide such an answer. According to authors – experts from the Center for Environmental Management and Sustainable Development, their opinion is precise having in mind that the air condition is satisfactory judging by the Report on the environmental situation in the Republic of Serbia for 2014. Namely, in 2014, 68.8 percent of Serbia's population had clean or slightly polluted air (The Agency for Environmental Protection, 2014).

Figure 2. The forecasting results for question "When will the measures for prevention and reduction of air pollution, while at the same time improving air quality, meet 50 percent of the European standards?"

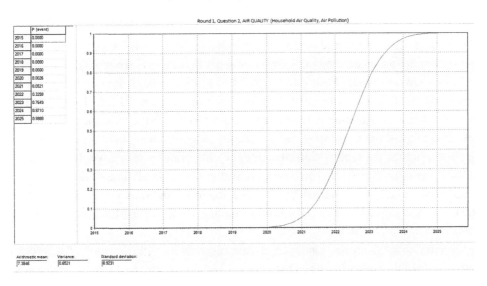

Figure 3. The forecasting results for question "When will the rates of reduction of diarrheal diseases by using advanced sanitation forms reach 90 percent?"

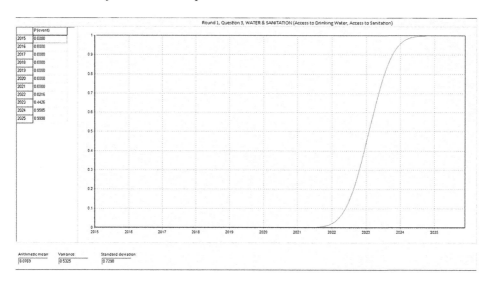

Speaking of EPI category referring to Water & Sanitation and the question 'When will the rate of reduction of diarrheal diseases by using advanced sanitation forms reach 90 percent?', it is evident that the highest agreement to this question was obtained with respondents in comparison to previous two questions (even though high percentage of forecasting improvement is present, the same as in the question under ordinal number 1). In this way, the respondents agreed that the progress will occur in 2023 (P=0.4426). The deviation in agreement is 0.5325, i.e. the standard deviation is 0.7298. This is to be expected due to the fact that estimates given in European Union membership Chapter 27 in the process of accession of Serbia to the European Union, show that Serbia will need around 10.6 billion euros by 2030 simply for reaching the environmental standards set by the EU. Out of this sum, around 5.9 billion euros will go to Water sector, which is more than half of the projected funds planned for investment in this EPI category (UETS, 2014).

According to the 2014 Environmental Performance Index, results for the Republic of Serbia are shown in Table 2.

Based on The 2014 Environmental Performance Index ranking of the Republic of Serbia, the members of the design group assigned the ranks for the nine EPI categories (round 8). Ranks were assigned based on The 2014 Environmental Performance Index ranking accomplished by the Republic of Serbia in all nine categories that were the object of examination. For the year 2014, EPI was calculated for 175 countries in nine categories. Ranking is based on the extent in which the countries fulfill the obligations and the level of accomplishment countries have in these categories. The more the country accomplishes in the category the higher the rank within that category the country will have. Ranks assigned by the members of the design group are based on how well Serbia ranked in all nine of these categories by EPI. The higher Serbia is ranked in a specific EPI category, the lower the rank was assigned. This is because the lower the country is ranked by The 2014 Environmental Performance Index that means more has to be done in this category on the national level.

Finally, assigned ranks from the round eight were compared with the ranks from the round five. Table 3 shows the absolute rank differences between ranked postgraduate students' attitudes and ranking

Table 2. Serbia 2014 ranking according to EPI methodology out of 175 countries

Environmental Performance Index Categories	Serbia Ranking According to EPI Methodology Out of 175 Countries
Health Impacts (Child Mortality)	61
Air Quality (Household Air Quality, Air Pollution)	157
Water and Sanitation (Access to Drinking Water, Access to Sanitation)	42
Climate and Energy (Trend in CO_2 Emissions, Change of Trend in Carbon Intensity, Trend in Carbon Intensity)	29
Biodiversity and Habitat (National Biome Protection, Global Biome Protection, Marine Protected Areas, Critical Habitat Protection)	10
Fisheries (Coastal Shelf Fishing Pressure, Fish Stocks)	/
Forests (Change in Forest Cover)	1
Agriculture (Agricultural Subsidies, Pesticide Regulation)	1
Water Resources (Wastewater Treatment)	93

Table 3. The absolute rank differences between ranked postgraduate students' attitudes and ranking based on 2014 Serbia EPI methodology results

Environmental Performance Index Categories	Rank	Rank According to EPI Methodology Results	Absolute Rank Difference
Health Impacts (Child Mortality)	1	4	3
Air Quality (Household Air Quality, Air Pollution)	2	2	0
Water and Sanitation (Access to Drinking Water, Access to Sanitation)	3	5	2
Agriculture (Agricultural Subsidies, Pesticide Regulation)	4	8.5	4.5
Climate and Energy (Trend in CO2 Emissions, Change of Trend in Carbon Intensity, Trend in Carbon Intensity)	5	6	1
Water Resources (Wastewater Treatment)	6	3	3
Biodiversity and Habitat (National Biome Protection, Global Biome Protection, Marine Protected Areas, Critical Habitat Protection)	7.5	7	0.5
Forests (Change in Forest Cover)	7.5	8.5	1
Fisheries (Coastal Shelf Fishing Pressure, Fish Stocks)	9	1	8

based on the 2014 Serbia's EPI methodology results while Figure 4 shows the ranks according to the postgraduate students' attitudes and according to the EPI methodology results.

DISCUSSION

Based on the comparison made in the round nine of the research, several issues came to attention as potential discussion topics. Once comparison was made, we can distinguish three groups of environmental issues based on the absolute rank of difference between the rank gained out of postgraduate students' responses and ranks based on the EPI methodology.

Firstly, when we compare students' rank and the EPI rank of the nine categories, we can note those postgraduate students' attitudes toward more than half of the categories do not differ by more than two ranks, which we can note as a high environmental awareness portrayed by students undergoing the research. Moreover, for four out of nine categories the absolute rank difference is 0 to 1 rank. These four categories include Air Quality, Climate & Energy, Biodiversity & Habitat, and Forests. We can state that these categories form the group of environmental issues with which students are well informed on, when the state of the environment in the Republic of Serbia is concerned. Their attitudes toward these issues correspond well and have the highest correlation to the reality portrayed by The 2014 Environmental Performance Index rank of the same categories. Additionally we can note that reasons for this concurrence in rankings is a result of - firstly, these students being enrolled at the Environmental Management and Sustainable Development studies at the Master program at the University of Belgrade – Faculty of Organizational Sciences, the Republic of Serbia, and, secondly, as a result of this program having well established up to date postgraduate curriculum.

Figure 4. Ranks according to the postgraduate students' attitudes and according to the EPI methodology results

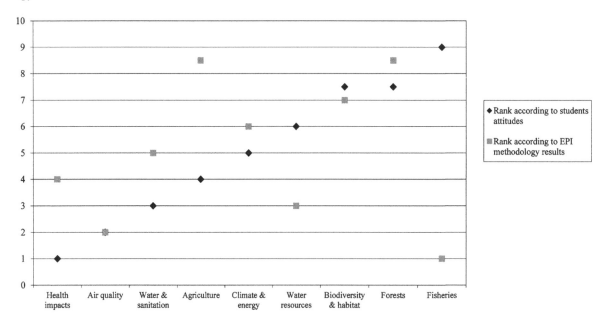

Second group of issues we can distinguish are issues with absolute rank difference higher than 2 and lower than 5, which would make a group of issues with medium postgraduate students' environmental awareness. This group includes issues that relate to Water Resources, Agriculture, and Health Impacts. We can note that issues like these that relate to Health, Food, and Water are generally the issues that are, not only by students of Environmental Management and Sustainable Development but general public as well, considered to be of the highest and constant importance no matter how well the country deals with them. Therefore, the perception is that they should be constantly of highest importance in the country's environmental agenda. This is why these issues rank high in the postgraduate students' attitudes and simultaneously rank low when objective measures are applied such as The 2014 Environmental Performance Index methodology.

Third instance that we can distinguish, out of the comparison made in the round nine of the research, are issues with low students' environmental awareness. These would be the issues with absolute rank difference higher than five. In the research conducted, this is only one category of issues, more specifically category relating to Fisheries (Coastal Shelf Fishing Pressure Fish Stocks). This is because this is the only category observed for which there is no data provided for the Environmental Performance Index. Meaning that this is the issue in which the Republic of Serbia should do the most, not only in the sense of quality monitoring and gaining results but in raising public awareness on the importance of this environmental category as well.

SOLUTIONS AND RECOMMENDATIONS

Several issues come to be noted when the matter of future research directions are analyzed. Firstly, it can be noted that the research on awareness and attitudes towards environmental performance of a country in the eyes of the public, as well as research on the same issue but in the eyes of postgraduate students in different vocations, should be done, in order to evaluate general environmental awareness in the Republic of Serbia.

Secondly, another idea for further research should be to see whether or not the Environmental Performance Index could be developed to measure a country's accomplishment within these nine environmental categories independently of each other. More specifically, although the Republic of Serbia ranked first out of 175 countries in two categories, it does not mean that Serbia as a country could not do more in regards to further fulfillment of goals within these two categories. In addition, such high ranking could act as a deterrence factor, creating such a scenario in which countries are reluctant to provide continuous environmental improvements within the categories where it found itself ranked high.

Finally, if sustainable development as a concept is becoming a globally pursuable goal and if the Environmental Performance Index methodology provides us with a tool for the measurement of success of accomplishing that goal, the question that arises is, if all of the countries that undergo The 2014 Environmental Performance Index ranking would perform a certain level of fulfillment of environmental policies, such as the level presented out of the top ranking countries, of all nine categories, would sustainable development be achieved. Answering this question is also an answer to the question of purposefulness of the Environmental Performance Index methodology.

FUTURE RESEARCH DIRECTIONS

Future research will be directed mainly toward expanding the use of the Delphi method in improving environmental education and education for sustainable development not only in the sense of active and practical studying and learning, but as well as a method that can give valuable feedback on the need of improving specific scientific and practical fields in the domain of environmental protection, national sustainable development strategy, harmonizing environmental laws with EU laws, and the needs for improving certain environmental categories in the specific condition in which a country such as the Republic of Serbia is. Having in mind that the environmental component is one third of the complex model of sustainable development, surely future research should be directed in a path to introducing indicators that are referring to the economic and social pillars of sustainable development. More precisely, the concrete situation that could arise in practice is that we develop policies and strategies that are not harmonized well with the objective situation and with crucial issues in our practice of implementation of sustainable development, and that we consequently address the issues that are not of the highest priority. This could lead to implementation of such strategies, to actions that do not correspond to the urgent needs in the domains of sustainable development. This means loss in financial, time, human, creative, material resources and could produce a wave of distrust and doubt in the efforts towards sustainable development.

On the other hand, when it comes to the educators in the field of environmental studies and studies for sustainable development, they need to be motivated and ready to enable effective learning and to engage all of their students in the newest worlds' results and research in the field of environmental performances such as in this case The 2014 Environmental Performance Index is.

CONCLUSION

The results shown in this paper are based on the perspectives of conceptual reflection in literature and are based on methods of analysis and synthesis, of interpretation and relevant comparisons. According to the authors of this research, the presented Delphi survey can be a useful tool for gaining the results of judgment in ranking categories of Environmental Performance Index by postgraduate students in circumstances where certain limits exist in:

- Their knowledge about Environmental Performance Index,
- Existing empirical methods and data,
- Their practical environmental knowledge and knowledge for sustainable development.

Despite these limitations, we believe that the proposed model has the potential to provide helpful information for future broader refining and ranking of priorities of national Environmental Performance Index for the Republic of Serbia. Moreover, our research starts with an investigation of an environmental basic pillar of sustainable development, i.e. the environmental dimension through the activities of the academia, more specifically of the postgraduate students' contribution to evaluating The 2014 Environmental Performance Index. Hence, in the future it must include research from broader perspective of sustainable development encompassing social and economic dimensions as well.

REFERENCES

Archibugi, D., Filippetti, A., & Frenz, M. (2013). Economic crisis and innovation: Is destruction prevailing over accumulation? *Research Policy*, *42*(2), 303–314. doi:10.1016/j.respol.2012.07.002

Bardy, R., & Massaro, M. (2013). Eco-social business in developing countries: the case for sustainable use of resources in unstable environments. In J. R. McIntyre, S. Ivanaj, & V. Ivanaj (Eds.), *Strategies for Sustainable Technologies and Innovations*. London: Edward Elgar. doi:10.4337/9781781006832.00018

Becker, T. (2008). The Business behind Green, Eliminating fear, uncertainty, and doubt. *APICS Magazine, 18*(2).

Bonnett, M. (2007). Environmental Education and the Issue of Nature. *Journal of Curriculum Studies*, *39*(6), 707–721. doi:10.1080/00220270701447149

Bramwell, L., & Hykawy, E. (1999). The Delphi technique: A possible tool for predicting future events in nursing education. *Canadian Journal of Nursing Research*, *30*(4), 47–58. PMID:10603776

Brown, B. B. (1968). *Delphi process: A methodology used for the elicitation of opinions of experts (No. RAND-P-3925)*. Santa Monica, CA: RAND CORP.

Cetin, G., & Nisanci, S. H. (2010). Enhancing students' environmental awareness. *Procedia: Social and Behavioral Sciences*, *2*(2), 1830–1834. doi:10.1016/j.sbspro.2010.03.993

Ćirović, M., Petrović, N., & Slović, D. (2012). Towards sustainable organization: measuring environmental performance indicators, *Proceedings of 31ˢᵗ International Conference on Organizational Science Development QUALITY. INNOVATION. FUTURE.*

Cirovic, M., Petrovic, N., & Slovic, D. (2014). EPI: Environmental Feedback on the Organization's Sustainability. In M. Levi Jakšić, S. Barjaktarović Rakočević, & M. Martić (Eds.), *Innovative Management and Firm Performance: An Interdisciplinary Approach and Cases* (pp. 122–138). Palgrave Macmillan. doi:10.1057/9781137402226_6

Conserve Energy Future – CEF. (2015). *Current environmental problems*. Retrieved from http://www.conserve-energy-future.com/15-current-environmental-problems.php

Cross, R. T., & Price, R. F. (1999). The social responsibility of science and the public understanding of science. *International Journal of Science Education*, *21*(7), 775–785. doi:10.1080/095006999290435

Dalkey, N., & Helmer, O. (1963). An experimental application of the Delphi method to the use of experts. *Management Science*, *9*(3), 458–467. doi:10.1287/mnsc.9.3.458

Daly, H. E., Cobb, J. B., & Cobb, C. W. (1994). *For the common good: Redirecting the economy toward community, the environment, and a sustainable future*. Beacon Press.

Delanghe, H., & Muldur, U. (2014). Research and experimental development (R&D) and technological innovation policy. In S. N. Durlauf & L. E. Blume (Eds.), *The New Palgrave Dictionary of Economics*. Online Edition.

Earth Summit. (2002). Retrieved from http://www.earthsummit2002.org/Es2002.pdf

Emerson, J., Esty, D. C., Levy, M. A., Kim, C. H., Mara, V., de Sherbinin, A., & Srebotnjak, T. (2010). *Environmental performance index*. New Haven, CT: Yale Center for Environmental Law and Policy.

Emerson, J. W., Hsu, A., Levy, M. A., de Sherbinin, A., Mara, V., Esty, D. C., & Jaiteh, M. (2012). *Environmental performance index and pilot trend environmental performance index*. New Haven, CT: Yale Center for Environmental Law and Policy.

Emil, S. (1994). *The challenge of sustainable consumption as seen from the South*. In *Symposium: Sustainable Consumption*, Oslo, Norway.

Environmental Performance Index (EPI). (2015). *Global Metrics for The Environment*. Retrieved from http://epi.yale.edu/

Epstein, M. J., & Roy, M. J. (2001). Sustainability in Action: Identifying and Measuring the Key Performance Drivers. *Long Range Planning, 34*(5), 584–604. doi:10.1016/S0024-6301(01)00084-X

Eskandari, H., Sala-Diakanda, S., Furterer, S., Rabelo, L., Crumpton-Young, L., & Williams, K. (2007). Enhancing the undergraduate industrial engineering curriculum: Defining desired characteristics and emerging topics. *Education+ Training, 49*(1), 45-55.

Esty, D. C., Levy, M. A., Srebotnjak, T., de Sherbinin, A., Kim, C. H., & Anderson, B. (2006). *Pilot 2006 environmental performance index*. New Haven, CT: Yale Center for Environmental Law & Policy.

Europian Commission - EC. (2003). *EMAS – guidance*. Retrieved from http://ec.europa.eu/environment/emas/pdf/guidance/guidance08_en.pdf

Faculty of Organizational Sciences – FOS. (2015a). *Master Studies – Management*. Retrieved from http://www.fon.bg.ac.rs/eng/studies/master-and-specialized-studies/management/

Faculty of Organizational Sciences – FOS. (2015b). *Master Studies – Management – Curriculum*. Retrieved from http://www.fon.bg.ac.rs/downloads/2014/04/Knjiga-predmeta.pdf (In Serbian)

Field, B. C., & Field, M. K. (2006). *Environmental Economics: An Introduction*. New York: McGrawHill/Urwin.

Flood, R. L., & Carson, E. (2013). *Dealing with complexity: an introduction to the theory and application of systems science*. Springer Science & Business Media.

Garetz, W. V. (1993). *Current concerns regarding the implementation of risk-based management: how real are they? In Comparative Environmental Risk* (pp. 11–31). Boca Raton, FL: Lewis Publishing.

Grossman, G. M., & Krueger, A. B. (1994). *Economic growth and the environment (No. w4634)*. National Bureau of Economic Research. doi:10.3386/w4634

Grubb, M., Koch, M., Thomson, K., Munson, A., & Sullivan, F. (1993). *The earth summit agreements: a guide to assessment*. An analysis of the Rio'92 UN Conference on Environment and Development.

Hsu, A., Emerson, J., Levy, M., de Sherbinin, A., Johnson, L., Malik, O., & Jaiteh, M. (2014). *The 2014 environmental performance index*. New Haven, CT: Yale Center for Environmental Law and Policy.

Kardos, M.Research on European Union Countries. (2012). The relationship between entrepreneurship, innovation and sustainable development. Research on European Union Countries. *Procedia Economics and Finance, 3*, 1030–1035. doi:10.1016/S2212-5671(12)00269-9

Klemenovic, J. (2004). Factors of environmental education. *Pedagoška stvarnost, 50*(5-6), 366-381. (In Serbian)

Lester, B. J., Ma, L., Lee, O., & Lambert, J. (2006). Social activism in elementary science education: A science, technology, and society approach to teach global warming. *International Journal of Science Education, 28*(4), 315–333. doi:10.1080/09500690500240100

Levi Jakšić, M. (2011). Sustainable Technology and Innovation Management. In Recent Economic Crisis and Future Development Tendencies. ASECU.

Levi Jakšić, M. (2012). Innovation Entrepreneurship for Sustainable Development. In D. Tipurić & M. Dabić (Eds.), *Management, Governance and Entrepreneurship – New Perspectives and Challenges* (pp. 487–508). London: Access Press.

Levi Jakšić, M. (2015). Sustainable Innovation of Technology and Business Models: steps towards rethinking technology and business strategy.*ASECU Conference Proceedings*.

Levi Jakšić, M., Barjaktarović Rakočević, S., & Martić, M. (Eds.). (2014). *Innovative management and Firm Performance-an interdisciplinary approach*. London: Palgrave Macmillan. doi:10.1057/9781137402226

Levi Jakšić, M., Marinković, S., & Petković, J. (2015). *Management of innovation and technology development*. Belgrade: Faculty of Organizational Sciences. (In Serbian)

Levi Jakšić, M., Stošić, B., Marinković, S., & Obradović, J. (2007). Sustainable management of technology and innovation. In Modern trends in the development of management. Belgrade: Faculty of Organizational Sciences. (In Serbian)

Linstone, A., & Turoff, M. (2002). *The Delphi Method: Technique and Applications*. Retrieved from http://www.is.njit.edu/pubs/delphibook/

Linstone, H. A., & Turoff, M. (Eds.). (1975). *The Delphi method: Techniques and applications* (Vol. 29). Reading, MA: Addison-Wesley.

Makridakis, S., Wheelwright, S. C., & Hyndman, R. J. (1998). *Forecasting Methods and Applications*. New York: Wiley.

Martino, J. P. (1993). *Technological Forecasting for Decision Making* (3rd ed.). New York: North-Holland.

Mason, L., & Santi, M. (1998). Discussing the greenhouse effect: Children's collaborative discourse reasoning and conceptual change. *Environmental Education Research, 4*(1), 67–68. doi:10.1080/1350462980040105

Mcrt, M. (2006). *Determination of consciousness level of high school students on the environmental education and solid wastes topics* (Master's Thesis). Hacettepe University.

Mulloen, P. M. (2003). Delphi: Myths and reality. *Journal of Health Organization and Management, 17*(1), 37–52. doi:10.1108/14777260310469319 PMID:12800279

Obradović, J. (2004). *Technology forecasting - Delphi method: a case study in Germany*. New trends in production and services in our society, II Conference of scientists and entrepreneurs, Belgrade. (In Serbian)

Olsthoorn, X., Tyteca, D., Wehrmeyer, W., & Wagner, M. (2001). Environmental indicators for business: A review of the literature and standardisation methods. *Journal of Cleaner Production*, 9(5), 453–463. doi:10.1016/S0959-6526(01)00005-1

Organization for Economic Cooperation and Development (OECD). (1991). *The State of the Environment*. Paris: OECD.

Panjabi, R. K. (1997). *The Earth Summit at Rio: politics, economics and the environment*. Northeastern University Press.

Pavlovic, V. (2011). Sustainable development and higher education. In V. Pavlovic (Ed.), *University and sustainable development* (pp. 13–30). Belgrade: Faculty of Political Sciences. (In Serbian)

Petrovic, N. (2010). Development of higher environmental education program. *Management - Časopis za teoriju i praksu menadžmenta, 15*(56), 35-41.

Petrović, N. (2012). *Environmental Management* (2nd ed.). Belgrade: Faculty of Organizational Sciences. (In Serbian)

Petrović, N. (2013). *Management of the environmental suitability of products*. Belgrade: Foundation Andrejević. (In Serbian)

Petrovic, N., Jeremic, V., Petrovic, D., & Cirovic, M. (2014). Modeling the Use of Facebook in Environmental Higher Education. In G. Mallia (Ed.), *The Social Classroom: Integrating Social Network Use in Education* (pp. 100–119). Hershey, PA: Information Science Reference; doi:10.4018/978-1-4666-4904-0.ch006

Petrović, N., & Slović, D. (2011): Environmental performance indicators of organizations. *SPIN 2011, VIII Conference of scientists and entrepreneurs – Operations management in the function of sustainable economic development of Serbia 2011-2020*, (pp 463-467). University of Belgrade, Serbian Chamber of Commerce, Belgrade. (In Serbian)

Petrović, N., Slović, D., & Ćirović, M. (2012). Environmental Performance Indicators as Guidelines Towards Sustainability. *Management*, (64).

Popper, R. (2008). How is foresight methods selected? *Foresight, 10*(6).

Porter, A. L., Cunningham, S. W., Banks, J., Roper, A. T., Mason, T. W., & Rossini, F. A. (2011). *Forecasting and Management of Technology*. New York: John Wiley&Sons.

Radojicic, Z., Isljamovic, S., Petrovic, N., & Jeremic, V. (2012). A Novel Approach to Evaluating Sustainable Development (Nowe podejście do waloryzacji rozwoju zrównoważonego). *Problemy Ekorozwoju–Problems of Sustainable Development, 7*(1), 81–85.

Riha, S., Levitan, L., & Hutson, J. (1996). Environmental impact assessment: The quest for a holistic picture. In *Proceedings of the Third National IPM Symposium/Workshop*, (pp. 40-58).

Rowe, G., & Wright, G. (1999). The Delphi technique as a forecasting tool: Issues and analysis. *International Journal of Forecasting, 15*(4), 353–375. doi:10.1016/S0169-2070(99)00018-7

Sackman, H. (1974). *Delphi assessment: Expert opinion, forecasting, and group process (No. RAND-R-1283-PR)*. Santa Monica, CA: RAND CORP.

Sakac, M. D., Cveticanin, S., & Sucevic, V. (2012). Possibilities of organization of the education process in environmental protection.[In Croatian]. *Socijalna Ekologija (Zagreb), 21*(1), 89–98.

Sempels, C., & Hoffman, J. (2013). *Sustainable Innovation Strategy - creating value in a world of finite resources*. London: Palgrave Macmillan. doi:10.1057/9781137352613

Symth, J. (2004). Environment and education: A view of a changing scene. *Environmental Education Research, 12*(4), 247–264.

The Agency for Environmental Protection. (2014). *Report on environmental conditions in the Republic of Serbia – 2014*. Retrieved from http://www.sepa.gov.rs/download/Izvestaj2014.pdf. (In Serbian)

Trumic, M., Petrovic, N., & Radojicic, Z. (2009). Environmental aweraness in formal elementary education in the Republic of Serbia. In N. Mladenović & D. Urošević (Eds.), *Proceedings of the XXXVI operational research conference - SYM-OP-IS 2009* (pp. 14-17). Belgrade: Mathematical institute SANU. (In Serbian)

Tyteca, D. (1996). On the measurement of the environmental performance of firms – a literature review and a productive efficiency perspective. *Journal of Environmental Management, 46*(3), 281–308. doi:10.1006/jema.1996.0022

Union of Engineers and Technicians of Serbia (UETS). (2014). *Report from the 35th International conference "Water supply and sewerage system"*. Retrieved from http://www.sits.org.rs/include/data/docs1106.pdf (In Serbian)

United Nations Sustainable Development (UNSD). (1992). *Agenda 21*. United Nations Conference on Environment & Development, Rio de Janeiro, Brazil. Retrieved from https://sustainabledevelopment.un.org/content/documents/Agenda21.pdf

United Nations Conference on Environment and Development (UNCED). (1992). Retrieved from http://www.un.org/geninfo/bp/enviro.html

United Nations Organization for Education, Science, and Culture (UNESCO). (2012). *Education for sustainable development*. Retrieved from http://www.unesco.org/new/en/education/themes/leading-the-international-agenda/education-for-sustainable-development/education-for-sustainable-development/

United Nations (UN). (1972). *Action Plan for The Human Environment.United Nations Conference on the Human Environment*, Stockholm, Sweden.

United Nations (UN). (2015). *Sustainable development goals*. Retrieved from http://www.un.org/sustainabledevelopment/sustainable-development-goals/

World Commission on Environment and Development (WCED). (1987). *Our Common Future*. Oxford, UK: Oxford University Press.

Young, J. L. M. (2009). *All education is environmental education*. Published Master's Thesis, Ontario, Canada.

ADDITIONAL READING

Adams, S. J. (2001). Projecting the next decade in safety management: A Delphi technique study. *Professional Safety*, *46*(10), 26–29.

Adler, M. (1996). *Gazing into the oracle: the Delphi method and its application to social policy and public health*. Jessica Kingsley Pub.

Albright, R. (2002). What can past technology forecast tell us about the future? *Technological Forecasting and Social Change*, *69*(5), 443–464. doi:10.1016/S0040-1625(02)00186-5

Albright, R. (2002). What can past technology forecast tell us about the future. *Technological Forecasting and Social Change*, *69*(5), 443–464. doi:10.1016/S0040-1625(02)00186-5

Altschuld, J. W. (2003). *Delphi technique. Lecture, Applied evaluation design*. The Ohio State University.

Applied Catalysis B: Environmental (ISSN: 0926-3373).

Armstrong, J. S. (2005). The forecasting canon: Nine generalizations to improve forecast accuracy, FORESIGHT. *The International Journal of Applied Forecasting*, *1*(1), 29–35.

Barrow, J. C. (1999). *Environmental management: Principles and Practice*. London: Routledge. doi:10.4324/9780203272817

Bary, J. (2007). *Environment and social theory*. New York: Routledge.

Coates, V., Faroque, M., Klavins, R., Lapid, K., Linstone, H. A., Pistorius, C., & Porter, A. L. (2001). On the future of technological forecasting. *Technological Forecasting and Social Change*, *67*(1), 1–17. doi:10.1016/S0040-1625(00)00122-0

Current Opinion in Environmental Sustainability. (ISSN: 1877-3435).

Dabić, M. (Ed.), *Management, Governance and Entrepreneurship – New Perspectives and Challenges* (pp. 487–508). London: Access Press.

EcoSummit 2016 (2016). Ecological Sustainability: Engineering Change. The 5th International EcoSummit Congress, 29 August - 1 September 2016 I Le Corum, Montpellier, France. Retrieved from: http://www.ecosummit2016.org/

EcoSummit 2016 (2016). Ecological Sustainability: Engineering Change. The 5th International EcoSummit Congress, 29 August - 1 September 2016 I Le Corum, Montpellier, France. Retrieved from: http://www.ecosummit2016.org/

Environment International, A Journal of Environmental Science (ISSN: 0160-4120).

Environmental Development (ISSN: 2211-4645).

Environmental Impact Assessment Review (ISSN: 0195-9255).

Environmental Research (ISSN: 0013-9351).

Firat, A. K., Madnick, S., & Won, L. W. (2008). *Technology forecasting - A review. Sloan School of Management, Room E53-320* (p. 02142). MA: Cabridge.

Gendron, C. (2013). Sustainable development through innovation? A social challenge. In J. R. McIntyre, S. Ivanaj, & V. Ivanaj (Eds.), *Strategies for Sustainable Technologies and Innovations*. London: Edward Elgar. doi:10.4337/9781781006832.00013

Georghiou, L., Harper, J. C., Keenan, M., Miles, I., & Popper, R. (2008). *The handbook of technology foresight: Concepts and Practice*. Edward Elgar Publishing Limited.

Goldfisher, K. (1992). Modified Delphi: A concept for new product forecasting. *The Journal of Business Forecasting*, *11*(4), 10.

Holsapple, P., & Joshi, K. (2002). Knowledge manipulation activities: Results of a Delphi study. *Information & Management*, *39*(6), 477–490. doi:10.1016/S0378-7206(01)00109-4

Hsu, C. C., & Sandford, B. A. (2007). The Delphi technique: Making sense of consensus. *Practical Assessment, Research & Evaluation*, *12*(10), 1–8.

International Chamber of Commerce - ICC. (2000). *The Business Charter for Sustainable Development*. Retrieved from http://www.iccwbo.org/Advocacy-Codes-and-Rules/Document-centre/2000/The-Business-Charter-for-Sustainable-Development/2000

International Journal of Sustainable Built Environment (ISSN: 2212-6090).

Janisch, E. (1966). *Tehnological Forecasting in Perspective*. Paris: Organization for Economic Cooperation and Developments.

Journal for Nature Conservation (ISSN: 1617-1381).

Journal of Cleaner Production (ISSN: 0959-6526).

Journal of Environmental Management (ISSN: 0301-4797).

Kaushik, P., & Kaushik, A. (2010). *Basic of environment and ecology*. New Delhi: New Age International Lt Publishers.

Meadows, D. (1998). *Indicators and Information Systems for Sustainable Development, A Report to the Balaton Group*. The Sustainability Institute.

Miller, L. E. (2006, October). *Determining what could/should be: The Delphi technique and its application*. Paper presented at the meeting of the 2006 annual meeting of the Mid-Western Educational Research Association, Columbus, Ohio.

Miller, P. E., & Swinehart, K. D. (2011). *Technological forecasting: A Strategic Imperative*. USA: Department of Management and Marketing, College of Business and Technology East Tennessee State University.

Okoli, C., & Pawlowski, S. D. (2004). The Delphi method as a research tool: An example, design considerations and applications. *Information & Management, 42*(1), 15–29. doi:10.1016/j.im.2003.11.002

Porter, A. L., Cunningham, S. W., Banks, J., Roper, A. T., Mason, T. W., & Rossini, F. A. (2011). *Forecasting and Management of Technology*. New York: John Wiley&Sons.

Quarrie, J. (1992). Earth Summit'92.*The United Nations Conference on Environment and Development*, Rio de Janeiro1992.

Schmidt, R. C., Lyytinen, K., Keil, M., & Cule, P. (2001). Identifying software project risks: An international Delphi study. *Journal of Management Information Systems, 17*(4), 5–36.

Science of the Total Environment (ISSN: 0048-9697).

Skulmoski, G. J., Hartman, F. T., & Krahn, J. (2007). The Delphi Method for Graduate Research. *Journal of Information Technology Education, 6*, 1–21.

Sustainable Cities and Society (ISSN: 2210-6707).

Sustainable Development Conference 2016. Green technology, Renewable energy and Environmental protection.

Sustainable Production and Consumption (ISSN: 2352-5509).

The Organisation for Economic Co-operation and Development – OECD. (2015). *OECD and the Sustainable Development Goals: Delivering on universal goals and targets*. Retrieved from http://www.oecd.org/dac/sustainable-development-goals.htm

The Organisation for Economic Co-operation and Development – OECD. (2015). *Environmental indicators, modeling and outlooks*. Retrieved from http://www.oecd.org/environment/indicators-modelling-outlooks/

The Sustainable Development 2015 (2015). *The Sustainable Development 2015*. Retrieved from http://www.sustainabledevelopment2015.org/

The World Bank. (2015). *Sustainable Development*. Retrieved from http://www.worldbank.org/en/topic/sustainabledevelopment

The World Bank. (2015). *Environment*. Retrieved from http://www.worldbank.org/en/topic/environment

United Nations Development Programme – UNDP. (2015). *Sustainable Development Goals (SDGs)*. Retrieved from http://www.undp.org/content/undp/en/home/mdgoverview/post-2015-development-agenda.html

United Nations Environment Programme – (UNEP). (2015). United Nations conference on climate change - The 2015 Paris Climate Conference - COP21. 2015, November 30 to December 11 – PARIS. Retrieved from http://www.cop21.gouv.fr/en

United Nations – UN. (2012). Rio+20 Conference – United Nations Conference on Sustainable Development. 20-22 June 2012, in Rio de Janeiro, Brazil.

World Health Organization – WHO. (2015). *Environmental health*. Retrieved from http://www.who.int/topics/environmental_health/en/

Woudenberg, F. (1991). An evaluation of Delphi. *Technological Forecasting and Social Change, 40*(2), 131–150. doi:10.1016/0040-1625(91)90002-W

Yokum, J. T., & Armstrong, J. S. (1995). Beyond accuracy: Comparison of criteria used to select forecasting methods. *International Journal of Forecasting, 11*(4), 591–597. doi:10.1016/0169-2070(95)00615-X

Young, S. J., & Jamieson, L. M. (2001). Delivery methodology of the Delphi: A comparison of two approaches. *Journal of Park and Recreation Administration, 19*(1), 42–58.

KEY TERMS AND DEFINITIONS

Delphi Method: One of the best-known qualitative methods of forecasting. It is being applied for forecasting probability and timeframe of future events. In order to set a forecast, a group of experts identifies and defines the subject event, the probability of its occurrence, and possible time of future event. Experts fill out the question form independently, which gives this method a character of impartiality in predicting. The outcome of a Delphi sequence is nothing but opinion. The results of the sequence are only as valid as the opinions of the experts who made up the panel. Delphi method often fails to give final forecasts, but rather serves as an additional source of information to planners regarding the structure of a certain problem in the future.

Ecosystem Vitality: The Environmental Performance Index category that measures ecosystem health and protection and natural resource management. It includes six themes (issues): water resources, agriculture, forests, fisheries, biodiversity and habitat, and climate and energy. The ecosystem vitality index can be used to reflect the environmental condition of the countries.

Environmental Health: World Health Organization definition of Environmental health states that it refers to all the environmental factors: physical, chemical, and biological, and the assessment and control of their potentially influence of health in order to prevent disease and creating health-supportive environments.

Environmental Metrics and Indicators: An environmental metric is a single quantitative measure or derivation from two or more measures that cannot be interpreted by it. It can be used for comparison of the similar entities but it is difficult to use for the different entities comparison in the sense of their relative environmental impact. An environmental indicator is a characteristic that indicates a quality or state of a system. It combines several metrics, observations or both, in the way that it can be used for the comparison of the environmental performance of the diverse entities: location, facilities, companies, industries, and countries.

Environmental Performance Index (EPI): Constructed through the calculation and aggregation of indicators reflecting national-level environmental data. It is a quantifiable metric comprising of nine environmental categories calculated based on data collection and analysis of 20 environmental performance indicators, used to evaluate environmental performance of a country. EPI indicators use a "proximity-to-target" methodology, which assesses how close a particular country is to an identified policy target.

Environmental Problems: Environmental problems have reached their critical point in the 21st century and they continue to rapidly grow: global warming, worsening of living conditions, deterioration of the ozone layer, conservation influences, solid waste growth, nuclear pollution, destruction of forests, extinction of plant and animal species, etc. In parallel, the rise of the world's population has brought forward the increase of the inefficient consumption of natural resources. The First conference of the United Nations on the environment was held in Stockholm in 1972, and having in mind that this is the first time that the environmental problems were the most important topic of the world agenda - it represents a turn point in the relationship between mankind and the environment. Further on, the growing public environmental awareness and the care for the protection of the environment have led to the conclusion that the issues and environmental problems cannot be solved at a national level but instead must be worked on at an international level, and that the actions that affect the governments to enact environmental laws, policies and standards, must be carried out.

Forecasting: A research activity that fully takes place in the present moment with the goal of measuring the uncertainty of future events. The forecasting helps at establishing narrow relation between theory and empirical research. Today, it is used in all spheres of social and economic life. By applying modern methods and forecasting techniques, it is possible to reveal future chances, point out to possible dangers in the future, and allow for easier choice of expected future.

Sustainable Development: The most complex model of development, which demystifies technology, and the current understanding of nature and progress. The concept of this model is based on the principles of intergenerational justice, which is defined as meeting the needs of the present generations without impairing the ability of future generations to meet their needs. This principle addresses the necessity of the right to inherit the same state of the environment from one generation to another. Further on, sustainable development is development that comprises out of three basic pillars: social, economic and environmental.

Chapter 12
How Age-Friendly Are Cities?
Measuring Age-Friendliness with a Composite Index

Lucie Vidovićová
Masaryk University, Czech Republic

ABSTRACT

The chapter introduces the Age-friendly City Index as a way of measuring the age-friendliness of urban environments. The proposed index assesses the dimensions of outdoor spaces and transportation as they are perceived and evaluated by older people, residents of the fourteen biggest towns in the Czech Republic. The dimensions and items included in the index are constructed upon the theoretical framework proposed by the World Health Organisation Global Age-friendly Cities Project. Validation of the results of the index is based on experimental open-ended question analysis. The resulting categories confirm the importance of greenery and aesthetics for the age-friendly concept, and confirm the rankings of cities obtained via the composite index. In addition, comparison with similar measures tested in Canada and Hong Kong are discussed, and the necessity of backing up index measures with policy analysis and general structural support is argued for.

INTRODUCTION

In recent decades there has been a "senior friendly boom" (Lui et al., 2009, p. 116): an increase in interest in the strategies, practices, services, products, and processes that reflect the specific needs of ageing people and which should help to increase their quality of life. The environment, a factor mediating the experience of aging and a key component of a positive approach to managing the challenges of population aging at the aggregate level, is also a prominent feature in such a list. Various sources talk about towns and communities friendly to every age (age-friendly cities / communities), liveable communities, elder-friendly communities, a lifetime house or lifetime housing, lifetime neighbourhoods (Lui et al., 2009; Harding 2007; Pynoos, Caraviello, & Cicero, 2009), and even an age-friendly world (see www.agefriendlyworld.org). These concepts serve as umbrella terms for building a favourable environment (especially, but not only) for older people (Lindenberg, & Westendorp, 2015; Moulaert, & Garon, 2015).

DOI: 10.4018/978-1-5225-0714-7.ch012

They are built on a consensus on the need to support aging individuals so that they can remain (age) in their natural communities as long as they want to, or for as long as it is possible (Scharlach, 2009), providing that such support has positive effects, both economic and social, on the individual and societal levels. The idea of "age friendliness" is at the same time an expression of socially inclusive policies which not only provide a place of care and support services, but also guarantee a space in which positive public opinion is constructed and non-discriminatory attitudes affecting the well-being of seniors are strengthened. Its characteristic feature is its multidimensionality, which includes the physical and social environment, ideally integrated with each other by means of appropriate policies, services, and structures. At least within Western (or Global Northern) societies there is a reasonable consensus on what features constitute the age–friendliness of a particular place (Levasseur et al. 2015; Lui, Everingham, Warburton, Cuthill, & Bartlett, 2009; Lindenberg & Westendorp, 2015). The World Health Organisation Guide "Global Age-friendly Cities" (2002) sorts these essential features into eight dimensions: housing, social participation, respect and social inclusion, civic participation, communication, community support and health services, outdoor spaces and buildings, and transportation.

However a more critical perspective on what has been termed 'age-friendly cities and communities' has recently been adopted by academia (Buffel, Phillipson, & Scharf, 2012) along with other important bodies and platforms, such as the International Federation on Ageing (2015). They call for increasing awareness of the profound changes in population and the need to increase the quality of life of individuals by shifting the focus from questions such as 'What is an ideal city/community for older people?' to the question of 'How age-friendly are cities and communities?'. Research into the environmental determinants of quality of life in later life is abundant (Menec, & Novicki 2014; Burton, Mitchell, & Stride, 2011; Bowling, & Stafford, 2007; Bramson, Pretty, & Chipuer, 2002; Wight, Ko, & Aneshensel 2011; Beard et. al., 2009; cf. recent overview by Levasseur et al. 2015), but studies assessing the actual physical environment as a subject are much rarer (cf. Moulaert, & Garon, 2015), especially those using a quantitative approach (Wong, Chau, Cheung, Phillips, & Woo, 2015; "*Age-friendly Cities*", 2009), and those within the context of environmental gerontology (Wahl, & Weisman, 2003; Kendig, 2003). In this chapter, we propose using a composite index measure to answer the question "How age-friendly are cities?" in a comparative manner, using a nation-wide and representative survey of older residents of the fourteen biggest cities in the Czech Republic.

BACKGROUND

Age-Friendliness as a Behind-Policy Concept

Everything that happens, happens somewhere, in some place (Gieryn, 2000), and as about half of the world´s population lives in urban areas, the "somewhere" for many is a city. In Europe, this trend is even more pronounced, as, in 2030, about 80% of Europeans will live in cities ("State of World", 2007).With the co-occurring unprecedented ageing of the world´s population, it could be said without much exaggeration that the future belongs to older people in cities (Phillipson, 2010). Since the preference of older people tends to be for ageing in place (Lanspery, 2002), the nature of the immediate social and physical environment is of increasing importance (Wahl,& Lang, 2003; Wiles, Leibing, Guberman, Reeve, & Allen, 2011; Bowling, & Dieppe, 2005; Fernández-Carro, & Evandrou, 2014), both for empirical study and the praxis of policymakers and care providers (Kendig, 2003). The concept of age-friendliness has been adopted by many cities and municipalities in order to provide a springboard for defining policies and setting goals ("Measuring the Age-friendliness", 2015) in the attempt to prepare for the challenges and opportunities of demographic change.

The declared aim of the age-friendly concept is to promote active aging, a process of optimizing opportunities for health, participation, and security in order to enhance the quality of life of people as they grow older ("Active aging", 2002). Governments of nation states and international organizations such as the World Health Organization (WHO) and the International Federation on Ageing (IFA, 2015) appeal to cities and local governments to develop policies in the spirit of this goal and to provide adequate support for mobility, security, health and social services, and economic and civic participation. The attainment of these goals is being promoted as a competitive advantage in the face of ongoing global demographic changes (Kresl, & Ietri, 2010).

The concept of "age-friendliness" became highly relevant in 2002, when the World Health Organization released a list of the essential features of age-friendly cities. This list was drawn up on the basis of results of consultations and focus group interviews with older people in 33 cities across 22 countries, conducted as part of the "WHO Global Age-friendly Cities Project". In total, there are eighty-four items of varying levels of complexity on the list, divided into eight general areas: outdoor spaces and buildings; transport; housing; social participation; communication and information; respect and social inclusion; civic participation and employment; and community support and health services. All the variables are built on three key principles: inclusion, participation, and security. The list was created with the aim of each city evaluating its strengths and weaknesses in terms of its "friendliness" to residents regardless of their age; however, the WHO Guide (2002) also speaks explicitly about the establishment of a universal model for a city friendly to seniors.

WHO, as an organization with global operations, does not primarily seek a comparison between towns, since the understanding of the concept of "age-friendliness" may be subject to cultural and social variation. Rather, the list should serve as an assessment tool for the mapping of development and progress. The preamble of this key document requires the evaluation to be done in consultation with older people themselves, so that features of age-friendliness would be in accordance with their own experience of the characteristics of the city.

Until very recently, there was no coordinated action plan, no universal standard tool agreed, in order to quantify the progress cities are making in becoming more age-friendly (Wong, Chau, Cheung, Phillips, & Woo, 2015). The new approach proposed by WHO in "Measuring the Age-Friendliness of Cities: A Guide to Using Core Indicators" (2015) suggests following four types of indicators: input indicators, output indicators, outcome indicators, and impact indicators. It makes use of a "general framework which shows how certain resources and structures (the inputs) enable interventions in the form of policies, services and programmes (the outputs) that help improve the age-friendliness of the physical and social environment (the outcomes), which, in turn, contribute to improving the health and wellbeing of older residents and of the population as a whole (the impact)" (Wong, Chau, Cheung, Phillips, & Woo, 2015, p.12). The inputs focus on resources and structures which act as key enabling factors and include indicators of high-level political commitment, collaboration between multiple stake holder groups, the shared ownership of older people, and financial and human resources. Outputs, i.e. interventions to create an age-friendly environment, are split between the physical and social environments. In the first group, issues such as planning and land use, the design of public spaces, housing design and cost options, and transportation design are followed. In the second group, the issues include culture and recreational programmes, communication and advocacy, health and social care services, and employment and business opportunities. Also, outcomes, the short- or medium-term changes achieved in creating an age-friendly environment, can be followed separately with respect to the physical and social environments. Walkability, the accessibility of public spaces, buildings and transport, the affordability of housing, and safety can be operationalized within physical environment outcomes, while chiefly volunteer activity and participation can be operationalized within social environment outcomes. Long-term changes achieved as a result of improving the age-friendliness of an environment are labelled as impacts and followed by indicators of health and wellbeing. Additionally, equity indicators require the disaggregation of data by social stratifiers such as gender, age, wealth, and neighbourhood. This comprehensive framework is, however, again only a proposal of what to measure, showing possible data sources, such as demographic and institutional data, and suggesting surveys of older residents as relevant data sources.

A crucial element within the evaluation process is the inclusion of older people's views in the definition of aspects constituting age-friendliness and the participation of a wide variety of local actors, including senior´s advocacy groups, in the design, implementation, and evaluation of derived age-friendly policies. This holds true especially at the local and regional level, since it is the regional government that is often responsible for providing a wide range of public services, as well as the context in which civil society organizations participate most efficiently (Hollbach-Grömig, & Trapp, 2006).

Approaches to Measuring Age-Friendliness: An Example from Canada and Hong Kong

As already stated, there are few examples of empirical (quantitative) insight into the satisfaction of seniors with the level of age-friendliness in the context of transportation, affordable housing, high-quality pedestrian environments, and the availability of social services and health care, as the effort to provide policy makers and other stakeholders with a simple metric was not practically supported until the publication of the WHO guide to the use of core indicators in 2015 ("Measuring the Age-Friendliness", 2015). One example worth quoting, however, is a study conducted in Canadian cities by the activist group CARP – A New Vision of Aging for Canada" ("Age-friendly Cities", 2009). Their respondents assessed the extent to which it is easy to live in their city and to meet their needs in the areas concerned. Roughly three-quarters of Canadian respondents identified living in cities as very easy, or at least easy. However, even in cities considered as very easy to live in, the use of vehicles in the city, the availability of affordable housing, pedestrian mobility, and access to home care were regarded as difficult by the vast majority of respondents. Nevertheless, these results varied between the cities; for example, Winnipeg and Montreal were positively assessed owing to the relative availability of adequate housing, while other cities, such as Calgary and Kelowna were downgraded due to problems with transportation. A list of the key demands of seniors with respect to improving the age-friendliness of cities was topped by a request for the provision of more health and social care services (almost 30%), followed by the demand for an advisory body for "age-friendly" issues at local government level (17%) and support for the involvement of seniors in activities (13%). Only about ten percent of respondents talked about improving infrastructural aspects, such as instituting "Stop on request" bus services, longer green traffic lights, and more public toilets. Less than five percent of respondents identified a lack of access ramps in public buildings as a problem, or demanded better visibility of traffic signs and more benches. Thus, in this particular survey, the idea of age-friendly places was much more connected to personalized services than about physical infrastructure. One can assume that these results reflect the prioritization of individual needs, the principle of subsidiarity, and areas where the greatest shortcomings are felt.

The second example of the empirical assessment of age friendliness we will quote here compared the age friendliness of two Hong Kong districts using a standardised questionnaire inspired by the WHO Guide and addressed to residents aged 50 years and older (Wuong, Chau, Cheung, Phillips, & Woo, 2015). District-wide differences in age-friendliness were compared on the basis of eight domain scores and showed that one district (Sha Tin) achieved significantly lower scores in outdoor spaces and buildings, transportation, social participation, respect and social inclusion, civic participation and employment, communication, and information. The second district (Tuen Mun) had a significantly lower score only in the housing domain, while differences in the community and health services domains were insignificant. The authors also used multiple linear regression to examine associations with demographic and socio-economic characteristics, and objective measures such as numbers of services and amenities available within districts to help explain the differences in domain scores. While many of the socio-demographic factors such as age group, gender, area of residence, type of housing, employment status, self-rated health and income were associated with domain scores, variations in the provision of services and amenities were not. What the authors found interesting was that the Sha Tin district had better services and infrastructure and a generally higher socio-economic status among its residents, but a lower level of age-friendliness. This warrants detailed research into the psychosocial factors that may influence residents' perceptions of local environments. Overall, Wuong, Chau, Cheung, Phillips, and Woo (2015) conclude that it would be more appropriate to study neighbourhoods or subareas instead of whole districts, because of the wide variations within each district.

Both of the abovementioned examples used a standardised questionnaire to assess the age friendliness of particular areas, as we did in our study, and compared them using these results. However, even though the methods and questionnaires are not presented in detail in these sources, the evaluations seems to be rather complex, relying on non-representative samples/sample techniques and rather small numbers of respondents and/or small numbers of areas for comparison. In our own study, which we introduce below, we were able to overcome some of these shortcomings. In the following section, we will first introduce the project and survey we conducted, and then describe the evaluation of fourteen large Czech cities by means of the Age-friendly City Index. We use the degree of satisfaction with the particular dimensions of transportation and the outdoor environment in order to illustrate how the index tool can be constructed and used for comparative evaluation.

DEVELOPING AN AGE-FRIENDLY CITY INDEX IN THE CZECH REPUBLIC

Data Collection

As was already mentioned, we took an alternative approach to assessing the age friendliness of a city by measuring the availability of, and satisfaction with output features, not by looking at the outcome indicators, such as the health or quality of life of older residents. That is, it is not the *life* in the urban area that is measured, but the perceived qualities of the urban features as such. By such an approach we arrive at an evaluation of particular urban areas and are thus able to compare them. We stand on the social constructionist paradigm. We understand the social reality, including perceptions of the physical reality, as constructed by the social actor. As the classic Thomas theorem puts it, if men define situations as real, they are real in their consequences, and the interpretation of a situation causes (or inhibits) the action. Therefore, in our approach we rely on a survey of older people's perceptions of the (selected aspects of) age-friendliness of a given urban area.

The assessment of the age-friendliness of Czech cities presented in this chapter was part of a broader survey of older people living in large urban areas in the Czech Republic. The data collection was split into two parts. The first part of the survey "The quality of life of older people in the City" (hereinafter "QinCity") was conducted from May 5 to July 9, 2011 in urban populations of the Czech Republic aged 60 years and older. The oldest respondent was 96 years old. The data were collected by an outsourced specialised agency in fourteen major cities representing each of the regions of the Czech Republic – namely, České Budějovice, Kladno, Plzeň, Karlovy Vary, Ústí nad Labem, Liberec, Hradec Králové, Pardubice, Jihlava, Brno, Olomouc, Zlín, Ostrava, and Prague, the capital. These cities also serve as administrative centres of the respective regions.

The first part of the survey was conducted as a face-to-face computer assisted interview (CAPI) with a total of 1,001 respondents. Quota sampling was used with selection quotas set for the city, sex, education, and the proportions of younger (60-69 years) and older seniors (70+ years). Only populations living in the central areas of cities were included for the interviews; seniors from suburban and peripheral areas were excluded from the sample. The boundaries were based on district borders, and the predominant types of buildings and their density were taken into account, as discussed in various spatial analyses (Ouředníček, Pospíšilová, Špačková, Temelová, & Novák, 2011; Mulíček, & Olšová, 2002). Since the research focused mainly on the quality of life of seniors as perceived by the seniors themselves on the basis of the quality of the outdoor environment, interviews were carried out only with respondents who had left their homes at least once in the previous six months. If the respondent did not fulfil this condition, the interviewer was instructed to end the interview.

In the second part, we repeated the survey in the population aged 60 years and older, but the selection of respondents was made only in designated central locations in Prague, Brno and Ostrava. In addition, the structured questionnaire was slightly adjusted, in that some questions were omitted and some were added; however, the core indicators remained the same and, thus, these two questionnaires were generally comparable. With respect to quotas, cross sampling quotas were set to age and gender, and free quotas for education in each of the cities. Within the period from November 10th to December 11th 2011 data from an additional 921 interviews were collected. Both datasets were subsequently merged and weighted to represent the population of older people living in major Czech cities. In this merged and weighted file there were 1922 complete interviews.

The answers "do not know" and "other" were labelled as missing and were omitted in the analysis if they represented less than 5% of all responses. Interviewing respondents was rated by interviewers as fairly simple or even very simple in 57% of cases (in the first part) and in 67% of cases (in the second part), which does not deviate from other research on similar topics in the older population (Petrová Kafková, 2012). The average duration of each interview was 56 minutes (st.dev. 14 minutes).

Given that our file was not based on a random sample, it should be regarded as representative only with respect to the known characteristics of the population. For this reason, the broad application of advanced statistical methods available in IBM SPSS 21.0, which was used for the analysis, was limited.

The environment was here defined in terms of both social and physical dimensions. The questionnaire included separate sections on housing, neighbours, mobility, the availability of services, the frequency of economic and social activities, the perception of changes in the immediate living environment, and experience with selected aspects of spatial ageism. By collecting the views of older people living in dynamically changing areas we simulated the consultation process required in the process of assessing age-friendliness. For the specific purpose of creating the index, only selected items from the questionnaire were used; these are described in more detail below.

Construction of the Age-Friendly City Index

When preparing the questionnaire, selected factors listed in the WHO Guide were operationalized ad hoc into indicators of outdoor accessibility and mobility. The focus was only on the two areas developed most in detail, i.e. outdoor spaces and buildings, and transportation. The result of operationalization process of transferring selected characteristics of the environment into measurable indicators is summarized in Table 1. Here, the features listed in the WHO Guide are shown in the left column and the corresponding survey items are listed in the column on the right. Respondents rated their feelings towards the statements shown in the right column of Table 1. either on a 5-point Likert scale, ranging from 1 ("fully agree") to 5 ("fully disagree"), or on scales representing the intensity or frequency of the given feature (see also legend in note to Table 2).

For the evaluation of age friendliness, only the share of positive feelings was taken into account; indecisive answers and negative evaluations were removed from the analysis (hence the use of a reverse scale in the aesthetic (non)quality index). The scales constructed from sub-indices (aesthetic (non)quality, green environment, and satisfaction with public transport) were represented by averages and ranked from the best results to the worst, as were the percentages representing the share of positive answers. The numerical results for each city, for each statement and index included, were collected into a table (see Table 2a.) and then replaced by the ranking from the best (1st place receiving a value of 1) to the worst (14th place receiving a value of 14) (see Table 3 for an example of the procedure).

For example, the people of Kladno were most satisfied with the proximity of shops and other services (85%; cf. Table 2, column B); therefore, Kladno achieved 1st place in this area and received the value 1 (Table 3, column B). Meanwhile, Karlovy Vary was ranked lowest in this regard (43%), achieving last (i.e. 14th) place and receiving a value of 14. In the next step, all the obtained indicator rankings for each of the cities were added up, the arithmetic average calculated, and the results ordered (see last column of the Table 3) Thus, we achieved an average ranking for each of the cities within our sample, and, according to this theoretically driven approach, Plzeň was identified as the most age-friendly Czech city. With 4.9 index points, it is closest to the ideal position of three points or less, which would mean that the city achieved one of "the medal positions" in all the assessed areas (having a value of 3 or less in all the evaluated indicators). The problem preventing Plzeň from having an even better score is mostly the non-availability of parking places and its non-walkability. If this problematic aspect were disregarded, Plzeň would achieve 4.0 points. Sometimes, as we show also below, the omission of an indicator may change the overall position of the city. However, this adjustment (i.e. disregarding the issue of parking), would not change the positions of Brno or Pardubice, which are at the very bottom of our rankings. Brno ranked tenth or worst in nine out of the ten evaluated features, and Pardubice in seven out of ten. Pardubice attained last position in several major aspects of age-friendliness, especially the amount of night street lighting, the presence of safe crossings, and the availability of green spaces (seniors´ criticisms of poor aesthetics and high levels of vandalism are also quoted in Toušek (2012)). In Brno, meanwhile, besides reservations about the lack of green spaces and about the generally poor aesthetic qualities of city infrastructure, the most problematic issue concerning residents seems to be the lack of public toilets and the non-availability of "ordinary" shops and services in the city centre.

Table 1. Operationalisation of checklist of essential features of age-friendly cities

WHO Essential Feature	QinCity Indicator
Dimension: Outdoor Spaces and Buildings	
Public areas are clean and pleasant.	(Sub-index of aesthetic (non)quality (a reversed scale)) [a] Our street is often full of garbage. In my neighbourhood there are a lot of unknown and homeless people. There are a lot of old and derelict houses with no tenants. It is dangerous to walk outside even during the day. (*fully disagree + disagree*).
Green spaces and outdoor seating are sufficient in number, well maintained and safe.	(Sub-index of green environment)[b] There are pleasant benches in sufficient numbers around here. There is enough greenery around here. There are nice places I can see from my window. (*fully agree + agree*)
Pavements are well-maintained, free of obstructions and reserved for pedestrians.	The majority of the streets in our surroundings have well maintained pavements. (*fully agree + agree*)
Pedestrian crossings are sufficient in number and safe for people with different levels and types of disability, with non-slip markings, visual and audio cues and adequate crossing times.	In our streets there are enough pedestrian crossings, so I can safely cross the road. (*fully agree + agree*)
Outdoor safety is promoted by good street lighting, police patrols and community education.	The streets are well lit during the night. (*fully agree + agree*)
	We can often see the police patrolling around here. (*fully agree + agree*)
Services are situated together and are accessible.	Most shops and services that I require are here in my neighbourhood. (*fully agree + agree*)
Public toilets outdoors and indoors are sufficient in number, clean, well-maintained and accessible.	There are enough public toilets in the city centre. (*fully agree + agree*)
Dimension: Transportation	
Public transport costs are consistent, clearly displayed and affordable.	(Sub-index transportation) [c] Taking in to account my current needs, public transport is well organised. The time tables are usually clearly readable. The vehicles of public transportation are usually easily accessible. The transport stop is close to my home. (*fully agree + agree*)
Vehicles are clean, well-maintained, accessible, not overcrowded and have priority seating that is respected.	
Transport stops and stations are conveniently located, accessible, safe, clean, well-lit and well-marked, with adequate seating and shelter.	
Parking and drop-off areas are safe, sufficient in number and conveniently located.	Is there a convenient possibility to park a car in the vicinity of your home? (*yes, always + most of the time*)

Source: (WHO, 2002)

Note: For the items with upper index letters, the average value of the sum of sub-indices is used for the evaluation instead of the sum of the share of answers "fully agree and agree". The indices of ([a]) aesthetic (non)quality (Cronbach´s $\alpha = 0.68$) and ([b]) green environment (Cronbach´s $\alpha = 0.56$) were defined with the help of factor analysis from a detailed battery of questions with the opening statement "In the vicinity of my home/in my neighbourhood there is/are...". Sub-index ([c]) satisfaction with public transport (Cronbach´s $\alpha = 0.80$).

Alternating the Age-Friendly City Index: "A Restricted Model"

Although the WHO Guide states that the index is not primarily to be used for comparison, but for self-assessment and progress mapping, the comparison of cities of roughly the same size occurring within a single nation-state and subject to similar legislative measures and levels of local government responsibil-

Table 2. Results for each of the age-friendly feature by the city (in % and average)

City	Indicators (See the Legend)									
	A	B	C	D	E	F	G	H	I	J
	%							Sub-Index Average		
Prague	33	78	48	80	71	64	37	1.7	2.8	2.4
Kladno	31	85	59	94	68	67	75	1.6	3.0	2.7
České Budějovice	24	79	52	88	70	88	68	2.1	3.1	2.8
Plzeň	35	72	41	96	87	90	52	1.8	3.3	2.8
Karlovy Vary	47	43	48	81	58	75	89	2.0	3.1	2.7
Ústí nad Labem	46	45	56	72	65	72	69	1.9	3.0	2.9
Liberec	13	73	45	89	78	84	67	1.4	3.3	2.5
Hradec Králové	16	74	30	94	68	65	80	1.4	3.4	2.7
Pardubice	28	61	32	65	48	69	62	1.9	3.0	2.3
Jihlava	54	69	35	72	63	88	65	1.7	3.1	2.7
Brno	15	57	35	77	63	71	59	1.9	3.0	2.5
Olomouc	9	72	38	82	83	80	59	1.9	3.1	2.6
Zlín	28	75	26	89	75	54	86	1.7	3.4	2.9
Ostrava	23	65	52	78	63	72	54	2.0	2.9	2.6
Total:	28	67	43	82	69	74	64	1.7	2.8	2.6

Note: Values are rounded.

A: In the city centre there are enough public toilets (fully agree + agree)

B: Most shops and services which I require are here in my area (fully agree + agree)

C: We can often see the police patrolling around here (fully agree + agree)

D: The streets are well lit during the night (fully agree + agree)

E: In our streets there are enough pedestrian crossings and traffic lights; I can safely cross the street (fully agree + agree)

F: Most of the streets in our neighbourhood have well-maintained pavements (fully agree + agree)

G: Near my residence is the possibility of convenient parking (always + mostly)

H: Index of satisfaction with public transport (1= very satisfied; 4 = very unsatisfied)

I: Index of aesthetic (non)quality (1= low quality / negative rating; 4 = high quality / positive rating)

J: Index of greenery (1 = not enough green spaces; 4 = a lot of green spaces)

ity can be a beneficial exercise. The ranking of cities can in many ways underline possible examples of good practice on the one hand, and, on the other, draw attention to areas in which there are deficiencies with respect to age-related agendas. Of course, we have to bear in mind that, here, we are dealing with the subjective evaluations of older inhabitants, and that we are not evaluating any policy outcomes or related contexts or structures directly.

Already, from the results summarized in Table 2 and Table 3, it is obvious that the cities' achievements in different respects vary considerably. For example, almost half of seniors are satisfied with the availability of public toilets in the city centre in Jihlava and Karlovy Vary, but just about every tenth respondent in Olomouc. Karlovy Vary is, in contrast, criticized for its lack of conventional grocery stores and services, the availability of which was positively evaluated in a number of other cities. One can interpret this feature as a result of the orientation of the city's economy on generally exclusive health and spa tourism catering for a mainly foreign clientele, and such infrastructure may not suit older-residents.

Table 3. Results for each of the age-friendly feature by the city – rankings

	A	B	C	D	E	F	G	H	I	J	Sum	Average	Final Ranking
Prague	5	3	6	9	5	13	14	6	14	13	88	8.8	11
Kladno	6	1	1	2	7	11	4	3	12	8	55	5.5	2
České Budějovice	9	2	4	6	6	3	6	14	7	4	61	6.1	4
Plzeň	4	8	8	1	1	1	13	7	3	3	49	4.9	1
Karlovy Vary	2	14	5	8	13	6	1	13	6	5	73	7.3	9
Ústí nad Labem	3	13	2	13	9	7	5	9	10	1	72	7.2	7
Liberec	13	6	7	5	3	4	7	2	4	11	62	6.2	5
Hradec Králové	11	5	13	3	8	12	3	1	1	7	64	6.4	6
Pardubice	8	11	12	14	14	10	9	10	9	14	111	11.1	14
Jihlava	1	9	10	12	12	2	8	5	8	6	73	7.3	8
Brno	12	12	11	11	11	9	10	11	11	12	110	11.0	13
Olomouc	14	7	9	7	2	5	11	8	5	9	77	7.7	10
Zlín	7	4	14	4	4	14	2	4	2	2	57	5.7	3
Ostrava	10	10	3	10	10	8	12	12	13	10	98	9.8	12

However, this explanation does not hold for Prague, another city with intensive touristic activity – and yet, here, complaints about the non-availability of services were much less frequent. Another interesting comparison can be made in the evaluation of the quality of mobility infrastructure. From the perspective of older people, not all the city centres that boast safe pedestrian crossings also have well maintained pavements. Zlín would be an example of such an inconsistency, while, in Jihlava, the opposite seems to be true: there is significantly greater satisfaction with the maintenance of sidewalks, but the crossings are evaluated as not very satisfactory. It is clear that various aspects of the recommendations included in the WHO Guide may not be directly associated. As the proposed index was developed from a theoretical framework based on the preferences of older people in various parts of the world living in various urban and social contexts, it was necessary to verify its functionality in the specific national context. Here, this was done simply by means of correlations, for which the results are shown in Table 4.

On the basis of correlation coefficients, it seems that individual items are relatively well associated and all contribute to the resulting index (Cronbach´s α = 0.618; statistical significance is not considered due to the aggregate level of analysis). It is interesting that the age friendliness concept is predicted most strongly by two of the features: the presence of functional street lighting in the night, used as a proxy for safe outdoor space, and by satisfaction with the presence of large and high-quality green spaces, relaxation zones, and pleasing visual aesthetics. Conversely, the weakest links in the test of the reliability of the summation index are the "police patrols" and "availability of toilets" items. These two items reduce the value of Cronbach´s α to below the acceptable threshold of 0.7 (Pallant, 2004). Therefore, we suggest computing the restricted model of the Age-friendly City Index without these two items. The results obtained from this computation are more statistically robust, with Cronbach´s α = 0.71. In Table 5, they are compared with those of the original model, as the rankings of some of the cities change in the restricted model.

Table 4. Correlation of selected age-friendliness indicators in the Czech Republic

	(A) toilets	(B) services	(C) police patrol	(D) night lighting	(E) safe crossings	(F) pavements	(G) parking	(H) public transport satisfaction	(I) aesthetic (non) quality index	(J) greenery index
B	-0.22									
C	0.26	0.04								
D	-0.17	0.64	-0.01							
E	-0.31	0.60	0.01	0.70						
F	0.13	-0.25	0.24	-0.00	0.14					
G	0.18	0.03	-0.03	0.22	-0.24	-0.22				
H	-0.08	0.50	-0.31	0.49	0.40	-0.29	0.17			
I	-0.17	0.10	-0.56	0.55	0.40	0.20	0.42	0.37		
J	0.50	-0.01	0.14	0.32	0.22	0.28	0.50	-0.02	0.46	

Note: See the legend in note to Table 2.

Hradec Králové, Olomouc, Brno, Zlín, Liberec, and Pardubice improve their positions in the simplified model by two or more index points, which, on a fourteen point scale, represents a 14% to 17% improvement. In other words, using the basic model, the low visibility of police patrols and the lack of public toilets comparatively worsened the position of these six towns by almost a fifth. Using the restricted model, the overall average decreases by 1.5 points to a value of 6 points. The restricted model-based

Table 5. Results for the theoretically driven model and the restricted model – comparison

	Theoretically Driven Model		Restricted Model		Change in	
	Average	Final Ranking	Average	Final Ranking	Average	Ranking
Prague	8.8	11	7.7	11	-1.1	0
Kladno	5.5	2	4.8	5	-0.7	+3
České Budějovice	6.1	4	4.8	6	-1.3	+2
Plzeň	4.9	1	3.7	2	-1.2	+1
Karlovy Vary	7.3	9	6.6	9	-0.7	0
Ústí nad Labem	7.2	7	6.7	10	-0.5	+3
Liberec	6.2	5	4.2	4	-2.0	-1
Hradec Králové	6.4	6	4.0	3	-2.4	-3
Pardubice	11.1	14	9.1	14	-2.0	0
Jihlava	7.3	8	6.2	8	-1.1	0
Brno	11.0	13	8.7	13	-2.3	0
Olomouc	7.7	10	5.4	7	-2.3	-3
Zlín	5.7	3	3.6	1	-2.1	-2
Ostrava	9.8	12	8.5	12	-1.3	0

rankings improve the positions of Liberec, Hradec Králové, Olomouc, and Zlín; worsen the rankings of Kladno, České Budějovice, Plzeň, and Ústí nad Labem; and leave six town´s rankings unchanged. Thus, the question may be which of the index models – the theoretically based model, which takes into account all suggested features, or the more restricted, but more coherent model – is better fitted for further use. On the basis of our results, we would suggest the second model. Not only the analysis of the internal reliability of the index (i.e. increased Cronbach´s alpha), but also further analyses prove that the restricted model describes the data somehow better, since it shows closer correlations with other variables than the basic model index. The level of age-friendliness can influence (and/or be influenced by) various factors: In the cities ranked as more age-friendly, the seniors are generally more satisfied (Pearson´s r = 0.17; p. <0.01); the city feels more like "home" (Pearson´s r = 0.19; p. <0.01); and the seniors tend to like the city centre more in general (Pearson´s r = 0.19; p. <0.01). The coefficients also tentatively suggest that in cities that are not so age-friendly, older people are less happy, feel more lonely, and claim to have higher levels of disability (measured by the Instrumental Activities of Daily Living (IADL) scale) (Pearson´s r = 0.07; 0.09; resp.0.08; all p. <0.01). In such cities, older people are less likely to engage in activities such as visiting friends, pursuing leisure activities, or doing "big" shopping; at the same time, they visit doctors more frequently than older people in cities which are perceived to have more age-friendly outdoor spaces and transportation. From a statistical standpoint, however, these correlations are rather weak, mediated by the higher levels of disability of respondents in lower-ranked cities. Even though demanding activities such as employment or lifelong learning, and various social indicators such as satisfaction with neighbourly ties seem to be unrelated to (or uninfluenced by) evaluation of the age-friendliness of a city, the above presented findings confirm that the concept of "age-friendliness" is indeed substantive for the older population and relevant for policy makers.

Controlling Reliability and Validity of the Index Ranking

One way to control whether the results (rankings) obtained substantially reflect the reality is to compare them with the results obtained by a different approach. In this section we will describe a triangulation technique that facilitates the validation of our data through cross verification. The different sources needed for triangulation are represented here not by different data sources, but by different indicators used in the same survey. An open ended question, the so-called "magic ring" method, was used in the QinCity survey to assess the most problematic aspects of urban environments for senior users.

We used it only in the second phase of the QinCity project, so only data on Prague, Brno, and Ostrava were available. The question was presented to respondents as follows: "If you had a "magic ring" and by just putting it on your finger you could change one thing in your neighbourhood, what would it be?" The question is based on the presupposition of shared cultural knowledge of a fairytale featuring such a "magic ring" (the TV series "Arabela", first broadcast from 1979 to 1981) and was designed to provoke a creative approach to thinking about change, regardless of the real or perceived ability to influence these factors, i.e. to overcome the risk of decreasing agency in older age (Fischer, 1973; Lachman, 1986; Ryan, 2005; Oswald, Wahl, Schilling, &, Iwarsson 2007). The question was answered by 82% of respondents (n=756; only one respondent explicitly said, "*I would never have such ring, so I don't know*"), which could be regarded as a satisfactory response rate for an open ended question. Respondents who answered "*nothing*", either because of overall satisfaction, or indecision ("*I cannot think of anything*") were excluded from the analysis. Substantive responses were coded into topical categories, counted, and grouped into more general topic groups. We would expect the rankings obtained according to the numbers of problems identified in each of the cities to be similar to the rankings obtained from the Age-friendly City Index, as the cities in which older people wished for considerably more change would also be the cities which were not yet regarded as truly age-friendly.

Let us now give an example of the analytical procedure just described by reproducing the results of the two most frequent topical areas. The most populated category with respect to changes within the neighbourhood brought about by the "magic ring" was "greenery" (19% in total; Prague 25%; 17% in Ostrava, 15% in Brno). The desires included in this category were for more benches and for more areas in which to relax, tidier and more accessible parks, and the replanting of trees and shrubs which had been removed. The degree of importance was probably best reflected in answers such as (hereinafter quotations from the questionnaire are given in *italics*): *"Shut down the Brno–Prague highway and replace it with greenery; I wish for a little more good health and more green spaces; I would plant flowers everywhere and built fountains and ponds..."*. The second most pressing problem which senior urban dwellers would solve by magic was the issue of cars and traffic in general (11% in total; 16% in Brno, 10% in Ostrava, and 9% in Prague), including associated noise (3% in total; 4% in Prague, 2% in Brno and Ostrava) and smog, and related problems with parking (3% in total; 4% in Brno, 3% in Prague, 2% in Ostrava). Their wishes were *"to limit, exclude, take away, not let in, get rid of, remove and cancel the traffic, keep it away from houses (including public transport, noisy trams, and railways), build the bypasses, introduce roundabouts, solve the lack of parking spaces and, by that, resolve the issue of non-accessible sidewalks."* Although the desire to limit traffic predominated, the positively formulated desire for mobility options to be strengthened – *"to have transport from anywhere; to have more frequent bus service"* – was also expressed, but with much less frequency.

We see from the above examples that the issue of greenery was most frequently mentioned in Prague, and the issue of traffic in Brno. Altogether, Brno leads with the number of desired changes in seven categories (housing, transportation, walkability, sidewalk maintenance, parking, the problem of dog excrement, the availability of services); Ostrava is overrepresented in five topic categories (children, owners, people from the Roma community, the quality of air, relationships); and Prague only in four (cleanliness, noise, greenery, and time). This mechanism of comparison therefore shows identical results to those of the above-presented model of age-friendliness, in which Prague is in 11th position, Ostrava in 12th, and Brno in 13th.

Although the question using the metaphor of a "magic ring" was a specific stimulus within the questionnaire, the results obtained were consistent with other parts of the study (Vidovićová, Galčanová, Petrová Kafková, & Sýkorová, 2013). The quantitative results may be partially an artefact of the questioning process itself; the respondents may only have re-emphasized the topics previously discussed in the survey, which could be illustrated by the relative narrow-mindedness and feasibility of the expressed wishes. The wish for *"oil gushing everywhere"* was a singular exception. However, the key position of greenery and the environmental aesthetic was also strongly present in other parts of the study, including the age-friendliness index results. Consequently, this reflection of the fidelity of the results to the underlying theoretical framework and the lay actors´ understanding of the indicators of an age-friendly environment gives us confidence in the validity and reliability of the index measure and obtained results.

Limitations of the Interpretation of the Index Measure

Despite the simplicity and descriptiveness of this tool for measuring the level of the perceived age-friendliness of cities, a few points must be highlighted with respect to trying to interpret the results.

Firstly, what is measured here is only a selection of the essential features of the age-friendly cities checklist proposed by WHO for assessing the quality of life of older people in cities. This proposed index is eclectic not only in terms of domains – here, the focus was primarily on the environmental viewpoint –, but also in terms of the indicators used. As was shown above, only a small change in the number or type of indicators selected for calculation of the index may lead to a more significant change in the obtained results and ultimately the rankings. This is a problem inherent to this methodology and similar challenges are discussed, for example, by the authors of the Active Ageing Index (Zaidi et al., 2012), which ranks countries according to the untapped potential of active aging within them. We could also argue that the included indicators do not all carry the same importance (for different socio-economic groups, policy agendas, city councils, etc.), and do not exhibit the same degree of variance. For some older people and/or some cities the availability of parking spaces may be a more critical issue than, for example, the quality and reliability of public transport. When evaluating cities using indices, one has to keep in mind that the individual preferences of seniors may vary, and these preferences may also potentially work against each other. For example, while, for some respondents, noisy and smelly cars, buses and trams within the city centre are bothersome, others call for more car parks or parking spaces or the possibility to access public transportation closer to their homes. Inevitably, therefore, the evaluation is necessarily simplified and generalized to a significant degree. This issue cannot be resolved by statistical methods, however, as the key issues must be decided either within the theoretical concept, or, even better, in this particular context, by methods involving consultation with the users and beneficiaries. These methods may include focus groups with different stakeholders or expert consultations with policy makers.

Further, cities are compared to each other while the question of how big the "real" distances are between cities with different rankings remains unanswered. Also, this exercise should be regarded as the analysis of subjective assessments given by the respondents living in city centres – that is, assessments evaluating their own immediate living environments; therefore, they should not be generalized to the city as whole. Respondents could also put more emphasis on particular features, reflecting current problems or an ongoing public debate on a particular topic, and/or personal experience. One may also argue that, rather than the "reality", the index rankings reflect the (high, and perhaps unrealistic) expectations of the evaluators, expressed in terms of the attitude "there is always room for improvement." These possibly interfering externalities are not explicitly represented in the QinCity dataset; therefore it is not possible to detect the degree of influence they may have on the presented results and interpretations. Unfortunately, the index results do not go far beyond simple description.

Lui and colleagues (2009) reviewed criticism applied to the concept of age-friendly cities in general, and such criticism can also be applied to the index measure, namely that the monitored indicators tend not to have a predictive value for suburban areas, and are not sensitive to the complex heterogeneity of individual senior lifestyles. Signing up to the legacy of active aging, which is criticized with growing vehemence for its normativity (Katz, 2005), such a construction of an Age-friendly City Index may also overemphasize social involvement and economically productive outdoor activities at the expense of individual diversity in values and preferences, i.e. it may overlook more housebound older residents or those who remain at home by choice.

The limitations mentioned here, however, do not undermine the general purpose of the Age-friendly City Index, which is to support knowledge-based policy making. As the new WHO Guide puts it: "indicators are, by definition, succinct measures which describe a complex phenomenon, typically produced by processing and simplifying a large amount of raw data. A few good indicators should be able to provide a fairly comprehensive picture without unnecessary detail. In general, a well-crafted, parsimonious indicator set is often preferred in practice because it has the advantage of efficiency and of focusing attention. This is especially the case when the purpose of the indicators is to obtain an overview of a situation and to set strategic directions by key decision makers or by multistakeholder, multisectoral groups" ("Measuring the Age-friendliness", 2015, p.15). And this is the role that the Age-friendly City Index could play within rapidly demographically changing societies.

DISCUSSION AND RECOMMENDATIONS

The measurement of age friendliness in urban areas is highly relevant for policy makers who aim to design supportive physical and social environments within ageing societies. On the basis of our research we would recommend further development of the Age-friendly City Index, taking on board other dimensions proposed within the WHO Guide. The approach tested in the above project, i.e. the ranking of cities or particular geographical areas, might help to identify sources of good practice when formulating age-friendly policies. Age-friendly in this context encapsulates not only particular reference to older residents and their specific needs, but also employment of the life-course approach (Lindenberg & Westendorp, 2015). The users of index-based measurement such as this benefit even more from the tool if there is an available framework for comparison. Therefore, if at all possible, the survey should be based on representative nationwide (or area wide, if smaller geographical units are to be evaluated) samples of appropriate size, which would allow for further analysis by age group and/or other characteristics.

From the methodological point of view, we would further propose careful interpretation of the results in the light of the theoretical framework in order to prevent misinterpretation. In our case, for example, the statistical results pointed out the ambiguity of the "police patrolling" indicator: the presence of police patrols may induce a feeling of security, i.e. that help is readily available if needed; it may also suggest the presence of crime and disorder which needs to be surveilled/monitored by armed force. That is, one has to come back and re-assess the theoretical framework regardless of the risk of losing some information in order to arrive at sounder rankings. Also, cross-checking results with more objective measures could be an interesting add on. Wong et al. (2015) did so with the availability of services, even though their study showed no association between the subjective measure of age friendliness and the objective availability of the services. They, however, used only a convenience (non-probabilistic) sample of relatively small N, which could have influenced the results. Menenc, Newall and Nowicki (2014) compared residents´ assessments with those of municipal officials, warning that the more "objective" measures (i.e. those of the municipal officials) may not adequately reflect residents' views and as such may be less adequate for the purposes of community development, etc. The ideal would be indicators which resonate with target audiences and are technically sound (Brown, 2009).

The preferences (older) residents and/or policy makers may have could also be reflected in the index design by introducing weights for domains or even individual indicators. This could, however, decrease nationwide comparability if introduced only at the city level. Such a risk could of course be reduced or removed by various methods of coordination of the surveys used for the Index computation and for the method of computation itself. National coordinators responsible for ageing-related policies may already have experience of similar projects.

The translation of numerical results (i.e. the proportions of agreement with particular statements or sub-indices averages) into rankings within given indicators seems to be useful for inter-city comparison, as it allows easier navigation through the results and the easier identification of cities which perform better or lag behind in each given indicator. Additionally, standard deviations from the average would provide information on the overall performance of a city by showing the (in)consistency of the overall result.

As already mentioned, indices which would quantify the age friendliness of cities or any other geographical units are not widely available, even less so in time sequences. Ensuring the possibility to repeat surveys with the same selected indicators over time would make an important contribution to assessing the validity and reliability of such composite indices.

CONCLUSION

People from many neighbourhoods discussed poorly lit and poorly maintained sidewalks; sidewalks that are crowded with people, dogs, litter, bicycles, and construction; and streets and sidewalks that are slippery and full of puddles after a heavy snow or rain. (...) particular mention was made of cars parked on the sidewalks (...) These obstacles make it difficult for older people with poor vision, poor balance, or who use wheelchairs or walkers to get around comfortably. (...) The lack of benches along public walkways was also often mentioned ... (as well as) ... the lack of public toilets ...

This paragraph could be a further quotation from the study presented in this chapter, yet is an excerpt from a report on the evaluation of age-friendliness of New York City edited by The New York Academy of Medicine ("Toward an Age-friendly", 2008, p. 40). A very similar list of grievances is presented by Valenčak (2012) and Slavuj (2012) for southern European cities, and certainly other examples can be found for other parts of Europe and the world. Such similarity leads to the idea that many of the aspects of "age-friendliness" – features that make a place "age-friendly" – could be presented almost as anthropological constants, emerging with repeated urgency in different cultures around the world. Age-friendliness, however, should not be treated as a fixed state which is supposed to be achieved, but rather as a continuum between exclusion and inclusion, between barriers and accessibility.

This chapter focused on the evaluation of the outdoor environment and the accessibility of certain urban areas and amenities, which is only a small part of the complex and comprehensive concept of age-friendliness. Considerable variability among Czech towns in these respects was highlighted. Discussions and consultations with various stakeholders at the national level conducted during the course of the QinCity project suggested that the cities in leading positions have pro-active policy actors working at the level of local government and social policy departments, who maximise the use of their vested authority and political support for the development and innovation of social services and support for various forms of active ageing activity in their cities. It can only be a speculation, but this environment of "interest about the citizen" may also result in more satisfied older citizens, who cope better with the surrounding environment and are more positive in their subjective evaluation of it. In order to prove that this is the case, age-friendly index measurement would need to be matched with policy analysis and repeated over time in order to understand the dynamics of both physical and social development within the city.

ACKNOWLEDGMENT

This chapter is based on data collected within the Czech Scientific Agency Grant project No. P404-10-1555 "Ageing in the environment: gentrification and social exclusion as new issues for environmental gerontology" (2010-2012).

REFERENCES

Active ageing. A Policy Framework. (2002). Retrieved September 10, 2015, from http://whqlibdoc.who.int/hq/2002/WHO_NMH_NPH_02.8.pdf

Age-friendly Cities Poll Report. (2009). Retrieved September 10, 2015, from: http://www.carp.ca/o/pdf/age-friendly%20cities%20poll%20report%20web%20copy.pdf

Beard, J. R., Blaney, S., Cerda, M., Frye, V., Lovasi, G. S., Ompad, D., & Vlahov, D. et al. (2009). Neighbourhood characteristics and disability in older adults. *The Journals of Gerontology. Series B, Psychological Sciences and Social Sciences, 64*(2), 252–257. doi:10.1093/geronb/gbn018 PMID:19181694

Bowling, A., & Stafford, M. (2007). How do objective and subjective assessments of neighbourhood influence social and physical functioning in older age? Findings from a British survey of ageing. *Social Science & Medicine, 64*(12), 2533–2549. doi:10.1016/j.socscimed.2007.03.009 PMID:17433509

Bramston, P., Pretty, G., & Chipuer, H. (2002). Unravelling Subjective Quality of Life: An Investigation of Individual and Community Determinants. *Social Indicators Research, 59*(3), 261–274. doi:10.1023/A:1019617921082

Brown, D. (2009). *Good practice guidelines for indicator development and reporting.* Busan: OECD. Retrieved September 10, 2015, from http://www.oecd.org/site/progresskorea/43586563.pdf

Buffel, T., Phillipson, C., & Scharf, T. (2012). Ageing in urban environments: Developing "age-friendly" cities. *Critical Social Policy, 32*(4), 597–617. doi:10.1177/0261018311430457

Burton, E. J., Mitchell, L., & Stride, C. B. (2011). Good places for ageing in place: Development of objective built environment measures for investigating links with older people's wellbeing. *BMC Public Health, 11*(1), 839. doi:10.1186/1471-2458-11-839 PMID:22044518

Feldman, P. H., & Oberlink, M. R. (2003). Developing community indicators to promote the health and well-being of older people. *Family & Community Health, 26*(4), 268–274. doi:10.1097/00003727-200310000-00004 PMID:14528133

Fernández-Carro, C., & Evandrou, M. (2014). Staying Put: Factors Associated with Ageing in One's 'Lifetime Home'. Insights from the European Context. *RASP - Research on Ageing and Social Policy, 2*(1). Retrieved from http://www.hipatiapress.com/hpjournals/index.php/rasp/article/view/1053

Fischer, C. S. (1973). On Urban Alienations and Anomie: Powerlessness and Social Isolation. *American Sociological Review, 38*(3), 311–326. doi:10.2307/2094355 PMID:4711439

Gieryn, T. F. (2000). A Space for Place in Sociology. *Annual Review of Sociology, 26*(1), 463–469. doi:10.1146/annurev.soc.26.1.463

Harding, E. (2007). *Towards Lifetime Neighbourhoods: Designing Sustainable Communities for All. A Discussion Paper*. London: International Longevity Centre UK. Retrieved September 10, 2015, from http://www.lifetimehomes.org.uk/data/files/Lifetime_Neighbourhoods/towards_lifetime_neighbourhoods_ilc_discussion_paper.pdf

Hollbach-Grömig, B., & Trapp, J. H. (2006). *The Impact of Demographic Change on Local and Regional Government – Research Project*. Paris: Council of European Municipalities and Regions.

IFA –International Federation on Aging. (2015). *Age - Friendly Cities and Communities –"Creating Enabling Environments" (The Conference Plenary Panel Abstract)*. Retrieved September 10, 2015, from http://www.ifa-fiv.org/wp-content/uploads/2015/06/Day-2-Plenary-Panel-Abstract.pdf

Katz, S. (2000). Busy Bodies: Activity, Aging, and the Management of Everyday Life. *Journal of Aging Studies, 14*(2), 135–152. doi:10.1016/S0890-4065(00)80008-0

Kendig, H. (2003). Directions in environmental gerontology: A multidisciplinary field. *The Gerontologist, 43*(5), 611–615. doi:10.1093/geront/43.5.611 PMID:14570957

Kresl, P., & Ietri, D. (2010). *The Aging Population and the Competitiveness of Cities: Benefits to the Urban Economy*. Cheltenham, UK: Edward Elgar Publishers. doi:10.4337/9781849806930

Lachman, M. E. (1986). Locus of control in aging research: A case for multidimensional and domain-specific assessment. *Psychology and Aging, 1*(1), 34–40. doi:10.1037/0882-7974.1.1.34 PMID:3267376

Lanspery, S. (2002). Aging in Place. In D. J. Ekerdt (Ed.), *Encyclopedia of Aging* (pp. 49–51). New York: Macmillan Reference.

Levasseur, M., Généreux, M., Bruneau, J.-F., Vanasse, A., Chabot, É., Beaulac, C., & Bédard, M.-M. (2015). Importance of proximity to resources, social support, transportation and neighbourhood security for mobility and social participation in older adults: Results from a scoping study. *BMC Public Health, 15*(1), 503. doi:10.1186/s12889-015-1824-0 PMID:26002342

Lindenberg, J., & Westendorp, R. G. J. (2015). Overcoming Old in Age-Friendliness. *Journal of Social Work Practice, 29*(1), 85–98. doi:10.1080/02650533.2014.993949 PMID:26028795

Lui, C.-W., Everingham, J.-A., Warburton, J., Cuthill, M., & Bartlett, H. (2009). What makes a community age-friendly: A review of international literature. *Australasian Journal on Ageing, 28*(3), 116–121. doi:10.1111/j.1741-6612.2009.00355.x PMID:19845650

Menec, V. H., Newall, N. E. G., & Nowicki, S. (2014). *Assessing Communities' Age-Friendliness: How Congruent Are Subjective Versus Objective Assessments? Journal of Applied Gerontology*. doi:10.1177/0733464814542612

Menec, V. H., & Nowicki, S. (2014). Examining the relationship between communities' 'age-friendliness' and life satisfaction and self-perceived health in rural Manitoba, Canada. *Rural and Remote Health, 14*, 2594. PMID:24437338

Moulaert, T., & Garon, S. (2015). *Age-friendly Cities and Communities in International Comparison: Political Lessons, Scientific Avenues, and Democratic Issues.* Springer.

Mulíček, O., & Olšová, I. (2002). Město Brno a důsledky různých forem urbanizace. *Urbanismus a územní rozvoj, 5*(6), 17–21.

OECD. (2015). *Ageing in Cities.* Paris: OECD Publishing; doi:10.1787/9789264231160-en

Oswald, F., Wahl, H.-W., Schilling, O., & Iwarsson, S. (2007). Housing-related control beliefs and independence in activities of daily living in very old age. *Scandinavian Journal of Occupational Therapy, 14*(1), 33–43. doi:10.1080/11038120601151615 PMID:17366076

Ouředníček, M., Pospíšilová, L., Špačková, P., Temelová, J., & Novák, J. (2012). Prostorová typologie a zonace Prahy. In M. Ouředníček & J. Temelová (Eds.), *Sociální proměny pražských čtvrtí* (pp. 268–297). Praha: Academia.

Pallant, J. (2004). *SPSS Survival Manual.* Open University Press.

Petrová Kafková, M. (2012). Vliv věku a pohlaví tazatele a respondenta na náročnost výběrového šetření v seniorské populaci. *Data a výzkum - SDA Info, 6*(2), 113-127.

Phillipson, C. (2011). Developing Age-friendly Communities: New Approaches to Growing Old in Urban Environments. In J. L. Angel & R. Settersten (Eds.), *Handbook of the Sociology of Aging* (pp. 279–296). New York: Springer Verlag. doi:10.1007/978-1-4419-7374-0_18

Pynoos, J., Caraviello, R., & Cicero, C. (2009). Lifelong Housing: The Anchor in Aging-friendly Communities. *Generations (San Francisco, Calif.), 33*(2), 26–32.

Ryan, R. L. (2005). Exploring the Effects of Environmental Experience on Attachment to Urban Natural Areas. *Environment and Behavior, 37*(1), 3–42. doi:10.1177/0013916504264147

Scharlach, A. E. (2009). Creating Aging-friendly Communities. *Generations (San Francisco, Calif.), 33*(2), 5–11.

Slavuj, L. (2012). Evaluacija kvalitete urbanoga susjedstva – prednosti i nedostaci neposrednoga životnog prostora. *Sociologija i proctor, 5*(2), 183–201.

State of World Population 2007 | UNFPA - United Nations Population Fund. (n.d.). Retrieved 16 January 2016, from http://www.unfpa.org/publications/state-world-population-2007

Toušek, L. (2012). *Kvantitativní analýza pocitu bezpečí města Pardubice.* 2012. Plzeň: FF ZČU. Retrieved September 10, 2015, from http://www.antropologie.org/cs/component/docman/doc_download/42-kvalitativni-analyza-pocitu-bezpei-oban-msta-pardubic

Toward an age-friendly New York City: A Findings Report. (2008). New York, NY: The New York Academy of Medicine.

Tracking the Development of Universal Metrics to Help cities and Communities Compare and Contrast Their Progress on the Design and Implementation of Age-friendly Policies, Strategies and Interventions. (2012). Active Age Discussion Paper. Retrieved September 10, 2015, from: http://library.constantcontact.com/download/get/file/1101901198311-1153/Age+Friendly+Paper.pdf

Valenčak, S. (2012). Kaj je v Sloveniji starosti prijazno in kaj ne? *Kakovostna starost, 15*(1), 3–19.

Vidovićová, L., Galčanová, L., Petrová Kafková, M., & Sýkorová, D. (2013). *Stáří ve městě, město v životě seniorů*. Praha: Sociologické nakladatelství.

Wahl, H.-W., & Lang, F. R. (2004). Aging in context across the adult life: Integrating physical and social research perspectives. In H.-W. Wahl, R. Scheidt, & P. G. Windley (Eds.), *Aging in context: Socio-physical environments* (pp. 1–33). New York: Springer.

Wahl, H.-W., & Weisman, G. D. (2003). Environmental gerontology at the beginning of the new millennium: Reflections on its historical, empirical, and theoretical development. *The Gerontologist, 43*(5), 616–627. doi:10.1093/geront/43.5.616 PMID:14570958

Walker, A. C. (2010). Ageing and Quality of Life in Europe. In D. Dannefer & C. Phillipson (Eds.), *The SAGE Handbook of Social Gerontology* (pp. 571–586). Los Angeles, CA: SAGE Publications. doi:10.4135/9781446200933.n44

WHO - World Health Organisation. (2002). *Global Age-friendly Cities. A Guide*. Retrieved September 10, 2015, from http://www.who.int/ageing/publications/Global_age_friendly_cities_Guide_English.pdf

Wight, R. G., Ko, M. J., & Aneshensel, C. S. (2011). Urban Neighbourhoods and Depressive Symptoms in Late Middle Age. *Research on Aging, 33*(1), 28–50. doi:10.1177/0164027510383048 PMID:21572903

Wiles, J. L., Leibing, A., Guberman, N., Reeve, J., & Allen, R. E. S. (2012). The meaning of 'aging in place' to older people. *The Gerontologist, 52*(3), 357–366. doi:10.1093/geront/gnr098 PMID:21983126

Wong, M., Chau, P. H., Cheung, F., Phillips, D. R., & Woo, J. (2015). Comparing the Age-Friendliness of Different Neighbourhoods Using District Surveys: An Example from Hong Kong. *PLoS ONE, 10*(7), e0131526. doi:10.1371/journal.pone.0131526 PMID:26132156

World Health Organisation (WHO). (2015.) *Measuring the Age-friendliness of Cities: A Guide to Using Core Indicators*. Retrieved January 10, 2016, from: http://apps.who.int/iris/bitstream/10665/203830/1/9789241509695_eng.pdf

Zaidi. (2012). *Active Ageing Index: Concept, Methodology and Final Results*. Retrieved September 10, 2015, from http://www1.unece.org/stat/platform/download/attachments/76287849/Methodology-Paper-as-of-10th_March-2013-FINAL.pdf?version=1&modificationDate=1367589733309

KEY TERMS AND DEFINITIONS

Active Ageing: A way of supporting the quality of life as people grow older by supporting health, participation in society and the economy, and security.

Age-Friendly: A characteristic that takes into account the different needs of people of different ages, but often understood with respect to the needs of older people in particular (i.e. "ageing-friendly"). It can relate to environments, policies, services, things, processes, etc.

Age-Friendly City: Urban areas which have broadly defined infrastructures fulfilling the needs of people of different ages.

Greenery: Green environments, such as parks, grassy areas, trees, bushes, plants.

Physical Environment: the manmade environment that consists of physical objects. includes land, air, water, buildings, roads, and other manmade infrastructure or things; can be outdoor or indoor.

Quality of Life: The general wellbeing of individuals, usually influenced by wealth, employment, the environment, physical and mental health, education, recreation and leisure time, and feelings of social belonging.

Social Environment: The part of the human environment that consists of social relationships with other people; includes social networks, family, friends, neighbors, and other human institutions in the immediate surroundings of a person.

Chapter 13
Using Data Envelopment Analysis to Construct Human Development Index

Paulo Nocera Alves Junior
University of São Paulo (USP), Brazil

Enzo Barberio Mariano
São Paulo State University (UNESP), Brazil

Daisy Aparecida do Nascimento Rebelatto
University of São Paulo (USP), Brazil

ABSTRACT

This chapter addresses problems related to methodological issues, such as data normalization, weighting schemes, and aggregation methods, encountered in the construction of composite indicators to measure socio-economic development and quality of life. It also addresses the use of several Data Envelopment Analysis (DEA) models to solve these problems. The models are discussed and applied in constructing a Human Development Index (HDI), derived from the most recent raw and normalized data, using arithmetic and geometric means to aggregate the indices. Issues related to data normalization and weighting schemes are emphasized. Kendall Correlation was applied to analyze the relationship between ranks obtained by DEA models and HDI. Recommendations regarding the advantages and disadvantages of using DEA models to construct HDI are offered.

INTRODUCTION

This chapter describes problems related to methodological issues in constructing composite indices. It also assesses the use of data envelopment analysis (DEA), a quantitative method, to solve them. Many factors can influence the construction of composite indicators. These include data normalization and weighting schemes. Accordingly, if the methods used to construct composite indicators are inconsistent, they may well lead to diverse rankings, thus increasing the probability of erroneous results (Booysen, 2002).

DOI: 10.4018/978-1-5225-0714-7.ch013

Many methods can be used to construct composite indicators, but DEA is one of the principal quantitative methods suitable for this purpose, because it enables nonarbitrary weighting, avoiding this methodological issue (although it comes from the application of a constrained optimization algorithm and this application of that algorithm itself is arbitrary), and it is invariant to the measurement unit, then DEA does not require data normalization (Cherchye, 2006). The DEA application used to construct composite indicator is known as the benefit of the doubt (BOD) model and it is be described at the "Data Envelopment Analysis and Composite Indicators" section.

While there are several composite indicators used to measure socio-economic development and quality of life (QOL), the most frequently used is the human development index (HDI). A general practical implication of composite QOL indices is its usefulness for decision makers, e.g., making political decisions based on the evolution of composite indicators over the past years or establishing residency on a place with higher QOL (Hagerty & Land,2007).

Focusing on the HDI together with its weights for each indicator of each country, other practical implications are that it shows the priorities of the countries, it can attract external investment and orientate the concession of international help. Also, it can help policy makers to prioritize public expenditures to improve QOL of the population, stimulating government policies about human development.

As presently constructed, HDI's data normalization and weighting schemes are arbitrary, giving rise to substantive criticism (Neumayer, 2001; Klugman, Rodríguez, & Choi, 2011). Since 1990 when HDI was first created, its calculation methods have been revised constantly, as shown in the survey conducted by Morse (2014). The most radical methodological alteration, a change in its aggregation method of indices, from an arithmetic to a geometric mean in 2010, did not save the index from further controversy (Klugman et al., 2011). The HDI construction and some other detail are presented at the "Data Envelopment Analysis and Composite Indicators" section.

With this history in mind, it is important to note that a slack-based measure (SBM) DEA model was not previously used to recalculate the HDI (Mariano, Sobreiro, & Rebelatto, 2015), so it is used in this regard, comparing its results to HDI's, where it lays the main contribution of this chapter, and those of other DEA models, viz., Charnes, Cooper and Rhodes (CCR) and geometric/multiplicative, in their standard and inverted forms.

The chapter describes and correlates the results of DEA models in calculating the HDI and provides recommendations regarding their respective advantages and disadvantages in constructing socio-economic composite indicators.

DATA ENVELOPMENT ANALYSIS AND COMPOSITE INDICATORS

The first data envelopment analysis model was created by Charnes, Cooper, and Rhodes (1978). The CCR model is a nonparametric mathematical programming method used to measure the relative efficiency of decision-making units (DMUs) in a system with multiple inputs and outputs. The original was an input-oriented fractional programming model formulated as follows:

$$\max P_0 = \frac{\sum_{i=1}^{m} u_i y_{i0}}{\sum_{j=1}^{n} v_j x_{j0}}$$

s.t.:

$$\frac{\sum_{i=1}^{m} u_i y_{ik}}{\sum_{j=1}^{n} v_j x_{jk}} \leq 1; k = 1, 2, \ldots, z$$

$$u_i, v_j \geq 0$$

where y_{i0} is the amount of the *ith* output of the analyzed DMU; x_{j0}, the amount of its *jth* input; y_{ik} is the amount of the *ith* output of the *kth* DMU; x_{jk}, the amount of its *jth* input; u_i is the weight of the *ith* output; v_j, the weight of the *jth* input; m is the number of analyzed outputs; n, the number of analyzed inputs; and z, the number of analyzed DMUs.

The linear form of CCR model, known as the standard CCR input-oriented multipliers model, is shown as follows:

$$\max \sum_{i=1}^{m} u_i y_{i0}$$

s.t.:

$$\sum_{j=1}^{n} v_j x_{j0} = 1$$

$$\sum_{i=1}^{m} u_i y_{ik} - \sum_{j=1}^{n} v_j x_{jk} \leq 0; k = 1, 2, \ldots, z$$

$$u_i, v_j \geq 0$$

Following the creation of the CCR model, several other DEA models were developed, which take into account assumptions related to their orientation, i.e., input, output, or non-oriented; whether or not they are radial; the relations between liner or nonlinear inputs and outputs; and the type of returns to scale, i.e., constant, variable, or hybrid (Mariano et al., 2015).

It is noteworthy, that given a level of outputs, models oriented to inputs seek to reduce inputs, and given a level of inputs, models oriented to outputs seek to increase outputs, while nonoriented models are nonradial and seek to reduce inputs and increase outputs simultaneously (Mariano et al., 2015).

DEA may be applied to generate an efficiency frontier by calculating the best nonarbitrary weights for each component of the composite indicator and a single performance measure between 0 and 1. As the chapter concerns the construction of indices, only models with input orientation and constant returns to scale (CRS) will be discussed, considering several output variables with raw or normalized data and setting the input variable as equal to 1. This DEA application, known as the benefit of the doubt (BOD) model, was proposed by Melyn and Moesen (1991) and reviewed by Cherchye, Moesen, Rogge, and Puyenbroeck (2007). It is worth noting that several countries could be ranked first and thereby deemed "efficient" in DEA terms. In constructing a human development composite indicator, all these models will be in the form of input-oriented multipliers, according to the methodology of Despotis (2005b).

The five DEA-BOD models used in this chapter are:

1. The standard input-oriented CCR multipliers model (Despotis, 2005a, 2005b; Melyn & Moesen, 1991):

$$\max \sum_{i=1}^{m} u_i y_{i0}$$

s.t.:

$$\sum_{i=1}^{m} u_i y_{ik} \leq 1; k = 1, 2, \ldots, z$$
$$u_i \geq 0; i = 1, 2, \ldots, m$$

2. The inverted (INV) input-oriented CCR model (Zhou, Ang, & Poh, 2007):

$$\min \sum_{i=1}^{m} u_i y_{i0}$$

s.t.:

$$\sum_{i=1}^{m} u_i y_{ik} \geq 1; k = 1, 2, \ldots, z$$
$$u_i \geq 0; i = 1, 2, \ldots, m$$

3. The geometric (GEO) model proposed by P. Zhou, Ang, and D. Zhou (2010):
    a. GEO (original form):

$$\max \prod_{i=1}^{m} \left(y_{i0} \right)^{u_i}$$

s.t."

$$\prod_{i=1}^{m} \left(y_{ik} \right)^{u_i} \leq e; k = 1, 2, \ldots, z$$
$$u_i \geq 0; i = 1, 2, \ldots, m$$

b.   GEO (linearized form):

$$\max \sum_{i=1}^{m} u_i \cdot \ln\left(y_{i0}\right)$$

s.t.:

$$\sum_{i=1}^{m} u_i \cdot \ln\left(y_{ik}\right) \leq 1; k = 1, 2, \ldots, z$$
$$u_i \geq 0; i = 1, 2, \ldots, m$$

4.   And the inverse geometric (GINV) model proposed by Zhou et al. (2010):
   a.   GINV (original form):

$$\min \prod_{i=1}^{m} \left(y_{i0}\right)^{u_i}$$

s.t.:

$$\prod_{i=1}^{m} \left(y_{ik}\right)^{u_i} \geq e; k = 1, 2, \ldots, z$$
$$u_i \geq 0; i = 1, 2, \ldots, m$$

   b.   GINV (linearized form):

$$\min \sum_{i=1}^{m} u_i \cdot \ln\left(y_{i0}\right)$$

s.t.:

$$\sum_{i=1}^{m} u_i \cdot \ln\left(y_{ik}\right) \geq 1; k = 1, 2, \ldots, z$$
$$u_i \geq 0; i = 1, 2, \ldots, m$$

5.   The SBM multipliers model (BOD model adapted from Tone, 2001):

$$\max \theta$$

s.t.:

$$\theta - \sum_{i=1}^{m} u_i y_{i0} = 0$$

$$\sum_{i=1}^{m} u_i y_{ik} \leq 1; k = 1, 2, \ldots, z$$

$$u_i \geq \frac{\theta}{m y_{i0}}; i = 1, 2, \ldots, m$$

All these models have the terms $\sum_{i=1}^{m} u_i y_{i0}$ or θ that refers to the efficiency of the analyzed DMU and the "max" of the objective function searches for the best practices of the DMUs and indicates the maximization of the efficiency, while $u_i \geq 0$ indicates that the weights which multiply outputs are positive (nonnegative). The constraints indicate the efficiencies of all DMUs are smaller or equal to 1. These constraints also serve as normalization tool.

The term "ln" of the geometric models (GEO and GINV) refers to the natural logarithm, used to linearize the geometric aggregation with a logarithmic scale. The constraint with $\geq$ signal together with the MIN of the objective function of the inverted models (INV and GINV) indicates a search of the worst practices of the DMUs and result in an inverted ranking that needs to be reversed. The $u_i \geq \theta/m y_{i0}$ SBM constraint indicates that the weights must be greater than an amount proportional to the efficiency of the DMU and inversely proportional to the number of output and to the outputs values, so that efficient DMUs do not have slacks. This constraint is better explained in the solutions and recommendation section.

These models can be used to construct a composite indicator for both raw and normalized data, according to the HDI calculation method, introduced as a measurement of human development by the United Nations Development Programme (UNDP) in 1990. The method uses maximum and minimum values, and the natural logarithm of the values in the case of GDP per capita, to normalize socio-economic indicators. Since 2010, HDI is calculated as summarized in Table 1, adapted from Despotis (2005b).

Table 2 depicts variations of the BOD-DEA models described in this chapter that can be used to construct HDI from both raw and normalized data.

The most recent HDI ranks 187 nations based on national data and UNDP-assigned equal weights, as shown in the last Human Development Report that is from 2014 (United Nations Development Programme [UNDP], 2015). Data available on the UNDP site and updated yearly. The Kendall Correlation, developed by Kendall (1938), is described by Taylor (1987) as a nonparametric method used to assess correlation between two ordinal variables, was applied to analyze the relationship between ranks obtained by the DEA models and HDI, inasmuch as that relationship may not be linear.

CONSTRUCTION OF COMPOSITE INDICES: WEIGHTS AND RANKINGS

Issues, Controversies, and Problems

According to Hagerty and Land (2007), there are some problems and barriers to construct composite QOL indices, like the too general concept of QOL and the heterogeneity in subjective weights. They also addresses other issues, like the little agreement among researchers about the best aggregation method to

Table 1. HDI calculations

Dimension	Indicator	Index	Composite Index
Health (Longevity)	Life expectancy at birth (LEB)	Life expectancy index (LEI) $$LEI = \frac{LEB - 20}{85 - 20}$$	Human Development Index (HDI) $$HDI = \sqrt[3]{LEI \cdot EDI \cdot GDPI} = LEI^{1/3} \cdot EDI^{1/3} \cdot GDPI^{1/3}$$
Education	Mean of years of schooling for adults aged 25 years (MSA)	Educational index (EDI) $$EDI = \frac{1}{2} \cdot \frac{MSA}{15} + \frac{1}{2} \cdot \frac{ESC}{18}$$	
	Expected years of schooling for children of school entering age (ESC)		
Standard of living	GDP per capita (GDP)	Adjusted GDP index (GDPI) $$GDPI = \frac{\ln(GDP) - \ln(100)}{\ln(75000) - \ln(100)}$$	

Note: Data from UNDP, 2015

Table 2. BOD-DEA model variations with HDI variables

Model	Normalized Data	Raw Data
CCR	max $u_{LEI} \cdot LEI_{i0} + u_{EDI} \cdot EDI_{i0} + u_{GDPI} \cdot GDPI_{i0}$ s.t.: $u_{LEI} \cdot LEI_{ik} + u_{EDI} \cdot EDI_{ik} + u_{GDPI} \cdot GDPI_{ik} \leq 1$ $u_{LEI}, u_{EDI}, u_{GDPI} \geq 0$	max $u_{LEB} \cdot LEB_{i0} + u_{MSA} \cdot MSA_{i0} + u_{ESC} \cdot ESC_{i0} + u_{GDP} \cdot GDP_{i0}$ s.t.: $u_{LEB} \cdot LEB_{ik} + u_{MSA} \cdot MSA_{ik} + u_{ESC} \cdot ESC_{ik} + u_{GDP} \cdot GDP_{ik} \leq 1$ $u_{LEB}, u_{MSA}, u_{ESC}, u_{GDP} \geq 0$
INV	min $u_{LEI} \cdot LEI_{i0} + u_{EDI} \cdot EDI_{i0} + u_{GDPI} \cdot GDPI_{i0}$ s.t.: $u_{LEI} \cdot LEI_{ik} + u_{EDI} \cdot EDI_{ik} + u_{GDPI} \cdot GDPI_{ik} \geq 1$ $u_{LEI}, u_{EDI}, u_{GDPI} \geq 0$	min $u_{LEB} \cdot LEB_{i0} + u_{MSA} \cdot MSA_{i0} + u_{ESC} \cdot ESC_{i0} + u_{GDP} \cdot GDP_{i0}$ s.t.: $u_{LEB} \cdot LEB_{ik} + u_{MSA} \cdot MSA_{ik} + u_{ESC} \cdot ESC_{ik} + u_{GDP} \cdot GDP_{ik} \geq 1$ $u_{LEB}, u_{MSA}, u_{ESC}, u_{GDP} \geq 0$
GEO	max $u_{LEI} \cdot \ln(LEI_{i0}) + u_{EDI} \cdot \ln(EDI_{i0}) + u_{GDPI} \cdot \ln(GDPI_{i0})$ s.t.: $u_{LEI} \cdot \ln(LEI_{ik}) + u_{EDI} \cdot \ln(EDI_{ik}) + u_{GDPI} \cdot \ln(GDPI_{ik}) \leq 1$ $u_{LEI}, u_{EDI}, u_{GDPI} \geq 0$	max $u_{LEB} \cdot \ln(LEB_{i0}) + u_{MSA} \cdot \ln(MSA_{i0}) + u_{ESC} \cdot \ln(ESC_{i0}) + u_{GDP} \cdot \ln(GDP_{i0})$ s.t.: $u_{LEB} \cdot \ln(LEB_{ik}) + u_{MSA} \cdot \ln(MSA_{ik}) + u_{ESC} \cdot \ln(ESC_{ik}) + u_{GDP} \cdot \ln(GDP_{ik}) \leq 1$ $u_{LEB}, u_{MSA}, u_{ESC}, u_{GDP} \geq 0$
GINV	min $u_{LEI} \cdot \ln(LEI_{i0}) + u_{EDI} \cdot \ln(EDI_{i0}) + u_{GDPI} \cdot \ln(GDPI_{i0})$ s.t.: $u_{LEI} \cdot \ln(LEI_{ik}) + u_{EDI} \cdot \ln(EDI_{ik}) + u_{GDPI} \cdot \ln(GDPI_{ik}) \geq 1$ $u_{LEI}, u_{EDI}, u_{GDPI} \geq 0$	min $u_{LEB} \cdot \ln(LEB_{i0}) + u_{MSA} \cdot \ln(MSA_{i0}) + u_{ESC} \cdot \ln(ESC_{i0}) + u_{GDP} \cdot \ln(GDP_{i0})$ s.t.: $u_{LEB} \cdot \ln(LEB_{ik}) + u_{MSA} \cdot \ln(MSA_{ik}) + u_{ESC} \cdot \ln(ESC_{ik}) + u_{GDP} \cdot \ln(GDP_{ik}) \geq 1$ $u_{LEB}, u_{MSA}, u_{ESC}, u_{GDP} \geq 0$
SBM	max θ s.t.: $\theta - u_{LEI} \cdot LEI_{i0} - u_{EDI} \cdot EDI_{i0} - u_{GDPI} \cdot GDPI_{i0} = 0$ $u_{LEI} \cdot LEI_{ik} + u_{EDI} \cdot EDI_{ik} + u_{GDPI} \cdot GDPI_{ik} \leq 1$ $u_{LEI} \geq \frac{\theta}{3LEI_{i0}}, \; u_{EDI} \geq \frac{\theta}{3EDI_{i0}}, \; u_{GDPI} \geq \frac{\theta}{3GDPI_{i0}}$	max θ s.t.: $\theta - u_{LEB} \cdot LEB_{i0} - u_{MSA} \cdot MSA_{i0} - u_{ESC} \cdot ESC_{i0} - u_{GDP} \cdot GDP_{i0} = 0$ $u_{LEB} \cdot LEB_{ik} + u_{MSA} \cdot MSA_{ik} + u_{ESC} \cdot ESC_{ik} + u_{GDP} \cdot GDP_{ik} \leq 1$ $u_{LEB} \geq \frac{\theta}{4LEB_{i0}}, \; u_{MSA} \geq \frac{\theta}{4MSA_{i0}}, \; u_{ESC} \geq \frac{\theta}{4ESC_{i0}}, \; u_{GDP} \geq \frac{\theta}{4GDP_{i0}}$

construct a composite QOL indices; and among individuals, policy makers and researchers on the best weighting scheme for social indicators. The most common is the equally-weighted social index scheme after normalization, used not only by the HDI, but by many other indicators, like the index of social health and the value based index of national quality of life. Another common procedure is the factor analysis, but the calculated weights of that method just make reference to common weights of each principal component instead of all the weight of each object of analysis and it is based on the explained variance of indicators.

As previously noted, the methodological problems encountered in HDI, which are also the problems of other composite indicators, arise from a number of factors and have led to frequent revisions that may well affect the relative position of countries in subsequent rankings. Among these factors are data normalization based on theoretical minimum and maximum parameters used as cut-off values, equally-weighted sub-index schemes, and aggregation methods, all of which can raise or lower the ranks of countries. These issues and potential biases can be addressed through DEA (Mahlberg & Obersteine, 2001; Despotis (2005a, 2005b); Zhou et al., 2010; Tofallis, 2013).

Summarizing, the main problem is about arbitrariness. It is common to choose any data normalization, e.g., it can be based on theoretical minimum and maximum values or only on relative maximum, to assign equal weights without justifying, and choosing any aggregation method without worrying about the perfect substitution and complementary of the indicators. They all need to be justified.

The DEA method does not need prior normalization, because it is based on its own weighting scheme, resulting on a final value between 0 and 1, the different aggregation methods can be addressed by different DEA models. Unlike factor analysis, DEA does not need any parameter, as explained variance and all nonarbitrary weights are calculated based on nonparametric constrained optimization.

SOLUTIONS AND RECOMMENDATIONS

As the revision or reconstruction of composite indicators use diverse calculations methods, different DEA models can be applied to address different needs. Additive and multiplicative models, with standard or inverted frontiers and common weights have been proposed (Mahlberg & Obersteiner, 2001; Despotis, 2005a, b; Zhou et al., 2010; Tofallis, 2013). Other DEA models, such as SBM, have not been reported in this regard prior to the present study.

To corroborate the theoretical premise regarding the use of diverse DEA models to calculate HDI, an empirical test was conducted applying different models to the most recent HDI (UNDP, 2014). In this application, calculated weights, based on raw (life expectancy, adult literacy rate, combined gross enrollment ratios, and GDP per capita) and normalized variables (longevity, education and standard of living indices calculated according to criteria established by UNDP),were obtained and analyzed.

For each application, two variations were employed, one with and one without virtual DMUs with theoretical minimum and maximum values as set in the 2014 HDI. It is important to note that, because of problems involving $1/0$ and $1/\log(1)$, inverted frontier models cannot be applied to virtual DMUs and normalized data between 0 and 1.

For normalized data, i.e., values between 0 and 1, the multiplicative model must be adapted, e.g., by considering values as percentages, rather than decimals, as its behavior is inverted and presents weighting problems for end values in the 0-to-1 range.

Analyze of the Contributions

In analyzing weights and contributions, using a virtual DMUs with theoretical extreme values to calculate absolute efficiency, instead of relative efficiency, makes only the virtual DMU becomes truly efficient, and other efficient DMUs will have slacks, then DMUs without all the optimal values assigns a weigh of 100% to the highest value, i.e. it would be sufficient to look at the greatest value and assigning an weight of 1 to the indicator.

Accordingly, in such cases, only DMUs that exceed the cut-off value in at least one component are deemed "efficient." In regard to HDI sub-indices, this requires a per capita GDP above $75,000, GDPI equal to 1, or more than 18 expected years of schooling for children of school entering age. On the other hand, most countries deemed "inefficient" assign 100% weight for life expectancy. Table 3 presents the mean relative contribution for each indicator for each DEA model.

Analyzing the means of relative contributions, it can be seen that with normalized data and virtual DMUs with theoretically optimal values, the SBM model tends to seek equal weights, i.e., efficient countries obtain weights equal to 1/n, wherein n indicates the number of dimensions of the composite indicator, viz., 1/3 for standardized data and 1/4 for raw data. Accordingly, among the DEA models studied, SBM most closely approximates HDI.

This SBM model tends to search equal weights due to the fact that its envelopment model define efficient DMU based on the slack equal to 0, for example, two DMUs (DMU1 and DMU2) are considered efficient by the CCR model, but DMU1 has all the slacks equal to 0, while DMU2 has a slack different of 0 in one variable, so DMU2 is not efficient in the SBM model, i. e. this slack optimization of SBM envelopment model are converted into minimum weights greater than 0 and inversely proportional to the number of variables in the multipliers SBM, and consequently the model starts to seek more central weights to not assign weight 0 for no one variable.

Table 3. Mean relative contribution for each indicator

Model	Virtual DMU	Normalized Data			Raw Data			
		LEI	EDI	GDPI	LEB	MSA	ESC	GDP
CCR	No	75.66%	12.05%	12.29%	81.02%	8.25%	8.30%	2.43%
	Yes	81.29%	3.74%	14.97%	84.49%	0%	13.37%	2.4%
GEO	No	76.22%	11.83%	11.95%	89.38%	4.13%	3.24%	3.25%
	Yes	81.28%	3.74%	14.98%	93.01%	0%	3.76%	3.23%
GINV	No	74.64%	8.37%	16.99%	83.88%	0.58%	0.8%	14.76%
	Yes	-	-	-	100%	0%	0%	0%
INV	No	64.91%	15.07%	20.02%	87.80%	2.11%	7.51%	2.58%
	Yes	-	-	-	100%	0%	0%	0%
SBM	No	34.60%	31.77%	33.64%	26.02%	25.43%	25.56%	22.99%
	Yes	33.30%	33.39%	33.31%	24.37%	25.18%	24.63%	25.82%

MODELS WITH COMMON WEIGHTS

While other DEA models vary, they all give priority to a single dimension, in other words, one single variable represents 100% of the contribution. One way to compare the DEA's ranking with HDI's is to apply a subsequent method using the same optimal efficiencies, but with equal weights. The formulation for this model adapted from Despotis (2005a, 2005b), which minimizes deviations, in the case of CCR is as follows:

$$\min \sum_{k=1}^{z} d_k$$

s.t.:

$$\sum_{i=1}^{m} u_i y_{ik} + d_k = \theta_k; k = 1, 2, \ldots, z$$
$$u_i \geq 0; i = 1, 2, \ldots, m$$

where θ_k is the previously calculated efficiency of the *kth* DMU; y_{ik}, the *ith* output of the *kth* DMU; u_i, the weight of the *ith* output; m, the number of analyzed outputs; z, the number of analyzed DMUs, and d_k is the deviation of the *kth* DMU in regard to the original.

Other models should keep their constraints and properties, for example, SBM model should keep the weight constraints and geometric model should keep the logarithm of the data.

Table 4 presents the indicators for each DEA model, using equal weights.

Table 4. Equal weights for each indicator for each DEA model

Model	Virtual DMU	Normalized Data			Raw Data			
		LEI	EDI	GDPI	LEB	MSA	ESC	GDP
CCR	No	1.0225	0	0	0.0120	0	0	0
	Yes	1.0000	0	0	0.0118	0	0	0
GEO	No	0.2182	0	0	0.2259	0	0	0
	Yes	0.2171	0	0	0.0023	0	0	0
GINV	No	0.1763	0	0	0.0020	0	0	0
	Yes	-	-	-	0.0015	0	0	0
INV	No	0.0002	0.1307	0.0771	0.0001	0.0059	0	0
	Yes	-	-	-	0.0090	0	0	0
SBM	No	0.2163	0.4366	0.3439	0.0001	0.0038	0.0003	0
	Yes	0.2009	0.4283	0.3136	0.0001	0.0039	0.0003	0

Analysis of the Rankings

Analyzing the HDI rankings provided in Table 6 of the Appendix, it is possible to see that the ranks have been relatively stable in regard to ranking changes among years with the same applied methodology, as it happened in recent years, for example, it had no change exceeding five positions between 2013 and 2014. Accordingly, the stability among DEA models was compared in terms of deviation of five or less positions.

Comparing the effect of adding the virtual DMUs between Geometric/Multiplicative and standard CCR Models: With normalized data, with or without virtual DMU, no countries exceeded the deviation of five positions. With raw data, with and without virtual DMUs, only 7.02% and 10.16%, respectively, changed more than five positions. Thus the study finds that these DEA models are analogous in this regard to HDI, as does the Kendall Correlation matrix (see Table 5).

Comparing the effect of changing data type between Geometric/Multiplicative and standard CCR Models: With virtual DMUs, using raw or normalized data, at least 80% of countries varied at most five positions; without virtual DMU compliance, using raw or normalized data, the deviation ranged from 69.52% to 79.68%. Thus it appears that in the absence of a virtual DMU the use of raw versus normalized data may affect rankings. Moreover, when comparing DEA models using the same input data, the greatest ranking changes occurred when raw data were used.

In general, inverted frontier models, viz., CCR and geometric inverted models, present different values than their standard forms, with countries changing as much as 80 positions in the case of the former. When compared using raw data, the rankings of CCR and geometric inverted models are similar. Given such similar results and the complexities and limitations of the geometric model, it would appear to be more efficient to use the CCR model in its standard and inverted forms in lieu of the geometric models in the absence of a compelling contrary rationale. Comparing the rankings of SBM models with or without virtual DMUs, using the same type of data, i.e., raw or normalized, results in holding 95.2% to 95.7% of the positions, but the SBM rankings compared with other DEA models, regardless of data type, ranged from 19.9% to 40.9%.

The Kendall Correlation matrix measures correlations among HDI and DEA model rankings as can be seen in Table 5. The correlation of models ranged from 0.647 (between SBM and inverted geometric models, using raw data and virtual DMUs) to 0.998 (between CCR and geometric models, with normalized data and virtual DMUs). In comparisons restricted to HDI and DEA models, the correlation ranged from 0.726 (between HDI and the inverted Geometric with raw data and virtual DMUs) to 0.989 (between HDI and SBM with normalized data and without virtual DMUs). This further illustrates the apparently greater effect of data type on rankings than virtual DMU use.

The minimum correlation of 0.726 and maximum of 0.989 between HDI and DEA models found in this paper is consistent with previous findings, as it could be seen at Hagerty and Land (2007), they found that even opposed weights would have QOL indices that have quite high correlation.

So the surprise in this paper was not about the correlations themselves, but about the correlations associated with the behavior of DEA models (GEO has a lower correlation with the HDI than the SBM has). Based on the behavior of the models and empirical evidences, it is possible to make a hypothesis about the causes of these correlations, based on what most affects the rankings, involving the calculation of the HDI (which is calculated with normalized data, equal weights and geometric mean). As for any type of data, and with or without the virtual DMU, GEO has a lower correlation with the HDI than SBM has, so the main cause could be aggregation method or weighting scheme.

Table 5. Kendall's correlation matrix between HDI/DEA model rankings

Model		HDI	Normalized Data and Virtual DMUs			Normalized Data without Virtual DMUs					Raw Data and Virtual DMUs					Raw Data without Virtual DMUs				
			CCR	GEO	SBM	CCR	INV	GEO	GINV	SBM	CCR	INV	GEO	GINV	SBM	CCR	INV	GEO	GINV	SBM
HDI		1.000	0.756	0.757	0.986	0.799	0.874	0.797	0.856	0.989	0.754	0.728	0.733	0.726	0.848	0.790	0.784	0.761	0.757	0.842
Normalized data and virtual DMUs	CCR	0.756	1.000	0.998	0.745	0.945	0.838	0.947	0.851	0.747	0.921	0.913	0.930	0.912	0.719	0.899	0.867	0.918	0.894	0.718
	GEO	0.757	0.998	1.000	0.745	0.944	0.838	0.946	0.851	0.747	0.921	0.912	0.928	0.911	0.719	0.898	0.866	0.917	0.893	0.718
	SBM	0.986	0.745	0.745	1.000	0.787	0.865	0.785	0.846	0.995	0.744	0.718	0.722	0.717	0.844	0.780	0.776	0.751	0.748	0.838
Normalized data without virtual DMUs	CCR	0.799	0.945	0.944	0.787	1.000	0.845	0.997	0.856	0.789	0.915	0.889	0.907	0.888	0.738	0.928	0.853	0.918	0.875	0.736
	INV	0.874	0.838	0.838	0.865	0.845	1.000	0.845	0.975	0.866	0.831	0.833	0.829	0.832	0.784	0.837	0.883	0.839	0.861	0.781
	GEO	0.797	0.947	0.946	0.785	0.997	0.845	1.000	0.856	0.787	0.915	0.890	0.908	0.890	0.737	0.928	0.855	0.918	0.876	0.735
	GINV	0.856	0.851	0.851	0.846	0.856	0.975	0.856	1.000	0.847	0.847	0.855	0.847	0.854	0.770	0.848	0.898	0.853	0.884	0.768
	SBM	0.989	0.747	0.747	0.995	0.789	0.866	0.787	0.847	1.000	0.746	0.719	0.724	0.718	0.848	0.781	0.777	0.752	0.749	0.842
Raw data and virtual DMUs	CCR	0.754	0.921	0.921	0.744	0.915	0.831	0.915	0.847	0.746	1.000	0.937	0.964	0.939	0.678	0.939	0.884	0.947	0.914	0.676
	INV	0.728	0.913	0.912	0.718	0.889	0.833	0.890	0.855	0.719	0.937	1.000	0.966	0.996	0.649	0.903	0.924	0.943	0.963	0.648
	GEO	0.733	0.930	0.928	0.722	0.907	0.829	0.908	0.847	0.724	0.964	0.966	1.000	0.967	0.666	0.922	0.898	0.963	0.933	0.665
	GINV	0.726	0.912	0.911	0.717	0.888	0.832	0.890	0.854	0.718	0.939	0.996	0.967	1.000	0.648	0.903	0.925	0.942	0.962	0.647
	SBM	0.848	0.719	0.719	0.844	0.738	0.784	0.737	0.770	0.848	0.678	0.649	0.666	0.648	1.000	0.706	0.689	0.687	0.673	0.989
Raw data without virtual DMUs	CCR	0.790	0.899	0.898	0.780	0.928	0.837	0.928	0.848	0.781	0.939	0.903	0.922	0.903	0.706	1.000	0.862	0.956	0.883	0.705
	INV	0.784	0.867	0.866	0.776	0.853	0.883	0.855	0.898	0.777	0.884	0.924	0.898	0.925	0.689	0.862	1.000	0.883	0.953	0.688
	GEO	0.761	0.918	0.917	0.751	0.918	0.839	0.918	0.853	0.752	0.947	0.943	0.963	0.942	0.687	0.956	0.883	1.000	0.911	0.685
	GINV	0.757	0.894	0.893	0.748	0.875	0.861	0.876	0.884	0.749	0.914	0.963	0.933	0.962	0.673	0.883	0.953	0.911	1.000	0.672
	SBM	0.842	0.718	0.718	0.838	0.736	0.781	0.735	0.768	0.842	0.676	0.648	0.665	0.647	0.989	0.705	0.688	0.685	0.672	1.000

At first, it could be stated that the GEO is more similar the HDI in the aggregation, while the SBM is more similar the HDI in the weights. While it may seem counterintuitive, the GEO aggregation method does not affect the scores as the weighting scheme does, because the main change to the geometric aggregation is about calculating the logarithm of the data, and not the weights, although these are affected by the data, but not by "scale changes", then it could be made an analogy to a change in the type of data that does not affect much the correlation, because instead of seeking equal weights, the GEO (linearized) behaves similarly to the CCR, seeking "extreme" weights rather than average ones, but on a logarithmic scale, i. e., on somehow it influences the weights more than the aggregation method, even in the GEO itself.

FUTURE RESEARCH DIRECTIONS

Regardless of critical views regarding the manner in which HDI normalizes variables, assigns their weighting, and sets their theoretical parameters, the rankings of the DEA models studied correlate significantly with HDI's to the point of being practically identical, in the case of SBM. Further research to evaluate the relative effectiveness of DEA and other alternative methods to those presently used to construct the Human Development Index should be undertaken to optimize its calculation. The fact that four of the five DEA models seek weights with 0 or 100% contribution merits further investigation, as do the research limitations arising from the problem of too many 0s.

CONCLUSION

The chapter contributions are regarding the use of SBM in constructing composite indicators, the empirical evidences that showed high correlations between HDI and SBM and low between HDI and GEO, and the counterintuitive behavior of the geometric model, which could be expected to have a high correlation with the HDI, because of the geometric aggregation.

Few differences in results were found among DEA models using the same form, i.e., standard or inverted, a finding that corresponds with the Kendall Correlation matrix. In comparing the results of the standard CCR and geometric models, for example, no substantive differences were found. The correlation among models ranged from 0.647 (between SBM and GINV) to 0.998 (between CCR and GEO), while restricted to HDI and DEA models, it ranged from 0.726 (between HDI and GEO) to 0.989 (between HDI and SBM).

Empirical evidences have shown that the aggregation method has the least influence and the weighting scheme has the most influence on the rankings, while data type has a greater effect on rankings than the use of virtual DMU.

These findings can be expected in the construction of any composite indicator, for example, the weighting schemes will have the most influence on the rankings, as well as it can be expected the same behavior of the models in regards to composite indicators, for example, the SBM results will be highly correlated to any composite indicator with equally-weighted scheme.

Given these facts, one should weigh other factors, such as complexities and limitations, in selecting the model used to construct a socio-economic composite indicator. Hence, our recommendation of the use of the CCR in lieu of the more complex and limited geometric model.

Another factor that could be considered in selecting a model is correlation with HDI rankings, in which the SBM model attains the closest approximation.

Finally, at several points, the findings suggested that the type of data used, i.e., raw or normalized, had a greater effect on rankings than the aggregation method or whether or not a virtual DMU was used, while it has less effect than the form in which the weighting scheme is calculated by the models. Moreover, the use of a virtual DMU with absolute values presents problems in its own right, as mentioned in the chapter. These are important factors to considerate in selecting and adapting a prospective alternative to the present methodology for calculating the Human Development Index.

REFERENCES

Booysen, F. (2002). An overview evaluation of composite indices of development. *Social Indicators Research*, *59*(2), 115–151. doi:10.1023/A:1016275505152

Charnes, A., Cooper, W. W., & Rhodes, E. (1978). Measuring the efficiency of decision-making units. *European Journal of Operational Research*, *2*(6), 429–444. doi:10.1016/0377-2217(78)90138-8

Cherchye, L., Moesen, W., Rogge, N., & Puyenbroeck, T. V. (2007). An Introduction to 'Benefit of the Doubt' Composite indicators. *Social Indicators Research*, *82*(1), 111–145. doi:10.1007/s11205-006-9029-7

Despotis, D. K. (2005a). Measuring human development via data envelopment analysis: The case of Asia and the Pacific. *Omega*, *33*(5), 385–390. doi:10.1016/j.omega.2004.07.002

Despotis, D. K. (2005b). A Reassessment of the Human Development Index Via Data Envelopment Analysis. *The Journal of the Operational Research Society*, *56*(8), 969–980. doi:10.1057/palgrave. jors.2601927

Hagerty, M. R., & Land, K. C. (2007). Constructing Summary Indices of Quality of Life: A Model for the Effect of Heterogeneous Importance Weights. *Sociological Methods & Research*, *35*(4), 455–496. doi:10.1177/0049124106292354

Kendall, M. G. (1938). A New Measure of Rank Correlation. *Biometrika*, *30*(2), 81–93. doi:10.1093/ biomet/30.1-2.81

Klugman, J., Rodríguez, F., & Choi, H. J. (2011). The HDI 2010: New controversies, old critiques. *The Journal of Economic Inequality*, *9*(2), 249–288. doi:10.1007/s10888-011-9178-z

Leta, F. R., Mello, J. C. C. B. S., Gomes, E. G., & Meza, L. A. (2005). Métodos de melhora de ordenação em DEA aplicados à avaliação estática de tornos mecânicos. *Investigação Operacional*, *25*, 229–242.

Mahlberg, B., & Obersteiner, M. (2001). *Remeasuring the HDI by Data Envelopment Analysis. Interim Report*. Laxenburg: International Institute for Applied Systems Analysis.

Mariano, E. B., Sobreiro, V. A., & Rebelatto, D. A. N. (2015). Human development and data envelopment analysis: A structured literature review. *Omega*, *54*, 33–49. doi:10.1016/j.omega.2015.01.002

Melyn, W., & Moesen, W. (1991). Towards a synthetic indicator of macroeconomic performance: Unequal weighting when limited information is available. *Public Economics Research Papers*, *17*(1), 1–24.

Morse, S. (2014). Stirring the pot. Influence of changes in methodology of the Human Development Index on reporting by the press. *Ecological Indicators*, *45*, 245–254. doi:10.1016/j.ecolind.2014.04.023

Neumayer, E. (2012). Human development and sustainability. *J. Human Dev. Capabil*, *13*(4), 561–579. doi:10.1080/19452829.2012.693067

Taylor, J. M. G. (1987). Kendall's and Spearman's Correlation Coefficients in the Presence of a Blocking Variable. *Biometrics*, *43*(2), 409–416. doi:10.2307/2531822 PMID:3607205

Tofallis, C. (2013). An automatic-democratic approach to weight setting for the new human development index. *Journal of Population Economics*, *26*(4), 1325–1345. doi:10.1007/s00148-012-0432-x

Tone, K. (2001). A slack-based measure of efficiency in data envelopment analysis. *European Journal of Operational Research*, *130*(3), 498–509. doi:10.1016/S0377-2217(99)00407-5

United Nations Development Programme. (2015). *Human Development Index (HDI)*. Retrieved May 06, 2015, from: http://hdr.undp.org/en/content/human-development-index-hdi

Yamada, Y., Matui, T., & Sugiyama, M. (1994). New analysis of efficiency based on DEA. *Journal of the Operations Research Society of Japan*, *37*, 158–167.

Zhou, P., Ang, B. W., & Poh, K. L. (2007). A mathematical programming approach to constructing composite indicators. *Ecological Economics*, *62*(2), 291–297. doi:10.1016/j.ecolecon.2006.12.020

Zhou, P., Ang, B. W., & Zhou, D. Q. (2010). Weighting and Aggregation in Composite indicators Construction: A Multiplicative Optimization Approach. *Social Indicators Research*, *96*(1), 169–181. doi:10.1007/s11205-009-9472-3 PMID:19966916

ADDITIONAL READING

Bernini, C., Guizzardi, A., & Angelini, G. (2013). DEA-Like Model and Common Weights Approach for the Construction of a Subjective Community Well-Being Indicator. *Social Indicators Research*, *114*(2), 405–424. doi:10.1007/s11205-012-0152-3

Blancard, S., & Hoarau, J. F. (2013). A new sustainable human development indicator for small island developing states: A reappraisal from data envelopment analysis. *Economic Modelling*, *30*, 623–635. doi:10.1016/j.econmod.2012.10.016

Cherchye, L., Lovell, C. A. K., Moesen, W., & Puyenbroeck, T. V. (2007). One market, one number? A composite indicator assessment of EU internal market dynamics. *European Economic Review*, *51*(3), 749–779. doi:10.1016/j.euroecorev.2006.03.011

Cherchye, L., Moesen, W., Rogge, N., & Puyenbroeck, T. V. (2011). Constructing composite indicators with imprecise data: A proposal. *Expert Systems with Applications*, *38*(9), 10940–10949. doi:10.1016/j.eswa.2011.02.136

Cherchye, L., Moesen, W., Rogge, N., Puyenbroeck, T. V., Saisana, M., Saltelli, A., & Tarantola, S. et al. (2008). Creating Composite Indicators with DEA and Robustness Analysis: The case of the Technology Achievement Index. *The Journal of the Operational Research Society*, *59*(2), 239–251. doi:10.1057/palgrave.jors.2602445

Cooper, W. W., Seiford, L. M., & Tone, K. (2006). *Data Envelopment Analysis: A comprehensive text with models, applications, references and DEA-Solver software* (2nd ed.). New York: Springer.

Dobos, I., & Vörösmarty, G. (2014). Green supplier selection and evaluation using DEA-type composite indicators. *International Journal of Production Economics*, *157*, 273–278. doi:10.1016/j.ijpe.2014.09.026

Filippetti, A., & Peyrache, A. (2011). The patterns of technological capabilities of countries: A dual approach using Composite Indicators and Data Envelopment Analysis. *World Development*, *39*(7), 1108–1121. doi:10.1016/j.worlddev.2010.12.009

Fusco, E. (2015). Enhancing non-compensatory composite indicators: A directional proposal. *European Journal of Operational Research*, *242*(2), 620–630. doi:10.1016/j.ejor.2014.10.017

Gaaloul, H., & Khalfallah, S. (2014). Application of the ''Benefit-Of-the-Doubt'' Approach for the Construction of a Digital Access Indicator: A Revaluation of the ''Digital Access Index''. *Social Indicators Research*, *118*(1), 45–56. doi:10.1007/s11205-013-0422-8

Hatefi, S. M., & Torabi, S. A. (2010). A common weight MCDA– DEA approach to construct composite indicators. *Ecological Economics*, *70*(1), 114–120. doi:10.1016/j.ecolecon.2010.08.014

Kortelainen, M. (2008). Dynamic environmental performance analysis: A Malmquist index approach. *Ecological Economics*, *64*(4), 701–715. doi:10.1016/j.ecolecon.2007.08.001

Lee, H. S., Lin, K., & Fang, H. H. (2006). A Fuzzy Multiple Objective DEA for the Human Development Index. *Proceedings of the International Conference on Knowledge-Based and Intelligent Information and Engineering Systems: Lecture Notes In Artificial Intelligence* (vol. 4252, pp. 922-928). Bournemouth: Springer. doi:10.1007/11893004_118

Martinez, E. R. (2013). Social and Economic Wellbeing in Europe and the Mediterranean Basin: Building an Enlarged Human Development Indicator. *Social Indicators Research*, *111*(2), 527–547. doi:10.1007/s11205-012-0018-8

Martinez, E. R., Limon, J. A. G., & Tadeo, A. J. P. (2011). Ranking farms with a composite indicator of sustainability. *Agricultural Economics*, *42*(5), 561–575. doi:10.1111/j.1574-0862.2011.00536.x

Mizobuchi, H. (2014). Measuring World Better Life Frontier: A Composite Indicator for OECD Better Life Index. *Social Indicators Research*, *118*(3), 987–1007. doi:10.1007/s11205-013-0457-x

Organization for Economic Cooperation and Development, European Commission, Joint Research Centre. (2008). *Handbook on constructing composite indicators: Methodology and user guide*. Retrieved August 28, 2015, from http://www.oecd.org/std/42495745.pdf

Prasetyo, A. D., & Zuhdi, U. (2013). The Government Expenditure Efficiency towards the Human Development. *Procedia Economics and Finance*, *5*, 615–622. doi:10.1016/S2212-5671(13)00072-5

Rogge, N. (2012). Undesirable specialization in the construction of composite policy indicators: The Environmental Performance Index. *Ecological Indicators, 23,* 143–154. doi:10.1016/j.ecolind.2012.03.020

Sayed, H., Hamed, R., Ramadan, M. A. G., & Hosny, S. (2015). Using Meta-goal Programming for a New Human Development Indicator with Distinguishable Country Ranks. *Social Indicators Research, 123*(1), 1–27. doi:10.1007/s11205-014-0723-6

Serrano, M. D., & Blancas, F. J. (2011). A Gender Wellbeing Composite Indicator: The Best-Worst Global Evaluation Approach. *Social Indicators Research, 102*(3), 477–496. doi:10.1007/s11205-010-9687-3

Shen, Y., Hermans, E., Brijs, T., & Wets, G. (2013). Data Envelopment Analysis for Composite Indicators: A Multiple Layer Model. *Social Indicators Research, 114*(2), 739–756. doi:10.1007/s11205-012-0171-0

United Nations Development Programme. (2011). Uncertainty and Sensitivity Analysis of the Human Development Index. *Human Development Reports Research Paper.* Retrieved August 28, 2015, from http://hdr.undp.org/sites/default/files/hdrp_2010_47.pdf

Witte, K. D., & Rogge, N. (2010). To publish or not to publish? On the aggregation and drivers of research performance. *Scientometrics, 85*(3), 657–680. doi:10.1007/s11192-010-0286-5 PMID:21057573

Witte, K. D., Rogge, N., Cherchye, L., & Puyenbroeck, T. V. (2013). Economi es of scope in rese arch and teaching: A non-para metric investig ation. *Omega, 41*(2), 305–314. doi:10.1016/j.omega.2012.04.002

Wu, P. C., Fan, C. W., & Pan, S. C. (2014). Does Human Development Index Provide Rational Development Rankings? Evidence from Efficiency Rankings in Super Efficiency Model. *Social Indicators Research, 116*(2), 647–658. doi:10.1007/s11205-013-0285-z

Zanella, A., Camanho, A. S., & Dias, T. G. (2015). Undesirable outputs and weighting schemes in composite indicators based on data envelopment analysis. *European Journal of Operational Research, 245*(2), 517–530. doi:10.1016/j.ejor.2015.03.036

KEY TERMS AND DEFINITIONS

CI: Composite indicator is a set of indicators measuring many dimensions of a phenomenon, but these are aggregated into a single multidimensional composite indicator.

DEA: Data envelopment analysis is a nonparametric mathematical programming method used to measure the relative efficiency of DMUs considering a system with multiple inputs and outputs.

DMU: Decision Making Unit is the system that transforms inputs into outputs.

EDI: Educational Index is related to the dimension of education of the HDI and it is measured based on combined education and literacy rates of adults.

GDPI: Adjusted GDP Index is related to the dimension of standard of living of the HDI and it is measured based on gross national income per capita.

HDI: Human Development Index is a measure that summarizes the level of human development achieved by a country based on three dimensions (health, education and standard of living).

Inputs: Inputs are the material that will be transformed on a process (expressed in units or financial form), as the amount of raw material and costs, i.e. everything that the system receives from the outside to start the process.

LEI: Life Expectancy Index is related to the dimension of health of the HDI and it is measured based on life expectancy at birth.

Outputs: Outputs are the products of a transformation process, as the amount of final goods and profit, i.e. everything that is released by the system involving the process after conclusion.

SBM: Slack Based Measure is a non-oriented DEA model, where efficiency is calculated based on the slacks and the amounts of both inputs and outputs to be reduced or increased are not equiproportional, it is an average.

APPENDIX: TABLE OF THE HDI/DEA RANKINGS

Table 6. HDI/DEA rankings

Country/Model	HDI	Normalized Data and Virtual DMUs			Normalized Data without Virtual DMUs					Raw Data and Virtual DMUs					Raw Data without Virtual DMUs				
		CCR	GEO	SBM	CCR	INV	GEO	GINV	SBM	CCR	INV	GEO	GINV	SBM	CCR	INV	GEO	GINV	SBM
#Vmax	-	0	0	0	-	-	-	-	-	0	0	0	0	0	-	-	-	-	-
Norway	1	7	7	1	1	5	1	5	1	11	12	15	14	1	1	13	1	14	1
Australia	2	11	12	2	2	6	2	6	2	1	4	1	4	7	2	4	2	4	7
Switzerland	3	9	9	3	3	3	3	4	3	12	3	13	3	5	3	3	3	3	5
Netherlands	4	26	26	4	16	16	17	16	4	8	18	8	18	10	15	17	15	18	10
United States	5	21	21	5	22	26	22	28	5	39	36	39	36	4	4	35	4	36	4
Germany	6	28	27	6	21	17	21	18	6	24	21	25	20	9	5	19	5	21	8
New Zealand	7	25	25	7	11	21	11	20	7	2	2	2	16	23	6	16	6	16	22
Canada	8	20	20	8	17	12	16	10	8	20	13	21	13	14	19	14	20	12	14
Singapore	9	4	4	12	4	2	4	2	11	14	6	9	6	2	7	6	7	6	2
Denmark	10	40	40	9	31	28	31	29	9	34	34	37	34	13	34	33	31	34	12
Ireland	11	29	29	10	25	23	25	24	10	3	20	3	21	26	8	20	8	20	26
Sweden	12	16	16	11	13	7	13	7	12	18	10	18	11	15	20	11	19	10	15
Iceland	13	15	15	13	12	11	12	9	13	4	7	4	7	27	9	8	9	7	27
United Kingdom	14	31	32	14	26	24	26	25	14	28	25	26	24	21	25	23	27	25	21
Hong Kong, China (SAR)	15	8	8	18	5	1	5	1	17	10	2	11	2	11	10	2	10	2	11
Korea (Republic of)	16	19	19	15	18	19	18	19	15	19	14	20	12	28	21	12	21	13	28
Japan	17	6	6	16	6	4	6	3	16	9	1	10	1	22	11	1	11	1	23
Liechtenstein	18	1	1	20	7	8	7	15	19	5	28	5	28	3	12	29	12	30	3
Israel	19	18	18	17	15	18	15	17	18	17	9	19	10	30	18	9	18	11	29
France	20	17	17	19	19	13	19	11	20	16	11	17	9	24	22	10	22	9	24
Austria	21	24	24	22	24	14	24	14	22	22	16	23	17	16	26	15	25	17	16
Belgium	22	30	30	21	28	20	28	21	21	27	23	29	25	19	29	21	30	23	18
Luxembourg	23	10	10	24	23	10	23	12	24	25	24	27	22	6	23	22	24	24	6
Finland	24	32	31	23	29	22	29	23	23	26	22	28	23	25	27	24	28	22	25
Slovenia	25	39	39	25	33	33	33	34	25	37	33	36	33	33	33	32	33	33	32
Italy	26	13	13	26	14	9	14	8	26	13	5	14	5	31	17	5	17	5	30

continued on following page

Table 6. Continued

Country/Model	HDI	Normalized Data and Virtual DMUs			Normalized Data without Virtual DMUs					Raw Data and Virtual DMUs					Raw Data without Virtual DMUs				
		CCR	GEO	SBM	CCR	INV	GEO	GINV	SBM	CCR	INV	GEO	GINV	SBM	CCR	INV	GEO	GINV	SBM
Spain	27	14	14	27	20	15	20	13	27	15	8	16	8	32	16	7	16	8	33
Czech Republic	28	44	44	28	42	39	42	38	28	43	40	41	41	37	37	38	41	40	39
Greece	29	27	28	29	32	29	32	30	29	23	19	24	19	41	24	18	26	19	37
Brunei Darussalam	30	5	5	31	10	25	10	26	30	29	37	12	37	12	31	36	23	37	13
Qatar	31	2	2	33	8	27	8	27	31	6	38	6	38	8	13	37	13	38	9
Cyprus	32	37	37	30	37	31	37	31	32	36	32	34	32	36	35	31	34	32	35
Estonia	33	60	60	32	44	56	44	57	33	41	75	77	75	42	44	70	65	75	42
Saudi Arabia	34	22	22	36	35	38	35	40	36	61	57	59	57	18	56	55	52	57	19
Lithuania	35	51	51	35	34	72	34	80	35	40	103	58	104	40	30	99	40	104	41
Poland	36	54	54	34	53	45	53	47	34	55	52	53	52	45	52	50	49	52	47
Andorra	37	23	23	39	27	30	27	22	39	21	15	22	15	29	28	45	29	15	31
Slovakia	38	61	62	37	56	47	56	50	37	63	58	60	58	38	60	56	59	59	36
Malta	39	38	38	38	41	32	41	32	38	35	31	35	31	39	40	30	38	31	40
United Arab Emirates	40	12	11	43	30	36	30	36	40	51	47	48	47	17	49	44	43	47	17
Chile	41	35	34	41	38	35	40	35	42	31	26	31	27	50	36	26	35	27	52
Portugal	42	34	35	40	39	34	39	33	41	32	30	32	30	46	32	28	32	28	44
Hungary	43	75	75	42	64	57	65	58	43	77	74	76	71	48	69	67	72	72	49
Bahrain	44	52	52	45	52	40	52	39	44	52	49	50	48	34	55	47	54	49	34
Cuba	45	42	42	44	43	37	43	37	45	38	35	38	35	52	41	34	39	35	54
Kuwait	46	3	3	49	9	43	9	48	49	7	79	7	78	20	14	73	14	76	20
Croatia	47	50	50	46	50	41	50	44	46	50	46	47	46	54	53	43	51	46	56
Latvia	48	100	100	47	60	76	62	82	47	100	102	103	102	43	77	98	100	102	46
Argentina	49	56	56	48	55	49	55	51	48	47	53	54	53	58	54	51	50	53	59
Uruguay	50	49	49	52	54	42	54	45	52	49	45	46	45	61	46	42	46	45	60
Bahamas	51	66	65	51	66	52	66	54	50	67	63	66	64	51	67	61	68	64	48
Montenegro	52	73	72	50	68	61	68	62	51	71	68	69	69	69	70	65	70	67	71

continued on following page

Table 6. Continued

Country/Model	HDI	Normalized Data and Virtual DMUs			Normalized Data without Virtual DMUs					Raw Data and Virtual DMUs					Raw Data without Virtual DMUs				
		CCR	GEO	SBM	CCR	INV	GEO	GINV	SBM	CCR	INV	GEO	GINV	SBM	CCR	INV	GEO	GINV	SBM
Belarus	53	96	96	53	59	98	59	99	53	82	115	114	114	62	76	109	113	112	63
Romania	54	89	90	54	83	64	84	69	54	91	86	87	86	60	88	83	89	86	61
Libya	55	63	64	55	67	51	67	53	55	57	62	63	62	55	61	58	58	60	53
Oman	56	41	41	63	45	54	45	43	60	53	48	49	49	35	57	46	53	48	38
Russian Federation	57	98	98	56	85	102	85	107	56	129	127	127	127	47	66	122	115	124	43
Bulgaria	58	93	93	57	87	71	87	76	57	94	90	91	90	66	93	86	92	89	68
Barbados	59	62	61	58	65	59	64	59	58	62	59	61	59	73	63	57	63	58	73
Palau	60	106	106	59	92	87	95	89	59	104	100	101	100	74	42	95	61	100	78
Antigua and Barbuda	61	57	57	60	61	50	60	52	61	58	54	55	54	59	64	52	57	54	58
Malaysia	62	69	69	62	72	55	72	55	62	69	66	68	66	53	75	63	73	66	50
Mauritius	63	91	91	61	89	66	90	71	63	92	88	90	89	64	86	85	84	88	65
Trinidad and Tobago	64	79	79	64	98	91	97	94	64	119	114	115	115	44	117	110	117	113	45
Lebanon	65	33	33	68	36	46	36	42	67	30	27	30	26	70	38	25	36	26	69
Panama	66	46	47	66	48	48	48	46	66	45	42	43	42	67	48	48	45	42	67
Venezuela	67	74	74	65	78	60	78	61	65	78	71	74	74	65	78	69	78	70	64
Costa Rica	68	36	36	69	40	44	38	41	69	33	29	33	29	80	39	27	37	29	80
Turkey	69	65	66	70	70	58	70	56	70	65	61	62	61	63	68	60	66	62	62
Kazakhstan	70	111	110	67	105	109	105	111	68	114	135	135	135	56	120	127	134	129	57
Mexico	71	47	46	72	49	53	49	49	72	46	43	44	43	71	50	40	47	43	72
Seychelles	72	84	82	71	93	62	93	66	71	98	93	96	94	49	103	101	96	95	51
Saint Kitts and Nevis	73	92	92	76	97	63	98	67	75	93	89	89	88	57	96	84	91	87	55
Sri Lanka	74	80	81	73	79	81	79	83	76	80	77	79	79	96	82	74	82	77	98
Iran	75	83	84	74	88	70	88	74	73	85	81	83	81	78	83	77	81	82	79
Azerbaijan	76	118	118	75	114	95	114	96	74	116	111	112	111	68	105	107	107	109	70
Jordan	77	88	87	77	91	78	91	81	77	87	84	85	85	83	92	81	87	85	85
Serbia	78	82	83	79	86	77	86	79	78	84	80	81	80	84	89	76	85	80	86

continued on following page

Table 6. Continued

Country/Model	HDI	Normalized Data and Virtual DMUs			Normalized Data without Virtual DMUs					Raw Data and Virtual DMUs					Raw Data without Virtual DMUs				
		CCR	GEO	SBM	CCR	INV	GEO	GINV	SBM	CCR	INV	GEO	GINV	SBM	CCR	INV	GEO	GINV	SBM
Brazil	79	86	86	80	94	69	92	73	80	89	83	84	84	77	85	79	83	84	75
Georgia	80	81	80	81	74	88	74	88	81	81	78	80	77	114	43	72	64	78	114
Grenada	81	102	102	78	103	89	103	92	79	74	96	97	96	92	95	91	94	96	92
Peru	82	72	73	82	76	67	77	70	82	73	67	72	68	88	80	66	75	68	89
Ukraine	83	110	111	83	81	111	82	112	83	109	122	122	122	105	98	119	119	121	106
Belize	84	87	88	84	95	85	94	87	84	88	85	86	83	98	91	80	88	83	99
Macedonia	85	67	67	85	71	68	71	64	85	66	64	65	63	85	72	62	69	63	84
Bosnia and Herzegovina	86	55	55	87	58	65	58	60	86	56	51	52	51	100	59	49	56	51	100
Armenia	87	76	77	86	80	83	80	84	87	75	73	75	72	109	74	68	77	71	111
Fiji	88	121	121	88	106	108	108	109	88	83	116	116	116	112	104	112	116	114	112
Thailand	89	78	78	90	84	80	83	77	89	79	76	78	76	81	87	71	80	74	81
Tunisia	90	59	59	91	63	73	63	68	91	60	55	56	56	95	62	53	60	55	95
China	91	64	63	93	69	79	69	72	93	64	60	64	60	90	71	59	67	61	90
Saint Vincent and the Grenadines	92	105	105	89	108	92	107	93	90	103	99	100	99	93	107	94	102	99	94
Algeria	93	115	115	92	117	97	117	97	92	111	109	108	109	82	112	104	109	107	83
Dominica	94	45	45	96	47	74	47	63	96	44	41	42	40	104	47	41	44	41	104
Albania	95	48	48	97	51	75	51	65	97	48	44	45	44	102	51	100	48	44	103
Jamaica	96	94	94	94	99	90	99	90	94	95	91	92	91	108	97	87	93	90	109
Saint Lucia	97	71	71	95	77	82	76	78	95	72	69	70	67	101	81	64	76	69	102
Colombia	98	85	85	98	90	86	89	85	98	86	82	82	82	91	90	78	86	81	91
Ecuador	99	53	53	99	57	84	57	75	99	54	50	51	50	97	58	54	55	50	97
Suriname	100	114	114	101	115	96	115	95	100	112	108	109	108	75	114	105	110	106	74
Tonga	101	103	103	100	104	101	104	102	102	101	97	98	97	122	101	92	99	97	124
Dominican Republic	102	95	95	104	100	94	100	91	104	96	92	93	92	94	99	88	95	91	93
Maldives	103	43	43	106	46	93	46	86	105	42	39	40	39	103	45	39	42	39	101

continued on following page

Table 6. Continued

Country/Model	HDI	Normalized Data and Virtual DMUs			Normalized Data without Virtual DMUs					Raw Data and Virtual DMUs					Raw Data without Virtual DMUs				
		CCR	GEO	SBM	CCR	INV	GEO	GINV	SBM	CCR	INV	GEO	GINV	SBM	CCR	INV	GEO	GINV	SBM
Mongolia	104	135	134	103	132	113	132	116	103	115	131	130	130	107	119	123	128	126	107
Turkmenistan	105	139	139	102	139	119	139	123	101	139	139	139	139	86	139	134	139	135	88
Samoa	106	99	99	105	101	100	101	101	106	97	94	95	93	129	100	90	98	93	131
Palestine, State of	107	97	97	108	102	99	102	98	109	99	95	94	95	126	102	89	97	94	126
Indonesia	108	117	117	109	119	104	119	104	108	117	112	111	112	106	116	106	112	110	105
Botswana	109	123	123	107	129	122	129	126	107	143	143	143	143	76	144	137	143	139	76
Egypt	110	113	113	110	116	105	116	103	110	110	107	107	107	99	113	102	108	105	96
Paraguay	111	107	107	111	109	103	109	100	112	105	101	102	101	113	108	97	103	101	113
Gabon	112	120	120	112	122	127	122	131	111	148	146	146	147	72	146	139	147	141	66
Bolivia	113	137	137	113	135	124	135	124	113	133	132	132	132	120	132	126	132	127	123
Moldova	114	126	126	114	123	115	123	118	114	122	120	119	119	128	122	115	121	117	129
El Salvador	115	104	104	118	107	107	106	106	117	102	98	99	98	115	106	93	101	98	115
Uzbekistan	116	131	131	115	127	117	127	120	115	128	126	126	126	125	126	121	127	123	125
Philippines	117	127	127	116	126	112	126	113	116	124	121	121	121	116	125	117	123	119	117
South Africa	118	138	138	117	133	147	133	149	118	154	168	168	168	87	145	154	168	160	87
Syrian Arab Republic	119	77	76	119	82	106	81	105	119	76	72	73	73	121	84	82	79	73	120
Iraq	120	122	122	121	121	128	121	121	121	120	117	117	117	89	121	132	118	116	82
Guyana	121	143	143	120	143	125	143	127	120	138	137	138	138	118	137	133	137	132	119
Viet Nam	122	58	58	123	62	110	61	108	122	59	56	57	55	132	65	75	62	56	133
Cape Verde	123	68	68	125	73	114	73	110	124	68	65	67	65	124	73	103	71	65	122
Micronesia (Federated States of)	124	124	124	122	124	120	124	122	123	121	118	118	118	139	123	114	120	120	139
Guatemala	125	108	108	127	110	123	110	119	127	106	104	104	103	117	109	116	104	103	116
Kyrgyzstan	126	134	135	124	134	131	134	133	126	131	129	129	129	143	133	125	130	130	143
Namibia	127	146	146	126	145	130	145	132	125	142	142	142	142	110	143	136	142	137	108
Timor-Leste	128	133	133	128	137	133	137	129	128	132	130	131	131	111	134	124	131	125	110

continued on following page

Table 6. Continued

Country/Model	HDI	Normalized Data and Virtual DMUs			Normalized Data without Virtual DMUs					Raw Data and Virtual DMUs					Raw Data without Virtual DMUs				
		CCR	GEO	SBM	CCR	INV	GEO	GINV	SBM	CCR	INV	GEO	GINV	SBM	CCR	INV	GEO	GINV	SBM
Honduras	129	90	89	130	96	118	96	115	130	90	87	88	87	138	94	96	90	92	138
Morocco	130	116	116	131	118	129	118	125	129	113	110	110	110	119	115	108	111	108	118
Vanuatu	131	112	112	129	113	116	113	114	131	108	106	106	106	151	111	120	106	115	151
Nicaragua	132	70	70	133	75	121	75	117	132	70	70	71	70	136	79	111	74	79	136
Kiribati	133	125	125	132	125	126	125	128	133	123	119	120	120	152	124	118	122	128	152
Tajikistan	134	136	136	134	138	134	138	134	134	134	133	133	133	156	131	128	133	136	156
India	135	141	141	135	141	135	141	135	135	136	136	136	136	132	136	129	136	131	132
Bhutan	136	130	130	138	130	137	131	136	138	126	125	124	125	127	128	140	126	138	127
Cambodia	137	109	109	137	111	132	111	130	137	107	105	105	105	148	110	113	105	111	148
Ghana	138	159	159	136	159	141	159	141	136	159	157	157	157	141	160	141	157	145	141
Lao People's Democratic Republic	139	129	129	141	131	138	130	138	141	127	124	125	124	137	129	135	125	122	137
Congo	140	169	169	139	168	144	168	145	139	167	164	165	165	134	166	147	165	154	134
Zambia	141	171	171	140	163	150	163	150	140	145	167	167	167	146	152	150	166	155	146
Bangladesh	142	119	119	143	120	136	120	137	143	118	113	113	113	153	118	131	114	118	153
Sao Tome and Principe	143	142	142	142	142	139	142	139	142	137	138	137	137	145	138	130	138	134	145
Equatorial Guinea	144	101	101	144	112	163	112	165	144	179	177	177	177	77	177	169	177	169	77
Nepal	145	128	128	146	128	140	128	140	146	125	123	123	123	159	127	138	124	133	159
Pakistan	146	140	140	149	140	145	140	142	149	135	134	134	134	135	135	152	135	143	135
Kenya	147	156	156	145	156	142	156	143	145	156	154	154	154	158	156	143	154	149	158
Swaziland	148	165	165	147	166	176	167	178	147	178	186	186	186	127	180	176	186	178	128
Angola	149	162	162	148	165	169	164	170	148	177	179	179	179	123	178	170	179	171	121
Myanmar	150	144	144	150	144	148	144	146	150	140	140	140	140	140	140	145	140	140	140
Rwanda	151	147	147	153	147	143	147	144	153	144	144	144	144	169	142	146	144	147	171
Cameroon	152	178	178	151	176	162	177	162	151	173	173	173	173	155	173	161	173	165	155
Nigeria	153	168	168	152	172	165	172	168	152	180	178	178	178	131	179	168	178	170	130

continued on following page

321

Table 6. Continued

Country/Model	HDI	Normalized Data and Virtual DMUs			Normalized Data without Virtual DMUs					Raw Data and Virtual DMUs					Raw Data without Virtual DMUs				
		CCR	GEO	SBM	CCR	INV	GEO	GINV	SBM	CCR	INV	GEO	GINV	SBM	CCR	INV	GEO	GINV	SBM
Yemen	154	150	150	159	150	157	150	156	156	149	148	149	149	142	150	151	149	148	142
Madagascar	155	145	145	155	146	146	146	147	155	141	141	141	141	173	141	144	141	146	174
Zimbabwe	156	164	164	156	164	153	165	155	157	163	161	161	161	175	163	156	161	161	175
Papua New Guinea	157	153	153	160	153	154	153	153	158	152	151	151	151	157	153	148	151	144	157
Solomon Islands	158	132	132	162	136	149	136	148	164	130	128	128	128	170	130	142	129	142	172
Comoros	159	161	161	158	161	151	161	152	160	160	159	159	159	167	158	160	158	159	167
Tanzania (United Republic of)	160	158	157	157	158	152	158	151	159	158	156	156	156	162	159	149	156	153	163
Mauritania	161	157	158	163	157	160	157	159	162	157	155	155	155	150	157	158	155	150	149
Lesotho	162	181	181	154	179	174	179	175	154	181	185	185	185	149	181	174	185	176	150
Senegal	163	149	149	164	149	156	149	154	163	147	147	147	146	159	148	155	146	151	160
Uganda	164	167	167	161	169	155	169	157	161	165	163	163	163	172	165	157	163	163	173
Benin	165	166	166	165	167	159	166	160	165	164	162	162	162	164	164	159	162	157	164
Sudan	166	154	154	170	154	166	154	163	169	153	152	152	152	145	154	166	152	158	144
Togo	167	173	173	166	173	164	173	166	166	169	169	169	169	177	169	167	169	168	177
Haiti	168	151	151	167	151	158	151	158	167	150	149	148	148	165	149	162	148	156	165
Afghanistan	169	160	160	168	160	161	160	161	168	161	158	158	158	161	161	153	159	152	161
Djibouti	170	155	155	171	155	167	155	164	171	155	153	153	153	148	155	171	153	167	147
Côte d'Ivoire	171	182	182	169	182	172	182	173	170	183	181	181	181	154	183	173	181	173	154
Gambia	172	170	170	172	170	170	170	169	172	166	165	164	164	166	167	165	164	164	166
Ethiopia	173	148	148	173	148	168	148	167	173	146	145	145	145	176	147	163	145	162	176
Malawi	174	176	176	174	177	171	176	172	174	172	172	172	172	185	172	172	172	172	185
Liberia	175	163	163	176	162	173	162	171	176	162	160	160	160	183	162	164	160	166	183
Mali	176	177	177	175	178	177	178	174	175	174	174	174	174	171	174	175	174	174	170
Guinea-Bissau	177	179	179	178	180	179	180	177	178	175	175	175	175	180	175	177	175	175	180
Mozambique	178	184	184	177	184	181	184	181	177	184	182	182	182	181	184	179	182	179	181

continued on following page

322

Table 6. Continued

Country/Model	HDI	Normalized Data and Virtual DMUs			Normalized Data without Virtual DMUs					Raw Data and Virtual DMUs					Raw Data without Virtual DMUs				
		CCR	GEO	SBM	CCR	INV	GEO	GINV	SBM	CCR	INV	GEO	GINV	SBM	CCR	INV	GEO	GINV	SBM
Guinea	179	175	175	180	175	180	175	179	179	171	171	171	171	179	171	180	171	180	179
Burundi	180	180	180	179	181	175	181	176	180	176	176	176	176	184	176	178	176	177	184
Burkina Faso	181	174	174	182	174	182	174	182	182	170	170	170	170	174	170	181	170	181	169
Eritrea	182	152	152	184	152	178	152	180	184	151	150	150	150	178	151	182	150	182	178
Sierra Leone	183	187	187	181	187	186	187	186	181	187	187	187	187	163	187	183	187	186	162
Chad	184	183	183	183	183	184	183	183	183	182	180	180	180	168	182	184	180	184	168
Central African Republic	185	185	185	185	185	183	185	184	185	185	183	183	183	186	186	185	183	185	186
Congo (Democratic Republic of the)	186	186	186	186	186	185	186	185	186	186	184	184	184	187	185	186	184	186	187
Niger	187	172	172	187	171	187	171	187	187	168	166	166	166	182	168	187	167	187	182
#Vmin	-	188	188	188	-	-	-	-	-	188	188	188	188	188	-	-	-	-	-

Chapter 14
Statistical Approach for Ranking OECD Countries Based on Composite *GICSES* Index and I–Distance Method

Maja Mitrović
University of Belgrade, Serbia

Maja Marković
University of Belgrade, Serbia

Stefan Zdravković
University of Belgrade, Serbia

ABSTRACT

This chapter will explore the impact of cognitive skills on education. In the case of OECD (Organisation for Economic Co-operation and Development) countries, it will be examined the relation between the level of education to the economic situation of a state. Case study work is based on a statistical approach of OECD countries ranking, based on The Global Index of Cognitive Skills and Educational Attainment (GICSES) and Ivanovic distance (I-distance). The chapter will be presented to rank these countries based on the value of the global index. Using I-distance method it will be formed a new order, and then it will be carried out a comparative analysis of these two ways of ranking. The aim of the chapter is to present a new approach to the evaluation of a composite indicator based on the multivariate statistical analysis.

DOI: 10.4018/978-1-5225-0714-7.ch014

INTRODUCTION

There were, throughout history, many theories about the reforms which lead to the economic growth in general (Scully, 2014). Besides changes in government and politics, a lot of different factors influenced some countries to became world powers and others to still be in a developing state (Balcerowicz, 2014; Aghion & Durlauf, 2005). Some of the newer factors that also happened to benefit economic growth are knowledge and education (Machlup, 2014).

The importance of education is on the list of priorities for economic development and progress in every country (Carlson, 1999). As shown in numerous studies (Benos & Zotou, 2014), education correlates with economic growth. In addition to being based on the adoption of series of rules and social values acquired through schooling, education reflects in knowledge and skills. By analyzing the economic outcomes, The Organisation for Economic Co-operation and Development (*OECD*) estimates that better skills lead to the economic growth in a half of the developing countries in the last decade (*OECD*, 2013). The difference is that the developing nations build their national infrastructures and create rewarding skilled jobs because current education systems are often proven to be inadequate (Lee & Chung, 2015). Success lies in having students learn basic cognitive skills which affect labor markets and aid economic growth substantially. World's leading countries represent a learning model for other countries, regarding learning outcomes (Koraneekij & Khlaisang, 2015), performance improvement (Nuchwana, 2012), and student's satisfaction (Aziz et al., 2012). The goal of these efforts is to make a contribution on how to improve teaching, learning, and the performance of the education systems (Gudeva et al., 2012). From another point of view, Bowles and Gintis (2011) insist that higher levels of education and economic success (income) tend to go together. Intellectual skills and the skills developed or validated in the schools give only a small causal contribution to the economic progress of the people (Bowles et al., 2001).

For many indices, education is just a part of the measurement. For example, Human Development Index (*HDI*) includes *School life expectancy* of children of school-entrance age and *Mean years of schooling* of adults as its new educational indicator (Hidalgo, 2010). Better life index (*BLI*) has identified Education as essential to comparing well-being across the countries (Lind, 2014). Just a few indices measure the real influence of the education output on the economic growth. One of them is The Efficiency Index that demonstrates which inputs funded by the governments substantially make a difference, and how countries are combining these inputs to produce the best educational outcomes (Dolton, Marcenaro-Gutiérrez & Still, 2014). However, the main limitation of the previously mentioned approaches is that they consider only one measurement for evaluation of the educational performance.

One of the potential alternative measures of the education output is Global Index of Cognitive Skills and Educational Attainment (*GICSES*), created by The Economist Intelligence Unit (*EIU*). The *GICSES* is a composite index that analyzes member countries of the *OECD* and ranks them based on the value of the global index using z-score normalization method. The *GICSES* contains comparative data divided into two categories: *Cognitive Skills (CS)* and *Educational Attainment (EA)*. It measures more than just the education output to determine if a country is making economic growth through it (Petrosillo et al., 2013). *GICSES* explores the concepts of cognitive science and cognitive skills, the way education is viewed through the term of a learning curve, and how these terms are related. Pearson learning curve leads to greater efficiency, emphasizing the importance of the outputs of all products and services, in order to safely contribute to an efficient education system performance in the 21st century (Waldron & Kaminer, 2004).

In order to understand the ranking, it is necessary to focus on the notion of the composite index (Amdt et al., 2013; Guttorp & Kim, 2013; Saisana et al., 2011). As an instrument for comparing the effects between countries, the composite has become predominantly frequent (Saisana & Tarantola, 2002; Saisana & D'Hombres, 2008). It is used to synthesize information included in the selected set of indicators and variables (Paruolo et al., 2013), as well as to measure a multi-criteria performance. The result is a composite index of outcomes that indicates the relative state performance set of selected countries (Brügermann & Patil, 2011).

It is important to choose the right methodology to capture and summarize all of the interactions among the individually included indicators (Saisana & Tarantola, 2002; Saisana & D'Hombres, 2008), in order to create an appropriate composite index. New literature on methodology and improvements in composites is being published every month (Benito & Romera, 2011). Improvement of the composite index results in the quality enhancement. The composite index improvement depends, not only on the quality of the methods of proper theoretical basis but also on the data (Saisana et al., 2011). It should be mentioned that, besides choosing the appropriate indicators, it is necessary to assign a weight to each indicator, based on its impact on education. Therefore, a composite index represents only the size of similarities (Saltelli 2007; Paruolo et al., 2013), which often leads to an unstable assessment. Results and values of the composite index significantly depend on the indicator weights and are often the subject of controversy (Paruolo et al., 2013; Salteli, 2007). In the majority of the existing approaches, the final rank is calculated as an average of all obtained values, which is one of the biggest shortcomings.

The *GICSES* is also based on the equally important indicators, and country's overall rank is calculated as an average of all obtained values. To reduce subjectivity and to improve the ranking method, the authors applied the I-distance methodology on the GICSES values and in that way created new ranks. The I-distance methodology presents a metric distance in an n-dimensional space. The approach was originally defined by Ivanovic (Ivanovic, 1977). Initially, he devised this method to rank the countries according to their development level based on several indicators, which is one of the perks of the proposed method. One of the principal issues was how to incorporate them all into a single index. This was successfully implemented in many studies (Jeremic, 2012; Dobrota et al., 2015; Dobrota et al., 2016).

By employing the I-distance method, we will be able to point out potential shortcomings of subjectively chosen weighting factors of *GICSES* ranking methodology. Then, we will compare the rankings of the *OECD* countries obtained using the *GICSES* and the I-distance method. With the obtained results, it will be possible to penetrate the essential components of the dynamics of ranking countries, with the aim of determining the reasons for the appearance of differences in ratings. In this regard, we applied the I-distance method through seven iterations, to present the most significant indicators that have the strongest influence on the rank formation. In the end, we compared the *GICSES* ranks with the I-distance ranks for carefully chosen countries.

The paper is organized as follows. Firstly, the fundamental concept of the *GICSES* index is described. The I-distance method will be elaborated in detail in Section 2 – Methodology. Discussion in Section 3 has three parts: first part emphasizes the differences in rankings based on the initial category set used both in *GICSES* and I-distance methodology; second part presents the results and differences in ranking before and after the variable (indicators) ejection and the third part summarizes the rankings obtained through the I-distance method. The concluding remarks are presented in the final chapter.

EMPIRICAL EXAMPLE

GICSES is the index, which shows economic prosperity of a country through the school system's treatment. As well as an overall rank, the *GICSES* provides separate standings for *CS* and *EA*. For the *CS* category, the composite index is based on the latest data retrieved from the Programme for International Student Assessment *(PISA)*, Trends in International Mathematics and Science Study (*TIMSS*) and Progress in International Reading Literacy Study *(PIRLS*) databases. For the *EA* category, the literacy rate is based on upper secondary and tertiary, University level.

For the entire European Union (EU) and many other countries, *PISA* data are used as indicators for assessing and monitoring progress in efficiency, equity and quality of education (European Commission, 2010). Indicators should provide adequate measurements of the developments in the area they are designed for – from educational reporting to tools for self-evaluation in individual schools (Rode & Michelsen, 2008).

Viewing the structure of GICSES in Table 1, we can see which indicators are used for the CS and EA categories, means and standard deviations used for z-score normalization process, as well as their Category weights and the overall GICSES weight.

The overall index score is the weighted sum of the underlying category scores. Within the CS GICSES it is calculated by the following formula: two-thirds go to CS plus one-third to EA. Because of this, the greater impact on the final score is given for CS category. Within the CS category, the Grade 8 tests' score considers for 60% while the Grade 4 tests' score considers for 40% (Reading, Maths, and Science all account for equal weights). Likewise, the category scores are the weighted sum of the underlying indicator scores. Each indicator score is calculated on the basis of a z-score normalization process. A z-score indicates how many standard deviations an observation is above or below the mean. To compute the z-score, each indicator's mean and standard deviation should be calculated using the

Table 1. Indicators and main categories

Category	Indicator		Mean	Standard Deviation	Category Weight	*GICSES* Weight
Cognitive skills	Grade 8 (*PISA* results)	Overall reading literacy	485	41		
		Mathematics literacy	481	49		
		Science literacy	488	44	0,6	
	Grade 8 (*TIMSS* results)	Mathematics Achievement	511	52		
		Science Achievement	513	44		2/3
	Grade 4 (*PIRLS* results)	Reading Literacy Achievement	507	59		
	Grade 4 (*TIMSS* results)	Mathematics Achievement	483	54	0,4	
		Science Achievement	488	50		
Educational attainment	*OECD* results	Literacy rate (15 and over), %	98	2	0,33	
		Graduation rate at upper secondary level	79	16	0,33	1/3
		Graduation rate at tertiary level	38	12	0,33	

data for the countries, followed by the distance of the observation from the mean in terms of standard deviations (Unit, 2014).

Indicators Descriptions

Overall Reading Literacy

In the *PISA* project, it was adopted that "reading literacy is understanding, using and reflecting on written texts in order to achieve personal goals, develop skills and potential and to participate in community life" (OECD, 2013). The concept relies on cognitive concepts that emphasize the interactive nature and constructivist, creative nature of the process of understanding. Cognitivists believe that the meaning of the text is constructed in the interaction between the text and the reader (Thomson et al., 2013).

Reading literacy plays an important role, starting with the individual aspirations of obtaining qualifications or finding a job, to less concrete, such as encountering the challenges of modern society with the aim of enriching the quality of life (Baucal & Pavlovic Babic, 2010).

Mathematics Literacy

Mathematical literacy focuses on solving problems in the real world and involves the integration of creativity and knowledge of mathematical terminology, facts, and mathematical methods, as well as the skills necessary to perform certain operations and the usage of certain methods of responding to the demands imposed on the external situation (OECD, 2009). It is stated in three important research that the comparative analysis report on the mathematics literacy concept is the assessment of the contents (Neidorf et al., 2006).

Science Literacy

Scientific literacy involves the possession of scientific knowledge and its application in identifying scientific issues, acquiring new knowledge, explaining scientific phenomena and drawing evidence-based conclusions about relevant science issues. The primary purpose is to understand the world we live in and contribution to decision-making, concerning nature and man's relationship with it (OECD, 2009). The students are expected to understand the nature of science-based knowledge.

Mathematics, Science, and Reading Achievement

Since 1960, the relative score of the average achievement on state tests has begun to have a significant impact on the development of the education national policy. The political responsibility of the EU Member States is to reduce the scale of small results (achievements). Guidelines for education should be carefully applied to some important factors that are not in the area of development education policy, which affects the success and usually differ from country to country (Mullis et al., 2012).

The *TIMSS* and *PIRLS* achievement scales summarize students' performance on large numbers of test items designed to measure the level of understanding and cognitive processing in mathematics, science, and reading, respectively. At each grade, the achievement results are reported in the mathematics, science, and reading achievement scales, each with a range of 0—1,000. Students' performance typically ranges between 300 and 700 (Data et al., 2013).

Graduation Rate (Upper Secondary Level and Tertiary Level)

"Graduation rates refer to the total number of graduates (the graduates may be of any age) at the specified level of education divided by the population at the typical graduation age from the specified level." In many countries, defining a typical age of graduation is difficult, because graduates are dispersed over a wide range of ages (OECD, 2002).

Graduation rates added value in assessing the impact of the national educational system. There is a universal recognition that national education systems have a goal for their citizens to acquire educational qualifications, particularly at the secondary level. Moreover, common sense suggests that a graduation rate can be a simple, standard measure that is easy to calculate.

METHODOLOGY

For a selected set of variables $X^T = \left(X_1, X_2, ..., X_k \right)$ that are chosen to explain the objects, the I-distance between the two entities and $e_r = \left(x_{1r}, x_{2r}, ..., x_{kr} \right)$ and $e_s = \left(x_{1s}, x_{2s}, ..., x_{ks} \right)$ is defined as

$$D(r,s) = \sum_{i=1}^{k} \frac{\left| d_i(r,s) \right|}{\sigma_i} \prod_{j=1}^{i-1} \left(1 - r_{ji.12...j-1} \right) \tag{1}$$

where $d_i = (r,s)$ is the distance between the values of available X_i for e_r and e_s, e.g. the discriminating effect,

$$d_i(r,s) = x_{ir} - x_{is} \ i \in \left\{ 1, ...k \right\} \tag{2}$$

σ_i the standard deviation of X_i, and $r_{ji.12...j-1}$ is a partial coefficient of the correlation between X_i and X_j, $(j < i)$ (Radojicic et al., 2012; Jeremic et al., 2013). It should be mentioned that the negative coefficient of correlation can occur when it is impossible to achieve the same direction of variables. In order to overcome the problem, it is appropriate to use the square I-distance (Jeremic et al., 2011). It is given as:

$$D^2(r,s) = \sum_{i-1}^{k} \frac{d_i^2(r,s)}{\sigma_i^2} \prod_{j=1}^{i-1} \left(1 - r_{ji.12...j-1}^2 \right) \tag{3}$$

The I-distance method is based on calculating distances between the entities being processed, which are later compared to one another in order to generate a rank (Seke et al., 2013). Also, it is necessary to fix one object as a reference. The ranking of objects in the set is formed according to the calculated distance from the referent object (Jovanovic et al., 2012).

RESULTS AND DISCUSSION

As previously explained, our approach to scrutinize the *GICSES* is multiple. Firstly, we applied the I-distance method on the indicators of each category to show the differences in rankings based on the initial category set used both in *GICSES* and the I-distance method. Secondly, the most significant indicators will be presented, as well as the change in ranks, as a result of the least important indicators ejection. Third part summarizes the rankings obtained through the I-distance value. Using the I-distance method a new order will be formed, and consequently, a comparative analysis of these two ways of ranking will be shown. Statistical methods and techniques used in the analysis, as well as procedures for the successful implementation of these methods, will be explained in the following.

The analysis shown in Table 2 was conducted on the official *Pearson Learning Curve* dataset for the year 2014 (Pearson, 2014). The dataset was incomplete for *EA* category, so we were able to analyze all 40 countries covered by the index for *CS* category. If the latest data for specific Indicators are five years older compared to the most recently available data, then those data will not be included in analyzes.

The best ranked countries are Singapore, Korea, Hong Kong, and Japan. It is interesting to note that the biggest positive change in ranks occurs in Switzerland, Israel, and Italy, which, according to the I-distance methodology take up to seven places higher rank in relation with ranking in *GICSES* index. By contrast, Ireland worsened its ranking by eight positions, and it's followed by France, which has a negative rank change of five positions. Other 14 countries have the same ranking in both comparisons.

Comparing the two methods of ranking, "Asian countries" do not have any change in ranks. As they are "Confucian" education nations, their education systems exhibit a unique developmental dynamics (Marginson, 2011).

Due to the public policies on educational financing in Singapore (Khan, 2001) and other political ethics (Englehart, 2000), the parents of students could play a significant role. They will always support the child during the course of education. It is not surprising if one takes into account the level of tuition fees. Statistically speaking, 97% of children are attending school in Singapore; more than in South Korea and Hong Kong (which rank just behind Singapore) with a 90% share respectively (Cheung et al., 2011). Whatever the reason is, parents are allowed to become part of the tuition fees system, so the education of students is directly dependent on the number of hours spent in the education system, which is covered by tuition (Liu et al., 2005; Albright & Luke, 2010).

Morris and Adamson (2010) argued that a change occurred when the Confucian system was implemented for young learners instead of adults. That was the beginning of the pressure, faced by Hong Kong families, which has increased in a competitive society. There is so-called shadow education system of supplementary tutoring. Families with adequate incomes have provided additional classes for their children, as a way of giving them extra help to keep up with their peers. Among the ingredients shaping demand in Hong Kong are social competition in an urban environment and a Confucian-style work ethic that emphasizes effort (Bray, 2011).

On the other hand, Education development in Korea is well aligned with economic development thanks to government policy initiatives. Korean higher education and economic development mutually reinforce one another. That means that the well trained human resources accelerated the economic productivity

Table 2. Ranks obtained by the I-distance, GICSES ranking, and changes in ranking (Category - CS)

Country	Category Cognitive Skills						
	I-Distance	*GICSES*	**Change in Ranks**	**Country**	**I-Distance**	*GICSES*	**Change in Ranks**
Singapore	1	1	0	Austria	21	22	1
Korea	2	2	0	Czech Republic	22	20	-2
Hong Kong	3	3	0	France	23	18	-5
Japan	4	4	0	Sweden	24	25	1
Russia	5	9	4	New Zealand	25	21	-4
Finland	6	5	-1	Portugal	26	26	0
Israel	7	14	7	Slovakia	27	29	2
Canada	8	6	-2	Norway	28	27	-1
USA	9	11	2	Spain	29	28	-1
United Kingdom	10	8	-2	Bulgaria	30	30	0
Netherlands	11	7	-4	Romania	31	31	0
Australia	12	13	1	Turkey	32	32	0
Hungary	13	19	6	Greece	33	33	0
Germany	14	12	-2	Thailand	34	35	1
Belgium	15	15	0	Chile	35	34	-1
Switzerland	16	23	7	Colombia	36	36	0
Italy	17	24	7	Indonesia	37	37	0
Ireland	18	10	-8	Mexico	38	38	0
Denmark	19	17	-2	Brazil	39	39	0
Poland	20	16	-4	Argentina	40	40	0

Figure 1. I-distance rank and GICSES index rank for the category cognitive skills

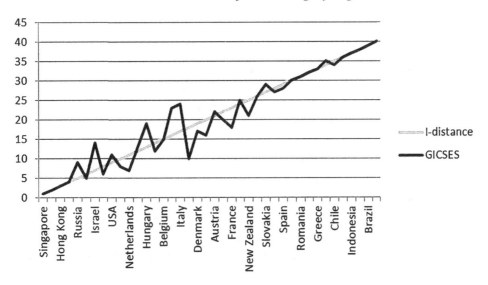

so that economic development can generate resources to invest in higher education development. The demand for education and the policy response were interrelated and encouraged upward development from elementary to graduate education (Shin, 2012).

In the previous graph, we can see a comparative view of the two methods of ranking based on the development of *CS*. What we can see is that the oscillations and deviations of *GICSES* method from I-distance method, watching the first four and the last five countries, do not exist. In other analyzed cases, oscillations are either negligible or considerably large. Based on the previous, the better-ranked countries, or those with higher literacy rate in observed areas, are also ranked in both methods. The influence of subjectively formed weight coefficients is observed in countries with the greatest fluctuation in range.

Hanushek and Woessmann (2012) said that variations in cognitive skills can arise from various influences - families, culture, health, and ability. Results indicate that schools and, institutional structures of school systems, are one way of improvement that is available to policymakers. There is a dynamic complementary of investments such that further schooling has a larger impact on skills if it builds on a wider base developed earlier (Cunha & Heckman, 2007).

Switzerland shows, on average, the highest level of professionalism associated with part-year of schooling at the secondary level (Bieber & Martens, 2011). It also shows the sharpest difference in average for each year of education after high school (Mak & Kennedy, 2012). The percentage of adults who have completed high school is 50% while 37% of them are university educated (Italy 42/16%, Israel 38/46%), which is 4% higher than the average in the *OECD* member states (*OECD* 44/33%). In Switzerland, even 15.9% of public expenditure is used to contribute the education, more than in Italy (8.62%) and Israel (13.46%). Israel occupies the highest rank due to the influence of the percentage of adult education and under the influence of other indicators that are included in the ranking. Also, the education system in Israel consists of five main types of schools (Friedler & Tamir, 1990). Public education includes religious schools - both same-sex institutions and separate classes for girls and boys at coeducational schools (Avissar, 2012; Tsameret & Zameret, 2012). Friedler and Tamir (1990) found considerable differences between male and female high school students. Feniger (2011) shows the difference between boys and girls in Israel education system and how it is connected with achievement in math and science.

On the other hand, Italy shows that the impact of different characteristics, such as family, university inputs and the labor market affect the time taken to get a degree. Comprehensive policy intervention is needed to increase the number of students graduating within the minimum period (Aina et al., 2011).

Ireland (Moloney, 2010) has a significant change in the ranking due to many reasons. As children acquire language skills in the early stages of life, their cognitive skills are progressing and allowing easier adoption of other materials in the same language. This directly affects the absorption of the curriculum in mathematics, as well as the development of skills for solving problems (Mak & Kennedy, 2012; Kernan & Devine, 2010). Keane (2011) in his study suggests the need for significant system-wide change, assessment, and teacher and academic staff development for future development of education.

As already mentioned, one of the primary goals of this chapter is to present a new approach to rank the *OECD* countries. The I-distance method uses the same indicator set and puts them in a particular order of importance using Pearson correlation coefficient, which is calculated to determine the significance of input indicators for I-distance value of each variable. However, the I-distance method gives more insight of those indicators which have higher Pearson correlation coefficient, instead giving the same importance to indicators based on the same weights in original *GICSES* methodology. That allows a better understanding of the results of ranking, as well as a better understanding of the difference between the comparisons of these rankings.

For this purpose, it is necessary to establish the order of importance of indicators. From Table 3 it can be seen that the most influential indicator is *Achievement in mathematics* for students in the Grade 8. What has the most impact on this indicator are home conditions in which the students work (whether the parents are educated, how often is the television watched), as well as the characteristics of the state, including demographic characteristics, public expenditure on education, and education system organization (Beaton et al., 1996).

It can be concluded from Table 3 that all indicators are important for the ranking because the correlation coefficients are greater than 0.5. Also, achievements have more significant impact than the literacy. The reason is that, although the success in education depends on the adoption and demonstration of cognitive skills, the effect at the end is influenced by other factors.

The role of metacognition in education, particularly in mathematics, is significant, which is directly connected with students' achievements. Numerous intervention studies have demonstrated that "standard" learners, as well as those with extraordinarily low mathematics performance, do substantially better from metacognitive instruction procedures (Schneider & Artelt, 2010).

Variables Ejection: Model Improvement

In the first iteration, all indicators are used. The I-distance methodology rank is based on their values. In the second iteration, indicators of less importance are ejected from the study and the new ranking is based on the values of remaining indicators. Following the same principle, in each subsequent iteration, the least important indicators will be selected for ejection. Finally, we came to the last, 7th iteration, where the states are ranked considering just two indicators (with the highest coefficient of determination). Next iteration would lead to a situation where the model would not be improved because the determination coefficient becomes smaller. Accordingly, in the 7th iteration, indicators exclusion stops.

Table 4 represents changes in ranks of the OECD countries between the first and the last iteration. In the top 10 countries, Singapore and Korea changed their places, as well as Finland and Israel, while

Table 3. Correlation coefficients for the indicators in the category cognitive skills obtained by the I-distance methodology

Indicators Cognitive Skills	r
TIMSS - Achievement in mathematics, Grade 8	0.968
TIMSS - Achievement in mathematics, Grade 4	0.880
TIMSS – Science achievement, Grade 8	0.868
PISA - Mathematics literacy, Grade 8	0.847
TIMSS - Science achievement, Grade 4	0.804
PISA – Science literacy, Grade 8	0.803
PISA – Reading literacy, Grade 8	0.797
PIRLS – Reading achievement, Grade 4	0.687

Table 4. I-distance methodology iterations, change in ranks between first and last iteration

Country	I-Distance Iterations for the Category Cognitive Skills				
	1st Iteration	**2nd Iteration**	**...**	**7th Iteration**	**Change in Rank**
Singapore	1	1	...	2	-1
Korea	2	2	...	1	1
Hong Kong	3	3	...	3	0
Japan	4	4	...	4	0
Russia	5	5	...	5	0
Finland	6	6	...	7	-1
Israel	7	7	...	6	1
Canada	8	8	...	10	-2
USA	9	9	...	8	1
United Kingdom	10	10	...	9	1
Netherlands	11	11	...	11	0
Australia	12	12	...	13	-1
Hungary	13	15	...	14	-1
Germany	14	16	...	16	-2
Belgium	15	14	...	12	3
Switzerland	16	13	...	15	1
Italy	17	17	...	17	0
Ireland	18	19	...	19	-1
Denmark	19	20	...	18	1
Poland	20	18	...	21	-1
Austria	21	21/22	...	22	-1
Czech Republic	22	23	...	24	-2
France	23	21/22	...	20	3
Sweden	24	25	...	23	1
New Zealand	25	24	...	26	-1
Portugal	26	26	...	25	1
Slovakia	27	28	...	28	-1
Norway	28	27	...	27	1
Spain	29	29	...	29	0
Bulgaria	30	30	...	30	0
Romania	31	31	...	31	0
Turkey	32	32	...	32	0
Greece	33	33	...	33	0
Thailand	34	34	...	34	0
Chile	35	35	...	35	0
Colombia	36	36	...	36	0
Indonesia	37	37		37	0
Qatar	38	39		39	-1
Mexico	39	38		38	1
Brazil	40	40		40	0
Argentina	41	41		41	0

Hong Kong, Japan, and Russia took the same ranks. The greatest progress has been noticed in Belgium and France, which have three places lower ranking in the first iteration, compared to the last iteration. This means that the expulsion of the indicators improves the quality of the educational system model. Behind them are Canada, Germany, and the Czech Republic. The other countries have the same or a place higher or lower ranking than in the first iteration.

After all these iterations, France is in the top twenty countries. Belgium and France both allocate over 10% of public expenditure on education. In addition, there is a large number of studies that indicate a correlation between academic concepts about themselves and school achievement (Marsh, Byrne, & Shavelson, 1988), as well as the significant positive association between indicators of mathematical concepts and achievement in mathematics (Marsh, 1994). The education systems in these countries are highly regulated.

In some countries, the percentage of pupils who have reached the two highest levels of *Reading literacy achievement* (indicator ejected in the first iteration) ranges between 10% and 20%. In the most European countries the percentage ranges between 5 and 10% (Gasic-Pavisic & Stankovic, 2011).

It is interesting that, with the release of indicator *Scientific achievements*, Korea was replaced by Singapore at the first position in the ranking. The reason should be sought in the perception of the learning environment; students do not have sufficient support from their teachers in Korea (Kim et al., 2000) while in Singapore the favor of teachers towards students is friendly and their engagement in the field of technological breakthroughs is outstanding (Awang & Fah, 2013).

In Grade 8, most European-like educational systems were Czech, Hungarian, Lithuanian, Slovenian, and the United Kingdom (England). Students in Turkey had much worse results than all other European countries. The results were significantly lower than the EU average in Bulgaria, Italy, Cyprus, Romania, and Norway.

Investing the improvement of the educational system, greater parental involvement, and teacher's better approach will lead to the better results in Mathematics and thus better economic indicators of the country. Economic development depends on the achievement in mathematics, technological discoveries, and individual incomes in high-rated countries (Hanushek et al., 2007; Ramirez et al., 2006).

Choosing of the appropriate variable can be very difficult. It is important to discover the bounds between the expected number of variables with the lowest probability of the base selection procedure, and the expected number of high selection probability variables that are excluded by other selection procedure (Shah & Samworth, 2011). Guyon (2003) explains in his study that correlation between variables does not mean the absence of variable complementarity which means that variables can be useless by themselves, but they can be more useful together.

Summary of Country Rankings Obtained through the I-Distance Method

For the *EA* category, there is an incomplete data in a database used for forming *GICSES* index (*TIMSS* and *PIRLS* base). Since the I-distance method does not give the satisfactory results if there are missing data, all those countries with the missing data are not included in the analysis and the I-distance was calculated for the remaining states.

Compared to the obtained results, a new rank was formed by the I-distance method, and we compared it with the *GICSES* index range. Table 5 presents the values of the ranks by the I-distance method for the following countries.

Table 5. Summary of ranks by I-distance method for all three categories

Country	Ranks by I-Distance Method		Total
	Category		
	Cognitive Skills	Educational Attainment	
Japan	1	3	1
Finland	2	2	2
United Kingdom	6	1	3
Poland	7	4	4
Netherlands	3	6	5
Denmark	11	5	6
Ireland	5	8	7
Germany	4	9	8
Norway	15	7	9
Slovakia	17	10	10
Czech Republic	9	13	11
Hungary	12	11	12
USA	8	14	13
Portugal	14	12	14
Sweden	16	15	15
Italy	13	16	16
Austria	10	17	17
Turkey	18	18	18
Mexico	19	19	19

The table is prepared as follows: there is a composite index for all variables of the first category and separately for all other categories. Then the two composite indices are viewed as a part of the overall composite index that is calculated by the I-distance method. Depending on the correlation indication that they have, their value will affect the ultimate value and, therefore, the result of the overall index. According to this ranking, Japan is ranked first, followed by Finland, United Kingdom, Poland, and the Netherlands. It is also interesting to point out that countries such as Austria, Turkey, and Mexico do not move from the last position. We can see that the first five countries and the last three slightly vary in range when categories are viewed separately and together. Particular attention should be paid to Slovakia, which, regardless of the value for Category *CS,* is still positioned seven ranks higher in the global I-distance index.

Kawamoto (et al., 2011) shows that the relationship among factors is of crucial importance in designing effective platforms for science communication, such as social education in Japan. Cummings (2014) describes all of the above-mentioned factors. Regarding cognitive equality, he mentioned the Bloom theory, which means breaking down curriculum into simple learning tasks while techniques have to be combined with attention to the entry characteristics of the learners. Japanese teachers are looking at other nations' pedagogic systems, using it in the best way, so the learners can profit from it in a short time and have the best results, which makes cognitive capabilities stronger. It is noticed that

Figure 2. The result of two phase approach to the I-distance method, review of the major indicators, key categories, and corresponding correlation coefficients

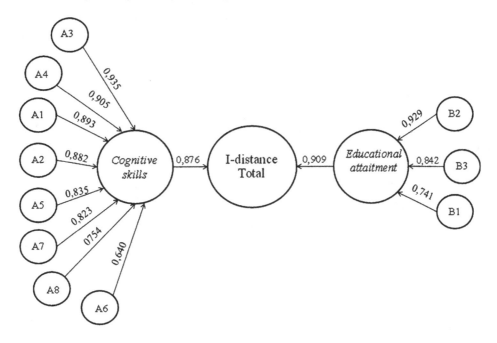

Japan has improved its position. The average score in the test *TIMSS* 2011 for Grade 4 is 570 points in mathematics (same as 2007) and 558 points in science while the average score of all countries is 500 points (Thompson et al., 2013).

An interesting case is presented by Finland, which occupies the 2nd ranking place in all criteria. When you allocate only European countries, it can be seen that the highest level of development competence is troubleshooting the pupils from Finland. Also, Austria occupies the middle of the cognitive skills list, but is at the end of the list, despite observing all the variables listed.

Pekarrinen (et al., 2009) studied how the Finnish comprehensive school reform had a small positive effect on the average arithmetic or logical reasoning results, which significantly reduced the degree of heterogeneity in the Finnish primary and secondary education. Results of his study indicate that the effects of school tracking on cognitive skills tend to be small, but the effects of tracking other later-in-life outcomes, such as earnings, completed schooling or college enrollment play a significant role. The reform increases the scores for students whose parents had only primary education.

Wößmann (2005) presented cross-country evidence on the effectiveness of public-private partnerships in providing cognitive skills to students. He characterized the opposite systems of sole public responsibility in Finland (100% public funding and 97% publicly operated schools). Consequently, practically all children go to publicly funded schools governed by the national curriculum, thus receiving a similar education and related services based on multicultural education for immigrant groups (Holm & Londen, 2010). Furthermore, there is a connection between educational attainment and crime, income, and employment (Kirkegaard, 2014). Population change and regional diversification are one of the most important variables watching the social impact on educational attainment (Svensson, 2011).

Based on the current frame of graduation rates, 82% of young people in the *OECD* countries will complete upper secondary level of education after 25 years. This is common in Denmark, Finland, Iceland, and Norway - North European countries. This level provides the foundation for advanced learning and training opportunities. The fact is that the young women reached this level of education in almost all the *OECD* countries. The highest growth was recorded in Portugal (Wright, 2012). However, this indicator does not take into account the quality of educational success (Educational outcome).

To provide a comparative view of countries identified by the analysis of *GICSES* index, we used data from nineteen countries. The results are presented in Table 6.

Countries are ranked in ascending order according to *GICSES* method created for all indicators. Also, it is possible to see the positions for the two categories in which variables are located, changes in ratings for each category, as well as the overall index. The highest ranking change was recorded in Slovakia (in the ranks by I-distance method six positions higher, while the United States ranked four positions lower). Seven countries did not change their ranks.

This leads to the fact that Japan ranks first while the states that follow it behave as follows: Finland ranked second by all criteria, whereas the UK, the Netherlands, and Ireland occupy the remaining

Table 6. Summary of ranks by the method GICSES index for both categories and total

Country	Ranks by *GICSES*		Total
	Category		
	Cognitive Skills	**Educational Attainment**	
Japan	1	5	1
Finland	2	3	2
United Kingdom	4	1	3
Netherland	3	6	4
Ireland	5	8	5
Poland	8	2	6
Denmark	9	4	7
Germany	7	10	8
USA	6	13	9
Czech Republic	11	11	10
Norway	16	7	11
Hungary	10	14	12
Sweden	14	12	13
Italy	13	15	14
Austria	12	16	15
Slovakia	17	9	16
Portugal	15	17	17
Turkey	18	18	18
Mexico	19	19	19

three places in the global index. Improvements in these countries are characterized by a high culture of community-oriented education, where every participant handles a large number of targets.

It is a 'mixed' effect for the Scandinavian countries, which tend to be "guiding stars" in the field of education. Finland has lost its leading position to Japan mainly because it is significantly below the average performance in the latest *PISA* tests. The performance of Sweden in tests also declined, leading to the drop to the 13th position and thereby encouraging criticism of the public education policy. Denmark is still in the top ten while Norway is in the 11th position. It can be pointed out that the maximum deviation in the *CS* category is with Germany, three positions while for graduates fluctuated the most in Portugal (Wright, 2012), only five positions less. Sweden is ranked three positions lower. All other states show no significant changes in ranks (up to a maximum of 2 positions).

International and national research and reports indicate that the motivation for mathematics is decreasing over the years; therefore, measures to prevent this situation must be developed. Some states have implemented the strategies and initiatives that seek to increase involvement, the interest of students, as well as their active participation in mathematics from an early age. These include innovative teaching methods, school partnerships with universities, and companies along with extracurricular activities related to talented students. Several countries have started the implementation of these activities already with preschool age children (Kaushal, Magnuson & Waldfogel, 2011).

In Table 7, we can see the changes in ranks from both I-distance method and GICSES index, obtained for categories CS and EA, as well as their Total value.

Countries with the biggest positive changes in ranks are colored green while those with the biggest negative changes in ranks are colored red. We can see that Germany has the biggest positive change in rank, 3 positions for Category *CS*. Portugal counts a 5 positions positive change in rank for *EA* category while Slovakia and the USA are top 2 for positive and negative changes in ranks, respectively. Japan, Finland, and the United Kingdom are the best ranked according to the Total I-distance and *GICSES* index.

CONCLUSION

Organizational solutions in various educational systems highlight major differences in terms of nature and duration (Meyer & Thomsen, 2012) of the educational cycle in compulsory pre-school education (Anders et al., 2011). Over the past years, it has been proven that establishing the basic skill level becomes relevant to enable the economic development with the penetration of the labor market (Hanushek & Woessmann, 2010). However, recent studies show that basic cognitive skills - reading, writing, and mathematics, though necessary, are not sufficient. "Understanding the environment" became the basis of the new ranking, which the intellectuals call the 'XXI century skills,' including communication, teamwork, and problem-solving (Brunello & Schlotter, 2011). Each state should possess a unique framework and methodology for developing these skills in order to improve economic progress.

Economy in the world does not pay more for the people who know, but for those who know what to do with what you know. (Andreas Schleicher, Deputy Director for Education, OECD)

As mentioned before, the *GICSES* uses results of *Cognitive skills* and *Educational Attainment* to measure the performance of educational systems in the economic development of the country. The *OECD* countries are ranked based on the results of investment in education by the concept of a composite index.

Table 7. Summary of changes in ranks obtained through the I-distance and GICSES index, for categories CS, EA, and Total

Country	A Change in the Range between I-Distance and *GICSES* Index								
	Cognitive Skills			**Educational Attainment**			**Total**		
	I-Distance	*GICSES*	**Change**	**I-Distance**	*GICSES*	**Change**	**I-Distance**	*GICSES*	**Change**
Japan	1	1	0	3	5	2	1	1	0
Finland	2	2	0	2	3	1	2	2	0
United Kingdom	6	4	-2	1	1	0	3	3	0
Poland	7	8	1	4	2	-2	4	6	2
Netherland	3	3	0	6	6	0	5	4	-1
Denmark	11	9	-2	5	4	-1	6	7	1
Ireland	5	5	0	8	8	0	7	5	-2
Germany	4	7	3	9	10	1	8	8	0
Norway	15	16	1	7	7	0	9	11	2
Slovakia	17	17	0	10	9	-1	10	16	6
Czech Republic	9	11	2	13	11	-2	11	10	-1
Hungary	12	10	-2	11	14	3	12	12	0
USA	8	6	-2	14	13	-1	13	9	-4
Portugal	14	15	1	12	17	5	14	17	3
Sweden	16	14	-2	15	12	-3	15	13	-2
Italy	13	13	0	16	15	-1	16	14	-2
Austria	10	12	2	17	16	-1	17	15	-2
Turkey	18	18	0	18	18	0	18	18	0
Mexico	19	19	0	19	19	0	19	19	0

Indicators used in the composite index are integrated in order of their evaluation, according to an equal weighting scheme. We decided to apply an I-distance method, a multivariate statistical analysis which is an alternative to *GICSES*, in order to improve the objective ranking of the observed countries. The I-distance, as a method of composite index modeling, covers a large part of the variability and largely eliminates subjectivity in ranking.

The goal of the chapter is multiple: (i) by applying the I-distance method we were able to point out potential shortcomings of subjectively chosen weighting factors of the *GICSES* ranking methodologies. (ii) Our approach provides detailed information on how each of the *GICSES* indicators contributes to the final positions and emphasizes crucial indicators in the process of classification. We try to provide a response to the issue: *"What are the essential skills to perform education?"* The answer allows for an enhanced understanding of what remarkably drives the education of people and nations and what should be done to achieve greater progress for all. Moreover, the obtained results can act as a catalyst for governments, nonprofits, and civil society to work together on the main indicators in order to improve the overall rank of their country. (iii) We have presented the highest quality of the model (model with the highest coefficient of determination) obtained by excluding one by one indicator, according to their significance. The maximum quality model includes the two most important indicators. It is necessary to make an effort and focus activities primarily on developing the most important individual indicators, in order to improve the final ranking.

The approach could be the basis for monitoring the progress of educational systems over time, every two years (when new data are available). The results also indicate that the I-distance method brings some improvements, and the obtained values can be used as a basis for comparison with other works that evaluate the same phenomenon using another method.

FUTURE RESEARCH DIRECTIONS

In future research, our aim will be to determine if the differences exist in the quality of education, not only among the OECD countries but also among other countries around the world. Some of the studies that have been done in Serbia can also be taken into consideration (Stamenkovic et al., 2015). In addition, we will examine the most important component(s) between analyzed variables. The I-distance method will be used to determine which components are the most important for a respective country in the set of analyzed countries. Moreover, component loadings, as the correlations between quality of education and educational components, will provide an in-depth overview of the most significant characteristics.

REFERENCES

Aghion, P., & Durlauf, S. (Eds.). (2005). *Handbook of economic growth* (Vol. 1). Amsterdam, The Netherlands: Elsevier.

Aina, C., Baici, E., & Casalone, G. (2011). Time to degree: Students' abilities, University characteristics or something else? Evidence from Italy. *Education Economics*, *19*(3), 311–325. doi:10.1080/0964529 2.2011.585016

Albright, J., & Luke, A. (Eds.). (2010). *Pierre Bourdieu and Literacy education*. New York: Routledge.

Anders, Y., Sammons, P., Taggart, B., Sylva, K., Melhuish, E., & Siraj-Blatchford, I. (2011). The influence of child, family, home factors and pre-school education on the identification of special educational needs at age 10. *British Educational Research Journal*, *37*(3), 421–441. doi:10.1080/01411921003725338

Arndt, S., Acion, L., Caspers, K., & Blood, P. (2013). How reliable are county and regional health rankings? *Prevention Science*, *14*(5), 497–502. doi:10.1007/s11121-012-0320-3 PMID:23400846

Avissar, G. (2012). Inclusive education in Israel from a curriculum perspective: An exploratory study. *European Journal of Special Needs Education*, *27*(1), 35–49. doi:10.1080/08856257.2011.613602

Awang, R., & Fah, L. Y. (2013). An Analysis on the Selected Factors Contributing to Science and Mathematics Achievement Among Secondary Students in Two SEAMEO Member Countries. *Jurnal Teknologi*, *63*(2). doi:10.11113/jt.v63.2020

Aziz, A. A., Yusof, K. M., & Yatim, J. M. (2012). Evaluation on the Effectiveness of Learning Outcomes from Students' Perspectives. *Procedia: Social and Behavioral Sciences*, *56*, 22–30. doi:10.1016/j.sbspro.2012.09.628

Balcerowicz, L. (Ed.). (2014). *Puzzles of Economic Growth*. Washington, DC: World Bank Publications. doi:10.1596/978-1-4648-0325-3

Baucal, A., Pavlović-Babić, D. (2010) *Čitalačka pismenost kao mera kvaliteta obrazovanja - procena na osnovu PISA 2009 podataka*. Beograd: Ministarstvo prosvete Republike Srbije.

Beaton, A. E. (1996). Mathematics Achievement in the Middle School Years. IEA's Third International Mathematics and Science Study (TIMSS). Boston College, Center for the Study of Testing, Evaluation, and Educational Policy.

Benito, M., & Romera, R. (2011). Improving quality assessment of composite indicators in university rankings: A case study of French and German universities of excellence. *Scientometrics*, *89*(1), 153–176. doi:10.1007/s11192-011-0419-5

Benos, N., & Zotou, S. (2014). Education and economic growth: A meta-regression analysis. *World Development*, *64*, 669–689. doi:10.1016/j.worlddev.2014.06.034

Bieber, T., & Martens, K. (2011). The OECD PISA study as a soft power in education? Lessons from Switzerland and the US. *European Journal of Education*, *46*(1), 101–116. doi:10.1111/j.1465-3435.2010.01462.x

Bowles, S., & Gintis, H. (2011). *A cooperative species: Human reciprocity and its evolution*. Princeton, NJ: Princeton University Press.

Bowles, S., Gintis, H., & Osborne, M. (2001). The determinants of earnings: A behavioral approach. *Journal of Economic Literature*, *39*(4), 1137–1176. doi:10.1257/jel.39.4.1137

Bray, M. (2011). Facing the shadow education system in Hong Kong. *The Newsletter*, *56*, 20.

Brüggemann, R., & Patil, G. P. (2011). *Ranking and prioritization for multi-indicator systems: Introduction to partial order applications*. Springer Science & Business Media. doi:10.1007/978-1-4419-8477-7

Brunello, G., & Schlotter, M. (2011). *Non-cognitive skills and personality traits: Labour market relevance and their development in education & training systems*. Academic Press.

Carlson, B. A. (1999). *Social dimensions of economic development and productivity: inequality and social performance*. CEPAL.

Cheung, A. C., Yuen, T. W., Yuen, C. Y., & Cheong Cheng, Y. (2011). Strategies and policies for Hong Kong's higher education in Asian markets: Lessons from the United Kingdom, Australia, and Singapore. *International Journal of Educational Management*, *25*(2), 144–163. doi:10.1108/09513541111107579

Cummings, W. K. (2014). *Education and equality in Japan*. Princeton University Press.

Cunha, F., & Heckman, J. (2007). The technology of skill formation. *American Economic Review*, *97*(2), 31–47. doi:10.1257/aer.97.2.31

Data, S. P. S. S., Data, S. A. S., & Data, R. D. (2013). *TIMSS and PIRLS 2011: Relationships among reading, mathematics, and science achievement at the fourth grade—Implications for early learning.* Academic Press.

Dobrota, M., Bulajic, M., Bornmann, L., & Jeremic, V. (2016). A new approach to the QS university ranking using the composite I-distance indicator: Uncertainty and sensitivity analyses. *Journal of the Association for Information Science and Technology, 67*(1), 200–211. doi:10.1002/asi.23355

Dobrota, M., Jeremić, V., Bulajić, M., & Radojičić, Z. (2015). Uncertainty and Sensitivity Analyzes of PISA Efficiency: Distance Based Analysis Approach. *Acta Polytechnica Hungarica, 12*(3).

Dolton, P., Marcenaro-Gutiérrez, O., & Still, A. (2014). *The efficiency index: Which education systems deliver the best value for money?* London: GEMS Education Solutions.

Englehart, N. A. (2000). Rights and culture in the Asian values argument: The rise and fall of Confucian ethics in Singapore. *Human Rights Quarterly, 22*(2), 548–568. doi:10.1353/hrq.2000.0024

European Commission. (2010). *Europe 2020: A European strategy for smart, sustainable and inclusive growth.* Brussels: European Commission.

Feniger, Y. (2011). The gender gap in advanced math and science course taking: Does same-sex education make a difference? *Sex Roles, 65*(9-10), 670–679. doi:10.1007/s11199-010-9851-x

Friedler, Y., & Tamir, P. (1990). Sex differences in science education in Israel: An analysis of 15 years of research. *Research in Science & Technological Education, 8*(1), 21–34. doi:10.1080/0263514900080103

Gasic-Pavisic, S., Stanković, D. (2011). *Obrazovna postignuća učenika iz Srbije u istraživanju TIMSS 2011.* Beograd: Institut za pedagoška istraživanja. doi:.10.2298/ZIPI1202243G

Gudeva, L. K., Dimova, V., Daskalovska, N., & Trajkova, F. (2012). Designing descriptors of learning outcomes for Higher Education qualification. *Procedia: Social and Behavioral Sciences, 46,* 1306–1311. doi:10.1016/j.sbspro.2012.05.292

Guttorp, P., & Kim, T. Y. (2013). Uncertainty in ranking the hottest years of U.S. surface temperatures. *Journal of Climate, 26*(17), 6323–6328. doi:10.1175/JCLI-D-12-00760.1

Guyon, I., & Elisseeff, A. (2003). An introduction to variable and feature selection. *Journal of Machine Learning Research, 3,* 1157–1182.

Hanushek, E. A., & Woessmann, L. (2007). *The Role of Education Quality for Economic Growth.* Washington, DC: World Bank. doi:10.1596/1813-9450-4122

Hanushek, E. A., & Woessmann, L. (2010). Education and Economic Growth. In D. J. Brewer & P. J. McEwan (Eds.), *Economics of Education.* Amsterdam: Elsevier. doi:10.1016/B978-0-08-044894-7.01227-6

Hanushek, E. A., & Woessmann, L. (2012). Do better schools lead to more growth? Cognitive skills, economic outcomes, and causation. *Journal of Economic Growth, 17*(4), 267–321. doi:10.1007/s10887-012-9081-x

Hidalgo, C. A. (2010). *Graphical statistical methods for the representation of the human development index and its components.* Human Development Reports Research Paper, 39.

Holm, G., & Londen, M. (2010). The discourse on multicultural education in Finland: Education for whom? *Intercultural Education, 21*(2), 107–120. doi:10.1080/14675981003696222

Huang, Y. (2012). *Confucius: a guide for the perplexed*. New York: Bloomsbury.

Ivanovic, B. (1977). *Classification theory*. Belgrade: Institute for Industrial Economic.

Jeremić, V. (2012). *Statistički model efikasnosti zasnovan na Ivanovićevom odstojanju. Doktorska disertacija, Fakultet organizacionih nauka*. Beograd: Univerzitet u Beogradu.

Jeremic, V., Isljamovic, S., Petrovic, N., Radojicic, Z., Markovic, A., & Bulajic, M. (2011). Human development index and sustainability: What's the correlation? *Metalurgia international, 16*(7), 63-67.

Jeremic, V., Milenkovic, M. J., Radojicic, Z., & Martic, M. (2013). Excellence with leadership: the crown indicator of Scimago Institutions Rankings Iber Report. *El profesional de la información, 22*(5), 474-480.

Jovanovic, M., Jeremic, V., Savic, G., Bulajic, M., & Martic, M. (2012). How does the normalization of data affect the ARWU ranking? *Scientometrics, 93*(2), 319–327. doi:10.1007/s11192-012-0674-0

Kaushal, N., Magnuson, K., & Waldfogel, J. (2011). *How is family income related to investments in children's learning?*. Russell Sage Foundation.

Kawamoto, S., Nakayama, M., & Saijo, M. (2011). A survey of scientific literacy to provide a foundation for designing science communication in Japan. *Public Understanding of Science (Bristol, England), 0963662511418893*. doi:10.1177/0963662511418893 PMID:23885051

Keane, E. (2011). Dependence-deconstruction: Widening participation and traditional-entry students transitioning from school to higher education in Ireland. *Teaching in Higher Education, 16*(6), 707–718. doi:10.1080/13562517.2011.570437

Kernan, M., & Devine, D. (2010). Being confined within? Constructions of the good childhood and outdoor play in early childhood education and care settings in Ireland. *Children & Society, 24*(5), 371–385. doi:10.1111/j.1099-0860.2009.00249.x

Khan, H. (2001). *Social Policy in Singapore: A Confucian model?* Washington, DC: World Bank Institute.

Kim, H. B., Fisher, D. L., & Fraser, B. J. (2000). Classroom environment and teacher interpersonal behavior in secondary science classes in Korea. *Evaluation and Research in Education, 14*(1), 3–22. doi:10.1080/09500790008666958

Kirkegaard, E. O. (2014). *Crime, income, educational attainment and employment among immigrant groups in Norway and Finland*. Open Differential Psychology.

Koraneekij, P., & Khlaisang, J. (2015). Development of Learning Outcome Based E-Portfolio Model Emphasizing on Cognitive Skills in Pedagogical Blended E-Learning Environment for Undergraduate Students at Faculty of Education, Chulalongkorn University. *Procedia: Social and Behavioral Sciences, 174*, 805–813. doi:10.1016/j.sbspro.2015.01.664

Lee, K. W., & Chung, M. (2015). Enhancing the link between higher education and employment. *International Journal of Educational Development, 40*, 19–27. doi:10.1016/j.ijedudev.2014.11.014

Lind, N. (2014). Better Life Index. In *Encyclopedia of Quality of Life and Well-Being Research* (pp. 381–382). Springer Netherlands. doi:10.1007/978-94-007-0753-5_3623

Liu, W. C., Wang, C. K. J., & Parkins, E. J. (2005). A longitudinal study of students' academic self-concept in a streamed setting: The Singapore context. *The British Journal of Educational Psychology*, *75*(4), 567–586. doi:10.1348/000709905X42239 PMID:16318679

Machlup, F. (2014). Knowledge: its creation, distribution and economic significance: Vol. I. *Knowledge and knowledge production*. Princeton, NJ: Princeton University press.

Mak, A. S., & Kennedy, M. (2012). Internationalizing the student experience: Preparing instructors to embed intercultural skills in the curriculum. *Innovative Higher Education*, *37*(4), 323–334. doi:10.1007/s10755-012-9213-4

Marginson, S. (2011). Higher education in East Asia and Singapore: Rise of the Confucian model. *Higher Education*, *61*(5), 587–611. doi:10.1007/s10734-010-9384-9

Marsh, H. W. (1994). Using the National Longitudinal Study of 1988 to evaluate theoretical models of self-concept: The Self-Description Questionnaire. *Journal of Educational Psychology*, *86*(3), 439–456. doi:10.1037/0022-0663.86.3.439

Marsh, H. W., Byrne, B. M., & Shavelson, R. J. (1988). A multifaceted academic self-concept: Its hierarchical structure and its relation to academic achievement. *Journal of Educational Psychology*, *80*(3), 366–380. doi:10.1037/0022-0663.80.3.366

Martin, L. M. (2004). An emerging research framework for studying informal learning and schools. *Science Education*, *88*(S1), S71–S82. doi:10.1002/sce.20020

Meyer, T., & Thomsen, S. L. (2012). *How important is secondary school duration for post-school education decisions? Evidence from a natural experiment* (No. 509). Diskussionspapiere der Wirtschaftswissenschaftlichen Fakultät, Universität Hannover, Deutschland. Retrieved September 22, 2015, from http://hdl.handle.net/10419/73103

Moloney, M. (2010). Professional identity in early childhood care and education: Perspectives of preschool and infant teachers. *Irish Educational Studies*, *29*(2), 167–187. doi:10.1080/03323311003779068

Morris, P., & Adamson, B. (2010). *Curriculum, schooling and society in Hong Kong* (Vol. 1). Hong Kong: Hong Kong University Press. doi:10.5790/hongkong/9789888028016.001.0001

Mullis, I. V., Martin, M. O., Foy, P., & Arora, A. (2012). TIMSS 2011 international results in mathematics. International Association for the Evaluation of Educational Achievement.

Neidorf, T. S., Binkley, M., Gattis, K., & Nohara, D. (2006). *Comparing Mathematics Content in the National Assessment of Educational Progress (NAEP), Trends in International Mathematics and Science Study (TIMSS), and Program for International Student Assessment (PISA) 2003. U.S. Department of Education*. Washington, DC: National Center for Education Statistics.

Nuchwana, L. (2012). How to link teaching and research to enhance students' learning outcomes: Thai University Experience. *Procedia: Social and Behavioral Sciences*, *69*, 213–219. doi:10.1016/j.sbspro.2012.11.401

OECD. (2002). *Education at a Glance 2002*. Paris: OECD Publications Glossary.

OECD. (2009). *Learning Mathematics for Life: A Perspective from PISA*. Paris: OECD Publishing.

OECD. (2013). *Assessing Scientific, Reading and Mathematical Literacy – A Framework for PISA 2015*. Paris: OECD Publications.

OECD. (2013). *Education at a Glance 2013*. Paris: OECD Publications.

Paruolo, P., Saisana, M., & Saltelli, A. (2013). Ratings and rankings: Voodoo or science? *Journal of the Royal Statistical Society. Series A, (Statistics in Society), 176*(3), 609–634. doi:10.1111/j.1467-985X.2012.01059.x

Pearson. (2014). *Pearson learning curve*. Retrieved August 25, from http://thelearningcurve.pearson.com/data-hub

Pekkarinen, T., Uusitalo, R., & Pekkala Kerr, S. (2009). *School tracking and development of cognitive skills. Discussion paper series. No. 4058*. Bonn, Germany: IZA.

Petrosillo, I., Costanza, R., Aretano, R., Zaccarelli, N., & Zurlini, G. (2013). The use of subjective indicators to assess how natural and social capital support residents' quality of life in a small volcanic island. *Ecological Indicators, 24*, 609–620. doi:10.1016/j.ecolind.2012.08.021

Radojicic, Z., & Jeremic, V. (2012). Quantity or quality: What matters more in ranking higher education institutions. *Current Science, 103*(2), 158–162.

Ramirez, F. O., Luo, X., Schofer, E., & Meyer, J. W. (2006). Student achievement and national economic growth. *American Journal of Education, 113*(1), 1–29. doi:10.1086/506492

Rode, H., & Michelsen, G. (2008). Levels of indicator development for education for sustainable development. *Environmental Education Research, 14*(1), 19–33. doi:10.1080/13504620701843327

Saisana, M., & D'Hombres, B. (2008). Higher education rankings: Robustness issues and critical assessment. How much confidence can we have in Higher Education Rankings? EUR23487. Italy: Joint Research Centre, Publications Office of the European Union. doi:10. 2788/92295

Saisana, M., D'Hombres, B., & Saltelli, A. (2011). Rickety numbers: Volatility of university rankings and policy implications. *Research Policy, 40*(1), 165–177. doi:10.1016/j.respol.2010.09.003

Saisana, M., & Tarantola, S. (2002). *State-of-the-art report on current methodologies and practices for composite indicator development EUR report20408EN*. Italy: European Commission, JRC-IPSC.

Saltelli, A. (2007). Composite Indicators between analysis and advocacy. *Social Indicators Research, 81*(1), 65–77. doi:10.1007/s11205-006-0024-9

Schneider, W., & Artelt, C. (2010). Metacognition and mathematics education. *ZDM, 42*(2), 149–161. doi:10.1007/s11858-010-0240-2

Scully, G. W. (2014). *Constitutional environments and economic growth*. Princeton, NJ: Princeton University Press.

Seke, K., Petrovic, N., Jeremic, V., Vukmirovic, J., Kilibarda, B., & Martic, M. (2013). Sustainable development and public health: Rating European countries. *BMC Public Health*, *13*(77), 1–7. doi:10.1186/1471-2458-13-77 PMID:23356822

Shah, R. D., & Samworth, R. J. (2013). Variable selection with error control: Another look at stability selection. *Journal of the Royal Statistical Society. Series B, Statistical Methodology*, *75*(1), 55–80. doi:10.1111/j.1467-9868.2011.01034.x

Shin, J. C. (2012). Higher education development in Korea: Western university ideas, Confucian tradition, and economic development. *Higher Education*, *64*(1), 59–72. doi:10.1007/s10734-011-9480-5

Stamenković, M., Anić, I., Petrović, M., & Bojković, N. (2015). An ELECTRE approach for evaluating secondary education profiles: Evidence from PISA survey in Serbia. *Annals of Operations Research*, 1–22.

Svensson, J. (2011). *Social Impact Assessment in Finland, Norway, and Sweden: A descriptive and comparative study. Unpublished degree project SoM EX 2011-30, KTH*. Stockholm, Sweden: Royal Institute of Technology.

Thomson, S., Hillman, K., & De Bortoli, L. (2013*). A teacher's guide to PISA reading literacy*. Retrieved August 20, 2015, from http://research.acer.edu.au/ozpisa/12

Tsameret, T., & Zameret, Z. (2012). *The Melting Pot in Israel: The Commission of Inquiry Concerning the Education of Immigrant Children During the Early Years of the State*. SUNY Press.

Unit, E. I. (2014). *The Learning Curve: Education and Skills for Life. A Report*. Pearson London.

Waldron, H. B., & Kaminer, Y. (2004). On the learning curve: The emerging evidence supporting cognitive – behavioral therapies for adolescent substance abuse. *Addiction (Abingdon, England)*, *99*(s2), 93–105. doi:10.1111/j.1360-0443.2004.00857.x PMID:15488108

Wößmann, L. (2005). *Public-private partnerships in schooling: cross-country evidence on their effectiveness in providing cognitive skills. Prepared for the conference: "Mobilizing the Private Sector for Public Education"*. Program on Education Policy and Governance, Research Paper PEPG, 05-09.

Wright, T. P. (2012). Factors affecting the cost of airplanes. *Journal of the Aeronautical Sciences*, *3*(4). doi:10.2514/8.155

ADDITIONAL READING

Išljamović, S., Jeremić, V., Petrović, N., & Radojičić, Z. (2014). Colouring the socio-economic development into green: I-distance framework for countries' welfare evaluation. *Quality & Quantity*, *49*(2), 617–629. doi:10.1007/s11135-014-0012-0

Jeremic, V., Bulajic, M., Martic, M., & Radojicic, Z. (2011). A fresh approach to evaluating the academic ranking of world universities. *Scientometrics*, *87*(3), 587–596. doi:10.1007/s11192-011-0361-6

Mullis, I. V., Martin, M. O., Foy, P., & Drucker, K. T. (2012b). PIRLS 2011 International Results in Reading. International Association for the Evaluation of Educational Achievement. Herengracht 487, Amsterdam, 1017 BT, The Netherlands.

Mullis, I. V. S., Martin, M. O., & Foy, P. (2008). *TIMSS 2007 International Mathematics Report*. Chestnut Hill, MA: TIMSS & PIRLS International Study Center, Boston College.

Munda, G., & Nardo, M. (2003). *On the methodological foundations of composite indicators used for ranking countries*. Ispra, Italy: Joint Research Centre of the European Communities.

Munda, G., & Nardo, M. (2009). Noncompensatory/nonlinear composite indicators for ranking countries: A defensible setting. *Applied Economics*, *41*(12), 1513–1523. doi:10.1080/00036840601019364

Nardo, M., Saisana, M., Saltelli, A., & Tarantola, S. (2005). *Tools for composite indicators building*. Ispra: European Comission.

Saltelli, A., Nardo, M., Saisana, M., &Tarantola, S. (2005). Composite indicators: the controversy and the way forward. *Statistics, Knowledge and Policy Key Indicators to Inform Decision Making: Key Indicators to Inform Decision Making*, 359.

Santos, A. (2012). The World Bank's Uses of the'Rule of Law'Promise in Economic Development. The new law and economic development: A critical appraisal, 253-300.

Scully, G. W., & Slottje, D. J. (1991). Ranking economic liberty across countries. *Public Choice*, *69*(2), 121–152. doi:10.1007/BF00123844

Tarantola, S., Saltelli, A. (2007). Composite indicators: the art of mixing apples and oranges. Presented on Composite Indicators – Boon or Bane. StatistischesBundesamt. JRC43341.

Zhou, P., Ang, B. W., & Poh, K. L. (2006). Comparing aggregating methods for constructing the composite environmental index: An objective measure. *Ecological Economics*, *59*(3), 305–311. doi:10.1016/j.ecolecon.2005.10.018

KEY TERMS AND DEFINITIONS

Cognitive Skills: Humans' ability to process information, remember, and relate them.

Composite Index: A group of indicators, indexes or other factors combined in a standardized way, which provides a useful statistical measure.

Educational Attainment: The highest level of schooling that a person has reached (the number of grades completed or degrees obtained).

GICSES: Global Index of Cognitive Skills and Educational Attainment, is a composite index that analyzes member countries of the *OECD* and ranks them based on the value of the global index using z-score normalization method.

I-Distance Method: Methodology which calculates distances between the entities, and after that, they are compared to one another in order to generate a rank.

OECD Countries: 34 countries which create an organization dedicated to economic development.

Ranking of Countries: Comparing countries to one another, based on the same index, and putting them in adequate positions.

Compilation of References

Abdalla Alfaki, I. M., & Ahmed, A. (2013). Technological readiness in the United Arab Emirates towards global competitiveness. World Journal of Entrepreneurship. *Management and Sustainable Development, 9*(1), 4–13.

Abdul Wahab, A. (2003). *A complexity approach to national IT policy making: The case of Malaysia's Multimedia Super Corridor (MSC).* (Doctoral thesis). School of Information Technology and Electrical Engineering (ITEE), University of Queensland, Queensland, Australia.

Ackerman, B. P., & Brown, E. D. (2010). Physical and psychological turmoil in the home and cognitive development. In G. W. Evans & T. D. Wachs (Eds.), *Chaos and its Influence on Children's Development* (pp. 35–47). Washington, DC: American Psychological Association.

Acs, Z. J., Desai, S., & Hessels, J. (2008). Entrepreneurship, economic development and institutions. *Small Business Economics, 31*(3), 219–234. doi:10.1007/s11187-008-9135-9

Acs, Z. J., Szerb, L., & Autio, E. (2015). *Global Entrepreneurship Index.* Powered by GEDI.

Active ageing. A Policy Framework. (2002). Retrieved September 10, 2015, from http://whqlibdoc.who.int/hq/2002/WHO_NMH_NPH_02.8.pdf

Adams, R., Bessant, J., & Phelps, R. (2006). Innovation management measurement: A review. *International Journal of Management Reviews, 8*(1), 21–47. doi:10.1111/j.1468-2370.2006.00119.x

Afsa, C., Blanchet, D., Marcus, V., Pionnier, P-A., & Rioux, L. (2008). *Survey of existing approaches to measuring socio-economic progress.* Study prepared for Commission on the Measurement of Economic Performance and Social Progress, INSEE/OECD.

Age-friendly Cities Poll Report. (2009). Retrieved September 10, 2015, from: http://www.carp.ca/o/pdf/age-friendly%20cities%20poll%20report%20web%20copy.pdf

Aghion, P., & Durlauf, S. (Eds.). (2005). *Handbook of economic growth* (Vol. 1). Amsterdam, The Netherlands: Elsevier.

Ahmed, E. M. (2008). ICT and human capital intensities effects on Malaysian productivity growth. *International Research Journal of Finance and Economics,* (13), 152-161.

Aina, C., Baici, E., & Casalone, G. (2011). Time to degree: Students' abilities, University characteristics or something else? Evidence from Italy. *Education Economics, 19*(3), 311–325. doi:10.1080/09645292.2011.585016

Alam, M., Dupras, J., & Messier, C. (2016). A framework towards a composite indicator for urban ecosystem services. *Ecological Indicators, 60,* 38–44. doi:10.1016/j.ecolind.2015.05.035

Al-Atawi, A. M., Kumar, R., & Saleh, W. (in press). Transportation sustainability index for Tabuk city in Saudi Arabia: An analytic hierarchy process. *Transport.* doi:10.3846/16484142.2015.1058857

Albright, J., & Luke, A. (Eds.). (2010). *Pierre Bourdieu and Literacy education*. New York: Routledge.

Al-Hawamdeh, S., & Hart, T. L. (2002). *Information and knowledge society*. Singapore: McGraw-Hill.

Alkire, S., & Santos, M. E. (2010). *Acute multidimensional poverty: A new index for developing countries*. Human Development Research Paper, 11.

Alkire, S., & Santos, M. E. (2013). A multidimensional approach: Poverty measurement & beyond. *Social Indicators Research, 112*(2), 239–257. doi:10.1007/s11205-013-0257-3

Ames, A., Ames, A., Houston, J., & Angioloni, S. (2016). Does Financial Literacy Contribute to Food Security? *International Journal of Food and Agriculture Economics, 4*, 21–34.

Andersen, P., & Petersen, N. C. (1993). A procedure for ranking efficient units in data envelopment analysis. *Management Science, 39*(10), 1261–1274. doi:10.1287/mnsc.39.10.1261

Anders, Y., Sammons, P., Taggart, B., Sylva, K., Melhuish, E., & Siraj-Blatchford, I. (2011). The influence of child, family, home factors and pre-school education on the identification of special educational needs at age 10. *British Educational Research Journal, 37*(3), 421–441. doi:10.1080/01411921003725338

Andreis, S. (2012). *QUARS – Regional quality of development index: Building alternative measures for development/ quality of life*. Project Wealth Kick-off Convention.

Andréosso-O'Callaghan, B. (2002). *Human Capital Accumulation and Economic Growth in Asia. National Europe Centre Paper No. 29*. Australian National University.

Antony, G. M., & Rao, K. V. (2007). A composite index to explain variations in poverty, health, nutritional status and standard of living: Use of multivariate statistical methods. *Public Health, 121*(8), 578–587. doi:10.1016/j.puhe.2006.10.018 PMID:17467017

ARCADIS. (2015). *Sustainable Cities Index 2015*. Retrieved November 21, 2015, from http://www.worldurbancampaign. org/resources/partners-resources/

Archibugi, D., & Coco, A. (2004). A new indicator of technological capabilities for developed and developing countries (ArCo). *World Development, 32*(4), 629–654. doi:10.1016/j.worlddev.2003.10.008

Archibugi, D., Denni, M., & Filippetti, A. (2009). The technological capabilities of nations: The state of the art of synthetic indicators. *Technological Forecasting and Social Change, 76*(7), 917–931. doi:10.1016/j.techfore.2009.01.002

Archibugi, D., Filippetti, A., & Frenz, M. (2013). Economic crisis and innovation: Is destruction prevailing over accumulation? *Research Policy, 42*(2), 303–314. doi:10.1016/j.respol.2012.07.002

Arndt, S., Acion, L., Caspers, K., & Blood, P. (2013). How reliable are county and regional health rankings? *Prevention Science, 14*(5), 497–502. doi:10.1007/s11121-012-0320-3 PMID:23400846

Arsoy, A. P., Arabaci, O., & Ciftcioğlu, A. (2012). Corporate social responsibility and financial performance relationship: The case of Turkey. *The Journal of Accounting and Finance, 53*, 159–176.

Atabek, A., Cosar, E. E., & Sahinoz, S. (2005). A new composite leading indicator for Turkish economic activity. *Emerging Markets Finance and Trade, 41*(1), 45–64. doi:10.1080/1540496X.2005.11052597

ATK/FP. (2007). *The Globalization Index 2007*. A.T. Kearney / Foreign Policy Magazine.

Atkinson, R. D., & Correa, D. K. (2007). *The 2007 State New Economy Index: Benchmarking Economic Transformation in the States*. The Information Technology and Innovation Foundation.

Aurino, E. (2014). *Selecting a Core Set of indicators for Monitoring Global Food Security. A Methodological Proposal.* FAO Statistics Division Working Papers 14-06.

Avissar, G. (2012). Inclusive education in Israel from a curriculum perspective: An exploratory study. *European Journal of Special Needs Education*, *27*(1), 35–49. doi:10.1080/08856257.2011.613602

Awang, R., & Fah, L. Y. (2013). An Analysis on the Selected Factors Contributing to Science and Mathematics Achievement Among Secondary Students in Two SEAMEO Member Countries. *Jurnal Teknologi, 63*(2). doi:10.11113/jt.v63.2020

Aziz, A. A., Yusof, K. M., & Yatim, J. M. (2012). Evaluation on the Effectiveness of Learning Outcomes from Students' Perspectives. *Procedia: Social and Behavioral Sciences*, *56*, 22–30. doi:10.1016/j.sbspro.2012.09.628

Badawy, A. M. (2009). Technology management simply defined: A tweet plus two characters. *Journal of Engineering and Technology Management*, *26*(4), 219–224. doi:10.1016/j.jengtecman.2009.11.001

Bakanligi, K. (2013). *Bolgesel Gelisme Ulusal Stratejisi (2014-2023)*. Ankara: Kalkınma Bakanligi.

BAKBasel Economics, (2008). *Top technology region benchmarking report 2008*. Basel: BAK Basel Economics.

Balcerowicz, L. (Ed.). (2014). *Puzzles of Economic Growth*. Washington, DC: World Bank Publications. doi:10.1596/978-1-4648-0325-3

Bandura, R. (2008). *A survey of composite indices measuring country performance: 2008 Update*. New York: Office of Development Studies.

Bandura, R. (2008). *A survey of composite indices measuring country performance: 2008 update*. New York: United Nations Development Programme.

Bandura, R. (2008). *A Survey of Composite Indices Measuring Country Performance: 2008 Update*. UNDP.

Bandura, R. (2008). *A survey of composite indices measuring country performance: 2008 Update. United Nations Development Programme*. Office of Development Studies.

Banker, R. D., Charnes, A., & Cooper, W. W. (1984). Some models for estimating technical and scale inefficiencies in data envelopment analysis. *Management Science*, *30*(9), 1078–1092. doi:10.1287/mnsc.30.9.1078

Bardy, R., & Massaro, M. (2013). Eco-social business in developing countries: the case for sustainable use of resources in unstable environments. In J. R. McIntyre, S. Ivanaj, & V. Ivanaj (Eds.), *Strategies for Sustainable Technologies and Innovations*. London: Edward Elgar. doi:10.4337/9781781006832.00018

Barney, J. B. (2004). Firm Resources and sustained competitive advantage. *Journal of Management*, *17*(1), 99–120. doi:10.1177/014920639101700108

Bartlett, M. S. (1954). A note on the multiplying factors for various chi square approximations. *Journal of the Royal Statistical Society, 16*(Series B), 296-8.

Baucal, A., Pavlović-Babić, D. (2010) *Čitalačka pismenost kao mera kvaliteta obrazovanja - procena na osnovu PISA 2009 podataka*. Beograd: Ministarstvo prosvete Republike Srbije.

Bawumia, M., & Appiah-Adu, K. (Eds.). (2015). *Key Determinants of National Development: Historical Perspectives and Implications for Developing Economies*. Gower Publishing, Ltd.

Bax, C., Wesemann, P., Gitelman, V., Shen, Y., Goldenbeld, C., Hermans, E., Doveh, E., Hakkert, S., Wegman, F., & Aarts, L. (2012). *Developing a road safety index*. Deliverable 4.9 of the EC FP7 project DaCoTA.

Beard, J. R., Blaney, S., Cerda, M., Frye, V., Lovasi, G. S., Ompad, D., & Vlahov, D. et al. (2009). Neighbourhood characteristics and disability in older adults. *The Journals of Gerontology. Series B, Psychological Sciences and Social Sciences, 64*(2), 252–257. doi:10.1093/geronb/gbn018 PMID:19181694

Beaton, A. E. (1996). Mathematics Achievement in the Middle School Years. IEA's Third International Mathematics and Science Study (TIMSS). Boston College, Center for the Study of Testing, Evaluation, and Educational Policy.

Beavers, A. S., Lounsbury, J. W., Richards, J. K., Huck, S. W., Skolits, G. J., & Esquivel, S. L. (2013). Practical considerations for using exploratory factor analysis in educational research. *Practical Assessment, Research & Evaluation, 18*(6), 1–13.

Becker, T. (2008). The Business behind Green, Eliminating fear, uncertainty, and doubt. *APICS Magazine, 18*(2).

Becker, G. (1962). Investment in human capital: A theoretical analysis. *Journal of Political Economy, 70*(5, Part 2), 9–49. doi:10.1086/258724

Becker, G. (1964). *Human Capital: A Theoretical and Empirical Analysis, with Special Reference to Education*. National Bureau of Economic Research; doi:10.7208/chicago/9780226041223.001.0001

Beckerman, W., & Bacon, R. (1966). International comparisons of income levels: A suggested new measure. *The Economic Journal, 76*(303), 519–536. doi:10.2307/2229519

Bedner, A. (2010). An Elementary Approach to the Rule of Law. *Hague Journal on the Rule of Law, 2*(1), 48–74. doi:10.1017/S1876404510100037

Ben-Gal, I. (2005). Outlier detection. In O. Maimon & L. Rockach (Eds.), *Data mining and knowledge discovery handbook: A complete guide for practitioners and researchers*. Boston: Kluwer Academic. doi:10.1007/0-387-25465-X_7

Beniger, J. R. (1986). *The control revolution: Technological and economic origins of the information society*. Harvard University Press.

Benito, M., & Romera, R. (2011). Improving quality assessment of composite indicators in university rankings: A case study of French and German universities of excellence. *Scientometrics, 89*(1), 153–176. doi:10.1007/s11192-011-0419-5

Bennett, M. K. (1951). International disparities in consumption levels. *The American Economic Review, 41*(4), 632–649.

Benos, N., & Zotou, S. (2014). Education and economic growth: A meta-regression analysis. *World Development, 64*, 669–689. doi:10.1016/j.worlddev.2014.06.034

Bergek, A., & Bruzelius, M. (2010). Are patents with multiple inventors from different countries a good indicator of international R&D collaboration? The case of ABB. *Research Policy, 39*(10), 1321–1334. doi:10.1016/j.respol.2010.08.002

Bergman, M. (2012). The Rule, the Law, and the Rule of Law: Improving Measurement and Content Validity. *Justice System Journal, 33*(2), 174–193. doi:10.1080/0098261X.2012.10768010

Berkman, L. F., & Kawachi, I. (2000). *Social Epidemiology*. New York: Oxford University Press.

Bersch, K., & Botero, S. (2014). Measuring Governance: Implications of conceptual choices. *European Journal of Development Research, 26*(1), 124–141. doi:10.1057/ejdr.2013.49

Bieber, T., & Martens, K. (2011). The OECD PISA study as a soft power in education? Lessons from Switzerland and the US. *European Journal of Education, 46*(1), 101–116. doi:10.1111/j.1465-3435.2010.01462.x

Black, J. A., Paez, A., & Suthanaya, P. A. (2002). Sustainable urban transportation: Performance indicators and some analytical approaches. *Journal of Urban Planning and Development, 128*(4), 184–209. doi:10.1061/(ASCE)0733-9488(2002)128:4(184)

Boarini, R., d'Ercole, M. M., & Liu, G. (2012). *Approaches to Measuring the Stock of Human Capital: A Review of Country Practices (No. 2012/4)*. OECD Publishing. doi:10.1787/18152031

Boelhouwer, J., & Stoop, I. (1999). Measuring well-being in the Netherlands: The SCP index from 1974 to 1997. *Social Indicators Research, 48*(1), 51–75. doi:10.1023/A:1006931028334

Bolch, B. W., & Huang, C. J. (1974). *Multivariate Statistical Methods for Business and Economics*. Englewood Cliffs, NJ: Prentice Hall.

Bonnett, M. (2007). Environmental Education and the Issue of Nature. *Journal of Curriculum Studies, 39*(6), 707–721. doi:10.1080/00220270701447149

Booysen, F. (2000). *The development of economic development: Alternative composite indices*. (Unpublished doctoral dissertation). University of Stellenbosch.

Booysen, F. (2002). An overview and evaluation of composite indices of development. *Social Indicators Research, 59*(2), 115–151. doi:10.1023/A:1016275505152

Bornstein, M. H., Hahn, C., Suwalsky, J. T. D., & Haynes, O. M. (2003). Socioeconomic status, parenting, and child development: The Hollingshead four-factor index of social status and the socioeconomic Index of occupations. In M. H. Bornstein & R. H. Bradley (Eds.), *Socioeconomic Status, Parenting, and Child Development* (pp. 29–82). Mahwah, NJ: Lawrence Erlbaum Associates.

Boschmann, E. (2011). Job access, location decision, and the working poor: A qualitative study in the Columbus, Ohio metropolitan area. *Geoforum, 42*(6), 671–682. doi:10.1016/j.geoforum.2011.06.005

Botero, J. C., & Ponce, A. (2011). *Measuring the Rule of Law*. doi: 10.2139/ssrn.1966257

Bowen, H. P., & Moesen, W. (2009). Composite Competitiveness Indicators With Endogenous Versus Predetermined Weights: An Application To The World Economic Forum's Global Competitiveness Index. *Competitiveness Review: An International Business Journal Incorporating Journal of Global Competitiveness, 21*(2), 129–151.

Bowles, S., & Gintis, H. (2011). *A cooperative species: Human reciprocity and its evolution*. Princeton, NJ: Princeton University Press.

Bowles, S., Gintis, H., & Osborne, M. (2001). The determinants of earnings: A behavioral approach. *Journal of Economic Literature, 39*(4), 1137–1176. doi:10.1257/jel.39.4.1137

Bowling, A., & Stafford, M. (2007). How do objective and subjective assessments of neighbourhood influence social and physical functioning in older age? Findings from a British survey of ageing. *Social Science & Medicine, 64*(12), 2533–2549. doi:10.1016/j.socscimed.2007.03.009 PMID:17433509

Bradley, R. H., & Corwyn, R. F. (2002). Socioeconomic status and child development. *Annual Review of Psychology, 53*(1), 371–399. doi:10.1146/annurev.psych.53.100901.135233 PMID:11752490

Braithwaite, J., & Pettit, P. (1990). *Not just deserts: A republican theory of criminal justice*. Oxford, UK: Clarendon Press.

Bramston, P., Pretty, G., & Chipuer, H. (2002). Unravelling Subjective Quality of Life: An Investigation of Individual and Community Determinants. *Social Indicators Research, 59*(3), 261–274. doi:10.1023/A:1019617921082

Bramwell, L., & Hykawy, E. (1999). The Delphi technique: A possible tool for predicting future events in nursing education. *Canadian Journal of Nursing Research*, *30*(4), 47–58. PMID:10603776

Braveman, P. A., Cubbin, C., Egerter, S., Chideya, S., Marchi, K. S., Metzier, M., & Posner, S. (2005). Socioeconomic status in health research: One size does not fit all. *Journal of the American Medical Association*, *294*(22), 2879–2888. doi:10.1001/jama.294.22.2879 PMID:16352796

Bray, M. (2011). Facing the shadow education system in Hong Kong. *The Newsletter*, *56*, 20.

British Columbia. (2009). *British Columbia Regional Socio-Economic Indicators: Methodology*. British Columbia: Ministry of Labor & Citizens Services.

Britz, J. J., Lor, P. J., Coetzee, I. E. M., & Bester, B. C. (2006). Africa as a knowledge society: A reality check. *The International Information & Library Review*, *38*, 25–40.

Bronfenbrenner, U. (1977). Toward an experimental psychology of human development. *The American Psychologist*, *32*(7), 513–532. doi:10.1037/0003-066X.32.7.513

Brown, D. (2009). *Good practice guidelines for indicator development and reporting*. Busan: OECD. Retrieved September 10, 2015, from http://www.oecd.org/site/progresskorea/43586563.pdf

Brown, B. B. (1968). *Delphi process: A methodology used for the elicitation of opinions of experts (No. RAND-P-3925)*. Santa Monica, CA: RAND CORP.

Brown, T. E., & Ulijn, J. M. (Eds.). (2004). *Innovation, entrepreneurship and culture: the interaction between technology, progress and economic growth*. Edward Elgar Publishing. doi:10.4337/9781845420550

Brüggemann, R., & Patil, G. P. (2011). *Ranking and prioritization for multi-indicator systems: Introduction to partial order applications*. Springer Science & Business Media. doi:10.1007/978-1-4419-8477-7

Brunello, G., & Schlotter, M. (2011). *Non-cognitive skills and personality traits: Labour market relevance and their development in education & training systems*. Academic Press.

Bryant, F. B., & Yarnold, P. R. (1995). Principal-components analysis and exploratory and confirmatory factor analysis. In L. G. Grimm & P. R. Yarnold (Eds.), *Reading and understanding multivariate statistics* (pp. 99–136). Washington, DC: American Psychological Association.

Bucken-Knapp, G. (2001). Just a train-ride away, but still worlds apart: Prospects for the Øresund region as a binational city. *GeoJournal*, *54*(1), 51–60. doi:10.1023/A:1021188631424

Bucken-Knapp, G. (2002). Testing our borders: Questions of national and regional identity in the Øresund region. *Journal of Baltic Studies*, *33*(2), 199–219. doi:10.1080/01629770200000051

Buffel, T., Phillipson, C., & Scharf, T. (2012). Ageing in urban environments: Developing "age-friendly" cities. *Critical Social Policy*, *32*(4), 597–617. doi:10.1177/0261018311430457

Bühler, K. G. (2008). The Austrian Rule of Law Initiative 2004-2008. *The Panel Series, the Advisory Group and the Final Report on the UN Security Council and the Rule of Law. Max Planck UNYB*, *12*, 409.

Bulbul, S., & Kose, A. (2010). Turkiye'de bolgelerarasi ic goc hareketlerinin cok boyutlu olcekleme yontemi ile incelenmesi. *Istanbul Universitesi Isletme Fakultesi Dergisi*, *39*(1), 75-94. Retrieved from http://www.journals.istanbul.edu.tr/iuisletme/index

Burton, E. J., Mitchell, L., & Stride, C. B. (2011). Good places for ageing in place: Development of objective built environment measures for investigating links with older people's wellbeing. *BMC Public Health*, *11*(1), 839. doi:10.1186/1471-2458-11-839 PMID:22044518

Bygvrå, S., & Wetlund, H. (2005). Shopping behaviour in the Øresund region before and after the establishment of the fixed link between Denmark and Sweden. *GeoJournal*, *61*(1), 41–52. doi:10.1007/s10708-005-0876-6

Byrne, B. M. (2001). *Structural equation modelling with AMOS: Basic concepts, applications and programming*. Mahwah, NJ: Lawrence Erlbaum Associates.

Cafiero, C. (2013). *What do we really know about food security?* National Bureau of Economic Research. doi:10.3386/w18861

Cafiero, C., Melgar-Quiñonez, H. R., Ballard, T. J., & Kepple, A. W. (2014). Validity and reliability of food security measures. *Annals of the New York Academy of Sciences*, *1331*(1), 230–248. doi:10.1111/nyas.12594 PMID:25407084

Camagni, R., Gibelli, M. C., & Rigamonti, P. (2002). Urban mobility and urban form: The social and environmental costs of different patterns of urban expansion. *Ecological Economics*, *40*(2), 199–216. doi:10.1016/S0921-8009(01)00254-3

Camp & Speidel. (1987). The military burden, economic growth, and the human suffering index: Evidence from the LDCs. *Cambridge Journal of Economics*, *13*(4), 497–515.

Canadian Institute for Health Information (2005). *Developing a healthy community's index: A collection of papers*. Author.

Caracciolo, F., & Santeramo, F. G. (2013). Price Trends and Income Inequalities: Will Sub-Saharan Africa Reduce the Gap? *African Development Review*, *25*(1), 42–54. doi:10.1111/j.1467-8268.2013.12012.x

Carletto, C., Zezza, A., & Banerjee, R. (2013). Towards better measurement of household food security: Harmonizing indicators and the role of household surveys. *Global Food Security*, *2*(1), 30–40. doi:10.1016/j.gfs.2012.11.006

Carlson, B. A. (1999). *Social dimensions of economic development and productivity: inequality and social performance*. CEPAL.

Caro, D. H. (2009). Socio-economic status and academic achievement trajectories from childhood to adolescence. *Canadian Journal of Education*, *32*(3), 558–590.

Carvalho, N., Carvalho, L., & Nunes, S. (2015). A methodology to measure innovation in European Union through the national innovation system. *International Journal of Innovation and Regional Development*, *6*(2), 159–180. doi:10.1504/IJIRD.2015.069703

Castellacci, F., & Natera, J. M. (2013). The dynamics of national innovation systems: A panel cointegration analysis of the coevolution between innovative capability and absorptive capacity. *Research Policy*, *42*(3), 579–594. doi:10.1016/j.respol.2012.10.006

Catell, R. B. (1966). The scree test for numbers of factors. *Multivariate Behavioral Research*, *1*(2), 245–276. doi:10.1207/s15327906mbr0102_10 PMID:26828106

Cetin, G., & Nisanci, S. H. (2010). Enhancing students' environmental awareness. *Procedia: Social and Behavioral Sciences*, *2*(2), 1830–1834. doi:10.1016/j.sbspro.2010.03.993

Chang, Y.-J., Schneider, L., & Finkbeiner, M. (2015). Assessing child development: A critical review and the Sustainable Child Development Index (SCDI). *Sustainability*, *7*(5), 4973–4996. doi:10.3390/su7054973

Charnes, A., Cooper, W. W., & Rhodes, E. (1978). Measuring the efficiency of decision making units. *European Journal of Operational Research*, *2*(6), 429–444. doi:10.1016/0377-2217(78)90138-8

Chen, E. (2007). Why socioeconomic status affects the health of children: A psychosocial perspective. *American Psychological Society*, *13*(3), 112–114.

Cherchye, L., Moesen, W., Rogge, N., & van Puyenbroeck, T. V. (2007). An introduction to 'benefit of the doubt' composite indicators. *Social Indicators Research*, *82*(1), 111–145. doi:10.1007/s11205-006-9029-7

Cherchye, L., Moesen, W., Rogge, N., & van Puyenbroeck, T. V. (2011). Constructing composite indicators with imprecise data: A proposal. *Expert Systems with Applications*, *38*(9), 10940–10949. doi:10.1016/j.eswa.2011.02.136

Cherchye, L., Moesen, W., Rogge, N., Van Puyenbroeck, T., Saisana, M., Saltelli, A., & Tarantola, S. (2008). Creating composite indicators with DEA and robustness analysis: The case of the Technology Achievement Index. *The Journal of the Operational Research Society*, *59*(2), 239–251. doi:10.1057/palgrave.jors.2602445

Cheung, A. C., Yuen, T. W., Yuen, C. Y., & Cheong Cheng, Y. (2011). Strategies and policies for Hong Kong's higher education in Asian markets: Lessons from the United Kingdom, Australia, and Singapore. *International Journal of Educational Management*, *25*(2), 144–163. doi:10.1108/09513541111107579

Ćirović, M., Petrović, N., & Slović, D. (2012). Towards sustainable organization: measuring environmental performance indicators, *Proceedings of 31ˢᵗ International Conference on Organizational Science Development QUALITY. INNOVATION. FUTURE.*

Cirovic, M., Petrovic, N., & Slovic, D. (2014). EPI: Environmental Feedback on the Organization's Sustainability. In M. Levi Jakšić, S. Barjaktarović Rakočević, & M. Martić (Eds.), *Innovative Management and Firm Performance: An Interdisciplinary Approach and Cases* (pp. 122–138). Palgrave Macmillan. doi:10.1057/9781137402226_6

Clarke, M. (2003). e-Development? Development and the new economy. In UNU World Institute for Development Economics Research. Policy Brief No. 7. Helsinki: United Nations University.

Coenen, L., Moodysson, J., & Asheim, B. (2004). Nodes, networks and proximities: On the knowledge dynamics of the Medicon Valley biotech cluster. *European Planning Studies*, *12*(7), 1003–1018. doi:10.1080/0965431042000267876

Cohen, D., & Prusak, L. (2001). *In good company: How social capital makes organizations work*. Boston: Harvard Business School Press.

Commission of the European Communities. (1984). *The regions of Europe: Second periodic report on the social and economic situation of the regions of the community, together with a statement of the regional policy committee*. Luxembourg: OPOCE.

Conserve Energy Future – CEF. (2015). *Current environmental problems*. Retrieved from http://www.conserve-energy-future.com/15-current-environmental-problems.php

Coob, J., & Daly, H. (1989). *For the common dood. Redirecting the economy toward community, the environment and a sustainable future*. Boston: Beacon Press.

Cooper, W. W., Ruiz, J. L., & Sirvent, I. (2009). Selecting non-zero weights to evaluate effectiveness of basketball players. *European Journal of Operational Research*, *195*(2), 563–574. doi:10.1016/j.ejor.2008.02.012

Cooper, W., Seiford, M. S., & Tone, K. (2000). *Introduction to Data Envelopment Analysis and its uses: With DEA-solver software and references*. New York: Springer.

Cornell University, INSEAD, & WIPO. (2014). *The Global Innovation Index 2014: The Human Factor In innovation*. Fontainebleau, Ithaca, and Geneva: Cornell University, INSEAD, WIPO.

Creswell, J. W. (2003). *Research design: Qualitative, quantitative and mixed methods approaches* (2nd ed.). London: SAGE Publications.

Crosnoe, R. (2007). Early child care and the school readiness of children from Mexican immigrant families.[Spring]. *IMR, 41*(1), 152–181.

Cross, R. T., & Price, R. F. (1999). The social responsibility of science and the public understanding of science. *International Journal of Science Education, 21*(7), 775–785. doi:10.1080/095006999290435

Cummings, W. K. (2014). *Education and equality in Japan.* Princeton University Press.

Cunha, F., & Heckman, J. (2007). The technology of skill formation. *American Economic Review, 97*(2), 31–47. doi:10.1257/aer.97.2.31

Cunningham, S. W., & Kwakkel, J. (2011). Innovation forecasting: A case study of the management of engineering and technology literature. *Technological Forecasting and Social Change, 78*(2), 346–357. doi:10.1016/j.techfore.2010.11.001

Dalkey, N., & Helmer, O. (1963). An experimental application of the Delphi method to the use of experts. *Management Science, 9*(3), 458–467. doi:10.1287/mnsc.9.3.458

Daly, H. E., Cobb, J. B., & Cobb, C. W. (1994). *For the common good: Redirecting the economy toward community, the environment, and a sustainable future.* Beacon Press.

Data, S. P. S. S., Data, S. A. S., & Data, R. D. (2013). *TIMSS and PIRLS 2011: Relationships among reading, mathematics, and science achievement at the fourth grade—Implications for early learning.* Academic Press.

Davey Smith, G., Ben-Shlomo, Y., & Hart, C. (1999). Use of census-based aggregate variables to proxy for socioeconomic group: Evidence from national samples. *American Journal of Epidemiology, 150*(9), 996–997. doi:10.1093/oxfordjournals.aje.a010109 PMID:10547146

Davis, K. E. (2004). What can the Rule of Law variable tell us about Rule of Law reforms? *NYU Law and Economics Research Paper,* 4-26. doi: 10.2139/ssrn.595142

Davis, K. E., & Kruse, M. B. (2007). Taking the measure of law: The case of the Doing Business project. *Law & Social Inquiry, 32*(4), 1095–1119. doi:10.1111/j.1747-4469.2007.00088.x

Davis, P., McLeod, K., Ransom, M., Ongley, P., Pearce, N., & Howden-Chapman, P. (1999). The New Zealand Socioeconomic Index: Developing and validating an occupationally-derived indicator of socioeconomic status. *Australian and New Zealand Journal of Public Health, 23*(1), 27–33. doi:10.1111/j.1467-842X.1999.tb01201.x PMID:10083686

De la Fuente, A., & Doménech, R. (2006). Human capital in growth regressions: How much difference does data quality make? *Journal of the European Economic Association, 4*(1), 1–36. doi:10.1162/jeea.2006.4.1.1

De la Fuente, A., & Doménech, R. (2015). Educational attainment in the OECD, 1960–2010. Updated series and a comparison with other sources. *Economics of Education Review, 48,* 56–74. doi:10.1016/j.econedurev.2015.05.004

De Sousa, L. (2013). Understanding European cross-border cooperation: A framework for analysis. *Journal of European Integration, 35*(6), 669–687. doi:10.1080/07036337.2012.711827

Decancq, K., & Lugo, M. A. (2013). Weights in multidimensional indices of wellbeing: An overview. *Econometric Reviews, 32*(1), 7–34. doi:10.1080/07474938.2012.690641

Decoville, A., Durand, F., Sohn, C., & Walther, O. (2013). Comparing cross-border metropolitan integration in Europe: Towards a functional typology. *Journal of Borderland Studies, 28*(2), 221–237. doi:10.1080/08865655.2013.854654

Delanghe, H., & Muldur, U. (2014). Research and experimental development (R&D) and technological innovation policy. In S. N. Durlauf & L. E. Blume (Eds.), *The New Palgrave Dictionary of Economics*. Online Edition.

Della Porta, D., & Vannucci, D. (1999). *Corrupt exchanges: Actors, Resources, and Mechanisms of Political corruption*. New York: Walter de Gruyter.

Demir, N., Yasa, S., & Dagdemir, V. (2013). Duzey 1 Bolgelerine Gore Yoksulluk ve Goc Durumu. *Journal of the Faculty of Agriculture, 44*(1), 99–102. Retrieved from http://dergipark.ulakbim.gov.tr/ataunizfd/

Desai, M., Fukuda-Parr, S., Johansson, C., & Sagasti, F. (2002). Measuring the technology achievement of nations and the capacity to participate in the network age. *Journal of Human Development, 3*(1), 95–122. doi:10.1080/14649880120105399

Despotis, D. K. (2005). A reassessment of the human development index via data envelopment analysis. *The Journal of the Operational Research Society, 56*(8), 969–980. doi:10.1057/palgrave.jors.2601927

Despotis, D. K. (2005). Measuring human development via data envelopment analysis: The case of Asia and the Pacific. *Omega, 33*(5), 385–390. doi:10.1016/j.omega.2004.07.002

Diener, E. (1995). A value based index for measuring national quality of life. *Social Indicators Research, 36*(2), 107–127. doi:10.1007/BF01079721

Diez-Roux, A. V. (2003). Residential environments and cardiovascular risk. *Journal of Urban Health, 80*(4), 569–589. doi:10.1093/jurban/jtg065 PMID:14709706

Dobrota, M., Bulajic, M., Bornmann, L., & Jeremic, V. (2016). A new approach to the QS University ranking using the composite I-distance indicator: Uncertainty and sensitivity analyses. *Journal of the Association for Information Science and Technology, 67*(1), 200–211. doi:10.1002/asi.23355

Dobrota, M., Jeremić, V., Bulajić, M., & Radojičić, Z. (2015). Uncertainty and Sensitivity Analyzes of PISA Efficiency: Distance Based Analysis Approach. *Acta Polytechnica Hungarica, 12*(3).

Dobrota, M., Martic, M., Bulajic, M., & Jeremic, V. (2015). Two-phased composite I-distance indicator approach for evaluation of countries' information development. *Telecommunications Policy, 39*(5), 406–420. doi:10.1016/j.telpol.2015.03.003

Dobrota, M., Savic, G., & Bulajic, M. (2015). A new approach to the evaluation of countries' educational structure and development: The European study. *European Review (Chichester, England), 23*(4), 553–565. doi:10.1017/S1062798715000277

Dolton, P., Marcenaro-Gutiérrez, O., & Still, A. (2014). *The efficiency index: Which education systems deliver the best value for money?* London: GEMS Education Solutions.

Dragu, T., & Polborn, M. (2014). The rule of law in the fight against terrorism. *American Journal of Political Science, 58*(2), 511–525. doi:10.1111/ajps.12061

Dreger, C., Erber, G., & Glocker, D. (2009). *Regional measures of human capital in the European Union* (No. 3919). IZA Discussion Papers. doi: 10.2139/ssrn.1285563

Dreher, A., Gaston, N., & Martens, P. (2008). *Measuring globalization - Gauging its consequences*. New York: Springer.

Drucker, P. F. (1993). *Post-capitalist society*. New York: HarperCollins.

Duff, A. S. (2000). *Information society studies*. London: Routledge.

Dunteman, G. H. (1989). *Principal Components Analysis*. Newbury Park, CA: SAGE Publications, Inc.; doi:10.4135/9781412985475

Durand, F., & Nelles, J. (2014). Binding cross-border regions: An analysis of cross-border governance in Lille-Kortrijk-Tournai Eurometropolis. *Tijdschrift voor Economische en Sociale Geografie, 105*(5), 573–590. doi:10.1111/tesg.12063

Dutta, S., & Mia, I. (2009). *The global information technology report 2008–2009: Mobility in a networked world.* Geneva: World Economic Forum & INSEAD.

Earth Summit. (2002). Retrieved from http://www.earthsummit2002.org/Es2002.pdf

ECMap. (2012). *Fact sheet.* Retrieved December 19, 2015, from http://www.ecmap.ca/images/ECMap_FactSheets/ECMap_Communities_FactSheet_20120914.pdf

ECMap. (2014). *How are our young children doing? Final Report of the Early Child Development Mapping Project (ECMap) Alberta.* Retrieved December 19, 2015, from http://www.ecmap.ca/images/ECMap_Reports/ECMap_Final_Report_20141118.pdf

Economic Planning Unit Malaysia. (2001). *The third outline perspective plan 2001 - 2010.* Prime Minister's Department.

Economic Planning Unit Malaysia. (2005). *International comparison: The knowledge-based economy development index 2000/2004.* Retrieved from http://www.epu.gov.my/html/themes/epu/images/common/pdf/ME_2005_chapt_ 13.pdf

Eibner, C., & Sturm, R. (2006). US-based indices of area-level deprivation: Results from health care for communities. *Social Science & Medicine, 62*(2), 348–359. doi:10.1016/j.socscimed.2005.06.017 PMID:16039764

Eisner, R. (1985). The Total Incomes System of Accounts. *Survey of Current Business, 65*(1), 24–48. doi:10.1111/j.1475-4991.1991.tb00385.x

EIU. (2008). *E-readiness rankings 2008: Maintaining momentum.* A white paper from the Economist Intelligence Unit.

EIU. (2009). *Country forecast Eastern Europe.* London: Economist Intelligence Unit.

Emerson, J. W., Hsu, A., Levy, M. A., de Sherbinin, A., Mara, V., Esty, D. C., & Jaiteh, M. (2012). *Environmental performance index and pilot trend environmental performance index.* New Haven, CT: Yale Center for Environmental Law and Policy.

Emerson, J., Esty, D. C., Levy, M. A., Kim, C. H., Mara, V., de Sherbinin, A., & Srebotnjak, T. (2010). *Environmental performance index.* New Haven, CT: Yale Center for Environmental Law and Policy.

Emil, S. (1994). *The challenge of sustainable consumption as seen from the South.* In *Symposium: Sustainable Consumption,* Oslo, Norway.

Englehart, N. A. (2000). Rights and culture in the Asian values argument: The rise and fall of Confucian ethics in Singapore. *Human Rights Quarterly, 22*(2), 548–568. doi:10.1353/hrq.2000.0024

Ensminger, M. E., & Fothergill, K. (2003). A decade of measuring SES: What it tells us and where to go from here? In M. H. Bornstein & R. H. Bradley (Eds.), *Socioeconomic Status, Parenting, and Child Development.* Lawrence Erlbaum Associates.

Environmental Performance Index (EPI). (2015). *Global Metrics for The Environment.* Retrieved from http://epi.yale.edu/

Epstein, M. J., & Roy, M. J. (2001). Sustainability in Action: Identifying and Measuring the Key Performance Drivers. *Long Range Planning, 34*(5), 584–604. doi:10.1016/S0024-6301(01)00084-X

Eryigit, S. B., Eryigit, K. Y., & Selen, U. (2012). The long-run linkages between education, health and defence expenditures and economic growth: Evidence from Turkey. *Defence and Peace Economics, 23*(6), 559–574. doi:10.1080/10242694.2012.663577

Eskandari, H., Sala-Diakanda, S., Furterer, S., et al. (2007). Enhancing the undergraduate industrial engineering curriculum, Defining desired characteristics and emerging topics. *Education + Training, 49*(1), 45-55.

Eskandari, H., Sala-Diakanda, S., Furterer, S., Rabelo, L., Crumpton-Young, L., & Williams, K. (2007). Enhancing the undergraduate industrial engineering curriculum: Defining desired characteristics and emerging topics. *Education+ Training, 49*(1), 45-55.

Esteban, G. G., Lopez-Pueyo, C., & Sanaú, J. (2015). Human capital measurement in OECD countries and its relation to GDP growth and innovation. *Revista de economía mundial, 39*, 77-108. Retrieved from http://rabida.uhu.es/dspace/handle/10272/10697

Estes, R. J. (1998). Trends in world social development, 1970-95: Development prospects for a new century. In P. K. Nandi & S. M. Shahidullah (Eds.), *Globalization and the evolving world society* (pp. 11–39). Leiden: Brill.

Esty, D. C., Levy, M. A., Srebotnjak, T., de Sherbinin, A., Kim, C. H., & Anderson, B. (2006). *Pilot 2006 environmental performance index*. New Haven, CT: Yale Center for Environmental Law & Policy.

Esty, D. C., Levy, M., Srebotnjak, T., & de Sherbinin, A. (2005). *2005 environmental sustainability index: Benchmarking national environmental stewardship*. New Haven, CT: Yale Center for Environmental Law and Policy.

Esty, D., Levy, M., Kim, C., de Sherbinin, A., Srebotnjak, T., & Mara, V. (2008). *2008 environmental performance index*. New Haven, CT: Yale Center for Environmental Law and Policy.

Etemad, H., & Séguin Dulude, L. (1987). Patenting patterns in 25 large multinational enterprises. *Technovation, 7*(1), 1–15. doi:10.1016/0166-4972(87)90043-5

Etlie, J. E. (2000). *Managing Technological Innovation*. John Wiley & Sons.

European Comission, Directorate-General for Internal Market, Industry, Entrepreneurship and SMEs. (2015). *Innovation Union Scoreboard Report 2015*. Available at: http://ec.europa.eu/growth/industry/innovation/facts-figures/scoreboards/files/ius-2015_en.pdf

European Commission. (2005). *Sustainable development indicators to monitor the implementation of the EU sustainable development strategy*. Brussels: Commission of the European Communities.

European Commission. (2005). *Towards a European research area – science, technology and innovation – key figures 2005*. Luxembourg: Office for Publications of the European Communities.

European Commission. (2010). *Europe 2020: A European strategy for smart, sustainable and inclusive growth*. Brussels: European Commission.

European Commission. (2015). *Clean transport, Urban transport*. Retrieved July 10, 2015, from http://ec.europa.eu/transport/themes/urban/urban_mobility/index_en.htm

European Commission. (2015). *CORDIS: Community Research and Development Information Service*. Retrieved November 25, 2015, from http://cordis.europa.eu/home_en.html

European Foundation for the Improvement of Living and Working Conditions. (2004). *European knowledge society foresight: The Euforia project synthesis*. Retrieved from http://www.eurofound.europa.eu/pubdocs/2004/04/en/1/ef0404en.pdf

Europian Commission - EC. (2003). *EMAS – guidance*. Retrieved from http://ec.europa.eu/environment/emas/pdf/guidance/guidance08_en.pdf

Eurostat. (2008). *Feasibility study on the measure of wellbeing presentation of Eurostat work*. Brussels: Eurostat/Strategic Development Group.

Eurostat. (2015). *Statistics explained: Patent statistics.* Retrieved November 25, 2015, http://ec.europa.eu/eurostat/statistics-explained/index.php/Patent_statistics

Evans, G. W., & Wachs, T. D. (Eds.). (2010). Chaos and its Influence on Children's Development. Washington, DC: American Psychological Association.

Evans, G. W. (2004). The environment of childhood poverty. *The American Psychologist, 59*(2), 77–92. doi:10.1037/0003-066X.59.2.77 PMID:14992634

Evans, G. W. (2006). Child development and the physical environment. *Annual Review of Psychology, 57*(1), 423–451. doi:10.1146/annurev.psych.57.102904.190057 PMID:16318602

Evans, P. B., & Wurster, T. S. (1997). Strategies and the new economics of information. *Harvard Business Review,* (September), 71–82. PMID:10170332

Evers, H. (2001). *Towards a Malaysian knowledge society.* Paper read at The 3rd International Malaysian Studies Conference (MSC3), Bangi, Selangor.

Faculty of Organizational Sciences – FOS. (2015a). *Master Studies – Management.* Retrieved from http://www.fon.bg.ac.rs/eng/studies/master-and-specialized-studies/management/

Faculty of Organizational Sciences – FOS. (2015b). *Master Studies – Management – Curriculum.* Retrieved from http://www.fon.bg.ac.rs/downloads/2014/04/Knjiga-predmeta.pdf (In Serbian)

FAO. (2013). *New metrics to measure and monitor performance in agriculture and food security.* Paper presented at the FAO conference, Rome, Italy.

Feldman, P. H., & Oberlink, M. R. (2003). Developing community indicators to promote the health and well-being of older people. *Family & Community Health, 26*(4), 268–274. doi:10.1097/00003727-200310000-00004 PMID:14528133

Feniger, Y. (2011). The gender gap in advanced math and science course taking: Does same-sex education make a difference? *Sex Roles, 65*(9-10), 670–679. doi:10.1007/s11199-010-9851-x

Fernández-Carro, C., & Evandrou, M. (2014). Staying Put: Factors Associated with Ageing in One's 'Lifetime Home'. Insights from the European Context. *RASP - Research on Ageing and Social Policy, 2*(1). Retrieved from http://www.hipatiapress.com/hpjournals/index.php/rasp/article/view/1053

Field, A. (2000). *Discovering statistics using SPSS for Windows: Advanced techniques for beginners (Introducing Statistical Methods series).* Sage Publications.

Field, B. C., & Field, M. K. (2006). *Environmental Economics: An Introduction.* New York: McGrawHill/Urwin.

Filiztekin, A. (2012). *Bolgesel Buyume, Es-Hareketlilik ve Sektorel Yapı* (No. 2012/61). Discussion Paper, Turkish Economic Association.

Fischer, C. S. (1973). On Urban Alienations and Anomie: Powerlessness and Social Isolation. *American Sociological Review, 38*(3), 311–326. doi:10.2307/2094355 PMID:4711439

Flood, R. L., & Carson, E. (2013). *Dealing with complexity: an introduction to the theory and application of systems science.* Springer Science & Business Media.

Foa, R., & Tanner, J. (2012). *Methodology of the Social Development Indices.* International Institute for Social Studies Working Paper # 2012-04. The Hague: International Institute of Social Studies.

Folloni, G., & Vittadini, G. (2010). Human capital measurement: A survey. *Journal of Economic Surveys, 24*(2), 248–279. doi:10.1111/j.1467-6419.2009.00614.x

Forum for the Future. (2007). *The sustainable cities index, ranking the largest 20 British cities.* Retrieved August 1, 2015, from http://www.forumforthefuture.org.uk

Foth, N., Manaugh, K., & El-Geneidy, A. (2013). Towards equitable transit: Examining transit accessibility and social need in Toronto, Canada 1996-2006. *Journal of Transport Geography, 29*, 1–10. doi:10.1016/j.jtrangeo.2012.12.008

Fotso, J., & Kuate-defo, B. (2005). Measuring socioeconomic status in health research in developing countries: Should we be focusing on households, communities, or both? *Social Indicators Research, 72*(2), 189–237. doi:10.1007/s11205-004-5579-8

Fraumeni, B. M. (2008, November). *Human capital: From indicators and indexes to accounts.* Fondazione Giovanni Agnelli/OECD Workshop on the Measurement of Human Capital, Turin, Italy.

Frenken, K. (2002). A new indicator of European integration and an application to collaboration in scientific research. *Economic Systems Research, 14*(4), 345–361. doi:10.1080/0953531022000024833

Freudenberg, M. (2003). *Composite Indicators of Country Performance: A Critical Assessment.* OECD Science, Technology and Industry Working Papers, 2003/16. OECD Publishing. 10.1787/405566708255

Freudenberg, M. (2003). Composite indicators of country performance: A critical assessment. *OECD STI Working Papers, 2003*(16).

Freudenberg, M. (2003). *Composite indicators of country performance: A critical assessment.* STI working paper 2003/16. Paris: Organization for Economic Co-operation and Development (OECD).

Friedler, Y., & Tamir, P. (1990). Sex differences in science education in Israel: An analysis of 15 years of research. *Research in Science & Technological Education, 8*(1), 21–34. doi:10.1080/0263514900080103

Fukuda, Y., Nakamura, K., & Takano, T. (2007). Higher mortality in areas of lower socioeconomic position measured by a single index of deprivation in Japan. *Public Health, 121*(3), 163–173. doi:10.1016/j.puhe.2006.10.015 PMID:17222876

Furceri, D., & Mourougane, A. (2010). *Structural Indicators: A Critical Review.* OECD Publishing.

Gabbert, S., & Weikard, H. (2001). How widespread is undernourishment? A critique of measurement methods and new empirical results. *Food Policy, 26*(3), 209–228. doi:10.1016/S0306-9192(00)00043-9

Gadrey, J., & Jany-Catrice, F. (2007). *Les Nouveaux Indicateurs de Richesse.* Repères-La Découverte.

Gao, S. (2005). China's transformation into a knowledge-based economy. In *WBI Global Innovation Policy Dialogue: India and China.* Washington DC: World Bank Institute.

Garetz, W. V. (1993). *Current concerns regarding the implementation of risk-based management: how real are they? In Comparative Environmental Risk* (pp. 11–31). Boca Raton, FL: Lewis Publishing.

Gasic-Pavisic, S., Stanković, D. (2011). *Obrazovna postignuća učenika iz Srbije u istraživanju TIMSS 2011.* Beograd: Institut za pedagoška istraživanja. doi:.10.2298/ZIPI1202243G

GEDI. (2014). *The Global Entrepreneurship & Development Index.* Retrieved from http://www.thegedi.org/research/gedi-index/(Accessed 19 September 2015

Genn, H. (1997). Understanding Civil Justice. *Current Legal Problems, 50*(1), 155–187. doi:10.1093/clp/50.1.155

Gerke, S., & Evers, H. (2005). Local and global knowledge on Southeast Asia. In T. Menkhoff, H. Evers, & Y. W. Chay (Eds.), *Governing and managing knowledge in Asia*. London: World Scientific.

Gieryn, T. F. (2000). A Space for Place in Sociology. *Annual Review of Sociology, 26*(1), 463–469. doi:10.1146/annurev.soc.26.1.463

Gillham, B. (2000). *Developing a questionnaire*. London: Continuum.

Ginsburg, N., Osborn, J., & Blank, G. (1986). *Geographic perspectives on the wealth of nations*. Department of Geography Research Paper No. 220. University of Chicago.

Gisselquist, R. M. (2014). Developing and evaluating governance indexes: 10 questions. *Policy Studies, 35*(5), 513–531. doi:10.1080/01442872.2014.946484

Glaeser, E., LaPorta, R., Lopez-de-Silanes, F., & Shleifer, A. (2004). Do institutions cause growth? *Journal of Economic Growth, 9*(3), 271–303. doi:10.1023/B:JOEG.0000038933.16398.ed

Godfray, H. C. J., Beddington, J. R., Crute, I. R., Haddad, L., Lawrence, D., Muir, J. F., & Toulmin, C. et al. (2010). Food security: The challenge of feeding 9 billion people. *Science, 327*(5967), 812–818. doi:10.1126/science.1185383 PMID:20110467

Goedkoop, M. & Spriensma, R. (2001). *The eco-indicator 99: A damage oriented method for life cycle assessment - methodology report*. Amersfoort: PRé Consultants.

Goossens, Y., Mäkipää, A., Schepelmann, P., de Sand, I., Kuhndt, M., & Herrndorf, M. (2007). *Alternative progress indicators to gross domestic product (GDP) as a means towards sustainable development. Study provided for the European Parliament's Committee on the Environment, Public Health and Food Safety*. PDESP/European Parliament.

Graham, J. W., & Webb, R. H. (1979). Stocks and depreciation of human capital: New evidence from a present-value perspective. *Review of Income and Wealth, 25*(2), 209–224. doi:10.1111/j.1475-4991.1979.tb00094.x

Graymore, M. (2005). *Journey of sustainability: Small regions, sustainable carrying capacity and sustainability assessment methods*. (Unpublished doctoral dissertation). Griffith University.

Gregersen, F. (2003). Factors influencing the linguistic development in the Øresund region. *International Journal of the Sociology of Language*, (159), 139–152. doi:10.1515/ijsl.2003.003

Grönlund, A., Svärdsten, F., & Öhman, P. (2011). Value for money and the rule of law: The (new) performance audit in Sweden. *International Journal of Public Sector Management, 24*(2), 107–121. doi:10.1108/09513551111109026

Grootaert, C., Narayan, D., Jones, V. N., & Woolcock, M. (2004). *Measuring social capital: An integrated questionnaire*. The World Bank. Retrieved from http://books.google.com.my/books?id=2PLkjetXoC&dq='What+is+Social+Capital+world+bank+1999&printsec=frontcover&source=in&hl=en&ei=JsBmSqTFMZCG6AP8qajACQ&sa=X&oi=book_result&ct=result&resnum=12

Grossman, G. M., & Krueger, A. B. (1994). *Economic growth and the environment (No. w4634)*. National Bureau of Economic Research. doi:10.3386/w4634

Grubb, M., Koch, M., Thomson, K., Munson, A., & Sullivan, F. (1993). *The earth summit agreements: a guide to assessment*. An analysis of the Rio'92 UN Conference on Environment and Development.

Grupp, H., & Mogee, M. (2004). Indicators for national science and technology policy: How robust are composite indicators? *Research Policy, 33*(9), 1373–1384. doi:10.1016/j.respol.2004.09.007

Grupp, H., & Schubert, T. (2010). Review and new evidence on composite innovation indicators for evaluating national performance. *Research Policy*, *39*(1), 67–78. doi:10.1016/j.respol.2009.10.002

Guan, J., & Chen, K. (2012). Modeling the relative efficiency of national innovation systems. *Research Policy*, *41*(1), 102–115. doi:10.1016/j.respol.2011.07.001

Gudeva, L. K., Dimova, V., Daskalovska, N., & Trajkova, F. (2012). Designing descriptors of learning outcomes for Higher Education qualification. *Procedia: Social and Behavioral Sciences*, *46*, 1306–1311. doi:10.1016/j.sbspro.2012.05.292

Guttorp, P., & Kim, T. Y. (2013). Uncertainty in ranking the hottest years of U.S. surface temperatures. *Journal of Climate*, *26*(17), 6323–6328. doi:10.1175/JCLI-D-12-00760.1

Guyon, I., & Elisseeff, A. (2003). An introduction to variable and feature selection. *Journal of Machine Learning Research*, *3*, 1157–1182.

Gwartney, J., & Lawson, R. (2007). Economic freedom of the world: 2007 annual report. Vancouver: Fraser Institute.

Hagedoorn, J., & Cloodt, M. (2003). Measuring innovative performance: Is there and advantage in using multiple indicators? *Research Policy*, *32*(8), 1365–1379. doi:10.1016/S0048-7333(02)00137-3

Hagén, H.-O. (2004). *Background facts on economic statistics 2004:15 - Comparing welfare of nations*. Stockholm: Department of Economic Statistics, Statistics Sweden.

Hagerty, M. R., & Land, K. C. (2007). Constructing Summary Indices of Quality of Life: A Model for the Effect of Heterogeneous Importance Weights. *Sociological Methods & Research*, *35*(4), 455–496. doi:10.1177/0049124106292354

Haggard, S., & Tiede, L. (2011). The rule of law and economic growth: Where are we? *World Development*, *39*(5), 673–685. doi:10.1016/j.worlddev.2010.10.007

Hair, J. F., Black, W. C., Babin, B. J., & Anderson, R. E. (2010). *Multivariate data analysis* (7th ed.). Upper Saddle River, NJ: Pearson Prentice Hall.

Hamid, N. A. (2011). *Development and validation of a knowledge society model and indicators in the Malaysian context*. (Unpublished Doctoral Thesis). Universiti Kebangsaan Malaysia.

Hansen, T. (2013). Bridging regional innovation: Cross-border collaboration in the Øresund region. *Geografisk Tidsskrift – Danish Journal of Geography*, *113*(1), 25–38. doi:10.1080/00167223.2013.781306

Hansen, T., & Hansen, R. (2006). Integration of the scientific community as exemplified by the biotech sector: An analysis based on bibliometric indicators in the Danish–Swedish border region. *GeoJournal*, *67*(3), 241–252. doi:10.1007/s10708-007-9057-0

Han, T. S., Lin, C. Y. Y., & Chen, M. Y. C. (2008). Developing human capital indicators: A three-way approach. *International Journal of Learning and Intellectual Capital*, *5*(3-4), 387–403. doi:10.1504/IJLIC.2008.021018

Hanushek, E. A., & Woessmann, L. (2007). *The Role of Education Quality for Economic Growth*. Washington, DC: World Bank. doi:10.1596/1813-9450-4122

Hanushek, E. A., & Woessmann, L. (2010). Education and Economic Growth. In D. J. Brewer & P. J. McEwan (Eds.), *Economics of Education*. Amsterdam: Elsevier. doi:10.1016/B978-0-08-044894-7.01227-6

Hanushek, E. A., & Woessmann, L. (2012). Do better schools lead to more growth? Cognitive skills, economic outcomes, and causation. *Journal of Economic Growth*, *17*(4), 267–321. doi:10.1007/s10887-012-9081-x

Harding, E. (2007). *Towards Lifetime Neighbourhoods: Designing Sustainable Communities for All. A Discussion Paper.* London: International Longevity Centre UK. Retrieved September 10, 2015, from http://www.lifetimehomes.org.uk/data/files/Lifetime_Neighbourhoods/towards_lifetime_neighbourhoods_ilc_discussion_paper.pdf

Hatefi, S. M., & Torabi, S. A. (2010). A common weight MCDA–DEA approach to construct composite indicators. *Ecological Economics, 70*(1), 114–120. doi:10.1016/j.ecolecon.2010.08.014

Havard, S., Deguen, S., Bodin, J., Louis, K., Laurent, O., & Bard, D. (2008). A small-area index of socioeconomic deprivation to capture health inequalities in France. *Social Science & Medicine, 67*(12), 2007–2016. doi:10.1016/j.socscimed.2008.09.031 PMID:18950926

Haveman, R., & Wolfe, B. (1984). Schooling and economic well-being: The role of non-markets effects. *The Journal of Human Resources, 19*(3), 377–407. doi:10.2307/145879

Hawkins, D. (1980). *Identification of outliers.* London: Chapman and Hall. doi:10.1007/978-94-015-3994-4

Health Canada. (1996). *Toward a Common Understanding: Clarifying the Core Concepts of Population Health.* Ottawa: Health Canada.

Hermans, E. (2009). *A methodology for developing a composite road safety performance index for cross-country comparison.* (Doctoral Dissertation). Hasselt University, Belgium.

Hermans, E., Van den Bossche, F., & Wets, G. (2008). Combining road safety information in a performance index. *Accident; Analysis and Prevention, 40*(4), 1337–1344. doi:10.1016/j.aap.2008.02.004 PMID:18606264

Hertel, T. W. (2016). Food security under climate change. *Nature Climate Change, 6*(1), 10–13. doi:10.1038/nclimate2834

Hidalgo, C. A. (2010). *Graphical statistical methods for the representation of the human development index and its components.* Human Development Reports Research Paper, 39.

Hoff, E., Laursen, B., & Bridges, K. (2012). Measurement and model building in studying the influence of socioeconomic status on child development. In L. Mayes & M. Lewis (Eds.), *The Cambridge Handbook of Environment in Human Development* (pp. 590–606). New York: Cambridge University Press. doi:10.1017/CBO9781139016827.033

Hollbach-Grömig, B., & Trapp, J. H. (2006). *The Impact of Demographic Change on Local and Regional Government – Research Project.* Paris: Council of European Municipalities and Regions.

Holmes, K. R., Feulner, E. J., & O' Grady, M. A. (2008). *2008 index of economic freedom.* Washington, DC: The Heritage Foundation & Dow Jones & Company, Inc.

Holm, G., & Londen, M. (2010). The discourse on multicultural education in Finland: Education for whom? *Intercultural Education, 21*(2), 107–120. doi:10.1080/14675981003696222

Hooper, D. (2012). Exploratory Factor Analysis. In H. Chen (Ed.), *Approaches to Quantitative Research – Theory and its Practical Application: A Guide to Dissertation Students.* Cork, Ireland: Oak Tree.

Horwitch, M., & Stohr, E. A. (2012). Transforming technology management education: Value creation-learning in the early twenty-first century. *Journal of Engineering and Technology Management, 29*(4), 489–507. doi:10.1016/j.jengtecman.2012.07.003

Hospers, G.-J. (2006). Borders, bridges and branding: The transformation of the Øresund region into an imagined space. *European Planning Studies, 14*(8), 1015–1033. doi:10.1080/09654310600852340

Hotelling, H. (1933). Analysis of a complex of statistical variables into principal components. *Journal of Educational Psychology, 24*(6), 417–441. doi:10.1037/h0071325

Houweling, T. A. J., Kunst, A. E., & Mackenbach, J. P. (2003). Measuring health inequality among children in developing countries: Does the choice of the indicator of socioeconomic status matter? *International Journal for Equity in Health*, *2*(1), 8. doi:10.1186/1475-9276-2-8 PMID:14609435

Howell, D. C. (2008). The analysis of missing data. In W. Outhwaite & S. Turner (Eds.), *Handbook of social science methodology*. London: Sage.

Hsu, A., Emerson, J., Levy, M., de Sherbinin, A., Johnson, L., Malik, O., & Jaiteh, M. (2014). *The 2014 environmental performance index*. New Haven, CT: Yale Center for Environmental Law and Policy.

Huang, Y. (2012). *Confucius: a guide for the perplexed*. New York: Bloomsbury.

Hurley, A. E., Scandura, T. A., Schriesheim, C. A., Brannick, M. T., Seers, A., Vandenberg, R. J., & Williams, L. J. (1997). Exploratory and confirmatory factor analysis: Guidelines, issues, and alternatives. *Journal of Organizational Behavior*, *18*(6), 667–683. doi:10.1002/(SICI)1099-1379(199711)18:6<667::AID-JOB874>3.0.CO;2-T

IFA –International Federation on Aging. (2015). *Age - Friendly Cities and Communities – "Creating Enabling Environments" (The Conference Plenary Panel Abstract)*. Retrieved September 10, 2015, from http://www.ifa-fiv.org/wp-content/uploads/2015/06/Day-2-Plenary-Panel-Abstract.pdf

IMD. (2008). *IMD world competitiveness yearbook 2008*. Lausanne: International Institute for Management Development.

IMD. (2014). *IMD world competitiveness yearbook 2014*. Lausanne: International Institute for Management Development.

Isljamovic, S., Jeremic, V., Petrovic, N., & Radojicic, Z. (2015). Colouring the socio-economic development into green: I-distance framework for countries' welfare evaluation. *Quality & Quantity*, *49*(2), 617–629. doi:10.1007/s11135-014-0012-0

Ivanovic, B. (1977). *Classification theory*. Belgrade: Institute for Industrial Economics.

Jacobs, R., Smith, & Goddard. (2004). *Measuring performance: an examination of composite performance indicators*. Centre for Health Economics, Technical Paper Series 29.

Janus, M., & Offord, D. (2007). Development and psychometric properties of the early development instrument (EDI): A measure of children's school readiness. *Canadian Journal of Behavioural Science*, *39*(1), 1–22. doi:10.1037/cjbs2007001

Jeremic, V., Isljamovic, S., Petrovic, N., Radojicic, Z., Markovic, A., & Bulajic, M. (2011). Human development index and sustainability: What's the correlation? *Metalurgia international*, *16*(7), 63-67.

Jeremic, V., Milenkovic, M. J., Radojicic, Z., & Martic, M. (2013). Excellence with leadership: the crown indicator of Scimago Institutions Rankings Iber Report. *El profesional de la información*, *22*(5), 474-480.

Jeremić, V. (2012). *Statistički model efikasnosti zasnovan na Ivanovićevom odstojanju. Doktorska disertacija, Fakultet organizacionih nauka*. Beograd: Univerzitet u Beogradu.

Jeremic, V., & Jovanovic-Milenkovic, M. (2014). Evaluation of Asian university rankings: Position and perspective of leading Indian higher education institutions. *Current Science*, *106*(12), 1647–1653.

Jeremic, V., Jovanovic-Milenkovic, M., Martic, M., & Radojicic, Z. (2013). Excellence with Leadership: The crown indicator of SCImago Institutions Rankings IBER Report. *El Profesional de la Informacion*, *22*(5), 474–480. doi:10.3145/epi.2013.sep.13

Johnson, R. A., & Wichern, D. W. (2014). *Applied multivariate statistical analysis*. Essex, England: Pearson Prentice Hall.

Joliffe, I. T. (2002). *Principal Component Analysis* (2nd ed.). New York: Springer-Verlag, New York, Inc.; doi:10.1007/b98835

Jolliffe, I. (2002). *Principal component analysis* (2nd ed.). New York: Springer.

Jones, B. F. (2014). The Human Capital Stock: A Generalized Approach. *The American Economic Review*, *104*(11), 3752–3777. doi:10.1257/aer.104.11.3752

Jorgenson, D. W., & Fraumeni, B. M. (1989). Investment in education. *Educational Researcher*, *18*(4), 35–44. doi:10.3102/0013189X018004035

Jorgenson, D. W., & Fraumeni, B. M. (1992a). Investment in education and US economic growth. *The Scandinavian Journal of Economics*, *94*, 51–70. doi:10.2307/3440246

Jorgenson, D. W., & Fraumeni, B. M. (1992b). The output of the education sector. In *Output measurement in the service sectors* (pp. 303–341). University of Chicago Press.

Jovanovic, M., Jeremic, V., Savic, G., Bulajic, M., & Martic, M. (2012). How does the normalization of data affect the ARWU ranking? *Scientometrics*, *93*(2), 319–327. doi:10.1007/s11192-012-0674-0

Jovanovic-Milenkovic, M., Brajovic, B., Milenkovic, D., Vukmirovic, D., & Jeremic, V. (2015). (in press). Beyond the equal-weight framework of the Networked Readiness Index A multilevel I-distance methodology. *Information Development*. doi:10.1177/0266666915593136

Kaiser, H. (1970). A second generation little jiffy. *Psychometrika*, *35*(4), 401–415. doi:10.1007/BF02291817

Kaiser, H. (1974). An index of factorial simplicity. *Psychometrika*, *39*(1), 31–36. doi:10.1007/BF02291575

Karahan, O. (2012). Input-output indicators of knowledge-based economy and Turkey. *Journal of Business Economics and Finance*, *1*(2), 21–36. Retrieved from http://dergipark.ulakbim.gov.tr/jbef/index

Kardos, M.Research on European Union Countries. (2012). The relationship between entrepreneurship, innovation and sustainable development. Research on European Union Countries. *Procedia Economics and Finance*, *3*, 1030–1035. doi:10.1016/S2212-5671(12)00269-9

Katz, S. (2000). Busy Bodies: Activity, Aging, and the Management of Everyday Life. *Journal of Aging Studies*, *14*(2), 135–152. doi:10.1016/S0890-4065(00)80008-0

Kaufmann, D., Kraay, A., & Mastruzzi, M. (2007). *The worldwide governance indicators: Answering the critics*. World Bank Policy Research Working Paper No. 4149. Washington, DC: World Bank.

Kaufmann, D., Kraay, A., & Mastruzzi, M. (2008). *Governance matters VII: Aggregate and individual governance indicators for 1996–2007*. World Bank Policy Research Working Paper No. 4654. Washington, DC: World Bank.

Kaushal, N., Magnuson, K., & Waldfogel, J. (2011). *How is family income related to investments in children's learning?*. Russell Sage Foundation.

Kawamoto, S., Nakayama, M., & Saijo, M. (2011). A survey of scientific literacy to provide a foundation for designing science communication in Japan. *Public Understanding of Science (Bristol, England)*, *0963662511418893*. doi:10.1177/0963662511418893 PMID:23885051

Keane, E. (2011). Dependence-deconstruction: Widening participation and traditional-entry students transitioning from school to higher education in Ireland. *Teaching in Higher Education*, *16*(6), 707–718. doi:10.1080/13562517.2011.570437

Kendall, M. G. (1938). A New Measure of Rank Correlation. *Biometrika*, *30*(2), 81–93. doi:10.1093/biomet/30.1-2.81

Kendig, H. (2003). Directions in environmental gerontology: A multidisciplinary field. *The Gerontologist*, *43*(5), 611–615. doi:10.1093/geront/43.5.611 PMID:14570957

Kendrick, J. (1976). *The Formation and Stocks of Total Capital.* New York: Columbia University Press for NBER.

Kernan, M., & Devine, D. (2010). Being confined within? Constructions of the good childhood and outdoor play in early childhood education and care settings in Ireland. *Children & Society, 24*(5), 371–385. doi:10.1111/j.1099-0860.2009.00249.x

Kershaw, P., Irwin, L., Trafford, K., & Hertzman, C. (2005). *The British Columbia Atlas of Child Development* (Vol. 40). Human Early Learning Partnership, Western Geographical Press.

Khan, H. (2001). *Social Policy in Singapore: A Confucian model?* Washington, DC: World Bank Institute.

Kim, H. B., Fisher, D. L., & Fraser, B. J. (2000). Classroom environment and teacher interpersonal behavior in secondary science classes in Korea. *Evaluation and Research in Education, 14*(1), 3–22. doi:10.1080/09500790008666958

King's Fund. (2001). *The sick list 2000, the NHS from best to worst.* Retrieved December 2, 2014, from http://www.fulcrumtv.com/sick%20list.htm

Kirkegaard, E. O. (2014). *Crime, income, educational attainment and employment among immigrant groups in Norway and Finland.* Open Differential Psychology.

Kiryushin, P., Mulloth, B., & Iakovleva, T. (2013). Developing cross-border regional innovation systems with clean technology entrepreneurship: The case of Øresund. *International Journal of Innovation and Regional Development, 5*(2), 179–195. doi:10.1504/IJIRD.2013.055237

Kleinknecht, A., van Montfort, K., & Brouwer, E. (2002). The non-trivial choice between innovation indicators. *Economics of Innovation and New Technology, 11*(2), 109–121. doi:10.1080/10438590210899

Klemenovic, J. (2004). Factors of environmental education. *Pedagoška stvarnost, 50*(5-6), 366-381. (In Serbian)

Klugman, J., Rodríguez, F., & Choi, H. J. (2011). The HDI 2010: New controversies, old critiques. *The Journal of Economic Inequality, 9*(2), 249–288. doi:10.1007/s10888-011-9178-z

Knowles, R. (2006). Transport impacts of the Øresund (Copenhagen to Malmö) fixed link. *Geography (Sheffield, England), 91*(3), 227–240.

Knowles, R., & Matthiessen, C. (2009). Barrier effects of international borders on fixed link traffic generation: The case of Øresundsbron. *Journal of Transport Geography, 17*(3), 155–165. doi:10.1016/j.jtrangeo.2008.11.001

Knudsen, M., & Rich, J. (2013). Ex post socio-economic assessment of the Oresund Bridge. *Transport Policy, 27*(1), 53–65. doi:10.1016/j.tranpol.2012.12.002

Koraneekij, P., & Khlaisang, J. (2015). Development of Learning Outcome Based E-Portfolio Model Emphasizing on Cognitive Skills in Pedagogical Blended E-Learning Environment for Undergraduate Students at Faculty of Education, Chulalongkorn University. *Procedia: Social and Behavioral Sciences, 174*, 805–813. doi:10.1016/j.sbspro.2015.01.664

Kozłowski, J. (2015). Innovation indices: The need for positioning them where they properly belong. *Scientometrics, 104*(3), 609–628. doi:10.1007/s11192-015-1632-4 PMID:26257448

Krajnc, D., & Glavic, P. (2005). A model for integrated assessment of sustainable development. *Resources, Conservation and Recycling, 43*(2), 189–208. doi:10.1016/S0921-3449(04)00120-X

Kresl, P., & Ietri, D. (2010). *The Aging Population and the Competitiveness of Cities: Benefits to the Urban Economy.* Cheltenham, UK: Edward Elgar Publishers. doi:10.4337/9781849806930

Krieger, N., Chen, J. T., & Waterman, P. D. (2002). Geocoding and monitoring of US socioeconomic inequalities in mortality and cancer incidence: Does the choice of area-based measure and geographic level matter? *American Journal of Epidemiology*, *156*(5), 471–482. doi:10.1093/aje/kwf068 PMID:12196317

Krishnan, V. (2010, May). *Early child development: A conceptual model*. Presented at the Early Childhood Council Annual Conference 2010, Christchurch, New Zealand.

Krishnan, V. (2011). *Introducing a School Preparedness Index for a Canadian sample of preschoolers without special needs*. Retrieved January 26, 2016, from http://www.cup.ualberta.ca/wp-content/uploads/2013/04/IntroducingSPICUP Website_10April-13.pdf

Krishnan, V. (2013). *The Early Child Development Instrument (EDI) An item analysis using Classical Test Theory (CTT) on Alberta's data*. Retrieved January 26, 2016, from http://www.cup.ualberta.ca/wp-content/uploads/2013/04/ItemAn alysisCTTCUPWebsite_10April13.pdf

Krishnan, V. (2015). Development of a Multidimensional Living Conditions Index (LCI). *Social Indicators Research*, *120*(2), 455–481. doi:10.1007/s11205-014-0591-0 PMID:25774072

Krušinskas, R., & Bruneckienė, J. (2015). Measurement of intellectual capital of Lithuanian cities by a composite index. *Journal of Business Economics and Management*, *16*(3), 529–541. doi:10.3846/16111699.2012.729155

Kwon, D. B. (2009). Human capital and its measurement. In *The 3rd OECD World Forum on 'Statistics, Knowledge and Policy' Charting Progress, Building Visions, Improving Life Busan*. OECD World Forum.

La Porta, R., Lopez-de-Silanes, F., Shleifer, A., & Vishny, R. (1998). Law and finance. *Journal of Political Economy*, *106*(6), 1113–1155. doi:10.1086/250042

Lachman, M. E. (1986). Locus of control in aging research: A case for multidimensional and domain-specific assessment. *Psychology and Aging*, *1*(1), 34–40. doi:10.1037/0882-7974.1.1.34 PMID:3267376

Lai, D. (2003). Principal component analysis on human development indicators of China. *Social Indicators Research*, *61*(3), 319–330. doi:10.1023/A:1021951302937

Lalloue, B., Monnez, J. M., Padilla, C., Kihal, W., Le Meur, N., Zmirou-Navier, D., & Deguen, S. (2013). A statistical procedure to create a neighborhood socioeconomic index for health inequalities analysis. *International Journal for Equity in Health*, *2*(1), 12–21. PMID:23537275

Lamb, V. L., & Land, K. C. (2013). Methodologies Used in the Construction of Composite Child Well-Being Indices. In A. Ben-Arieh (Ed.), *Handbook of Child Well-Being*. New York: Springer.

Lanspery, S. (2002). Aging in Place. In D. J. Ekerdt (Ed.), *Encyclopedia of Aging* (pp. 49–51). New York: Macmillan Reference.

Laroche, M., Toffoli, R., Kim, C., & Muller, T. E. (1996). The influence of culture on pro-environmental knowledge, attitudes, and behavior: A Canadian perspective. *Advances in Consumer Research. Association for Consumer Research (U. S.)*, *23*, 196–202.

Lata, R., Scherngell, T., & Brenner, T. (2013). Observing integration processes in European R&D networks: A comparative spatial interaction approach using project based R&D networks and co-patent networks. In T. Scherngell (Ed.), *The geography of networks and R&D collaboration* (pp. 131–150). Cham: Springer International Publishing. doi:10.1007/978-3-319-02699-2_8

Lata, R., Scherngell, T., & Brenner, T. (2015). Integration processes in European research and development: A comparative spatial interaction approach using project based research and development networks, co-patent networks and co-publication networks. *Geographical Analysis*, *47*(4), 349–375. doi:10.1111/gean.12079

Lebas, M. (1995). Performance measurement and performance management. *International Journal of Production Economics*, *41*(1-3), 23–35. doi:10.1016/0925-5273(95)00081-X

Lee, B. J. (2014). Mapping domains and indicators of children's well-being. In A. Ben-Arieh, F. Casas, I. Frønes, & J. E. Korbin (Eds.), *The Handbook of Child Well-Being—Theories, Methods and Policies in Global Perspective* (pp. 2797–2805). Dordrecht, The Netherlands: Springer.

Lee, K. W., & Chung, M. (2015). Enhancing the link between higher education and employment. *International Journal of Educational Development*, *40*, 19–27. doi:10.1016/j.ijedudev.2014.11.014

Lester, B. J., Ma, L., Lee, O., & Lambert, J. (2006). Social activism in elementary science education: A science, technology, and society approach to teach global warming. *International Journal of Science Education*, *28*(4), 315–333. doi:10.1080/09500690500240100

Le, T., Gibson, J., & Oxley, L. (2005). *Measures of human capital: A review of the literature (No. 05/10)*. New Zealand Treasury.

Leta, F. R., Mello, J. C. C. B. S., Gomes, E. G., & Meza, L. A. (2005). Métodos de melhora de ordenação em DEA aplicados à avaliação estática de tornos mecânicos. *Investigação Operacional*, *25*, 229–242.

Levasseur, M., Généreux, M., Bruneau, J.-F., Vanasse, A., Chabot, É., Beaulac, C., & Bédard, M.-M. (2015). Importance of proximity to resources, social support, transportation and neighbourhood security for mobility and social participation in older adults: Results from a scoping study. *BMC Public Health*, *15*(1), 503. doi:10.1186/s12889-015-1824-0 PMID:26002342

Levi Jaksic, M. (2007). Technology Innovation Management for Sustainable Business Development. In Contemporary Challenges of Theory and Practice in Economics, Section: Management and Marketing Under Globalization. University of Belgrade, Faculty of Economics.

Levi Jakšić, M. (2011). Sustainable Technology and Innovation Management. In Recent Economic Crisis and Future Development Tendencies. ASECU.

Levi Jakšić, M., Stošić, B., Marinković, S., & Obradović, J. (2007). Sustainable management of technology and innovation. In Modern trends in the development of management. Belgrade: Faculty of Organizational Sciences. (In Serbian)

Levi Jakšić, M. (2012). Innovation Entrepreneurship for Sustainable Development. In D. Tipurić & M. Dabić (Eds.), *Management, Governance and Entrepreneurship – New Perspectives and Challenges* (pp. 487–508). London: Access Press.

Levi Jakšić, M. (2015). Sustainable Innovation of Technology and Business Models: steps towards rethinking technology and business strategy.*ASECU Conference Proceedings*.

Levi Jakšić, M., Barjaktarović Rakočević, S., & Martić, M. (Eds.). (2014). *Innovative management and Firm Performance-an interdisciplinary approach*. London: Palgrave Macmillan. doi:10.1057/9781137402226

Levi Jaksic, M., Jovanovic, M., & Petkovic, J. (2015). Technology Entrepreneurship in the Changing Business Environment – A Triple Helix Performance Model. *Amfiteatru Economic*, *17*(38), 422–440.

Levi Jaksic, M., & Marinkovic, S. (2012). *Menadžment održivog razvoja*. Beograd: FON.

Levi Jaksic, M., Marinkovic, S., & Kojic, J. (2014a). Technology Innovation Education in Serbia. In M. Levi Jaksic, S. Barjaktarovic Rakocevic, & M. Martic (Eds.), *Innovative Management and Firm Performance* (pp. 57–63). London: Palgrave, McMillan. doi:10.1057/9781137402226_2

Levi Jaksic, M., Marinkovic, S., & Kojic, J. (2014b). Open Innovation and Sustainable Technology Entrepreneurship. In M. Baćović (Ed.), *Entrepreneurship and Innovation as Precondition for Economic Development* (pp. 45–60). Podgorica: University of Montenegro.

Levi Jakšić, M., Marinković, S., & Petković, J. (2015). *Management of innovation and technology development*. Belgrade: Faculty of Organizational Sciences. (In Serbian)

Levi Jaksic, M., & Trifunovic, M. (2010). Leading Innovation Based on Knowledge Entrepreneurship. *Scientific Conference Proceedings, Fakulteta za organizacijske vede, Univerza v Mariboru*.

Lindahl, M., & Krueger, A. B. (2001). Education for Growth: Why and for Whom? *Journal of Economic Literature*, *39*(4), 1101–1136. doi:10.1257/jel.39.4.1101

Lindenberg, J., & Westendorp, R. G. J. (2015). Overcoming Old in Age-Friendliness. *Journal of Social Work Practice*, *29*(1), 85–98. doi:10.1080/02650533.2014.993949 PMID:26028795

Lind, N. (2014). Better Life Index. In *Encyclopedia of Quality of Life and Well-Being Research* (pp. 381–382). Springer Netherlands. doi:10.1007/978-94-007-0753-5_3623

Linstone, A., & Turoff, M. (2002). *The Delphi Method: Technique and Applications*. Retrieved from http://www.is.njit.edu/pubs/delphibook/

Linstone, H. A., & Turoff, M. (Eds.). (1975). *The Delphi method: Techniques and applications* (Vol. 29). Reading, MA: Addison-Wesley.

Liu, H., Shah, S., & Jiang, W. (2004). On-line outlier detection and data cleaning. *Computers & Chemical Engineering*, *28*(9), 1635–1647. doi:10.1016/j.compchemeng.2004.01.009

Liu, W. C., Wang, C. K. J., & Parkins, E. J. (2005). A longitudinal study of students' academic self-concept in a streamed setting: The Singapore context. *The British Journal of Educational Psychology*, *75*(4), 567–586. doi:10.1348/000709905X42239 PMID:16318679

Liu, X., & Lu, K. (2008). Student performance and family socioeconomic status. *Chinese Education & Society*, *41*(5), 70–83. doi:10.2753/CED1061-1932410505

Lor, P. J., & Britz, J. J. (2007). Is a knowledge society possible without freedom of access to information? *Journal of Information Science*, *33*(4), 387–397. doi:10.1177/0165551506075327

Lucas, R. E. Jr. (1988). On the mechanics of economic development. *Journal of Monetary Economics*, *22*(1), 3–42. doi:10.1016/0304-3932(88)90168-7

Lui, C.-W., Everingham, J.-A., Warburton, J., Cuthill, M., & Bartlett, H. (2009). What makes a community age-friendly: A review of international literature. *Australasian Journal on Ageing*, *28*(3), 116–121. doi:10.1111/j.1741-6612.2009.00355.x PMID:19845650

Lundquist, K.-J., & Trippl, M. (2009). Towards cross-border innovation spaces: A theoretical analysis and empirical comparison of the Öresund region and the Centrope area. *Institut für Regional- und Umweltwirtschaft Discussion Papers, 2009*(5).

Lundquist, K.-J., & Trippl, M. (2013). Distance, proximity and types of cross-border innovation systems: A conceptual analysis. *Regional Studies*, *47*(3), 450–460. doi:10.1080/00343404.2011.560933

Lundquist, K.-J., & Winther, L. (2006). The interspace between Denmark and Sweden: The industrial dynamics of the Öresund cross-border region. *Geografisk Tidsskrift – Danish Journal of Geography*, *106*(1), 115–129. doi:10.1080/00 167223.2006.10649549

Lustig, S. L. (2010). An ecological framework for the refugee experience: What is the impact on child development? In G. W. Evans & T. D. Wachs (Eds.), *Chaos and its Influence on Children's Development* (pp. 239–251). Washington, DC: American Psychological Association. doi:10.1037/12057-015

Luukkonen, T., Tijssen, R., Persson, O., & Sivertsen, G. (1993). The measurement of international scientific collaboration. *Scientometrics*, *28*(1), 15–36. doi:10.1007/BF02016282

Machlup, F. (1962). *The production and distribution of knowledge in the United States*. Princeton, NJ: Princeton University Press.

Machlup, F. (2014). Knowledge: its creation, distribution and economic significance: Vol. I. *Knowledge and knowledge production*. Princeton, NJ: Princeton University press.

Mahadevan, R., & Hoang, V. (2015). Is There a Link Between Poverty and Food Security? *Social Indicators Research*, 1–21.

Mahlberg, B., & Obersteiner, M. (2001). *Remeasuring the HDI by Data Envelopment Analysis, IR-01-069*. Luxemburg, Austria: International Institute for Applied System Analysis.

Mahlberg, B., & Obersteiner, M. (2001). *Remeasuring the HDI by Data Envelopment Analysis. Interim Report*. Laxenburg: International Institute for Applied Systems Analysis.

Mak, A. S., & Kennedy, M. (2012). Internationalizing the student experience: Preparing instructors to embed intercultural skills in the curriculum. *Innovative Higher Education*, *37*(4), 323–334. doi:10.1007/s10755-012-9213-4

Makkonen, T. (2015). National innovation system capabilities among leader and follower countries: Widening gaps or global convergence? *Innovation and Development*, *5*(1), 113–129. doi:10.1080/2157930X.2014.992818

Makkonen, T., & van der Have, R. P. (2013). Benchmarking regional innovation performance: Composite measures and direct innovation counts. *Scientometrics*, *94*(1), 247–262. doi:10.1007/s11192-012-0753-2

Makridakis, S., Wheelwright, S. C., & Hyndman, R. J. (1998). *Forecasting Methods and Applications*. New York: Wiley.

Mallick, D. N., & Chaudhury, A. (2000). Technology management education in MBA programs: A comparative study of knowledge and skill requirements. *Journal of Engineering and Technology Management*, *17*(2), 153–173. doi:10.1016/S0923-4748(00)00019-9

Mansell, R., & When, U. (1998). *Knowledge societies: Information technology for sustainable development*. New York: United Nations Commission on Science and Technology for Development.

Manuel, A. (2015). *Sustainable city index 2015*. The Hague, The Netherlands: Sustainable Society Foundation.

Marginson, S. (2011). Higher education in East Asia and Singapore: Rise of the Confucian model. *Higher Education*, *61*(5), 587–611. doi:10.1007/s10734-010-9384-9

Mariano, E. B., Sobreiro, V. A., & Rebelatto, D. A. (2015). Human development and data envelopment analysis: A structured literature review. *Omega*, *54*, 33–49. doi:10.1016/j.omega.2015.01.002

Maricic, M., Bulajic, M., Dobrota, M., & Jeremic, V. (2016). Redesigning the Global Food Security Index: A Multivariate Composite I-Distance Indicator Approach. *International Journal of Food and Agricultural Economics, 4*(1), 69-86.

Maricic, M., Bulajic, M., Martic, M., & Dobrota, M. (2015). Measuring the ICT Development: The Fusion of Biased and Objective Approach. In *Proceedings of the XII Balkan Conference on Operational Research (BALCOR 2015).*

Maricic, M., & Kostic-Stankovic, M. (2016). Towards an impartial Responsible Competitiveness Index: A twofold multivariate I-distance approach. *Quality & Quantity, 50*(1), 1–18. doi:10.1007/s11135-014-0139-z

Markovic, M., Zdravkovic, S., Mitrovic, M., & Radojicic, A. (2016). An Iterative Multivariate Post Hoc I-Distance Approach in Evaluating OECD Better Life Index. *Social Indicators Research, 126*(1), 1–19. doi:10.1007/s11205-015-0879-8

Marks, N., Abdallah, S., Simms, A., & Thompson, S. (2006). *The (un)happy planet index: An index of human well-being and environmental impact.* London: New Economics Foundation.

Marshall, A. (1890). *Principles of political economy.* New York: Maxmillan.

Marshall, K. (2006). Converging gender roles. *Perspectives on Labour and Income, 18*(3), 7–19.

Marsh, H. W. (1994). Using the National Longitudinal Study of 1988 to evaluate theoretical models of self-concept: The Self-Description Questionnaire. *Journal of Educational Psychology, 86*(3), 439–456. doi:10.1037/0022-0663.86.3.439

Marsh, H. W., Byrne, B. M., & Shavelson, R. J. (1988). A multifaceted academic self-concept: Its hierarchical structure and its relation to academic achievement. *Journal of Educational Psychology, 80*(3), 366–380. doi:10.1037/0022-0663.80.3.366

Martić, M., & Savić, G. (2001). An application of DEA for comparative analysis and ranking of regions in Serbia with regards to social-economic development. *European Journal of Operational Research, 132*(2), 343–356. doi:10.1016/S0377-2217(00)00156-9

Martin, L. M. (2004). An emerging research framework for studying informal learning and schools. *Science Education, 88*(S1), S71–S82. doi:10.1002/sce.20020

Martino, J. P. (1993). *Technological Forecasting for Decision Making* (3rd ed.). New York: North-Holland.

Mason, L., & Santi, M. (1998). Discussing the greenhouse effect: Children's collaborative discourse reasoning and conceptual change. *Environmental Education Research, 4*(1), 67–68. doi:10.1080/1350462980040105

Masuda, Y. (1980). *The information society as a post-industrial society.* World Future Society.

Matthiessen, C. (2004). The Öresund area: Pre- and post-bridge cross-border functional integration: The bi-national regional question. *GeoJournal, 61*(1), 31–39. doi:10.1007/s10708-005-5234-1

Mazziotta, M., & Pareto, A. (2013). Methods For Constructing Composite Indices: One For All Or All For One? RIEDS-Rivista Italiana di Economia, Demografia e Statistica-Italian Review of Economics. *Demography and Statistics, 67*(2), 67–80.

McGranahan, D. V., Richard-Proust, C., Sovani, N. V., & Subramanian, M. (1972). *Contents and measurement of socioeconomic development.* New York: Praeger.

Meier, K. J., Favero, N., & Compton, M. (2016). Social Context, Management, and Organizational Performance: When human capital and social capital serve as substitutes. *Public Management Review, 18*(2), 258–277. doi:10.1080/14719037.2014.984621

Melyn, W., & Moesen, W. (1991). Towards a synthetic indicator of macroeconomic performance: Unequal weighting when limited information is available. *Public Economics Research Papers, 17*(1), 1–24.

Menec, V. H., Newall, N. E. G., & Nowicki, S. (2014). *Assessing Communities' Age-Friendliness: How Congruent Are Subjective Versus Objective Assessments? Journal of Applied Gerontology*. doi:10.1177/0733464814542612

Menec, V. H., & Nowicki, S. (2014). Examining the relationship between communities' 'age-friendliness' and life satisfaction and self-perceived health in rural Manitoba, Canada. *Rural and Remote Health*, *14*, 2594. PMID:24437338

Merkel, W. (2012). Measuring the Quality of Rule of Law. In M. Zurn, A. Nollkaemper, & R. Peerenboom (Eds.), *Rule of Law Dynamics: In an Era of International and Transnational Governance*. Cambridge University Press. doi:10.1017/CBO9781139175937.004

Merry, S. E. (2009, March). Measuring the world: indicators, human rights, and global governance. In *Proceedings of the 103rd Annual Meeting* (vol. 103, pp. 239-243). American Society for International Law.

Merry, S. E., Davis, K., Kingsbury, B., & Fisher, A. (2015). *The Quiet Power of Indicators: Measuring Governance, Corruption, and Rule of Law*. Cambridge University Press.

Mert, M. (2006). *Determination of consciousness level of high school students on the environmental education and solid wastes topics* (Master's Thesis). Hacettepe University.

Messer, L. C., Vinikoor, L. C., Laraia, B. A., Kaufman, J. S., Eyster, J., Holzman, C., & O'Campo, P. et al. (2008). Socioeconomic domains and associations with preterm birth. *Social Science & Medicine*, *67*(8), 1247–1257. doi:10.1016/j.socscimed.2008.06.009 PMID:18640759

Metcalfe, S. (1995). The economic foundations of technology policy: equilibrium and evolutionary perspectives. In P. Stoneman (Ed.), *Handbook of the Economics of Innovation and Technological Change* (pp. 409–512). London: Blackwell.

Meyer, T., & Thomsen, S. L. (2012). *How important is secondary school duration for post-school education decisions? Evidence from a natural experiment* (No. 509). Diskussionspapiere der Wirtschaftswissenschaftlichen Fakultät, Universität Hannover, Deutschland. Retrieved September 22, 2015, from http://hdl.handle.net/10419/73103

Michener, G. (2015). Policy Evaluation via Composite Indexes: Qualitative Lessons from International Transparency Policy Indexes. *World Development*, *74*, 184–196. doi:10.1016/j.worlddev.2015.04.016

Middendorf, T. (2006). Human capital and economic growth in OECD countries. *Jahrbucher fur Nationalokonomie und Statistik*, 670–686.

Mihyeon Jeon, C., & Amekudzi, A. (2005). Addressing sustainability in transportation systems: Definitions, indicators, and metrics. *Journal of Infrastructure Systems*, *11*(1), 31–50. doi:10.1061/(ASCE)1076-0342(2005)11:1(31)

Miles, M. B., & Huberman, A. M. (1994). *Qualitative data analysis: An expanded sourcebook* (2nd ed.). California: SAGE.

Mill, J. S. (1848). *Principles of Political Economy with Some of Their Applications to Social Philosophy*. Manchester, UK: George Routledge and Sons.

Mioara, M. S. (2012). The impact of technological and communication innovation in the knowledge-based society. *Procedia: Social and Behavioral Sciences*, *51*, 263–267. doi:10.1016/j.sbspro.2012.08.156

Miringoff, M.-L., & Opdycke, S. (2007). *America's social health: Putting social issues back on the public agenda*. Armonk, NY: M.E. Sharpe.

Mohamad, M. (1991). *Malaysia: The way forward*. Kuala Lumpur: Centre for Economic Research & Services, Malaysian Business Council. Retrieved from http://www.digitalibrary.my/dmdocuments/malaysiakini/007_malaysia_the%20way%20forward.pdf

Mokyr, J. (2005). Long-term economic growth and the history of technology.Handbook of Economic Growth, 1, 1113-1180. doi:10.1016/S1574-0684(05)01017-8

Møller, J., & Skaaning, S. E. (2011). On the limited interchangeability of rule of law measures. *European Political Science Review*, *3*(3), 371–394. doi:10.1017/S1755773910000421

Moloney, M. (2010). Professional identity in early childhood care and education: Perspectives of pre-school and infant teachers. *Irish Educational Studies*, *29*(2), 167–187. doi:10.1080/03323311003779068

Moodysson, J., & Jonsson, O. (2007). Knowledge collaboration and proximity: The spatial organization of biotech innovation projects. *European Urban and Regional Studies*, *14*(2), 115–131. doi:10.1177/0969776407075556

Moon, H.-S., & Lee, J.-D. (2005). A fuzzy set theory approach to national composite S&T indices. *Scientometrics*, *64*(1), 67–83. doi:10.1007/s11192-005-0238-7

Moore, K. A., Murphey, D., Bandy, T., & Lawner, E. (2014). Indices of child well-being and developmental contexts. In A. Ben-Arieh, F. Casas, I. Frønes, & J. E. Korbin (Eds.), *The Handbook of Child Well-Being—Theories, Methods and Policies in Global Perspective* (pp. 2807–2822). Dordrecht, The Netherlands: Springer. doi:10.1007/978-90-481-9063-8_139

Moore, K. A., Theokas, C., Lippman, L. H., Bloch, M., Vandivere, S., & O'Hare, W. P. (2008). A microdata child well-being index: Conceptualization, creation, and findings. *Child Indicators Research*, *1*(1), 17–50. doi:10.1007/s12187-007-9000-4

Moreira, S. B., Simões, N., & Crespo, N. (2012). Composite indicators of development – The importance of dimensional weights. *Global Economics and Management Review*, *2*(September), 79–95.

Mori, K., & Christodoulou, A. (2012). Review of sustainability indices and indicators: Towards a new City Sustainability Index (CSI). *Environmental Impact Assessment Review*, *32*(1), 94–106. doi:10.1016/j.eiar.2011.06.001

Morris, M. D. (1979). *Measuring the condition of the world's poor: The physical quality of life index*. New York: Pergamon Press.

Morris, P., & Adamson, B. (2010). *Curriculum, schooling and society in Hong Kong* (Vol. 1). Hong Kong: Hong Kong University Press. doi:10.5790/hongkong/9789888028016.001.0001

Morris, R., & Castairs, V. (1991). Which deprivation? A comparison of selected deprivation indices. *Journal of Public Health Medicine*, *13*, 318–326. PMID:1764290

Morse, S. (2004). *Indices and indicators in development*. London: Earthscan Publications Ltd.

Morse, S. (2014). Stirring the pot. Influence of changes in methodology of the Human Development Index on reporting by the press. *Ecological Indicators*, *45*, 245–254. doi:10.1016/j.ecolind.2014.04.023

Moulaert, T., & Garon, S. (2015). *Age-friendly Cities and Communities in International Comparison: Political Lessons, Scientific Avenues, and Democratic Issues*. Springer.

Mousavi, A., & Krishnan, V. (2014). *Socioeconomic status as a determinant of early child developmental outcomes: A multi-level analysis on Early Development Instrument (EDI) data, ECMap, CUP*. Faculty of Extension, University of Alberta.

Mulíček, O., & Olšová, I. (2002). Město Brno a důsledky různých forem urbanizace. *Urbanismus a územní rozvoj*, *5*(6), 17–21.

Mulligan, C. B., & Sala-i-Martin, X. (1997). A labor income-based measure of the value of human capital: An application to the states of the United States. *Japan and the World Economy*, *9*(2), 159–191. doi:10.1016/S0922-1425(96)00236-8

Mullis, I. V., Martin, M. O., Foy, P., & Arora, A. (2012). TIMSS 2011 international results in mathematics. International Association for the Evaluation of Educational Achievement.

Mulloen, P. M. (2003). Delphi: Myths and reality. *Journal of Health Organization and Management, 17*(1), 37–52. doi:10.1108/14777260310469319 PMID:12800279

Munda, G. (2005). Multi-criteria decision analysis and sustainable development. In J. Figueira, S. Greco, & M. Ehrgott (Eds.), *Multiple-criteria decision analysis: State of the art surveys* (pp. 953–986). New York: Springer.

Munda, G. (2008). *Social multi-criteria evaluation for a sustainable economy.* Berlin: Springer. doi:10.1007/978-3-540-73703-2

Munda, G. (2012). Choosing aggregation rules for composite indicators. *Social Indicators Research, 109*(3), 337–354. doi:10.1007/s11205-011-9911-9

Munda, G., & Nardo, M. (2009). Non-compensatory/non-linear composite indicators for ranking countries: A defensible setting. *Applied Economics, 41*(12), 1513–1523. doi:10.1080/00036840601019364

Mustard, C. A., Derksen, S., Berthelot, J. M., & Wolfson, M. (1999). Assessing ecologic proxies for household income: A comparison of household and neighborhood level income measures in the study of population health status. *Health & Place, 5*(2), 157–171. doi:10.1016/S1353-8292(99)00008-8 PMID:10670997

Nardo, M., Saisana, M., Saltelli, A., Tarantola, S., Hoffman, A., & Giovannini, E. (2005b). *Handbook on constructing composite indicators.* Academic Press.

Nardo, M., Saisana, M., Saltelli, A., & Tarantola, S. (2005a). *Input to Handbook of Good Practices for Composite Indicators' Development.* Ispra, Italy: Joint Research Centre.

Nardo, M., Saisana, M., Saltelli, A., & Tarantola, S. (2005b). *Tools for composite indicators building.* Ispra: European Comission.

Nardo, M., Saisana, M., Saltelli, A., Tarantola, S., Hoffman, A., & Giovannini, E. (2005a). *Handbook on constructing composite indicators: methodology and user guide (No. 2005/3).* OECD Publishing. doi:10.1787/533411815016

Nardo, M., Saisano, M., Saltelli, A., & Tarantola, S. (2005). *Tools for Composite Indicators Building.* European Commission Joint Research Centre, Institute for the Protection and Security of the Citizen Econometrics and Statistical Support to Antifraud Unit.

National Economic Advisory Council (NEAC). (2010). *New economic model for Malaysia 2010.* Retrieved from http://www.neac.gov.my/content/download-option-new-economic-model-malaysia-2010

National research Council. (1987). *Management of Technology: the hidden competitive advantage.* Washington, DC: National Academy press.

Nauwelaers, C., Maguire, K., & Ajmone Marsan, G. (2013). The case of Oresund (Denmark-Sweden). *OECD Regional Development Working Papers, 2013*(21).

Nehru, V., Swanson, E., & Dubey, A. (1995). A new database in human capital stock in developing industrial countries: Sources, methodology and results. *Journal of Development Economics, 46*(2), 379–401. doi:10.1016/0304-3878(94)00054-G

Neidorf, T. S., Binkley, M., Gattis, K., & Nohara, D. (2006). *Comparing Mathematics Content in the National Assessment of Educational Progress (NAEP), Trends in International Mathematics and Science Study (TIMSS), and Program for International Student Assessment (PISA) 2003. U.S. Department of Education.* Washington, DC: National Center for Education Statistics.

Nelles, J. (2011). *Cooperation in crisis? An analysis of cross-border intermunicipal relations in the Detroit-Windsor region. Articulo – Journal of Urban Research*, (6). doi:10.4000/articulo.2097

Neumayer, E. (2012). Human development and sustainability. *J. Human Dev. Capabil, 13*(4), 561–579. doi:10.1080/19452829.2012.693067

Nicoletti, G., Scarpetta, S., & Boylaud, O. (2000). *Summary indicators of product market regulation with an extension to employment protection legislation.* Economics department working papers No. 226. Paris: OECD. Retrieved Jan 20, 2016, from http://www.oecd.org/eco/eco100

NISTEP. (2004). *Science and technology indicators: 2004 – A systematic analysis of science and technology activities in Japan.* Japan: National Institute of Science and Technology Policy.

Nordhaus, W., & Tobin, J. (1972). Is growth obsolete? National Bureau of Economic Research, General Series No. 96.

Nuchwana, L. (2012). How to link teaching and research to enhance students' learning outcomes: Thai University Experience. *Procedia: Social and Behavioral Sciences, 69*, 213–219. doi:10.1016/j.sbspro.2012.11.401

Nye, J. (1969). Regional integration: Concept and measurement. *International Organization, 22*(4), 855–880. doi:10.1017/S0020818300013837

Oakes, J. M., & Rossi, P. H. (2003). The measurement of SES in health research: Current practice and steps toward a new approach. *Social Science & Medicine, 56*(4), 769–784. doi:10.1016/S0277-9536(02)00073-4 PMID:12560010

Obradović, J. (2004). *Technology forecasting - Delphi method: a case study in Germany.* New trends in production and services in our society, II Conference of scientists and entrepreneurs, Belgrade. (In Serbian)

OECD & EC. (2008). Handbook on constructing composite indicators: Methodology and user guide. Paris & Ispra: OECD (the Statistics Directorate and the Directorate for Science, Technology and Industry) & European Commission (the Econometrics and Applied Statistics Unit of the Joint Research Center).

OECD. (2000). *Education at a Glance: OECD Indicators.* Paris: OECD. doi: 10.1787/eag-2015-en

OECD. (2002). *Education at a Glance 2002.* Paris: OECD Publications Glossary.

OECD. (2008). The OECD REGPAT database: A presentation. *OECD STI Working Papers, 2008*(2).

OECD. (2009). *Learning Mathematics for Life: A Perspective from PISA.* Paris: OECD Publishing.

OECD. (2013). *Assessing Scientific, Reading and Mathematical Literacy – A Framework for PISA 2015.* Paris: OECD Publications.

OECD. (2013). *Education at a Glance 2013.* Paris: OECD Publications.

OECD. (2013). *Regions and innovation: Collaborating across borders.* Paris: OECD Publishing.

OECD. (2015). *Ageing in Cities.* Paris: OECD Publishing; doi:10.1787/9789264231160-en

OECD. (2015). *Better Life Index 2015: Definitions and medata.* OECD Statistics Online.

OECD. (2015). *OECD member countries*. Retrieved from http://www.oecd.org/about/membersandpartners/list-oecd-member-countries.htm

Okonny-Myers, I. (2010). *The Interprovincial Mobility of Immigrants in Canada*. Ottawa: Citizenship and Immigration Canada. Retrieved January 27, 2016, from http://www.cic.gc.ca/english/pdf/research-stats/interprov-mobility.pdf

Olsthoorn, X., Tyteca, D., Wehrmeyer, W., & Wagner, M. (2001). Environmental indicators for business: A review of the literature and standardisation methods. *Journal of Cleaner Production, 9*(5), 453–463. doi:10.1016/S0959-6526(01)00005-1

Örestat. (2013). *Øresund trends 2012*. Arbetsförmedlingen Scania, Employment Region Copenhagen & Zealand, Interreg Project Jobs & Education, Malmö City, Landskrona City, Lund Municipality, Helsingborg City, Capital Region, Region Zealand, Region Sania, Wonderful Copenhagen and Öresundskomiteen.

Örestat. (2015). *Öresundsdatabasen (engelsk)*. Retrieved November 25, 2015, from http://www.orestat.se/en/oresunds-databasen-engelsk

Öresundskomiteen. (2010). *Oresund regional development strategy*. Copenhagen: Öresundskomiteen.

Öresundskomiteen. (2013). *The Oresund integration index*. Copenhagen: Öresundskomiteen.

Öresundskomiteen. (2015). *Öresundskomiteens integrationsindeks JUNI 2015*. Copenhagen: Öresundskomiteen.

Organization for Economic Cooperation and Development (OECD). (1991). *The State of the Environment*. Paris: OECD.

Organization for Economic Co-operation and Development (OECD). (2008). *Handbook on constructing composite indicators: Methodology and user guide*. Paris: OECD.

Oswald, F., Wahl, H.-W., Schilling, O., & Iwarsson, S. (2007). Housing-related control beliefs and independence in activities of daily living in very old age. *Scandinavian Journal of Occupational Therapy, 14*(1), 33–43. doi:10.1080/11038120601151615 PMID:17366076

Ouertani, E. (2016). Food Security in Tunisia within Water Scarcity the Relative Importance of the Meat Sector. *International Journal of Food and Agricultural Economics, 4*(1), 35-54.

Ouředníček, M., Pospíšilová, L., Špačková, P., Temelová, J., & Novák, J. (2012). Prostorová typologie a zonace Prahy. In M. Ouředníček & J. Temelová (Eds.), *Sociální proměny pražských čtvrtí* (pp. 268–297). Praha: Academia.

Oxley, L., Trinh, L., & John, G. (2008). Measuring Human Capital: Alternative Methods and International Evidence. *The Korean Economic Review, 24*(2), 283-344. Retrieved from http://www.kereview.or.kr/main/?load_popup=1&filter=on

Paasi, A. (2002). Regional transformation in the European context: Notes on regions, boundaries and identity. *Space and Polity, 6*(2), 197–201. doi:10.1080/1356257022000003626

Paas, T., & Poltimäe, H. (2012). Consistency between innovation indicators and national innovation performance in the case of small economies. *Eastern Journal of European Studies, 3*(1), 101–121.

Pallant, J. (2004). *SPSS Survival Manual*. Open University Press.

Pallant, J. (2007). *SPSS Survival Manual: A Step by Step Guide to Data Analysis Using SPSS for Windows* (3rd ed.). New York: McGraw Hill, Open University Press.

Pallant, J. (2007). *SPSS survival manual: A step by step guide to data analysis using SPSS*. Allen & Unwin.

Pampalon, R., Hamel, D., & Gamache, P. (2009). A comparison of individual and area-based socioeconomic data for monitoring social inequalities in health (Statistics Canada, Catalogue no. 82-003-XPE). *Health Reports, 20*(3), 85–94. PMID:20108609

Pampalon, R., & Raymond, G. (2000). A deprivation index for health and welfare planning in Quebec. *Chronic Diseases in Canada*, *21*, 104–113. PMID:11082346

Panjabi, R. K. (1997). *The Earth Summit at Rio: politics, economics and the environment.* Northeastern University Press.

Paruolo, P., Saisana, M., & Saltelli, A. (2013). Ratings and rankings: Voodoo or science? *Journal of the Royal Statistical Society. Series A, (Statistics in Society)*, *176*(3), 609–634. doi:10.1111/j.1467-985X.2012.01059.x

Pavlovic, V. (2011). Sustainable development and higher education. In V. Pavlovic (Ed.), *University and sustainable development* (pp. 13–30). Belgrade: Faculty of Political Sciences. (In Serbian)

Pearson. (2014). *Pearson learning curve.* Retrieved August 25, from http://thelearningcurve.pearson.com/data-hub

Pearson, K. (1901). On lines and planes of closest fit to systems of points in space. *Philosophical Magazine*, *2*(6), 559–572. doi:10.1080/14786440109462720

Pekkarinen, T., Uusitalo, R., & Pekkala Kerr, S. (2009). *School tracking and development of cognitive skills. Discussion paper series. No. 4058.* Bonn, Germany: IZA.

Performance Management and Delivery Unit (PEMANDU) Malaysia. (2010). Retrieved from http://www.pemandu.gov.my/en/rural-basic-infrastructure/620.html

Performance Management and Delivery Unit (PEMANDU). (2012). *Government Transformation Programme.* Retrieved from http://www.pemandu.gov.my/gtp/

Perreira, K. M., & Smith, L. (2007). A cultural-ecological model of migration and development: Focusing on Latino immigrant youth. *Prevention Researcher*, *14*(4), 6–9.

Petrosillo, I., Costanza, R., Aretano, R., Zaccarelli, N., & Zurlini, G. (2013). The use of subjective indicators to assess how natural and social capital support residents' quality of life in a small volcanic island. *Ecological Indicators*, *24*, 609–620. doi:10.1016/j.ecolind.2012.08.021

Petrová Kafková, M. (2012). Vliv věku a pohlaví tazatele a respondenta na náročnost výběrového šetření v seniorské populaci. *Data a výzkum - SDA Info*, *6*(2), 113-127.

Petrovic, N. (2010). Development of higher environmental education program. *Management - Časopis za teoriju i praksu menadžmenta*, *15*(56), 35-41.

Petrović, N., & Slović, D. (2011): Environmental performance indicators of organizations. *SPIN 2011, VIII Conference of scientists and entrepreneurs – Operations management in the function of sustainable economic development of Serbia 2011-2020*, (pp 463-467). University of Belgrade, Serbian Chamber of Commerce, Belgrade. (In Serbian)

Petrović, N., Slović, D., & Ćirović, M. (2012). Environmental Performance Indicators as Guidelines Towards Sustainability. *Management*, (64).

Petrović, N. (2012). *Environmental Management* (2nd ed.). Belgrade: Faculty of Organizational Sciences. (In Serbian)

Petrović, N. (2013). *Management of the environmental suitability of products.* Belgrade: Foundation Andrejević. (In Serbian)

Petrovic, N., Jeremic, V., Petrovic, D., & Cirovic, M. (2014). Modeling the Use of Facebook in Environmental Higher Education. In Ġ. Mallia (Ed.), *The Social Classroom: Integrating Social Network Use in Education* (pp. 100–119). Hershey, PA: Information Science Reference; doi:10.4018/978-1-4666-4904-0.ch006

Petty, W. (1899). *Political Arithmetick* (London, 1690). *Economic Writings*, *1*, 245.

Phillipson, C. (2011). Developing Age-friendly Communities: New Approaches to Growing Old in Urban Environments. In J. L. Angel & R. Settersten (Eds.), *Handbook of the Sociology of Aging* (pp. 279–296). New York: Springer Verlag. doi:10.1007/978-1-4419-7374-0_18

Pinstrup-Andersen, P. (2009). Food security: Definition and measurement. *Food Security, 1*(1), 5–7. doi:10.1007/s12571-008-0002-y

Planning Commission. (1993). *Report on the Expert Group on Estimation of Proportion and Number of Poor.* New Delhi: Perspective Planning Division.

Popper, R. (2008). How is foresight methods selected? *Foresight, 10*(6).

Porter, M. E. (2002). *Enhancing the Microeconomic Foundations of Prosperity: The Current Competitiveness Index.* World Economic Forum.

Porter, M. E., & Schwab, K. (2008). *The global competitiveness report 2008-2009.* Geneva: World Economic Forum.

Porter, A. L., Cunningham, S. W., Banks, J., Roper, A. T., Mason, T. W., & Rossini, F. A. (2011). *Forecasting and Management of Technology.* New York: John Wiley&Sons.

Porter, M. E., & Stern, S. (2004). Ranking national innovative capacity: Findings from the national innovative capacity index. In X. Sala-i-Martin (Ed.), *The Global competitiveness report 2003-2004* (pp. 91–116). New York: Oxford University Press.

Porter, M. E., Stern, S., & Green, M. (2015). *Social progress index 2015: Executive summary.* Social Progress Imperative.

Prajogo, D. I., & Sohal, A. S. (2006). The integration of TQM and technology/R&D management in determining quality and innovation performance. *Omega, 34*(3), 296–312. doi:10.1016/j.omega.2004.11.004

Prescott-Allen, R. (2001). *The wellbeing of nations: A country-by-country index of quality of life and the environment.* Washington, DC: Island Press.

Program Effectiveness Data Analysis Coordinators of Eastern Ontario. (2009). *Early Childhood Risks, Resources, and Outcomes in Ottawa.* Retrieved January 18, 2016, from http://parentresource.on.ca/DACSI_ e.html

Psacharopoulos, G., & Arriagada, A. M. (1986). The educational composition of the labour force: An international comparison. *International Labour Review, 125*(5), 561–574.

Public Health Agency of Canada. (2015). Retrieved March 7, 2016, from http://www.phac-aspc.gc.ca/ph-sp/determinants/index-eng.php

Puolamaa, M., Kaplas, M., & Reinikainen, T. (1996). *Index of environmental friendliness: A methodological study.* Eurostat.

Putnam, R. D., & Goss, K. A. (2002). Introduction to democracies. In R. D. Putnam (Ed.), *Democracies in flux: The evolution of social capital in contemporary society.* Oxford, UK: Oxford University Press. doi:10.1093/0195150899.003.0001

Pynoos, J., Caraviello, R., & Cicero, C. (2009). Lifelong Housing: The Anchor in Aging-friendly Communities. *Generations (San Francisco, Calif.), 33*(2), 26–32.

Radojicic, Z., Isljamovic, S., Petrovic, N., & Jeremic, V. (2012). A Novel Approach to Evaluating Sustainable Development (Nowe podejście do waloryzacji rozwoju zrównoważonego). *Problemy Ekorozwoju–Problems of Sustainable Development, 7*(1), 81–85.

Radojicic, Z., & Jeremic, V. (2012). Quantity or quality: What matters more in ranking higher education institutions. *Current Science, 103*(2), 158–162.

Radovanović, S., Radojicić, M., & Savić, G. (2014). Two-phased DEA-MLA approach for predicting efficiency of NBA players. *Yugoslav Journal of Operational Research, 24*(3), 347–358. doi:10.2298/YJOR140430030R

Rai, H. B., van Lier, T., & Macharis, C. (2015). Towards data-based mobility policies in Flemish cities: creating an inclusive sustainability index. In *Proceedings of the BIVEC/GIBET Transport Research Days 2015* (pp. 104-116).

Ramirez, F. O., Luo, X., Schofer, E., & Meyer, J. W. (2006). Student achievement and national economic growth. *American Journal of Education, 113*(1), 1–29. doi:10.1086/506492

Ram, R. (1982). Composite indices of physical quality of life, basic needs fulfilment, and income: A principal component representation. *Journal of Development Economics, 11*(2), 227–247. doi:10.1016/0304-3878(82)90005-0

Ramsey, P. H. (1989). Critical values for Spearman's rank order correlation. *Journal of Educational and Behavioral Statistics, 14*(3), 245–253. doi:10.3102/10769986014003245

Randolph, J. (2001). *G-Index: Globalisation measured. Global Insight.* World Markets Research Center.

Reed, B. A., Habicht, J. P., & Niameogo, C. (1996). The effects of maternal education on child nutritional status depend on socio-environmental conditions. *International Journal of Epidemiology, 25*(3), 585–592. doi:10.1093/ije/25.3.585 PMID:8671560

Riha, S., Levitan, L., & Hutson, J. (1996). Environmental impact assessment: The quest for a holistic picture. In *Proceedings of the Third National IPM Symposium/Workshop*, (pp. 40-58).

Rios-Figueroa, J., & Staton, J. (2008). *Unpacking the rule of law: A review of Judicial independence measures.* Committee on concepts and measures working paper series. International Political Science Association.

Roberts, S. (2002). *A statistical framework for describing a knowledge-based economy/society.* In IAOS Conference 2002. Organised by Office for National Statistics, UK. London, UK.

Rode, H., & Michelsen, G. (2008). Levels of indicator development for education for sustainable development. *Environmental Education Research, 14*(1), 19–33. doi:10.1080/13504620701843327

Rohrbach, D. (2007). The development of knowledge societies in 19 OECD countries between 1970 and 2002. *Social Sciences Information. Information Sur les Sciences Sociales, 46*(4), 655–689. doi:10.1177/0539018407082596

Romer, P. M. (1989). *Human capital and growth: theory and evidence.* NBER Working Paper Series, 3173. doi: 10.3386/w3173

Romer, P. M. (1986). Increasing returns and long-run growth. *Journal of Political Economy, 94*(5), 1002–1037. doi:10.1086/261420

Ronchi, E., Federico, A., & Musmeci, F. (2002). A system oriented integrated indicator for sustainable development in Italy. *Ecological Indicators, 2*(1-2), 197–210. doi:10.1016/S1470-160X(02)00045-6

Roodman, D. (2008). *The commitment to development index: 2008 edition.* Washington, DC: Center for Global Development.

Rowe, G., & Wright, G. (1999). The Delphi technique as a forecasting tool: Issues and analysis. *International Journal of Forecasting, 15*(4), 353–375. doi:10.1016/S0169-2070(99)00018-7

Rubin, D. B. (1987). *Multiple imputation for non-response in surveys.* New York: John Wiley & Sons. doi:10.1002/9780470316696

Ruggerio, J., & Vitaliano, D. F. (1999). Assessing the efficiency of public schools using data envelopment analysis and frontier regression. *Contemporary Economic Policy, 17*(3), 321–331. doi:10.1111/j.1465-7287.1999.tb00685.x

Ryan, R. L. (2005). Exploring the Effects of Environmental Experience on Attachment to Urban Natural Areas. *Environment and Behavior*, *37*(1), 3–42. doi:10.1177/0013916504264147

Rygel, L., O'Sullivan, D., & Yarnal, B. (2006). A method for constructing a social vulnerability index: An application to hurricane storm surges in a developed country. *Mitigation and Adaptation Strategies for Global Change*, *11*(3), 741–764. doi:10.1007/s11027-006-0265-6

Saaty, T. L. (1980). *The analytic hierarchy process*. New York: McGraw-Hill.

Saaty, T. L. (2001). *Decision Making for Leaders: The Analytic Hierarchy Process for Decisions in a Complex World. 1999/2000 Edition* (Vol. 2). RWS publications.

Sackman, H. (1974). *Delphi assessment: Expert opinion, forecasting, and group process (No. RAND-R-1283-PR)*. Santa Monica, CA: RAND CORP.

Saisana, M. (2008). *List of composite indicators*. Retrieved July 23, 2015, from http://composite-indicators.jrc.ec.europa.eu/

Saisana, M. (2008). The 2007 Composite Learning Index: Robustness Issues and Critical Assessment. Report 23274. European Commission, JRC-IPSC.

Saisana, M., & D'Hombres, B. (2008). Higher Education Rankings: Robustness Issues and Critical Assessment. How much confidence can we have in Higher Education Rankings? EUR23487, Joint Research Centre, Publications Office of the European Union. doi:10.2788/92295

Saisana, M., & D'Hombres, B. (2008). Higher education rankings: Robustness issues and critical assessment. How much confidence can we have in Higher Education Rankings? EUR23487. Italy: Joint Research Centre, Publications Office of the European Union. doi:10. 2788/92295

Saisana, M., & Tarantola, S. (2002). *State-of-the-art report on current methodologies and practices for composite indicator development*. EUR 20408 EN Report. Ispra: The Joint Research Center of European Commission.

Saisana, M., & Tarantola, S. (2002). State-of-the-art report on current methodologies and practices for composite indicator development. European Commission, Joint Research Centre, Institute for the Protection and the Security of the Citizen, Technological and Economic Risk Management Unit.

Saisana, M., D'Hombres, B., & Saltelli, A. (2011). Rickety numbers: Volatility of university rankings and policy implications. *Research Policy*, *40*(1), 165–177. doi:10.1016/j.respol.2010.09.003

Saisana, M., & Saltelli, A. (2014). JCR statistical audit of the WJP Rule of Law index 2014. In *World Justice Project* (pp. 188–197). The World Justice Project Rule of Law Index.

Saisana, M., & Tarantola, S. (2002). *State-of-the-art report on current methodologies and practices for composite indicator development EUR report20408EN*. Italy: European Commission, JRC-IPSC.

Saisana, M., & Tarantola, S. (2002). *State-of-the-art report on current methodologies and practices for composite indicator development*. Joint Research Center, European Commission.

Saisana, M., Tarantola, S., & Saltelli, A. (2005). Uncertainty and sensitivity techniques as tools for the analysis and validation of composite indicators. *Journal of the Royal Statistical Society A*, *168*(2), 307–323. doi:10.1111/j.1467-985X.2005.00350.x

Sakac, M. D., Cveticanin, S., & Sucevic, V. (2012). Possibilities of organization of the education process in environmental protection.[In Croatian]. *Socijalna Ekologija (Zagreb)*, *21*(1), 89–98.

Saltelli, A., Nardo, M., Saisana, M., & Tarantola, S. (2004). *Composite indicators-The controversy and the way forward.* OECD World Forum on Key Indicators, Palermo.

Saltelli, A. (2007). Composite indicators between analysis and advocacy. *Social Indicators Research, 81*(1), 65–77. doi:10.1007/s11205-006-0024-9

Samara, E., Georgiadis, P., & Bakouros, I. (2012). The impact of innovation policies on the performance of national innovation systems: A system dynamics analysis. *Technovation, 32*(11), 624–638. doi:10.1016/j.technovation.2012.06.002

Samuels, K. (2006). Rule of Law in Post-Conflict Countries. Operational Initiatives and Lessons Learnt. Social Development Papers (37). Conflict Prevention and Reconstruction (CPR) Unit in the Social Development of the Sustainable Development Network of the World Bank.

Santeramo, F. G. (2014). *On the composite indicators for food security: Decisions matter!* MPRA Paper.

Santeramo, F. G. (2015a). On the composite indicators for food security: Decision matter! *Food Reviews International, 1*(1), 63–73. doi:10.1080/87559129.2014.961076

Santeramo, F. G. (2015b). Food security composite indices: Implications for policy and practice. *Development in Practice, 25*(4), 594–600. doi:10.1080/09614524.2015.1029439

Santeramo, F. G. (2015c). Indicatori compositi di Food Security: Quali implicazioni per i policymaker? *AgriregioniEuropa, 41*, 102–104.

Santeramo, F. G. (2016). Il consumo di calorie, micro e macro nutrienti: Cosa insegnano le elasticità al reddito? *AgriregioniEuropa, 44*, 101–102.

Santeramo, F. G., Di Pasquale, J., Contò, F., Tudisca, S., & Sgroi, F. (2012). Analyzing risk management in Mediterranean Countries: The Syrian perspective. *New Medit, 11*(3), 35–40.

Santeramo, F. G., & Shabnam, N. (2015). The income-elasticity of calories, macro-and micro-nutrients: What is the literature telling us? *Food Research International, 76*, 932–937. doi:10.1016/j.foodres.2015.04.014

Sarosa, S. (2007). *The information technology adoption process within Indonesian small and medium enterprises.* (Doctoral thesis). University of Technology Sydney.

Sbilanciamoci! (2006). *The QUARS: Assessing the quality of development in Italian regions.* Roma: Lunaria.

Scharlach, A. E. (2009). Creating Aging-friendly Communities. *Generations (San Francisco, Calif.), 33*(2), 5–11.

Scheerens, J., Luyten, H., & van Ravens, J. (2011). Measuring educational quality by means of indicators. In *Perspectives on Educational Quality* (pp. 35–50). Springer Netherlands; doi:10.1007/978-94-007-0926-3_2

Schmidt, T. D. (2005). Cross-border regional enlargement in Øresund. *GeoJournal, 64*(3), 249–258. doi:10.1007/s10708-006-6874-5

Schneider, W., & Artelt, C. (2010). Metacognition and mathematics education. *ZDM, 42*(2), 149–161. doi:10.1007/s11858-010-0240-2

Schultz, T. W. (1961). Investment in Human Capital. *The American Economic Review, 51*(1), 1–17.

Schwab, K. (2014). *The global competitiveness report 2014-2015.* Geneva: World Economic Forum.

Scully, G. W. (2014). *Constitutional environments and economic growth.* Princeton, NJ: Princeton University Press.

Seke, K., Petrovic, N., Jeremic, V., Vukmirovic, J., Kilibarda, B., & Martic, M. (2013). Sustainable development and public health: Rating European countries. *BMC Public Health*, *13*(77), 1–7. doi:10.1186/1471-2458-13-77 PMID:23356822

Sekhar, C. C., Indrayan, A., & Gupta, S. M. (1991). Development of an Index of Need for Health Resources for Indian States Using Factor Analysis. *International Journal of Epidemiology*, *20*(1), 246–250. doi:10.1093/ije/20.1.246 PMID:2066229

Sempels, C., & Hoffman, J. (2013). *Sustainable Innovation Strategy - creating value in a world of finite resources*. London: Palgrave Macmillan. doi:10.1057/9781137352613

Shah, R. D., & Samworth, R. J. (2013). Variable selection with error control: Another look at stability selection. *Journal of the Royal Statistical Society. Series B, Statistical Methodology*, *75*(1), 55–80. doi:10.1111/j.1467-9868.2011.01034.x

Sharma, S. (1996). *Applied multivariate techniques*. New York: John Wiley and Sons.

Sharpe, A. (2001). *The development of indicators for human capital sustainability*. Annual Meeting of the Canadian Economics Association, Montreal, Canada.

Shavers, V. L. (2007). Measurement of socioeconomic status in health disparities research. *Journal of the National Medical Association*, *99*(9), 1013–1023. PMID:17913111

Shen, Y., Hermans, E., Bao, Q., Brijs, T., Wets, G., & Wang, W. (2015). Inter-national benchmarking of road safety: State of the art. *Transportation Research Part C, Emerging Technologies*, *50*, 37–50. doi:10.1016/j.trc.2014.07.006

Shen, Y., Hermans, E., Brijs, T., & Wets, G. (2013). Data envelopment analysis for composite indicators: A multiple layer model. *Social Indicators Research*, *114*(2), 739–756. doi:10.1007/s11205-012-0171-0

Shen, Y., Hermans, E., Brijs, T., & Wets, G. (2013). Fuzzy data envelopment analysis in composite indicator construction. In *Performance Measurement with Fuzzy Data Envelopment Analysis* (pp. 89–100). Springer Berlin Heidelberg.

Shen, Y., Hermans, E., Ruan, D., Wets, G., Brijs, T., & Vanhoof, K. (2011). A generalized multiple layer data envelopment analysis model for hierarchical structure assessment: A case study in road safety performance evaluation. *Expert Systems with Applications*, *38*(12), 15262–15272. doi:10.1016/j.eswa.2011.05.073

Shen, Y., Ruan, D., Hermans, E., Brijs, T., Wets, G., & Vanhoof, K. (2011). Modeling qualitative data in data envelopment analysis for composite indicators. *International Journal and System Assurance and Engineering Management*, *2*(1), 21–30.

Shen, Y., Ruan, D., Hermans, E., Brijs, T., Wets, G., & Vanhoof, K. (2011). Modeling qualitative data in data envelopment analysis for composite indicators. *International Journal of Systems Assurance Engineering and Management*, *2*(1), 21–30. doi:10.1007/s13198-011-0051-z

Shin, J. C. (2012). Higher education development in Korea: Western university ideas, Confucian tradition, and economic development. *Higher Education*, *64*(1), 59–72. doi:10.1007/s10734-011-9480-5

Sikdar, S. K., Sengupta, D., & Harten, P. (2012). More on aggregating multiple indicators into a single index for sustainability analyses. *Clean Technologies and Environmental Policy*, *14*(5), 765–773. doi:10.1007/s10098-012-0520-3

Singh, G. K., Miller, B. A., & Hankey, B. F. (2002). Changing area socioeconomic patterns in U.S. cancer mortality, 1950-1998: Part II-Lung and colorectal cancers. *Journal of the National Cancer Institute*, *94*(12), 916–925. doi:10.1093/jnci/94.12.916 PMID:12072545

Singh, R. K., Murty, H. R., Gupta, S. K., & Dikshit, A. K. (2012). An overview of sustainability assessment methodologies. *Ecological Indicators*, *15*(1), 281–299. doi:10.1016/j.ecolind.2011.01.007

Sirin, S. R. (2005). Socioeconomic status and academic achievement: A meta-analytic review of research. *Review of Educational Research*, *75*(3), 417–453. doi:10.3102/00346543075003417

Sjöö, K., Taalbi, J., Kander, A., & Ljungberg, J. (2014). SWINNO: A database of Swedish innovations, 1970–2007. *Lund Papers in Economic History, 2014*(133).

Skanning, S. (2009). Measuring the rule of law. *Political Research Quarterly, 63*(2), 449–460. doi:10.1177/1065912909346745

Skare, M., & Lacmanovic, S. (2015). Human capital and economic growth: a review essay. *Amfiteatru Economic, 17*(39), 735-760. Retrieved from http://www.amfiteatrueconomic.ro/temp/Article_2422.pdf

Slavuj, L. (2012). Evaluacija kvalitete urbanoga susjedstva – prednosti i nedostaci neposrednoga životnog prostora. *Sociologija i proctor, 5*(2), 183–201.

Slottje, D. J. (1991). Measuring the quality of life across countries. *The Review of Economics and Statistics, 73*(4), 684–693. doi:10.2307/2109407

Smart, W. J. (2009). *Information system success: Evaluation of a carbon accounting and sequestration system.* (Doctoral thesis). School of Commerce and Management, Southern Cross University, Lismore, Australia.

Smith, A. (1776). *An inquiry into the nature and causes of the wealth of nations.* London: George Routledge and Sons. doi:10.1093/oseo/instance.00043218

Smith, J. (2003). *Guide to the construction and methodology of the index of economic well-being.* Ottawa: Center for the Study of Living Standards.

Soares, J. Jr, & Quintella, R. H. (2008). Development: An analysis of concepts, measurement and indicators. *Brazilian Administration Review, 5*(2), 104–124. doi:10.1590/S1807-76922008000200003

Social Indicators Department. (n.d.). *Calculation of composite index of individual living conditions.* Mannheim: Social Indicators Department, Center for Survey Research and Methodology (ZUMA), Leibniz Institute for the Social Sciences (GESIS).

Sohn, C. (2014). The border as a resource in the global urban space: A contribution to the cross-border metropolis hypothesis. *International Journal of Urban and Regional Research, 38*(5), 1697–1711. doi:10.1111/1468-2427.12071

Sorn-Friese, H., & Sørensen, J. (2005). Linkage lock-in and regional economic development: The case of the Øresund medi-tech plastics industry. *Entrepreneurship & Regional Development, 17*(4), 267–291. doi:10.1080/08985620500218695

Spangenberg, J. H. (2005). Will the information society be sustainable? Towards criteria and indicators for a sustainable knowledge society. *International Journal of Innovation and Sustainable Development, 1*(1/2), 85–102. doi:10.1504/IJISD.2005.008082

Stamenković, M., Anić, I., Petrović, M., & Bojković, N. (2015). An ELECTRE approach for evaluating secondary education profiles: Evidence from PISA survey in Serbia. *Annals of Operations Research*, 1–22.

State of World Population 2007 | UNFPA - United Nations Population Fund. (n.d.). Retrieved 16 January 2016, from http://www.unfpa.org/publications/state-world-population-2007

Staton, J. K., & Moore, W. H. (2011). Judicial power in domestic and international politics. *International Organization, 65*(03), 553–587. doi:10.1017/S0020818311000130

StC. (2008). *State of the world's mothers 2008: Closing the survival gap for children under 5.* Westport, CT: Save the Children.

Steenland, K., Henley, J., Calle, E., & Thun, M. (2004). Individual-and area-based socioeconomic status variables as predictors of mortality in a cohort of 179,383 persons. *American Journal of Epidemiology, 159*(11), 1047–1056. doi:10.1093/aje/kwh129 PMID:15155289

Stehr, N. (1994). *Knowledge societies*. London: SAGE Publications.

Stiftung, B. (2008). *Bertelsmann transformation index 2008: Political management in international comparison*. Gütersloh: Bertelsmann Stiftung Verlag.

Stiftung, B. (2014). Transformation index. In *Political management in international comparison*. Gütersloh: Bertelsmann Stiftung Verlag.

Stiglitz, J. E., Sen, A. & Fitoussi, J.-P. (2009). *Report by the commission on the measurement of economic performance and social progress*. Academic Press.

Stroombergen, A., Rose, W. D., & Nana, G. (2002). *Review of the statistical measurement of human capital*. Statistics New Zealand working paper.

Subramanian, S. V., Chen, J. T., Rehkopf, D. H., Waterman, P. D., & Krieger, N. (2006). Comparing individual and area-based socioeconomic measures for the surveillance of health disparities: A multilevel analysis of Massachusetts births, 1989-1991. *American Journal of Epidemiology*, *164*(9), 823–834. doi:10.1093/aje/kwj313 PMID:16968866

Svedberg, P. (2011). How Many People are Malnourished? *Annual Review of Nutrition*, *31*(1), 263–283. doi:10.1146/annurev-nutr-081810-160805 PMID:21756133

Svensson, J. (2011). *Social Impact Assessment in Finland, Norway, and Sweden: A descriptive and comparative study. Unpublished degree project SoM EX 2011-30, KTH*. Stockholm, Sweden: Royal Institute of Technology.

Symth, J. (2004). Environment and education: A view of a changing scene. *Environmental Education Research*, *12*(4), 247–264.

Tabachnick, B. G., & Fedell, L. S. (2007). *Using Multivariate Statistics* (5th ed.). Boston: Pearson Education.

Tabachnick, B., & Fidell, L. (2007). *Using multivariate statistics* (5th ed.). Boston: Pearson Education, Inc.

Talberth, J., Cobb, C., & Slattery, N. (2007). *The genuine progress indicator 2006: A tool for sustainable development*. Oakland, CA: Redefining Progress.

Tarantola, S., Saisana, M., & Saltelli, A. (2002). *Internal market index 2002: Technical details of the methodology*. European Commission Joint Research Center.

Taylor, J. M. G. (1987). Kendall's and Spearman's Correlation Coefficients in the Presence of a Blocking Variable. *Biometrics*, *43*(2), 409–416. doi:10.2307/2531822 PMID:3607205

Teitelbaum, S., & Beckley, T. (2006). Hunted, harvested and homegrown: The prevalence of self-provisioning in rural Canada. *Journal of Rural and Community Development*, *1*(2), 114–130.

The Agency for Environmental Protection. (2014). *Report on environmental conditions in the Republic of Serbia – 2014*. Retrieved from http://www.sepa.gov.rs/download/Izvestaj2014.pdf. (In Serbian)

The Economist. (2004). *The economist intelligence unit's quality-of-life index*. Economist Online.

Thompson Reuters. (2015). *Web of science*. Retrieved November 25, 2015, from http://wokinfo.com/products_tools/multidisciplinary/webofscience/

Thomson, S., Hillman, K., & De Bortoli, L. (2013*). A teacher's guide to PISA reading literacy*. Retrieved August 20, 2015, from http://research.acer.edu.au/ozpisa/12

Todorovic, M., Levi Jaksic, M., & Marinkovic, S. (2011). Sustainable technology management indicators: Objectives matrix approach. *African Journal of Business Management*, *5*(28), 11386–11398.

Tofallis, C. (2013). An automatic-democratic approach to weight setting for the new human development index. *Journal of Population Economics*, *26*(4), 1325–1345. doi:10.1007/s00148-012-0432-x

Tone, K. (2001). A slack-based measure of efficiency in data envelopment analysis. *European Journal of Operational Research*, *130*(3), 498–509. doi:10.1016/S0377-2217(99)00407-5

Toušek, L. (2012). *Kvantitativní analýza pocitu bezpečí města Pardubice*. 2012. Plzeň: FF ZČU. Retrieved September 10, 2015, from http://www.antropologie.org/cs/component/docman/doc_download/42-kvalitativni-analyza-pocitu-bezpei-oban-msta-pardubic

Toward an age-friendly New York City: A Findings Report. (2008). New York, NY: The New York Academy of Medicine.

Tracking the Development of Universal Metrics to Help cities and Communities Compare and Contrast Their Progress on the Design and Implementation of Age-friendly Policies, Strategies and Interventions. (2012). Active Age Discussion Paper. Retrieved September 10, 2015, from: http://library.constantcontact.com/download/get/file/1101901198311-1153/Age+Friendly+Paper.pdf

Trippl, M. (2010). Developing cross-border regional innovation systems: Key factors and challenges. *Tijdschrift voor Economische en Sociale Geografie*, *101*(2), 150–160. doi:10.1111/j.1467-9663.2009.00522.x

Trumic, M., Petrovic, N., & Radojicic, Z. (2009). Environmental aweraness in formal elementary education in the Republic of Serbia. In N. Mladenović & D. Urošević (Eds.), *Proceedings of the XXXVI operational research conference - SYM-OP-IS 2009* (pp. 14-17). Belgrade: Mathematical institute SANU. (In Serbian)

Tsameret, T., & Zameret, Z. (2012). *The Melting Pot in Israel: The Commission of Inquiry Concerning the Education of Immigrant Children During the Early Years of the State*. SUNY Press.

Tsoukalas, S., & Mackenzie, A. (2003). *The personal security index, 2003 - five years later*. Ottawa: Canadian Council on Social Development.

Turner, C., & Martin, E. (1985). *Surveying Subjective Phenomena*. Russell Sage Foundation.

Tyteca, D. (1996). On the measurement of the environmental performance of firms – a literature review and a productive efficiency perspective. *Journal of Environmental Management*, *46*(3), 281–308. doi:10.1006/jema.1996.0022

UN, EC, IMF, OECD, &World Bank. (2003). Handbook of national accounting: integrated environmental and economic accounting 2003. Studies in Methods, Series F, No.61, Rev.1, United Nations, European Commission, International Monetary Fund, Organisation for Economic Co-operation and Development and World Bank.

UN. (2015). *The Universal Declaration of Human Rights*. Retrieved September 15, 2015, from http://www.un.org/en/documents/udhr/

UN. (2015). *Transforming our world: The 2030 agenda for sustainable development*. United Nations.

UNDP Oslo Governance Centre. (2006). *How informal justice systems can contribute*. Oslo: United Nations.

UNDP. (2001). *Human development report 2001*. New York: Oxford University Press.

UNDP. (2001). *Human Development Report, Making New Technologies Work for Human Development*. Oxford, UK: Oxford University Press.

UNDP. (2007). *Human development report 2007*. New York: Oxford University Press.

UNESCO. (2005). *World Report: Towards knowledge societies*. UNESCO Publishing. Retrieved from http://unesdoc.unesco.org/images/ 0014/001418/141843e.pdf

Union of Engineers and Technicians of Serbia (UETS). (2014). *Report from the 35th International conference "Water supply and sewerage system"*. Retrieved from http://www.sits.org.rs/include/data/docs1106.pdf (In Serbian)

Unit, E. I. (2014). *The Learning Curve: Education and Skills for Life. A Report*. Pearson London.

United Nations (UN). (1972). *Action Plan for The Human Environment.United Nations Conference on the Human Environment*, Stockholm, Sweden.

United Nations (UN). (2015). *Sustainable development goals*. Retrieved from http://www.un.org/sustainabledevelopment/sustainable-development-goals/

United Nations Conference on Environment and Development (UNCED) . (1992). Retrieved from http://www.un.org/geninfo/bp/enviro.html

United Nations Development Programme. (2015). *Human Development Index (HDI)*. Retrieved May 06, 2015, from: http://hdr.undp.org/en/content/human-development-index-hdi

United Nations Organization for Education, Science, and Culture (UNESCO). (2012). *Education for sustainable development*. Retrieved from http://www.unesco.org/new/en/education/themes/leading-the-international-agenda/education-for-sustainable-development/education-for-sustainable-development/

United Nations Sustainable Development (UNSD). (1992). *Agenda 21*. United Nations Conference on Environment & Development, Rio de Janeiro, Brazil. Retrieved from https://sustainabledevelopment.un.org/content/documents/Agenda21.pdf

United Nations, Department of Economic and Social Affairs, Population Division (2014). *World urbanization prospects: The 2014 revision, Highlights*. ST/ESA/SER.A/352.

United Nations. (2012). *Fostering innovative entrepreneurship: challenges and policy options / United Nations Economic Commission for Europe*. Geneva: United Nations New York.

UNU-MERIT. (2009). *European innovation scoreboard 2008: Comparative analysis of innovation performance*. Maastricht Economic and Social Research and Training Center on Innovation and Technology, Inno Metrics, Pro Inno Europe.

Ura, K., Alkire, S., Zangmo, T., & Wangdi, K. (2012). *A short guide to gross national happiness index*. Bhutan: The Center for Bhutan Studies.

Uslaner, E. M. (2005, November). The bulging pocket and the rule of law: Corruption, inequality, and trust. In *Conference on The Quality of Government: What It Is, How to Get It, Why It Matters* (pp. 17-19).

Valenčak, S. (2012). Kaj je v Sloveniji starosti prijazno in kaj ne? *Kakovostna starost, 15*(1), 3–19.

van Audenhove, F., Korniichuk, O., Dauby, L., & Pourbaix, J. (2014). *The future of urban mobility 2.0, Arthur D. Little and UITP*. Retrieved August 5, 2015, from http://www.adl.com/FUM2.0

van de Kerk, G., & Manuel, A. (2008). *Sustainable society index SSI-2008*. Netherlands: Sustainable Society Foundation.

van de Kerk, G., & Manuel, A. (2014). *Sustainable society index 2014*. The Hague, The Netherlands: Sustainable Society Foundation.

van Houtum, H. (2000). An overview of European geographical research on borders and border regions. *Journal of Borderland Studies, 15*(1), 56–83. doi:10.1080/08865655.2000.9695542

van Lier, T., Rai, H. B., & Macharis, C. (2015). Sustainable logistics in urban areas: What gets measured, gets managed. In *Proceedings of the NECTAR City Logistics and Sustainable Freight Transport Workshop* (pp. 1-37).

Vidovićová, L., Galčanová, L., Petrová Kafková, M., & Sýkorová, D. (2013). *Stáří ve městě, město v životě seniorů*. Praha: Sociologické nakladatelství.

Vos, R. (1996). *Educational indicators: What's to be measured?* INDES Working Papers I-1. Washington, DC: Inter-American Development Bank.

Vyas, S., & Kumaranayake, L. (2006). Constructing socioeconomic status indices: How to use principal components analysis. *Advance Access Publication, 9*, 459–468.

Wahl, H.-W., & Lang, F. R. (2004). Aging in context across the adult life: Integrating physical and social research perspectives. In H.-W. Wahl, R. Scheidt, & P. G. Windley (Eds.), *Aging in context: Socio-physical environments* (pp. 1–33). New York: Springer.

Wahl, H.-W., & Weisman, G. D. (2003). Environmental gerontology at the beginning of the new millennium: Reflections on its historical, empirical, and theoretical development. *The Gerontologist, 43*(5), 616–627. doi:10.1093/geront/43.5.616 PMID:14570958

Waldron, H. B., & Kaminer, Y. (2004). On the learning curve: The emerging evidence supporting cognitive – behavioral therapies for adolescent substance abuse. *Addiction (Abingdon, England), 99*(s2), 93–105. doi:10.1111/j.1360-0443.2004.00857.x PMID:15488108

Walker, A. C. (2010). Ageing and Quality of Life in Europe. In D. Dannefer & C. Phillipson (Eds.), *The SAGE Handbook of Social Gerontology* (pp. 571–586). Los Angeles, CA: SAGE Publications. doi:10.4135/9781446200933.n44

Warner, R. M. (2013). *Applied Statistics: from Bivariate through Multivariate Techniques* (2nd ed.). Thousand Oaks, CA: Sage Publications, Inc.

Warren, E. M. (2004). What does corruption mean in a democracy? *American Journal of Political Science, 48*(2), 328–343. doi:10.1111/j.0092-5853.2004.00073.x

Webster, F. (1995). *Theories of the information society*. London: Routledge.

Wefering, F., Rupprecht, S., Buhrmann, S., & Bohler-Baedeker, S. (2014). *Guidelines-developing and implementing a sustainable urban mobility plan*. Brussels: European Platform on Sustainable Urban Mobility Plans.

Weingast, B. R. (2008). Why developing countries prove so resistant to the rule of law. In Global Perspectives on the Rule of Law. Routledge.

Weisbrod, B. A. (1961). The valuation of human capital. *Journal of Political Economy, 69*(5), 425–436. doi:10.1086/258535

Welch, E. W., & Hinnant, C. C. (2003, January). Internet use, transparency, and interactivity effects on trust in government. In *Proceedings of the 36th Annual Hawaii International Conference on System Sciences*. IEEE. doi:10.1109/HICSS.2003.1174323

Westlund, H., & Bygvrå, S. (2002). Short-term effects of the Öresund Bridge on crossborder interaction and spatial behavior. *Journal of Borderland Studies, 17*(1), 57–77. doi:10.1080/08865655.2002.9695582

Wheeler, T., & von Braun, J. (2013). Climate change impacts on global food security. *Science, 341*(6145), 508–513. doi:10.1126/science.1239402 PMID:23908229

White, A. (2007). A global projection of subjective well-being: A challenge to positive psychology? *Psychtalk, 56*, 17–20.

WHO - World Health Organisation. (2002). *Global Age-friendly Cities. A Guide*. Retrieved September 10, 2015, from http://www.who.int/ageing/publications/Global_age_friendly_cities_Guide_English.pdf

Wight, R. G., Ko, M. J., & Aneshensel, C. S. (2011). Urban Neighbourhoods and Depressive Symptoms in Late Middle Age. *Research on Aging*, *33*(1), 28–50. doi:10.1177/0164027510383048 PMID:21572903

Wiles, J. L., Leibing, A., Guberman, N., Reeve, J., & Allen, R. E. S. (2012). The meaning of 'aging in place' to older people. *The Gerontologist*, *52*(3), 357–366. doi:10.1093/geront/gnr098 PMID:21983126

Wilmots, B., Shen, Y., Hermans, E., & Ruan, D. (2011). *Missing data treatment: Overview of possible solutions*. Diepenbeek: Policy Research Centre Mobility and Public Works, track Traffic Safety, RA-MOW-2011-002.

WJP. (2014). *The World Justice Project Rule of Law Index 2014*. The World Justice Project.

Wong, M., Chau, P. H., Cheung, F., Phillips, D. R., & Woo, J. (2015). Comparing the Age-Friendliness of Different Neighbourhoods Using District Surveys: An Example from Hong Kong. *PLoS ONE*, *10*(7), e0131526. doi:10.1371/journal.pone.0131526 PMID:26132156

World Bank. (2006). *Where is the wealth of nations? Measuring capital for the 21st century*. Washington, DC: The World Bank.

World Bank. (2012). *Knowledge Economy Index (KEI) 2012 Rankings*. Retrieved from http://www.siteresources.worldbank.org/INTUNIKAM/.../2012.pdf

World Commission on Environment and Development (WCED). (1987). *Our Common Future*. Oxford, UK: Oxford University Press.

World Economic Forum. (2014). *Global Competitiveness Report 2014-15*. Retrieved from http://www3.weforum.org/docs/WEF_GlobalCompetitivenessReport_2014-15.pdf

World Health Organisation (WHO). (2015.) *Measuring the Age-friendliness of Cities: A Guide to Using Core Indicators*. Retrieved January 10, 2016, from: http://apps.who.int/iris/bitstream/10665/203830/1/9789241509695_eng.pdf

Wößmann, L. (2005). *Public-private partnerships in schooling: cross-country evidence on their effectiveness in providing cognitive skills. Prepared for the conference: "Mobilizing the Private Sector for Public Education"*. Program on Education Policy and Governance, Research Paper PEPG, 05-09.

Wright, T. P. (2012). Factors affecting the cost of airplanes. *Journal of the Aeronautical Sciences*, *3*(4). doi:10.2514/8.155

Yamada, Y., Matui, T., & Sugiyama, M. (1994). New analysis of efficiency based on DEA. *Journal of the Operations Research Society of Japan*, *37*, 158–167.

Yigitcanlar, T., & Dur, F. (2010). Developing a sustainability assessment model: The sustainable infrastructure, land-use, environment and transport model. *Sustainability*, *2*(1), 321–340. doi:10.3390/su2010321

Yin, R. (2003). *Case study research: Design and methods* (2nd ed.). Thousand Oaks, CA: Sage Publications.

Young, J. L. M. (2009). *All education is environmental education*. Published Master's Thesis, Ontario, Canada.

Zagorski, K. (1985). Composite measures of social, economic, and demographic regional differentiation in Australia: Application of multi-stage principal component methods to aggregate data analysis. *Social Indicators Research*, *16*, 131–156. doi:10.1007/BF00574614

Zaidi. (2012). *Active Ageing Index: Concept, Methodology and Final Results*. Retrieved September 10, 2015, from http://www1.unece.org/stat/platform/download/attachments/76287849/Methodology-Paper-as-of-10th_March-2013-FINAL.pdf?version=1&modificationDate=1367589733309

Zanella, A., Camanho, A. S., & Dias, T. G. (2015). Undesirable outputs and weightings schemes in composite indicators based on data envelopment analysis. *European Journal of Operational Research, 245*(2), 517–530. doi:10.1016/j.ejor.2015.03.036

Zhang, M. (2002). *Measuring urban sustainability in China.* (Doctoral Dissertation). Erasmus University, The Netherlands.

Zhou, P., & Ang, B. W. (2009). Comparing MCDA aggregation methods in constructing composite indicators using the Shannon-Spearman measure. *Social Indicators Research, 94*(1), 83–96. doi:10.1007/s11205-008-9338-0

Zhou, P., Ang, B. W., & Poh, K. L. (2007). A mathematical programming approach to constructing composite indicators. *Ecological Economics, 62*(2), 291–297. doi:10.1016/j.ecolecon.2006.12.020

Zhou, P., Ang, B. W., & Zhou, D. Q. (2010). Weighting and aggregation in composite indicators construction: A multiplicative optimization approach. *Social Indicators Research, 96*(1), 169–181. doi:10.1007/s11205-009-9472-3 PMID:19966916

Zhou, P., Fan, L. W., & Zhou, D. Q. (2010). Data aggregation in constructing composite indicators: A perspective of information loss. *Expert Systems with Applications, 37*(1), 360–365. doi:10.1016/j.eswa.2009.05.039

Zolotas, X. (1981). *Economic growth and declining social welfare.* New York: New York University Press.

Zornic, N., Bornmann, L., Maricic, M., Markovic, A., Martic, M., & Jeremic, V. (2015). Ranking institutions within a university based on their scientific performance: A percentile-based approach. *El Profesional de la informacion, 24*(5), 551-566. doi: 10.3145/epi.2015.sep.05

About the Contributors

Paulo Nocera Alves, Jr. is currently a doctoral student at Production Engineering from University of São Paulo (USP) - School of Engineering of São Carlos (EESC). Master's at Production Engineering from São Paulo State University (UNESP) - College of Engineering of Bauru (FEB), 2014, and Bachelor's at Production Engineering from University of Franca (UNIFRAN), 2011. The author has experience in Production Engineering, acting on the following subjects: inventory control, optimal control, data envelopment analysis, multivariate analysis and quantitative methods.

Sibel Bali graduated from the Uludag University, Faculty of Economics and Administrative Sciences, Department of Business Administration in 2000. She received her PhD from the Uludag University, Institute of Social Sciences and the topic of her thesis was "The Institutional of Determinants of Financial Development: A Cross-Country Analysis". Bali Eryigit works at Uludag University, Department of Economics as a Dr. Assistant. The research interests of Bali Eryigit research interests are institutional economics, financial development, economic growth, monetary economics, defense economics and demographic economics, and her presentations, projects and published works cover these areas as well.

Milica Bulajic graduated from Faculty of Mathematics, University of Belgrade in 1981. She received her PhD in 2002 at the Faculty of Organizational Sciences where she works since 2003 as a full professor for the scientific field of computational statistics. She is engaged in probability theory, statistics, econometric methods, data analysis and other subjects of the Department of Operations Research and Statistics. She is a member of the Statistical Society of Serbia. She speaks English, Italian and French.

Marko Cirovic works as a teaching assistant at the University of Belgrade, Faculty of Organizational Sciences, Belgrade, the Republic of Serbia. He graduated with a degree in Management in 2010, and got his master degree in 2012. He is currently enrolled in doctoral studies at the Faculty of Organizational Sciences. His area of interest includes: environmental management, eco-marketing, environmental risk assessment.

Nuno Crespo (PhD) is Professor of Economics at the ISCTE Business School Economics Department, Instituto Universitário de Lisboa (ISCTE - IUL) and a researcher of BRU - IUL (Business Research Unit, Economics Group). He is the Director of the Economics Department and was the Director for several years of the Master in Health Services Management (ISCTE - IUL) and the Master in Portuguese Economy and International Integration (ISCTE - IUL). His recent work has been published in Journal of Economic

Surveys, World Development, Empirical Economics, Journal of Common Market Studies, Economics Letters, World Economy, Review of World Economics and Papers in Regional Science, among others.

Norsiah Abdul Hamid is a Senior Lecturer at the School of Multimedia Technology and Communication, Universiti Utara Malaysia. She holds a PhD in Information Science from Universiti Kebangsaan Malaysia. Her focus areas of teaching, student supervision, research and publications among others are the impact of ICT and media on society, information and knowledge society, and studies on women and gender. She has been involved in various research projects and publications at the university and national levels. Current research projects include the development of social media model for women and girls, as well as publication of books related to social media in Malaysia.

Elke Hermans is associate professor at Hasselt University in Belgium. She works at the Transportation Research Institute (IMOB) where she coordinates the Centre on Travel and Tourism Research. Moreover, she is involved in the Bachelor (Dutch) and Master (Dutch and English) programme in Transportation Sciences as well as a lecturer in the inter-university Master in Tourism (Dutch) programme. In fact, her current research and educational skills relate to mobility, travel and tourism. She has a Master degree in Commercial Engineering (obtained in 2004) and a PhD degree in transportation sciences (obtained in 2009). During her career, Elke Hermans published her research in various scientifically ranked journal articles (for example Accident Analysis and Prevention, Transportation Research Record, Knowledge-Based Systems, etc) and conference proceedings (such as Annual Meeting of the Transportation Research Board, International Road Traffic and Accident Database Conference, International Conference on Sensitivity Analysis of Model Output, etc). At the same time, she has been involved in the supervision of PhD students and the execution and coordination of a number of research projects.

Mohd Sobhi Ishak, Ph.D., is a Senior Lecturer at the School of Multimedia Technology and Communication, College of Arts and Sciences, Universiti Utara Malaysia. He holds a PhD in Mass Communication and Master of Science in Communication Technology from Universiti Putra Malaysia, and Bachelor of Information Technology (Hons) from Universiti Utara Malaysia. His research interests focus on the influence and impact of media on religious, society, and politics. He has also presented numerous papers at national and international conferences, and contributes articles in journals and chapters in books on media. He also participates as a researcher for various national Grant (LRGS, FRGS, and RAGS). His expertise is quantitative research methods and advanced statistical analysis of Structural Equation Modeling (SEM) using AMOS and SmartPLS.

Maja Levi Jaksic, PhD, is full professor at Faculty of Organizational Sciences, and Head of Department for Technology, Innovation and Development Management. Prof Levi Jaksic has published more than 200 works, among which more than 20 books and monographs and had been engaged fundamental and applied research projects. She has been teaching as visiting professor at universities in Greece, United Kingdom, Japan, and France and is the program leader of the dual diploma Academic Master program in International Business and Management with Middlesex University from London. She is member of Editorial Board of Technovation.

Milica Jovanovic, MSc., works as a teaching assistant at the Faculty of Organizational Sciences, Department for Technology, Innovation and Development Management. She is completing her PhD studies at the Faculty of Organizational Sciences, University of Belgrade - Information systems and management. She has been involved in 3 consulting projects and 1 strategic project funded by the Ministry of education, science and technological development of the Republic of Serbia. Her main research interests include: technology and innovation management, quantitative management, sustainable development and performance management.

Vijaya Krishnan is a researcher at the School of Public Health at the University of Alberta, Edmonton. She is specialized in technical demography and has written and published widely in health and early child development. Vijaya received her Masters' in Mathematics and Masters' in Demography from the University of Kerala. She received her doctorate in Demography from the University of Alberta in 1989. Since then, she held various positions in government, academia and the private sector, which includes Alberta Health, Simon Fraser University, and the University of Botswana. She is the recipient of several research grants and scholarship. She is widely travelled and has presented her research at various international conferences.

Dragana Makajic-Nikolic works as Assistant Professor at the Faculty of Organizational Sciences at the University of Belgrade, where she lectures in Operations Research courses. Her research interests are related to Mathematical Modeling, Optimization methods, Reliability and Risk Analysis.

Teemu Makkonen holds a PhD and a Title of Docent in Economic Geography (University of Helsinki). He is currently working as a Marie Curie Research Fellow at the School of Hospitality and Tourism Management (University of Surrey). He is also an Assistant Professor (on a leave of absence) at the Department of Border Region Studies (University of Southern Denmark). His research interests include border regions, economic geography, innovation and statistical methods.

Enzo Barberio Mariano, assistant professor at the Universidade Estadual Paulista Production Engineering department "Júlio de Mesquita Filho", Campus Bauru - SP. Master's mentor at the Postgraduate program in industrial engineering in the area of applied quantitative methods. He graduated in Production Engineering from Universidade de São Paulo - USP (2005) and Pedagogy from the Federal University of São Carlos - UFSCar (2011). It is also the master (2008) and Ph.D. (2012) in Production Engineering from the University of Sao Paulo.

Milica Maricic is a teaching associate at the Department of Operations Research and Statistics at the Faculty of Organizational Sciences, University of Belgrade (UB). After graduation in 2014 at the Faculty of Organizational Sciences, she enrolled in post-graduate studies at the same Faculty, where she is specializing in business statistics. In 2015, she enrolled in a post-graduate program at the UB, which is part of the Tempus project Incoming, where she is specializing in social sciences and computing.

Sanja Marinkovic, PhD, is an assistant professor at Faculty of organizational sciences, Department for Technology, Innovation and Development Management. She is an author and co-author of several books and more than 60 scientific papers. She is a lecturer at dual award master programme International Business and Management, validated by Middlesex University London. Her research and teaching interests are in the fields of technology and innovation management, sustainable development and SMEs development.

Maja Marković, Education: Master of Biostatistics, Erasmus University, Rotterdam (2015-) Master of Computational Statistics, Faculty of Organizational Sciences, Belgrade University (2013 - 2014) Bachelor of Management, Faculty of Organizational Sciences, Belgrade University (2009-2013) Work experience: Doing research on data operations and computational statistics, writing papers, assisting professors in research, reviewing papers. Being a member review team for "Social Indicators Research" journal. Organizing events and conferences trough student organization ESTIEM.

Milan Martic received his M.Sc. degree in 1989 and his Ph.D. in 1999 from the University of Belgrade, Faculty of Organizational Sciences in the area of Operations Research. Currently, he is Full Professor and dean of Faculty of Organizational Sciences, University of Belgrade. He lectures courses in the Operations Research field. His research interests are related to Mathematical Modeling, Efficiency evaluation and DEA theory and application. He is the author or co-author of over 60 papers and co-author of two books in the OR area. His papers have been published in journals including European Journal of Operational Research, Expert Systems with Application, Scientometrics and Higher Education.

Maja Mitrović, Education: PhD Studies – Quantitative Management, Faculty of Organizational Sciences, Belgrade University (2015-); Master of Computational Statistics, Faculty of Organizational Sciences, Belgrade University (2013 - 2014) Bachelor of Operations Management, Faculty of Organizational Sciences, Belgrade University (2009-2013) Work experience: Ministry of Finance, Republic of Serbia (2014-2015) Doing research on data operations and computational statistics, writing papers, assisting professors in research. Organizing events and conferences through student organization ESTIEM. Participating trainings as a volunteer of Olimpic Comitee of Serbia.

Sandrina B. Moreira (PhD) is Professor of Economics at the Instituto Politécnico de Setúbal (ESCE - IPS) and a researcher of BRU - IUL (Business Research Unit, Economics Group). She is the Vice-President of the Management and Economics Department and the School Coordinator of International Mobility. Her broad research and teaching interests are Macroeconomics, Economic Growth and Development, and International Economics. Her recent work has been published in Journal of Economic Surveys, Empirical Economics, International Journal of Social Economics, International Review of Applied Economics, RPER / Portuguese Review of Regional Studies, among others.

Jasna Petkovic is an Assistant Professor at the Faculty of Organizational Sciences, University of Belgrade, Serbia, where she got her MSc and Phd degrees. She is an author and co-author several books and more than 60 scientific papers. Her research and teaching interests are in the fields of technology management, technology forecasting and SMEs development.

Natasa Petrovic is a Full Professor at the University of Belgrade - Faculty of Organizational Sciences, the Republic of Serbia, where she acquired her M.Sc. (1999) and Ph.D. (2002) degrees in Environmental management. Areas of her research include: Environmental management, Environmental science, Sustainable development, Green marketing, Environmental education and Education for sustainable development, Environmental risk management, Energy efficiency, Management skills for environmental managers, Public participation in environmental protection.

Jovana Rakicevic, MSc, works as a teaching assistant at the University of Belgrade, Faculty of Organizational Sciences, Department for Technology, Innovation and Development Management. She is currently enrolled in PhD studies – Information Systems and Quantitative Management. She is author and co-author of about 20 scientific papers. Her research and teaching area of interest includes Technology and Innovation Management at micro and macro level, Performance Measurement, SMEs Development, Sustainable Development and Technology Entrepreneurship.

Daisy Aparecida do Nascimento Rebelatto graduated in Civil Engineering from the Universidade Federal de São Carlos, master's degree in Industrial Engineering from the Universidade de São Paulo and PhD in Mechanical Engineering from the Universidade de São Paulo. Currently, is associate professor at the Universidade de São Paulo and has experience in Production Engineering with emphasis in Economic Engineering, acting on the following topics: energy, productive infrastructure and efficiency analysis.

Fabio Gaetano Santeramo, Ph.D., is Assistant Professor at the University of Foggia, Italy. He has served as consultant in Economics for several International Organization (FAO, CIHEAM, IFPRI). His area of research concerns agricultural economics, applied econometrics, and development economics. His articles have been published in Agricultural Economics, Journal of Policy Modeling, African Development Review, Tourism Economics, Food Reviews International, European Review of Agricultural Economics, Agribusiness: An International Journal, Food Research International, Journal of Agricultural Economics.

Gordana Savic received her M.Sc. degree in 2006 and her Ph.D. in 2012 from the University of Belgrade, Faculty of Organizational Sciences (area - Operations Research). Currently, she is Assistant Professor at the Faculty of Organizational Sciences, University of Belgrade, where she lectures courses in the Operations Research field. Her research interests are related to Mathematical modeling, Optimization methods and software, Advance planning and Scheduling, DEA theory and application. She is the author or co-author of over 40 papers and co-author of two books in the OR area. Her papers have been published in journals including European Journal of Operational Research, Expert Systems with Application, Scientometrics and Higher Education.

Yongjun Shen is an assistant professor at the Transportation Research Institute (IMOB) of Hasselt University in Belgium. He received his Ph.D. in Transportation Sciences from Hasselt University. His current research interests are traffic safety and sustainability, travel behavior modeling and risk analysis, driving simulator research, data mining and decision making. He has participated in several EU and Flemish projects, and has published over 60 articles in scientific peer-reviewed journals, books, and conferences, such as Transportation Research Part C, Accident Analysis and Prevention, Expert Systems with Applications, etc. He currently serves as a guest editor of several Special Issues on transportation research, and as International Program Committee Member of several international conference series.

Milica Vasilijevic graduated from Faculty of Organizational Sciences, University of Belgrade in 2014. Her subjects of interest are Applied Statistics and Government indices. She speaks English.

Lucie Vidovićová, PhD., is a sociologist. Her long-term research interests include sociology of ageing, environmental gerontology, age discrimination, and active ageing. She is also involved in research projects in the field of family and social policy. She conducts research for national as well as European bodies and works as a consultant on a number of implementation projects such as Ageing in the media. Lucie also cooperates with different governmental and NGO bodies in the field of senior advocacy. Her experience includes involvement with the European projects DIALOG, ActivAge, MOPACT, and co-operation with EUROFOUND. She is also part of the UNECE Task Force for Ageing-related statistics. Recent projects she has been involved in include surveys of older consumers, age discrimination (www. ageismus.cz), ageing in big cities (http://starnuti.fss.muni.cz), and the issue of role overload in active ageing grandparents (http://ups.fss.muni.cz). Lucie also serves as serves at the Executive Committee of RC 11 Sociology of Ageing at the International Sociological Association (ISA).

Norhafezah Yusof, PhD, is an Associate Professor in Department of Communication, School of Multimedia Technology and Communication. She read her PhD in Nottingham Trent University, UK. She has completed her post-doctorate at Nanyang Technological University (NTU), Singapore. Her expert area is communication management. The specific areas include space and culture, change, women and media.

Hamilah Badioze Zaman, PhD, is currently a Professor and Director at the Institute of Visual Informatics (IVI), Universiti Kebangsaan Malaysia (UKM). She received her undergraduate, Master and PhD education in United Kingdom. She is an active researcher in the field of computer science and ICT specifically in Visual Informatics. She has worked extensively in the areas of visual informatics namely, virtual reality, e-learning and virtual learning, augmented reality, virtual Islamic banking, haptic & multi-touch applications, and voice recognition system for the visually impaired. She is also involved in social computing research related to knowledge society and sentiment analysis of the social media and visualization of big data. She holds many positions that has contributed to the formulation of ICT policies in the country. She is currently Head of the ICT Cluster, National Professor's Council; a Fellow of the Academy of Sciences Malaysia (ASM) in the Engineering and Computer Science Discipline; Chairperson of the Expert Working Group on Computer Science and ICT, National Science Research Council (NSRC); Chairperson of the Expert Working Group on Technology and Innovation Ecosystem, National Information Technology Council (NITC) and President of the Malaysian Information Technology Malaysia (MITS).

Index

Printed in the United States
By Bookmasters